UNDERSTANDING SALES AND LEASES OF GOODS

UNDERSTANDING SALES AND LEASES OF GOODS

SECOND EDITION

William H. Henning
Distinguished Professor of Law
The University of Alabama School of Law

William H. Lawrence
Professor of Law
University of San Diego School of Law

Library of Congress Cataloging-in-Publication Data

Henning, William H., 1947-
    Understanding sales and leases of goods / William H. Henning, William H. Lawrence. -- 2nd ed.
      p. cm.
    Lawrence's name appears first on the earlier edition.
    Includes index.
    ISBN: 978-1-4224-2249-6 (softbound)
   1. Sales--United States. 2. Industrial equipment leases--United States. I. Lawrence, William H. II. Title.
    KF915.L395 2009
    346.7307'2--dc22

                                           2009028702

This publication is designed to provide accurate and authoritative information in regard to the subject matter covered. It is sold with the understanding that the publisher is not engaged in rendering legal, accounting, or other professional services. If legal advice or other expert assistance is required, the services of a competent professional should be sought.

LexisNexis and the Knowledge Burst logo are registered trademarks and Michie is a trademark of Reed Elsevier Properties Inc., used under license. Matthew Bender and the Matthew Bender Flame Design are registered trademarks of Matthew Bender Properties Inc.

NOTE TO USERS

To ensure that you are using the latest materials available in this area, please be sure to periodically check the LexisNexis Law School web site for downloadable updates and supplements at www.lexisnexis.com/lawschool.

Editorial Offices
121 Chanlon Rd., New Providence, NJ 07974 (908) 464-6800
201 Mission St., San Francisco, CA 94105-1831 (415) 908-3200
www.lexisnexis.com

MATTHEW◆BENDER

                                                   (2009–Pub.065)

To the two little joys of my life, Emma and Ayden. —WHH

In honor of the memory of my good friend and colleague, Dick Speidel, who tended these same vineyards with such care. —WHL

PREFACE

This book is designed exclusively as a student text. Although it covers both sales of goods under Article 2 of the Uniform Commercial Code and leases of goods under Article 2A, the primary focus is on Article 2. The decision to pursue this approach is based in part on the fact that many commercial law courses contain little or no coverage of Article 2A. Even in courses that devote significant time to leases, the main focus generally is on sales. Thus, concentrating primarily on sales best meets the needs of most students.

Another reason for the book's approach is that much of Article 2A is based on Article 2 as a statutory analogue, and thus the primary focus on Article 2 is often an efficient means of presenting both articles. The case law is much more developed with respect to Article 2, and a study of cases interpreting that article is generally beneficial in interpreting the comparable provisions of Article 2A, which are cross-referenced to facilitate access to them. The major discussions devoted to Article 2A focus on those provisions that deviate from the statutory analogue, and the text discusses the differences between sales and lease transactions that caused the drafters of Article 2A to adopt a different statutory approach.

The organization of the subject matter is also designed to correlate with a general course in contracts. This approach recognizes that, at many law schools, there is extensive treatment of Article 2, and sometimes Article 2A, in the first-year course on contracts.

The Table of Contents includes section numbers for relevant provisions of Articles 2 and 2A. It does not contain the number for each and every section that might be relevant, but it does guide students to the most fundamental provisions relating to each topic. This approach should aid students because they can quickly find relevant discussion either by the language in the Table of Contents describing the topic or by locating the basic Code section numbers. The Index and the Table of Statutes and Authorities will facilitate a more detailed search.

This second edition represents more than a routine update. So much has happened since the first edition was published that nothing more than a thorough rewrite, coupled with an expansion of coverage, would suffice. Articles 2 and 2A were amended in 2003, and some coverage of the amendments is necessary even though the Code's sponsors have not yet been successful in getting the state legislatures to adopt them. A study of the amendments will help students better understand problem areas in the original articles, but a full-scale treatment of them is not warranted at this time. Thus, each chapter contains a separate section that discusses the amendments relevant to the subject matter of the chapter. Similarly, each chapter contains a section that discusses the relevant provisions of the Convention on the International Sale of Goods (CISG). Given the shrinking nature of our world and the dramatic increase in international transactions, no book on sales law would be complete without a discussion of the CISG.

Other changes of note from the first edition include a detailed discussion of the effects on Articles 2 and 2A of state and federal laws validating electronic contracting; with regard to warranty rights, expanded discussions of the federal Magnuson-Moss Act, federal preemption, and state consumer-protection laws; and an expanded discussion of issues relating to the scope of Articles 2 and 2A, especially the extent to which the articles are applicable to transactions involving products that combine goods and computer programs.

PREFACE

Professor Henning gratefully acknowledges the support provided by the University of Alabama Law School Foundation, which supports his scholarship.

Professor Lawrence gratefully acknowledges the support provided by a summer research grant from the University of San Diego School of Law.

May 2009

William H. Henning
William H. Lawrence

TABLE OF CONTENTS

TABLE OF CONTENTS

TABLE OF CONTENTS

TABLE OF CONTENTS

TABLE OF CONTENTS

TABLE OF CONTENTS

TABLE OF CONTENTS

TABLE OF CONTENTS

TABLE OF CONTENTS

TABLE OF CONTENTS

Chapter 1

HISTORY AND SCOPE OF ARTICLES 2 AND 2A

[C] **Exclusions**

[D] **Construing the CISG**

§ 1.01 BRIEF HISTORY OF COMMERCIAL LAW PRIOR TO THE UNIFORM COMMERCIAL CODE

Much of modern commercial law can be traced to the Law Merchant, a body of rules and principles developed in medieval Europe by merchants for the purpose of regulating mercantile transactions.[1] As trade expanded markets and fairs based on unfettered principles of free trade became established in European locations. These markets benefitted all parties: The merchants enjoyed the profits, the local rulers collected taxes, and the community attained increased employment and desired goods from other locations.

Over time the Law Merchant developed into a system that regulated the business dealings of merchants generally, including such activities as negotiating contracts, entering into partnerships, and buying and selling goods. It was truly merchants' law rather than a regulatory scheme imposed as an exercise of local or regional sovereign authority. Values were determined in accordance with commercial custom and usage as reflected in dynamic trade relationships. Even the methods of resolving disputes reflected the practical needs of commerce: The Law Merchant was administered by specialized courts established along trade routes, in cities, and at trade fairs, and the judges were usually merchants themselves. Procedures were kept informal and disputes were resolved quickly and efficiently.

With the emergence of national interests, the Law Merchant gradually became more and more incorporated into national legal systems. European nations on the continent essentially codified it into commercial codes. England largely subjugated it to the strict proceedings of the common law. England's position as a world trading power, however, meant that the English courts could not ignore trade customs and usages completely. Lord Mansfield recognized this reality and successfully sought to free commercial law from many of the common-law restraints in order to allow it to reflect the realities of the marketplace. Although tremendous advances were made in this respect, the English courts insisted on the use of formal methods to establish the existence of customs and usages. For example, a party seeking to use a trade custom in litigation had to prove that it had been in effect since time immemorial.

The principles of the Law Merchant re-emerged as a powerful influence in the United States. Trade custom and usage has been recognized as a primary source of U.S. commercial law, with legal rules generally being premised on business practices. The constraints of formality generally have been rejected in American law. Current commercial legislation, particularly the Uniform Commercial Code (UCC), continues these traditions. The UCC recognizes and elevates the role of custom and usage, and it rejects any requirement that for custom to be relevant

---

[1] The Law Merchant first developed in the 11th century, primarily as a means of protecting foreign traders not eligible for protection under local law. For an excellent and thorough explanation, see L. Trakman, The Law Merchant: The Evolution of Commercial Law (1983).

it must have been in effect since time immemorial.[2] Indeed, one of the purposes and policies of the Code is to "permit the continued expansion of commercial practices through custom, usage, and agreement of the parties."[3]

§ 1.02   THE PROMULGATION OF ARTICLES 2 AND 2A

[A]   Initial Promulgation

The Uniform Commercial Code was not the initial codification of commercial law in the United States. The National Conference of Commissioners on Uniform State Laws, more commonly known today as the Uniform Law Commission (ULC), had previously promulgated several uniform acts dealing with areas of commercial law. The most relevant of these early acts to the subject matter of this book was the Uniform Sales Act, drafted by Professor Samuel Williston, promulgated in 1906, and ultimately adopted by about two-thirds of the states.

Interest in reforming commercial law heightened by 1940 and the various uniform acts were no longer thought to be sufficient. Commercial law practices had changed, leaving the acts inadequate to resolve new issues. The failure of some states to enact some of the acts and non-uniform amendments adopted in various enacting jurisdictions undercut uniformity. In 1940 the ULC adopted a bold plan to prepare a single commercial code,[4] and in 1944 the American Law Institute agreed to co-sponsor the project. Professor Karl Llewellyn was appointed as the Chief Reporter and also served as the principle reporter for Article 2. The establishment of a Permanent Editorial Board (PEB) helped the sponsors oversee the project.

The first Official Text of the Code was promulgated in 1951. It consisted of nine Articles, including Article 2 on sales. Pennsylvania in 1953 became the first state to enact the Code, but further enactments bogged down when the legislature and governor in New York referred it to the New York Law Revision Commission. Based on recommendations of the Commission and other authorities, including an independent study undertaken by the PEB, the Code was revised in 1957 and then amended in 1958 and 1962. State enactments followed quickly after the promulgation of the 1962 Official Text and by 1968 all of the states[5] as well as Guam, the District of Columbia, and the U.S. Virgin Islands, had adopted the Code.

---

[2] "A usage of trade under [UCC § 1-303(c)] must have the 'regularity of observance' specified. The ancient English tests for 'custom' are abandoned in this connection. Therefore, it is not required that a usage of trade be 'ancient or immemorial,' 'universal,' or the like." UCC § 1-303, cmt. 4.

[3] UCC § 1-103(a)(2).

[4] Mr. William A. Schnader generally is recognized as having conceived of the project.

[5] Because of its civil law tradition, Louisiana initially enacted only some of the articles. It has still not adopted either Article 2 or Article 2A.

[B] Article 2A

The initial Code project understandably did not deal with leases of goods because leasing activity was relatively insignificant during the late 1940s and the 1950s. The modern leasing industry can be traced to the enactment of certain favorable tax provisions in the mid-1950s and for the first few decades of its existence the governing law consisted of scattered fragments of the ancient law of bailments, isolated statutory provisions, application of Article 2 and real property law by analogy, and the general law of contracts. By the 1980s leasing of business equipment had become a multi-billion dollar industry that was expanding rapidly, and a burgeoning consumer leasing industry had emerged as well. The need for a comprehensive and uniform body of law became increasingly apparent.

Following a 1980 study by the American Bar Association, the ULC undertook a drafting project that culminated in 1985 with the promulgation of the Uniform Personal Property Leasing Act. Based on the recommendation of the PEB, the ULC and the ALI decided that the new act should be incorporated into the UCC and the drafting committee revised it into Article 2A, which the sponsoring organizations approved in 1987.[6] The new article was the first expansion of the Code's subject matter since its original promulgation.

Unlike the drafters of other Code articles, the drafters of Article 2A did not have a predecessor statute on which to base their work. They decided, therefore, to draw on Articles 2 and 9 to the extent that their provisions were compatible with lease transactions,[7] but to deviate from the statutory analogues when necessary.[8] They used Article 2 as the primary analogue because of the similarity of many aspects of sales and lease transactions and the desire of the drafters to perpetuate the freedom-of-contract principle embodied in that article.[9] A committee of the California State Bar Association subjected the newly promulgated Article 2A to an intense review and issued a report that identified several areas that needed revision in order to reflect better the realities of lease transactions.[10] Reluctant to reopen debate, the drafters responded with explanatory changes to the Comments, but the California Bar

---

[6] A more extensive discussion of the initial development of Article 2A is provided in A. Boss, *The History of Article 2A: A Lesson for Practitioner and Scholar Alike*, 39 Ala. L. Rev. 575 (1988).

[7] For a discussion of the major policy decisions facing the drafters, including the decision to use statutory analogues, see W. Lawrence & J. Minan, *Resolved: That the Kansas and Other State Legislatures Should Enact Article 2A of the Uniform Commercial Code*, 39 U. Kan. L. Rev. 95 (1990).

[8] The differences are highlighted in W. Lawrence & J. Minan, *Deviations from the Statutory Analogues: The New U.C.C. Article 2A*, 40 U. Kan. L. Rev. 531 (1992).

[9] "This codification was greatly influenced by the fundamental tenet of the common law as it has developed with respect to leases of goods: freedom of the parties to contract." UCC § 2A-101, cmt. (relationship of Article 2A to Other Articles).

[10] Preliminary Draft Report of the Uniform Commercial Code Committee of the Business Law Section of the State Bar of California on Proposed California Commercial Code Division 10 (Article 2A) (May 18, 1987).

committee rejected this approach as inadequate.[11] California ultimately enacted a version of Article 2A with several non-uniform provisions.

Recognizing that a number of states were prepared to follow California's lead, the Code's sponsors relented and in 1990 adopted a set of amendments that reflected much of the California criticism, as well as suggestions made in other bar-association studies and in a report of the New York Law Revision Commission. Article 2A today is as broadly enacted as Article 2.

[C] 2003 Amendments to Articles 2 and 2A

The advance of time and the evolution of new business practices, including electronic contracting and the integration of goods and software, led the PEB, based on a thorough study report,[12] to recommend that Article 2 be revised, and in 1991 the Code's sponsors appointed a drafting committee to accomplish the task. As the Article 2 drafting process proceeded, a separate drafting committee was appointed to determine the extent to which Article 2A should be revised to reflect the changes to Article 2.

The story of the effort to revise Article 2 is long and complicated and must be told in detail elsewhere.[13] Suffice it to say that it became entangled with another Code initiative — an effort to produce a new Article 2B dealing with software licensing — that became controversial because of an inability to reach consensus on certain issues, including notably the appropriate treatment of products that combine goods and software and the extent to which terms first revealed by a licensor after receiving payment should be effective. Eventually the sponsors determined that the lack of consensus would prevent the uniform adoption of Article 2B and the ALI withdrew from that part of the revision process, after which the ULC in 1999 promulgated the freestanding Uniform Computer Information Transactions Act.[14] Also in 1999, the scope of the Article 2 drafting project was reduced to the production of a discrete set of amendments rather than a wholesale revision, and a reconstituted drafting committee was appointed to prepare the amendments and also to prepare conforming amendments as appropriate to Article 2A. Amended Articles 2 and 2A were promulgated in 2003 but immediately ran into difficulty in the states, primarily because of the failure of the drafters to find a consensus resolution to the same issues that had made the Article 2B project so controversial. As of the time of the publication of this book, no state has adopted the amendments, but efforts continue. Whether the amendments ultimately succeed through enactment, they represent a significant improvement in the law and studying them sheds light on some of the problems in the original articles.

---

[11] Report of the Uniform Commercial Code Committee of the Business Law Section of the State Bar of California on Proposed California Commercial Code Division 10 (Article 2A) (Dec. 18, 1987).

[12] PEB Study Group: Uniform Commercial Code Article 2 (Preliminary Report, Mar. 1, 1990).

[13] *See* W. Henning, *Amended Article 2: What Went Wrong?*, 11 Duq. Bus. L. J. 131 (2009).

[14] The act has been adopted in Maryland and Virginia.

§ 1.03   SCOPE OF ARTICLE 2 [§ 2-102]

[A]   Sales

[1]   Direct Application

Section 2-102 states that "[u]nless the context otherwise requires, this Article applies to transactions in goods." At first blush the range of applicable transactions appears to be very broad and might include leases, bailments, and even gifts. This appearance is deceiving for two reasons. First, the proviso that the context might preclude application of the article must always be considered. More importantly, the short title of Article 2 is "Uniform Commercial Code — Sales"[15] and the scope of the article is largely restricted to sales transactions through the pervasive use in the substantive provisions of the terms "contract for sale,"[16] "sale,"[17] "buyer,"[18] and "seller."[19] Provisions of Article 2 that use any of these sales-related terms may not be applied directly to nonsales transactions, although as explained below, they might be applicable by analogy.[20] The only Article 2 provision that refers directly to a transaction that is not a sale is Section 2-403 on entrustments.[21]

Not surprisingly, a few courts have ignored the limitations imposed by the Article 2 terminology and have held that other types of transactions are fully within the scope of the article. Most of these cases involved leases and were decided before the promulgation of Article 2A,[22] and even in that era a majority of courts recognized that direct application of Article 2 was largely limited to sales transactions.[23]

A sale "consists in the passing of title from the seller to the buyer for a price."[24] The signature feature of a sale is that the seller does not retain a

---

[15] UCC § 2-101.

[16] " 'Contract' for sale includes both a present sale of goods and a contract to sell goods at a future time." UCC § 2-106(1). The provision further states that "[i]n this Article unless the context otherwise requires 'contract' and 'agreement' are limited to those relating to the present or future sale of goods."

[17] "A 'sale' consists in the passing of title from the seller to the buyer for a price." UCC § 2-106(1).

[18] " 'Buyer' means a person who buys or contracts to buy goods." UCC § 2-103(1)(a).

[19] " 'Seller' means a person who sells or contracts to sell goods." UCC § 2-103(1)(d).

[20] *See* § 1.03[A][2] *infra.*

[21] Entrustments are discussed in § 10.01[B] *infra.*

[22] *See, e.g.*, Owens v. Patent Scaffolding Co., 354 N.Y.S.2d 778, 14 UCC Rep. Serv. 610 (Sup. Ct. 1974), *rev'd on other grounds*, 376 N.Y.S.2d 948, 18 UCC Rep. Serv. 699 (App. Div. 1975). For a case applying Article 2 directly to a transaction other than a lease, see *Wellmore Coal Co. v. Powell Const. Co., Inc.*, 600 F. Supp. 1042, 40 UCC Rep. Serv. 362 (W.D. Va. 1984) (construction of coal preparation plant and aerial tram refuse system).

[23] Pre-Article 2A cases denying direct applicability of Article 2 to contracts for the lease of goods include *W. R. Weaver Co. v. Burroughs Corp.*, 580 S.W.2d 76, 27 UCC Rep. Serv. 64 (Tex. Civ. App. 1979); *Bona v. Graefe*, 264 Md. 69, 285 A.2d 607, 10 UCC Rep. Serv. 47 (Md. Ct. App. 1972).

[24] UCC § 2-106(1). Although title is central to the concept of a sale, most of the provisions of Article 2 apply irrespective of its location. UCC § 2-401. Basing issues such as the allocation of risk

property interest in the goods once it completes its delivery obligations. This feature distinguishes sales from leases and other kinds of bailments, *i.e.*, transactions in which a person rightfully places goods in the possession of another person for a limited purpose such as repair, storage, or transport.[25] Gifts are not sales because, although title passes, donees do not pay a price.

Transfer of title also distinguishes sales from license transactions,[26] and courts have struggled to determine which category is appropriate for software transactions.[27] Software is typically copyrighted, and under federal copyright law the owner of a copyrighted work generally has the exclusive right to distribute copies of the work to the public.[28] Distribution by an unauthorized person generally constitutes an infringement; however, under the "first-sale" doctrine the owner's rights under copyright law "cease with respect to a particular copy . . . once [the owner] has parted with ownership of it," and the owner of the copy may "sell or otherwise dispose of the possession of that copy."[29] A software vendor may wish to prohibit a vendee from lawfully selling or otherwise distributing its copy,[30] but if the transaction in which the vendee acquired the copy is a sale, the first-sale doctrine exhausts the vendor's copyright protection with respect to the copy. The first-sale doctrine applies without regard to whether the copy constitutes goods,[31] and whether a transaction is a sale for purposes of copyright law is a federal, rather than an Article 2 question. However, if a court determines that a transaction constitutes a sale for purposes of copyright law and if the software constitutes goods, the conclusion that Article 2 governs the contract is almost inevitable.

To illustrate the sales/license dichotomy suppose that a vendee pays an electronics store for a copy of software on a CD, and then loads the copy onto a computer in its home or office. From the perspective of the vendee, the transaction seems like a sale — a lump-sum payment for unlimited use of the

---

of loss on the moment that title passes, as was done under Section 22 of the Uniform Sales Act, proved too complicated and uncertain and thus was largely abandoned as the relevant determinant in Article 2.

[25] *See* R. Brown, The Law of Personal Property § 10.1 (W. Raushenbush 3d ed. 1975).

[26] The Uniform Computer Information Transactions Act (UCITA) defines a license as "a contract that authorizes access to, or use, distribution, performance, modification, or reproduction of information or informational rights, but expressly limits the access or uses authorized or expressly grants fewer than all rights in the information, whether or not the licensee has title to a licensed copy." UCITA § 102(a)(41). UCITA has only been adopted in Maryland and Virginia, but its definition of license is consistent with the general usage of the term.

[27] On virtually identical facts, different conclusions were reached in *Adobe Systems, Inc. v. Stargate Software Inc.*, 216 F. Supp. 2d 1051, 48 UCC Rep. Serv. 2d 489 (N.D. Cal. 2002) (transfer of copies from Adobe to its distributor constituted license transaction) and *Softman Prods. Co., LLC v. Adobe Systems, Inc.*, 171 F. Supp. 2d 1075, 45 UCC Rep. Serv. 2d 945 (C.D. Cal. 2001) (transfer of copies from Adobe to its distributor constituted sales transaction).

[28] 17 U.S.C. § 106(3).

[29] 17 U.S.C. § 109(a).

[30] The terms "vendor" and "vendee" are used in order to avoid the terms "seller" and "buyer" on the one hand and "licensor" and "licensee" on the other.

[31] The copy might be embedded in a tangible medium such as a CD or it might be acquired by an Internet download. Whether a copy of software constitutes goods is discussed in § 1.03[B] *infra*.

copy — and many courts have so held.[32] The copyright owner, however, will argue for a license transaction in order to avoid the effect of the first-sale doctrine. Because the success of this argument precludes a transfer of copies from the owner to the electronics store in the form of a sale,[33] the contract between them will use terminology common to license agreements and provide that title to the copies remains in the owner. The copyright owner will have to convince the court that the vendee did not buy the copy but rather paid for the privilege of entering into a license agreement with the owner. To facilitate this argument the owner typically will require that the vendee click assent to the end-user license agreement (EULA) that pops up in a dialog box the first time the vendee runs the program. As a hedge against the risk that a court will hold that a sale has occurred and that the vendee has title to the copy, the EULA will contain a term that precludes the vendee from distributing the copy. Copyright protection may be enhanced by contract and even if distribution by the vendee does not constitute an infringement, the copyright owner can argue that it constitutes a breach of contract.[34]

Determining the law that governs the transaction in the preceding paragraph is complex. If it is a sales transaction and if the software constitutes goods, Article 2 governs. If it is a license transaction and the software is goods, it is a transaction in goods and potentially within the scope of Article 2, but the provisions of the article that use terms associated with sales can only be applied by analogy. If the software is not goods, the transaction is clearly outside the scope of Article 2 but the article's provisions might be applied by analogy.

[2]   Application by Analogy

The provisions of Article 2 may be applied by analogy to other types of transactions, whether they involve goods or not. Application by analogy is not a magic wand that simply dispenses with the scope limitations; rather, an appropriate basis for the analogy should be established before a court applies a provision by analogy.[35]

The kind of analysis commonly used by courts to establish a basis for applying a provision of Article 2 by analogy is illustrated by the decision in *Baker v. City of Seattle*,[36] in which the court refused to uphold a liability-disclaimer provision in a contract for the rental of a golf cart. The court held

---

[32] *See, e.g.*, Softman Prods. Co., LLC v. Adobe Systems, Inc., 171 F. Supp. 2d 1075, 45 UCC Rep. Serv. 2d 945 (C.D. Cal. 2001) (transfer of copies from Adobe to its distributor constituted sales transaction).

[33] A sale to the electronics store would invoke the first-sale doctrine and exhaust the copyright owners's protection under federal law.

[34] The same issues arise if the copyright owner uses a shrinkwrap license, meaning a written license placed inside the shrinkwrap packaging, or a browsewrap license, meaning a license accessible on the Internet but not requiring a clicked assent. The effectiveness of clickwrap, shrinkwrap, and browsewrap terms is discussed generally in § 2.05 *infra*.

[35] For an excellent discussion of argument by analogy with respect to the Code, see Murray, *Under the Spreading Analogy of Article 2 of the Uniform Commercial Code*, 39 Fordham L. Rev. 447 (1971).

[36] 79 Wash. 2d 198, 484 P.2d 405, 9 UCC Rep. Serv. 226 (1971).

that the lessor generally should be liable for an implied warranty of fitness,[37] that its attempt to disclaim the warranty was ineffective because it was not conspicuous as required by Section 2-316(2), and that its attempt to limit liability for personal injury to an individual caused by consumer goods was ineffective under Section 2-719(3). The court justified its application of the Article 2 provisions on the grounds that they reflected the public policy of the state with respect to attempts to avoid liability in consumer transactions.

In *Wivagg v. Duquesne Light Co.*[38] the jury found that a high-voltage surge caused a fire that damaged plaintiff's business but that the defendant public utility was not negligent. Because of the lack of negligence, the common-law of contracts did not provide protection for the plaintiffs, and thus they argued that Section 2-314's implied warranty of merchantability should apply.[39] The court agreed, basing its decision on the enterprise-liability policies that underlie the implied warranty. It emphasized that the utility had complete control of the electricity until it entered the building so that the plaintiffs were unable to protect themselves and that the utility was in a better position to absorb the loss.

A number of the cases applying Article 2 by analogy involve leases of goods, which are now governed by Article 2A. The aptness of the analogy is demonstrated by the fact that the drafters of Article 2A used Article 2 as the primary statutory analog. The analogy may be more or less persuasive depending on the type of transaction and the issue. *Hoffman v. Horton*[40] involved an auction sale of real estate and posed the issue of whether the auctioneer properly reopened the bidding after being informed that he had missed a bid before dropping the hammer. The court applied Section 2-326(2), which gives auctioneers discretion in such situations, by analogy. Although the court did not make the point directly, sales of real estate in the circumstances of the facts of the case are similar to sales of goods in that both categories involve the passage of title to an asset for a price, and auctions of real estate are similar to auctions of goods. The court in *I.Lan Systems, Inc. v. Netscout Service Level Corp.*[41] held that Article 2 by its terms did not apply directly to a license of computer software, but nevertheless in an unusually candid admission assumed that it applied given the lack of other viable law. The court noted that the law relating to software licenses is in flux and determined that, pending further developments, Article 2 was a better fit for the parties' expectations than the common law. Because the issues before the court with respect to software licensing often concern warranties, disclaimers, and limitations of remedies, the parties certainly can develop analogies to support the application of the Article 2 provisions on these topics.

---

[37] Although the court referred to a warranty of fitness, the facts indicate that an implied warranty of merchantability would have been the more precise Article 2 analogy. The implied warranties are discussed in § 5.02[B] (merchantability) and [C] (fitness) *infra.*

[38] 73 Pa. D. & C. 2d 694, 20 UCC Rep. Serv. 597 (1975).

[39] Merchantability is a strict-liability standard. *See* § 5.02[B][2] *infra.*

[40] 212 Va. 565, 186 S.E.2d 79, 10 UCC Rep. Serv. 338 (1972).

[41] 183 F. Supp. 2d 328, 46 UCC Rep. Serv. 2d 287 (D. Mass. 2002).

In contrast with *Hoffman* and *I.Lan*, the court in *Zapatha v. Dairy Mart, Inc.*[42] went out its way to emphasize the dissimilarity of the franchise agreement at issue from an ordinary sales contract. The franchisee in the case argued that the franchisor's termination of the agreement was unconscionable and in bad faith under the provisions of Article 2. The court noted that even though the franchisor sold some goods to the franchisee, the franchisee bought seventy percent of its goods from other sellers and the franchisor derived its profits from the franchise fee rather than the sale of goods. Nevertheless, the court stated as follows:

> We view the legislative statements of policy concerning good faith and unconscionability as fairly applicable to all aspects of the franchise agreement, not by subjecting the franchise relationship to the provisions of the sales article but rather by applying the stated principles by analogy. This basic common law approach, applied to statutory statements of policy, permits a selective application of those principles expressed in a statute that reasonably should govern situations to which the statute does not apply explicitly.[43]

Having imported the Article 2 concepts into the transaction, the court held that the franchisor had not acted unconscionably or in bad faith, and it reversed the trial court's judgment in favor of the franchisee.

[B]   Goods

However broadly or narrowly the courts choose to construe the Article 2 scope provision, the transaction must involve goods. Because of the key role played by goods, the definition of the term is set out in full:

> "Goods" means all things (including specially manufactured goods) which are moveable at the time of identification to the contract for sale other than money in which the price is to be paid, investment securities (Article 8) and things in action. "Goods" also includes the unborn young of animals and growing crops and other identified things attached to realty as described in the section on goods to be severed from realty (Section 2-107).[44]

Goods consist of tangible, moveable property whose value is determined by their physical properties and performance characteristics. Real property is immoveable and therefore excluded except as provided by Section 2-107.[45] Purely intangible personal property, such as contract and intellectual property rights, is excluded, as is money when it is used as a medium of exchange. However, money bought as a commodity constitutes goods.[46]

---

[42] 381 Mass. 284, 408 N.E.2d 1370, 29 UCC Rep. Serv. 1121 (1980).

[43] 381 Mass. at 290 (citation omitted).

[44] UCC § 2-105(1).

[45] The discussion at the end of this subsection explains Section 2-107.

[46] *See, e.g.*, Jalali v. M.G. Eagle Entertainment Corp., 52 UCC Rep. Serv. 2d 373 (Cal. Ct. App. 2003) (unpublished). The drafters of amended Article 2 took the position that a transaction in which dollars are physically exchanged for another currency is within the scope of Article 2, but Article 4A

Certain types of personal property consist of intangible rights that have been "reified" in the form of indispensable paper, meaning that the rights have been embedded in a writing and are customarily transferred by delivery of the writing to the transferee.[47] Examples include negotiable instruments, negotiable documents, and certificated securities (*e.g.*, stock certificates). Indispensable paper is tangible and moveable, but its value is determined not by its physical properties — it is just paper — but by the rights it embodies. A negotiable instrument such as a check or promissory note has value because of the obligation to pay money that it evidences.[48] A stock certificate has value because of the equity interest in an organization that it represents.[49] A negotiable document such as a bill of lading or warehouse receipt represents title to goods and its value is based on the value of those goods.[50]

An issue that has divided courts and legal experts in recent years is whether a physical medium like a CD that contains information in electronic form constitutes goods. The CD might contain a computer program (*i.e.*, software)[51] or it might contain other informational content such as music or a video, game, book, or database.[52] The drafters of the Uniform Computer Information Transactions Act concluded that a tangible medium that does nothing more than contain electronic information should be treated as part of the information and not as goods.[53] By contrast, Article 9 treats a computer program on a CD as software but treats the CD itself as goods.[54] The courts generally have held that "off-the-shelf" software, meaning software generally available to the public in a tangible medium as opposed to customized software created or adapted for the needs of a particular user, constitutes goods.[55] Some courts have concluded that

---

or other law applies to an exchange made by wire transfer or another means of transferring a credit balance. Amended UCC §§ 2-103(1)(i) (defining "foreign exchange transaction"), 2-103(1)(k) (excluding subject matter of foreign exchange transactions from definition of goods).

[47] The rights might be embedded today in an electronic record. Electronic contracting is discussed generally in § 2.06 *infra.*

[48] UCC Article 3 governs negotiable instruments.

[49] UCC Article 8 governs stock certificates and other securities.

[50] UCC Article 7 governs negotiable documents, but subject to significant federal preemption.

[51] A computer program consists of electronic statements or instructions that are used by a computer to produce a particular result. *See* UCITA § 102(a)(12) (defining "computer program"); ALI Principles of the Law of Software Contracts § 1.01(j) (Council Draft No. 3, Nov. 7, 2008) (defining "software"). UCC Article 9 uses the term "software" to refer to a computer program that is treated as an intangible asset. UCC §§ 9-102(a)(75) (defining "software"), 9-102(a)(42) (defining software as a subset of "general intangibles"). Article 9 contains a test to determine whether a computer program embedded in goods is part of the goods or is software. *See* UCC § 9-102(a)(44) (defining "goods").

[52] UCITA uses the term "informational content" to refer to electronic information that is intended to be communicated to or perceived by an individual [UCITA § 102(a)(37)], whereas the ALI Principles of Software Contracts use the term "digital content" and divide the category into "digital art" and a "digital database." ALI Principles n.53, § 1.01(f).

[53] UCITA refers to the medium that contains the information as a "copy," UCITA § 102(a)(20), and copies are part of "computer information." UCITA § 102(a)(10). The definition of goods in turn excludes computer information. UCITA § 102(a)(33).

[54] UCC § 9-102(a)(44).

[55] *See, e.g,* Olcott Int'l & Co. v. Micro Base Data Systems, Inc., 793 N.E.2d 1063, 51 UCC Rep.

a contract to develop custom software is a contract for services rather than a contract for goods,[56] but that conclusion does not determine whether a CD in which the program is embedded is goods.

The reference in the definition of goods to the time of identification to the contract for sale means the time when the buyer receives a special property and an insurable interest in the goods under Section 2-501(1).[57] Identification occurs at the earliest point in time at which the specific goods that the seller will tender to the buyer are so designated. If the buyer selects the specific goods at the time of contract formation, identification occurs then.[58] For example, if a buyer decides to buy a specific car from a dealer's lot, identification occurs when the parties enter into a contract. By contrast, the parties might contract for a quantity of standard catalog items that the seller keeps in inventory, in which case identification occurs when the seller ships them, marks them, or otherwise designates them as the goods to which the contract refers.[59]

Land cannot constitute goods because it is never moveable; however, an issue sometimes arises when an asset that is attached to land is the subject matter of a contract for sale. In the case of minerals or the like (including oil and gas) or of a structure or its materials (*e.g.*, a house or the bricks incorporated into it), the contract is for the sale of goods if the asset is to be severed by the seller, but not if it is to be severed by the buyer.[60] In the case of crops or an asset attached to land that is not a structure, meaning essentially a fixture, the contract is for the sale of goods without regard to which party will sever the asset.[61] A court occasionally has had to decide whether an asset is a structure or a fixture. For example, the parties in *Condon Brothers, Inc. v. Simpson Timber Co.*[62] entered into a contract for the sale of a five-mile stretch of rail line affixed to land and to be severed by the buyer. The court concluded that the asset was a structure and

---

Serv. 2d 352 (Ind. Ct. App. 2003) (contract for pre-existing, standardized software modules).

[56] The courts sometimes distinguish between transactions to develop custom software from scratch and transactions to customize existing software, with the former more likely to be classified as services contracts and the latter more likely to be classified as goods contracts. For cases involving software developed from scratch, see, e.g., *Pearl Investments, LLC v. Standard I/O, Inc.*, 257 F. Supp. 2d 326, 50 UCC Rep. Serv. 2d 377 (D. Maine 2003) (services contract); *Waterfront Properties, Inc. v. Xerox Connect, Inc.*, 58 UCC Rep. Serv. 2d 809 (W.D.N.C. 2006) (services contract). For cases involving customization of existing custom, see, e.g., *Micro Data Base Systems, Inc. v. Dharma Systems, Inc.*, 148 F.3d 648, 35 UCC Rep. Serv. 2d 747 (7th Cir. 1998) (goods contract); *Dealer Management Systems v. Design Automotive Group, Inc.*, 355 Ill. App. 3d 416, 290 Ill. Dec. 971, 822 N.E.2d 556, 55 UCC Rep. Serv. 2d 965 (2003) (goods contract). Intellectual property rights to software are not goods. *Architectronics, Inc. v. Control Systems, Inc.*, 935 F. Supp. 425, 33 UCC Rep. Serv. 2d 714 (S.D.N.Y. 1996).

[57] Goods must be both existing and identified before a property interest can pass from the seller to the buyer. UCC § 2-105(2). Goods that are not both existing and identified are "future" goods. *Id.*

[58] UCC § 2-501(1)(a).

[59] UCC § 2-501(1)(b). Special identification rules also apply to crops and the unborn young of animals. UCC § 2-501(1)(c).

[60] UCC § 2-107(1). Although not moveable at the time of identification to the contract for sale, minerals or a structure to be severed by the seller are within the definition of goods by virtue of the cross reference in the definition to the rules of Section 2-107.

[61] UCC § 2-107(2).

[62] 92 Wash. App. 275, 966 P.2d 355, 37 UCC Rep. Serv. 2d 547 (1998).

therefore the contract was not for the sale of goods. Had it concluded that the asset was a fixture, the contract would have been governed by Article 2.

[C]   Hybrid Transactions

Perhaps the most difficult issue related to the scope of Article 2 concerns the extent to which the article applies to hybrid transactions. These transactions involve sales of goods but they also include another contract category, such as the provision of services, the sale or lease of real property, or the sale or licensing of intellectual property. Faced with a hybrid transaction, a court might apply Article 2 in its entirety, apply the law applicable to the non-goods part of the transaction in its entirety, or bifurcate the transaction by applying Article 2 to the goods and other law to the non-goods parts.

Courts applying either Article 2 or other law in its entirety generally decide based on a "predominant-purpose" test; in other words, the court applies Article 2 if the goods aspect of the transaction predominates and other law if the non-goods aspect predominates. Courts that bifurcate the transaction use a "gravamen-of-the-action" test, applying both Article 2 and other law depending on the extent that the gravamen of the action relates to goods or to other aspects of the contract. The ease of applying the all-or-nothing approach of the predominant purpose test gives it a significant advantage. The gravamen-of-the-action test is ill-suited to resolve issues that affect the contract as a whole, such as contract formation, the statute of frauds, the parol evidence rule, and the statute of limitations. It may work better when applied to discreet performance-related issues, such as whether a merchant seller is bound by the strict-liability standard of Article 2's implied warranty of merchantability or is liable only if it performed in a negligent manner as provided in the common law, but even then common-law and Code issues may become intertwined. The overwhelming majority of courts apply the predominant-purpose test.

The case cited most often for the predominant-purpose test is *Bonebrake v. Cox*,[63] in which the court held that Article 2 applied to the entire contract for the sale of used bowling-alley equipment and lane beds, even though the contract also involved substantial labor to install the goods.[64] By contrast, the court in *Cork Plumbing Co. v. Martin Bloom Associates, Inc.*[65] applied only the common law to the contract, holding that the goods supplied were only an incidental part of a plumbing-construction contract that required the contractor to assemble and connect different plumbing materials into a completed system.[66]

---

[63] 499 F.2d 951, 14 UCC Rep. Serv. 1318 (8th Cir. 1974).

[64] *See also* Neibarger v. Universal Cooperatives, Inc., 439 Mich. 512, 486 N.W.2d 612, 18 UCC Rep. Serv. 2d 729 (1992) (installation and servicing obligations held to be incidental to the sale of automatic milking system).

[65] 573 S.W.2d 947, 25 UCC Rep. Serv. 1245 (Mo. Ct. App. 1978).

[66] *See also* Geotech Energy Corp. v. Gulf States Telecommunications & Information Systems, Inc., 788 S.W.2d 386, 12 UCC Rep. Serv. 2d 41 (Tex. Ct. App. 1990) (installation of telephone system and creation of software to customize it predominated).

Many courts applying the predominant-purpose test have focused on the percentage of the total contract price allocable to the purchase of the goods.[67] Other courts have held that the predominant purpose must be gleaned from a consideration of factors in addition to an allocation of costs.[68] The court in *Insul-Mark Midwest v. Modern Materials, Inc.*[69] described the latter approach as follows:

> To determine whether the predominant thrust of a mixed contract is to provide services or goods, one looks first to the language of the contract, in light of the situation of the parties and the surrounding circumstances. Specifically one looks to the terms describing the performance of the parties, and the words used to describe the relationship between the parties.
>
> Beyond the contractual terms themselves, one looks to the circumstances of the parties, and the primary reason they entered into the contract. One also considers the final product the purchaser bargained to receive, and whether it may be described as a good or a service.
>
> Finally, one examines the costs involved for the goods and services, and whether the purchaser was charged only for a good, or a price based on goods and services. If the cost of the goods is but a small portion of the overall contract price, such fact would increase the likelihood that the services portion predominates.[70]

The plaintiff's affiliate in *Insul-Mark* sent roofing fasteners to the defendant for the application of a fluorocarbon coating warranted to increase the rust resistance of the fasteners' screws, and the litigation stemmed from the alleged failure of the coating to meet the appropriate standard. Rather than using language of sale, the contract referred to a "process" by which a layer of wax would be stripped away and a coating of defendant's product applied. Moreover, the contract based the price on the number of pounds of screws coated, not on the cost of the coating material. Not surprisingly, the court held that Article 2 did not apply.

How thin the line can be between a goods contract and a services contract can be illustrated by *National Historic Shrines v. Dali*,[71] a case in which the famous surrealist painter Salvador Dali agreed to appear on a televised program and raise funds for the plaintiff by painting a picture of the Statue of Liberty. When he backed out and the plaintiff sued claiming that the painting would have been

---

[67] *See, e.g.*, Baker v. Compton, 455 N.E.2d 382, 38 UCC Rep. Serv. 10 (Ind. Ct. App. 1983) (predominant purpose measured in part by relationship of cost of the goods to the total contract price); Monetti, S.P.A. v. Anchor Hocking Corp., 931 F.2d 1178, 14 UCC Rep. Serv. 2d 706 (7th Cir. 1991) (contemplated sales volume outweighed intangibles sold in exclusive distributorship agreement).

[68] *See, e.g.*, Urban Indus. of Ohio, Inc. v. Tectum, Inc., 81 Ohio App. 3d 768, 612 N.E.2d 382, 20 UCC Rep. Serv. 2d 1193 (1992); Standard Structural Steel Co. v. Debron Corp., 515 F. Supp. 803, 32 UCC Rep. Serv. 393 (D. Conn. 1980).

[69] 612 N.E.2d 550, 21 UCC Rep. Serv. 2d 219 (Ind. 1993).

[70] 612 N.E.2d, 555.

[71] 4 UCC Rep. Serv. 71 (N.Y. Sup. Ct. 1967).

worth $25,000, Dali raised the Article 2 statute of frauds as a defense. Denying Dali's motion for summary judgment, the court indicated that the transaction was predominantly for services and thus Article 2 did not apply. Had Dali simply promised to sell a completed painting at a low price so that the plaintiff could resell it to raise money, the transaction undoubtedly would have been governed by Article 2. The court would have faced a harder issue if the plaintiff had commissioned the painting at a low price and Dali was to complete it off-camera and deliver it in time for the television program. In that case the court might have applied Article 2 by determining that the painting constituted specially manufactured goods and the service aspect did not predominate, or it might have decided that having the services of a famous painter predominated. Dali's agreement to appear on camera, thereby attracting viewers, differentiated the actual case from the hypothetical situations posited above.

The case most often cited for the gravemen-of-the-action test is *Anthony Pools v. Sheehan*,[72] a case in which the defendant designed and installed a swimming pool and a diving board from which the plaintiff slipped and fell, injuring himself. The court determined that an Article 2 implied warranty of merchantability covered the diving board even though the contract, viewed as a whole, no doubt was predominantly for services.

The decision in *TK Power, Inc. v. Textron, Inc.*[73] provides an interesting amalgamation of the predominant-purpose and gravamen-of-the-action tests. The contract in the case called for the plaintiff to develop and produce high-speed on-board battery chargers for electric golf carts. The first stage of the contract called in part for the development of a software code to operate the microprocessor installed in the battery and the production of five prototypes for testing and evaluation. The contract allocated $39,000 to developing proprietary software codes and $20,000 to producing the prototypes. The second stage of the contract called for the plaintiff to produce and sell roughly 75,000 units per year. The project ran into trouble at the development stage and the defendant sought to cancel under rights provided in Article 2.[74] The court divided the contract into its stages and, using the predominant purpose test, applied the common law to the first stage. Although not called upon to decide the matter, the court indicated that Article 2 would govern the second stage.

The law is in its nascent development with respect to hybrid transactions in which the subject matter of the contract is a product that combines goods and one or more computer programs. The Uniform Computer Information Transactions Act (UCITA) generally takes a gravamen-of-the-action approach with respect to contracts that combine computer information and a subject matter other than goods. In the case of goods UCITA often defers entirely to Articles 2 and 2A The basic idea is that computer programs that operate as ordinary parts of standard goods, such as the anti-lock brake system of a car or a chip that regulates the settings of a microwave oven, are part of the goods for all purposes and UCITA is irrelevant. By contrast, UCITA reverts to the general approach

---

[72] 295 Md. 285, 455 A.2d 434, 35 UCC Rep. Serv. 408 (1983).

[73] 433 F. Supp. 2d 1058 (N.D. Cal. 2006).

[74] *See* UCC § 2-601; § 7.04[A] *infra*.

of the gravamen of the action if the program runs on a computer or computer peripheral or if gaining access to or use of the program is a material part of ordinary transactions in goods of the type, as with a diagnostic program used in connection with an MRI machine.[75]

The American Law Institute Principles of Software Contracting reject the latter UCITA test (computer program a material part of ordinary transactions) as too vague[76] and apply the predominant-purpose test when software is "embedded" in goods.[77] The Comments explain that "[e]mbedded software is built or integrated into goods so that the user cannot easily separate the software from the goods. In addition, the user cannot easily replace embedded software without the aid of a technician."[78] As a general rule Article 2 or 2A will govern entirely, but the Principles will govern entirely if "a reasonable transferor would believe the transferee's predominant purpose for engaging in the transfer is to obtain the software."[79]

The law in this area obviously is enormously complex and the courts will struggle with it for some time to come. The drafters of amended Article 2 attempted to craft an appropriate test, but ultimately failed to reach consensus and simply revised the definition of goods to exclude information and drafted a Comment that they hoped will be helpful to the courts.[80] The failure to reach consensus on this issue is the single most important reason for the inability of the amendments to gain traction in the state legislatures.

§ 1.04   SCOPE OF ARTICLE 2A [§ 2A-102]

[A]   Lease Defined [§ 2A-103(1)(j)]

Article 2A establishes scope much more directly than Article 2 does. Section 2A-102 simply states that the article "applies to any transaction, regardless of form, that creates a lease," and a lease is defined as "a transfer of the right to possession and use of goods for a term in return for consideration, but a sale or retention of a security interest is not a lease."[81] Thus, Article 2A applies only to leases of goods, although the range of such transactions extends from the rental of a tool or a punch bowl for a few hours to a sophisticated lease of industrial

---

[75] UCITA § 103(b)(1).

[76] ALI Principles of the Law of Software Contracts § 1.07, Reporter's Notes, cmt. b (Council Draft No. 3, Nov. 7, 2008).

[77] UCITA uses "computer program" and the ALI Principles use "software." The terms mean essentially the same thing.

[78] ALI Principles of the Law of Software Contracts § 1.07, cmt. (Council Draft No. 3, Nov. 7, 2008).

[79] ALI Principles of the Law of Software Contracts § 1.07(a) (Council Draft No. 3, Nov. 7, 2008). The Principles also deal with mixed transfers involving non-embedded software and any combination of goods, digital content other than software (e.g., music, a game, a multimedia program built into a cell phone), and services. Principles § 1.08(b).

[80] *See* discussion § 1.06 *infra.*

[81] UCC § 2A-103(1)(j).

equipment for a number of years.[82]

[1] Distinguishing Sales

A sale is easy to distinguish from a lease. A sale transfers title to the goods from the seller to the buyer.[83] The seller does not retain a property interest in the goods, and if a buyer accepts the goods but does not make payment the seller may recover the contract price but generally may not recover the goods themselves.[84] The seller in effect has traded the goods for a promise and may do no more than enforce the promise. By contrast, a lessee acquires only the right to the use and enjoyment of the goods for the duration of the lease term. Title does not pass; rather, the lessor retains it in the form of a residual interest in the goods which reverts to the lessor when the lease term expires or the lessor justifiably cancels the lease because of a default by the lessee.[85]

[2] Distinguishing Secured Transactions [§ 1-201(37)]

The essential characteristics of secured transactions and leases are also easy to distinguish. A credit seller that retains a security interest in goods delivered to a buyer passes title to the goods. The retained security interest gives the seller the right to repossess the goods in the event of default by the buyer.[86] Upon repossession the seller/secured party must dispose of the goods and apply the proceeds to the outstanding indebtedness.[87] Any surplus proceeds belong to the buyer/debtor.[88] A lessor also retains an interest in goods it delivers to the lessee. Like a secured party, a lessor can repossess the goods following a default.[89] Unlike the secured party, however, the lessor does not have to dispose of the goods following repossession or to pay over to the lessee any of the proceeds from a disposition of the lessor's choosing.[90] The lessor owns the residual interest.

Distinguishing leases and secured transactions in actual practice has proven to be difficult and has led to some of the most pervasive litigation under the

---

[82] UCC § 2A-102, cmt.

[83] UCC § 2-106(1). "Unless otherwise explicitly agreed title passes to the buyer at the time and place at which the seller completes his performance with reference to the physical delivery of the goods." UCC § 2-401(2).

[84] Although a seller does not retain a property interest in goods after delivering them to a buyer, two narrow circumstances permit the seller to reclaim them from the buyer: 1) if a check given in payment is dishonored; and 2) if a credit buyer is insolvent when it receives the goods. UCC §§ 2-507(2), 2-511(3) (dishonored check), 2-702(2) (insolvent credit buyer). *See* discussion § 9.08[C] *infra.*

[85] UCC § 2A-103(1)(q) ("lessor's residual interest" defined).

[86] UCC § 9-609(a).

[87] UCC §§ 9-610(a); 9-615(a).

[88] UCC § 9-615(d)(1).

[89] UCC § 2A-525(2).

[90] UCC § 2A-527.

Code.[91] The similarity of some of the attributes of the transactions contributes to the problem. An even more significant factor is that, for a variety of reasons related to taxes, accounting, or bankruptcy, parties sometimes disguise a secured transaction by calling it a lease. For example, suppose that a dealer delivers a piece of equipment to a user pursuant to a written contract binding the user to make twenty-four equal monthly payments of $1,000 each. The writing, which refers to the transaction as a "lease," the installments as "lease payments," and the parties as "lessor" and "lessee," provides that the user will have the option to purchase the equipment for $10 at the end of the "lease term" even though the parties anticipate that it will have significantly more value at that time. Because any rational economic actor will exercise the option and become the owner, the transaction is the economic equivalent of a sale. Further, the "lessor's" right to repossess the "leased property" in the event of default operates as a security device. The Code directs the courts to look through the parties' terminology and sweeps the security aspects of the transaction into Article 9.[92] This means that the "lessor" will have to follow Article 9's disposition rules after repossession and will have to perfect its interest under Article 9 (usually by a public filing[93]) to obtain priority against third parties that might acquire a competing interest in the goods.[94]

Inadequate legal standards have played a significant role in blurring the boundaries. The original definition of "security interest" included a sentence directed toward distinguishing leases and secured transactions which proved woefully inadequate.[95] The revised test is extremely long and complex,[96] but it does provide an effective standard based on functional considerations. Rather than continuing the original test's unworkable central standard relying on the parties' intent, the current test focuses on the economics of the transaction. The basic economic reality of a lease is that the lessor has retained a meaningful residual interest. The test thus focuses on determining whether the terms of the transaction actually compensate the purported lessor for the residual interest, as well as for the use of the goods during the lease term.

The new guidelines include a two-part test for distinguish a security interest from a lease.[97] A transaction creates a security interest if (1) the lessee does not have a right to terminate the lease before its stated expiration date, and (2) any one of several enumerated factors is present. If the lessee has a right to

---

[91] See the extensive case law citations in W. Lawrence & J. Minan, The Law of Personal Property Leasing 2-6 to 2-21 (1993).

[92] UCC § 9-109(a)(1).

[93] Article 9 provides that a lessor, concerned that a court might conclude that a transaction called a lease in fact creates a disguised security interest, may make a protective filing, using the terms "lessor" and "lessee" instead of "secured party" and "debtor." UCC § 9-505(a). Such a filing, standing alone, is not an admission that the transaction is not a true lease. UCC § 9-505(b).

[94] With one optional provision for leased goods that become fixtures, UCC § 2A-309, a true lessor need not consider making a public filing to protect its residual interest. UCC § 2A-301.

[95] UCC § 1-201(37) (1962 Official Text). For a critique of the inadequacies of the original definition, see W. Lawrence & J. Minan, The Law of Personal Property Leasing 2-15 to 2-21 (1993).

[96] See UCC § 1-203 (lease distinguished from security interest).

[97] UCC § 1-203(b).

terminate the lease, the lessor retains a meaningful residual interest unless the right cannot be exercised until the lessor has been fully compensated for the economic value of the goods. The right to terminate unilaterally with no further financial obligations makes the transaction a true lease.

Assuming no right of termination, a transaction creates a security interest as a matter of law if any of the enumerated factors is present. One of these factors is that the original term of the lease equals or exceeds the remaining economic life of the goods.[98] The economic reality of such a transaction is that the purported lessor has not retained a meaningful residual interest in the goods but rather has sold the goods and retained a security interest in them against the outstanding obligation. The practical effect is precisely the same if a lessee that cannot terminate the lease is bound to renew it to the end of the economic life of the goods, or is bound to become the owner of the goods. The lessee is contractually obligated to pay for the remaining economic life of the goods, leaving no meaningful residual in the lessor.

The remaining factors address the role of options. They cover the circumstances in which a lessee, upon compliance with the terms of the lease, has the option to become the owner of the goods or to renew the lease for the remaining economic life of the goods. If the lessee can exercise either option for no additional consideration or for only nominal consideration,[99] the transaction is not a true lease but is rather a security interest. The purported rental payments in such a transaction obviously compensate the lessor not only for the lessee's use of the goods during the lease term but also for the residual value that remains in the goods following the lease term. Despite the labels applied by the parties to the transaction, the economic reality is that a lessor willing to allow a lessee to retain the goods for nominal or even no additional consideration has not retained a meaningful residual interest. Conversely, a lessor has retained the requisite interest for a true lease if the lessee must pay more than nominal additional consideration in order to exercise an option to purchase the goods or to renew the lease until the end of the economic life of the goods.

[B]   Finance Leases [§ 2A-103(1)(g)]

The lessor serves a unique role in "finance leases," a special category of lease under Article 2A. Unlike an ordinary lessor that leases goods from its inventory, a finance lessor facilitates a lessee's acquisition of goods by buying or leasing them from a supplier and then leasing or subleasing them to the lessee. The lessor is comparable to a bank that provides purchase-money financing to a person that buys goods on credit. The bank takes a security interest in the goods as collateral for the buyer's repayment obligation; the lessor retains a residual interest in the leased goods. Because finance leases involve a tripartite

---

[98] The remaining economic life of the goods must be determined based on the facts and circumstances that exist at the time the transaction is entered into. UCC § 1-203(e).

[99] The guidelines do not define nominal consideration. They provide "safe-harbor" rules that provide clear circumstances in section 1-203(d), but the courts have been left to resolve a significant grey area without much guidance. The various components of the test (reasonably predictable cost of performing, fair market rent or price) are to be determined based on the facts and circumstances that exist at the time that the parties enter the transaction. UCC § 1-203(e).

relationship among the supplier, the lessor, and the lessee, they do not fit the statutory analogue of Article 2, and thus the drafters created the special category.

To qualify as a finance lease, a transaction must be a true lease rather than a security interest[100] and must also satisfy three requirements.[101] First, the lessor may not participate in selecting, manufacturing, or supplying the goods; rather, its function is to facilitate the lessee's acquisition of the goods from the supplier.[102] Consequently, the lessee selects the desired goods and the lessor then enters into a supply contract with the supplier and a lease agreement with the lessee.[103] The supplier often delivers the goods directly to the lessee.

Isolating the finance lessor from direct participation in selecting or supplying the goods requires the lessee to look directly to the supplier, or perhaps to the manufacturer or the obligor on a third-party service contract, for recourse if the lessee experiences problems with the goods. Just as a financing bank is not responsible for the quality of goods bought with the proceeds of a loan, Article 2A relieves a finance lessor of such responsibility except in the unlikely event that the lessor chooses to make an express warranty of quality to the lessee.[104]

The second requirement for a finance lease is that the finance lessor's acquisition of the goods must be "in connection with the lease."[105] The lessor thus cannot acquire goods from a supplier and then later decide to lease them. The requirement further restricts the lessor to its role as financier. The limitation has one unfortunate effect: A re-lease of the goods by the finance lessor after the original lease has ended will not qualify as a finance lease.

The final requirement for a finance lease is that one of four stated methods must be used to give the lessee advance notification of applicable warranties and promises of the supplier or a third party.[106] A finance lessee that is dissatisfied with the goods must look to the supplier or third party and the requirement ensures that finance lessees are apprised of the obligations of these parties. The requirement is logical because the supplier's contract is with the lessor and the lessee might not otherwise be adequately informed of its rights.

Article 2A includes other provisions necessary to facilitate a finance lease. Because the lessee will not be in privity of contract with the supplier, an appropriate mechanism must cause the supplier's obligations with regard to the quality of the goods to flow to the lessee. Article 2A accomplishes this objective

---

[100] *See* § 1.04[A][2] *supra.*

[101] UCC § 2A-103(1)(g).

[102] "'Supplier' means a person from whom a lessor buys or leases goods to be leased under a finance lease." UCC § 2A-103(1)(x).

[103] "'Supply contract' means a contract under which a lessor buys or leases goods to be leased." UCC § 2A-103(1)(y).

[104] UCC § 2A-103, cmt. (g).

[105] UCC § 2A-103(1)(g)(ii).

[106] UCC § 2A-103(g)(iii). The methods are not equally revealing, and the least revealing method is not available if the finance lease is a consumer lease. UCC § 2A-103(g)(iii)(D).

through a provision that makes the lessee the beneficiary of any warranties and promises that the supply contract extends to the finance lessor.[107]

Except in a consumer lease,[108] a finance lessee loses something in exchange for the benefit of becoming a beneficiary of third-party warranties and promises: The lessee's promises under the lease contract "become irrevocable and independent upon the lessee's acceptance of the goods."[109] This provision deprives the lessee of any right to set off rents due under the lease for nonconforming goods or to claim excuse from the obligation to pay rent by justifiably revoking its acceptance against the supplier. It has the effect of an express "hell or high water" clause,[110] which makes the party against whom it operates irrevocably committed to perform its obligations. The approach again reflects the role of financing banks that can demand repayment of their secured loans even if the goods bought with the loan proceeds fail to perform as warranted. Once the finance lessee accepts the goods, any complaints about quality are between it and the supplier.

[C]   Consumer Leases [§ 2A-103(1)(e)]

Most of the drafting of Article 2 occurred in the late 1940s, long before the consumer-protection movement that first developed during the 1960s. Consequently, it is not surprising that Article 2 contains very few provisions that could be characterized as consumer-oriented.

Even though consumer protection was a much greater concern during the promulgation of Article 2A, the drafters faced a major policy decision. They ultimately decided to adhere for the most part to the Article 2 statutory analogue but to add a sprinkling of consumer-protection provisions. They chose not to make wholesale additions because of political implications. State legislatures have always been free to enact any consumer-protection measures they consider appropriate and, while some states have enacted extensive protections,[111] others have declined to do so. The drafters were concerned that the addition of too many consumer-protection provisions would create problems integrating the provisions of Article 2A with the more general consumer protections of state law, and they also feared legislative rejection in jurisdictions that had not previously adopted comparable consumer-protection measures.[112]

---

[107] UCC § 2A-209(1). In addition to giving the finance lessee a direct cause of action against the supplier, the provision extends to the finance lessee the benefit of any rights the finance lessor might have against a third party, such as a remote manufacturer or an obligor under a service contract, with which the finance lessee is not in privity. UCC § 2A-103(1)(x).

[108] See § 1.04[C] infra.

[109] UCC § 2A-407(1).

[110] The clause is so called because of its initial use in ship-charter contracts.

[111] See California Song-Beverly Consumer Warranty Act, Cal. Civ. Code §§ 1790–1795.8; Ann. Cal. Codes, Civil §§ 1790–1795.8 (1985 & Supp. 1992); Kansas Consumer Protection Act, Kan. Stat. Ann. §§ 50-623 to 50-644 (1983 & Supp. 1991). Eleven states have enacted all or part of the Uniform Consumer Credit Code (UCCC), which includes several provisions of consumer protection. UCCC (revised Official Text with Comments), 7A ULA 1 (1974).

[112] See F. Miller, Consumer Leases Under Uniform Commercial Code Article 2A, 39 Ala. L. Rev. 957, 962 (1988). The fear seems to have been justified. In 2001, the Uniform Law Commission

Except for a few modest measures, the article leaves the policy choice of the extent of consumer protection to the discretion of each state.

Article 2A includes a definition of "consumer lease" that draws heavily on the definition in the federal Consumer Leasing Act.[113] The term means "a lease that a lessor regularly engaged in the business of leasing or selling makes to a lessee who is an individual and who takes under the lease primarily for a personal, family or household purpose[, if the total payments to be made under the lease contract, excluding payments for options to renew or buy, do not exceed $ _____]."[114]

The most important of the protections provided for lessees in consumer leases is freedom from the statutory provision that makes the promises of finance lessees irrevocable and independent upon acceptance of the goods.[115] The Comments state that the section "does not address whether a 'hell or high water' clause . . . is enforceable if included in a finance lease that is a consumer lease or a lease that is not a finance lease."[116] Among the other important consumer-protection provisions is Section 2A-106, which makes unenforceable a choice-of-law clause that selects a jurisdiction other than where the lessee resides,[117] and a choice-of-forum clause that selects a forum that would not otherwise have jurisdiction over the lessee.

§ 1.05 SUPPLEMENTATION BY PRINCIPLES OF LAW AND EQUITY [§ 1-103(b)]

Articles 2 and 2A are not the exclusive sources of the law of sales and leases of goods. An important provision in Article 1 recognizes the continuing viability of general principles of law and equity. It provides in its entirety as follows:

> Unless displaced by the particular provisions of [the Uniform Commercial Code], the principles of law and equity, including the law merchant and the law relative to capacity to contract, principal and agent, estoppel, fraud, misrepresentation, duress, coercion, mistake, bankruptcy, and other validating or invalidating cause supplement its provisions.[118]

The Code was drafted against the existing backdrop of the common law and equity. Many of the provisions of Articles 2 and 2A were adopted to change the existing approach, or at least to provide a consistent approach to certain issues on which jurisdictions varied. The principles of law and equity may not displace

---

promulgated the Uniform Consumer Leases Act but as of the publication date of this book it had only been enacted in Connecticut.

[113] 15 U.S.C. § 1667(1) (1982).

[114] UCC § 2A-103(1)(e). The language in brackets is provided for states that wish to impose a monetary limitation to qualify as a consumer transaction.

[115] UCC § 2A-407(a). The provision is discussed in § 1.04[B] *supra*.

[116] UCC § 4-407, cmt. 6.

[117] UCC § 2A-106(1).

[118] UCC § 1-103(b).

a Code provision,[119] but as long as they are consistent with those provisions they remain relevant to transactions within the scope of the Code. Articles 2 and 2A in particular rely heavily on the common law of contracts.

§ 1.06 AMENDED ARTICLE 2

[A] Mixed Transactions Involving Goods and Information

One of the most difficult tasks facing the drafting committee was to define the scope of Article 2 as it relates to mixed transactions involving goods and information. The committee ultimately determined to leave Article 2's scope provision ("transactions in goods") alone, but to exclude "information" from the definition of goods. The drafters left the term "information" undefined but understood it to mean data of all kinds, whether or not protected by intellectual-property law, including *inter alia* text, images, sounds, and computer programs.[120] While original Article 2 does not explicitly exclude information, without doubt information is not goods and the amended definition thus does not represent a change in the law. The following Comment provides guidance to courts and is as valid under original Article 2 as under the amendments.

> The definition of "goods" in this article has been amended to exclude information not associated with goods. Thus, this article does not directly apply to an electronic transfer of information, such as the transaction involved in *Specht v. Netscape*, 150 F. Supp. 2d 585 (S.D.N.Y. 2001), *aff'd*, 306 F.3d 17 (2d. Cir. 2002). However, transactions often include both goods and information: some are transactions in goods as that term is used in Section 2-102, and some are not. For example, the sale of "smart goods" such as an automobile is a transaction in goods fully within this article even though the automobile contains many computer programs. On the other hand, an architect's provision of architectural plans on a computer disk would not be a transaction in goods. When a transaction includes both the sale of goods and the transfer of rights in information, it is up to the courts to determine whether the transaction is entirely within or outside of this article, or whether or to what extent this article should be applied to a portion of the transaction. While this article may apply to a transaction including information, nothing in this Article alters, creates, or diminishes intellectual property rights.

The first sentence of the Comment is accurate but understates the effect of the definition. Information is not goods even if the information is associated with goods. If a transaction does not include the acquisition of goods, Article 2 does

---

[119] The Comments indicate that the intent is not just to displace common-law and equitable principles that are inconsistent with the explicit provisions of the Code but also to displace any that are inconsistent with the Code's underlying purposes and policies as set forth in UCC § 1-103(a). UCC § 1-103, cmt. 2.

[120] For a useful definition of the term, see UCITA § 102(35).

not apply. Thus, as the Comment indicates, a download of a computer program or other information from the Internet is entirely outside the scope of the article.

The courts will have to determine the applicable law for an almost limitless variety of transactions in which information is associated with goods. The analysis should not be terribly difficult in most cases. At one extreme are transactions in which goods play such a trivial role that they should be ignored for purposes of determining the applicable law. A contract to custom design a computer program and deliver it over the Internet is not a goods transaction and the same should be true if the program is delivered on a tangible medium such as a CD. The Comment refers to an architect providing architectural plans to make the same point — before the computer age, no one would have considered the contract to be for the sale of goods merely because the plans were provided on paper, and the CD today serves the same function as the paper.

At the other extreme are products that the Comments call "smart goods." Smart goods in general are goods that use an embedded or associated computer program to perform a function that would, in an earlier age, have been performed mechanically. The Comments use a car as an example. Modern cars contain dozens of computer programs that operate systems like antilock brakes and cruise control, and no one could argue plausibly that the purchase of a car is not a transaction in goods. Although it is a mixed transaction involving goods and information, the manner in which the information is used necessitates its treatment as part of the goods. Of course, as the Comments indicate, application of Article 2 in no way creates, alters, or diminishes intellectual property rights. The buyer of a car thus does not acquire the right to infringe on the owner of the underlying patent or copyright. Between the extremes of these transactions that are entirely within or outside the scope of Article 2 are a range of transactions with which the courts must grapple to choose the appropriate law.

[B]   Consumer Protections

Amended Article 2 creates a new category of transactions — consumer contracts — and uses the category as a mechanism to add more consumer protection. A "consumer contract" is "a contract between a merchant seller and a consumer,"[121] and a "consumer" is "an individual who buys or contracts to buy goods that, at the time of contracting, are intended by the individual to be used primarily for personal, family, or household purposes."[122]

Perhaps the most important new consumer protections relate to warranty disclaimers. In both the original and amended articles, Section 2-316(2) sets forth "safe-harbor" language that, absent unconscionability, effectively disclaims the implied warranties of merchantability and fitness. The amended article contains special language for consumer contracts to make this effect more understandable.

---

[121] Amended UCC § 2-103(1)(d).

[122] Amended UCC § 2-103(1)(c). The definition generally tracks the definition in Article 9. *See, e.g.*, UCC § 9-102(a)(23) (consumer goods).

§ 1.07   CISG

On April 11, 1980 representatives from sixty-two nations at a diplomatic conference in Vienna approved the United Nations Convention for the International Sale of Goods (CISG). The CISG entered into force on January 1, 1988 and, as of January 2009, a total of seventy-two nations were parties. The United States Senate ratified the CISG in October 1986.[123] As part of the law of the United States pursuant to the treaty powers of Congress,[124] the CISG preempts the application of the UCC to contracts that fall within its scope.

[A]   Scope

Article 1(1) sets out the scope of the CISG as follows:

> This Convention applies to contracts of sale of goods between parties whose places of business are in different States:
>
> (a)   when the States are Contracting States; or
>
> (b)   when the rules of private international law lead to the application of the law of a Contracting State.[125]

A transaction must meet four basic requirements in order to fall within the scope of the CISG: (1) It must be international; (2) it must be a contract for sale; (3) it must be for a sale of goods; and (4) it must have a sufficient relationship with a Contracting State. The discussion below examines each of the requirements.

[1]   International Transaction

The CISG governs only international sales transactions. In determining internationality, the nationalities of the parties to the transaction are irrelevant; rather, the CISG provides that "[n]either the nationality of the parties nor the civil or commercial character of the parties or of the contract is to be taken into consideration in determining the application of this Convention."[126] The CISG thus does not apply merely because a contract for the sale of goods is between a corporation organized under the laws of an American state and a French individual. To be international the contract must be "between parties whose places of business are in different States."[127] If the business locations of the U.S. corporation and the French individual are both in the U.S., or France, or any other country, the contract is not international; their places of business must be in different countries to satisfy the requirement.[128]

---

[123] The United States deposited the ratification with UNCITRAL on December 11, 1986.

[124] U.S. Const. Art. VI.

[125] The CISG refers to scope as the sphere of application of the Convention.

[126] CISG Art. 1(3).

[127] CISG Art. (1)(1). "State" in the CISG refers to nations or countries, not to geographical subdivisions of a nation such as the states comprising the United States.

[128] The CISG addresses the multiple-office issue by providing the following: "If a party has more than one place of business, the place of business is that which has the closest relationship to the contract and its performance, having regard to the circumstances known to or contemplated by the parties at any time before or at the conclusion of the contract." CISG Art. 10(a). The fact that the

[2]   Contract for Sale

The CISG is limited to "contracts of sale." The term is not defined but its essence can be extrapolated from the provisions of the CISG that establish the respective obligations of the parties. A seller must deliver the goods and related documents and transfer the property interest in the goods,[129] and a buyer must take delivery of the goods and pay for them.[130] Thus, the signature features of a CISG transaction are comparable to those of a domestic sales transaction: a transfer of title to goods in exchange for a price. Transactions in goods that are not sales (*e.g.*, leases, bailments, gifts, and secured transactions) are not covered by the CISG.

The CISG excludes a number of sales transactions that would otherwise be within its scope, including sales "of goods bought for personal, family or household use. . . ."[131] The rationale is to avoid superceding domestic consumer-protection laws. The CISG also excludes sales by auction or on execution or otherwise by authority of law because many special local regulations govern such sales.[132]

[3]   Goods

A contract under the CISG must be for the sale of goods.[133] "Goods" is not defined but the meaning may be inferred from the exclusion of "stocks, shares, investment securities, negotiable instruments or money."[134] The elimination of these forms of property, all of which can be reduced to paper form but whose value consists of intangible rights, shows that goods are meant to be tangible, moveable assets whose value is determined by their physical characteristics.[135]

[4]   Relationship to a Contracting State

Even though a transaction for the sale of goods meets the internationality standard, the CISG does not apply in the absence of a significant relationship between the transaction and a Contracting State, meaning a country that has adhered to the Convention. Subsections (a) and (b) of Article 1(1) prescribe the nature of the relationship. Absent satisfaction of one of these subsections, the governing law will be determined by the private international choice-of-law rules of the State in which the tribunal sits. Even if the CISG would otherwise

---

reference draws upon the closest relationship to formation *and* performance creates difficult issues of application.

[129] CISG Art. 30.

[130] CISG Art. 53.

[131] CISG Art. 2(a). A buyer who purchases goods for the purpose of reselling the goods to consumers does not buy for personal, family or household use. This type of buyer purchases inventory to use in its business of reselling at the retail level.

[132] CISG Art. 2(b), (c).

[133] "The Convention applies to contracts of sale of goods. . . ." CISG Art. 1(1).

[134] CISG Art. 2(d).

[135] The CISG also excludes sales of ships, vessels, hovercraft, aircraft, and electricity because of the variety of rules and regulations on these types of goods that apply in many countries. CISG Art. 2(e), (f).

apply, the parties may opt out of it entirely or they may derogate from or vary the effect of its provisions.[136]

[a] Both Parties' Businesses Located in Contracting States

Under Article 1(1)(a), the CISG applies to contracts between parties whose places of business are in different States "when the States are Contracting States." For example, suppose a seller with its place of business in the United States agrees to sell goods to a buyer with its place of business in Germany. Because both countries are Contracting States, the CISG applies to the transaction. If litigation ensues in either of these countries, the tribunal should apply the CISG. If litigation takes place in a non-Contracting State, such as Great Britain, the tribunal will not be bound by treaty to apply the CISG. Instead, the tribunal will apply Great Britain's private international choice-of-law rules and, if under those rules the governing law is that of the United States or Germany, the tribunal should apply the CISG.

[b] Only One Party's Business Located in Contracting State

Under Article 1(1)(b), the CISG applies to contracts between parties whose places of business are in different States if "the rules of private international law lead to the application of the law of a Contracting State."[137] For example, suppose a seller in Germany, a Contracting State, enters into a contract for the sale of goods to a buyer in Great Britain, a non-Contracting State. If the private international choice-of-law rules of the forum State require application of German law or the law of another Contracting State, the tribunal should apply the CISG.

Article 1(1)(b) was controversial and, faced with the possibility that it would be deleted, the delegates struck a compromise that left each Contracting State with an opportunity to avoid its application. They added Article 95, which provides that "[a]ny State may declare at the time of the deposit of its instrument of ratification, acceptance, approval or accession that it will not be bound by subparagraph (1)(b) of article 1 of this Convention." The United States made the Article 95 declaration.[138] Thus, if a business located in the United States enters into a transaction with a business located in a non-Contracting State and the private international choice-of-law rules of the forum State require application of U.S. law, the governing law will be state law rather than the CISG, meaning the UCC in all states other than Louisiana.

---

[136] *See* § 1.07[B] *infra.*

[137] CISG Art. 1(1)(b).

[138] Other countries making the declaration were China, the Czech Republic, St. Vincent & Grenadines, Singapore, and Slovakia.

[B]   Opting Out

The CISG generally upholds the principle of party autonomy, and consistent with this principle Article 6 provides that "[t]he parties may exclude the application of this Convention or, subject to article 12, derogate from or vary the effect of any of its provisions." The parties thus have discretion to "opt-out" of the CISG, either at the time of contract formation or by subsequent modification.[139] The parties may also choose to derogate from or vary the effect of specific provisions instead of excluding the CISG in its entirety. The only nonvariable provision is Article 12, which empowers a Contracting State to retain its domestic law with respect to the requirement of a writing. The United States has not chosen to retain the statute-of-frauds provisions of UCC Article 2.[140]

Opting out of the CISG may require more than merely designating the law of a particular American state as the governing law because under our federal system the CISG is the law in every state. A contract term stating that the governing law is "the law of the state of Alabama other than the Convention on the International Sale of Goods" should suffice.

[C]   Exclusions

Even though a contract is generally governed by the CISG, exclusions in the Convention provide that certain issues will be resolved by domestic law. The exclusions cover issues upon which attaining a consensus among the delegates would have been extremely difficult because of the extent to which they involve sensitive areas of domestic policy.

Among the issues excluded is "the validity of the contract or of any of its provisions or of any usage."[141] Validity addresses whether a contract or any of its terms are enforceable. The CISG also does not apply "to the liability of the seller for death or personal injury caused by the goods to any person."[142] This exclusion is in deference to the varied approaches to products liability among the world's different legal systems and the rapid changes that have developed in this area. Notwithstanding the exclusion, damage to other property caused by the goods is economic loss that falls within the scope of the CISG.

[D]   Construing the CISG

The drafters intended for the CISG to constitute the exclusive embodiment of the legal principles applicable to international sales transactions. Put another way, they intended for the convention to be a self-contained, unifying force that transcends national legal systems. A significant impediment to realizing this

---

[139] If the parties opt out of the CISG but do not specify the governing law, the court will have to determine that law through the rules of private international law.

[140] *See* § 3.08 *infra.*

[141] CISG Art. 4(a).

[142] CISG Art. 5.

goal is what Professor Honnold calls "the homeward trend."[143] This trend is the natural tendency of judges and legal practitioners to place a gloss on the CISG that corresponds to their domestic sales law. It occurs because their training is often limited to their domestic legal system and they have little exposure to, or experience in, international or comparative law and analysis. It is almost inevitable that judges and practitioners will utilize the principles with which they are familiar in applying the CISG.[144]

Although understandable and perhaps inevitable, the homeward trend is not desirable. Construing the CISG through the multiple lenses of domestic laws precludes it from becoming the unifying force envisioned by the drafters, leaving its application so fragmented that it can serve only as a small step beyond reliance on domestic sales law in resolving disputes arising out of international sales transactions. Article 7(1) was drafted to counter the homeward trend and provides as follows: "In the interpretation of this Convention, regard is to be had to its international character and to the need to promote uniformity in its application. . . ."[145] The standards make clear that the CISG operates on a separate international plane with its own autonomous interpretation:[146] Its international character is to be the compass for interpretation, and uniformity in its application is to be promoted.

The standards set forth in Article 7(1) are lofty and some have criticized them as unattainable. Unquestionably, the drafters goal has not been realized consistently in actual practice. Nevertheless, the inclusion of the standards in the text of the CISG is both desirable and critical because they establish clear goals and undercut the legitimacy of the homeward trend. Lawyers and judges who ignore their mandate can and should be criticized.

---

[143] J. Honnold, Documentary History of the Uniform Law for International Sales 1 (1989).

[144] For example, the court in *Delchi Carrier SpA v. Rotorex Corp.*, 71 F.3d 1024 (2d Cir. 1995), recognized the standards of interpretation stated in Article 7(1) but then proceeded to ignore them by indicating that the principle of foreseeability stated Article 74 of the CISG is the same as the principle of foreseeability stated in *Hadley v. Baxendale*, 156 Eng. Rep. 145 (Ex. Ct. 1854), and incorporated into UCC § 2-715(2)(a).

[145] CISG Art. 7(1).

[146] Michael Van Alstine, *Dynamic Treaty Interpretation*, 146 U. Pa. L. Rev. 687, 731-32 (1998).

Chapter 2

THE AGREEMENT PROCESS

§ 2.01 AN OVERVIEW OF CONTRACT FORMATION UNDER THE CODE [§ 2-204; § 2A-204]

As late as the first half of the twentieth century, contract formation was a fairly rigid process. Most contracts were formed by communications between the parties that took the form of an offer and an acceptance. To serve as the basis for a contract, an offer had to address material terms common to contracts of the type and failure to address such terms generally resulted in the contract failing for indefiniteness. The acceptance had to mirror the offer perfectly and be communicated using the same medium as that chosen by the offeror. The court had to be able to pinpoint the precise moment of contract formation. An offer was freely revocable unless the offeree created an option contract by giving consideration for the privilege of having it held open, and modifications required separate consideration. The statute of frauds, when applicable, imposed a detailed writing requirement, and the parol evidence rule made supplementation of writings difficult.

By the time the Code was first promulgated, many progressive jurisdictions had begun to relax this formalism, and Article 2 greatly accelerated the trend. Section 2-204 provides that "[a] contract for sale of goods may be made in any manner sufficient to show agreement, including conduct of both parties which recognizes the existence of such a contract"[1] and that "[a]n agreement sufficient to constitute a contract for sale may be found even though the moment of its making is undetermined."[2] Permitting agreements to be based solely on the conduct of both parties and eliminating the requirement that a court be able to pinpoint the time of formation allows the courts, in appropriate cases, to dispense with the necessity of finding a formal offer and acceptance.[3]

Although an agreement based solely on the conduct of both parties is possible, it is relatively rare. In most cases, the courts still search for a discreet offer and acceptance. The Code does not define these terms, deferring for the most part to the common law;[4] nevertheless, much of the rigidity of the prior common law was eliminated. While the offeror is still the master of the offer and can insist on a particular manner or medium of acceptance, an ambiguous offer must be "construed as inviting acceptance in any manner and by any medium reasonable

---

[1] UCC § 2-204(1). Section 2A-204(1) is comparable.

[2] UCC § 2-204(2). Section 2A-204(2) is comparable.

[3] Contracts based solely on the conduct of both parties are commonly referred to as implied-in-fact contracts. Section 2-207(3) deals explicitly with a common situation involving such a contract. *See* § 2.04[D][2] *infra.*

[4] For definitions of offer and acceptance, see Restatement (Second) of Contracts §§ 24 (offer), 50 (acceptance). As with common-law contracts, courts generally hold that advertisements, circulars, and price quotes are not offers. *See, e.g.,* Master Palletizer Sys., Inc. v. T.S. Ragsdale Co., 725 F. Supp. 1525, 11 UCC Rep. Serv. 2d 1125 (D. Colo. 1989) (price quote sent to buyer); Corinthian Pharmaceutical Sys., Inc. v. Lederle Laboratories, 724 F. Supp. 605, 11 UCC Rep. Serv. 2d 463 (S.D. Ind. 1989) (price list circulated among prospective buyers). A number of cases also have held that a reservation in a communication that requires further approval by the sender makes it an invitation to deal rather than an offer. *See, e.g.,* McCarty v. Verson Allsteel Press Co., 89 Ill. App. 3d 498, 411 N.E.2d 936, 30 UCC Rep. Serv. 440 (1980) (clause requiring approval by home office prevented seller's proposal from being an offer).

in the circumstances."[5] This means that an offeree ordinarily can accept either by making a return promise or by commencing the requested performance, and a promissory acceptance need not be communicated using the same medium as that selected by the offeror.[6] Furthermore, in some circumstances a communication that does not mirror the offer can operate as an acceptance.[7]

Section 2-204(3) provides that "[e]ven though one or more terms are left open a contract for sale does not fail for indefiniteness if the parties have intended to make a contract and there is a reasonably certain basis for giving an appropriate remedy."[8] The provision lessens significantly the chances that a court will find that a contract is too indefinite to enforce. The first step in the search for a contract requires a determination that the parties intended to make one.[9] Intent here does not refer to the parties' subjective state of mind: What matters is their objective manifestations of an intent to be bound.[10] If the requisite intent is present, the question becomes whether the court has a reasonably certain basis for giving the aggrieved party an appropriate remedy. Deciding this issue requires an understanding of the distinction between "agreement" and "contract."

An "agreement" is "the bargain of the parties in fact."[11] It includes the terms upon which the parties have expressly agreed and any terms reasonably inferred from the factual matrix surrounding the transaction, including any relevant usage of trade, course of dealing, or course of performance.[12] The idea is that parties do not enter into contracts in a vacuum; rather, they proceed in a particular setting and they make a variety of assumptions based on that setting. For example, suppose both parties are members of a trade in which goods are always delivered on thirty-day credit. Their agreement will, unless they expressly agree to the contrary, contain a thirty-day credit term. The drafters elevated the surrounding circumstances to an exalted position in the contract formation process.[13]

A "contract" is "the total legal obligation that results from the parties' agreement as determined by the [Uniform Commercial Code] as supplemented

---

[5] UCC § 2-206(1)(a); *see* § 2.02[A] *infra.*

[6] UCC § 2-206(1)(a); *see* § 2.02[A] *infra.*

[7] UCC § 2-207(1); *see* § 2.04[B][1] *infra.*

[8] UCC § 2-204(3). Section 2A-204(3) is comparable.

[9] Group One, Ltd. v. Hallmark Cards, Inc., 254 F.3d 1041, 45 UCC Rep. Serv. 2d 88 (Fed. Cir. 2001), *cert. denied*, 534 U.S. 1127 (2002) (indefinite nature of communications and lack of specificity on price and quantity suggested parties were still negotiating).

[10] *See, e.g.*, Computer Network Ltd. v. Purcell Tire & Rubber Co., 747 S.W.2d 669, 6 UCC Rep. Serv. 2d 642 (Mo. Ct. App. 1988) (buyer who signed written agreement to purchase 21 computers held to that quantity notwithstanding evidence of subjective intent to purchase one computer for each of its 15 stores).

[11] UCC § 1-201(b)(3).

[12] UCC § 1-201(b)(3). See § 4.03 *infra* for a discussion of usage of trade, course of dealing, and course of performance.

[13] *See* UCC § 1-103(a)(2) (one of the purposes underlying the Code is "to permit the continued expansion of commercial practices through custom, usage and agreement of the parties.").

by any other applicable laws."[14] While legal obligations clearly can arise from the express and implied-in-fact terms that constitute the parties' agreement, additional obligations can arise as a result of provisions in Article 2 that commonly are known as "gap-fillers."[15] The reference is apt because the obligations apply only if the parties leave a gap in their agreement. Gap-fillers are not based on the actual or presumed intent of the parties but rather reflect the consensus of the drafters regarding the most appropriate default rules for situations as to which agreement has not been reached. In effect, the Code contains a smorgasbord of standard provisions that can kick in to supplement the agreement.[16]

The effect of Section 2-204(3) is thus clear. The fact that an agreement does not include a term material to a contract of the type will not cause a contract to fail for indefiniteness if a relevant implied-in-fact term or gap-filler provides a basis for giving the aggrieved party an appropriate remedy.

Article 2 contains additional provisions that reduce formalism and meet commercial expectations. For example, the role of consideration is reduced: Offers may be made irrevocable without consideration[17] and modifications are enforceable without separate consideration.[18] Also, the primacy of writings is reduced: A writing may satisfy the statute of frauds even though it is considerably less detailed than its common-law counterpart,[19] and the parol evidence rule has been liberalized to make it easier to supplement a writing.[20] The remainder of this chapter explains the Article 2 provisions on contract formation, Chapter 3 covers the statute of frauds, and Chapter 4 covers the parol evidence rule.

All in all, the process of contract formation under the Code looks very different from its antecedents. It had a profound influence on the Second Restatement and, therefore, on the development of the common law. Perhaps the best expression of the Code's philosophy is the following statement by the New York Court of Appeals in *Kleinschmidt Division of SCM Corp. v. Futuronics, Inc.*:[21]

> The basic philosophy of the sales article of the Uniform Commercial Code is simple. Practical business people cannot be expected to govern their actions with reference to nice legal formalisms. Thus, when there is basic agreement, however manifested and whether or not the precise moment of agreement may be determined, failure to articulate that

---

[14] UCC § 1-201(b)(12).

[15] See § 4.04 *infra* for a discussion of gap-fillers.

[16] *See, e.g.*, Jannusch v. Naffziger, 379 Ill. App. 3d 381, 883 N.E.2d 711, 65 UCC Rep. Serv. 2d 116 (2008) (oral agreement to sell concession business and its equipment enforceable even though agreement did not allocate price of equipment and good will, did not contain covenant not to compete common to contracts of the type, and did not include other common terms; contract may be enforced unless essential terms are so uncertain that there is no basis for deciding whether breach has occurred).

[17] UCC § 2-205; *see* § 2.03 *infra*.

[18] UCC § 2-209(1); *see* § 2.07 *infra*.

[19] UCC § 2-201(1); *see* § 302[C] *infra*.

[20] UCC § 2-202(a); *see* § 4.03[B] *infra*.

[21] 41 N.Y.2d 972, 395 N.Y.S.2d 151, 363 N.E.2d 701, 21 UCC Rep. Serv. 422 (1977).

agreement in the precise language of a lawyer, with every difficulty and contingency considered and resolved, will not prevent formation of a contract.[22]

§ 2.02   ACCEPTANCE [§ 2-206; § 2A-206]

[A]   Generally

An offeror has always had the power to impose an exclusive manner of acceptance, but if it failed to do so the pre-Code common-law courts generally had to decide whether the offer invited acceptance by rendering full performance (creating a unilateral contract) or by making a return express promise (creating a bilateral contract). Furthermore, a return promise had to be communicated using the same medium as that selected by the offeror to communicate the offer. A purported acceptance using the wrong manner or medium did not create a contract.

The Code effects a radical change. Unless the language or circumstances make it clear that the offeror is insisting on an exclusive manner or medium of acceptance, the offeree may accept in any manner and by any medium reasonable in the circumstances.[23] In cases of ambiguous offers, most offerees accept either by making a return promise or by commencing the requested performance.[24] Under supplementary common-law rules: (1) a return promise must be communicated to be effective unless the offeror dispenses with the requirement;[25] (2) a promissory acceptance is effective upon dispatch;[26] and (3) the commencement of performance operates as an implied-in-fact promise to complete the performance.[27]

Even though an offeree's conduct in commencing performance is treated as a return promise, it does not have to be communicated to be effective. The reason should be obvious: Treating the conduct of offerees as an acceptance encourages them to begin work quickly and it would be unfair to permit the offer to be revoked once performance begins. The approach protects the offeree's

---

[22] 41 N.Y.2d at 973, 363 N.E.2d at 701, 21 UCC Rep. Serv. at 423. The court affirmed the trial court's ruling that the evidence of assent could not satisfy even the Code's minimal requirements.

[23] UCC §§ 2-206(1)(a); 2A-206(1).

[24] *See, e.g.,* Shaw Environmental, Inc. v. Double D Transp., 63 UCC Rep. Serv. 2d 307 (Cal. Ct. App. 2007) (unpublished) (general contractor's purchase order offering to buy dirt accepted by seller's dispatch of truck hauling dirt; indemnity provision included in offer in effect at the time truck collided with freight train).

[25] *See* Restatement (Second) of Contracts § 56.

[26] *See* Restatement (Second) of Contracts § 63. The common law permits an offeror to preclude application of the "mailbox rule" by insisting that acceptance not be effective until received.

[27] *See* Restatement (Second) of Contracts § 62(2). Occasionally the language or circumstances make it clear that the offeror wants full performance; that is, the offer is for the formation of a unilateral contract. Because the offeror signals that it does not want a return promise, the commencement of performance does not bind the offeree. However, it creates an option contract, precluding the offeror from revoking, and thereby providing the offeree with an opportunity to complete the performance. Restatement (Second) of Contracts § 45.

reasonable reliance, but it can create problems for an offeror that needs to know if acceptance has occurred. Section 2-206(2) addresses this concern as follows: "Where the beginning of performance is a reasonable mode of acceptance an offeror who is not notified of acceptance within a reasonable time may treat the offer as having lapsed before acceptance."[28]

The overall effect of Section 2-206 is to balance the interests of the parties. It encourages offerees to begin performing quickly and protects their investment by precluding revocation once performance has commenced. Nevertheless, the offeree should notify the offeror within a reasonable time after commencing performance so that the offeror knows that it does not need to contract with someone else.[29] If the offeree waits too long to notify, the offeror cannot be bound. Conceptually, it is as if commencing performance creates a bilateral contract with the offeror's duty to perform subject to a condition precedent — timely notification by the offeree.

To illustrate, suppose on Tuesday morning a seller receives an order for equipment that needs to be specially manufactured. Neither the language nor the circumstances indicate an exclusive manner of acceptance. Later that day the seller begins work on the equipment but has not notified the buyer when, on Friday, the buyer calls and attempts to revoke the offer. During the conversation the seller insists on going through with the contract and informs the buyer that performance has already begun. On these facts the seller's conduct amounts to an acceptance and the buyer's attempted revocation is ineffective. The only issue is whether the three-day delay in giving notice was unreasonable. The cases to date give little guidance in determining a reasonable time[30] in this context but surely the courts will want to protect an offeror that, after waiting for a response for what seems an adequate time to the fact-finder, enters into a binding contract with a third party.

The Comments invite the courts to follow common-law precedents that make offers irrevocable in certain situations.[31] For example, suppose one party relies on an offer in a way other than by beginning performance.[32] The classic case involves a contractor that receives an offer to sell equipment from a subcontractor and then uses that offer in computing its bid on a project. If the contractor is awarded the project and the subcontractor subsequently revokes,

---

[28] UCC § 2A-206(2). Section 2A-206(2) is comparable.

[29] An offeree may not have to take affirmative steps to notify the offeror. "Notify" means "taking such steps as may be reasonably required to inform the other person in ordinary course, whether or not the other person actually comes to know of it." UCC § 1-202(d). Furthermore, "a person has 'notice' of a fact if the person: (1) has actual knowledge of it; (2) has received a notice or notification of it; or (3) from all the facts and circumstances known to the person at the time in question, the person has reason to know that it exists." UCC § 1-202(a)(2). Thus, no affirmative steps would be required to notify an offeror that knows or has reason to know that performance has commenced.

[30] "Whether a time for taking an action required by [the Uniform Commercial Code] is reasonable depends on the nature, purpose, and circumstances of the action." UCC § 1-205(a).

[31] UCC § 2-206, cmt. 3.

[32] If commencing performance operates as an acceptance, the offeree does not need the protection provided by this approach. A contract has been form and all the offeree needs to do is give timely notification to the offeror.

the contractor may suffer a loss, but its reliance does not constitute the commencement of performance and thus it is not protected by an existing contract. While some early cases provide to the contrary,[33] most later cases[34] and the Second Restatement[35] use the doctrine of promissory estoppel to create an option contract, meaning that the offer cannot be revoked pending timely acceptance by the offeree. Thus, upon being awarded the project, the contractor may accept until the offer lapses.

[B] Countering the Unilateral Contract Trick

Article 2 further implements its policy of permitting an offeree to accept in any reasonable manner by addressing a commonly recurring situation. Section 2-206(b) provides that:

> [a]n order or other offer to buy goods for prompt or current shipment shall be construed as inviting acceptance either by a prompt promise to ship or by the prompt or current shipment of conforming or non-conforming goods, but such a shipment of non-conforming goods does not constitute an acceptance if the seller seasonably notifies the buyer that the shipment is offered only as an accommodation to the buyer.

This provision prevents sellers from using what came to be called the "unilateral contract trick." Under pre-Code law, a seller that shipped nonconforming goods in response to an offer made a counteroffer. If the buyer kept the goods without objection, a contract to buy the nonconforming goods existed. If the buyer objected and claimed that the seller had breached, the seller could avoid liability because it had not accepted the buyer's offer. The seller had not accepted by promise, and it had not accepted by shipping the requested goods. Under Article 2, shipment by the seller constitutes acceptance without regard to whether the goods conform to the offer.[36] Accordingly, the same act that creates the contract can also constitute a breach.

The impact of the provision can be illustrated by the facts of *Corinthian Pharmaceutical Systems, Inc. v. Lederle Laboratories*,[37] in which the buyer

---

[33] *See, e.g.*, James Baird Co. v. Gimbel Bros., 64 F.2d 344 (2d Cir. 1933). In that case, Judge Learned Hand refused to deviate from the standard common-law rule making offers revocable until acceptance. Among other reasons, Judge Hand stated that the contractor could have protected itself by entering into an option contract with the subcontractor. In a true option contract, as opposed to one resting on estoppel principles, the offeree gives consideration to keep the offer open. Nothing in Article 2 prevents parties from using true option contracts. As an alternative, an offeree can insist on a "firm offer," discussed in § 2.03 *infra*.

[34] *See, e.g.*, Drennan v. Star Paving Co., 51 Cal. 2d 409, 333 P.2d 757 (1958); Montgomery Indus. Int'l v. Thomas Constr. Co., 620 F.2d 91 (5th Cir. 1980). A few cases, primarily in Massachusetts, have held that the contractor's mere use of the bid amounts to an acceptance, creating a contract subject to the condition that the contractor be awarded the project.

[35] *See* Restatement (Second) of Contracts § 87(2).

[36] Consistent with its usage in Section 2-504, "shipment" refers to sending the goods to the buyer by carrier. If the seller uses its own vehicle, a contract is formed if the court finds that the seller's conduct amounts to commencing performance as opposed to preparing to perform. UCC § 2-206, cmt. 2.

[37] 724 F. Supp. 605, 11 UCC Rep. Serv. 2d 463 (S.D. Ind. 1989).

offered to purchase 1,000 vials of vaccine at the seller's listed price one day before a price increase was due to take effect. The seller shipped fifty vials along with a letter stating that, as an accommodation, the buyer could have those vials for the old price but the balance would have to be at the new price. When the buyer sued for breach, the court sided with the seller. After all, the seller's nonconforming shipment had been accompanied by a letter stating that the vials were being sent as an accommodation.[38] The effect of the letter was to convert the shipment into a counteroffer.[39] Had the seller not sent the letter, its nonconforming shipment would have operated as an acceptance of the buyer's offer, obligating it to sell the full 1,000 vials at the old price. *Corinthian Pharmaceutical* involved a nonconforming tender rather than nonconforming goods, but the principle involved is the same.

§ 2.03 FIRM OFFERS [§ 2-205; § 2A-205]

A basic principle of contract law is that offers are freely revocable, even if the offeror has promised not to revoke and even if the revocation is made in bad faith.[40] The rationale for this strange rule is that promises by offerors to keep their offers open typically are not supported by consideration. The common law developed two basic exceptions to this doctrine. First came the option contract, in which an offeree gave consideration to keep an offer open.[41] More recently, courts have used principles of estoppel to make offers irrevocable.[42]

Although nothing prevents parties from using these devices in contracts for the sale or lease of goods, Articles 2 and 2A give parties another mechanism for creating an irrevocable offer. Section 2-205 provides for what are called "firm offers" as follows:

> An offer by a merchant to buy or sell goods in a signed writing which by its terms gives assurances that it will be held open is not revocable, for lack of consideration, during the time stated or if no time is stated for a reasonable time, but in no event may such period of irrevocability exceed three months; but any such term of assurance on a form supplied by the offeree must be separately signed by the offeror.[43]

A firm offer has much the same effect as the seal at common law. Promises made under seal were enforceable absent consideration, with the seal providing evidence of the promisor's seriousness of purpose. The law governing seals does

---

[38] The seller's shipment was nonconforming because of Section 2-307. Absent agreement to the contrary, a seller must deliver all the goods in a single lot rather than in installments.

[39] The buyer could accept the counteroffer for the fifty vials by keeping them without objection but presumably would have to communicate assent to accept as to the remaining vials.

[40] The Code's obligation of good faith applies to the performance and enforcement of contracts, not their formation. UCC § 1-304. *See* discussion § 4.05[B] *infra*.

[41] *See* Restatement (Second) of Contracts § 25. Even nominal consideration will suffice. *See, e.g.*, Board of Control v. Burgess, 45 Mich. App. 183, 206 N.W.2d 256 (1973). Restatement (Second) of Contracts § 87(1) goes even further, stating that an offer is irrevocable if it is in a signed writing that recites a purported consideration.

[42] *See* discussion § 2.02[A] *supra*.

[43] UCC § 2A-205 is comparable.

not apply to contracts formed under the Code[44] but offers can be made irrevocable by complying with the statute's requirements.

A firm offer must in the first instance constitute an offer. In addition, the offeror must be a merchant,[45] the offer must be in a signed writing,[46] and the writing must give assurances that it will be held open.[47] If the term giving assurances that an offer will be kept open is on a form provided by the offeree, it is not effective unless it is separately signed by the offeror. The statutory requirements are clear and have generated relatively little litigation.

Three months is the maximum period of irrevocability. A firm offer that states a period of irrevocability that exceeds three months can be accepted until the period expires, but it can be revoked after the first three months.[48] If a firm offer does not establish a definite period, it is irrevocable for a reasonable time. The courts have given little guidance here,[49] although surely the most important factors are the volatility of the product's price and whether the product is still available to the offeror.

§ 2.04   THE BATTLE OF THE FORMS [§ 2-207]

[A]   Introduction

At common law a purported acceptance that does not mirror the terms of the offer is treated as a counteroffer; that is, as a rejection of the offer coupled with a new offer by the original offeree.[50] This approach works well in many contexts, but the drafters thought it was unworkable as applied to certain situations involving the use of standard forms.[51]

---

[44] UCC §§ 2-203, 2A-203.

[45] *See* discussion § 3.03[B] *infra*.

[46] See § 3.02[A] *infra* for a discussion of what constitutes a signature and for the effect of statutes governing electronic contracting on the Code's writing and signature requirements. In regard to the latter issue, see also § 2.06 *infra*.

[47] The writing must do more than merely state that an offer exists. *See, e.g.,* Ivey's Plumbing & Elec. Co. v. Petrochem Maintenance, Inc., 463 F. Supp. 543, 26 UCC Rep. Serv. 621 (N.D. Miss. 1978) (no language of irrevocability); Lowenstern v. Stop & Shop Companies, 32 UCC Rep. Serv. 414 (Mass. Super. 1981) ("raincheck" allowing customer to purchase item from store at a later date constituted firm offer).

[48] UCC § 2-205, cmt. 3; *see also* Mid-South Packers, Inc. v. Shoney's, Inc., 761 F.2d 1117, 41 UCC Rep. Serv. 38 (5th Cir. 1985); Loranger Plastics Corp. v. Incoe Corp., 670 F. Supp. 145, 5 UCC Rep. Serv. 2d 58 (W.D. Pa. 1987).

[49] *See, e.g.,* Lowenstern v. Stop & Shop Companies, 32 UCC Rep. Serv. 414 (Mass. Super. 1981) (court gave no convincing rationale for holding that store's "raincheck" was irrevocable for 15 days).

[50] *See* Restatement (Second) of Contracts § 39. Perhaps the most graphic example of the rule is *Poel v. Brunswicke-Balke-Collender Co.*, 216 N.Y. 310, 110 N.E.2d 619 (1915), in which a buyer of rubber accepted the seller's offer and added that the seller had to send back a prompt acknowledgment. The court held that this addition made the acceptance conditional, converting it into a counteroffer.

[51] *See generally* Murray, *The Chaos of the "Battle of the Forms": Solutions*, 39 Vand. L. Rev. 1307 (1986); Baird & Weisberg, *Rules, Standards, and the Battle of the Forms: A Reassessment of § 2-207*, 68 Va. L. Rev. 1217 (1982); Brown, *Restoring Peace in the Battle of the Forms: A Framework for*

Their concern stemmed from abuses by sellers under the "mirror-image" rule. For example, suppose a buyer sent a standard purchase-order form that constituted an offer calling for the future delivery of goods and the seller responded with a standard acknowledgment form that did not mirror the offer and therefor constituted a counteroffer. If the price of the goods rose before the delivery date, the seller could back out. The seller, in effect, could speculate at the buyer's expense. Now suppose the goods were delivered and the buyer kept them without objection. The buyer's exercise of dominion over the goods constituted acceptance of the counteroffer,[52] resulting in a contract formed on the seller's terms. This "last-shot rule" overwhelmingly favored sellers because they typically sent the last form. Of course, the buyer arguably could have read the seller's form and objected to anything contained in it, but having purchasing agents spend their time poring over fine print is not efficient unless the contract is for a relatively large amount of money.

As discussed below, one of the assumptions underlying the approach of Section 2-207 is that each party will focus on certain terms that are typically written or typed near the top of a standard form but will not read the other party's "boilerplate," meaning the standard terms, often in fine print, that are not typically the subject of negotiation.[53] The section dispenses with the last-shot rule and replaces it with what might be called a "first-shot" rule, or at least a first-shot bias. As demonstrated below, an offeror has a decided advantage in shaping the terms of the agreement.

For obvious reasons, Section 2-207 has come to be known as the "battle-of-the-forms" provision. It has been somewhat successful in ending the abuses of the last-shot rule but has created a host of new problems. It is poorly drafted and virtually no aspect of this complicated area is free from conflicting court decisions. The confusion is so great that the drafters of Article 2A, who closely modeled their product on Article 2, would have no part of it. The amendments to Article 2 make radical departures from the original section.[54]

[B]   The Basic Rules

[1]   Definite and Seasonable Expressions of Assent

Section 2-207(1) states in full that:

A definite and seasonable expression of acceptance or a written confirmation which is sent within a reasonable time operates as an acceptance even though it states terms additional to or different from those offered or agreed upon, unless acceptance is made expressly conditional on assent to the additional or different terms.

Making Uniform Commercial Code § 2-207 Work, 69 N.C. L. Rev. 893 (1991).

[52] *See* Restatement (Second) of Contracts § 69(2).

[53] *See, e.g.*, Belden, Inc. v. American Electronic Components, Inc., 66 UCC Rep. Serv. 2d 399 (Ind. Ct. App. 2008) (UCC § 2-207 based on assumption that business people do not read preprinted forms).

[54] *See* § 2.08[B] *infra*.

The section deals with two types of communications: a definite and seasonable expression of acceptance, and a written confirmation. The existence of a written confirmation presupposes that a contract has already been formed and the issue is whether its terms can be modified by the terms in the confirmation. Discussion of written confirmations, and of the "unless" clause following the comma in the statute, are deferred until later.[55] The word "seasonable"[56] merely refers to the normal rule that acceptance must occur before an offer lapses and it will not be included in the following discussion.

Leaving out the material just mentioned, Section 2-207(1) provides that "[a] definite . . . expression of acceptance . . . operates as an acceptance even though it contains terms additional to or different from those offered. . . ." The provision abrogates the common law mirror-image rule: A communication that does not mirror an offer may nevertheless operate as an acceptance rather than a counteroffer.

Obviously, a "definite expression of acceptance" can differ from a common-law acceptance, but what does the undefined term mean? The consensus is that a qualifying communication should express an unequivocal commitment to go forward with a deal on the same negotiated, or "dickered," terms as those offered, but there is an inherent problem in determining which terms are for negotiation and which are not. If an offer is oral or is made in a letter that is not a standard form, presumably every proposed term is for negotiation. If the offer is made using a standard form — the classic battle-of-the-forms situation — the dickered terms usually will be those that the offeror has entered in spaces provided on the form, as opposed to the pre-printed boilerplate. Dickered terms are usually material but that is not necessarily the case; what matters is that the offeree know or have reason to know that the offeror considers them sufficiently important to raise them to the negotiation level.

If the offeree's response differs from the offer on dickered terms, it generally will be treated as a common-law counteroffer, not as a definite expression of acceptance.[57] For example, suppose a prospective buyer sends an e-mail to a car dealer offering to buy a particular car for $25,000. The seller responds with a standard-form acknowledgment indicating a willingness to sell a different car for $30,000. No one would argue that the seller's acknowledgment constitutes a definite expression of acceptance. The buyer should have noticed the discrepancies and, if the seller delivers the car described in its form and the buyer keeps it without objection, it should pay $30,000. If, on the other hand, the seller's acknowledgment mirrors the buyer's choice of car and price but in addition contains a set of standard terms that the seller uses in a wide range of transactions, the acknowledgment will constitute a definite expression of acceptance and operate as an acceptance even though it contains terms in addition to the ones in the offer. The same conclusion applies if the buyer had made its offer

---

[55] *See* § 2.04[B][2], [D] *infra*.

[56] UCC § 1-205(b) provides that "[a]n action is taken seasonably if it is taken at or within the time agreed or, if no time is agreed, at or within a reasonable time."

[57] *See, e.g.,* Dubrofsky v. Messer, 1981 Mass. App. Div. 55, 31 UCC Rep. Serv. 907 (1981) (difference as to quantity); Alliance Wall Corp. v. Ampat Midwest Corp., 17 Ohio App. 3d 59, 477 N.E.2d 1206, 41 UCC Rep. Serv. 377 (1984) (difference as to delivery date).

on a form containing its own standard terms, with the description of the car and the price set out in spaces reserved for that purpose at the top of the form. As long as the seller's acknowledgment refers to the same car and price, it operates as an acceptance even though it may contain terms both additional to and different from those proposed in the offer.[58]

The consequence that a definite expression of acceptance operates as an acceptance means that the resulting contract is formed, at least in the first instance, on the offeror's terms. This approach might be referred to as a "first-shot" rule and it gives offerors a significant advantage. An offeree that wants to avoid this result has two choices: It can read the offer carefully and insist on express agreement to the additional or different terms that it considers important before entering into a contract, or it can take advantage of the clause at the end of Section 2-207(1) by stating in its response that no contract will be formed unless the offeror agrees to all of its terms. The latter option is discussed in detail below.[59]

To illustrate the operation of the basic rule, suppose a buyer sends a seller a standard-form purchase order (assume an offer) with the desired subject matter, price, and quantity typed into spaces created for that purpose at the top of the form. The pre-printed boilerplate specifies that the buyer will make payment thirty days after delivery. The form is silent on the time of delivery and on how disputes will be resolved. Before the offer lapses, the seller responds with its standard acknowledgment form. The form indicates a willingness to go forward with a deal, mirrors the dickered terms of the offer, is silent on the time of delivery, specifies that payment is due on delivery, and further specifies that all disputes must be resolved through binding arbitration. The seller's form is a definite expression of acceptance, creating a contract generally on the buyer's terms. Three outstanding issues, however, remain: What is the time for delivery, when is payment due, and must disputes be arbitrated?

Because the forms of both parties are silent as to the time of delivery, the resolution of that issue requires searching elsewhere. Under the Code's normal contract formation rules, a relevant provision derived from a usage of trade, course of dealing, or course of performance becomes part of the agreement. In the absence of such a term, Section 2-309(a), which requires the seller to deliver within a reasonable time, fills the gap.[60]

The seller's arbitration clause is in addition to, not different from, the terms of the offer. To determine its fate, we turn to Section 2-207(2), which establishes that it is a proposal for addition to the contract. In other words, the seller has agreed to the buyer's offer and requested a modification. The term can become

---

[58] Some tolerance of variation even as to the dickered terms should be acceptable. Since failure of a response to qualify as a definite expression of acceptance means that it operates as a counteroffer, a seller should not be able to insert a minor variation as to a dickered term into its response and thereby invoke the common-law last-shot rule. For an example of a court that tolerated perhaps too much of a variation from the offeror's dickered terms, see *Southern Idaho Pipe & Steel Co. v. Cal-Cut Pipe & Supply, Inc.*, 98 Idaho 495, 567 P.2d 1246, 22 UCC Rep. Serv. 25 (1977) (response operated as acceptance notwithstanding variance in delivery date).

[59] *See* § 2.04[D] *infra.*

[60] *See* discussion § 4.04[C][3] *infra.*

effective in either of two ways: The buyer can assent to it or it can become part of the contract automatically under a rule that operates only if both parties are merchants.[61] If the seller delivers the goods and the buyer keeps them without objection, the buyer's exercise of dominion over the goods would not constitute assent to the additional term. Permitting such a result would simply reinstate the last-shot rule[62] and, in any event, the buyer's conduct would be ambiguous since keeping the goods would be consistent with a contract that contains the additional term and with a contract that does not contain it. The buyer might expressly agree to the term, as by signing and returning the seller's form. Alternatively, a court might infer assent from such circumstances as the buyer acting as if the term were part of the contract (*e.g.*, demanding arbitration on one occasion and denying enforceability of the clause on a later occasion)[63] or the buyer objecting to some of the seller's standard terms but not to the arbitration clause.[64]

The issue of the seller's different term — the time for payment — is more complicated because subsection (2) refers only to additional terms. A majority of courts have held that different terms cancel each other out, reasoning that to hold otherwise would be to take the offeror's first-shot advantage to an extreme.[65] These courts often cite Comment 6 to Section 2-207, which states that "[w]here clauses on confirming forms conflict each party must be assumed to object to a clause of the other conflicting with one on the confirmation sent by himself." Although the "knock-out" result is defensible on policy grounds, use of the Comment is inapt. Section 2-207(1) deals with both definite expressions of acceptance and written confirmations, and Comment 6 applies only to the latter.

Other courts take a literal approach, relying on the statement in subsection (1) that a definite expression of acceptance "operates as an acceptance."[66] Because the only thing it can operate as an acceptance *of* is the offer, the contract in the hypothetical must be on the buyer's terms. This reasoning means that the seller's different term is inoperative unless the buyer assents to it. Courts taking the literal approach do not apply the between-merchants rule of subsection (2) because that subsection refers only to additional terms.

A few courts have adopted a variation of the literal approach. They rely on Comment 3 to Section 2-207, which indicates that the drafters intended subsection (2) to apply to both different and additional terms, and they read the

---

[61] The rule is discussed in detail in § 2.04[C] *infra*.

[62] *See, e.g.*, Belden, Inc. v. American Electronic Components, Inc., 66 UCC Rep. Serv. 2d 399 (Ind. Ct. App. 2008).

[63] *See, e.g.*, Twin Disc v. Big Bud Tractor, Inc., 772 F.2d 1329, 41 UCC Rep. Serv. 1627 (7th Cir. 1985) (buyer invoked warranty in seller's form on several occasions).

[64] *See, e.g.*, Construction Aggregates Corp. v. Hewitt-Robins, Inc., 404 F.2d 505, 6 UCC Rep. Serv. 112 (7th Cir. 1968).

[65] *See, e.g.*, Daitom, Inc. v. Pennwalt, Inc., 741 F.2d 1569, 39 UCC Rep. Serv. 1203 (10th Cir. 1984); Vulcan Automotive Equip. Co. v. Global Marine Engine & Parts, Inc., 240 F. Supp. 2d 156, 49 UCC Rep. Serv. 2d 743 (D.R.I. 2003). Absent an implied-in-fact term, payment in the hypothetical case presented would be due on delivery under Section 2-310(a).

[66] *See, e.g.*, Valtrol, Inc. v. General Connectors Corp., 884 F.2d 149, 10 UCC Rep. Serv. 2d 1165 (4th Cir. 1989).

subsection as though it explicitly refers to different terms.[67] Under this approach a different term does not knock out its counterpart but rather is a proposal for addition to the contract that can become operative automatically under the between-merchants rule. The argument for this approach is weak. Under a standard rule of statutory construction, the reference in subsection (1) to both different and additional terms followed by the reference in subsection (2) to additional terms means that different terms were intended to be excluded from subsection (2).[68] Moreover, subsection (2) states that additional terms are proposals for addition to the contract; making a different term effective would change the contract rather than add to it. Finally, the only reason to read different terms into subsection (2) is to make them eligible for the between-merchants rule, but not even an additional term becomes enforceable under that rule if the offeror has given notification of objection to it. Notification of objection should be assumed for different terms.[69]

While the Code has solved some of the problems created by the common law's last-shot rule, its first-shot bias has created its own set of problems. For example, in *Technographics, Inc. v. Mercer Corp.*[70] a seller sent a buyer a price quotation on a form that conspicuously disclaimed all implied warranties and excluded consequential damages. The buyer responded with an order form that was silent on these matters and the seller delivered the equipment. When issues of quality arose the court concluded that the seller's disclaimers were ineffective. The price quotation was a mere invitation to deal; the buyer's purchase order constituted the offer. The seller's subsequent delivery of the machine constituted an acceptance of the buyer's offer under Section 2-206(1)(b). The decision is troubling. What could the seller have done? It could have extended an offer rather than a price-quotation, in which case the buyer's purchase order would have been a definite expression of acceptance and the contract would have been formed on the seller's terms. Another approach would have been to insist on the buyer's express assent to its terms, or at least to the disclaimer, before delivering the goods. For example, the seller could have responded to the buyer's purchase order with an acknowledgment form reiterating the seller's terms and containing a signature block for the buyer to indicate its assent. Had the seller refused to deliver the goods until it received the signed acknowledgment, it no doubt would have prevailed.

---

[67] *See, e.g.*, Steiner v. Mobil Oil Corp., 20 Cal. 3d 90, 141 Cal. Rptr. 157, 569 P.2d 751, 22 UCC Rep. Serv. 865 (1977).

[68] The rule is known by the Latin phrase "expressio unius est exclusio alterius" — the express mention of one thing excludes all others.

[69] Under UCC § 1-202(d), a person notifying another person must take "such steps as may be reasonably required to inform the other in ordinary course. . . ." The language of a different term in an acceptance should not constitute notification of objection; after all, one of the underlying rationales for UCC § 2-207 is that it is inefficient to spend time reading boilerplate. However, a reasonable offeree should assume that the offeror would object to the automatic displacement of any of its preferred term with something different and therefore the offeror would not have to take any steps to inform the offeree.

[70] 777 F. Supp. 1214, 16 UCC Rep. Serv. 2d 1035 (M.D. Pa. 1991).

[2]   Written Confirmations

Section 2-207(1) covers written confirmations as well as definite expressions of acceptance. It provides that "a written confirmation which is sent within a reasonable time . . . operates as an acceptance even though it states terms additional to or different from . . . those agreed upon." The language is problematic. A written confirmation can be sent only after a contract has been formed, meaning that acceptance has already occurred. Thus it is nonsensical to say that a written confirmation "operates as an acceptance." Further complicating the analysis, grammatically the "unless" clause at the end of the subsection modifies the rules for both definite expressions of acceptance and written confirmations, but logically it cannot apply to confirmations since acceptance has already occurred. For this reason the clause should be ignored.[71]

A written confirmation can best be understood as an attempt to modify an existing contract and the only relevant issue is what happens to additional and different terms if the recipient does not assent to them. Although the statute is silent on the point, if both parties send a confirmation and they coincide with regard to a particular term, the term should become part of the contract. Additional terms in a confirmation are treated exactly like additional terms in a definite expression of acceptance: They are proposals for addition to the contract and may become operative by assent or by operation of the between-merchants rule.[72]

The treatment of different terms is more problematic and should not parallel entirely the treatment of different terms in definite expressions of acceptance. If each party sends a written confirmation that differs as to a particular term, both terms drop out.[73] However, a term in a written confirmation that differs from a term of the contract should not knock out that term, even though some courts allow that result with a term in a definite expression of acceptance that differs from a term in the offer.[74] It is one thing to lessen the effect of Section 2-207's first-shot bias by using, in the contract-formation process, implied-in-fact terms and gap-fillers whenever possible. By contrast, permitting a party to an existing contract unilaterally to force a modification of a term it does not like merely by placing a different term in a written confirmation would give the party entirely too much power.

---

[71] *See, e.g.*, St. Charles Cable TV, Inc. v. Eagle Comtronics, Inc., 687 F. Supp. 820, 6 UCC Rep. Serv. 2d 659 (S.D.N.Y. 1988).

[72] *See* discussion § 2.04[C] *infra*.

[73] *See* UCC § 2-207, cmt. 6 ("[w]here clauses on confirming forms conflict each party must be assumed to object to a clause of the other conflicting with the one on the confirmation sent by himself"). To the same effect, see *Coorstek, Inc. v. Electric Melting Serv. Co., Inc.*, 64 UCC Rep. Serv. 2d 861 (E.D. Ark. 2008).

[74] *See* discussion § 2.04[B][1] *supra*.

[C]   The Between-Merchants Rule

Section 2-207(2) permits additional terms proposed by one party to become effective even though the other party has not assented to them.[75] The rule creates a presumption that all additional terms automatically become part of a contract between merchants[76] but limits the effect of the presumption by articulating three situations in which additional terms drop out. An offeror or a recipient of a written confirmation can control two of these situations. First, an offer that expressly limits acceptance to its terms prevents additional terms in a definite expression of acceptance from becoming effective automatically.[77] Although subsection (2) is not explicit on the point, presumably an express limitation in an offer carries through to written confirmations. Second, a notification of objection given by an offeror or a recipient of a written confirmation either before or within a reasonable time after notice of additional terms is received blocks the application of the between-merchants rule.[78] A notification of objection may refer to all additional terms or may target a specific term.

The third situation in which an additional term cannot become effective automatically is situational: The term may not materially alter the offer or contract.[79] What terms are material for purposes of Section 2-207(2)? The Comments provide some guidance by stating that a clause materially alters a contract if it would "result in surprise or hardship if incorporated without express awareness by the other party."[80] They continue with the following examples of material terms:[81]

- a clause disclaiming implied warranties of merchantability or fitness;

- a clause requiring a guaranty of quantity greater than the requirements in a relevant usage of trade;

- a clause giving the seller a right to cancel if the buyer fails to pay an invoice; and

- a clause requiring that complaints be made within a time period shorter than is customary or reasonable.

---

[75] Whether the between-merchants rule applies to different terms is discussed in the context of the treatment of definite expressions of acceptance [§ 2.04[B][1] *supra*] and written confirmations [§ 2.04[B][2] *supra*].

[76] For purposes of UCC § 2-207, "merchant" has the same meaning as it has for purposes of UCC § 2-201(2). See the discussion of that topic in § 3.03 [B] *infra*.

[77] UCC § 2-207(2)(a). *See, e.g.*, Curwood, Inc. v. Prodo-Pak Corp., 65 UCC Rep. Serv. 2d 333 (E.D. Wis. 2008) (offer stating that acceptance was expressly limited to its terms precluded additional term in definite expression of acceptance from becoming operative automatically in contract between merchants).

[78] UCC § 2-207(2)(c). Notice is received when a definite expression of acceptance or written confirmation is received.

[79] UCC § 2-207(2)(b).

[80] UCC § 2-207, cmt. 4.

[81] *Id.*

The Comments also give the following examples of nonmaterial clauses:[82]

- a clause providing for interest on overdue invoices that is within the range of trade practice;

- a clause setting a reasonable time for complaints;

- a clause giving the seller reasonable credit terms; and

- a clause limiting the buyer's right of rejection for defects that fall within trade tolerances for acceptance with adjustment.

The meaning and importance of "surprise" and "hardship" are not entirely clear, and two different approaches have emerged. One approach is illustrated by the decision in *Dale R. Hornung Co. v. Falconer Glass Industries, Inc.*,[83] in which the buyer, a glazing subcontractor on an office-building project, ordered glass for the building by phone. Before shipment, the seller sent a written confirmation with a clause excluding consequential damages. When the glass proved to be defective, the buyer sued to recover the consequential losses it incurred. The court held that for a clause to be effective under Section 2-207(2), it must cause neither hardship nor surprise. Surprise obviously refers to whether a clause catches a buyer unawares, and in this regard the court held that the buyer should not have been surprised because clauses excluding consequential damages were fairly common in its industry.[84] The court concluded that hardship refers to whether enforcement of a clause would impose a substantial economic detriment on the non-assenting party. Under this test any clause that shifts a substantial economic risk from one party to another is material. Using this approach, the court found that the clause at issue would cause the buyer to suffer a hardship and refused to enforce it. The court noted that the seller could have separately negotiated its limitation prior to shipping the glass.

The court in *Union Carbide Corp. v. Oscar Mayer Foods Corp.*[85] adopted a different approach. Union Carbide, which had been selling plastic sausage casings to Oscar Mayer, had printed on the back of its invoices a clause requiring the buyer to indemnify it for all sales-tax liability. Eventually, the Illinois taxing authority held that the seller owed additional sales taxes, placing at issue the enforceability of the indemnification clause. The decision, authored by Judge Posner, concluded that the only relevant test for materiality is surprise. If a term is so unusual that it would come as a surprise to the other party, that party's assent should not be presumed. Hardship is a consequence of surprise and, therefore, is not a separate criterion. If a term is so routine that it does not cause surprise, assent can be presumed and any hardship caused by it is legally insignificant unless it reaches such a level that it gives rise to a claim

---

[82] UCC § 2-207, cmt. 5.

[83] 730 F. Supp. 962, 11 UCC Rep. Serv. 2d 536 (S.D. Ind. 1990); *see also* Trans-Aire Int'l, Inc. v. Northern Adhesive Co., 882 F.2d 1254, 9 UCC Rep. Serv. 2d 878 (7th Cir. 1989).

[84] Apparently, the practice of excluding consequential damages was not so common that it rose to the level of a usage of trade. If it had done so, it would have been part of the contract from the outset.

[85] 947 F.2d 1333, 16 UCC Rep. Serv. 2d 46 (7th Cir. 1991).

of commercial impracticability.[86] Ultimately, the court found that the clause in question came as a surprise to the buyer, precluding its liability for the additional taxes.

An example of a clause that courts have routinely viewed as nonmaterial is one requiring the buyer to pay interest on past-due amounts.[87] At the other extreme, courts almost always find warranty disclaimers to be material,[88] although a contrary result was reached in *Graham Hydraulic Power, Inc. v. Stewart & Stevenson Power, Inc.*[89] The parties in that case held preliminary discussions regarding the sale of hydraulic pumps, and during the course of those discussions the seller gave the buyer a copy of its warranty disclaimer form. After the buyer submitted its purchase order, the seller responded with an acknowledgment that contained the disclaimer. The pumps were defective and the court found that the disclaimer caused neither hardship nor surprise and, therefore, was nonmaterial. Because both parties were merchants, it became operative automatically. The result is appropriate given the circumstances: Allowing the buyer, which knew about the disclaimer, to avoid the risk through a mechanical application of Section 2-207 would have violated the spirit of that section.

Graham Hydraulic Power demonstrates that materiality is best understood as an issue of fact that must be decided on a case-by-case basis, making inconsistent results inevitable.[90] While some cases have held that certain types of clauses, such as arbitration clauses, are material as a matter of law,[91] the better-reasoned decisions have adopted the case-by-case approach, focusing primarily on the extent to which the term at issue is used within the relevant industry.[92]

Two straightforward illustrations show the effect of materiality on the between-merchants rule. Suppose a buyer places a purchase order stating that payment will be due thirty days after delivery. The seller responds with an acknowledgment form that mirrors the buyer's dickered terms and has clauses in the boilerplate that require the buyer to pay interest on late payments and

---

[86] For discussion of commercial impracticability, see § 7.08[D] *infra*.

[87] *See, e.g.*, Advance Concrete Forms, Inc. v. McCann Constr. Specialties Co., 916 F.2d 412, 12 UCC Rep. Serv. 2d 1047 (7th Cir. 1990); Southwest Concrete Prod. v. Gosh Constr. Corp., 215 Cal. App. 3d 134, 263 Cal. Rptr. 387, 10 UCC Rep. Serv. 2d 73 (1989).

[88] *See, e.g.*, USEMCO, Inc. v. Marbro Co., Inc., 60 Md. App. 351, 483 A.2d 88, 39 UCC Rep. Serv. 1600 (1984); Boese-Hilburn Co. v. Dean Mach. Co., 616 S.W.2d 520, 31 UCC Rep. Serv. 830 (Mo. Ct. App. 1981).

[89] 797 P.2d 835, 12 UCC Rep. Serv. 2d 658 (Colo. App. 1990).

[90] *Compare* Burbic Constr. Co., Inc. v. Cement Asbestos Prod. Co., Inc., 409 So. 2d 1, 32 UCC Rep. Serv. 1406 (Ala. 1982) (limited-remedy clause nonmaterial), *with* Transamerica Oil Co. v. Lynes, Inc., 723 F.2d 758, 37 UCC Rep. Serv. 1076 (10th Cir. 1983) (limited-remedy clause material).

[91] *See, e.g.*, Windsor Mills, Inc. v. Collins & Aikman Corp., 25 Cal. App. 3d 987, 101 Cal. Rptr. 347, 10 UCC Rep. Serv. 1020 (1972).

[92] *See, e.g.*, Valmont Indus., Inc. v. Mitsui & Co. (USA), Inc., 419 F. Supp. 1238, 20 UCC Rep. Serv. 626 (D. Neb. 1976) (court should consider industry practices in deciding materiality of arbitration clause). An industry practice that is sufficiently widespread can constitute a usage of trade and become part of the agreement through implication.

that conspicuously disclaim implied warranties. The seller's response is a definite expression of acceptance and the parties' communications create a contract on the buyer's terms. Nonmaterial additional terms become part of the contract automatically; material additional terms do not. The probable result will be enforcement of the seller's interest clause but not of its disclaimer clause.

Now assume that the same parties agree by telephone on subject matter, quantity, price, and credit. The buyer sends a written confirmation calling for arbitration and the seller sends a written confirmation with its interest and disclaimer clauses. Again, the seller's interest clause will probably become part of the contract and its disclaimer clause probably will not. The buyer's arbitration clause will be a closer question, given the split among the courts, but the analysis remains the same. The clause will be included only if it is nonmaterial.

Because an additional term cannot become part of a contract automatically if it is material or if it is objected to, the between-merchants rule should have been relatively noncontroversial. Unfortunately, it has led to a never-ending stream of litigation over whether a particular term is material and must be considered a failure.

[D]   Expressly Conditional Acceptances

Section 2-207(1) states that a definite expression of acceptance that contains additional or different terms operates as an acceptance "unless acceptance is expressly made conditional on assent to the additional or different terms." The provision balances the first-shot bias of the subsection by giving an offeree a mechanism to opt out of it. The two basic issues in this area concern the language that triggers the "unless" clause and creates an expressly conditional acceptance, and the effect of such an acceptance.

[1]   Language Creating an Expressly Conditional Acceptance

The first major case to address the language issue was the infamous *Roto-Lith, Ltd. v. F.P. Bartlett & Co, Inc.*[93] The case presented one of the classic problems that Section 2-207 was designed to remedy: The buyer submitted a purchase order that was silent as to quality and the seller responded with an acknowledgment disclaiming implied warranties. The seller then delivered the goods, which the buyer kept without objection. When the goods proved to be defective, the buyer asserted a claim based on the implied warranty of merchantability and the seller raised its disclaimer as a defense.

The proper analysis would have been to treat the seller's acknowledgment as a definite expression of acceptance, forming a contract on the buyer's terms. The disclaimer was an additional term and therefore a proposal for addition to the contract. The buyer's conduct did not constitute assent to the proposal and, since the court held that the disclaimer was material, it did not become operative automatically under the between-merchants rule. This result, of

---

[93] 297 F.2d 497, 1 UCC Rep. Serv. 73 (1st Cir. 1962).

course, would have been inconsistent with the common law's mirror-image rule, and the court apparently could not conceive that the drafters had effected such a radical change. It held that because the disclaimer was material, it automatically triggered the "unless" clause of subsection (1) and thus the seller's acknowledgment did not operate as an acceptance. It also held that a response to an offer that comes within the "unless" clause operates as a counteroffer, which the buyer accepted by exercising dominion over the goods.

The decision in *Roto-Lith* effectively reinstated the last-shot rule and is indefensible as a matter of statutory construction. The court ignored the fact that the exception to the rule that a definite expression of acceptance operates as an acceptance requires the offeree's communication to *expressly* state that contract formation is conditional on the offeror's assent to its terms. The decision also conflicts with the Comment that states that a disclaimer is generally material for purposes of the between-merchants rule.[94] The Comment would be nonsensical if every term that materially alters an offer causes the communication containing the term to be treated like a counteroffer. Subsequent commentary and cases resoundingly rejected *Roto-Lith* and it was eventually overruled.[95]

Most courts insist on language that makes it clear that the offeree is not willing to contract unless the offeror assents to the offeree's terms. *Dorton v. Collins & Aikman Corp.*[96] set the standard, holding that the phrase "[t]he acceptance of your order is subject to all the terms & conditions on the face and reverse side hereof, including arbitration" did not make a seller's response expressly conditional. The court stated that the fact that a contract is not being formed must be "directly and distinctly stated rather than implied or left to inference."[97] The words "subject to" in the acknowledgment did not clearly reveal the seller's unwillingness to proceed with the transaction without the buyer's assent. In contrast with *Dorton*, the court in *Construction Aggregates, Inc. v. Hewitt-Robins, Inc.*[98] held that an acknowledgment stating that any final contract was "predicated on the following clarifications, additions or modifications to the [buyer's] order" did not operate as an acceptance. There is no real distinction between "subject to" and "predicated on," and the cases cannot be reconciled. A vast majority of cases have followed the *Dorton* approach.

Offerees sometimes try to have their cake and eat it too by using language that simply states that there is a contract and that their terms control. The court in *DTE Energy Technologies, Inc. v. Briggs Electric, Inc.*[99] properly held

---

[94] UCC § 2-207, cmt. 4.

[95] Ionics, Inc. v. Elmwood Sensors, Inc., 110 F.3d 184, 32 UCC Rep. Serv. 2d 1 (1st Cir. 1997).

[96] 453 F.2d 1161, 10 UCC Rep. Serv. 585 (6th Cir. 1972); *see also* Reaction Molding Technologies, Inc. v. General Electric Co., 588 F. Supp. 1280, 38 UCC Rep. Serv. 1537 (E.D. Pa. 1984); Step-Saver Data Sys., Inc. v. Wyse Technology, 912 F.2d 643, 12 UCC Rep. Serv. 2d 343 (3d Cir. 1990).

[97] 453 F.2d at 1168, 10 UCC Rep. Serv. at 594 (citing *Webster's Third International Dictionary*'s definition of "express").

[98] 404 F.2d 505, 6 UCC Rep. Serv. 112 (7th Cir. 1968).

[99] 62 UCC Rep. Serv. 2d 530 (E.D. Mich. 2007).

that such a notice did not have any effect. A statement attempting to impose a contract on the offeree's terms differs considerably from a statement indicating that there is no contract without the offeror's assent to those terms. There is a price for using the "unless" clause of subsection (1) — an offeree can insist on its own terms but doing so leaves the offeror free to deal with others. The seller in *Coastal & Native Plant Specialties, Inc. v. Engineered Textile Products, Inc.*[100] tried a variation on the theme with no greater success. Its acknowledgment stated, "Buyer shall be deemed to have assented to the provisions hereof in all respects by its acceptance of any goods shipped or by failure to give Seller written notice of objection within five business days of Buyer's receipt of this invoice." The court properly held the language to be ineffective and the seller got exactly what it tried to avoid — a contract on the buyer's terms.[101] To hold otherwise would have allowed reinstatement of the last-shot rule through clever drafting.

[2]   Consequences of an Expressly Conditional Acceptance

Numerous courts have held that an expressly conditional acceptance is a counteroffer. While the language of Section 2-207(1) does not mandate this result, the conclusion is reasonable. The original offeror can choose to assent to the counteroffer, thereby creating a contract on its terms, or to withhold assent, thereby leaving the parties without a contract.

Suppose a seller sends an expressly conditional acceptance and then ships the goods, which the buyer keeps without objection. If the court concludes that the buyer's conduct constitutes assent to the counteroffer — the *Roto-Lith* holding — it would improperly reinstate the lost-shot rule. Section 2-207(3) precludes such a result by providing as follows:

> Conduct by both parties which recognizes the existence of a contract is sufficient to establish a contract for sale although the writings of the parties do not otherwise establish a contract. In such case the terms of the particular contract consist of those terms on which the writings of the parties agree, together with any supplementary terms incorporated under any other provisions of this Act.

The reference to conduct by both parties that recognizes the existence of a contract must be read in conjunction with Section 2-204(1), which provides that a contract may be formed in any reasonable manner "including conduct by both parties which recognizes the existence of such a contract," and with Section 2-204(2), which provides that a contract can exist even though the moment of its making cannot be determined. Cases governed by Section 2-207(3) do not require a search for an offer and an acceptance; the conduct of both parties forms the

---

[100] 139 F. Supp. 2d 1326, 44 UCC Rep. Serv. 2d 75 (N.D. Fla. 2001).

[101] *See also* Polytop Corp. v. Chipsco, Inc., 826 A.2d 945, 50 UCC Rep. Serv. 2d 652 (R.I. 2003) (responsive communication stating that the offeree rejected additional or different terms in offer operated as acceptance); Curwood, Inc. v. Prodo-Pak Corp., 65 UCC Rep. Serv. 2d 333 (E.D. Wis. 2008) (neither the statement that acceptance is subject to terms and conditions nor the inclusion of integration clause in boilerplate created expressly conditional acceptance).

contract and the only relevant question is its terms. By contrast, if a buyer places an order for the prompt or current shipment of goods and in response the seller ships goods, a contract is formed under Section 2-206(1)(b) and Section 2-207(3) is irrelevant.[102] In such a case, the contract is not formed by the conduct of both parties; rather, it is formed by the buyer's express offer coupled with the seller's acceptance by conduct.[103]

In a case governed by Section 2-207(3), the search for the terms starts with the communications of the parties. Terms on which their communications agree are included; terms on which their communications do not agree, whether additional or different, are knocked out.[104] The resulting group of express terms is supplemented by "terms incorporated under any other provisions" of the UCC. This process of supplementation sweeps in terms derived from implied-in-fact sources,[105] including usage of trade, course of dealing, and course of performance. Gaps in the agreement are filled in to the extent possible with Article 2's standard gap-filler provisions.[106]

The court in *Dresser Industries, Inc. v. The Gradall Co.*[107] addressed the interplay between implied-in-fact terms and gap-fillers. The buyer bought a series of engines from the seller, with each sale initiated by a purchase order specifying that the buyer would receive all implied warranties plus a fifteen-month express warranty. The seller responded each time with an acknowledgment that disclaimed all implied warranties and gave a one-year express warranty. Each acknowledgment expressly conditioned any contract on assent to its terms. When litigation arose over a problem that developed in one engine between the twelfth and fifteenth months after its sale,[108] the court applied Section 2-207(3). The buyer, of course, argued that the resulting contract could be supplemented only by standard gap-fillers because it would receive the benefit of the implied warranty of merchantability. The court, however, sided with the seller, which wanted to show that the series of purchases established a course of

---

[102] Contract formation under UCC § 2-206(1)(b) is discussed in § 2.02[B] *supra*.

[103] The lines in this area are paper thin. If the seller sends a communication with the goods that, standing alone, would constitute a definite expression of acceptance, is the contract formed under Section 2-206(1)(b) with the communication constituting a written confirmation, or is it formed under Section 2-207(1)? And if the communication sent with the goods is an expressly conditional acceptance, is the contract formed under Section 2-206(1)(b) or does the analysis shift to Section 2-207(3)? The Code provides no answers.

[104] *See, e.g.*, McJunkin Corp. v. Mechanicals, Inc., 888 F.2d 481, 10 UCC Rep. Serv. 2d 712 (6th Cir. 1989); Scientific Components Corp. v. Isis Surface Mounting, Inc., 65 UCC Rep. Serv. 2d 408 (E.D.N.Y. 2008).

[105] UCC § 1-201(b)(3); *see In re* Cotton Yarn Antitrust Litigation, 505 F.3d 274, 64 UCC Rep. Serv. 2d 214 (4th Cir. 2007) (enforceable agreement to arbitrate based on usage of trade).

[106] *See* § 4.01 *infra*.

[107] 956 F.2d 1442, 18 UCC Rep. Serv. 2d 43 (9th Cir. 1992); *see also* Daitom, Inc. v. Pennwalt Corp., 741 F.2d 1569, 39 UCC Rep. Serv. 1203 (10th Cir. 1984).

[108] Suppose the problem had occurred in the tenth month after purchase and the seller had refused to honor its express warranty. The express warranty terms in the communications of the parties were at variance in terms of their duration but were not contradictory. Since each provided for at least twelve months of coverage, the court should conclude that the contract contained an express warranty of that duration. The buyer would lose only the additional three months of coverage that its term would have provided.

dealing because the buyer had been aware of the seller's terms for a long time. The seller also wanted to show that under a relevant trade usage buyers generally adopted their sellers' warranty terms. The court correctly held that the express terms on which the communications of the parties agreed could be supplemented by terms derived from implied-in-fact sources.[109]

While the knock-out rule of Section 2-207(3) is preferable to the common-law's last-shot rule, the parties must be aware of its impact and plan accordingly. For example, suppose a seller sends an offer that conspicuously disclaims implied warranties and the buyer responds with an expressly conditional acceptance that does not refer to implied warranties. The seller then ships the goods and the buyer uses them. If they prove to be defective, the buyer will have a claim for breach of the implied warranty of merchantability. Section 2-207(3) will determine the terms of the contract, knocking out the seller's disclaimer and filling the resulting gap with the implied warranty. An offeror that receives an expressly conditional acceptance should realize that its standard terms will not control if it performs without obtaining assent to those terms. Similarly, an offeree that sends an expressly conditional acceptance must act consistently with its statement that there is no contract without assent to its terms; if it acts otherwise, its terms will not control.

§ 2.05   TERMS FIRST DISCLOSED AFTER PAYMENT

Courts in recent years have increasingly been called on to resolve disputes involving terms first disclosed by a seller after a buyer has paid for goods. Many of the cases involve purchases of software and, although it is not clear that Article 2 applies to such transactions,[110] the principles involved clearly do. The problem typically arises when a buyer calls a toll-free telephone number or visits a website, selects the desired goods, pays for them by credit card, and later discovers a set of standard terms inside the packaging when the goods arrive.

The seminal case holding that undisclosed terms are unenforceable is *Step-Saver Data Systems, Inc. v. Wyse Technology*.[111] The court in that case held that the terms of a "box-top" license constituted a written confirmation of an existing contract and thus were subject to Section 2-207. That section treats additional terms in a confirmation as proposals for addition to an existing contract and as generally unenforceable absent assent, which may not be inferred from the mere exercise of dominion over the goods. An exception automatically makes immaterial terms part of a contract between merchants if the recipient of the confirmation does not object to them.[112] *Step-Saver* involved an unusual set of facts. After discussions between the parties that did not

---

[109] The court in *C. Itoh & Co. v. Jordan Int'l Co.*, 552 F.2d 1228, 21 UCC Rep. Serv. 353 (7th Cir. 1977), held incorrectly that supplementation was limited to gap-fillers.

[110] The discussion uses the terms buyer, seller, and goods even though a copy of software might not be goods and a transaction in which a person acquires a copy of software might constitute a license rather than a sale. The application of Article 2 to software transactions is discussed in § 1.03[B] and [C] *supra*.

[111] 939 F.2d 91 (3d Cir. 1991).

[112] The treatment of terms in a written confirmation is discussed generally in § 2.04[B][2] *supra*.

mention standard terms, the buyer placed an order by telephone for software and followed up with a purchase order. The seller shipped the box containing the software with an invoice that essentially tracked the terms of the purchase order. A license agreement printed on the box was inconsistent with the discussions of the parties, the purchase order, and the invoice because it disclaimed express and implied warranties and limited the purchaser's remedies. The court not surprisingly applied Section 2-207 and found on these facts that the terms could not become part of the contract automatically because they materially altered it. Other cases support more directly the proposition that terms first disclosed after payment are written confirmations under Section 2-207.[113]

The seminal case taking the opposite approach is *ProCD, Inc. v. Zeidenberg*,[114] Judge Easterbrook, in an opinion that has been both highly praised and roundly criticized, found that Section 2-207 did not apply to "shrinkwrap" terms[115] and that the buyer had assented to them by retaining the software after having had an opportunity to review the terms and return the software for a full refund. The rationale for finding Section 2-207 inapplicable was that the transaction involved only one form whereas *Step-Saver*, which the opinion distinguished, involved two forms. Judge Easterbrook subsequently applied the same rationale in *Hill v. Gateway 2000*,[116] a case clearly governed by Article 2 because it involved standard terms in the box that accompanied a computer that the buyer ordered and paid for over a toll-free number.

Judge Easterbrook's stated rationale is thoroughly unconvincing. During the telephone call in which the buyer in *Hill* specified the desired computer and paid by credit card, the seller's representative undoubtedly promised that the computer would be shipped. Whether the promise was an acceptance of the buyer's offer or an offer or counteroffer that the buyer accepted by payment,

---

[113] *See, e.g.*, Licitra v. Gateway, Inc. 189 Misc. 2d 721, 734 N.Y.S.2d 389, 47 UCC Rep. Serv. 2d 59 (N.Y. Civ. Ct. 2001); Klocek v. Gateway, Inc., 104 F. Supp. 2d 1332, 41 UCC Rep. Serv. 2d 1059 (D. Kan. 2000); Arizona Retail Sys., Inc. v. The Software Link, Inc., 831 F. Supp. 759, 22 UCC Rep. Serv. 2d 70 (D. Ariz. 1993); Lively v. IJAM, Inc., 114 P.3d 487, 58 UCC Rep. Serv. 2d 639 (Okla. Civ. Ct. App. 2005).

[114] 86 F.3d 1447, 29 UCC Rep. Serv. 2d 1109 (7th Cir. 1996).

[115] A "shrinkwrap" license gets its name from the fact that its terms cannot be seen without opening the plastic wrap in which software is commonly packaged. Software vendors today more commonly use "clickwrap" licenses. In a clickwrap license a person that downloads software is presented with a screen containing the license and must click an "agree" icon. Courts generally have enforced clickwrap licenses. *See, e.g.*, Person v. Google, Inc., 456 F. Supp. 2d 488 (S.D.N.Y. 2006); Siebert v. Amateur Athletic Union of U.S., Inc., 422 F. Supp. 2d 1033 (D. Minn. 2006); *see also* Davis, *Presume Assent: The Judicial Acceptance of Clickwrap*, 22 Berkeley Tech. L. J. (2007).

Another method used by vendors is a "browsewrap" license, which means that the terms are available online, usually via a hyperlink, but there is no requirement that a person click assent to them. Browsewrap terms are enforceable if they are presented in such a manner that they would come to the attention of a reasonable person against whom they are to operate. *See, e.g.*, Register.com, Inc. v. Verio, Inc., 126 F. Supp. 2d 238 (S.D.N.Y. 2000), *aff'd*, 356 F.3d 393 (2d Cir. 2004). In *Specht v. Netscape Communications Corp.*, 306 F.3d 17, 48 UCC Rep. Serv. 2d 761 (2d Cir. 2002), the court held that Netscape's license terms were not enforceable because the only way to find them was by scrolling down from the download button and then following a hyperlink that was labeled in such a way as to constitute a mere invitation to peruse the terms.

[116] 105 F.3d 1147, 31 UCC Rep. Serv. 2d 303 (7th Cir. 1997), *cert denied*, 522 U.S. 808 (1997).

under a traditional analysis a contract was formed on the terms discussed during the call as supplemented by implied-in-fact terms and gap-fillers. Under this analysis, the terms in the box could have been nothing other than a confirmation, and the statement that Section 2-207 does not apply to transactions in which only one party uses a standard form is ridiculous.

An alternative, and more plausible, rationale is that the parties entered into what has been called a "rolling" contract.[117] The theory is that buyers are or ought to be aware that sellers in mass-market transactions insist on their standard terms and thus their inclusion with the goods should not be a surprise. Even though the parties have agreed up front on the subject matter, price, and perhaps such other terms as the method of delivery and the duration of the express warranty, and even though the buyer has paid by credit card, the parties are still negotiating until the buyer receives the goods, has an opportunity to review the seller's standard terms, and decides whether to accept them by keeping the goods or reject them by returning the goods. If the buyer returns the goods, no contract is formed and the buyer is entitled to a refund of the amount charged.

The trend among the cases is to permit later terms to be effective,[118] although with some constraints. To get the benefit of the terms, courts have insisted that buyers that do not agree to them be given a reasonable amount of time to return goods. In *Defontes v. Dell Computers Corp.*,[119] the court held that the buyers had not knowingly consented to the seller's standard terms because they were not given sufficient notice of the method to reject them. A seller should also willingly give a refund, and anecdotal evidence indicates that many sellers do not comply.[120] A seller that insists there is a contract by refusing a buyer's timely request for a refund is acting inconsistently with the rolling-contract theory, and the courts should not infer the buyer's assent to the seller's standard terms from its retention of the goods.

The solution to the problem presented by later terms may in part lie in improvements in technology. One of the concerns expressed by Judge Easterbrook in *Hill* is that a typical buyer who calls a toll-free number does not want to listen to a seller's representative read the standard terms. Buyers today often use the Internet to research goods they are considering, and good business practice surely includes making standard terms readily accessible from the seller's website.[121] During a telephone order, the seller's representative can

---

[117] *See* Hillman, *Rolling Contracts*, 71 Fordham L. Rev. 743 (2002).

[118] *See, e.g.*, Arizona Cartridge Remanufacturers Ass'n, Inc. v. Lexmark Intern., Inc., 421 F.3d 981 (9th Cir. 2005); Meridian Project Sys., Inc. v. Hardin Const. Co., LLC, 426 F. Supp. 2d 1101 (E.D. Cal. 2006); Stenzel v. Dell, Inc., 870 A.2d 133 (Me. 2005); I-A Eqpt. Co. v. Icode, Inc., 2003 Mass. App. Div. 30 (2003); Westendorf v. Gateway, 41 UCC Rep. Serv. 2d 1110 (Del. Ch. Ct. 2000).

[119] 2004 R.I. Super LEXIS 32, 52 UCC Rep. Serv. 2d 795 (Jan. 29, 2004).

[120] *See* Tussey, *UCITA, Copyright, and Capture*, 21 Cardozo Arts & Ent. L.J. 319, 329 n. 51 (2003). The Uniform Computer Information Transactions Act (UCITA), which is effective in Virginia and Maryland, requires that a software vendor insisting on later terms provide a right of return. UCITA § 113(c).

[121] The Comments to UCITA indicate that among the rationales for providing a right of return is that it will encourage vendors to make pre-transaction disclosures. UCITA § 113, Comment 2(c).

inform the buyer that the goods shipped will include the seller's standard terms, available on its website, and that the buyer needs to return the goods if it does not wish to be bound by them. A seller that follows these practices will increase the chances that the courts will enforce its terms.

§ 2.06 ELECTRONIC CONTRACTING

Article 2 was drafted before the advent of electronic contracting and Article 2A was drafted while it was in its infancy. Electronic contracting is commonplace today and rules governing the practice as applied to sale and lease transactions are found generally in two sources — the state-enacted Uniform Electronic Transactions Act (UETA), and the federally enacted Digital Signatures in Global and National Commerce Act (commonly referred to as E-Sign).[122] A federal act ordinarily would preempt state law on the same topic but, with exceptions not relevant to this discussion, E-Sign specifically defers to UETA in states that have adopted it as promulgated by the National Conference of Commissioners on Uniform State Laws.[123]

Understanding UETA and E-Sign requires a familiarity with some basic terminology. Each act uses the term "record" and defines it as "information that is inscribed on a tangible medium or that is stored in an electronic or other medium and is retrievable in perceivable form."[124] The term applies to both physical and electronic documents. UETA defines "electronic signature" as "an electronic sound, symbol, or process attached to or logically associated with a record and executed or adopted by a person with the intent to sign the record"[125] and E-Sign's definition is substantially the same.[126] Although both UETA and E-Sign exclude application to the Uniform Commercial Code generally, both apply to Articles 2 and 2A.[127] Neither act requires the use of electronics, but they both level the playing field so that electronic records and signatures have the same legal effect as physical records and signatures.

The key provision of UETA is Section 7, which states as follows:

(a)   A record or signature may not be denied legal effect or enforceability solely because it is in electronic form.

The American Bar Association, in a report on UCITA, recommended that software vendors be required to make their terms available online before purchase. American Bar Association Working Group Report on the Uniform Computer Information Transactions Act ("UCITA"), Jan. 31, 2002, at 8.

[122] 15 U.S.C. §§ 7001-70031. The Uniform Computer Information Transactions Act also contains a comprehensive set of rules governing electronic contracting.

[123] 15 U.S.C. § 7002(a)(1). UETA has been enacted, sometimes with non-uniform amendments, in over 45 states. The effect of non-uniformity on preemption is not clear. It may cause E-Sign to preempt UETA entirely or preemption may be limited to the extent of the non-uniformity.

[124] UETA § 2(13); 15 U.S.C. § 7006(9). Article 1 of the UCC defines the term the same way but it is not used in Article 2 or Article 2A. UCC § 1-201(b)(31).

[125] UETA § 2(8).

[126] 15 U.S.C. § 7006(5).

[127] UETA § 3(b)(2); 15 U.S.C. § 7003(a)(3).

(b)   A contract may not be denied legal effect or enforceability solely because it is in electronic form.

(c)   If a law requires a record to be in writing, an electronic record satisfies the law.

(d)   If a law requires a signature, an electronic signature satisfies the law.

E-Sign's rules are substantially the same.[128]

UETA and E-Sign override any inconsistent provision in Article 2 or 2A. For example, Section 2-207 contains rules that apply to written confirmations.[129] "Writing" is defined in Article 1 as including any "intentional reduction to *tangible* form."[130] The word "tangible" excludes electronic records and thus as drafted Section 2-207 does not apply to electronic confirmations.[131] UETA and E-Sign override the limitation, meaning that electronic confirmations receive the same treatment under the Code as their written counterparts.

Under Section 2-205 a firm offer must be signed.[132] Like writings, the Code limits signatures to the physical world. Article 1 defines "signed" to mean a "symbol executed or adopted with present intention to adopt or accept a *writing*."[133] Because of UETA and E-Sign, a merchant clearly can give a firm offer in electronic form.

UETA and E-Sign differ in a significant way that can lead to unexpected results. UETA is an "opt-in" statute; its application is limited to "transactions between parties each of which has agreed to conduct transactions by electronic means."[134] The act makes it clear that the parties' agreement may be "determined from the context and surrounding circumstances, including the parties' conduct,"[135] and the Comments give several examples of situations in which a court might infer such an agreement.[136] They include acts as simple as a person giving out a business card that contains an e-mail address and as complex as an automobile manufacturer and a supplier entering into a formal agreement providing in detail for the conduct of their business by electronic means. By

---

[128]   15 U.S.C. § 7001(a)(1).

[129]   Written confirmations in the context of Section 2-207 are discussed generally in § 2.04[B][2] *supra*.

[130]   UCC § 1-201(a)(43) (emphasis supplied).

[131]   Recognizing that Article 2 was drafted before the electronic age, courts have occasionally overlooked the limitation. *See, e.g.*, Bazak Int'l Corp. v. Tarrant Apparel Group, 378 F. Supp. 2d 377 (S.D.N.Y. 2005) (e-mail may constitute written confirmation for purposes of UCC § 2-201(2)).

[132]   Firm offers are discussed generally in § 2.03 *supra*.

[133]   UCC § 1-201(a)(37) (emphasis supplied). Revised Article 1 did not change the definition to accommodate electronic signatures because Article 3 relies on the definition and that article does not recognize electronic negotiable instruments.

[134]   UETA § 5(b). The act makes it clear that nothing in the act requires the use of an electronic record or electronic signature. UETA § 5(a). It also makes clear that a person that agrees to conduct one transaction by electronic means may refuse to conduct another transaction by such means, and the right to refuse provided by the act may not be waived. UETA § 5(c).

[135]   *Id.*

[136]   UETA § 5, cmt. 4.

contrast, E-Sign is an "opt-out" statute[137] and applies unless the parties agree not to use electronics.[138]

The applicability of UETA and E-Sign is not always obvious. For example, suppose a prospective buyer receives a voice message in which the caller says "Hi, this is Sue Jones from the car dealership. We spoke earlier today. I can sell you that car we discussed for $22,000 and that price is firm until the end of the month." A voice message qualifies as an electronic record and the statement of the caller's name qualifies as an electronic signature.[139] Because the signed record is from a merchant and gives assurances that it will be held open, it is a firm offer and may not be revoked. The result might be different if the words had been sent in an instant message. Even though an IM uses an electronic medium, it might not be preserved in such a manner that it is retrievable in perceivable form and in such a case it would not constitute a record.

UETA contains other procedural rules that affect contract formation.[140] Section 14 on automated transactions is particularly important; E-Sign does not have a counterpart. In an automated transaction at least one party is represented by a machine functioning as an "electronic agent."[141] The Comments note that "[w]hen machines are involved, the requisite intention [to contract] flows from the programing and use of the machines."[142] Two electronic agents can create a contract without the involvement of a human being,[143] and a contract can also be formed by a human being interacting with an electronic agent.[144] The latter situation can include "an interaction that the individual is free to refuse to perform and which the individual knows or has reason to know will cause the electronic agent to complete the transaction or performance." This language validates what are called "click-through" transactions in which a person goes to a website and clicks assent. Section 10(2) is also important in such transactions, providing procedures that allow an individual that mistakenly clicks assent to get out of the transaction if the other person's electronic agent does not provide an opportunity to prevent or correct the mistake.

---

[137] 15 U.S.C. § 7001(a).

[138] It is possible for UETA to preempt E-Sign yet not apply to a transaction because the parties did not agree to the use of electronics, leaving the Code requirements of a physical document and signature in place.

[139] For a more thorough discussion of electronic signatures, see the discussion of the signed-writing requirement of the Code's statute-of-frauds provisions in § 3.02[A] *infra*.

[140] The discussion does not cover the rules of Section 15, which determine the time and place of sending and receipt of electronic records.

[141] UETA § 2(6) defines the term to mean "a computer program or an electronic or other automated means used independently to initiate an action or respond to electronic records or performances in whole or in part, without review or action by an individual."

[142] UETA § 14, cmt. 1.

[143] UETA § 14(1).

[144] UETA § 14(2).

§ 2.07 MODIFICATION [§ 2-209; § 2A-208]

Parties to a contract frequently need to modify their understandings in order to meet changing circumstances, but the common law made such modifications difficult. Under the pre-existing duty rule, a promise modifying a contract requires new consideration to be binding. *Lingenfelder v. Wainwright Brewery Co.*[145] demonstrates the problem the rule was designed to address. The defendant hired an architect to supervise the construction of a brewery. The architect was also the president of a company that sold refrigeration equipment and when he learned that the refrigeration subcontract had been given to a competitor, he walked off the job. He returned only after the defendant's president promised additional compensation. When the defendant later reneged, the architect sued. In holding for the defendant, the court stated that "[t]o permit plaintiff to recover under such circumstances would be to offer a premium upon bad faith, and invite men to violate their most sacred contracts that they may profit by their own wrong."[146]

While the pre-existing duty rule led to the right result in *Lingenfelder*, it is an obstacle for parties that face genuine hardships and wish to enter into good-faith modifications. The courts consequently sought ways to avoid its application. Some courts employed the legal fiction that the parties first rescinded the original contract and that the subsequent "modification" was in fact a new contract supported by new consideration.[147] Other courts found that the parties had altered the promisee's duties in some trivial way, thus providing nominal consideration to support the modification.[148]

A rule is seriously flawed when the courts have to resort to fictions to avoid its impact, and the drafters of the Code eliminated the consideration requirement for modifications. Section 2-209(1) provides simply that "[a]n agreement modifying a contract within this Article needs no consideration to be binding."[149] The Comments address the potential for abuse as follows:

> However, modifications made [under Section 2-209(1)] must meet the test of good faith imposed by this Act. The effective use of bad faith to escape performance on the original contract terms is barred, and the extortion of a "modification" without legitimate commercial reason is ineffective as a violation of the duty of good faith. Nor can a mere technical consideration support a modification made in bad faith.[150]

The Comments further note that "such matters as a market shift which makes performance come to involve a loss may provide [a legitimate reason for a

---

[145] 103 Mo. 578, 15 S.W. 844 (1891).

[146] 103 Mo. at 582, 15 S.W. at 848.

[147] *See, e.g.*, Schwartzreich v. Bauman-Basch, Inc., 231 N.Y. 196, 131 N.E. 887 (1921).

[148] *See, e.g.*, Jaffray v. Davis, 124 N.Y. 164, 26 N.E. 351 (1891).

[149] UCC § 2-209(1). Restatement (Second) of Contracts § 89(1) followed the lead of the Code to an extent by eliminating the consideration requirement for contracts that remain at least partially executory on each side "if the modification is fair and equitable in view of circumstances not anticipated by the parties when the contract was made."

[150] UCC § 2-209, cmt. 2.

modification] even though there is no such unforeseen difficulty as would make out a legal excuse from performance under Sections 2-615 and 2-616."[151] The Code's shift away from a rule of form gives the courts the flexibility to differentiate between modifications tinged with duress and those that make commercial sense.[152]

While abandoning the formalistic pre-existing duty rule, the drafters subjected modifications to the formal requirements of the statute of frauds and enhanced the enforceability of private statutes of frauds, meaning agreements that modifications must be evidenced by a signed writing. The topic is discussed in Chapter 3.[153]

§ 2.08 AMENDED ARTICLE 2

[A] Electronic Contracting

Amended Article 2 contains provisions on electronic contracting that are consistent with but go somewhat beyond the provisions of the Uniform Electronic Transactions Act (UETA) and the Digital Signatures in Global and National Commerce Act (E-Sign).[154] Amended Section 2-108(4) creates what is known as an "E-Sign shield;"[155] that is, it takes advantage of a provision in E-Sign that permits state law to modify, limit, or supersede E-Sign if the state law is consistent with Titles I and II of that act.[156] Amended Article 2 does not contain a provision that specifically displaces UETA, and thus UETA's provisions generally apply to transaction within the scope of the article. However, the amended article draws its definitions and most of its rules directly from UETA, thereby eliminating inconsistency between the acts.

Amended Section 2-204 has been expanded to cover certain limited aspects of electronic contract formation. Subsection (1), which states that a contract may be formed in any manner sufficient to show agreement, adds as examples "the interaction of electronic agents, and the interaction of an electronic agent and an individual."[157] Subsection (4), which is entirely new, provides as follows:

> Except as otherwise provided in Sections 2-211 through 2-213, the following rules apply:
>
> (a) A contract may be formed by the interaction of electronic agents of the parties, even if no individual was aware of or reviewed

---

[151] *Id.*

[152] *See generally* Hillman, *Policing Contract Modifications Under the UCC: Good Faith and the Doctrine of Economic Duress,* 64 Iowa L. Rev. 849 (1979). Good faith is discussed generally in § 4.05[B] *infra.*

[153] *See* § 3.06 *infra.*

[154] Article 2A contains comparable provisions. UETA and E-Sign are discussed generally in § 2.06 *supra.*

[155] UCC Amended §§ 2-108(4), 2A-104(4).

[156] 15 U.S.C. § 7002(a)(2).

[157] Amended Section 2A-204(1) is the same.

the electronic agents' actions or the resulting terms and agreements.

(b) A contract may be formed by the interaction of an electronic agent and an individual acting on the individual's own behalf or for another person. A contract is formed if the individual takes actions that the individual is free to refuse to take or makes a statement, and the individual has reason to know that the actions or statement will:

(i) cause the electronic agent to complete the transaction or performance; or

(ii) indicate acceptance of an offer, regardless of other expressions or actions by the individual to which the electronic agent cannot react.

The rules state expressly what has been implicit for years with the widespread use of vending machines and the other automated methods of contracting: The lack of human intention at the time of offer and acceptance does not prevent a contract from being formed.[158]

Amended Article 2 does not deal with the availability of equitable defenses, such as fraud and mistake. The Comments note that nothing in the text is intended to restrict the use of such defenses;[159] however, they do not provide guidance because the law in this area as it applies to electronic contracting is not sufficiently developed for a consensus. The Comments indicate that courts should consider the electronic environment in determining the availability of equitable defenses and should not assume that the rules should be the same as they are in the paper world.

Amended Section 2-211 provides that records, signatures, and contracts may not be denied legal effect solely because they are in electronic form.[160] The section does not create substantive rules of validity; rather, it creates an environment of medium neutrality in which parties may accomplish in electronic form whatever the law permits them to accomplish in paper form.

Amended Section 2-212 provides that an electronic record or electronic signature is attributed to the person that created it.[161] Although the section states the obvious, the intention is to avoid the determination that a record or signature is attributed to a machine as opposed to the person operating or programming the machine. Section 2-212 only provides for attribution of a record, not the legal effects of attribution. Whatever legal effects flow from attribution in the paper world will also flow from attribution in the electronic world.

Amended Section 2-213 sets forth two basic principles.[162] First, it provides that an electronic communication that would otherwise have a legal effect has

---

[158] Amended Section 2A-204(1) contains the same rules adapted to reflect leasing terminology.

[159] UCC Amended § 2-204, cmt. 6.

[160] Amended UCC Section 2A-222 is the same.

[161] Amended UCC Section 2A-223 is the same.

[162] Amended UCC Section 2A-224 is the same.

that effect even if the recipient is unaware of its receipt.[163] The analogy in the paper world is the recipient of a letter who does not take the time to read it. Nothing in the section provides that any communication has a legal effect: One must look elsewhere to make that determination. The section also does not state standards to determine when receipt occurs in the electronic context. The provisions of Article 1 provide the standards for receipt of notices.[164] For other communications (*e.g.*, an offer or acceptance), the Comments suggest that the same principles should apply.[165] However, courts need not apply the principle by analogy; UETA § 15(b) contains a rule governing receipt of electronic records generally that is consistent with Article 1 and that applies to transactions governed by Article 2.

The second basic principle of amended Section 2-213 is that receipt of an electronic acknowledgment of an electronic communication establishes receipt of the communication but does not establish its content. Without this provision, a party whose electronic system automatically responds to electronic communications might be bound to the content as sent even if it did match the content as received. The section places this risk on the sender.

[B]   Battle of the Forms

Amended Article 2 takes a different approach to the battle of the forms. It does not have a section entirely devoted to such transactions. Rather, its version of Section 2-207 describes the terms of all contracts, whether formed by an order for goods followed by a prompt promise to ship or their prompt shipment, an oral or record-form offer and an oral or record-form acceptance that mirrors the offer's terms, the interaction of electronic agents or of an electronic agent and an individual, an offer and a definite and seasonable expression of acceptance in a record that contains additional or different terms, or conduct by both parties which recognizes the existence of a contract. The section also deals with the terms of a contract that results when a contract formed in any manner is confirmed by a record that contains additional or different terms.

[1]   The Effect of a Definite and Seasonable Expression of Acceptance

One of the deficiencies of original Section 2-207 is that it conflates two distinct concepts — whether a contract is formed and, if so, the identification of its terms. Amended Article 2 clarifies the analysis by removing the concept of the definite expression of acceptance from Section 2-207 and placing it in Section 2-206. The change is appropriate given that the latter section deals generally with offer and acceptance. Amended Section 2-206 adds a new subsection that states that "[a] definite and seasonable expression of acceptance in a record operates

---

[163] The term "communication" is broader than "record." As noted in Comment 2, "[t]his section deals with electronic communications generally, and it is not limited to electronic records which must be retrievable in perceivable form."

[164] UCC § 1-202(e).

[165] UCC Amended § 2-213, cmt. 3.

as an acceptance even if it contains terms additional to or different from the offer."

The core concept does not differ between the original and the amended versions, but two changes are worth noting. First, while an offer can take any form, amended Section 2-206(3) does not apply unless the definite expression of acceptance is in a record. This limitation is implicit in original Article 2 since terms communicated orally must of necessity be the subject of negotiation. The second change is that the clause at the end of original Section 2-207(1) stating the effect of an expressly conditional acceptance has been eliminated. The Comments explain that the concept still remains viable.[166] Parties can always refuse to enter into deals on terms other than their own, and a record that clearly expresses that intent cannot be said definitely to contemplate an alternative deal.

Another more important reason for omitting the clause is that it focuses only on the offeree's ability to insist on its own terms. Yet what happens if an offer contains a statement that no contract is formed absent assent to its terms and the offeree responds with a definite expression of acceptance that contains additional or different terms? Under original Section 2-207, a contract is formed on the offeror's terms and the only effect of the statement is to preclude application of the between-merchants rule. Under the amendments courts should give such a notation by an offeror the same effect as an equivalent notation by an offeree — the communications of the parties standing alone generally should not result in a contract. A court nevertheless should have the freedom to determine that, notwithstanding the inclusion of such a notation by either or both of the parties, the variance between their communications is so immaterial that a reasonable person in the position of each would conclude that a contract exists. The statute frees the courts to deal with the effects of such notations in a more flexible manner.

[2]   Determining Terms of All Contracts (Including Those Resulting From a Battle of the Forms)

As indicated above, amended Section 2-207 describes the terms of a contract formed in any manner, as well as the terms of the contract that results if a contract formed in any manner is confirmed by a record that contains additional or different terms. The section provides in full as follows:

> Subject to Section 2-202, if (i) conduct by both parties recognizes the existence of a contract although their records do not otherwise establish a contract, (ii) a contract is formed by an offer and acceptance, or (iii) a contract formed in any manner is confirmed by a record that contains terms additional to or different from those in the contract being confirmed, the terms of the contract are:
>
> (a)   terms that appear in the records of both parties;

---

[166] UCC Amended § 2-206, cmt. 3.

(b)   terms, whether in a record or not, to which both parties agree; and

(c)   terms supplied or incorporated under any provision of this Act.

Paragraph (a) cannot apply unless each party uses a record in forming or confirming the contract. Terms that appear in both records obviously should be part of the contract. If neither party, or only one party, uses a record to create or confirm a contract, paragraph (a) does not apply and the terms of the contract are the ones agreed to by the parties and the ones supplied or incorporated under a provision of the Code. Outside the battle-of-the-forms context, this approach has always been applied to determine the terms of contracts. The statement that the parol evidence rule applies is obvious but worth stating.

Amended Section 2-207 does not revert back to the common-law's mirror-image rule with its last-shot bias, but neither does it perpetuate the tilt towards the offeror in the manner provided by original Section 2-207. For example, suppose a seller responds to a standard-form offer with a standard-form definite expression of acceptance that contains additional or different terms. Under original Section 2-207, a contract is formed and the baseline for determining its terms is the offer. Under amended Article 2, a contract is again formed but the baseline for the terms is not the offer. Instead, the result will be consistent with the effect of the knock-out rule of original Section 2-207(3): The contract will include terms that appear in both records, other terms agreed to by the parties, whether express[167] or implied-in-fact, and any gap fillers supplied or incorporated under a Code provision. Amended Section 2-207 is balanced because it permits neither a first-shot nor a last-shot advantage. If paragraph (a) does not apply, the terms are the ones agreed to by the parties plus gap-fillers.

Amended section 2-207 also deals with the terms that result when a contract formed in any manner is confirmed by a record that contains additional or different terms. It applies the same rules here as it applies to the original contract. Terms in a confirmation will not be operative unless they also appear in the other party's record or the parties have agreed to them. The Comments note that "[a]s with original Section 2-207, the courts will have to distinguish between 'confirmations' that are addressed in this section and 'modifications' that are addressed in Section 2-209."[168]

Finally, the amendments eliminate the between-merchants rule of original Section 2-207(2). The drafters judged that it had been the cause of entirely too much litigation and, because only immaterial terms became part of a contract under the rule, the litigation cost exceeded whatever marginal benefit the rule might provide.

---

[167] The admissibility of testimony of an express term not reflected in the parties' records must be determined under UCC Amended § 2-202 (the parol evidence rule).

[168] UCC Amended § 2-207, cmt. 2.

[3] Neutrality as to Terms First Supplied After Buyer Pays

The Comments to amended Section 2-207 indicate that the section takes no position on the effectiveness of terms first provided by the seller after the buyer has made payment.[169] As with other issues in this area, the question boils down to whether the parties have an agreement to the terms under paragraph (b). The Comments state as follows:

> The section omits any specific treatment of terms attached to the goods, or in or on the container in which the goods are delivered. This article takes no position on whether a court should follow the reasoning in *Step-Saver Data Systems, Inc. v. Wyse Technology*, 939 F.2d 91 (3d Cir. 1991) and *Klocek v. Gateway, Inc.* 104 F. Supp. 2d 1332 (D. Kan. 2000) (original 2-207 governs) or the contrary reasoning in *Hill v. Gateway 2000*, 105 F. 3d 1147(7th Cir. 1997) (original 2-207 inapplicable).

§ 2.09 CISG

The basics on contract formation under the CISG are mostly unremarkable. CISG provisions address the concepts of offer[170] and acceptance[171] and provide that neither is effective until it reaches the other party.[172] A purported acceptance that contains additions or modifications to an offer constitutes a counteroffer.[173] The discussion below addresses some of the more prevalent issues that have emerged concerning contract formation under the CISG.

[A] Contract Formation Without Identifiable Offer and Acceptance

Although contract formation through an identifiable offer and acceptance is readily apparent under the CISG, what about transactions in which the parties clearly have manifested contractual intent but a specific offer and acceptance cannot be identified? Given modern methods of easy and rapid communication, buyers and sellers often send back and forth numerous informal communications that do not yield an identifiable offer and acceptance but which nevertheless show their intent to be bound. Alternatively, they might engage in extensive negotiations, reaching agreement on several points as they proceed but never indicating a particular time as the defining moment of contract formation. Parties also often agree on certain aspects of their transaction and then, because of an unwillingness to invest additional time or cost, proceed directly to performance without forging an agreement on other aspects.

---

[169] UCC Amended § 2-207, cmt. 5.

[170] CISG Art. 14.

[171] CISG Art. 18.

[172] CISG Arts. 15(1), 18(2).

[173] CISG Art. 19(1).

The CISG does not include an explicit statement concerning agreements between parties that do not fit the traditional offer-acceptance construct. It only addresses contract formation in the context of an identifiable offer and acceptance, concluding that a contract is formed "at the moment when an acceptance of an offer becomes effective in accordance with the provisions of the Convention."[174] On the other hand, the CISG does not state categorically that contract formation is confined to cases of identifiable offer and acceptance, and if all of the relevant statements and the conduct of the parties taken together reflect their mutual intentions to be bound, the CISG arguably recognizes those intentions. Article 8 provides standards by which statements and conduct of the parties are to be interpreted. Article 8(3) requires expansive consideration in applying these standards, as "due consideration is to be given to all relevant circumstances of the case including the negotiations, any practices which the parties have established between themselves, usages and any subsequent conduct of the parties." At least from this perspective, if the parties speak and act as though they have a contract, it seems that the CISG recognizes their manifestations, thereby supporting the argument that it should not be necessary to identify a specific offer and acceptance in order to find that a contract exists.

[B]   Unstated Price

Article 14 provides that a proposal for concluding a contract must be sufficiently definite if it is to constitute an offer.[175] The article also amplifies on the standard for determining definiteness by providing that "[a] proposal is sufficiently definite if it indicates the goods and expressly or implicitly fixes or makes provision for determining the quantity and the price." This provision does not pose much difficulty with respect to flexible quantity terms; an offer that proposes the formation of a requirements or an output contract include s at least the means to determine the quantity. Article 65 is also helpful in this context because it recognizes the acceptability of a contact in which "the buyer is to specify the form, measurement and other features of the goods."[176]

The case of an unstated price is another matter. Unlike the approach of the common law and the Uniform Commercial Code, the law in some legal systems is not receptive to open-price contracts.[177] A communication that does not expressly or implicitly fix the price or provide a method for determining it is not sufficiently definite to qualify as an offer.[178] The question thus follows whether

---

[174] CISG Art. 23.

[175] CISG Art. 14(1).

[176] CISG Art. 65(1).

[177] *See* Civil Code Art. 1591 (France) (1908) (must agree upon price or method of establishing price). Socialist countries have generally required price specificity and developing nations have not favored open-price terms because of perceived vulnerability of its citizens to price changes for raw materials. *See* Alejandro Garro, *Reconciliation of Legal Traditions in the U.N. Convention on Contracts for the International Sale of Goods*, 23 Int'l Law. 443, 463 (1989).

[178] Trade usage and the practices of the parties should be consulted to determine whether they provide a source for determining the price. *See* CISG Art. 8(3).

satisfaction of the definiteness standard in the CISG is a prerequisite to contract formation.

An answer seems to be provided by Article 55, which states in its entirety as follows: "Where a contract has been validly concluded but does not expressly or implicitly fix or make provision for determining the price, the parties are considered, in the absence of any indication to the contrary, to have impliedly made reference to the price generally charged at the time of the conclusion of the contract for such goods sold under comparable circumstances in the trade concerned." The language suggests that a valid contract may be concluded even though it does not expressly or implicitly fix or make provision for determining the price. This construction suggests in turn that Article 14(1) does not have to be satisfied in order for a contract to be formed.

A contrary construction, however, also lurks. By its own terms, Article 55 can operate to fill a gap concerning price only "where a contract has been validly concluded." If Article 14(1) is a prerequisite to a valid contract under the CISG, Article 55 cannot be used as a bootstrap to provide the missing price term. The missing price term would prevent the contract from being formed and Article 55 would have no effect.

Several arguments undercut the latter construction. First, the construction makes Article 55 nearly redundant: It could play a role only when an Article 92 declaration of a Contracting State makes Article 14 inapplicable[179] *and* the applicable domestic law of that state determines that a contract was concluded validly despite the missing price term. That the drafters would have given so much attention to a provision that would have such a minimal effect seems unlikely. Second, Professor Honnold has demonstrated through legislative history that the intent with respect to the reference in Article 55 to a contract that has been validly concluded was to refer to the domestic law that would be applicable under rules of private international law.[180] His analysis is consistent with the reference in Article 55 to a contract that has *validly* been concluded without a provision for determining price. It suggests that open-price terms pose an issue of contract validity that is governed by domestic law.[181] In other words, Article 55 provides a basis for determining the price only if an open-price term in the parties' agreement would not defeat a valid contract under the applicable domestic law. Third, Article 14(1) states the requirements that must be satisfied in order for a proposal for concluding a contract to qualify as an *offer*. The only way that this provision could preclude an international sales contract because of the absence of the designated price term is to conclude that contract formation under the CISG requires an identifiable offer (and acceptance). As discussed above,[182] however, there is a strong argument that

---

[179] Article 92 allows a Contracting State to declare that it will not be bound by the provisions of the CISG that cover contract formation. Only Denmark, Finland, Norway and Sweden have made Article 92 declarations. The United States has not done so.

[180] J. Honnold, Uniform Law for International Sales Under the 1980 United Nations Convention 150-56 (3d ed. 1999).

[181] *See* CISG Art. 4(a); § 1.07[C] *supra*.

[182] *See* § 2.09[A] *supra*.

the CISG does not prevent contract formation just because a specific offer and an acceptance cannot be identified.

Although the issues concerning unstated price are largely academic, as most parties entering into an international sales contract include a price term, they pose significant risks in the rare case where the price is unstated. The danger is that a tribunal in a country that is hostile to unstated prices in contracts may be disposed to construe the CISG in a way that will satisfy those predispositions. For this reason, the parties should reach express agreement on pricing.

[C]   Revocability

An offer is not effective under the CISG until it reaches the offeree.[183] Because it is not effective any earlier, it can be withdrawn by the offeror if the withdrawal reaches the offeree either before or at the same time as the offer, and this is true even if the offer states that it is irrevocable.[184] Once an offer reaches the offeree, it becomes effective and the issue becomes whether it can be revoked as opposed to withdrawn. The starting point on revocation is that "[u]ntil a contract is concluded an offer may be revoked if the revocation reaches the offeree before he has dispatched an acceptance."[185]

Article 16 includes two rules that if applicable preclude revocation. The first rule provides that "an offer cannot be revoked . . . [i]f it was reasonable for the offeree to rely on the offer as being irrevocable and the offeree has acted in reliance on the offer."[186] Although the rule states principles that are recognized under U.S. domestic law,[187] the similarity does not mean that courts in the international context necessarily will apply it in a manner consistent with U.S. law. Many civil-law countries recognize a presumption that an offer is irrevocable long enough for the offeree to give it due consideration. The rule thus has the potential to raise very different expectations.

The other rule in Article 16 provides that "an offer cannot be revoked . . . [i]f it indicates, whether by stating a fixed time for acceptance or otherwise, that it is irrevocable."[188] Despite certain similarities to U.S. law,[189] a significant pitfall awaits legal advisers that rely on that law. Lawyers experienced in the common law would not consider a statement in an offer that fixes the time for acceptance as having an effect on the offer's revocability; rather, they would view the statement as fixing the time when the offer will lapse. They thus might be inclined to conclude that a statement directed toward lapse does not, in the words of the Article 16 rule, indicate that "by stating a fixed time for acceptance . . . that it [the offer] is irrevocable." In many civil-law systems, however, such a provision would be construed to make the offer irrevocable. Therefore, an

---

[183] CISG Art. 15(1).

[184] CISG Art. 15(2).

[185] CISG Art. 16(1).

[186] CISG Art. 16(2)(b).

[187] Restatement (Second) of Contracts § 87(b)(2).

[188] CISG Art. 16(2)(a).

[189] UCC § 2-205.

offeror that wishes to include a limited time for acceptance of the offer but also wishes to retain the power to revoke the offer prior to an acceptance should be careful to state its intentions precisely in the offer.

Chapter 3

THE REQUIREMENT OF A WRITING

§ 3.01 THE STATUTE OF FRAUDS: A BRIEF HISTORY

The statute of frauds has been a part of our legal tradition since its enactment by Parliament in 1677. Parties then could not testify on their own behalf, and judges had little control over arbitrary jury verdicts. These circumstances often tempted litigants to suborn perjured testimony to the effect that the other party had been overheard making a binding commitment.[1] This state of affairs led to the passage of the original "Act for Prevention of Frauds and Perjuries,"[2] which in Section 17 placed certain sales of goods within the scope of the act. Section 4 referred to five other classes of contracts.

During the three centuries of its existence, the statute of frauds has won widespread praise and generated more than its share of criticism.[3] Certainly the original conditions that contributed to its passage have changed: Parties are competent to testify and judges have a host of mechanisms available to control runaway juries. The statute came to be viewed as an anachronism in England, and in 1954 Parliament repealed all but the suretyship and land provisions.[4] The statute retains much of its original vigor in the United States, although many exceptions have evolved over the years. The primary modern justification for the statute is that a record[5] serves an evidentiary purpose in that it corroborates a party's assertion that a contract had been created. The statute also serves a cautionary function in that a party might reflect further on an undertaking before signing a record.[6]

Opponents of the statute counter these points by arguing that, now that the procedural conditions prevalent in the seventeenth century have changed, the statute actually serves to promote fraud by encouraging parties seeking to avoid liability to perjure themselves. They argue that juries today are well-equipped to determine the truth or falsity of a party's claim of an oral contract. The drafting committee responsible for the 2003 amendments to Article 2 initially followed the English example and deleted Section 2-201; however, virtually every constituency affected by the article objected and the committee reinstated the section in a somewhat amended form. Whatever its deficiencies, the statute of frauds will be with us for the foreseeable future.

§ 3.02   SPECIFIC STATUTE-OF-FRAUDS PROVISIONS [§ 2-201(1); § 2A-201(1)]

Section 2-201(1) provides as follows:

> Except as otherwise provided in this section a contract for the sale of goods for the price of $500 or more is not enforceable by way of action or defense unless there is some writing sufficient to indicate that a

---

[1]   See E.A. Farnsworth, Contracts § 6.1 (2d ed. 1990); 6 W. Holdsworth, History of English Law 379-397 (1924).

[2]   Stat. 29 Car. 2, c. 3.

[3]   Two classic law review articles stated the arguments for and against the statute nearly 80 years ago, and the arguments have changed little since then. The article supporting the statute is Vold, *The Application of the Statute of Frauds Under the Uniform Sales Act*, 15 Minn. L. Rev. 391 (1931). The article urging repeal is Willis, *The Statute of Frauds-a Legal Anachronism*, 3 Ind. L.J. 427 (1928).

[4]   Grunfeld Law Reform (Enforcement of Contracts) Act, 1954, 2 & 3 Eliz. 2, c. 34.

[5]   "Record" is used here rather than "writing," the term used in Articles 2 and 2A, to reflect the effects of modern statutes that override the UCC by creating a medium-neutral environment. However, in the remainder of this chapter, the traditional term "writing" is used except in the discussions of electronic contracting.

[6]   See the note preceding Restatement (Second) of Contracts § 110.

contract for sale has been made between the parties and signed by the party against whom enforcement is sought or his authorized agent or broker. A writing is not insufficient because it omits or incorrectly states a term agreed upon but the contract is not enforceable under this paragraph beyond the quantity of goods shown in the writing.

Similarly, Section 2A-201(1) requires a writing for leases, but the monetary threshold is raised to $1,000.[7] The section also includes some variations from Section 2-201 that are necessary to accommodate leases as opposed to sales.[8] For example, under Section 2-201(1) the only term that must appear in the writing is the quantity term, whereas Section 2A-201(1) requires that the writing also contain a description of the goods leased and the lease term.[9] The elements of a sufficient writing are discussed in ensuing subsections.

Noncompliance with a statute of frauds generally renders a contract unenforceable. This consequence differs from a finding that the contract is void or voidable. The contract exists and is not subject to rescission because of the noncompliance, but the party seeking to enforce it is denied a remedy. The Second Restatement makes the point as follows:

> "Where a contract within the Statute of Frauds is not enforceable against the party to be charged by an action against him, it is not enforceable by a set-off or counterclaim in an action brought by him, or as a defense to a claim by him."[10]

The difference between being void or voidable on the one hand and unenforceable on the other hand is significant. A void contract is an oxymoron — the contract does not exist for any purpose. A contract that is voidable exists but is subject to rescission, after which it will be as if it never existed. By contrast, a contract that is unenforceable may later become enforceable through the creation of a complying memorandum or through one of the exceptions to the memorandum requirement. The distinction has another important consequence: A party that has bestowed a benefit upon another may, subject to certain conditions, be entitled to a remedy based on the other's unjust enrichment,[11] and evidence that the parties entered into a contract, albeit unenforceable, is

---

[7] The $1,000 measure is for total payments to be made under the lease and excludes payments for options to renew or buy. UCC § 2A-201(1)(a).

[8] *See* § 3.02[D] *infra.* Similarly, UCC § 9-203(b)(3)(A) serves as a statute of frauds for secured transactions.

[9] Contrast these requirements with the requirements for common-law contracts within other statutes of frauds. Restatement (First) of Contracts § 207 required the writing to contain "the terms and conditions of all the promises constituting the contract and by whom and to whom the promises are made." Restatement (Second) of Contracts § 131 requires the writing to state the essential terms of the unperformed promises. In other words, the First Restatement required that the details of all the promises (whether performed or unperformed) be in the writing, while the Second Restatement is satisfied by a writing that establishes the broad outlines of the unperformed promises, even if it omits the details. Both of these approaches require far more information than do UCC §§ 2-201(1) and 2A-201(1).

[10] Restatement (Second) of Contracts § 138.

[11] *See* Restatement (Second) of Contracts § 375; Restatement of Restitution § 108.

admissible to show that the party did not bestow the benefit as a gift or as an officious intermeddler.[12]

The statute of frauds is an affirmative defense that must be pleaded in a timely manner in order to avoid being waived. A successful statute-of-frauds defense leads to the conclusion that even if the parties entered into a contract, it cannot be enforced because it is not supported by corroborative evidence sufficient to counter the defense. For purposes of judicial efficiency, determining whether the statute of frauds has been satisfied is a preliminary matter as it does not make sense to complete a trial if the alleged contract ultimately is unenforceable. If the court determines as a matter of law that the statute of frauds bars enforcement, it will dismiss a claim based on the alleged contract.[13] If the claimant satisfies the statute of frauds, by producing a sufficient writing or by demonstrating successfully that the transaction comes within an applicable exception,[14] the case will proceed to the substantive contract issues.

Neither the production of a sufficient writing nor the applicability of an exception establishes that the parties entered into a contract. The writing or exception will prevent the claim from being dismissed because of the affirmative defense. Having survived, however, the claimant must still prove that the parties entered into a contract, the relevant terms, breach by the other party, and any other facts required for the court to grant an appropriate remedy (*e.g.*, the resulting damages or circumstances entitling the claimant to specific performance). The defendant is at liberty to introduce evidence showing that, despite the writing or exception, the parties never in fact reached a binding agreement. For example, the fact that a seller introduces a signed memorandum indicating the sale of a certain quantity of goods will not preclude the buyer from attempting to show that the seller misunderstands the import of the memorandum. The statute of frauds does not address the substantive issues of a contract-based claim; rather, its objective is simply to require a claimant to support its claim with corroborative evidence of the contract's existence. Satisfaction of this objective does not establish that the parties entered into a contract, nor does it establish any of the purported contract's terms.[15]

[A]   The Signed Writing/Record Requirement

The primary evidence of a contract's existence required by Sections 2-201 and 2A-201 is the type of evidence required historically by all statutes of frauds: a sufficiently detailed writing signed by the party to be charged. The writing does not have to reflect the shared understanding of the parties and does not

---

[12] *See* Restatement (Second) of Contracts § 143, cmt. a, illus. 1.

[13] *See, e.g.*, Lee v. Voyles, 898 F.2d 76 (7th Cir. 1990) (oral contract to sell a Ferrari for $275,000 was unenforceable).

[14] *See* §§ 3.03–3.05 *infra*.

[15] The court in *American Bronze Corp. v. Streamway Products*, 8 Ohio App.3d 223, 456 N.E.2d 1295, 37 UCC Rep. Serv. 687 (1982), succinctly summarized the point as follows: "The only effect of meeting [section 2-201] requirements is to take away the statute of frauds as a defense to an oral contract. The burden of persuading the trier of fact that a contract was in fact made orally prior to any written agreement is unaffected." *See also* Atronic Intern., GmbH v. SAI Semispecialists of Am., Inc., 71 Fed. R. Evid. Serv. 300 (E.D.N.Y. 2006).

even have to have been signed as part of the contract-formation process. Indeed, it might be no more than a file memo prepared by a party who thinks that an oral understanding has been reached. In some states the memo does not even have to exist; the statute of frauds can be satisfied by a showing that it existed at one time but has since disappeared.[16]

Consistent with the approach taken with common-law contracts covered by a statute of frauds, the required elements may be found from a combination of writings.[17] For example, an unsigned writing could indicate that a contract had been entered into and the requisite signature could be found on a check given by the buyer to the seller as a down payment.[18] The pre-Code split among courts over the proof required to establish the relationship among multiple writings continues. For example, the court in *West Central Packing, Inc. v. A.F. Murch Co.*[19] allowed the jury to consider any combination of writings, while the court in *Horn & Hardart Co. v. Pillsbury Co.*[20] insisted that the writing showing that a contract existed had to be signed and that any unsigned writings used to satisfy the other requirements had to show on their face that they were part of the same transaction.

To be sufficient, a writing must be signed by the party to be charged. Article 1 treats the concept of "signed" broadly to include "any symbol executed or adopted by a party with present intention to authenticate a writing."[21] The courts have been quite liberal in construing this provision. For example, a pre-printed name on a letterhead has been held to satisfy the signature requirement[22] on the theory that the act of sending the letter constitutes an adoption of the name and shows the requisite intent to authenticate the letter. Courts have also validated a typed name,[23] a hand-printed name at the top of a

---

[16] *Cf.* Sebasty v. Perschke, 404 N.E.2d 1200, 29 UCC Rep. Serv. 39 (Ind. Ct. App. 1980) (proof of lost confirming memorandum admissible for merchant seeking to use UCC § 2-201(2)).

[17] *See, e.g.,* Waltham Truck Equip. Corp. v. Massachusetts Equip. Co., 7 Mass. App. 580, 389 N.E.2d 753, 26 UCC Rep. Serv. 613 (1979) (three writings combined to satisfy statute); Nebraska Builders Prods. Co. v. Industrial Erectors, Inc., 239 Neb. 744, 478 N.W.2d 257, 16 UCC Rep. Serv. 2d 568 (1992) (several letters considered together); Azevedo v. Minister, 86 Nev. 576, 471 P.2d 661, 7 UCC Rep. Serv. 1281 (1970) (multiple accounting statements sent by seller held sufficient).

[18] A check, standing alone, might be sufficiently complete to satisfy the statute. Also, the check could constitute a payment that would bring the contract within an exception to the statute. *See* UCC § 2-201(3)(c), discussed § 3.04[B] *infra*.

[19] 109 Mich. App. 493, 311 N.W.2d 404, 32 UCC Rep. Serv. 1361 (1981); *see also* Migerobe, Inc. v. Certina USA, Inc., 924 F.2d 1330, 14 UCC Rep. Serv. 2d 59 (5th Cir. 1991) (there must be a sufficiently strong connection to suggest that the writings relate to the same transaction).

[20] 703 F. Supp. 1062, 8 UCC Rep. Serv. 2d 354 (S.D.N.Y. 1989).

[21] UCC § 1-201(37).

[22] *See, e.g.,* First Valley Leasing, Inc. v. Goushy, 795 F. Supp. 693, 19 UCC Rep. Serv. 2d 1002 (D.N.J. 1992). Use of the paper with the letterhead by an unauthorized person, on the other hand, would not constitute the company's signature because the company did not have any intent to authenticate whatever was written.

[23] A & G Constr. Co., Inc. v. Reid Bros. Logging Co., Inc., 547 P.2d 1207, 19 UCC Rep. Serv. 37 (Alaska 1976).

memorandum,[24] a company name on a sales brochure,[25] and the minutes of a board of directors meeting.[26] In *Procyon Corp. v. Components Direct, Inc.*,[27] a buyer that directed its bank to issue a letter of credit was held to have adopted the bank's signature.

The use of electronics has raised numerous contracts-related issues, among them the validity of electronic documents and electronic signatures for the purpose of satisfying the statute of frauds. Articles 2 and 2A require a "writing," defined in Article 1 as including any "intentional reduction to *tangible* form."[28] The word "tangible" excludes electronic documents. Article 1 limits the definition of "signed" to physical signatures — a "symbol executed or adopted with present intention to adopt or accept a *writing*."[29] Without more, electronic documents and electronic signatures can satisfy Sections 2-201 and 2A-201 only if a court overlooks the limitations imposed by these definitions.[30]

In most instances the limitations imposed by the definitions will be overcome by one of two acts — the state-enacted Uniform Electronic Transactions Act (UETA) and the federally enacted Digital Signatures in Global and National Commerce Act (commonly referred to as E-Sign).[31] Neither act requires the use of electronics, but both level the playing field so that electronic records and signatures have the same legal effect as physical records and signatures. UETA provides that if a law requires either a physical writing or signature, the law will be satisfied with an electronic record or signature.[32] E-Sign's rules are substantially the same.[33] Both of these acts override the limitations in Sections 2-201 and 2A-201 to physical writings and signatures, validating in addition the use of electronic records and signatures.[34]

UETA and E-Sign both define the term "record" as "information that is inscribed on a tangible medium or that is stored in an electronic or other

---

[24] Southwest Eng'g Co. v. Martin Tractor Co., 205 Kan. 684, 473 P.2d 18, 7 UCC Rep. Serv. 1288 (1970).

[25] Barber & Ross Co. v. Lifetime Doors, Inc., 810 F.2d 1276, 3 UCC Rep. Serv. 2d 41 (4th Cir. 1987), *cert. denied*, 484 U.S. 823 (1987).

[26] Modern Mach. v. Flathead County, 202 Mont. 140, 656 P.2d 206, 36 UCC Rep. Serv. 395 (1982).

[27] 203 Cal. App. 3d 409, 249 Cal. Rptr. 813, 6 UCC Rep. Serv. 2d 655 (Cal. Ct. App. 1988).

[28] UCC § 1-201(a)(43) (emphasis supplied).

[29] UCC § 1-201(a)(37) (emphasis supplied). The definition was not changed in revised Article 1 to accommodate electronic signatures because Article 3 relies on the definition and that article does not recognize electronic negotiable instruments.

[30] *See, e.g.*, Ellis Canning Co. v. Bernstein, 348 F. Supp. 1212, 11 UCC Rep. Serv. 443 (D. Colo. 1972) (tape recording held sufficient to satisfy UCC § 2-201); Bazak International Corp. v. Tarrant Apparel Group, 378 F. Supp. 2d 377 (S.D. N.Y. 2005) (e-mail may constitute written confirmation for purposes of UCC § 2-201(2)).

[31] 15 U.S.C. §§ 7001–7031. For a more complete discussion of both acts in the context of contract formation and the interaction between the two acts, see § 2.06 *supra*.

[32] UETA § 7(c), (d).

[33] 15 U.S.C. § 7001(a)(1).

[34] Although both UETA and E-Sign exclude application to the Uniform Commercial Code generally, they both apply to Articles 2 and 2A.

medium and is retrievable in perceivable form."[35] The term applies to both physical and electronic documents. UETA defines "electronic signature" as "an electronic sound, symbol, or process attached to or logically associated with a record and executed or adopted by a person with the intent to sign the record"[36] and E-Sign's definition is substantially the same.[37]

The application of UETA, which is an "opt-in" statute, is limited to "transactions between parties each of which has agreed to conduct transactions by electronic means."[38] The parties' agreement may be "determined from the context and surrounding circumstances, including the parties' conduct,"[39] and the Comments give several examples of situations in which a court might infer such an agreement.[40] A party thus cannot simply assume that the use of electronics will be the equivalent of the use of paper; absent an agreement by the parties to the use of electronics, the Code requirements of a physical writing and signature will remain intact. By contrast, E-Sign is an "opt-out" statute[41] and, if applicable, overrides the Code requirements unless the parties agree not to use electronics.[42]

As with physical signatures, an electronic sound, symbol, or process might be a forgery. A signature, whether physical or electronic, need not identify the person signing. The fact finder must resolve any questions that arise as to the identity of the signer. If Jack forges Jill's signature on a physical document, he will have executed a symbol with present intent to authenticate the writing and the symbol will serve as his signature rather than Jill's. The same result follows in the electronic world, in which the term used to describe the authenticity of a signature is "attribution." In this regard, UETA provides as follows:

> An electronic record or electronic signature is attributable to a person if it was the act of he person. The act of the person may be shown in any manner, including the showing of the efficacy of any security procedure applied to determine the person to which the electronic record or electronic signature was attributable.[43]

Although a security procedure is not necessary for the creation of an electronic signature, parties that contract regularly in the electronic world often require such procedures in order to prove attribution more easily.

---

[35] UETA § 2(13); 15 U.S.C. § 7006(9). An e-mail obviously is an electronic record, but an instant message would not qualify unless it is stored in memory and retrievable in perceivable form.

[36] UETA § 2(8).

[37] 15 U.S.C. § 7006(5).

[38] UETA § 5(b).

[39] *Id.*

[40] UETA § 5, cmt. 4.

[41] 15 U.S.C. § 7001(a).

[42] For discussion on the choice of law between the federal and the state enactments, see § 2.06 *supra.*

[43] UETA § 9(a).

[B] Sufficient to Show a Contract

Sections 2-201(1) and 2A-201(1)(b) require that to satisfy the statute of frauds a writing must" "be sufficient to indicate that a contract [of sale or lease] has been made between the parties." The required level of specificity is unclear, but the fact that the statutes use the past tense strongly suggests, and perhaps even mandates, that the words of the writing, standing alone, demonstrate that a contract has come into existence. Many courts have followed this approach, holding that the requirement cannot be satisfied by a writing that constitutes an application,[44] a proposal,[45] a negotiating position,[46] or a statement that a future contract is intended.[47] In this same vein, quite a number of courts have refused to recognize a written offer as sufficient,[48] concluding that an offer does not indicate that a contract *has* been formed and that in any event allowing the writing to be supplemented by evidence that the offer was accepted would create the risk of perjury that led to adoption of the statute in the first place.[49]

The drafters of Section 2-201(1) likely did not intend that it be read so literally. They drafted the requirement with an awareness of prior experience, including the application of the statute of frauds to the various categories of common-law contracts.[50] Article 2A simply adopted the Article 2 approach and should be interpreted consistently with its counterpart. The overall goal of the Article 2 drafters was to relax the common law's writing requirements, and it would have been odd for them to have required a more explicit showing that a contract exists than was required at common law.[51] The Comments succinctly state their objective: "All that is required is that the writing afford a basis for believing that the offered oral evidence rests on a real transaction."[52] This statement, standing alone, suggests that the role of the writing is merely as corroboration that a contract for the sale of goods exists between the parties.

---

[44] *See, e.g.*, McClure v. Duggan, 674 F. Supp. 211, 5 UCC Rep. Serv. 2d 925 (N.D. Tex. 1987).

[45] *See, e.g.*, Added Extras, Inc. v. Party City Corp., 193 Misc. 2d 403, 749 N.Y.S.2d 647, 49 UCC Rep. Serv. 2d 409 (N.Y. Sup. Ct. 2002) (writings submitted showed proposals but did not include any documentary evidence of assent); Arcuri v. Weiss, 198 Pa. Super. 506, 184 A.2d 24, 1 UCC Rep. Serv. 45 (1962) (writing stated that agreement was tentative).

[46] Central Illinois Light Co. v. Consolidation Coal Co., 235 F. Supp. 2d 916, 49 UCC Rep. Serv. 2d 399 (C.D. Ill. 2002), *aff'd*, 349 F.3d 488, 52 UCC Rep. Serv. 2d 75 (7th Cir. 2003) (e-mail sent between the parties showed that they were part of the negotiations and did not evidence a contract).

[47] *See, e.g.*, John H. Wickersham Eng'g & Constr., Inc. v. Arbutus Steel Co., 1 UCC Rep. Serv. 49 (Pa. Ct. C.P. 1962) (writing stated intent to award contract).

[48] *See, e.g.*, Howard Constr. Co. v. Jeff-Cole Quarries, Inc., 669 S.W.2d 221, 37 UCC Rep. Serv. 1040 (Mo. Ct. App. 1983); Conaway v. 20th Century Corp., 491 Pa. 189, 420 A.2d 405, 29 UCC Rep. Serv. 1387 (1980).

[49] *See, e.g.*, Bazak Int'l Corp. v. Mast Indus., Inc., 73 N.Y.2d 113, 538 N.Y.S.2d 503, 535 N.E.2d 633, 7 UCC Rep. Serv. 2d 1380 (1989).

[50] *See, e.g.*, Tymon v. Linoki, 16 N.Y.2d 293, 213 N.E.2d 661 (1965) (signed offer to sell land sufficient in action against offeror); *see also* Restatement (Second) of Contracts § 133, illus. 2, § 131, cmt. f.

[51] *See* Monetti, S.P.A. v. Anchor Hocking Corp., 931 F.2d 1178, 14 UCC Rep. Serv. 2d 706 (7th Cir. 1991) (suggesting that, notwithstanding the verb tense chosen by the drafters, it is unlikely that they would have weakened the writing requirement generally yet strengthened it in this respect).

[52] U.C.C. § 2-201, cmt. 1.

The statement, however, does not stand alone. The following language can be read to suggest that the drafters did indeed intend that the requirement be strictly applied: "Only three definite and invariable requirements as to the memorandum are made by this subsection. First, it must evidence a contract for the sale of goods. . . ."[53]

Seeing an apparent inconsistency, some courts and commentators have ignored the first statement in the Comments and applied the statute literally. However, the two statements are not inconsistent if the purpose of the second statement is merely to stress that the writing must relate to a "contract for the sale of goods" rather than a contract that is a loan, lease, or bailment of goods, or that involves property other than goods. Reading the Comments in this manner, an offer to buy or sell goods, and some other preliminary writings, would be sufficient in that they would provide corroboration for the claimant's assertion that a contract of sale had come into existence by the time of trial. A strong policy justification supports this approach: Because the statute of frauds does not address whether the parties in fact have a contract, requiring that a writing demonstrate unequivocally the existence of a contract raises the bar too high and blurs the distinction between the statute's reach and the claimant's substantive case.

A number of cases have refused to apply the statute literally. Their approach is illustrated by *Barber & Ross Co. v. Lifetime Doors, Inc,*[54] where the seller sent the buyer sales literature promising that the seller would be able to meet all of the buyer's demands for doors if the buyer would agree to purchase exclusively from the seller. The court held that the writing, in conjunction with the buyer's evidence that the parties later reached an oral agreement, was sufficient to lower the bar of the statute because, citing the Comments, it provided "a basis for believing that the offered oral evidence rests on a real transaction." Satisfaction of the statute of frauds, however, did not preclude the seller from attempting to prove at trial that, notwithstanding the buyer's evidence, the parties' discussions never ripened into a contract.

[C]   The Quantity Term

The requirements for the Articles 2 and 2A statutes of frauds differ most drastically from the statutes that govern particular categories of common-law contracts with respect to the terms that must be included for the writing to be sufficient. Writings for the common-law contracts must include at least the essential terms of the unfulfilled promises.[55] Section 2-201(1) rejects the common law's level of specificity by stating that "[a] writing is not insufficient because it omits or incorrectly states a term agreed upon." The section continues by providing that "the contract is not enforceable under this

---

[53] *Id.*

[54] 810 F.2d 1276, 3 UCC Rep. Serv. 2d 41 (4th Cir. 1987); *see also* Impossible Elec. Techniques, Inc. v. Wackenhut Protective Systems, Inc., 669 F.2d 1026, 33 UCC Rep. Serv. 806 (5th Cir. 1982) (permitting evidence of oral understanding to be introduced to connect purchase order to contract).

[55] *See* note 9 *supra.*

paragraph beyond the quantity of goods shown in such writing."[56] Virtually all of the cases have held that the section requires a written quantity term,[57] and this approach finds support in the Comments, which state that "[t]he only term which must appear is the quantity term which need not be accurately stated but recovery is limited to the amount stated."[58]

Of all the possible terms that might be in a contract of sale, why did the drafters insist upon the inclusion of a quantity term? Perhaps the reason relates to the type of evidence necessary to corroborate a dispute over quantity. With regard to other terms, the trier of fact can generally be provided objective evidence that will allow it to assess the reasonableness of the asserted term. However, an objective-reasonableness assessment may not be possible when the quantity of goods is in dispute.[59] The requirement that the writing state a quantity establishes an upper limit. In addition, knowing the quantity involved will often facilitate an evaluation of the reasonableness of other terms that may be asserted at trial, especially the price term.

A statement indicating a number of units is not the only way to satisfy the quantity-term requirement. Quantity may also be expressed in terms of the seller's output or the buyer's requirements.[60] For example, a letter indicating that a dealership agreement existed was sufficient even though it was totally silent as to quantity because a dealership is, by definition, a requirements contract.[61] Courts have also upheld writings from which the quantity could be derived by assessing other information in the writing.[62]

The unenforceability of a contract beyond the quantity shown in the writing is illustrated by *Ivey's Plumbing & Electric Co. v. Petrochem Maintenance,*

---

[56] Article 2A contains a comparable limitation. UCC § 2A-201(3).

[57] *See, e.g.*, Office Pavilion S. Florida, Inc. v. ASAL Prod., Inc., 849 So.2d 367, 51 UCC Rep. Serv. 2d 648 (Fla. Dist. Ct. App. 2003) (alleged contract for the sale of chairs was unenforceable because of the absence of a writing that indicated a quantity); MacSteel, Inc. v. Eramet N. Am., 61 UCC Rep. Serv. 2d 385 (E.D. Mich. 2006) (option addendum to a purchase order that did not specify a quantity of additional goods held unenforceable).

[58] UCC § 2-201, cmt. 1. The statute itself does not clearly mandate this result. It merely provides that if the writing contains a quantity term, the party seeking enforcement may not enforce a contract for a greater quantity. Nevertheless, this distinction has largely been lost on the courts, and as a practical matter the party seeking enforcement must show that the writing contains a quantity term.

[59] Many of the gap-filler provisions of Articles 2 and 2A incorporate a reasonableness standard. *See* § 4.04 *infra*. The only gap-fillers with respect to quantity concern output, requirements, and exclusive-dealing contracts (a type of requirements contract).

[60] *See, e.g.*, Riegle Fiber Corp. v. Anderson Gin Co., 512 F.2d 784, 16 UCC Rep. Serv. 1207 (5th Cir. 1975) ("all acceptable cotton" grown on a specified amount of acreage held sufficient); Marion Square Corp. v. Kroger Co., 873 F.2d 72, 8 UCC Rep. Serv. 2d 913 (4th Cir. 1989) (all equipment at a stated location held sufficient). Output and requirement contracts are discussed generally in § 4.04[B] *infra*.

[61] *See* Seaman's Direct Buying Serv. v. Standard Oil Co., 36 Cal.3d 752, 206 Cal. Rptr. 354, 686 P.2d 1158, 39 UCC Rep. Serv. 46 (1984).

[62] Simplex Supplies, Inc. v. Abhe & Svoboda, Inc., 586 N.W.2d 797, 39 UCC Rep. Serv. 2d 1068 (Minn. Ct. App. 1998) (writings showed that the price per ton was $145 and that the total price was $362,500, permitting the court to conclude that the contract was for 2,500 tons).

Inc.,[63] in which the seller unsuccessfully argued that the parties had actually agreed on five units when the writing indicated two. Conversely, if the writing had stated five, the statute would not have prevented one of the parties from arguing that the stated quantity was a mistake and that the actual agreement was for two units.[64]

Suppose parties enter into a contract that is similar to an output or requirements contract but does not technically qualify. For example, in order to reduce the cost of carrying components in stock, a manufacturer might arrange for a seller of the components to deliver them just in time for incorporation into a finished product. To effectuate their intent, the parties might execute a master agreement that requires the seller to fill orders as they are received, but it is clear that the seller will not be the only supplier of the components and thus the contract is not a requirements contract. Does the fact that the parties are unable to provide a quantity term in the master agreement render it unenforceable? "Just-in-time" contracts serve an important commercial function and the law should not interpose a requirement for enforceability that cannot be met, yet that will be the outcome if Section 2-201(1) is applied literally. Although not directly on point, the case of *PMC Corp. v. Houston Wire and Cable Co.*[65] may offer help. In that case, a writing indicated that the buyer would treat the seller as a preferred supplier of a thermocouple product and would buy "the major portion of this product" from it. The court held that the writing satisfied the statute, citing this sentence from the Comments: "The required writing need not contain all the material terms of the contract and such terms as are stated need not be precisely stated."[66] It is not at all clear that this sentence was intended to apply to the quantity term, which is dealt with separately in the Comments. Nevertheless, the case stands for the proposition that the quantity-term requirement may be relaxed in order to enforce a contract that is in the nature of a requirements contract.

[D]   Terms Describing the Goods and Duration — Leases

In addition to the quantity term, Article 2A requires the writing to "describe the goods leased and the lease term."[67] Because a lease gives the lessee the right to use the goods for a period of time, duration is as crucial to a lease transaction as quantity is to a sales transaction. Accordingly, Article 2A treats

---

[63] 463 F. Supp. 543, 26 UCC Rep. Serv. 621 (N.D. Miss. 1978).

[64] If the written memorandum qualified as a final writing for purposes of the parol evidence rule, any extrinsic evidence of a different quantity would be excluded except for the purpose of showing that the writing should be reformed. Just because a writing satisfies the statute of frauds does not mean that it is also final for purposes of the parol evidence rule. A final writing requires the parties to agree on the form of expression. A written memorandum may be no more than one party's recollection of a conversation. The parol evidence rule is discussed in general in § 4.02 *infra*. The requirements for a final writing are discussed in § 4.02[B][1], and the use of reformation to overcome the rule is discussed in § 4.02[C][3].

[65] 797 A.2d 125 (N.H. 2002). The case is referenced approvingly in amended UCC § 2-201, cmt. 1.

[66] UCC § 2-201, cmt. 1.

[67] UCC § 2A-201(1)(b).

the duration term the same as it does the quantity term: The contract is not enforceable beyond the duration shown in the writing.[68]

The requirement that the goods be described serves a function comparable to Article 9's requirement that a security agreement include a description of the collateral — providing evidence of the goods that are to be returned to the lessor at the end of the lease term.[69] Article 2A is consistent with Article 9 in providing that the description of the goods or the lease term is sufficient "whether or not it is specific, if it reasonably identifies what is described."[70]

§ 3.03 THE WRITTEN-CONFIRMATION STATUTORY EXCEPTION [§ 2-201(2)]

[A] Policy

The drafters of Article 2 faced a paradox. They recognized that buyers and sellers of some goods, such as commodities, often enter into contracts over the telephone. A desirable business practice in such circumstances is for one of the parties promptly to send a written[71] confirmation to the other. If the confirmation conflicts in any respect with the other party's understanding of the agreement, that party should respond with its concerns. The paradox is that the party that sends the confirmation provides the other party with a writing that satisfies the statute of frauds against the sender but, because the confirmation is not signed by the other party, the sender may not itself be able to enforce the contract. This gives the recipient a strategic advantage in that it can enforce the contract if market conditions are favorable and can hide behind the statute of frauds if they are unfavorable. In this manner Section 2-201(1) can work to the detriment of a party that observes the good business practice of sending written confirmations.

The drafters developed a statutory exception to the signature requirement that deals specifically with the paradox. It is exclusive to Article 2, as there is nothing similar in other statutes of frauds and the drafters of Article 2A chose not to replicate it.[72] The exception is stated in Section 2-201(2) as follows:

> Between merchants if within a reasonable time a writing in confirmation of the contract and sufficient against the sender is received and the party receiving it has reason to know its contents, it satisfies the requirements of subsection (1) against such party unless written notice of objection to its contents is given within 10 days after it is received.

---

[68] UCC § 2A-201(3).

[69] UCC § 9-203(b)(3)(A).

[70] UCC § 2A-201(2) (based on UCC § 9-108(a)).

[71] Today, the confirmation might consist of an electronic record. The use of electronic records and signatures in the context of the statute of frauds is discussed in § 3.02[A] *supra*.

[72] The drafters of Article 2A considered it superfluous because of the limited use of written confirmations in the leasing industry. *See* UCC § 2A-201, cmt.

Put simply, a writing that satisfies the statute of frauds as to the merchant that signed it might also satisfy the statute as to another merchant that has not signed it. Section 2-201(2) thus operates as a partial exception to the statute of frauds: A sufficient signed writing is still required, but the writing does not have to be signed by the party to be charged.

[B]   Requirements

Section 2-201(2) applies only when both parties are merchants, but courts should be careful in handling this issue. The term "merchant" is defined as someone "who by his occupation holds himself out as having knowledge or skill peculiar to the practices or goods involved in the transaction."[73] Note carefully that the merchant's expertise need not be with the type of goods involved in the transaction; it may instead relate to the business practices involved. The Comments explain the point regarding business practices as follows:

> Sections 2-201(2), 2-205, 2-207 and 2-209 rest on normal business practices which are or ought to be typical of and familiar to any person in business. For purposes of these sections almost every person in business would, therefore, be deemed to be a "merchant" under [the definition] since the practices involved in the transactions are non-specialized business practices such as answering mail.[74]

In other words, "merchant" is a flexible term that means different things in different contexts. If a hospital orders a computer and receives a written confirmation from the seller, it is a merchant and may lose its statute-of-frauds defense by virtue of Section 2-201(2). If the same hospital later sells the computer as used goods, it is probably not a merchant for purposes of the implied warranty of merchantability since it has no particular expertise in computer products.[75]

To be effective under Section 2-201(2), a writing must have two distinct attributes. Initially, it must be sufficient against the sender. In other words the writing must satisfy Section 2-201(1) for purposes of an action against the sender,[76] meaning that it must indicate the existence of a sales contract between the parties, provide a quantity term, and contain the sender's signature. Unless the sender provides the recipient with a writing that satisfies the statute of frauds against the sender, the paradox behind the exception will not arise.[77] The only other attribute required of the writing is that it must confirm the contract. The very idea of a confirmation presupposes the existence of a contract and thus

---

[73] UCC § 2-104(1).

[74] UCC § 2-104, cmt. 2.

[75] See UCC § 2-104, cmt. 2. Under UCC § 2-314(1), there is an implied warranty of merchantability only if the seller is a merchant "with respect to goods of that kind." See also § 5.02[B][1] infra.

[76] Trident Const. Co., Inc. v. Austin Co., 2272 F. Supp. 2d 566, 51 UCC Rep. Serv. 2d 638 (D.S.C. 2003), aff'd, 93 Fed. Appx. 509 (4th Cir. 2004) (letter that would be insufficient to satisfy the statute of frauds against the sender does not satisfy Section 2-201(2)).

[77] See § 3.03[A] supra.

the exception applies only if the writing confirms a contract previously formed by the parties.[78] This limitation again restricts the availability of Section 2-201(2) to the circumstances of the paradox.[79]

The mailbox rule, used with respect to the effectiveness of an acceptance, does not apply to written confirmations. Unless the other party receives the confirmation, it does not have a writing that satisfies Section 2-201(1) and the paradox will not arise unless the court allows the claimant to prove that it once existed but has been lost.[80] Another reason for requiring receipt is that the other party must receive the confirmation in order to learn of its contents and decide whether to object to them. The time of receipt can be an issue, and the Code provides guidance on this point.[81]

Section 2-201(2) requires that receipt occur within a reasonable time.[82] Recall that the primary rationale for the exception is to eliminate the opportunity for the recipient of a confirmation to speculate at the sender's expense as market prices change. Requiring that the confirmation be received within a reasonable time precludes the sender from comparable speculation. Given this objective and the ease of preparing a written confirmation, the courts are likely to allow only a relatively short period to get the writing to the other party, particularly in volatile markets where there are rapid price fluctuations.[83]

The statute requires that the merchant receiving the written confirmation have reason to know its contents, but business people generally have actual knowledge of the contents of their mail because they read it. Merchants that fail to read their mail do so at their peril. Nevertheless, a merchant might not have reason to know the contents of a letter if the envelope would make it appear to a reasonable merchant to be junk mail, and a similar problem can arise with e-mail that appears to be spam.[84]

---

[78] At least one court has suggested that a written confirmation must have additional language that expressly states that it is a confirmation. *See* Trilco Terminal v. Prebilt Corp., 167 N.J. Super. 449, 400 A.2d 1237 (1979) (dictum). Such a requirement goes well beyond the language of Section 2-201(2) and should be rejected.

[79] Audio Visual Assoc., Inc. v. Sharp Electronics Corp., 210 F.3d 254, 41 UCC Rep. Serv. 2d 430 (4th Cir. 2000) (purchase order sent by the plaintiff was a writing intended to form a contract, not one in confirmation of an existing contract). *But see* Melford Olsen Honey, Inc. v. Adee, 452 F.3d 956, 60 UCC Rep. Serv. 2d 331 (8th Cir. 2006) (buyer satisfied the requirement of the merchant's exception by sending a purchase order that memorialized the terms for a sale of honey).

[80] See text accompanying note 16 *supra*.

[81] UCC § 1-202(e) states that "a person 'receives' a notice or notification when: (1) it comes to that person's attention; or (2) it is duly delivered in a form reasonable under the circumstances at the place of business through which the contract was made or at another location held out by that person as the place for receipt of such communications." *See also* Thompson Printing Mach. Co. v. B.F. Goodrich Co., 714 F.2d 744, 36 UCC Rep. Serv. 737 (7th Cir. 1983) (receipt occurs even if mail-room personnel mishandle confirmation).

[82] UCC § 1-205 provides that whether a time for taking an action is reasonable "depends on the nature, purpose, and circumstances of the action."

[83] Bureau Serv. Co. v. King, 308 Ill. App.3d 835, 721 N.E.2d 159, 42 UCC Rep. Serv. 2d 906 (Ill. Ct. App. 1999) (in light of volatility of the grain market, eight months held to be an unreasonable period of time in which to send confirmatory memorandum).

[84] *See, e.g.*, Bazak International Corp. v. Tarrant Apparel Group, 378 F. Supp. 2d 377 (S.D.N.Y.

The Code does not make the contents of the written confirmation binding on the recipient. Section 2-201(2) specifies that the effect of a written confirmation is to satisfy against the recipient the requirements of Section 2-201(1), thus defeating a statute-of-frauds defense. The recipient is free to introduce extrinsic evidence and to use substantive contract law to prove that no contract was ever formed or that a contract was formed but its terms differ significantly from those contained in the confirmation.[85] The recipient can even prevent the written confirmation from eliminating its statute-of-frauds defense by giving, within ten days after receipt of the confirmation, written notice of objection to its contents. This provision is within the framework of the targeted paradox because a prudent business person should register an objection to an erroneous claim of an oral contract and thereby undercut any continuing reliance by the claimant. Moreover, even if the statute of frauds is satisfied against the sender, a recipient objecting to a confirmation could not credibly maintain an action to enforce the contract or, if the objection went to a term, to hold the sender to that term.

§ 3.04 OTHER STATUTORY EXCEPTIONS [§ 2-201(3); § 2A-201(4)]

Articles 2 and 2A contain three statutory exceptions to the writing requirement of their respective statutes of frauds. Each of these exceptions provides a form of corroborative evidence that the drafters considered to be at least as good as the traditional required writing. Because the objective of the statute of frauds can be just as readily satisfied through these forms of corroborative evidence, the exceptions provide complete alternatives that are sufficient to defeat a statute-of-frauds defense. The exceptions are discussed in the ensuing subsections. Unlike the partial exception of Section 2-201(2) in which a writing is required but not the signature of the party to be charged, these full exceptions apply to sellers, buyers, lessors, and lessees without regard to whether they are merchants.

Application of the exceptions poses a unique problem in the context of Article 2A. Enforcement of a lease is dependent upon knowing the duration of the lease, and the Article 2A statute of frauds thus requires that the writing include a description of the lease term in order to be sufficient. The lease term will not always be apparent when the statutory exceptions are applied, and thus the drafters of Article 2A provided as follows:

> The lease term under a lease contract referred to in [the statutory exception provision] is: (a) if there is a writing signed by the party against whom enforcement is sought or by that party's authorized agent specifying the lease term, the term so specified; (b) if the party against

---

2005) (whether recipient had reason to know contents of e-mail that it claimed appeared to be spam raised an issue of fact to be resolved by jury).

[85] The court in *Milltex Industries Corp. v. Jacquard Lace Co., Ltd.*, 557 So. 2d 1222, 12 UCC Rep. Serv. 2d 44 (Ala. 1990), held incorrectly that the buyer's failure to object meant that it had acquiesced in the seller's price. The buyer's failure to object did no more than preclude the buyer from using the statute of frauds as a defense.

whom enforcement is sought admits in that party's pleading, testimony, or otherwise in court a lease term, the term so admitted; or (c) a reasonable lease term.[86]

This language is troubling in that it appears to preclude the party that did not sign the writing or make the admission from attempting to prove that the lease term is actually shorter than the written or admitted term. In Article 2, the quantity term in the writing sets the upper limit for enforcement, and if a party against whom enforcement is sought makes a judicial admission, the admitted quantity sets the upper limit. Presumably, the Article 2A provision functions similarly and does not preclude a party from arguing that the agreed duration was shorter.

[A]   Admissions in Judicial Proceedings [§ 2-201(3)(b); § 2A-201(4)(b)]

The most obvious functional substitute for a writing is the exception based on an admission in judicial proceedings. Section 2-201(3)(b) provides as follows:

> A contract which does not satisfy the requirements of subsection (1) but which is valid in other respects is enforceable . . . if the party against whom enforcement is sought admits in his pleading, testimony or otherwise in court that a contract for sale was made, but the contract is not enforceable under this provision beyond the quantity of goods admitted.[87]

An admission by the party to be charged provides strong corroborative evidence with respect to the transaction. The exception undercuts the "laughing defendant" approach whereby a defendant could take the witness stand, admit that the parties formed a contract, but still rely successfully on the statute of frauds to prevent enforcement. As with the writing requirement, the drafters sought to avoid disputes over quantity by limiting the exception only to the quantity of goods admitted.[88]

With one caveat, admissions contained in depositions, affidavits, responses to interrogatories, or requests to admit satisfy the statute.[89] Purely procedural admissions, such as the negative inference to be drawn from a failure to respond to a request to admit, do not qualify[90] — an affirmative statement by the defendant is required. Notwithstanding some pre-Code authority to the con-

---

[86] UCC § 2A-201(5).

[87] Article 2A includes a comparable exception. UCC § 2A-201(4)(b).

[88] Acemo, Inc. v. Olympic Steel Lafayette, Inc., 2005 Mich. App. LEXIS 2656 (Oct. 27, 2005) (unpublished) (the exception did not apply because the admission in a deposition did not state any quantity of goods).

[89] See, e.g., Oskey Gasoline & Oil Co. v. Continental Oil Co., 534 F.2d 1281, 19 UCC Rep. Serv. 61 (8th Cir. 1976) (deposition); Jackson v. Meadows, 153 Ga. App. 1, 264 S.E.2d 503, 28 UCC Rep. Serv. 990 (1980) (affidavit attached to motion for summary judgment).

[90] See, e.g., Anthony v. Tidwell, 560 S.W.2d 908, 23 UCC Rep. Serv. 561 (Tenn. 1977) (inference drawn from filing motion to dismiss rather than raising affirmative defense insufficient to invoke UCC § 2-201(3)(b)).

trary, it seems settled that an involuntary admission elicited under cross-examination satisfies the statute.[91] An admission of facts that support contract formation can invoke the exception even though a defendant denies the existence of a contract; after all, the existence of a contract is a legal conclusion to be drawn from the facts in evidence. The exception merely requires that the defendant admit to statements or actions that reasonably lead to the conclusion that a contract was formed.[92]

Perhaps the most intriguing question presented by this exception is the extent to which the trial judge should allow the plaintiff to pursue discovery, or even go to trial, in an attempt to force the defendant to make an admission. Suppose the defendant raises the statute of frauds as an affirmative defense and then files a motion for summary judgment. In response to the motion, the plaintiff asks the judge for an opportunity to depose the defendant in the hope of gaining a useful admission. Most courts will allow the plaintiff this opportunity,[93] although there is some authority to the contrary. For example, the court in *DF Activities Corp. v. Brown*[94] held that the plaintiff could not depose a defendant who had attached to her motion to dismiss a sworn affidavit stating that there was no contract between the parties. The court reasoned that the chance that the defendant would contradict her affidavit under cross-examination was too remote to justify requiring her deposition.

Should a plaintiff whose discovery attempts fail be allowed to go to trial in order to cross-examine the defendant on the witness stand? On this issue, both the courts and commentators have split.[95] The argument favoring trial is that a defendant is most likely to admit the truth when faced with the majesty of the courtroom setting. The argument against is based on efficiency: A trial is unlikely to produce results that discovery has not yielded, yet the defendant will have been forced to go to the expense of mounting a courtroom defense and the resources of the judicial system will have been needlessly utilized.

---

[91] *Lewis v. Hughes*, 276 Md. 247, 346 A.2d 231, 18 UCC Rep. Serv. 52 (1975), contains an excellent discussion of the issue and an extensive listing of authorities.

[92] *See* Guy v. Starwood Hotels & Resorts Worldwide, Inc., 2005 D. N.H. 126, 58 UCC Rep. Serv. 2d 699 (2005) (admission of facts supporting contract formation sufficient to overcome bar of statute of frauds even though layperson who testified to the facts denied the existence of a contract).

[93] *See, e.g.*, Migerobe, Inc. v. Certina USA, Inc., 924 F.2d 1330, 14 UCC Rep. Serv. 2d 59 (5th Cir. 1991) (plaintiff entitled to enough discovery to determine whether defendant has internal documents that would satisfy the statute).

[94] 851 F.2d 920, 7 UCC Rep. Serv. 2d 1396 (7th Cir. 1988); *see also* Triangle Mkt'g, Inc. v. Action Indus., Inc., 630 F. Supp. 1578, 1 UCC Rep. Serv. 2d 36 (N.D. Ill. 1986).

[95] The cases requiring trial appear to be more numerous. *See, e.g.*, Theta Prods., Inc. v. Zippo Mfg. Co., 81 F. Supp. 2d 346, 39 UCC Rep. Serv. 2d 670 (D.R.I. 1999); Franklin County Coop. v. MFC Services, 441 So. 2d 1376, 37 UCC Rep. Serv. 1465 (Miss. 1983). *Contra*, Farmland Service Coop., Inc. v. Klein, 196 Neb. 538, 244 N.W.2d 86, 19 UCC Rep. Serv. 1063 (1976).

[B]   Goods Accepted or Payment Made [§ 2-201(3)(c); § 2A-20 1(4)(c)]

Another full exception to the Article 2 statute of frauds states that no writing is required "with respect to goods for which payment has been made and accepted or which have been received and accepted."[96] Unilateral action by one party is not sufficient. Both parties must act: one party by tendering delivery or payment and the other party by accepting the tender. The concept is simple: A buyer's receipt and acceptance of tendered goods or a seller's receipt and acceptance of tendered payment constitutes sufficient corroborative evidence of a contractual relationship to allow elimination of the usual writing requirement. The corroborative force of such evidence follows because most sellers will not keep a payment in the absence of a contract with the payor, just as most buyers will not keep goods they have received in the absence of a contract. Of course, either party is still free to prove that no contract really exists — for example, by trying to show that a gift was intended — but doing so will be an uphill struggle.

Under the Uniform Sales Act, part performance took away the entire statute of frauds defense, just as it still does in contracts for the transfer of an interest in real estate.[97] Under Article 2, part performance renders the contract enforceable only as to the quantity of goods accepted by the buyer or the quantity for which the seller has accepted payment.[98] For example, in *Howard Construction Co. v. Jeff-Cole Quarries, Inc.*[99] the seller delivered base rock, for which the buyer paid. The buyer then sought to prove that the oral agreement also called for the seller to deliver asphaltic rock. The court correctly held that the exception did not lower the bar of the statute of frauds for rock that was neither paid for nor delivered.

An issue arises when a buyer makes a partial payment towards the purchase of a single, indivisible item. For example, the buyer in *Lockwood v. Smigel*[100] made a $100 down payment and later sued for breach of an oral contract for the sale of a 1961 Rolls-Royce Silver Shadow for $11,400. The court held that the partial payment fully satisfied the exception, reasoning that limiting the exception to goods for which payment has been made is based on the objective of avoiding disputes over quantity. The seller's acceptance of the money indicated that a contract existed, and the indivisible nature of the goods precluded a dispute over quantity.

Receipt of goods can indicate a bailment rather than a contract for sale, a possibility that created a difficult issue in *Joseph Heiting & Sons v. Jacks Bean Co.*[101] In that case, a grain elevator regularly purchased beans for its own use

---

[96] UCC § 2-201(3)(c). The exception in Article 2A differs somewhat, as is explained *infra*.

[97] *See* Restatement (Second) of Contracts § 129.

[98] Omega Eng'g, Inc. v. Eastman Kodak Co., 908 F. Supp. 1084, 30 UCC Rep. Serv. 2d 194 (D. Conn. 1995) (partial performance cannot provide an exception to enforce an alleged requirements contract because it applies only with respect to what has already been performed).

[99] 669 S.W.2d 221, 37 UCC Rep. Serv. 1040 (Mo. Ct. App. 1983).

[100] 18 Cal. App. 3d 800, 96 Cal. Rptr. 289, 9 UCC Rep. Serv. 452 (1971).

[101] 236 Neb. 765, 463 N.W.2d 817, 13 UCC Rep. Serv. 2d 336 (1990).

and also received beans as bailee, storing them for the producers. When sued by a producer for failing to pay for beans that it had allegedly purchased, the elevator operator raised the statute of frauds as a defense and argued that its receipt of the beans amounted to a mere bailment. The producer argued that by taking and keeping the beans, the operator had lost the protection of the statute of frauds and that it could make its bailment argument to the jury. The court remanded the case, instructing the trial judge to focus on three factors: 1) whether the beans were out of the producer's control;[102] 2) whether the operator exercised complete control; and 3) whether the particular beans could be returned to the producer.[103] In other words, the trial judge was instructed to make a preliminary determination as to whether the transaction looked more like a sale or a bailment. If it looked like a sale, the operator could not use the statute of frauds because of its receipt and acceptance of the beans, although it could still try to convince the jury that, despite appearances, the parties had agreed to a bailment. If it looked like a bailment, the statute created a complete defense and the producer could gain nothing more than the return of its beans (after paying for their storage).

The court made too much of the issue. The Comments state as follows:

> The overt actions of the parties make admissible evidence of the other terms of the contract necessary to a just apportionment. This is true even though the actions of the parties are not inconsistent in themselves with a different transaction such as a consignment for resale or a mere loan of money.[104]

In other words, the mere fact that the operator received and kept the beans should have been sufficient to lower the bar of the statute. The operator could then have tried to convince the jury that the agreement was in fact a bailment rather than a sale, presumably focusing on the factors discussed by the court.

Article 2A deviates from its statutory analogue by excluding the Article 2 exception for goods for which payment has been made and accepted.[105] The drafters reasoned that "[u]nlike a buyer in a sales transaction, the lessee does not tender payment in full for goods delivered, but only payment of rent for one or more months."[106] They concluded that lease payments were not a sufficient substitute for a signed writing. This reasoning is unpersuasive. As the *Lockwood* case discussed previously so ably demonstrates, partial payment for the purchase of an indivisible item has been upheld as sufficient under the Article 2 exception because it meets the underlying objective of providing corroborative evidence of a sale while avoiding a dispute over the quantity of goods sold. When limited to a single item, an advance payment of rent serves precisely the same objective.

---

[102] For example, the producer might have received a warehouse receipt giving it continuing control over the beans (or a fungible portion of commingled beans).

[103] It appeared that the beans had been commingled and, therefore, could not be returned.

[104] UCC § 2-201, cmt. 2.

[105] The exception is retained for goods that have been received and accepted by the lessee. UCC § 2A-201(4)(c).

[106] UCC § 2A-201, cmt.

[C]   Specially Manufactured Goods [§ 2-201(3)(a); § 2A-201(4)(a)]

Another full exception to the Article 2 statute of frauds provides that no writing is required if

> . . . the goods are to be specially manufactured for the buyer and are not suitable for sale to others in the ordinary course of the seller's business and the seller, before notice of repudiation is received and under circumstances which reasonably indicate that the goods are for the buyer, has made either a substantial beginning of their manufacture or commitments for their procurement.[107]

This provision is commonly referred to as the specially-manufactured-goods exception, but the reference is over-broad. It is true that the exception only applies if the goods are to be specially manufactured for the buyer, but that is only the first of several elements that must be satisfied.

To qualify for the exception, the goods cannot be suitable for sale to others in the ordinary course of the seller's business.[108] This requirement is central to the rationale for providing this exception to the normal signed-writing requirement. Sellers are unlikely to commence the manufacture of specialty goods that they cannot readily sell to others unless they have a prior contractual commitment from a buyer. This business reality corroborates a seller's claim that a contract exists.

The exception further requires the seller to have made either a substantial beginning of the manufacture of the goods or a commitment for their procurement,[109] and either of these undertakings must have been initiated by the seller before receipt of a notification of repudiation from the buyer. The exception thus protects the seller's reasonable reliance.[110] It is akin to the "part performance" exception for contracts transferring interests in realty.[111] Because the goods are not suitable for sale to others, the seller's only recourse, absent the exception, would be to scrap them, often at a significant sacrifice. With the protection of the specially-manufactured-goods exception, the seller will have an adequate remedy: If the buyer repudiates while the goods are unfinished, the seller can pursue

---

[107]   UCC § 2-201(3)(a). Article 2A contains an equivalent exception. UCC § 2A-201(4)(a).

[108]   The court in *Impossible Elec. Techniques, Inc. v. Wackenhut Protective Systems, Inc.*, 669 F.2d 1026, 33 UCC Rep. Serv. 806 (5th Cir. 1982), rejected the seller's claim that this requirement is met if the goods have to be custom made outside the seller's normal processes. The criteria is resaleability, not usual manufacturing procedures.

[109]   Because another part of the exception limits it to goods to be specially manufactured for the buyer, merely procuring standard goods or merely procuring standard parts for later assembly does not qualify.

[110]   A restitutionary cause of action would not work here because the buyer has not received a benefit.

[111]   *See* Restatement (Second) of Contracts § 129.

a lost-profit recovery;[112] if the buyer breaches after they have been finished, the seller can recover the contract price.[113]

Determining the level of reliance necessary to invoke the exception can be tricky. In *Chambers Steel Engraving Corp. v. Tambrands, Inc.,*[114] the seller alleged that the buyer had repudiated a contract for the purchase of at least 20 embossing machines. The seller argued that its reliance in building a prototype was sufficient to satisfy the exception but the court disagreed, requiring at least some evidence of an expenditure on the actual goods. The decision is correct since it is not uncommon for a prototype to be built to induce a buyer to enter into a contract.

Some commentators, and an occasional court, have read the specially-manufactured-goods exception as dispensing with Section 2-201(1)'s limitation of enforcement to the quantity indicated in a signed writing.[115] They point out that the other exceptions in Section 2-201(3) contain explicit quantity limitations, and such a limitation is obvious for the exception for written confirmations in Section 2-201(2) since a qualifying confirmation must be sufficient against the sender. This makes the failure to refer to a quantity term in the specially-manufactured-goods exception all the more conspicuous, leading to the conclusion that the drafters did not intend a limitation. Thus, with sufficient reliance to overcome the bar of the statute of frauds, there is no reason why the parties should not be as free to introduce evidence regarding quantity as they are to introduce evidence regarding any other term.

The contrary position relies on the fact that the exceptions in Section 2-201(3) were created as functional substitutes for the signed-writing requirement and thus the specially-manufactured-goods exception should apply only to goods which the seller has substantially begun to manufacture or procure; otherwise the prospect for disputes over quantity inevitably can arise. Applying this reasoning, the court in *Epprecht v. IBM Corp.*[116] held that the seller could recover for the 7,000 parts that it had begun work on but not for the remaining 43,000 parts that it claimed were also part of the contract.[117]

A final requirement significantly limits the availability of the specially-manufactured-goods exception. Just as the signed-writing requirement and all the other exceptions require evidence that the alleged transaction is between the parties before the court, this exception requires that the seller's commencement of manufacturing or procurement must be "under circumstances which reasonably indicate that the goods are for the buyer." In *Smith-Scharff Paper Co. v.*

---

[112] See UCC Section 2-708(2) and the discussion in § 9.03 *infra.* The seller would not ordinarily be able to finish the goods and then sue for the price under UCC Sections 2-703(e) and 2-709(1)(b) because of the lack of a market for them.

[113] See UCC Section 2-709(1)(b) and the discussion in § 9.04[A][3] *infra.*

[114] 895 F.2d 858, 10 UCC Rep. Serv. 2d 1152 (1st Cir. 1990).

[115] LTV Aerospace Corp. v. Bateman, 492 S.W.2d 703 (Tex. Civ. Ct. App. 1973).

[116] 36 UCC Rep. Serv. 391 (E.D. Pa. 1983).

[117] *See also* Vision Sys. Inc. v. Emc Corp., 56 UCC Rep. Serv. 2d 875 (Mass. Super. Ct. 2005) (substantial-beginning requirement satisfied for units that had been produced but not for other units allegedly included in oral contract).

P.N. Hirsch & Co. Stores, Inc.,[118] the seller clearly satisfied the exception by manufacturing paper bags imprinted with the buyer's logo. By contrast, the court in *Jones v. Wide World of Cars, Inc.*[119] correctly held that a limited-production, high-quality sports car, although not *readily* resalable, was suitable for sale to others and refused to enforce an alleged oral contract because the circumstances did not reasonably indicate that the car was being manufactured for the alleged buyer. Sellers can face a substantial burden in tying the goods to the defendant.

§ 3.05   NONSTATUTORY EXCEPTIONS: EQUITABLE AND PROMISSORY ESTOPPEL

Equitable estoppel, or estoppel *in pais*, traditionally has been viewed as an exception to the statute of frauds and many courts today also accept promissory estoppel as an exception. An equitable estoppel generally requires a misrepresentation or concealment of existing facts, whereas promissory estoppel requires a promise regarding future facts. In either case, reasonable reliance by the party seeking to use the doctrine is a prerequisite.

Courts applying the common law have been quite strict about the facts that will support an estoppel claim. Equitable estoppel is generally available, but the plaintiff must show that the defendant made one of the following affirmative representations: 1) that the statute of frauds had been satisfied; 2) that the defendant would prepare a signed writing in the future; or 3) that the statute of frauds would not be used as a defense.[120] The use of promissory estoppel in this context is a more recent phenomenon, and courts applying the doctrine have often required a great deal of reliance. In one of the early cases, the California Supreme Court held that to overcome the statute of frauds, the promisee's reliance must amount to an unconscionable injury.[121] The Restatement (Second) of Contracts recognizes promissory estoppel as an exception to the statute of frauds but suggests that the promisee's reliance must be "definite and substantial"[122] and that other remedies, such as cancellation and restitution, must be insufficient to mitigate the harm.[123]

Section 2-201(1) begins with the phrase "[e]xcept as otherwise provided in this section," leading some courts to preclude exceptions other than those articulated in the section.[124] However, most courts that have addressed the issue have

---

[118] 754 S.W.2d 298, 7 UCC Rep. Serv. 2d 38 (Mo. Ct. App. 1988); *see also* Pharmaceutical Corp. v. Ivax Pharmaceuticals, Inc., 322 F. Supp. 2d 406, 54 UCC Rep. Serv. 2d 130 (S.D. N.Y. 2004) (bottles that were silk-screened and labeled for the buyer qualified for the exception).

[119] 820 F. Supp. 132, 21 UCC Rep. Serv. 2d 27 (S.D.N.Y. 1993).

[120] Even though the second and third affirmations amount to promises of future conduct, the courts lumped them in with equitable estoppel. *See* Restatement of Contracts § 178, cmt. f.

[121] Monarco v. Lo Greco, 35 Cal. 2d 621, 220 P.2d 737 (1950).

[122] *See* Restatement (Second) of Contracts § 139(2)(b).

[123] *See* Restatement (Second) of Contracts § 139(2)(a).

[124] *See, e.g.*, Futch v. James River-Norwalk, Inc., 722 F. Supp. 1395, 10 UCC Rep. Serv. 2d 684 (S.D. Miss. 1989); Golden Plains Feedlot, Inc. v. Great W. Sugar Co., 588 F. Supp. 985, 39 UCC Rep. Serv. 785 (D.S.D. 1984).

concluded that the statutory exceptions are not exclusive. These courts cite Article 1 for the proposition that the Code is supplemented by common-law and equitable principles and have concluded that the introductory phrase to Section 2-201(1) is insufficient to demonstrate an intent that these principles be displaced.[125] For example, in *R. S. Bennett & Co. v. Economy Mechanical Industries, Inc.*[126] the plaintiff, who wanted to sell equipment to be used in a water reclamation project, made initial offers to three general contractors that were bidding on the project. Just before the bidding deadline, the plaintiff told each contractor that it would reveal a lower price if the contractor agreed to buy from it in the event that the contractor was awarded the project. Each contractor agreed, but when the defendant won the project it refused to deal with the plaintiff, which then brought suit. The plaintiff argued that if the defendant had not agreed to buy from it, it would never have revealed the lower price and another contractor would have won the competition and purchased the equipment from it. Even though the Illinois Supreme Court had ruled some 25 years earlier that promissory estoppel could not be used to overcome the statute of frauds,[127] the Seventh Circuit Court of Appeals concluded that the use of promissory estoppel had become so commonplace in the interim that the court, if faced with the issue again, would change its mind.[128]

Even courts that have accepted estoppel as an exception to the Article 2 statute of frauds have often found that the level of injury suffered by the plaintiff was insufficient to cause the bar to be lowered. For example, the court in *Columbus Trade Exchange, Inc. v. AMCA Int'l Corp.*[129] indicated that it was receptive to the use of promissory estoppel but that the plaintiff had not shown that it had suffered such an injury that failure to enforce the contract would amount to a manifest inequity. The court gave little indication of what it would have considered sufficient, although it did cite Section 139 of the Second Restatement with approval. Another, somewhat older example is *Sacred Heart Farmers Cooperative v. Johnson*,[130] where the court held that to work an estoppel the conduct must be unconscionable or akin to fraud.

---

[125] *See* UCC § 1-103(b).

[126] 606 F.2d 182, 27 UCC Rep. Serv. 345 (7th Cir. 1979).

[127] *See* Ozier v. Haines, 411 Ill. 160, 103 N.E.2d 485 (1952).

[128] *See also* Hitzke v. Easterday, 285 Wis. 2d 807, 701 N.W.2d 654 (Ct. App. 2005); Adams v. Petrade Int'l, Inc., 754 S.W.2d 696, 7 UCC Rep. Serv. 2d 369 (Tex. Civ. App. 1988); Massey v. Hardcastle, 753 S.W.2d 127, 7 UCC Rep. Serv.2d 661 (Tenn. Ct. App. 1988); Allen M. Campbell Co. v. Virginia Metal Indus., 708 F.2d 930, 36 UCC Rep. Serv. 384 (4th Cir. 1983).

[129] 763 F. Supp. 946, 15 UCC Rep. Serv. 2d 51 (S.D. Ohio 1991).

[130] 305 Minn. 324, 232 N.W.2d 921, 17 UCC Rep. Serv. 901 (1975); *see also* Casazza v. Kiser, 313 F.3d 414, 49 UCC Rep. Serv. 2d 342 (8th Cir. 2002) (reliance was not such that applying the statute of frauds would allow defendant to perpetrate a fraud).

§ 3.06 MODIFICATIONS AND THE STATUTE OF FRAUDS

The drafters feared that abandoning the pre-existing duty rule would enable a dissatisfied party to invent a modification.[131] Accordingly, they subjected modifications to Article 2's statute of frauds and sanctioned the creation of private statutes of frauds — contractual provisions requiring that modifications be evidenced by a signed writing. They also provided a mechanism — waiver — for circumventing these rules. Section 2-209(2) through (5) state in full as follows:

> (2) A signed agreement which excludes modification or rescission except by a signed writing cannot be otherwise modified or rescinded, but except as between merchants such a requirement on a form supplied by the merchant must be separately signed by the other party.

> (3) The requirements of the statute of frauds section of this Article (Section 2-201) must be satisfied if the contract as modified is within its provisions.

> (4) Although an attempt at modification or rescission does not satisfy the requirements of subsection (2) or (3) it can operate as a waiver.

> (5) A party who has made a waiver affecting an executory portion of the contract may retract the waiver by reasonable notification received by the other party that strict performance will be required of any term waived, unless the retraction would be unjust in view of a material change of position in reliance on the waiver.

These provisions have led to great confusion and uncertainty, as will be shown in the ensuing discussion.

[A]   Applying the Code's Statute of Frauds to Modifications

Section 2-209(3) requires that Article 2's statute-of-frauds provision must be satisfied "if the contract as modified is within its provisions." The statute presents difficult problems of interpretation. Perhaps it applies only if a modification brings a contract within the statute of frauds for the first time. An example would be a modification raising the price term to at least $500. This interpretation is implausible because it would limit application of the section to relatively insignificant contracts. Another possibility is that the section applies whenever a modification calls for the purchase of additional goods costing $500 or more. The text, which refers to the "contract as modified" rather than the subject matter of the modification, suggests otherwise.

A more plausible interpretation is that a signed writing is not necessary unless a modification changes the quantity term. The text supports this approach. Section 2-209(3) does *not* expressly state that all of the terms of a modification must be in a signed writing; rather, it says that Section 2-201 must be satisfied and quantity is the only term mandated by that section. Subject to

---

[131] UCC § 2-209, cmt. 3. For discussion on abrogation of the pre-existing duty rule, see § 2.07 *supra*.

the parol evidence rule in the case of a final writing, all other terms may be proved by extrinsic evidence. If the parties modified the price but not the quantity, a new writing that reiterated the quantity term but omitted any reference to the price would satisfy Section 2-201. The problem with this approach is that it renders Section 2-209(1) inapplicable to the vast majority of modifications, which is likely contrary to the drafter's intention.

Under the most common approach, the courts have imposed a signed writing requirement for modifications that is more stringent than the requirements of Section 2-201(1) for original contracts. Courts following this approach have held that all the essential terms of the modification must be expressed with reasonable certainty in a signed writing,[132] a standard similar to the requirements of the Second Restatement for original contracts.[133] The approach finds some support in the Comments, which state that a modification "for the future cannot therefore be conjured up by oral testimony if the price involved is $500.00 or more since such modification must be shown at least by an authenticated memo."[134] A broad application of Section 2-209(3) is consistent with the drafters' desire to substitute a formal writing requirement for the common law's consideration requirement.

If the signed writing requirement of Section 2-201(1) is not met, are the exceptions set out in Section 2-201(2) and (3) available to the party seeking to enforce the modification? Because Section 2-209(3) does not refer to a specific subsection of Section 2-201, the answer should be yes. For example, in *Starry Construction Co., Inc. v. Murphy Oil USA, Inc.*[135] the parties initially agreed to a contract for the sale of 20,000 tons of asphalt cement oil and then changed the quantity to 25,000 tons. Six months later, Iraq invaded Kuwait and the buyer, concerned about the seller's ability to perform, sent a signed confirmation of the modification to the seller. The seller later breached and raised Section 2-209(3) as a defense. The court held that the written- confirmation exception of Section 2-201(2) can be used to satisfy Section 2-209(3) but that the buyer's confirmation had not been sent within a reasonable time after the modification. Accordingly, the modification was unenforceable.

[B]   No-Oral-Modification (NOM) Clauses

Parties frequently provide that their contracts may not be modified except by a signed writing, and Section 2-209(2) validates such private statutes of frauds. The clauses are commonly referred to as "no-oral-modification," or NOM, clauses. To be enforceable a NOM clause must be in a signed agreement, but the

---

[132] *See, e.g.,* In re Atkins, 139 B.R. 39, 19 UCC Rep. Serv. 2d 18 (Bankr. M.D. Fla. 1992) (alleged oral agreement modifying the financing aspects of the contract unenforceable); Cooley v. Big Horn Harvestore Sys., Inc., 767 P.2d 740, 7 UCC Rep. Serv. 2d 1051 (Colo. Ct. App. 1988) (alleged oral agreement by seller to broaden its warranty liability unenforceable).

[133] *See* Restatement (Second) of Contracts § 131(c) (signed writing must state "with reasonable certainty the essential terms of the unperformed promises").

[134] UCC § 2-209, cmt. 3.

[135] 785 F. Supp. 1356, 17 UCC Rep. Serv. 2d 353 (D. Minn. 1993), *aff'd,* 986 F.2d 503 (8th Cir. 1993).

statute does not indicate which party needs to sign the agreement. Analogizing to Section 2-201, the NOM clause should be enforced if the agreement creating it has been signed by the party seeking to avoid enforcement of the oral modification. Section 2-209(3) provides non-merchants with an added layer of protection. A NOM clause on a form supplied by a merchant is not enforceable unless the non-merchant signs separately at the place on the form where the clause appears.[136] The rule does not apply if both parties are merchants.

[C] Waiver

While subsections (2) and (3) of Section 2-209 create hurdles for a party seeking to enforce an oral modification, subsections (4) and (5) invoke the doctrine of waiver to provide a way around those hurdles. Waiver is a notoriously elusive concept. Historically the term has been used most often to refer to a voluntary relinquishment of the right to assert a condition. For example, an owner might waive the right to an architect's certificate as a condition to the release of a progress payment. The courts generally required new consideration only if the condition being waived was a material part of the agreed exchange.[137]

Conditions may be waived in several ways. For example, a party may express in advance an intent not to enforce a condition. Such a waiver may be retracted until the time for the condition has passed or the other party has materially relied on the waiver. Another example, called an "election" waiver, occurs when a party proceeds to perform knowing that its performance has been excused by the failure of a condition. An election waiver may not be retracted. Finally, a party may be estopped to enforce a condition. For example, in *Universal Builders, Inc. v. Moon Motor Lodge, Inc.*[138] an owner asked a contractor to do work not covered in the original plans. The court held the owner liable for payment notwithstanding a clause requiring all modifications to be approved by the owner in a signed writing.

The cases do not reflect this logical and orderly analysis. Many common-law courts use the waiver doctrine indiscriminately, applying it to situations that conceptually should be viewed as modifications. If these courts characterize an event as a modification, they must refuse to enforce the modification in the absence of consideration. They can avoid this requirement by instead characterizing the event as a waiver. Moreover, in cases with repeated occasions for performance, characterizing conduct as a waiver allows the original contract term to be reinstated for the future, whereas characterizing it as a modification does not. The courts unsurprisingly gravitate towards the waiver concept given the flexibility that it provides.

---

[136] *See, e.g.*, Knoxville Rod & Bearing, Inc. v. Bettis Corp. of Knoxville, Inc., 672 S.W.2d 203, 39 UCC Rep. Serv. 415 (Tenn. Ct. App. 1984).

[137] *See* Restatement (Second) of Contracts § 84(1). *See, e.g.*, Rennie & Laughlin, Inc. v. Chrysler Corp., 242 F.2d 208 (9th Cir. 1957). UCC Section 2-209(1) dispenses with the consideration requirement for modifications but is silent regarding waivers. Because waivers affecting material conditions really have the same effect as modifications, consideration should not be required.

[138] 430 Pa. 550, 244 A.2d 10 (1968).

Section 2-209(4) states that an attempt at modification *can* operate as a waiver even though it does not satisfy the statute-of-frauds rules of subsections (2) and (3), but it does not define when such a waiver occurs. For example, suppose a contract contains a NOM clause and the seller, after having initially agreed to a particular delivery date, encounters difficulties and requests an extension. The buyer grants the extension orally and the seller relies by ceasing what had been frantic efforts to meet the original date. The parties have orally agreed to a modification, but has the buyer waived the NOM clause? If not, the modification is not enforceable.

One early case held that a NOM clause cannot be waived unless the parties expressly addressed the clause.[139] In other words, the buyer had to say something like "I hereby waive our agreement requiring that modifications be in writing and I also agree to your requested modification." This approach is unreasonable. Parties that orally agree on a modification are unlikely to take the time to expressly waive a NOM clause, and an overly technical insistence on formalities can cause substantial injustice.

Wisconsin Knife Works v. National Metal Crafters[140] represents a different approach. The buyer agreed to purchase spade-bit blanks that were to be manufactured into finished spade bits pursuant to a contract that contained a NOM clause. When the seller failed to make timely delivery, the buyer sued for damages. The seller claimed that by its conduct the buyer had agreed to a new delivery schedule, and the buyer raised Section 2-209(2) as a defense. Writing for the majority, Judge Posner held that an attempted modification acts as a waiver of a NOM clause only if there has been reliance. The opinion states as follows:

> The path of reconciliation with subsection (4) is found by attending to its precise wording. It does not say that an attempted modification "is" a waiver; it says that "it can operate as a waiver." It does not say in what circumstances it can operate as a waiver; but if an attempted modification is effective as a waiver only if there is reliance, then both 2-209(2) and 2-209(4) can be given effect. Reliance, if reasonably induced and reasonable in extent, is a common substitute for consideration in making a promise legally enforceable, in part because it adds something in the way of credibility to the mere say-so of one party.[141]

Judge Easterbrook argued in a compelling dissent that the majority mischaracterized the relationship between Sections 2-209(4) and (5). Subsection (4) provides that an attempted modification may operate as a waiver, and subsection (5) provides that a waiver of an executory part of a contract that has not been materially relied upon may be retracted. If every waiver requires reliance, subsection (5) is meaningless. Although the majority suggests that subsection (4) applies only to a subset of waivers — attempted modifications and rescissions —

---

[139] C.I.T. Corp. v. Jonnet, 3 UCC Rep. Serv. 321 (Pa. C.P. 1965), *aff'd*, 419 Pa. 435, 214 A.2d 620, 3 UCC Rep. Serv. 968 (1965).

[140] 781 F.2d 1280, 42 UCC Rep. Serv. 830 (7th Cir. 1986); *see also* Thomas Knutson Shipbuilding Corp. v. George W. Rogers Constr. Co., 6 UCC Rep. Serv. 323 (N.Y. Sup. Ct. 1969).

[141] 781 F.2d at 1287, 42 UCC Rep. Serv. at 837.

and not *inter alia* to express waivers, the dissent argued that the two subsections cover the same domain. They apply to all attempted modifications, whether oral, written, or implied from conduct, that do not satisfy the formal requirements of subsections (2) and (3), and therefore "waiver" should mean the same thing in both sections.[142] In the absence of a "material change of position in reliance on the waiver," it may be retracted under subsection (5).

In order to retract a waiver of a term affecting an executory portion of a contract that has not induced material reliance, the retracting party must reasonable notify the other party that it is insisting on strict performance of the term.[143] By limiting the provision to executory parts of a contract, the Code recognizes that election waivers may not be retracted. In other words, a party that proceeds to perform even though aware that performance has been excused by the failure of a condition irrevocably waives the condition.

§ 3.07 AMENDED ARTICLE 2

Despite the elimination of the statute-of-frauds provision early in the drafting process, the drafters reinstated the provision with only a few adjustments. The most important change is that the threshold amount in Section 2-201(1) was increased from $500 to $5,000.

The amendments delete the introductory phrase to Section 2-201(1) ("[e]xcept as otherwise provided in this section"). The purpose of removing the phrase was to preclude courts from holding that the section displaces principles of law and equity, thereby opening the door to broader use of promissory and equitable estoppel.

Original Section 2-201(3)(b) provides that the statute is satisfied by an admission in pleading, testimony, or otherwise in court. Considering the phrasing to be too restrictive, the drafters amended the subsection to permit the exception to be satisfied by any admission made under oath (*e.g.*, an affidavit).

Finally, a new Section 2-201(4) precludes application of a statute-of-frauds provision predicated on the time for performance (*e.g.*, the "one-year" rule) to a contract that is governed by Article 2 and is enforceable under Section 2-201. Curiously, other common-law statute-of-frauds provisions that might in an unusual circumstance be applicable to a contract of sale (*e.g.*, a promise to pay the debt of another in exchange for goods) were not precluded, leaving the courts to decide whether to treat them as cumulative with Section 2-201.

---

[142] *Accord* BMC Indus., Inc. v. Barth Indus., Inc., 160 F.3d 1322, 37 UCC Rep. Serv. 2d 63 (11th Cir. 1998) (reliance not required for attempted modification to constitute waiver under UCC § 2-209(4); notwithstanding NOM clause, eyeglass manufacturer waived delivery date for equipment because, after date passed, it accepted promise of seller's parent company to ensure "timely" delivery and in return agreed to increase price and continue to work with seller; after waiver, delivery was due within reasonable time).

[143] *See* Double-E Sportswear Corp. v. Girard Trust Bank, 488 F.2d 292, 13 UCC Rep. Serv. 577 (3d Cir. 1973) (whether notice of retraction is reasonable is an issue of fact).

§ 3.08 CISG

The CISG rejects the imposition of formal requirements that can impair the enforceability of sales contracts. It specifically deletes any requirement that a contract be in writing. It provides that "[a] contract of sale need not be concluded in or evidence by writing and is not subject to any other requirement as to form."[144] The imposition of a variety of formal requirements that have been recognized under different domestic legal regimes would overly burden international contracting. Thus, unlike the law in the United States, the CISG does not include a statute of frauds.[145]

The absence of a statute of frauds in the draft of the CISG caused considerable consternation in the former U.S.S.R., as its laws on foreign-trade contracts included strict formal requirements. Although most of the delegates felt that such requirements were not consistent with current commercial trade practices, they agreed to a compromise. A declaration can be made by "[a] Contract State whose legislation requires contracts of sale to be concluded in or evidenced by writing."[146] The effect of such a declaration is spelled out as follows in Article 12:

> Any provision of article 11, article 29 or Part II of this Convention that allows a contract of sale or its modification or termination by agreement or any offer, acceptance or other indication of intention to be made in any form other than in writing does not apply where any party has his place of business in a Contracting State which has made a declaration under article 96 of this Convention. The parties may not derogate from or vary the effect of this article.[147]

Only nations whose domestic law requires sales contracts to be in writing are eligible to make the Article 96 declaration. A declaration once made removes only the effect of the exclusion in Article 11 of a writing requirement.

---

[144] CISG Art. 11.

[145] The parties remain free to impose whatever formal requirement that they wish in order to govern their contract formation. Offerors, for example, often include a requirement in their offers that an acceptance be made in writing. The parties can also agree that any modifications to their contract will be in writing. CISG Art. 29(2).

[146] CISG Art. 96.

[147] Such a declaration has been made by Argentina, Belarus, Chile, China, Estonia, Hungary, the Russian Federation, and Ukraine. The United States chose not to do so.

Chapter 4

CONTRACT TERMS

§ 4.01 INTRODUCTION

Determining the terms of a contract under the Uniform Commercial Code requires first an understanding of the distinction between "agreement" and "contract." Article 1 provides that " '[a]greement,' as distinguished from 'contract,' means the bargain of the parties in fact, as found in their language or inferred from other circumstances, including course of performance, course of dealing, or usage of trade as provided in Section 1-303."[1] Although terms may be implied from any factual matrix, the three most common sources of implied-in-fact terms are those listed in the definition of agreement. Contract, by contrast, means "the total legal obligation that results from the parties' agreement as determined by [the Uniform Commercial Code], as supplemented by any other applicable laws."[2] The agreement is the sole source of a contract's "terms" but is not the sole source of contractual obligations. As used in the Code, "[t]erm means a portion of an *agreement* that relates to a particular matter."[3] The contract, however, includes other legal obligations, and these are found in the "gap-fillers" and supereminent principles that will be discussed below.

Express terms are those that are expressly stated, whether orally or in a record. The parties may actually bargain over them or they may be found in the boilerplate of one party's standard form. A term derived from a usage of trade,

---

[1] UCC § 1-201(b)(3).

[2] UCC § 1-201(b)(12).

[3] UCC § 1-201(b)(40) (emphasis supplied).

course of dealing, or course of performance is "background music," meaning that the parties should assume it is part of their agreement without articulating that assumption. In addition to being a potential source of terms,[4] a usage of trade, course of dealing, or course of performance may be relevant in interpreting an express term.[5]

Unlike express and implied-in-fact terms, gap-fillers are not based on the stated or presumed intent of the parties but were instead thought by the drafters to be appropriate for contracting parties that have not reached agreement on a particular point. Colloquially, gap-fillers might be thought of as terms, but their exclusion from the definition of "term" is not an accident. For an example of a situation in which the distinction matters, a term in a definite and seasonable expression of acceptance that contradicts a gap-filler in an offer will be treated under Section 2-207 as an additional, not a different, term.[6]

Gap-fillers are a statutory standardized set of obligations that fill the gaps left in the parties' agreement. The drafters have provided the parties with a set of boilerplate provisions that flesh out the contract on points on which there is no agreement. Under Articles 2 and 2A a contract will not fail for indefiniteness if the parties have manifested an intention to enter into the contract and there is a reasonably certain basis for providing an appropriate remedy if a dispute occurs.[7] Gap-fillers often provide that basis and thus reduce the number of cases in which a contract will fail for indefiniteness. They also reduce transaction costs by reducing the number of potential issues as to which bargaining may be thought necessary. Note, however, that a gap-filling rule will not apply if an agreement covers the subject matter of the rule. Many of the gap-filling provisions state explicitly that they apply unless the parties have agreed otherwise, but the same limitation applies even if the relevant provision is not explicit on the point. Consistent with the principle of freedom of contract, "the effect of provisions of [the Uniform Commercial Code] may be varied by agreement."[8] Moreover, "[t]he presence in certain provisions [of the Code] of the phrase 'unless otherwise agreed . . . does not imply that the effect of other provisions may not be varied by agreement. . . ."[9] Accordingly, a term in the agreement of the parties, whether express or implied-in-fact, will exclude application of a gap-filler relevant to the same issue.

Supereminent principles also establish contractual obligations but are not terms.[10] Like gap-fillers, they are implied in law; unlike gap-fillers, they may not be displaced and they even override an agreement's terms. They are over-arching, pervasive standards recognized as exceptions to the general concept of freedom of contract, and this principle is stated as follows: "The obligations of

---

[4] UCC § 1-303(d).

[5] *Id.*

[6] Notwithstanding this technical exclusion of gap-fillers as terms to the contract, they are commonly designated as implied-in-law terms.

[7] UCC §§ 2-204(3), 2A-204(3).

[8] UCC § 1-302(a).

[9] UCC § 1-302(b).

[10] The concept of supereminent principles was developed by drafters of codes in western Europe.

good faith, diligence, reasonableness, and care prescribed by [the Uniform Commercial Code] may not be disclaimed by agreement."[11] The discussion in this chapter of supereminent principles focuses on the concepts of unconscionability and good faith.

§ 4.02   THE PAROL EVIDENCE RULE [§ 2-202; § 2A-202]

[A]   Statement of the Rule

Subject to the limitations imposed by the statute of frauds, contracts need not be in a writing to be enforceable. Express terms thus may be oral or written. Parties frequently choose to reduce some or all of their understandings to written form, and when they do the parol evidence rule might preclude their ability to introduce evidence of terms not reflected in the writing. The parol evidence rule comes into play during litigation when one of the parties seeks to introduce evidence for the purpose of establishing a term other than as appears in the writing.[12] Application of the rule might cause the court to preclude admission of the evidence.

Because an understanding of the Code's version of the parol evidence rule requires some familiarity with the rule's long and tortured common-law history, references to the common law intersperse our discussion of the Code. The common-law rule has been stated many ways,[13] but the following is a reasonable distillation of the approach generally taken by the courts:

> If parties to a contract have reduced their agreement to a writing which they intend to be a final expression of at least some of their understandings, they may not introduce evidence of prior oral or written terms, or contemporaneous oral terms, that contradict the writing. They may, however, attempt to supplement the writing by introducing evidence of consistent additional terms unless they intended that the writing be both final and complete, in which case even evidence of consistent additional terms will be excluded.

A writing is final if the parties have gone beyond the negotiating stage and have agreed that the language in the writing represents at least some of the terms of their agreement. The Second Restatement uses the term "partial integration" to refer to a writing that is intended by each of the parties to be final with respect to some express terms but is not intended to be a complete statement of all such terms.[14] A writing is complete and exclusive (or, in the

---

[11] UCC § 1-302(b).

[12] For discussion the introduction of extrinsic evidence for other purposes that are not affected by the parol evidence rule, see § 4.02[C] *infra*.

[13] *See, e.g.*, Restatement of Contracts §§ 237, 240; Restatement (Second) of Contracts §§ 210, 213; A. Corbin, 3 Contracts § 573 (rev. ed. 1960); S. Williston, 4 Contracts § 631 (3d ed. 1961); J. Wigmore, 9 Evidence § 2425 (3d ed. 1940).

[14] Restatement (Second) of Contracts § 210(2).

language of the Second Restatement, a "complete integration")[15] if the parties also intend that it represent *all* of the express terms of their agreement.

Section 2-202 provides, in part, as follows:

> Terms . . . set forth in a writing intended by the parties as a final expression of their agreement with respect to such terms as are included therein may not be contradicted by evidence of any prior agreement or of a contemporaneous oral agreement but may be . . . supplemented . . .
>
> (a)   by course of performance, course of dealing, or usage of trade (Section 1-303), and
>
> (b)   by evidence of consistent additional terms unless the court finds the writing to have been intended also as a complete and exclusive statement of the terms of the agreement.[16]

As to express terms, the provision simply reiterates the traditional rule: If a writing is final, it may not be contradicted by evidence of a term agreed to, whether orally or in writing, before the writing was created, or of an oral term agreed to contemporaneously with the creation of the writing.[17] Evidence of a consistent additional term is admissible, unless the court finds that the writing was also intended to be complete and exclusive.[18] Section 2-202 goes beyond the traditional statement of the rule, however, in its treatment of terms implied from a course of performance, course of dealing, or usage of trade.[19]

The reasons for the parol evidence rule are eminently sensible. If the parties agreed on something before or at the time they reduced their agreement to writing, why didn't they include it in the writing? If they intended their written version of a particular term to be the final word with regard to that term, a court should not allow the jurors to be confused by allegations that the parties had actually agreed on something quite different. And if they intended the writing to

---

[15] Restatement (Second) of Contracts § 210(1).

[16] Section 2A-202 is identical.

[17] The parol evidence rule does not bar the admissibility of evidence for the purpose of proving that a contract was modified by a post-writing term. Muther-Ballenger v. Griffin Electronic Consultants, Inc., 100 N.C. App. 505, 397 S.E.2d 247, 13 UCC Rep. Serv. 2d 353 (1990) (oral modifications of writing not barred).

[18] The Code's parol evidence rule also applies to "[t]erms with respect to which the confirmatory memoranda of the parties agree." For example, assume that the parties enter into a contract on the telephone and each subsequently sends to the other a confirmatory memorandum of their agreement. Terms that are the same in both memoranda become part of the contract under UCC § 2-207 and are appropriately treated as part of a final writing under the parol evidence rule. *See also* BNE Swedbank, S.A. v. Banker, 794 F. Supp. 1291, 20 UCC Rep. Serv. 2d 35 (S.D.N.Y. 1992) (parol evidence rule inapplicable where the only writing was a confirmatory memorandum sent by one party).

[19] As with express terms, evidence of a contradictory term implied from these sources is precluded. On the other hand, extrinsic evidence to prove consistent additional terms from these sources is admissible even if the final writing is also complete and exclusive. For an explanation of these sources of terms and their relationship with the parol evidence rule, see § 4.03[B] *infra*.

be a statement of all the express terms[20] of their agreement, why should they be allowed later to claim that there were, in fact, agreed terms that were left out?

The term "parol evidence rule" is misleading in several respects. The word "parol," for example, means oral, but the parol evidence rule operates to exclude evidence of both oral and written terms. Further, the rule is not a rule of evidence but operates instead as a rule of substantive law. A rule of evidence deals with the appropriate method of proving a question of fact, and evidence is excluded if it is not relevant, is subject to serious credibility problems, or is susceptible to misuse by the jury. The parol evidence rule, by contrast, excludes evidence on policy grounds even when it meets the ordinary tests for admissibility. The Second Restatement takes the position that the parties, by adopting a final writing, intended to discharge those agreements that are excluded by the rule.[21]

Because it excludes evidence of extrinsic terms (those not reflected in the writing), the rule allows judges to control juries by keeping out evidence that they consider to be suspect in some way.[22] As we shall see, however, it often does so at the expense of the true agreement of the parties, and to that extent it can subvert the goal of fairly adjudicating a particular dispute. The tension between these policy goals has led to such inconsistent results that some commentators have despairingly concluded that the parol evidence rule lacks the certainty necessary to make it a "rule."[23]

[B]   Application of the Rule

Because the parol evidence rule is directed toward the admissibility of evidence, the court must make certain preliminary determinations in deciding whether to apply it. Both the common-law and UCC versions of the rule focus on the intent of the parties at the time the writing was created. Determining whether the writing was intended to be final with respect to the terms contained in it and, if so, whether it was also intended to be complete and exclusive, are fact questions, but they are reserved for the court rather than the jury.[24] Before making a determination, the court should allow the parties to present evidence

---

[20] The rationale also applies in the rare case of a term that is implied from the surrounding circumstances but does not fit into the categories of usage of trade, course of dealing, or course of performance.

[21] Restatement (Second) of Contracts § 213 states that an integrated agreement "discharges prior agreements to the extent that it is inconsistent with them" and a completely integrated agreement discharges prior agreements to the extent that they are within its scope." The Comments do not indicate whether the Code's parol evidence rules are based on this policy.

[22] *See* McCormick, *The Parol Evidence Rule as a Procedural Device for the Control of the Jury*, 41 Yale L.J. 365 (1932).

[23] *See, e.g.,* Broude, *The Consumer and the Parol Evidence Rule: Section 2-202 of the Uniform Commercial Code*, 1970 Duke L.J. 881, 884 ("even these leading academic commentators cannot agree about what the rule is, what it purports to exclude, and what evidence may be admitted despite its restrictions").

[24] *See* Restatement (Second) of Contracts § 209(2) & cmt. c. UCC § 2-202 is silent on this point, but it expressly allocates the issue of completeness and exclusivity to the court. Unless the court also handles the issue of finality, the evidence that it ultimately may have to exclude will be heard by the jury.

concerning their intent with respect to the writing.[25]

[1]   Determining Finality and Completeness

The first step in determining whether to invoke the parol evidence rule is to ascertain whether the parties intended to adopt a particular writing as a final expression of at least part of their agreement. One party may have made a memorandum of an oral agreement, but a writing prepared unilaterally will not be considered final even if it is sufficient to satisfy the statute of frauds. The reason is that the other party never assented to the form of expression used in the writing.[26] Likewise, although the parties may have exchanged various writings during the course of their negotiations, a draft advanced by one party but not assented to by the other will not be considered final. Without a final writing, either party is free to introduce evidence tending to show that the parties agreed to a term. If the other party denies that it agreed to the term, the jury will make a factual determination.[27]

Because a consistent additional term agreed to by the parties can supplement even a writing that is determined to be final, the court's next step is to determine whether a writing that it finds to be final is also complete and exclusive. If the writing is obviously skeletal in nature, the judge can easily find that it is only a partial integration. Difficult issues arise, however, when the writing appears on its face to be complete. The Code's approach to the issue can be understood only in light of its common-law antecedents.

In an early common-law approach, the courts essentially took a shortcut in the analysis. If a writing appeared to be complete, a court would presume that it was complete. The court made its decision on the "four corners" of the document and neither party could convince it that what they actually intended was a partial integration. Even under this restrictive approach, a party was free to show that the agreement represented by the writing was not the only contract between the parties. No matter how complete it may appear, a writing can cover only so much ground. For example, a writing covering the sale of a wagon could not preclude one party from trying to show that the parties had also orally agreed to the sale of a shotgun. An independent contract with a separate subject matter and a separate consideration would not be affected by the writing. Suppose, however, that the writing referred to the sale of a wagon for $100 and the buyer wanted to show that the seller had orally agreed to replace the wheels for an extra $25. Should this understanding, which is really collateral to the main contract, be treated as if it were truly independent, thereby clearing the

---

[25] Middletown Concrete Produts, Inc. v. Black Clawson Co., 802 F. Supp. 1135, 20 UCC Rep. Serv. 2d 815 (D. Del. 1992) (court should consider the writing, the intent of the parties, and the surrounding circumstances of the transaction).

[26] Brewster of Lynchburg, Inc. v. Dial Corp., 33 F.3d 355, 24 UCC Rep. Serv. 2d 738 (4th Cir. 1994) (seller never agreed to buyer's Purchase and Change Order but rather objected to specific terms).

[27] Although often referred to as a jury-control mechanism, the parol evidence rule is also applicable in bench trials, where the judge makes preliminary determinations and, if required to do so by the rule, will ignore the evidence of the extrinsic term in deciding the case.

path for the introduction of extrinsic evidence? Over time, a series of tests developed to resolve this issue.

One of the most influential cases, *Mitchill v. Lath*,[28] concerned the buyer of a farm who wanted to show that the seller had orally agreed to remove an unsightly icehouse that the seller owned on an adjoining piece of land. This alleged oral agreement was not mentioned in the writing, which appeared complete on its face, nor was it supported by a separate consideration. Nevertheless, the court held that the evidence would be admissible if the term was one that a reasonable person "would not ordinarily be expected to embody in the writing."[29] A majority of the court ultimately concluded that, had the parties actually agreed on the proffered oral term, a reasonable person would ordinarily have included it in the writing, and thus the evidence was excluded. Even though the buyer lost, however, the case is noteworthy because it created the possibility that evidence of an agreement not obviously part of a separate contract might be admissible to supplement the terms of a facially complete writing.

Under the *Mitchill* approach, a judge could not consider the circumstances surrounding the transaction in deciding the parties' intent. The judge might well believe that the parties actually agreed on an omitted term but still keep evidence of it from the jury by concluding that a reasonable person, not in the circumstances but in the abstract, would not ordinarily be expected to include the term in the writing. Judges applying other early approaches listened to evidence of the general circumstances surrounding the contract (the status and sophistication of the parties, their purposes in entering into the transaction, etc.) but refused to listen to evidence regarding the disputed term itself (how it first came up, why it was not included in the writing, etc.).

Professor Corbin criticized both of these approaches on the ground that a judge can hardly decide what a reasonable person would have done without listening to evidence of *all* the surrounding circumstances.[30] For example, suppose the omitted term was an afterthought that the parties, who were not sophisticated in legal matters and were not represented by counsel, agreed to after the writing had been prepared but before it had been signed. Surely this fact should be relevant in deciding whether a reasonable person would have gone to the effort of modifying the writing. In direct response to Professor Corbin's concerns, a Comment to the Second Restatement provides that: "A writing cannot of itself prove its own completeness, and wide latitude must be allowed for inquiry into circumstances bearing on the intention of the parties."[31]

Under Section 209(3) of the Second Restatement, a writing that because of its scope and specificity appears complete must be accepted by the judge as a complete integration absent evidence that the parties intended otherwise. Section 216(2) addresses the kind of evidence that would establish a contrary

[28] 247 N.Y. 377, 160 N.E. 646, 68 A.L.R. 239 (1928).

[29] 247 N.Y. at 381, 160 N.E. at 647.

[30] A. Corbin, Contracts § 582 (rev. ed. 1960).

[31] Restatement (Second) of Contracts § 210 cmt. b.

intent and provides that a writing is not completely integrated if it "omits a consistent additional agreed term which is (a) agreed to for a separate consideration, or (b) such a term as in the circumstances might naturally be omitted from the writing." Thus, with separate consideration, the only inquiry is consistency. Without separate consideration, a reasonable-person test must be applied, although the Second Restatement's requirement that all the surrounding circumstances be considered means that the test will be applied in a manner that differs from the approach taken by the court in *Mitchill*.

Section 2-202 also rejects the four-corners approach, stating in the Comments that "[a]ny assumption that because a writing has been worked out which is final on some matters, it is to be taken as including all the matters agreed upon."[32] Thus, the judge must consider evidence of the circumstances that led to the omission of the term. The following Comment also suggests that the door of admissibility should be more open than it is under the Second Restatement, which requires that evidence of an extrinsic term be excluded unless, in the circumstances, a reasonable person might naturally have omitted the term from the writing:

> Under paragraph (b) consistent additional terms, not reduced to writing, may be proved unless the court finds that the writing was intended by both parties as a complete and exclusive statement of all the terms. If the additional terms are such that, if agreed upon, they would certainly have been included in the document in the view of the court, then evidence of their alleged making must be kept from the trier of fact.

Unless the proffered term would "certainly" have been included in the writing by a reasonable person, taking into consideration the surrounding circumstances, evidence of the term must be admitted.[33] The scope of the evidence regarding the surrounding circumstances that a judge should consider in applying the "certainly" test is unclear, although Corbin's analysis seems to be the most appropriate. Surely the judge should listen to evidence of all the surrounding circumstances, including evidence relating to the term itself, before deciding whether a reasonable person would certainly have included the disputed term in the writing.[34]

---

[32] UCC § 2-202, cmt. 1(a). *See, e.g.*, Northwest Cent. Pipeline Corp. v. JER Partnership, 943 F.2d 1219, 16 UCC Rep. Serv. 2d 1004 (10th Cir. 1991) (Section 2-202 creates a presumption that a writing is not fully integrated unless the court makes an explicit finding to the contrary); Century Ready-Mix Co. v. Lower & Co., 770 P.2d 692, 10 UCC Rep. Serv. 2d 705 (Wyo. 1989), *app. after remand*, 816 P.2d 795 (Wyo. 1991) (Code eliminates any presumption of completeness).

[33] Sagent Tech., Inc. v. Micros Sys., Inc., 276 F. Supp. 2d 464, 51 UCC Rep. Serv. 2d 59 (D. Md. 2003) (evidence was not admissible because any agreement by the seller to help resell the computer software or to grant a full refund for unsold products was so significant that it certainly would have been included in the writing had the parties actually agreed on these terms); Braund, Inc. v. White, 486 P.2d 50 (Alaska 1971) (because the trial court had not made a finding either that the parties intended the written agreement to be complete or that the offered term would certainly have been included if the parties had agreed to it, the trial court's grant of summary judgment was premature).

[34] *See, e.g.*, Alaska Northern Dev., Inc. v. Alyeska Pipeline Serv. Co., 666 P.2d 33, 36 UCC Rep. Serv. 1527 (Alaska 1983), *cert. denied* 464 U.S. 1041 (1984) (trial court correctly considered evidence of a wide range of surrounding circumstances).

Parties often seek to control the issue of completeness and exclusivity by stating an intent in the writing itself, most commonly by a clause stating that the writing represents their entire agreement. If such a clause, commonly called a merger clause, is given effect, the writing may not be supplemented by evidence of consistent additional terms.[35] At one time, merger clauses were routinely enforced without further analysis, something that still often happens in commercial contracts between merchants of relatively equal bargaining strength.[36] Merger clauses, however, have lost some of their vitality in other cases. Although courts typically state that a merger clause creates a strong inference that a writing is a complete and exclusive statement of the parties' agreement, they often refuse to enforce such clauses if they are convinced that the real intent of the parties was otherwise.[37] They follow this course most frequently when a consumer challenges a merger clause in a seller's boilerplate, but one court even agreed with a used-car dealer's challenge to its own boilerplate clause in a dispute with a conniving consumer.[38]

[2]   Determining Contradiction or Consistency

A partial integration may not be contradicted by evidence of any extrinsic terms but may be supplemented by evidence of terms drawn from a course of performance, course of dealing, or usage of trade and may also be supplemented by evidence of consistent additional terms drawn from other sources. What is a contradiction and when is an additional term consistent? The first major case to wrestle with these issues under the Code was *Hunt Foods & Industries v. Doliner*,[39] The case actually involved a contract for the sale of stock rather than goods, but the court nevertheless applied Section 2-202.

The plaintiff corporation in *Hunt Foods* wanted to buy the defendant's controlling stock in another corporation and the parties had agreed on the price when circumstances forced a temporary recess in the negotiations. Before the recess, the seller executed a writing giving the buyer an option to buy the stock at the agreed price. The writing did not disclose any conditions to the exercise of the option, but when the buyer attempted to do so the seller argued that the parties had agreed that it could be exercised only if the seller received an offer from a third party. In deciding that the alleged condition did not contradict the writing and was not inconsistent with it, the court stated, "To be inconsistent the

---

[35] Watkins & Son Pet Supplies v. The Iams Co., 254 F.3d 607, 44 UCC Rep. Serv. 2d 708 (6th Cir. 2001) (merger clause controlling on issue of completeness and exclusivity).

[36] *See, e.g.,* Ray Martin Painting, Inc. v. Ameron, Inc., 638 F. Supp. 768, 1 UCC Rep. Serv. 2d 713 (D. Kan. 1986) (court upheld merger clause, but only after explicitly finding that corporations had relatively equal bargaining strength). *Cf.* Sierra Diesel Injection Serv., Inc. v. Burroughs Corp., 890 F.2d 108 (9th Cir. 1989) (merger clause on preprinted form invalidated; form was prepared by sophisticated corporation and used in contract with small business being run by family members with limited educations).

[37] Morgan v. Stokely-Van Camp, Inc., 34 Wash. App. 801, 663 P.2d 1384 (1983) (merger clause merely some evidence of whether the parties intended writing to be complete and exclusive); *see also* Restatement (Second) of Contracts § 216, cmt. e (suggesting careful scrutiny of boilerplate merger clauses).

[38] Lopez v. Reynoso, 129 Wash. App. 165, 118 P.3d 398 (2005).

[39] 26 A.D.2d 41, 270 N.Y.S.2d 937, 3 UCC Rep. Serv. 597 (1966).

term must contradict or negate a term of the writing. A term or condition which has a lesser effect is provable."[40] Under this analysis, contradiction and inconsistency are equated, and extrinsic evidence is admissible unless a term that is expressed in the writing is directly negated. The *Hunt Foods* analysis was a dramatic contrast with many pre-Code cases, which typically held that to be consistent, a proffered term could not even vary the terms of the writing, much less contradict them.[41] A few of the early decisions applying the Code adopted the *Hunt Foods* approach.[42]

Hunt Foods represents the extreme, as most subsequent cases have been less hostile to the parol evidence rule. The emerging approach seems to be a "reasonable harmony" test first articulated in *Snyder v. Herbert Greenbaum & Associates.*[43] In *Snyder*, a buyer of carpeting tried to show through a course of dealing that it had a right to cancel the contract unilaterally. The court held that even though the contract was silent on cancellation, thus eliminating direct contradiction of an express term, the proffered understanding was not consistent because it was not in reasonable harmony with the writing. Obviously, a highly subjective standard like "reasonable harmony" gives judges great discretion, and, not surprisingly, the test has now been adopted by a number of courts.[44] It is possible, however, that some judges explain their decisions in terms of the reasonable-harmony test for consistency, and perhaps the certainly test for completeness as well, while the actual basis for those decisions is a negative assessment of the credibility of the proffered evidence.

[C]　Extrinsic Evidence Admissible Notwithstanding a Complete Writing

Even if a court finds that a writing is intended to be complete and exclusive, some extrinsic evidence can still be introduced. The most important situations are discussed below.

[1]　Invalidating Causes

The parol evidence rule precludes the introduction of certain evidence for the purpose of supplementing a writing. The very same evidence, however, may be admissible for the purpose of proving an invalidating cause that would render the contract voidable. Although the Code does not address this issue, the Second

---

[40] 26 A.D.2d at 43, 270 N.Y.S.2d at 940.

[41] Surprisingly, the Restatement (Second) of Contracts provides no guidance on this issue. Section 215 states that a partial integration cannot be contradicted, and Comment b to that section states that whether there is a contradiction depends on whether the proffered term is consistent or inconsistent with the writing.

[42] *See, e.g.*, Ace Supply, Inc. v. Rocky-Mountain Mach. Co., 96 Idaho 183, 525 P.2d 965, 15 UCC Rep. Serv. 324 (1974) (court admitted buyer's evidence that apparently unconditional sale of tractor was in fact conditioned on seller's inability to find another buyer).

[43] 38 Md. App. 144, 380 A.2d 618, 22 UCC Rep. Serv. 1104 (1977).

[44] *See, e.g.*, ARB, Inc. v. E-Sys., Inc., 663 F.2d 189, 30 UCC Rep. Serv. 949 (D.C. Cir. 1980); Alaska Northern Dev., Inc. v. Alyeska Pipeline Serv. Co., 666 P.2d 33, 36 UCC Rep. Serv. 1527 (Alaska 1983), *cert. denied* 464 U.S. 1041 (1984).

Restatement makes it clear that extrinsic evidence is admissible to prove "illegality, fraud, duress, mistake, lack of consideration or other invalidating cause."[45] Another invalidating cause, identified in the Code, is unconscionability.

The most commonly used invalidating cause is fraud. For example, in *Latham & Associates, Inc. v. William Raveis Real Estate, Inc.*,[46] the buyer of two computer systems sought to introduce evidence of certain express warranties made by the seller but not reflected in the writing. Had the buyer wanted to introduce the evidence in order to make the oral warranties part of the contract, the judge would have had to apply the parol evidence rule to decide whether to admit the evidence.[47] Instead, the buyer was seeking rescission of the contract and introduced the evidence to show the court that the seller had deliberately misrepresented its expertise in developing the systems. As the case did not involve supplementation of the writing, the parol evidence rule was irrelevant and the court properly admitted the evidence.

Extrinsic evidence can also be used to prove other invalidating causes. The Second Restatement uses an example in which a buyer and a seller enter into a completely integrated agreement for the sale of rifles. Extrinsic evidence would be admissible to show that the buyer had promised to buy the rifles to foment a rebellion, thereby making the contract illegal.[48] Although extreme, the example illustrates the point well.

[2]   Conditions Precedent

Section 2-202(b) precludes supplementation by consistent additional terms if a writing is complete and exclusive, and "term" means "that portion of an agreement that relates to a particular matter."[49] Although it is hard to argue that a condition precedent is not just another term for purposes of the parol evidence rule,[50] numerous common-law decisions and a few decisions under the Code have permitted the introduction of extrinsic evidence of a condition precedent even when there is a complete and exclusive writing.[51] The rationale is that a condition precedent operates like an invalidating cause. In other words, since the condition prevents the parties' duties from becoming enforceable, its effect is similar to the effect of the usual invalidating causes.[52]

Presumably, additional language in a merger clause specifying that there are no conditions precedent would be effective, assuming of course that the merger

---

[45] Restatement (Second) of Contracts § 214(d). The principles of common law and equity can, of course, be used to supplement the provisions of the Code. UCC § 1-103(b).

[46] 218 Conn. 297, 589 A.2d 337, 14 UCC Rep. Serv. 2d 394 (1991).

[47] *See* UCC § 2-316(1).

[48] Restatement (Second) of Contracts § 214, cmt. c, illus. 6.

[49] UCC § 1-201(b)(40).

[50] *See* Deck House, Inc. v. Scarborough, Sheffield & Gaston, Inc., 139 Ga. App. 173, 228 S.E.2d 142, 20 UCC Rep. Serv. 278 (1976).

[51] *See, e.g.*, Ace Supply, Inc. v. Rocky-Mountain Mach. Co., 96 Idaho 183, 525 P.2d 965, 15 UCC Rep. Serv. 324 (1974) (court admitted seller's proffered evidence that sale would be completed only if seller could not sell tractor elsewhere).

[52] *See* Restatement (Second) of Contracts § 217.

clause is enforced by the court. Even without a specific reference in a merger clause, evidence of an inconsistent condition precedent should not be admitted. Furthermore, if a writing specifies a number of conditions, it will be difficult for a party to convince the judge that there was, in fact, an additional one.

[3]   Reformation

In certain situations, a party faced with a final writing, even one that is complete and exclusive, may be able to convince the court that the writing should be reformed to show the true intent of the parties.[53] The predicate for this approach is that the parties agreed on the disputed term but then made a mistake in transcription.[54] The protection of the parol evidence rule is not considered necessary in these situations since a contract may not be reformed without "clear and convincing" evidence of the mistake.[55] If the issue is not within the scope of the reformation rule, the fact that there might be clear and convincing evidence that the parties agreed to a term will not be sufficient to overcome the parol evidence rule. For example, after proving by clear and convincing evidence that a written agreement contained clerical errors regarding delivery date and mode of shipment, the seller in *Luria Brothers & Co., Inc. v. Piellet Brothers Scrap Iron & Metal, Inc.*[56] sought to use the same evidentiary standard to prove in addition that the sale was conditioned on obtaining goods from a particular supplier. The court refused to admit the evidence, stating, "Allowing one party to use parol evidence to clarify a mistake in a writing, does not open the flood gates to any and all parol evidence bearing on the agreement."[57]

[4]   Interpretation

The parol evidence rule does not preclude extrinsic evidence introduced to explain an ambiguity in a final writing.[58] With one exception that will be discussed below, the rule applies only to attempts to supplement a writing. When the parties have included a term in their writing, evidence proffered for the purpose of explaining the term's meaning does not constitute an attempt at supplementation.

---

[53] *See* Braund, Inc. v. White, 486 P.2d 50, 9 UCC Rep. Serv. 183 (Alas. 1971) (parol evidence rule did not preclude granting remedy of reformation).

[54] *See, e.g.*, Ag Sales v. Klose, 199 Mont. 400, 649 P.2d 447, 34 UCC Rep. Serv. 1529 (1982) (extrinsic evidence admitted to show that the date stated in the written agreement was incorrect).

[55] *See* Kirkwood Motors, Inc. v. Conomon, 2001 Del. Super. LEXIS 15, 44 UCC Rep. Serv. 2d 355 (Feb. 5, 2001) (court determined that any mistake of the buyers in failing to notice that the value of their trade-in vehicle had been understated was attributable to their failure to read the contract).

[56] 600 F.2d 103, 26 UCC Rep. Serv. 1081 (7th Cir. 1979).

[57] 600 F.2d, at 110.

[58] Hessler v. Crystal Lake Chrysler-Plymouth, Inc., 338 Ill. App. 3d 1010, 788 N.E.2d 405, 50 UCC Rep. Serv. 2d 330 (Ill. Ct. App. 2003) (parol evidence rule did not preclude the admission of evidence to show the meaning of "ASAP"); Burroughs Corp. v. Macon Rubber Co., Inc., 154 Ga. App. 322, 268 S.E.2d 374 (1980) (extrinsic evidence admitted to show the parties' meaning of "under the same terms").

Because the line between interpretation and supplementation can be very thin, the judge's perspective can determine the outcome. If the judge concludes that the issue involves interpretation, extrinsic evidence is, subject to the plain-meaning rule discussed below, admissible. If the judge decides that the issue concerns supplementation, the very same evidence may be excluded by the parol evidence rule.

The court in *Alaska Northern Development, Inc. v. Alyeska Pipeline Service Co.*[59] explored the borderline between interpretation and supplementation. The buyer in that case had entered into a written agreement to buy all of the seller's inventory of Caterpillar parts "subject to the final approval of the [seller's] owner committee." The seller's committee subsequently refused to approve the sale for reasons unrelated to price. The buyer sought to prove the existence of an extrinsic understanding pursuant to which the owner's committee could disapprove the sale only if it concluded that the contract price was unfair. The court concluded that the issue was one of supplementation because the meaning that the buyer asserted — that the committee's discretion was limited — was not one to which the language of the writing was reasonably susceptible.

As noted above, the Code's parol evidence rule goes beyond supplementation in one respect. After providing that the terms of a final writing may not be contradicted, Section 2-202 states that they may be "explained" or supplemented. The word "explained" clearly refers to interpretation but it applies only to paragraph (a) dealing with course of performance, course of dealing, and usage of trade. It cannot apply to paragraph (b) because that paragraph deals with "additional" terms, a reference that limits it to supplementation. The curious injection of a rule of interpretation into the parol evidence rule is explained by the Comments, which state that Section 2-202 rejects "[t]he requirement that a condition precedent to the admissibility of the type of evidence specified in paragraph (a) is an original determination by the court that the language used is ambiguous." The effect of this rule is to cut back on the application of the plain-meaning rule, used by many courts to exclude extrinsic evidence relevant to the meaning of a term if the term appears, based only on the four corners of the writing, to be unambiguous.[60] Section 2-202 requires that before making a determination that a term is unambiguous, the court must at least consider relevant evidence as to its meaning drawn from a course of performance, course of dealing, or usage of trade.

Bayer Chemicals Corp v. Albermarle Corp.[61] illustrates the use of a course of performance for interpretation purposes and also illustrates how a course of dealing or usage of trade might be used similarly.[62] Bayer agreed to buy all its requirements of "C16-C18 alkenyl succinic anhydride" from Albermarle but

---

[59] 666 P.2d 33, 36 UCC Rep. Serv. 1257 (Alaska 1983), *cert. denied* 464 U.S. 1041 (1984).

[60] *See* W.W.W. Associates, Inc. v. Giancontieri, 77 N.Y.2d 157, 565 N.Y.S.2d 440, 566 N.E.2d 639 (1990) (extrinsic evidence not admissible to create an ambiguity where document complete, clear and unambiguous on its face).

[61] 171 Fed. Appx. 392 (3d Cir. 2006).

[62] *See also* Griffith v. Clear Lakes Trout Co., 143 Ida. 733, 152 P.3d 604, 61 UCC Rep. Serv. 2d 926 (2007) (the parties' performance over the first three years of the contract, their course of dealing prior to entering the current contract, and similar trade usage all supported the plaintiff's position

could seek other suppliers, subject to Albermarle's right of first refusal, if the need arose for it to use a reformulated product. After six years, during which time Albermarle consistently supplied a mixture that was 65% C16 and 35% C18, Bayer decided that it needed a mixture of 25% C16 and 75% C18 and triggered the reformulation provision of the contract. Albermarle argued that no combination of C16 and C18 could constitute a reformulation since the term describing the product did not specify percentages, but Bayer successfully argued that, while susceptible to Albermarle's interpretation at the contract's inception, the term had taken on a fixed meaning through the parties' course of performance.

[5]   Implied-in-Fact Terms

Evidence of a usage of trade, course of dealing, or course of performance often is used to aid in the process of interpreting ambiguous terms, but it also may be used to prove a term that supplements a writing.[63] Section 2-202(a) makes it clear that evidence of supplemental terms derived from these sources may be introduced even if there is a final writing — indeed, even if the writing is complete and exclusive. Because an understanding of this relationship between the parol evidence rule and the use of trade usage, course of dealing, and course of performance depends initially upon an understanding of these sources themselves, the sources must be defined. All of this discussion is included in the next section of this chapter, which also examines the problems that arise when there is an apparent clash between a writing's express terms and a proffered term implied from one of these sources.

§ 4.03   USAGE OF TRADE, COURSE OF DEALING, AND COURSE OF PERFORMANCE [§ 1-303]

The agreement of the parties may consist of more than express terms. As indicated in the preceding section on the parol evidence rule,[64] terms may also be derived from a usage of trade, course of dealing, or course of performance. In addition to providing a source of supplementary terms, evidence derived from these sources may be used to ascertain the meaning of the agreement or of a term of the agreement, and may even go so far as to qualify a term of the agreement. This section explains each of these potential sources, how they are used, their relationship to the parol evidence rule, and the issues that arise when a term implied from one of the sources conflicts with another term of the agreement.

---

that the parties' intended "market size" of raised trout to refer to fish that were approximately one pound live weight).

[63]   UCC § 1-303(d).

[64]   *See* § 4.02[C][5] *supra.*

[A]   Definitions

[1]   Usage of Trade

The Code defines a usage of trade as "any practice or method of dealing having such regularity of observance in a place, vocation or trade as to justify an expectation that it will be observed with respect to the transaction in question."[65] At its core, the idea is really quite simple: A person engaged in a business ought to be aware of the language and practices common to that business.

How deeply rooted must a usage of trade be? The Comments state that the Code has abandoned the ancient English tests for "custom" and that a party seeking to take advantage of a usage of trade need not prove that it is " 'ancient or immemorial,' 'universal' or the like."[66] The Comments also state that new usages may be proved, along with usages "currently observed by the great majority of decent dealers, even though dissidents ready to cut corners do not agree."[67] Of course, the usage must have enough "regularity of observance" to "justify an expectation that it will be observed."[68] Obviously, this flexible standard leaves the fact-finder with considerable discretion.[69] Further flexibility is suggested by Comment 8 to Section 1-303, which states that:

> In cases of a well established line of usage varying from the general rules of this Act where the precise amount of the variation has not been worked out into a single standard, the party relying on the usage is entitled, in any event, to the minimum variation demonstrated.

If, for example, a usage could be established pursuant to which sellers in a particular trade made delivery anywhere from five to eight days after receiving a purchase order, a buyer would be entitled to delivery no later than eight days after submitting an order.

The definition of usage of trade includes practices in a "place" as well as in a "vocation or trade,"[70] and it is effective against parties that are members of the vocation or trade or that are or should be aware of the usage.[71] A usage of trade may thus be effective against a party that is not a member of the particular trade, a fact that was demonstrated in *Nanakuli Paving & Rock Co. v. Shell Oil Co.*,

---

[65] UCC § 1-303(c).

[66] UCC § 1-303, cmt. 4. The common-law tests for establishing a "custom" were quite stringent. *See generally* Levie, *Usage of trade and Custom Under the Common Law and the Uniform Commercial Code*, 40 N.Y.U. L. Rev. 1101 (1965).

[67] UCC § 1-303, cmt. 4.

[68] UCC § 1-303(c).

[69] The Code allocates determinations about the existence and scope of a usage of trade to the trier of fact. However, if the usage is a part of a written trade code that requires interpretation, the meaning of the code is an issue for the court. UCC § 1-303(c).

[70] UCC § 1-303(c). Spurgeon v. Jamieson Motors, 164 Mont. 296, 521 P.2d 924 (1974) (implied warranties excluded by usage of trade).

[71] UCC § 1-303(d).

Inc.[72] Shell supplied asphalt to Nanakuli, which was a paving contractor on the island of Oahu. The contract provided that the price of asphalt would be Shell's posted price at the time of delivery, but Nanakuli tried to show that it was common on Oahu for parties selling supplies to paving contractors to offer "price protection." If effective, this usage would have qualified the express price term[73] by limiting Shell to the price in effect at the time Nanakuli entered into its contracts with third parties.

Only Shell and one other party sold asphalt on Oahu, and Nanakuli was unable to prove a usage in the business of buying and selling asphalt. It did, however, prove that price protection was regularly, indeed almost universally, observed in the asphalt paving business. The evidence supported the jury's conclusion that Shell should have been aware that asphalt pavers had to bid with government agencies at fixed prices because the agencies would not accept price escalation clauses and that as a result parties supplying materials, such as aggregate rock suppliers, provided the pavers with price protection. The usage of trade established for a place — Oahu — was binding on Shell even though it was not in the relevant trade. The Comments support this result, stating, "[t]he language used [by the parties] is to be interpreted as meaning what it may fairly be expected to mean to parties involved in the particular commercial transaction *in a given locality* or in a given vocation or trade."[74] Most trade usages nevertheless arise when both parties are members of a particular business or trade.[75]

The Code does not allocate the burden of proving a usage of trade but it surely must fall on the party that would benefit from its existence.[76] A party seeking to establish a usage of trade must give the other party sufficient notice to avoid unfair surprise.[77] Unlike course of performance and course of dealing, establishing a usage of trade is almost certain to require expert testimony.[78] A usage of trade may not be established unless the party against which it is to operate should have been aware of it, but the fact that the party did not actually know of it is irrelevant.[79]

---

[72] 664 F.2d 772, 32 UCC Rep. Serv. 1025 (9th Cir. 1981).

[73] Section 4.03[B] *infra* contains a discussion of the extent to which a term derived from a course of performance, course of dealing, or usage of trade may qualify an express term of the agreement, including a discussion of the *Nanakuli* court's analysis of that issue.

[74] UCC § 1-303, cmt. 3 (emphasis supplied). Although addressing the issue of interpretation, the Comment is equally relevant as applied to the issue of supplementation.

[75] *See, e.g.*, Graaf v. Bakker Bros. of Idaho, Inc., 85 Wash. App. 814, 934 P.2d 1228, 35 UCC Rep. Serv. 2d 126 (1997) (usage of trade established that germination testing of onion-seed crop was to be conducted after the seed was washed and cleaned); Warrick Beverage Corp. v. Miller Brewing Co., 170 Ind. App. 114, 352 N.E. 2d 496 (1976) (beer distributor allowed to show through usage of trade that only one local distributor would be appointed by brewing company).

[76] *See, e.g.*, Coleman v. Dupree, 1994 WL 8614 (Tex. Ct. App., Jan. 7, 1994).

[77] UCC § 1-303(g). *See, e.g.*, Western Int'l Forest Prods., Inc. v. Boise Cascade Corp., 63 Or. App. 475, 665 P.2d 1231 (1983) (plaintiff precluded from introducing evidence of a usage of trade because no advance notice given to defendant).

[78] *See, e.g.*, Western Indus., Inc. v. Newcor Canada, Ltd., 739 F.2d 1198, 38 UCC Rep. Serv. 1458 (7th Cir. 1984).

[79] *See, e.g.*, Aceros Prefabricados, S.A. v. TradeArbed, Inc., 282 F.3d 92, 46 UCC Rep. Serv. 2d 596 (2d Cir. 2002).

[2]   Course of Dealing

A course of dealing is "a sequence of conduct concerning previous transactions between the parties to a particular transaction that is fairly to be regarded as establishing a common basis of understanding for interpreting their expressions and other conduct."[80] As with a usage of trade, the idea is quite simple: A party to a current contract should expect that its terms will be consistent with the terms of previous comparable contracts with the same party. The pattern of conduct in the prior contracts provides a reasonable basis for assuming that same pattern of conduct will apply again.[81]

The existence of a course of dealing would seem to be a question of fact for the jury, although the Code is silent on this point.[82] The proof typically comes from a party's own experience; hence, no expert testimony is necessary. Because a course of dealing must be based on a sequence of conduct, a single occurrence cannot support a finding that the parties had an established course of dealing.[83] Evidence of a single occurrence might, however, be relevant in determining the parties' intent with regard to the transaction at issue and should, subject to the parol evidence rule and the normal rules of interpretation, be admissible for that purpose.[84]

[3]   Course of Performance

A course of performance is "a sequence of conduct between the parties to a particular transaction that exists if: (1) the agreement of the parties with respect to the transaction involves repeated occasions for performance by a party; and (2) the other party, with knowledge of the nature of the performance and opportunity for objection to it, accepts the performance or acquiesces in it without objection."[85] The major difference between the two concepts is that a course of dealing involves a sequence of conduct between the parties *prior to* the contract in question, whereas a course of performance involves a sequence of conduct *under* the contract in question. As with a course of dealing, more than one occasion for performance is required,[86] and even then the courts are

---

[80] UCC § 1-303(b).

[81] Koenen v. Royal Buick Co., 62 Ariz. 376, 783 P.2d 822 (1989) (course of dealing pursuant to which the buyer had always paid the dealer the manufacturer's sticker price for new cars); Vogel v. W.A. Sandri, Inc., 898 F. Supp. 254, 27 UCC Rep. Serv. 2d 1167 (D. Vt. 1995) (prior course of dealing established that the motor-fuel supply contract between the parties was a requirements contract that required the buyer to purchase all of its requirements from the seller).

[82] Arguably, since the existence of a usage of trade is expressly assigned to the jury, silence of the drafters with regard to a course of dealing implies that it is an issue for the judge. This argument is weak. The existence of a usage of trade is allocated to the jury in order to contrast the issue of interpretation of a trade code or similar record, which is assigned to the court. UCC § 1-303(c).

[83] Kalmes Farms, Inc. v. J-Star Industries, Inc., 52 UCC Rep. Serv. 2d 845 (D. Minn. 2004).

[84] *See, e.g.*, Bowdoin v. Showell Growers, Inc., 817F.2d 1543, 3 UCC Rep. Serv. 2d 1366 (11th Cir. 1987).

[85] UCC § 1-303(a); Mulberry-Fairplains Water Ass'n, Inc. v. Town of N. Wilkesboro, 105 N.C. App. 258, 412 S.E.2d 910, 17 UCC Rep. Serv. 2d 48 (N.C. Ct. App. 1992) (course of performance used to fix the price of extra water).

[86] *See* Palmer v. Idaho Peterbilt, Inc., 102 Ida. 800, 641 P.2d 346 (1982).

occasionally reluctant to find a course of performance. For example, in *John P. Saad & Sons v. Nashville Thermal Transfer Corp.*,[87] the court refused to find that the buyer's repeated pattern of accepting nonconforming oil in an installment contract amounted to a course of performance.

If one party regularly performs in a certain manner but the other party repeatedly objects, there is no course of performance.[88] Likewise, there is no course of performance if the nonperforming party is mistaken as to the requirements of the contract.[89] As with usage of trade and course of dealing, the burden of proof should be on the party that will benefit from the evidence, and the existence of a course of performance should be a question of fact for the jury.

It would be unusual for a writing to be supplemented by a term drawn from a course of performance since a course of performance cannot occur until after the parties have reached a contract. Accordingly, this source is most often used as an aid in interpretation or to show either a waiver or modification of an agreed term.

[B]   Relationship With the Parol Evidence Rule

As noted above, evidence of a usage of trade, course of dealing, or course of performance often is used to aid in the process of interpreting ambiguous terms,[90] but it may also be used to prove a term that supplements a writing.[91] Section 2-202(a) makes it clear that evidence of supplemental terms derived from these sources may be introduced even if there is a final writing — indeed, even if the writing is complete and exclusive.[92] The treatment of these sources when the writing is complete and exclusive is distinct because, even though Section 2-202(b) permits a writing to be supplemented by evidence of consistent additional terms drawn from other sources,[93] it denies admissibility if the writing is complete and exclusive. The reason for allowing the admission of

---

[87]   715 S.W.2d 41 (Tenn. 1986). *But see* Lancaster Glass Corp. v. Phillips ECG, Inc., 835 F.2d 652, 5 UCC Rep. Serv. 2d 1306 (6th Cir. 1987) (pattern of accepting nonconforming installments established a course of performance).

[88]   *See, e.g.*, A & G Constr. Co. v. Reid Bros. Logging Co., 547 P.2d 1207, 19 UCC Rep. Serv. 37 (Alaska 1976).

[89]   *See, e.g.*, Kern Oil & Refining Co. v. Tenneco Oil Co., 792 F.2d 1380, 1 UCC Rep. Serv. 2d 651 (9th Cir. 1986), *cert. denied*, 480 U.S. 906 (1987).

[90]   For discussion of the use of these sources as aids in interpretation, see § 4.02[C][4] *supra*.

[91]   In this respect Section 2-202 goes beyond the traditional statement of the parol evidence rule.

[92]   The discussion in § 4.02[C] addresses extrinsic evidence that is admissible notwithstanding a complete writing. Although it deferred the discussion of usage of trade, course of dealing, and course of performance and their relationship with the parol evidence rule in the interest of first explaining the implied-in-fact categories in this section, § 4.02[C][5] nevertheless noted the relevance of these concepts to the discussion in § 4.03. Extrinsic evidence concerning implied-in-fact terms derived from these sources can supplement a written agreement, even if it is a complete and exclusive statement of the express terms.

[93]   As a practical matter, UCC § 2-202(b) is limited to express terms, although it would also apply in the rare case of a term inferred from a factual matrix other than a usage of trade, course of dealing, or course of performance.

extrinsic evidence to prove a term based on usage of trade, course of dealing, or course of performance is perfectly understandable. Terms derived from these sources are the background music for the agreement — that is, the parties implicitly rely on them even if they are not articulated — and thus their omission from even a complete and exclusive writing is to be expected.

Comment 2 to Section 2-202 makes the point as follows:

> Such writings are to be read on the assumption that the course of prior dealings between the parties and the usages of trade were taken for granted when the document was phrased. Unless carefully negated they have become an element of the meaning of the words used.

In other words, if the parties want to preclude supplementation through evidence of implied-in-fact sources, the writing itself must contain an effective clause stating that such sources are out of bounds.

A writing could be supplemented by a term drawn from a course of performance only in highly unusual circumstances since a course of performance cannot occur until after the parties have reached a contract. Accordingly, this source is used most often as an aid in interpretation or to show a waiver or a modification of an agreed term.[94]

[C]   The Code's Hierarchy of Terms

A term implied from a usage of trade, course of dealing, or course of performance might contradict or be inconsistent with an express term. How should such a conflict be resolved? As noted in the discussion of the parol evidence rule,[95] Section 2-202 indicates that the implied-in-fact terms derived from these sources may not be used to contradict a term in a final writing although, unlike terms derived from other sources, there is no explicit requirement that an implied-in-fact term be consistent with the written term.[96]

Section 1-303(e), which creates a hierarchy for terms derived from different sources, supplies the missing requirement of consistency. The beginning of the section provides that express terms and terms derived from the three implied-in-fact sources must be construed whenever reasonable as consistent with each other, a process sometimes referred to as "practical construction." If such a construction is unreasonable, the hierarchy becomes applicable: An express term prevails over a term derived from the other three sources, a term derived from a course of performance prevails over a term derived from a course of dealing or a usage of trade, and a term derived from a course of dealing prevails over a term derived from a usage of trade. This hierarchical structure, which applies whether or not there is a final writing, is based on the assumption that the best indicator of the parties' intent is their expression on a particular subject, that their performance on the contract in dispute is a better indicator

---

[94] UCC § 1-303 (d), (f).

[95] *See* § 4.03[B] *supra.*

[96] Contrast paragraphs (a) and (b) of UCC § 2-202. Inconsistency in the context of UCC § 2-202(b) is discussed in § 4.02[B][2] *supra.*

than their performance on prior contracts, and that their performance on prior contracts is a better indicator than the generally accepted practices within their trade. Notwithstanding the hierarchy, however, Section 1-303(f) appropriately provides that a course of performance may be used to show that an inconsistent express term has been waived or modified.[97]

Curiously, Section 1-303(d), which states the ways in which the three implied-in-fact sources may be used other than waiver or modification by a course of performance, refers neither to contradiction nor inconsistency; rather, it provides that the sources may be used to ascertain the meaning of the agreement or a term of the agreement or to "supplement or qualify" the terms of the agreement. For purposes of Section 1-303, where is the line between a permissible qualification and an impermissible inconsistency?

One of the earliest cases to explore this borderland was *Division of Triple T Services, Inc. v. Mobil Oil Corp.*[98] The plaintiff, the lessee of a gasoline station, wanted to show a usage of trade that precluded termination by the lessor except for cause notwithstanding a written provision that the lease would "terminate at the end of any current period (original or renewal) by notice from either party to the other, given not less than 90 days prior to such termination."[99] The court refused to admit the evidence, relying on the Code's hierarchy.[100] The result is debatable. The writing did not expressly state that the lease was terminable at will; it was simply silent on that point. The decision did not explain why the alleged usage did more than qualify the right to terminate in a manner consistent with the writing.

The court in *Columbia Nitrogen Corp. v. Royster Co.*[101] took a more liberal approach. A written contract required the buyer to purchase at least 31,000 tons of phosphate per year for three years at a price that was subject to escalation if certain market conditions occurred but was silent regarding de-escalation. When the market price fell, the buyer refused to accept the quantity of goods provided for by the contract, arguing that the quantity term was a mere projection under both a course of dealing and a usage of trade. The trial judge's decision in favor of the seller was reversed, with the appellate court holding that the evidence was consistent with the contract. In support of the result the appellate court stressed that the writing did not exclude evidence of implied-in-

---

[97] See, *e.g.*, *Radiation Sys., Inc. v. Amplicon, Inc.*, 882 F. Supp. 1101, 26 UCC Rep. Serv. 2d 695 (D. D.C. 1995), where an express term required that the seller make delivery within ninety days of the purchase-order date and for each delivery provide the buyer with an acceptance certificate signed by the buyer's lessee on a form supplied by the buyer. Evidence that the buyer had accepted late deliveries and had paid for deliveries accompanied by forms not supplied by it was sufficient to preclude granting the buyer's motion for summary judgment.

[98] 60 Misc. 2d 720, 304 N.Y.S.2d 191, 6 UCC Rep. Serv. 1011 (Sup. Ct. 1969), *aff'd*, 34 A.D.2d 618, 311 N.Y.S.2d 961 (App. Div. 1970).

[99] *Id.*, 60 Misc. 2d at 722, 304 N.Y.S.2d at 194, 6 UCC Rep. Serv. at 1014.

[100] Several other decisions have relied on the hierarchy as the basis for upholding an express term. *See, e.g.*, Western Pet Wholesalers, Inc. v. Natura Pet Products, 2005 Cal. App. Unpub. LEXIS 7286 (Aug. 11, 2005); Hoover Universal, Inc. v. Brockway Imco, Inc., 809 F.2d 1039 (4th Cir. 1987); Southern Concrete Serv., Inc. v. Mableton Contractors, Inc., 407 F. Supp. 581 (N.D. Ga. 1975).

[101] 451 F.2d 3, 9 UCC Rep. Serv. 977 (4th Cir. 1971).

fact terms and was silent as to the effect of price declines. The court noted that the Code assigns to terms derived from the implied-in-fact sources "unique and important roles" and stated that "overly simplistic and overly legalistic interpretation of a contract should be avoided."[102] Notwithstanding the court's analysis, it is difficult not to conclude that the court permitted an express term to be contradicted, or so qualified as to be rendered virtually meaningless, by an implied-in-fact term.

Another case that arguably permitted an implied-in-fact term to contradict an express term is *Nanakuli Paving & Rock Co. v. Shell Oil Co., Inc,*[103] in which a written requirements contract called for the price of asphalt to be Shell's posted price at the time of delivery. After Shell raised its prices, Nanakuli tried to show that under a usage of trade Shell should have given it "price protection," meaning that Shell could only charge the price in effect at the time Nanakuli bound itself to perform paving work for a third party. The court concluded that the usage merely qualified the express term but, since Nanakuli was unlikely to order asphalt unless it had a binding contract, it is hard to escape the conclusion that the Court permitted a direct contradiction. In effect, the contract as construed by the court called for the price to be the posted price at the time Nanakuli contracted with a third party, not the posted price at the time of delivery. The decision need not be read as permitting a contradiction because, through additional evidence of a course of performance, the jury also found a modification of the written term. The evidence of the course of performance was somewhat weak because it consisted of only two occasions on which price protection had been provided, but coupled with the usage of trade it seems to have provided valuable corroboration that price protection was, in fact, the real intent of the parties all along notwithstanding the writing.

The cases in this area, many of which focus on only some of the relevant Code provisions, are difficult to reconcile. Notwithstanding occasional cases like *Columbia Nitrogen* and *Nanakuli*, most courts apply the hierarchical rules of Section 1-303 mechanically, without much analysis of the extent to which those rules result in an elevation of express terms at the expense of a thorough search for the real intent of the parties. Perhaps all that can be said is that the cases are inconsistent, differences in the drafting of Sections 2-202 and 1-303 raise questions regarding the extent to which their rules are parallel, and terms such as "qualify" and "consistent" are sufficiently indefinite to provide judges with a great deal of discretion. It is not surprising that judges in their exercise of that discretion vary in the rigor with which they apply the hierarchy.

---

[102] *Id.,* 451 F.2d at 10, 9 UCC Rep. Serv. at 987; *see also* Modine Mfg. Co. v. North E. Indep. School Dist., 503 S.W.2d 833, 14 UCC Rep. Serv. 317 (Tex. Ct. App. 1973) (6 percent deviation from express quantity term permitted under usage of trade); Heggblade-Marguleas-Tenneco, Inc. v. Sunshine Biscuit, Inc., 59 Cal. App. 3d 948, 131 Cal. Rptr. 183, 19 UCC Rep. Serv. 1067 (1976) (usage of trade used to show that fixed quantity term was a mere estimate).

[103] 664 F.2d 772, 32 UCC Rep. Serv. 1025 (9th Cir. 1981).

§ 4.04　GAP-FILLERS

Being limited to express and implied-in-fact terms, an agreement may fail to cover an area that later proves to be critical. At common law, failure to agree on a material term frequently meant that the courts would not enforce the agreement because of indefiniteness. Article 2 represents a dramatic shift from that approach. Recognizing that parties often reach agreement during a relatively short exchange (a phone conversation, for example), the drafters of Article 2 created what can best be understood as a default contract consisting of a set of standard provisions. If the parties intend to be bound but have not reached agreement on a matter covered by one these default provisions, the provision will supplement the agreement.[104] The default provisions, which are implied-in-law, are known as "gap-fillers."[105] Some of the most important of the gap-fillers are discussed in the ensuing subsections. Other gap-fillers are discussed elsewhere in this book in the context of the topic to which they relate.[106]

[A]　Open and Deferred Price [§ 2-305]

Section 2-305(1) provides that "[t]he parties if they so intend can conclude a contract for sale even though the price is not settled." The absence of an agreement on a term as important as price may well indicate that the parties never went beyond the negotiating stage, and a court should not supply a price term unless the party seeking to enforce the contract establishes that they intended to be bound.[107] Of course, the most obvious indication of such an intent would be tender of the goods by the seller and acceptance by the buyer. Short of such a showing, a court will no doubt be influenced by a desire to protect any significant, reasonable reliance by one of the parties. Absent a finding that the parties intended to be bound, however, the court should find that the parties never entered into a contract.

The parties rarely fail even to address the issue of price, and when they do, each party is likely to be gambling either that there will be a favorable market shift before the delivery date or that later negotiations on price will not pose a

---

[104] *See* UCC § 1-201(11) (contract means the total legal obligation resulting from the agreement as determined by the UCC as supplemented by other applicable laws). Gap-fillers create contractual obligations but are not technically "terms" of a contract. In this regard, see the discussion in § 4.01 *supra*. A colloquial reference to gap-fillers as creating implied-in-law terms is nonetheless prevalent and is used on occasion in this discussion.

[105] Due to the nature of lease transactions, which are typically set forth in a detailed writing intended to cover virtually every contingency, Article 2A does not include an expansive set of gap-fillers.

[106] See, for example, Chapter 5 on gap-fillers relating to the quality of the goods and Chapter 6 on gap-fillers relating to risk of loss.

[107] This observation restates for emphasis the basic principle of UCC § 2-204(3), which makes intent to be bound a prerequisite to gap-filling. *See, e.g.*, In re BTS, Inc., 104 B.R. 1009, 11 UCC Rep. Serv. 2d 444 (Bankr. W.D. Mo. 1989) (court should not supply price in the absence of evidence that the parties intended to go forward with the deal); D. R. Curtis Co. v. Mathews, 103 Idaho 776, 653 P.2d 1188, 35 UCC Rep. Serv. 1425 (Ct. App. 1982) (court must find intent to be bound before supplying missing price term).

problem. If a contract is completely silent as to price, the court will fill the gap with a "reasonable price." If the buyer is purchasing one of the seller's standard products, it is reasonable to infer that the buyer is willing to pay the seller's standard price. In other instances, a reasonable price may be the market price.[108] If market price would be the appropriate standard but the circumstances are so unusual as to preclude an objective method for measuring the market, the contract should fail for indefiniteness.[109]

Parties frequently discuss price without setting a specific amount. They may, for example, agree to agree on the price in the future (deferred pricing), or they may establish a mechanism for determining the price, such as a trade journal or a neutral third party. Prior to the Code, most courts held that agreements to agree on material terms were unenforceable,[110] and they also generally refused to enforce agreements establishing a pricing mechanism if the mechanism failed to produce a result.[111]

Section 2-305(1)(b) and (c) explicitly reverse such decisions by applying the reasonable-price standard. Before the court fills the gap with a reasonable price, however, it must make a separate determination that the parties intended to remain bound notwithstanding their failure to agree.[112] If they have a longstanding relationship and their pricing procedure fails, or if one of the parties has made a significant investment that cannot be recouped if the contract is not enforced, the court should not hesitate to fill the gap if it has an objective basis for doing so. If, however, the contract is entirely executory and neither party has relied to any significant degree, the best result is generally for the court to allow the parties to go their own ways. Of course, the parties are free to, and should, draft clauses expressing their intent on whether a gap should be filled if they fail to agree.

The parties sometimes agree that one of them will fix the price. In these circumstances, Section 2-305(2) requires that the price be fixed in good faith. A significant number of cases involve claims by gasoline dealers that their suppliers have violated the good-faith standard by fixing discriminatory prices designed to drive them out of business. Several cases have concluded that the supplier was not in good faith because it set prices arbitrarily, unreasonably, or capriciously with the intention of depriving the other party of its reasonably expected contractual benefits.[113] Other courts have held that a supplier's intent to drive a dealer out of business is irrelevant if the price it sets is within the range of charges of other suppliers in the area and is applied to its dealers

[108] *See, e.g.*, Spartan Grain & Mill Co. v. Ayers, 517 F.2d 214, 17 UCC Rep. Serv. 693 (5th Cir. 1975); Alamo Clay Prods., Inc. v. Gunn Tile Co., 597 S.W.2d 388, 29 UCC Rep. Serv. 31 (Tex. Ct. App. 1980).

[109] UCC § 2-204(3).

[110] *See, e.g.*, Taller & Cooper v. Illuminating Elec. Co., 172 F.2d 625 (7th Cir. 1949) (deferred pricing mechanism unenforceable for lack of mutuality of obligation).

[111] *See, e.g.*, Interstate Plywood Sales Co. v. Interstate Container Corp., 331 F.2d 449 (9th Cir. 1949) (contract held unenforceable when price-setting mechanism based on prices at five mills failed due to closure of some of the mills).

[112] UCC § 2-305(4).

[113] *See, e.g.*, Wilson v Amerada Hess Corp., 168 N.J. 236, 773 A.2d 1121 (2001).

uniformly.[114] The decisions are not inconsistent if one concludes that the setting of a price within the normal range is by definition not arbitrary, capricious, or unreasonable.

[B]   Open Quantity (Output and Requirements Contracts) [§ 2-306]

A requirements contract is one in which a buyer agrees to purchase all of its requirements for particular goods from a seller. An output contract is one in which a buyer agrees to purchase all of a seller's output of particular goods. Historically, these types of contracts often were invalidated for two reasons: lack of mutuality of obligation, and indefiniteness as to quantity. Even before enactment of the Code, however, most common-law courts had accepted the view that these contracts had great utility and ought to be enforced. Resort to the doctrine of good faith resolved the problems with mutuality and indefiniteness. Requirements and output contracts are clearly enforceable under the Code by virtue of Section 2-306.

Despite the general enforceability of these contracts, the lack of a specific quantity term can still present problems. For example, suppose a buyer in a requirements contract is purchasing a particular product for use in a manufacturing process. When the market price for the goods rises, the buyer suddenly begins ordering, at the lower contract price, more of the product than it can use in order to sell the excess on the spot market. Under pre-Code law, a court no doubt would have considered the buyer's order excessive under the good-faith doctrine. A court today would reach the same result under Section 2-306(1), which states:

> A term which measures the quantity by the output of the seller or the requirements of the buyer means such actual output or requirements as may occur in good faith, except that no quantity unreasonably disproportionate to any stated estimate or in the absence of a stated estimate to any normal or otherwise comparable prior output or requirements may be tendered or demanded.

Notice that the Code goes well beyond good faith in policing the appropriate quantity. In the example posed, the buyer's demand would have violated the duty of good faith because the buyer was in effect appropriating a business opportunity that had been implicitly allocated to the seller under their agreement. The buyer's demand might also have been stricken if it was unreasonably disproportionate to stated estimates or past orders.

The courts have struggled with the "unreasonably disproportionate" standard. A seller in a requirements contract should understand that risk is involved. If, for example, the buyer's business falls off, the seller will be selling fewer goods. If the buyer's business suddenly takes off, the seller may be called upon to provide goods in excess of its production capacity. In either case, the buyer's demands are consistent with its actual requirements and with the good-faith

[114] *See, e.g.*, Shell Oil Co. v. HRN, Inc., 144 S.W.3d 429, 54 UCC Rep. Serv. 2d 725 (Tex. 2004).

standard. Nevertheless, in either case, a fact-finder might conclude that the new demands are inappropriate because they are unreasonably disproportionate to the seller's actual expectations.

In requirements contracts, a number of courts have differentiated between an increase and a decrease in the buyer's demands. When they decrease, these courts have read the "unreasonably disproportionate" limitation out of the Code,[115] relying solely on good faith to police the transactions.[116] The reason is that the buyer is likely to have a valid business reason for a decrease and the good-faith doctrine will protect the seller in the rare case to the contrary. While eliminating the disproportionality requirement in cases of a decrease in quantity does violence to the language of the Code, it has become the trend.[117] The same analysis has been used to limit the obligation of a seller in an output contract that reduces its supply of goods.[118]

With an unexpected increase in the buyer's needs in a requirements contract, the seller may be caught off guard, unable either to expand capacity in a short period of time or to purchase the needed excess on the spot market. Many courts have been sympathetic with sellers in such cases and have bound the buyer by both the doctrine of good faith and the requirement of reasonable proportionality. In analyzing this latter requirement, the New York Court of Appeals in *Orange and Rockland Utilities v. Amerada Hess Corp.*[119] suggested that the following factors be considered:

> (1) the amount by which the requirements exceed the contract estimate; (2) whether the seller had any reasonable basis on which to forecast or anticipate the requested increase; (3) the amount, if any, by which the market price of the goods in question exceeded the contract price; (4) whether such an increase in market price was itself fortuitous; and (5) the reason for the increase in requirements.[120]

---

[115] *See, e.g.*, R.A. Weaver & Assocs. v. Asphalt Construction, Inc., 587 F.2d 1315, 25 UCC Rep. Serv. 388 (D.C. Cir. 1978); Empire Gas Corp. v. American Bakeries Co., 840 F.2d 1333, 5 UCC Rep. Serv. 2d 545 (7th Cir. 1988); Atlantic Track & Turnout Co. v. Perini Corp., 989 F.2d 541, 20 UCC Rep. Serv. 2d 426 (1st Cir. 1993) (output contract).

[116] UCC § 2-306, Comment 2 suggests that a buyer may not curtail demands in order to cut losses on the requirements contract itself; rather, the reduction must be related to the buyer's market for the finished product. *Vulcan Materials Co. v. Atofna Chem. Inc.*, 355 F. Supp. 2d 1214, 56 UCC Rep. Serv. 2d 278 (D. Kan. 2005), is illustrative. In *Vulcan*, the buyer closed its plant, thereby ending its need for the seller's goods, prior to the end of the contract term because the corporate enterprise of which the buyer was a part had determined that the plant was not competitive, primarily because of the price the buyer had to pay under the requirements contracts. The enterprise did not reduce its overall demand for the goods but instead entered into contracts with other suppliers at cheaper prices. The court held that the buyer had breached its duty of good faith.

[117] *See, e.g.*, Wisco, Inc. v. Johnson Controls, Inc., 59 UCC Rep. Serv. 2d 884 (6th Cir. 2005); Simcala, Inc. v. American Coal Trade, Inc., 821 So. 2d 197, 46 UCC Rep. Serv. 2d 369 (Ala. 2001); Dienes Corp. v. Long Island R. Co., 47 UCC Rep. Serv. 2d 941 (E.D.N.Y. 2002).

[118] *See* Atlantic Track & Turnout Co. v. Perini Corp., 989 F.2d 541, 20 UCC Rep. Serv. 2d 426 (1st Cir. 1993).

[119] 59 A.D.2d 110, 397 N.Y.S.2d 814, 22 UCC Rep. Serv. 310, 96 A.L.R.3d 1263 (1977).

[120] *Id.*, 397 N.Y.S.2d at 818–819, 59 A.D.2d at 115–116.

An exclusive-dealing agreement is a type of requirements contract in which the buyer agrees to buy all the goods it needs from the seller and the seller agrees not to sell those goods to any other dealer in a particular geographic area. As a requirements contract, all the rules discussed above involving good faith and disproportionality are applicable.[121] Section 2-306(2) is limited to "lawful" agreements, emphasizing that such agreements might cross the boundaries established by antitrust laws.

The difference between an ordinary requirements contract and an exclusive-dealing contract is that the parties in the latter type of transaction have a heightened obligation to use their best efforts to supply the goods (seller) and to promote their resale (buyer). The Comments describe the best-efforts requirement as follows:

> Under such contracts the exclusive agent is required, although no express commitment has been made, to use reasonable effort and due diligence in the expansion of the market or the promotion of the product, as the case may be. The principal is expected under such a contract to refrain from supplying any other dealer or agent within the exclusive territory.[122]

Thus, parties to an exclusive-dealing contract have a duty of good faith in determining quantity, a duty of good faith in the performance and enforcement of the contract,[123] and a heightened duty to use their best efforts in supplying the goods and promoting their resale.

[C]   Delivery

Section 2-301 states succinctly the essential duties of a seller: "The obligation of the seller is to transfer and deliver . . . in accordance with the contract." The reference to delivery relates to a seller's tender of the goods to the buyer, whereas the reference to transfer relates to a seller's transfer of title. These concepts are covered in the discussion below.

[1]   Combination of Express and Implied Delivery Terms [§ 2-503, § 2-504, § 2-319(1)]

Nearly every sales contract involves a combination of express terms and gap-fillers that establish the particulars of a seller's delivery obligation. If the parties are in different cities, for example, the agreement may authorize or require the seller to ship the goods by common carrier without spelling out every detail on how this is to be accomplished. If the parties are located in the same area, they may specify that the seller is to drop off the goods or that the buyer will pick them up, again without specifying the details. The gap-fillers provide the details.

Do not equate the seller's obligation of delivery with sending the goods to the buyer; indeed, the basic gap-filler for the place of delivery is the seller's place of

---

[121] UCC § 2-306, cmt. 5.

[122] *Id.*

[123] UCC § 1-304.

business or, if none, the seller's residence.[124] Delivery requires a tender of the goods[125] that conforms to the contract, and Section 2-503 provides guidance in this regard. The basic rule of the section requires the seller to "put and hold conforming goods at the buyer's disposition and give the buyer any notification reasonably necessary to enable him to take delivery."[126] The details — the manner, time, and place for tender — are determined by the agreement of the parties and any applicable gap-fillers,[127] but in particular: (1) the tender must be at a reasonable hour and the goods "must be kept available for the period reasonably necessary to enable the buyer to take possession;"[128] and (2) unless the parties agree otherwise "the buyer must furnish facilities reasonably suited to the receipt of the goods."[129]

If the contract requires the seller to send the goods to the buyer, or if it so authorizes the seller and the seller chooses to send them, the appropriate rules governing tender depend upon the characterization of the contract either as a shipment contract or as a destination contract. If it is a destination contract, the seller is responsible for getting the goods to a particular destination and tendering them there under the basic tender rule described above.[130] If it is a shipment contract, however, the seller is not responsible for getting the goods to a particular destination, but rather complies with its tender obligations by fulfilling the four requirements detailed in Section 2-504 for placing the goods in the hands of a carrier.[131] These requirements are that the seller (1) put the goods in the possession of a carrier that is reasonable given the nature of the goods and relevant circumstances,[132] (2) enter into a contract for transport of the goods that is reasonable given the nature of the goods and the circumstances of the case,[133] (3) obtain and promptly forward any documents

---

[124] UCC § 2-308(a). If the contract is for the sale of identified goods that to the knowledge of the parties at the time they enter into the contract are at a different location, that location is the place at which delivery must occur. UCC § 2-308(b).

[125] For the most part, "tender" in Article 2 refers to " 'due tender' which contemplates an offer coupled with a present ability to fulfill all the conditions resting on the tendering party and must be followed by actual performance if the other party shows himself ready to proceed." UCC § 2-503, cmt. 1. Section 2-503 also governs tender of the goods and tender of documents necessary to enable the buyer to obtain possession of the goods from a bailee.

[126] UCC § 2-503(1).

[127] Id.

[128] UCC § 2-503(1)(a).

[129] UCC § 2-503(1)(b).

[130] UCC § 2-503(3).

[131] UCC §§ 2-503(2), 2-504.

[132] A. M. Knitwear Corp. v. All America Export-Import Corp., 41 N.Y.2d 14, 390 N.Y.S.2d 832, 359 N.E.2d 342, 20 UCC Rep. Serv. 581 (N.Y. 1976) (in addition to loading the purchased yarn into the shipping container, the seller had to place the container into the possession of the carrier in order to complete delivery).

[133] La Casse v. Blaustein, 93 Misc. 2d 572, 403 N.Y.S.2d 440, 23 UCC Rep. Serv. 907 (N.Y.C. Civ. Ct. 1978) (seller that shipped calculators under shipment contract but did not insure them for their full value after the buyer had advanced sufficient funds for the insurance did not enter into a proper contract for their shipment).

necessary for the buyer to obtain possession of the goods,[134] and (4) notify the buyer of the shipment.[135] Proper tender in a shipment contract requires that each of these requirements be satisfied.

For example, in a shipment contract between a Seattle seller and a Miami buyer, the seller can meet its delivery obligation in Seattle.[136] If the parties have not agreed on a carrier, the seller must make an appropriate selection.[137] In the absence of a need for the buyer to receive the goods as soon as possible, shipment by air freight might be unreasonable in light of the higher rates for transport, whereas shipment by ocean carrier might be too slow. The seller must make all of the contractual arrangements with the carrier for transportation of the goods, and these arrangements must be reasonable. For example, the seller must provide the shipper the proper destination address, provide for extra services like refrigerated cars if the shipment is of perishable goods like fruits or vegetables,[138] and provide an appropriate level of insurance in the event the goods are lost or damaged in transit.[139] The seller must also select an appropriate method of notifying the buyer that the goods are on their way and an appropriate method, frequently through banking channels, of forwarding a bill of lading so that the buyer can obtain possession from the carrier when they arrive in Miami.

As noted above, in a destination contract the seller must make a conforming tender under the basic rules *at* a particular destination and may not fulfill its obligations just through its dealings with a carrier.[140] If the seller ships the goods by carrier, the carrier will serve as the seller's agent for purposes of making a conforming tender.[141] If the seller ships the goods in its own vehicle,

---

[134] Monte Carlo Shirt, Inc. v. Daewoo Internat'l (America) Corp., 707 F.2d 1054, 36 UCC Rep. Serv. 487 (9th Cir. 1983) (buyer rejected shirts that arrived in this country because the documents needed to take possession of the shipment arrived too late for the Christmas season).

[135] Ninth St. East, Ltd. v. Harrison, 5 Conn. Cir. Ct. 597, 259 A.2d 772, 7 UCC Rep. Serv. 171 (Conn. Cir. Ct. 1968) (notice properly given by forwarding invoices covering the shipped clothing).

[136] Sessa v. Riegle, 427 F. Supp. 760, 21 UCC Rep. Serv. 745 (E.D. Pa. 1977), *aff'd*, 568 F.2d 770 (3d Cir. 1978) (table) (after parties modified contract authorizing seller to ship horse to buyer but not requiring delivery at a particular destination, seller tendered delivery when it placed the horse into the possession of a carrier); Ninth St. East, Ltd. v. Harrison, 5 Conn. Cir. Ct. 597, 259 A.2d 772, 7 UCC Rep. Serv. 171 (1968) (seller not responsible for dispute between carrier and buyer over carrier's refusal to take goods inside buyer's store as seller tendered delivery of the goods in Los Angeles under a shipment contract).

[137] "In the absence of agreement, the provision of this Article on options and cooperation respecting performance gives the seller the choice of any reasonable carrier, routing and other arrangements." UCC § 2-504, cmt. 3 (referring to § 2-311(1)).

[138] Larsen v. A. C. Carpenter, Inc., 620 F. Supp. 1084, 2 UCC Rep. Serv. 2d 433 (E.D. N.Y. 1985) (seller of perishable potatoes had duty to procure refrigerated transportation for shipment to the buyer).

[139] "It is an improper contract . . . for the seller to agree with a carrier to a limited valuation below the true value and thus cut off the buyer's opportunity to recover from the carrier in the event of loss. . . ." UCC § 2-504, cmt. 3.

[140] The seller must make a conforming tender of the goods under UCC § 2-503(1) and also comply with UCC § 2-503(4) and (5) on tender of documents necessary to enable the buyer to obtain possession of the goods from the carrier.

[141] Lumber Sales, Inc. v. Brown, 63 Tenn. App. 189, 469 S.W.2d 888 (Tenn. Ct. App. 1971) (tender

its employee will serve as agent. As we have seen, the tender must be at a reasonable hour and the goods must be kept available long enough for the buyer to take possession of them.[142] Thus, tender would not be sufficient if the driver delivering the goods by truck to the buyer's plant made the tender at hours during which the plant did not operate or left before all of the goods reasonably could be unloaded.[143] Also, since the buyer must furnish facilities reasonably suited to receiving the goods,[144] a buyer may not defeat a seller's tender simply because it does not have sufficient warehouse capacity to store the goods.[145]

The parties often use a sort of commercial shorthand in their express terms to designate the manner in which the goods will be sent. One of the common designations is an agreement that the goods will be sent F.O.B. If the parties do not agree on another meaning,[146] Section 2-319(1) provides that "the term F.O.B. (which means 'free on board') at a named place, even though used only in connection with the stated price, is a delivery term." If the named place is the place of shipment, the contract is a shipment contract and the seller may tender delivery to a carrier at that place.[147] It must bear the expense and risk of putting the goods into the carrier's possession,[148] but the risk that the goods will be lost or damaged in transit falls on the buyer. If the named place is the destination, the contract is a destination contract and the seller must tender delivery at that place.[149] The expense and risk of getting the goods to the destination falls on the seller.[150]

For example, assume that a San Diego seller and a New York buyer enter into a contract that states "F.O.B. San Diego $10,000." Under this contract, as under any shipment contract, the seller will tender and thereby meet its delivery obligation by putting the goods into the possession of a carrier, making an appropriate contract for their transport, forwarding any necessary

---

occurred when buyer was notified by carrier that boxcar had been placed at designated siding); *cf.* Baumgold Bros., Inc. v. Allan M. Fox Co., East, 375 F. Supp. 807, 14 UCC Rep. Serv. 580 (N.D. Ohio 1973) (delivery did not occur when postman left package of diamonds on the counter of the buyer's unattended store).

[142] UCC § 2-503(1)(a).

[143] Heggblade-Marguleas-Tenneco, Inc. v. Norinsberg & Co., Inc., 12 UCC Rep. Serv. 1121 (Dept. of Ag. 1977) (buyer had more than a sufficient time in which to unload bell peppers as the seller's truck with the peppers remained at the buyer's dock for several days).

[144] UCC § 2-503(1)(b).

[145] Eades Commodities, Co. v. Hoeper, 825 S.W.2d 34, 17 UCC Rep. Serv. 2d 771 (Mo. Ct. App. 1992).

[146] In international transactions and increasingly in domestic transactions, the parties are likely to adopt the meaning ascribed to F.O.B. under the international trade terms known as Incoterms. Incoterms are discussed in § 4.07[C][2][a] *infra*.

[147] Pittsburgh Indus. Furnace Co. v. Universal Consol. Co., Inc., 789 F. Supp. 184, 18 UCC Rep. Serv. 2d 152 (W.D. Pa. 1991) (seller delivered upon compliance with section 2-504 under a contract that indicated "FOB points of shipment").

[148] UCC § 2-319(1)(a).

[149] In re Isis Foods, Inc., 38 B.R. 48, 38 UCC Rep. Serv. 1134 (W.D. Mo. 1983) (contract providing "F.O.B. St. Louis" when the buyer was located in St. Louis created a destination contract and required the seller to tender delivery there).

[150] UCC § 2-319(1)(b).

documents, and notifying the buyer.[151] If the contract had stated "F.O.B. New York $10,000," it would have been a destination contract and the seller could meet its delivery obligation only by tendering the goods in New York.[152] As between the two contract terms, the buyer will receive more for its $10,000 under the destination contract. Under the shipment contract, the seller would only have to pay the transportation costs needed to get the goods to the carrier in San Diego rather than also to transport them to New York. Furthermore, because the risk of loss remains on the seller under the destination contract until tender occurs in New York, it should insure against that risk. The risk of loss is on the buyer in a shipment contract, so insurance would be at its expense.[153] The parties, of course, should adjust their agreement on price to reflect these allocations of transportation and insurance expenses.

If the parties agree that the buyer will pay against a presentment of documents, they often use a C.I.F. term. A C.I.F. contract requires the seller to deliver conforming goods to a carrier, obtain a prepaid bill of lading covering the entire cost of transportation from the place of shipment, and obtain a prepaid certificate of insurance providing for payment to the buyer in the event of loss or damage in transit. The seller will then tender the bill of lading and certificate of insurance, along with an invoice, to the buyer.[154] The contract price reflected on the invoice will be a lump sum including the cost of the goods (C), insurance (I), and freight (F) to the named destination.[155] A C.I.F. contract is a shipment contract,[156] as it does not require the seller to deliver at a named destination, and the ordinary requirements regarding selection of an appropriate carrier, entering into a reasonable contract with the carrier, providing documents, and notifying the buyer of the shipment apply. Unless otherwise agreed, however, the buyer will have to pay when presented with the bill of lading and certificate of insurance even though the goods may not have arrived yet and the buyer has not had an opportunity to inspect them prior to making payment.[157]

Sometimes the parties agree that the seller will ship the goods without any additional indication of the manner in which it should be accomplished. In such cases a shipment contract is inferred. The Comments state that "[t]he seller is not obligated to deliver at a named destination and bear the concurrent risk of loss until arrival, unless he has specifically agreed so to deliver or the

---

[151] Travelnol Lab., Inc. v. Zotal, Ltd., 394 Mass. 95, 474 N.E.2d 1070, 40 UCC Rep. Serv. 487 (Sup. Jud. Ct. 1985) (seller selling to an Israeli buyer delivered in Massachusetts under a contract providing "F.O.B. Cambridge, Massachusetts").

[152] Ontario Hydro v. Zallea Sys., Inc., 569 F. Supp. 1261, 36 UCC Rep. Serv. 1222 (D. Del. 1983) (tender of delivery did not occur until the goods were delivered to the jobsite in a contract providing "F.O.B. Carrier, Jobsite, Douglas Point, Ont.").

[153] Because the seller must make a reasonable contract with the carrier and it would be unreasonable for the seller to enter into an agreement that limited the carrier's liability to less than the full value of the goods, the buyer may choose to rely on its right to recover from the carrier in lieu of purchasing insurance.

[154] UCC § 2-320(2).

[155] UCC § 2-320(1). The term C. & F. or C.F. is comparable in all respects, except that the lump sum covers only the cost of the goods and freight to the named destination. *Id.*

[156] UCC § 2-320, cmt. 1.

[157] UCC § 2-320(4).

commercial understanding of the terms used by the parties contemplates such delivery."[158]

If the contract is neither a shipment nor a destination contract, as when the buyer is to pick up the goods at the seller's place of business, the basic tender rule of Section 2-503(1) applies; that is, the seller must "put and hold conforming goods at the buyer's disposition and give the buyer any notification reasonably necessary to enable him to take delivery."[159] For example, if the parties agree that the seller needs a specific amount of time to prepare the goods for delivery, the seller would breach its duty to put and hold the goods at the buyer's disposition if it did not have them ready on the agreed turnover date.[160] If the preparation time was left indefinite, the seller would have to notify the buyer when they were ready.[161]

[2]   Place of Delivery [§ 2-308]

Although Section 2-308 is a gap-filler on the place of delivery, parties to commercial sales contracts seldom rely on it. Because delivery will impose transportation costs on one of the parties, they almost always address in their agreement aspects of delivery that cover the place where it will occur. For example, if delivery by a carrier is required or authorized and the contract is a shipment contract, Section 2-504 governs the place of delivery rather than Section 2-308.[162] The Comments acknowledge the narrow range of practical applicability of the gap-filler on the place of delivery, noting that it "provide[s] for those noncommercial sales and for those occasional commercial sales where no place or means of delivery has been agreed upon by the parties."[163]

The default rule of Section 2-308 is that "the place for delivery of goods is the seller's place of business or if he has none his residence."[164] In other words, the buyer must pick up the goods. This norm governs a vast multitude of transactions in which consumers make purchases from retailers. Buyers that want a seller to deliver the goods somewhere else must make an agreement to that effect. This is commonly done when goods are ordered through a toll-free telephone number or over the Internet. In those cases, it is understood that the

[158] UCC § 2-503, cmt. 5; *see, e.g.*, Morauer v. Deak & Co., Inc., 26 UCC Rep. Serv. 1142 (D.C. Super. Ct. 1979).

[159] *See* Martin v. Melland's Inc., 283 N.W.2d 76, 27 UCC Rep. Serv. 94 (N.D. 1979) (seller of goods being traded in on new goods was entitled to continue using the trade-in goods until the new goods were ready and did not tender them while using them).

[160] *Cf.* Schock v. Ronderos, 394 N.W.2d 697, 2 UCC Rep. Serv. 2d 1302 (N.D. 1986) (seller of used mobile home tendered delivery by preparing it for removal and disconnecting the electricity and gas hookups).

[161] Uchitel v. F. R. Tripler & Co., 107 Misc. 2d 310, 434 N.Y.S.2d 77, 30 UCC Rep. Serv. 933 (Sup. Ct. 1980) (tender of delivery occurred when seller notified buyer that clothing was ready for buyer to pick up at seller's store).

[162] *See also* Dura-Wood Treating Co. v. Century Forest Indus., Inc., 675 F.2d 745, 33 UCC Rep. Serv. 1201 (5th Cir. 1982) (court erred in applying UCC § 2-308 since evidence established industry practice of delivering at buyer's place of business).

[163] UCC § 2-308, cmt. 1.

[164] UCC § 2-308(a).

seller will ship the goods to an address provided by the buyer. Alternatively, a local retailer may advertise that it makes free deliveries or the buyer might pay an additional fee for the service.

An exception to the general default rule provides that "in a contract for sale of identified goods which to the knowledge of the parties at the time of contracting are in some other place, that place is the place for their delivery."[165] This situation generally arises when the seller is selling goods that are in the possession of a bailee. Because the cooperation of the bailee will be necessary for the buyer to take possession, the seller must, as part of its obligation to make a proper tender,[166] procure an acknowledgment by the bailee of the buyer's right to possession.[167]

[3]   Time for Delivery [§ 2-309]

Section 2-309(1) provides a gap-filler for the time performance is due.[168] Given the wide range of circumstances that can affect shipment and delivery, the implied term understandably uses the broad standard of reasonableness. The Comments state that "[t]he applicable principles . . . make it clear that surprise is to be avoided, good faith judgment is to be protected, and notice or negotiation to reduce the uncertainty to certainty is to be favored."[169] Thus, for example, the delivery of a sprinkler system too late to be used on an oat crop that had to be planted earlier did not constitute an unreasonable delivery because the parties did not have a specific agreement for an earlier delivery and the seller had never been informed of the buyer's special need.[170]

To reduce the uncertainty associated with the reasonableness standard, the Comments encourage the courts to require that the parties communicate with each other. Neither party should be able to establish a breach by the other party simply by allowing a clearly reasonable period of time to pass. Silence in this context should be viewed as a course of conduct that "may be viewed as enlarging the reasonable time for tender or demand of performance."[171] Moreover, the obligation of good faith requires reasonable notification before a sales contract can be treated as breached because of the passage of a reasonable time for performance.[172] Thus, one of the parties will have to initiate

---

[165] UCC § 2-308(b).

[166] UCC § 2-503(3), (4)(a).

[167] UCC § 2-308, cmt. 2; Goosic Constr. Co. v. City Nat'l Bank of Crete, 196 Neb. 86, 241 N.W.2d 521, 19 UCC Rep. Serv. 117 (1976) (seller in breach when bailee refused to release purchased goods because it claimed a storage lien). If the parties intend delivery through documents covering warehoused goods, Section 2-308(b) does not apply. Generally, a document of title must be delivered to the buyer's place of business, although Section 2-308(c) provides that they "may be delivered through customary banking channels."

[168] BMC Indus., Inc. v. Barth Indus., Inc., 160 F.3d 1322, 37 UCC Rep. Serv. 2d 63 (11th Cir. 1998) (after buyer waived express delivery date, gap-filler established delivery term).

[169] UCC § 2-309, cmt. 3.

[170] Beiriger & Sons Ir., Inc. v. Southwest Land Co., Inc., 705 P.2d 532, 41 UCC Rep. Serv. 1621 (Colo. Ct. App. 1985).

[171] UCC § 2-309, cmt. 5.

[172] Id.

communication about delivery and perhaps even propose a delivery date.[173]

The communication of a proposed delivery date calls for a response from the other party, and failure to respond constitutes acquiescence to the proposal.[174] The only instances in which a response to a proposed delivery date raises a question of breach is "when a party insists on undue delay or on rejection of the other party's reasonable proposal."[175] Since any other response that objects to the proposed time is neither an acquiescence nor a breach, the communications of the parties will not have fixed the delivery date. A party that wishes to press the issue may make a written demand for adequate assurances of performance under Section 2-609.[176]

[4]   Transfer of Title [§ 2-401]

Although Article 2 abandons the use of title in allocating the risk of loss and in other ways,[177] the concept nevertheless occupies a central role. The signature feature of a sale of goods is "the passing of title from the seller to the buyer for a price."[178] Subject to the provisions of Article 9 on secured transactions, the parties are free to agree on the manner in which title passes if the agreement is explicit.[179] In the absence of an explicit agreement, "title passes to the buyer at the time and place at which the seller completes his performance with reference to the physical delivery of the goods"[180] or, if the seller is to deliver a document of title and not move the goods, "at the time when and the place where he delivers such documents."[181] The gap-fillers thus tie the transfer of title to the delivery of the goods.

The proviso regarding Article 9 is an important limitation on the parties' right to agree on the time at which title passes. A credit seller might want to retain title pending payment of all or part of the price but the Code precludes

---

[173] Autonumerics, Inc. v. Bayer Indus., Inc., 144 Ariz. 181, 696 P.2d 1330, 39 UCC Rep. Serv. 802 (Ct. App. 1984) (contract was not breached when the seller waited to begin manufacturing until buyer informed it of desired delivery date and selected certain optional items).

[174] UCC § 2-309, cmt. 6.

[175] *Id.* Note the difference with respect to more general proposals: "When the time for delivery is left open, unreasonably early offers of or demands for delivery are intended to be read under this Article as expressions of desire or intention, requesting the assent or acquiescence of the other party, not as final positions which may amount without more to breach or to create breach by the other side." UCC § 2-309, cmt. 4.

[176] UCC § 2-309, cmt. 6; *see* Copylease Corp. of Am. v. Memorex Corp., 403 F. Supp. 625, 18 UCC Rep. Serv. 317 (S.D.N.Y. 1975) (prior to placing any delivery orders, buyer made a written demand for adequate assurances of performance; demand was justified in light of indications from the defendant that it was resolved to find a way out of the contract). For a discussion of demands for assurance of performance, see UCC § 2-609 and § 7.07[B] *infra*.

[177] "Each provision of this Article with regard to the rights, obligations and remedies of the seller, the buyer, purchasers or other third parties applies irrespective of title to the goods except where the provision refers to such title." UCC § 2-401. *See, e.g.*, § 6.01 *infra* (Article 2 abandonment of location of title as factor in loss-allocation principles).

[178] UCC § 2-106(1).

[179] UCC § 2-401(1).

[180] UCC § 2-401(2).

[181] UCC § 2-401(3)(a).

such an arrangement. Even if the parties explicitly agree on a title-retention provision, it will not be applied literally but instead will be limited in effect to a reservation by the seller of a security interest governed by Article 9.[182] The buyer will obtain title upon delivery and the seller will have the security it needs; however, the seller will have to comply with the formalities of Article 9 if it wishes its security interest to be enforceable against the buyer and to have priority against third parties. Those formalities are beyond the scope of this book.

[D]   Inspection and Payment [§ 2-310; § 2-511; § 2-513]

The basic obligation of a buyer is to accept and pay for the goods in accordance with the terms of the contract.[183] If the goods or the seller's tender of delivery do not conform to the contract, the buyer has a right to cancel the contract,[184] thereby excusing itself from all executory obligations while preserving its rights based on the seller's breach.[185] In order to maximize its right to cancel, the buyer needs an opportunity to inspect the goods prior to making payment.[186]

The parties may by agreement determine the scope of the buyer's right to inspect, but if they fail to do so the gap-filler gives the buyer a pre-payment right "to inspect [the goods] at any reasonable place and time and in any reasonable manner."[187] Because the expenses of inspection must be borne by the buyer,[188] Section 2-513(1) specifies that "[w]hen the seller is required or authorized to send the goods to the buyer, the inspection may be after their arrival."[189]

Although the parties often agree on how and when payment will be made,[190] Section 2-310(a) provides a straightforward gap-filler if they fail to do so:

---

[182] UCC § 2-401(1).

[183] UCC § 2-301.

[184] UCC §§ 2-601 (rejection), 2-608 (revocation of acceptance). For discussion of these concepts, see §§ 7.04 and 7.05 *infra*.

[185] "Tender of delivery is a condition to the buyer's duty to accept the goods and, unless otherwise agreed, to his duty to pay for them." UCC § 2-507(1).

[186] Although a buyer that pays before inspecting and finding a defect in the goods will still have remedies under Article 2, the buyer may have to initiate legal action for relief because the seller will have the buyer's money.

[187] UCC § 2-513(1); Furlong v. Alpha Chi Omega Sorority, 73 Ohio Misc. 2d 26, 657 N.E.2d 866, 28 UCC Rep. Serv. 2d 1194 (Mun. Ct. 1993) (sorority inspection of boxes of sweaters to determine whether they complied with the contract was reasonable as it was conducted on the same day that the sweaters were received from the seller).

[188] UCC § 2-513(2). The buyer may recover the expenses from the seller if the goods are rightfully rejected.

[189] *See* EPN-Delaval, S.A. v. Inter-Equip., Inc., 542 F. Supp. 238, 34 UCC Rep. Serv. 130 (S.D. Tex. 1982) (under a contract that required goods to be shipped to buyer's place of business outside Mexico City, the buyer was entitled to inspect the goods upon their arrival and was not required to inspect them at the place of delivery to the buyer's forwarding agent in Laredo, Texas).

[190] In re Bullet Jet Charter, Inc., 177 B.R. 59, 327 UCC Rep. Serv. 2d 1256 (N.D. Ill. 1995) (complying tender when the buyer deposited the purchase price in escrow with appropriate

"[P]ayment is due at the time and place at which the buyer is to receive the goods even though the place of shipment is the place of delivery." In other words, payment is due when the goods are physically delivered to the buyer and a buyer that wants credit or a seller that wants payment before delivery must bargain for it. An exception to this principle applies to shipment contracts, because delivery occurs when the seller turns the goods over to the carrier. Because the buyer generally should be permitted to inspect the goods after their arrival, Section 2-310(a) provides that payment need not be made upon the seller's delivery of the goods to the carrier.[191]

If a seller turns the goods over to the buyer directly, the seller's duty to deliver and the buyer's duty to pay are treated as concurrent conditions.[192] Thus, the seller must at a minimum make a conforming tender[193] before the buyer can be found in breach for failure to pay.[194] Likewise, the buyer must be ready, willing, and able to pay before the seller can be found in breach for failure to tender delivery.[195] This system protects both the seller, which does not need to part with the goods before payment has been made, and the buyer, which does not need to part with payment before having a chance to inspect. If the buyer refuses to make the payment, even though justified, the seller cannot be required to deliver the goods. Of course, if the seller's breach justified the buyer's refusal, the seller will be liable for compensatory damages.

When the goods are to be delivered by carrier to the buyer's location, the Code provides the parties with substantially the same level of protection. The seller can ship the goods under a negotiable bill of lading and forward it through banking channels to a representative located in the place of arrival. The buyer will be notified when the goods arrive and given an opportunity to inspect them before having to pay for the document, which it will need in order to obtain possession of the goods from the carrier.

A buyer can bargain away its right to pre-payment inspection.[196] For example, a buyer might agree to pay when a negotiable bill of lading issued by a carrier is presented even if the goods have not yet arrived. The seller will obtain the bill of lading at the time it delivers the goods to the carrier and

---

instructions in accordance with the requirements in the sales agreement); Cooper Alloy Corp. v. E.B.V. Sys., Inc., 206 A.2d 837, 13 UCC Rep. Serv. 2d 84 (R.I. 1973) (under applicable usage of trade foundries require payment for patterns before delivering them).

[191] In re Ault, 6 B.R. 58, 30 UCC Rep. Serv. 1714 (E.D. Tenn. 1980) (payment due when the goods arrive instead of when they are shipped).

[192] See UCC §§ 2-301, 2-507(1), 2-511(1).

[193] See generally UCC § 2-503(1); § 4.04[C][1] supra.

[194] June G. Ashton Interiors v. Stark Carpet Corp., 142 Ill. App. 3d 100, 491 N.E.2d 120, 2 UCC Rep. Serv. 2d 74 (Ct. App. 1986) (improper tender by the seller entitled the buyer to cancel the contract).

[195] Matsushita Elec. Corp. of Am. v. Sonus Corp., 362 Mass. 246, 284 N.E.2d 880, 10 UCC Rep. Serv. 1363 (1972) (buyer was justified in withholding payment because of incomplete delivery by the seller). Of course, an anticipatory repudiation would excuse either party from its duty to tender. See UCC § 2-610 and the discussion in § 7.07[A] infra.

[196] UCC § 2-513(3)(b). Payment is also due prior to inspection when, pursuant to the parties' agreement, the goods are delivered C.O.D. UCC § 2-513(3)(a).

forward it to the buyer along with a demand for payment.[197] If the buyer agrees to such a payment term, it can inspect the goods once they arrive and, if they are defective, reject them and pursue the seller for a refund.

If the parties do not agree on the manner in which payment is to be made, the governing gap-filler provides that "[t]ender of payment is sufficient when made by any means or in any manner current in the ordinary course of business."[198] This rule is subject to the caveat that the seller can defeat a tender of payment by check or other mechanism by demanding legal tender, meaning money. A seller that makes such a demand must give the buyer "any extension of time reasonably necessary to procure [legal tender]."[199]

Consistent with the provisions of Article 3 on negotiable instruments, a buyer's payment by check is only conditional until such time as the bank upon which the check is drawn makes final payment on it.[200] If the drawee bank dishonors the check, payment is defeated[201] and the seller has a right to reclaim the goods from the buyer.[202]

§ 4.05 SUPEREMINENT PRINCIPLES

While freedom of contract generally prevails under the Code, that freedom is constrained in some respects. The discussion below covers the two most important limitations on freedom of contract — unconscionability and good faith.

[A]   Unconscionability [§ 2-302; § 2A-108]

Although doctrines like misrepresentation (including fraud) and duress historically were considered sufficient to protect contracting parties, occasional cases of gross unfairness did not fit squarely within the black letter of these doctrines. The need to adjudicate such cases fairly gave rise to the concept of unconscionability.[203]

---

[197] Typically the seller will have its bank forward the document, together with a draft ordering the buyer to pay the amount due, through banking channels to a bank in the buyer's city. That bank will present the draft to the buyer and, upon receiving payment for the seller's account, deliver the document to the buyer. A buyer that does not pay breaches the contract, will not receive the document, and thus cannot obtain access to the goods from the carrier.

[198] UCC § 2-511(2).

[199] *Id.*

[200] UCC § 2-511(3).

[201] In re Amica, Inc., 135 B.R. 534, 17 UCC Rep. Serv. 2d 11 (N.D. Ill. 1992) (dishonor of tendered check entitled seller to cancel the contract and refuse to send the remaining software to the buyer). *But see* Myers v. Columbus Sales Pavilion, Inc., 575 F. Supp. 805, 37 UCC Rep. Serv. 1122 (D. Neb. 1983), *aff'd on op. below*, 723 F.2d 37, 37 UCC Rep. Serv. 2d 1128 (8th Cir. 1983) (dishonor does not revest title to the goods in the seller; seller's remedies are in Section 2-703 based on the failure of the buyer to pay).

[202] The seller's right of reclamation is discussed in § 9.08[C][1] *infra.*

[203] The earliest reference to the doctrine seems to have been by Lord Hardwicke in *Earl of Chesterfield v. Janssen*, 2 Ves. Sen. 125, 28 Eng. Rep. 82 (Ch. 1750). The development of the doctrine at common law is discussed in Spanogle, *Analyzing Unconscionability Problems*, 117 U. Pa. L. Rev. 931 (1969). Two classic law review articles have had a significant influence on the development of the

This kind of "policing" of contracts by the courts has become more common since the advent of standard-form contracts, particularly when they are offered to relatively unsophisticated customers on a take-it-or-leave-it basis. Because customers do not assent to the terms on these forms but rather are forced to adhere to them, the term "contract of adhesion" was coined to describe such forms. The courts were particularly likely to intervene when an entire industry began using such forms, essentially precluding customers from negotiating better terms by shopping around.

Despite increased use of the unconscionability doctrine, common-law courts often expressed reservations about it. It involved, after all, departing from traditional notions of *caveat emptor* and freedom of contract. By explicitly recognizing the doctrine,[204] the Code seems to have spurred the courts to overcome this reluctance.[205]

Several aspects of the Code's provisions on unconscionability are notable. Either party can raise the issue or the court can raise it *sua sponte.*[206] Whether there has been unconscionability is an issue for the court rather than the jury,[207] and once the issue has been raised, the court should hold a hearing to resolve it. *Johnson v. Mobil Oil Corp.*[208] contains an excellent discussion of the factors to be considered by the court. These factors include the parties' relative age, status, intelligence, business sophistication, bargaining power, the degree to which the party with greater bargaining strength has explained a suspect term, the intrinsic fairness of a suspect term, and the availability of alternatives in the marketplace.

The doctrine applies only if unconscionability was present at the time of contract formation.[209] Thus, the doctrine should be viewed as an invalidating cause, much like the related doctrines of misrepresentation and duress. Issues related to the performance stage are dealt with under the doctrine of good faith, which by its terms has no application to the contract formation stage.[210]

[1]   Procedural and Substantive Unconscionability

What makes a particular term unconscionable? The mere fact that a term is included in a standard form does not render it unenforceable. Standard forms provide an efficient method of doing business, and the courts generally enforce

doctrine under the Code. *See* Ellinghaus, *In Defense of Unconscionability*, 78 Yale L.J. 757 (1969); Leff, *Unconscionability and the Code—The Emperor's New Clause*, 115 U. Pa. L. Rev. 485 (1967).

[204] UCC § 2-302. Article 2A includes comparable provisions. UCC § 2A-108(1), (3).

[205] Only California failed to adopt UCC § 2-302. The state nevertheless recognizes the doctrine and applies it to sales cases. *See, e.g.*, Carboni v. Arrospide, 2 Cal. App. 4th 76, 2 Cal. Rptr. 2d 845, 16 UCC Rep. Serv. 2d 584 (1991) (applying Cal. Civ. Code § 1670.5, a virtual reproduction of UCC § 2-302, to sales cases).

[206] *See, e.g.*, Maxon Corp. v. Tyler Pipe Indus., Inc., 497 N.E.2d 570, 3 UCC Rep. Serv. 2d 52 (Ind. Ct. App. 1986) (issue raised by court *sua sponte*).

[207] UCC § 2-302, cmt. 3.

[208] 415 F. Supp. 264, 20 UCC Rep. Serv. 637 (E.D. Mich. 1976).

[209] For discussion of unconscionability in the context of limited remedies, see § 5.04[B] *infra*.

[210] *See* § 4.05[B] *infra*.

their terms. An attitude still prevails, after all, that one should read and understand a document before signing it. The Comments provide the courts with some guidance on the meaning of unconscionability:

> The basic test is whether, in the light of the general commercial background and the commercial needs of the particular trade or case, the clauses involved are so one-sided as to be unconscionable under the circumstances existing at the time of the making of the contract. Subsection (2) makes it clear that it is proper for the court to hear evidence upon these questions. The principle is the prevention of oppression and unfair surprise and not of disturbance of allocation of risks because of superior bargaining power.[211]

Obviously, the key principle seems to be that while some terms are so one-sided as to cause oppression and unfair surprise, many one-sided terms are to be enforced as the product of normal bargaining and risk allocation. Where do we draw the line?

Many courts have resolved the problem by dividing general unconscionability into two categories — procedural and substantive — and requiring that each be present before the doctrine can be invoked successfully. As the discussion below explains, procedural unconscionability addresses concern over unfair surprise, while substantive unconscionability deals with one-sidedness.

Procedural unconscionability refers to problems that taint the bargaining process. Evidence of procedural unconscionability includes gross inequality of bargaining power (typically exemplified by a lack of intelligence and/or sophistication on the part of the buyer),[212] creation by the seller of an atmosphere of haste, the use of high-pressure sales tactics, the use of confusing language, the use of small print, and the presence of a relationship that allows one party to exert undue influence. Procedural unconscionability deprives a party of any "meaningful choice."[213]

Substantive unconscionability refers to terms that are so grossly unfair and one-sided that they shock the conscience of the court. Without procedural problems, the suspect term is likely to be the product of normal risk allocation, even if it is one-sided. Without a substantive problem, the court has no reason to use this particular doctrine.

Numerous cases have discussed procedural and substantive unconscionability, although not always in those terms. In *Williams v. Walker-Thomas Furniture Co.*,[214] the buyer was a welfare recipient who had purchased a significant number of consumer items from the seller over a period of years. The buyer purchased each item on a secured-installment basis, and each installment sales contract

---

[211] UCC § 2-302, cmt. 1 (citation omitted).

[212] Of course, either party can make a claim of unconscionability, but the buyer or lessee most often asserts the doctrine against the seller or lessor respectively.

[213] This oft-repeated term comes from Judge Skelly Wright's opinion in the celebrated case of *Williams v. Walker-Thomas Furniture Co.*, 350 F.2d 445, 449, 2 UCC Rep. Serv. 955, 958 (D.C. Cir. 1965) (applying Code by analogy).

[214] *Id.*

contained what was referred to as a "cross-collateral" clause. This clause, which was drafted in nearly incomprehensible language, allowed each of the buyer's payments to be credited on a pro-rata basis to each item purchased, so that even though she had given the seller enough money to pay for her earlier purchases many times over, the seller was able to retain its security interest in those earlier items. The court emphasized the buyer's lack of sophistication and criticized the seller for displaying the clause in fine print. The court also noted that the very concept underlying the clause is so difficult that the average consumer could not understand it. Finally, the court stressed the unfairness of a term that allowed the seller to repossess items for which the buyer had given the seller the full price. The decision is debatable. The judge portrays the seller as preying on the poor but in fact cross-collateralization clauses were commonly used by national retailers at that time. Because the clause increased a credit seller's available collateral, it had the effect of lowering interest rates for consumers generally, and this redounded to the benefit of residents of the less affluent communities that the court sought to protect. Nevertheless, there is something unseemly about permitting a seller to take advantage of such a clause, and it is unlikely that the clause as worded would have been understood even by a relatively sophisticated consumer.

Although the decision does not speak in these terms, the judge in the *Williams* case found serious unconscionability of both the procedural and substantive varieties. That combination is not always present.[215] Sometimes the procedural unconscionability is slight, sometimes the substantive unconscionability is slight, sometimes both are slight, or sometimes one is missing. What relative weight should the court give to these factors? Many courts have followed a line of analysis first articulated in *Funding Systems Leasing Corp. v. King Louie International, Inc.*[216] The court in that case concluded that while both procedural and substantive unconscionability must be present for relief to be granted, a sliding scale should be used: Gross procedural unconscionability coupled with slight substantive unconscionability, or vice versa, would suffice.

Can the price term be attacked successfully as substantively unconscionable? Certainly it can be argued that price is always the product of ordinary bargaining and, no matter how unsophisticated, a buyer should be able to understand the price term and seek out alternatives. Nevertheless, a few cases have held a price term unconscionable. For example, in *Jones v. Star Credit Corp.*[217] the buyers,

---

[215] Sossamon v. Central Valley RV Outlet, Inc., 2004 Cal. App. Unpub. LEXIS 6071 (June 25, 2004) (despite finding substantive unconscionability in a clause that required the buyer to arbitrate but allowed the seller to litigate, the court refused to uphold the lower court's denial of the seller's petition to compel arbitration on the grounds that the buyer had not demonstrated procedural unconscionability).

[216] 597 S.W.2d 624 (Mo. Ct. App. 1979); *see also* Tacoma Boatbuilding, Inc. v. Delta Fishing Co., 28 UCC Rep. Serv. 26 (W.D. Wash. 1980); Freeman v. Wal-Mart Stores, Inc., 11 Cal. App. 4th 660, 3 Cal. Rptr. 3d 860 (2003).

[217] 59 Misc. 2d 189, 298 N.Y.S.2d 264, 6 UCC Rep. Serv. 76 (Sup. Ct. 1969). Other cases holding that the price term can be unconscionable include *American Home Improvement, Inc. v. MacIver*, 105 N.H. 435, 201 A.2d 886, 2 UCC Rep. Serv. 235, 14 A.L.R.3d 324 (1964); *Murphy v. McNamara*, 36 Conn. Supp. 183, 416 A.2d 170, 27 UCC Rep. Serv. 911 (1979). Virtually all of the cases declaring a price term unconscionable were decided before 1980. *See* Horowitz, *Reviving the Law of*

who like the plaintiff in *Williams* were welfare recipients, agreed to purchase a freezer worth a maximum of $300 for a total price, including interest and credit life and property insurance, of over $1,200. Aspects of procedural unconscionability were clearly present. The buyers were unsophisticated, and the salesman came to their home and apparently applied significant pressure. The court found that the price term was unconscionable and in effect reformed the term by allowing the buyers to keep the freezer with no further obligation even though they had paid only around $600.

Courts have occasionally found a contract term unconscionable on substantive grounds alone. In *Brower v. Gateway 2000, Inc.*,[218] the buyers purchased computer equipment and software from Gateway and subsequently sued for breach of warranty and various other alleged wrongs. Gateway had shipped the goods to the buyers and included with the shipment a copy of its standard terms and conditions, one of which required that disputes be arbitrated in Chicago pursuant to the Rules of Conciliation and Arbitration of the International Chamber of Commerce (ICC). The ICC was headquartered in France and not registered to do business in the United States, making it difficult to contact. More importantly, the ICC's rules required payment by the initiating party of an advance fee of $4,000 for claims under $15,000, with $2,000 being non-refundable even if the initiating party prevailed. The court determined that Gateway's standard terms and conditions were generally enforceable[219] and that the arbitration clause was spelled out with sufficient clarity to preclude a finding of procedural unconscionability. Nevertheless, the court struck that part of the clause requiring the use of the ICC, stressing that the excessive cost, which effectively barred consumers from seeking relief, rendered the requirement substantively unconscionability. Gateway clearly included the ICC requirement because it wanted to place reasonable remedies beyond the reach of the average consumer, not because adoption of the ICC's rules made commercial sense. Given the egregious nature of Gateway's conduct, it would have been appropriate for the court to have stricken the arbitration clause altogether.

If courts are going to enforce terms that the seller first discloses after a buyer has paid for the goods, they will have to develop appropriate policing techniques. If a purchase is made over the Internet or through a toll-free telephone number and the term at issue is expressed clearly in the documentation later provided to the buyer, it will be hard for a court that generally enforces such terms to find procedural unconscionability. Buyers often cite a relative lack of sophistication as a factor in determining whether procedural unconscionability is present, but that factor alone should be insufficient to show a procedural problem, particularly in the type of anonymous mass-market transaction exemplified by *Brower*. One way in which sellers in such transactions might reduce their exposure to claims of unconscionability is by conspicuously posting their standard terms on their

---

Substantive Unconscionability: Applying the Implied Covenant of Good Faith and Fair Dealing to Excessively Priced Consumer Credit Contracts, 33 UCLA L. Rev. 940 (1986) (surveying the cases and urging a shift from unconscionability to a good faith analysis).

[218] 246 A.D.2d 246, 676 N.Y.S.2d 569, 37 UCC Rep. Serv. 2d 54 (App. Div. 1998).

[219] For a discussion of the enforceability of terms first made available after a buyer has paid for goods, see § 2.05 *supra*.

website and notifying buyers, before accepting payment, that they can review the terms if they wish before making their purchase.[220]

[2]   Unconscionability in a Commercial Context

Courts applying the unconscionability doctrine often stress the status of the parties. Application of the doctrine is most common when the seller is a merchant and the buyer is a consumer.[221] It is virtually never successfully asserted when both parties are merchants with relative equality of bargaining strength.[222]

Use of the doctrine appears to be on the rise, however, when both parties are merchants but are unequal in their bargaining strength. In that context, the courts have focused on whether the disadvantaged party could have read and understood the suspect clause, whether that party had any meaningful alternatives readily available in the marketplace, and perhaps most importantly, whether the clause bears a reasonable relationship to the risks associated with the party seeking to enforce it.[223]

As might be expected, the cases in the commercial context have focused heavily on the procedural aspects of the transaction. Of course, the terms at issue are one-sided, but tolerance of one-sided terms seems to be greater outside the consumer area. This attitude is a natural outgrowth of our general reluctance to upset the risk-allocation system adopted by commercial entities. Several of the cases have involved indemnification clauses in fine print, not separated by headings from other portions of a long, standard-form contract.[224]

---

[220] The American Bar Association's review of the Uniform Computer Information Transactions Act recommended that the act require software publishers to make their standard terms available before purchase. American Bar Association Working Group Report on the Uniform Computer Information Transactions Act ("UCITA"), Jan. 31, 2002, at 8. For a discussion of the benefits of disclosure on a website, see Hillman, *On-Line Boilerplate: Would Mandatory Disclosure of E-Terms Backfire?*, 104 Mich. L. Rev. 837 (2006). Notifying prospective buyers about the availability of the additional terms prior to concluding a contract would, in addition, address many of the concerns that some courts and commentators have advanced concerning the inclusion of the terms in the contract.

[221] *See, e.g.*, Orlett v. Suburban Propane, 54 Ohio App. 3d. 127, 561 N.E.2d 1066, 13 UCC Rep. Serv. 2d 70 (1989) (clause in contract for the sale of liquid propane gas that disclaimed liability for merchant's ordinary negligence held to be unconscionable because of unequal bargaining power between consumer, who depended on gas for cooking and heating home, and merchant). Consumer buyers do not succeed in all cases. *See, e.g.*, Wilson v. World Omni Leasing, Inc., 540 So. 2d 713 (Ala. 1989) (court relied on lessee's educational background, work experiences, and line of employment in determining that parties were in equal bargaining position).

[222] *See, e.g.*, Royal Indem. Co. v. Westinghouse Elec. Co., 385 F. Supp. 520, 15 UCC Rep. Serv. 631 (S.D.N.Y. 1974) (court refused even to listen to plaintiff's argument that a particular term had not been read and understood).

[223] Geldermann & Co. v. Lane Processing, Inc., 527 F.2d 571, 18 UCC Rep. Serv. 294 (8th Cir. 1975); *see also* Pig Improvement Co., Inc. v. Middle States Holding Co., 943 F. Supp. 392, 31 UCC Rep. Serv. 2d 422 (D. Del. 1996) (court concluded that agreement was not unconscionable because buyer had not made any effort to negotiate a change in the contract terms and had actually invoked the challenged remedy provision on prior occasions).

[224] *See, e.g.*, Weaver v. American Oil Co., 257 Ind. 458, 276 N.E.2d 144 (1971); Maxon v. Tyler Pipe Indus., Inc., 497 N.E.2d 570, 3 UCC Rep. Serv. 2d 52 (Ind. Ct. App. 1986). *See generally* Mallor, *Unconscionability in Contracts Between Merchants*, 40 Sw. L.J. 1065 (1986).

Many other cases have involved exclusions of consequential damages, a topic discussed in the next chapter.[225]

[3] Forms of Relief Available

Articles 2 and 2A explicitly permit the courts to strike an entire contract because of unconscionability, or to strike an offending term and enforce the rest of the contract.[226] These options suggest that unconscionability can be used only defensively, not as a vehicle for the affirmative recovery of damages.[227] Nevertheless, a court that strikes an unconscionable clause can still proceed to award damages for breach of the remaining portion of the contract.[228] Also, conduct by a party attempting to enforce an unconscionable clause might constitute a breach of the duty of good faith, for which monetary damages are available.[229]

Although not expressly sanctioned by the Code,[230] some courts have used unconscionability to reform the terms of a contract. In the *Jones*[231] case discussed above, the court reformed the price term of a contract downward from $1,200 to $600. Similarly, in *Brower v. Gateway 2000, Inc.*,[232] which is discussed above,[233] after determining that a clause requiring that the parties arbitrate under the rules of a foreign organization was unconscionable, the court remanded the case to allow the parties to seek the appointment of an alternative organization.

[4] Additional Consumer Protection — Leases

Article 2A adds some provisions on unconscionability beyond those provided in the statutory analogue.[234] In each instance these additions apply only with respect to a consumer lease.[235] One of these provisions empowers a court to grant appropriate relief if a lease contract or a clause in the contract was induced by unconscionable conduct.[236] Procedural unconscionability is thus

---

[225] *See* § 5.04[C] *infra.*

[226] UCC §§ 2-302(1), 2A-108(1).

[227] *See, e.g.,* Cowin Equip. Co. v. General Motors Corp., 734 F.2d 1581, 38 UCC Rep. Serv. 1565 (11th Cir. 1984).

[228] *See, e.g.,* Langemeier v. Nat'l Oats Co., Inc., 775 F.2d 975, 41 UCC Rep. Serv. 1616 (8th Cir. 1985).

[229] *Cf.* Best v. United States Nat'l Bank, 303 Or. 557, 739 P.2d 554, 4 UCC Rep. Serv. 2d 8, 73 A.L.R.4th 1009 (1987).

[230] Section 2-302(1) does permit a court to "so limit the application of any unconscionable clause as to avoid any unconscionable result."

[231] Jones v. Star Credit Corp., 59 Misc. 2d 189, 298 N.Y.S.2d 264, 6 UCC Rep. Serv. 76 (Sup. Ct. 1969).

[232] 246 A.D.2d 246, 676 N.Y.S.2d 569, 37 UCC Rep. Serv. 2d 54 (App. Div. 1998).

[233] *See* § 4.05[A][1] *supra.*

[234] These additional provisions are based on Uniform Consumer Credit Code § 5.108(1), (2), (6) and 7A U.L.A. 167, 169.

[235] For a discussion of consumer leases, see § 1.04[C] *supra.*

[236] UCC § 2A-108(2).

sufficient for a court to grant relief in the absence of any substantive unconscionability, at least in the case of a consumer lease. Article 2A also allows courts to grant appropriate relief if the unconscionable conduct occurred in the collection of a claim that arose from a lease contract.[237]

Another provision unique to Article 2A deals with attorney's fees. A court that finds unconscionability in a consumer lease is required to award reasonable attorney's fees to the lessee.[238] This provision recognizes that a successful lessee will be excused from performing if the court cancels the contract but will often not be entitled to damages. An award of attorney's fees protects a consumer lessee by covering the cost of legal representation to press the unconscionability claim. To counter the tendency to assert clearly unwarranted claims, Article 2A also requires courts to award attorney's fees to a lessor against whom a consumer lessee asserts a claim of unconscionability that the lessee knows to be groundless.[239]

[B] The Duty of Good Faith [§ 1-304; § 1-201(20)]

Contract law during the previous century had increasingly come to recognize a general obligation to deal in good faith. This concept finds expression in Section 1-304 of the Code, which states that "[e]very contract or duty within this Act [the Uniform Commercial code] imposes an obligation of good faith in its performance and enforcement." Unlike the related doctrine of unconscionability, which presents issues to be decided by the judge, the determination of whether a party has acted in good faith is generally understood to be a factual inquiry that is within the province of the jury.[240]

Section 1-304 does not impose a duty of good faith in negotiating a contract — only in performing or enforcing one. The duty is an implied-in-law obligation that arises from the contract itself. Problems that occur during negotiations are typically handled under other doctrines, such as misrepresentation, duress, and unconscionability. That said, the parties may reach such an advanced stage in their negotiations that they are willing to accept a mutual commitment to bargain in good faith to reach a final agreement.[241]

While Section 1-304 establishes a broad principle, the Code gives courts very little guidance, an omission that is deliberate. The short Comment to the section notes that particular sections of the Code reiterate the duty of good faith in specific contexts.[242] It goes on to state that "the applicability of the duty is broader than merely these situations and applies generally, as stated in this

---

[237] *Id.*

[238] UCC § 2A-108(4)(a).

[239] UCC § 2A-108(4)(b).

[240] *See, e.g.,* Banner Iron Works, Inc. v. Amax Zinc Co., 621 F.2d 883 (8th Cir. 1980).

[241] *See* Teachers Ins. & Annuity Co. v. Tribune Co., 670 F. Supp. 491 (S.D.N.Y. 1987) (commitment letter represented binding preliminary agreement and obligated parties to negotiate in good faith to reach final agreement); Arcadian Phosphates, Inc. v. Arcadian Corp., 884 F.2d 69 (2d Cir. 1989) (evidence demonstrated that parties had not agreed to bargain in good faith).

[242] Examples include options to accelerate at will, UCC § 1-309, the right of cure, § 2-508, and the failure of presupposed conditions. UCC § 2-615.

section, to the performance or enforcement of every contract or duty within this Act." An articulation of a detailed standard for determining when the duty has been breached is almost impossible.

The Code defines "good faith" to mean "honesty in fact and the observance of reasonable commercial standards of fair dealing."[243] The definition includes both subjective and objective elements. The requirement of honesty in fact creates a purely subjective standard. It can be best understood in contrast to bad faith, which must involve a subjective intent to take advantage of another in some dishonest fashion.

The objective element is based on the reasonable standards of the marketplace but only as they implicate fair dealing. The Comments make this point as follows:

> Although "fair dealing" is a broad term that must be defined in context, it is clear that it is concerned with the fairness of conduct rather than the care with which an act is performed. This is an entirely different concept than whether a party exercised ordinary care in conducting a transaction. Both concepts are to be determined in the light of reasonable commercial standards, but those standards in each case are directed to different aspects of commercial conduct.[244]

Commentators have pointed out a moralistic tone to the duty of good faith. Terms such as honesty and fairness are themselves highly subjective and can only be understood as imposing some level of morality on contracting parties.[245] This minimum morality requires that each party avoid conduct that prevents the other from substantially realizing the bargained-for benefit.

Good faith can best be understood by employing an "excluder"[246] analysis. It excludes certain specific forms of bad conduct, but beyond that has no particular meaning. Thus, good faith can only be understood in context, and most of the discussion of good faith in this book is reserved for other sections.[247]

---

[243] UCC § 1-201(20). Prior to the 2001 revision of Article 1, the definition was limited to honesty in fact. Section 2-103(1)(b), however, provided that in the case of a merchant, good faith meant honesty in fact "and the observance of reasonable commercial standards in the trade." States adopting revised Article 1 as promulgated by the Code's sponsors have deleted this provision. Many states have adopted revised Article 1 without changing the definition of good faith, leaving the objective aspect of the good-faith obligation in Article 2 applicable only to merchants.

[244] UCC § 1-201, cmt. 20. For an excellent discussion of the concept of fair dealing, see Maine Family Federal Credit Union v. Sun Life Assurance Co. of Canada, 727 A.2d 335, 37 UCC Rep. Serv. 2d 875 (Me. 1999) (analyzing good faith in context of requirements for qualifying as holder in due course under Article 3).

[245] See generally Farnsworth, *Good Faith Performance and Commercial Reasonableness Under the Uniform Commercial Code*, 30 U. Chi. L. Rev. 666 (1963); Burton, *Good Faith Performance of a Contract Within Article 2 of the Uniform Commercial Code*, 67 Iowa L. Rev. 1 (1981); Summers, *The General Duty of Good Faith — Its Recognition and Conceptualization*, 67 Cornell L. Rev. 810 (1982).

[246] This term was first used in Summers, *"Good Faith" in General Contract Law and the Sales Provisions of the Uniform Commercial Code*, 54 Va. L. Rev. 195 (1968). Summers' analysis was further developed in his law review article cited in note 245 *supra*.

[247] See, e.g., § 2.07 *supra* (contract modification); § 7.08[D][1][a] *infra* (failure of presupposed

§ 4.06 AMENDED ARTICLE 2

[A] Parol Evidence Rule

The amendments break Section 2-202 (and Section 2A-202) into two subsections, with the parol evidence rule in subsection (1) and a rule related to interpretation in subsection (2). Other than the substitution of "record" for "writing," subsection (1)'s statement of the parol evidence is unchanged except for the omission of the word "explained." Subsection (2), which is based on that word and included intended more fully to implement the intent of the original drafters, states as follows:

> Terms in a record may be explained by evidence of course of performance, course of dealing, or usage of trade without a preliminary determination by the court that the language used is ambiguous.

As explained above,[248] the intent of the original drafters was to cut back on the application of the plain-meaning rule[249] by requiring a court, before making a determination that a term is unambiguous, to at least consider relevant evidence as to its meaning drawn from a usage of trade, course of dealing, or course of performance.

The only other change is in the Comments, which now address merger clauses as follows:

> This section is not intended to suggest what should be the evidentiary strength of a merger clause as evidence of the mutual intent that the record be final and complete. That determination depends upon the particular circumstances of each case.[250]

Although the comment purports to be neutral, the fact that it refers to the particular circumstances of each case indicates that merger clauses should not be enforced automatically but must instead be considered in context.

[B] Shorthand Shipping Terms

The Article 2 amendments repeal Sections 2-319 through 2-324 and designate those sections as "reserved."[251] The repealed sections cover delivery terms like F.O.B., C.I.F., and the like that parties commonly use with respect to shipment of goods, and they were eliminated because they are inconsistent with the way the terms are used in modern commercial practices.[252] The Comments indicate that in the absence of an express agreement on the meaning of these terms, the effect of their use "must be interpreted in light of any applicable usage of trade

---

condition); § 7.04 *infra* (rejection of goods); § 7.07[A] *infra* (anticipatory repudiation).

[248] *See* § 4.02[C][4] *supra.*

[249] The plain-meaning rule is discussed in § 4.02[C][4] *supra.*

[250] UCC Rev. § 2-202, cmt. 3.

[251] Reserving the section numbers allowed the drafters to retain the original numbering system for the sections of amended Article 2.

[252] UCC Rev. § 2-319 (Legislative Note).

and any course of performance or course of dealing between the parties."[253] The expectation is that the business and legal communities in the United States will gravitate towards the Incoterms adopted by the International Chamber of Commerce and discussed below in connection with the CISG.[254] With increased globalization, U.S. enterprises are becoming increasingly familiar with international standards and following those standards in both domestic and international transactions will increase efficiency.

§ 4.07   CISG

[A]   Parol Evidence Rule

Article 8(3) of the CISG directs that "[i]n determining the intent of a party or the understanding a reasonable person would have had, due consideration is to be given to all relevant circumstances of the case including the negotiations, any practices which the parties have established between themselves, usages and any subsequent conduct of the parties." The inclusion of the parties' negotiations among the factors for consideration has led several courts and commentators to conclude that the CISG rejects the parol evidence rule.[255] The conclusion is generally correct. The CISG clearly displaces the various tests and presumptions used in U.S. law for determining whether a writing is a complete integration of the express terms of an agreement. Whether the parties intended a writing to be a complete integration is to be resolved like any other question of intent and domestic rules that otherwise would apply are not recognized.

One aspect of the parol evidence rule is readily recognizable under the CISG.[256] Most commentators agree that a merger clause can preclude prior terms not covered by a writing from being included in a contract because the clause abrogates the requirement in Article 8(3) that the prior negotiations of the parties be consulted. Article 6 allows the parties to "derogate from or vary the effect of any of its [the CISG's] provisions" and a merger clause simply takes advantage of the freedom-of-contract principle.

---

[253] UCC Rev. § 2-319, cmt.

[254] International Chamber of Commerce, Incoterms 1990 (I.C.C. Pub. No. 460) (1990). For discussion of Incoterm provisions, see §§ 4.07[C][2][a] and 6.05[A][1] *infra*.

[255] *See, e.g.*, MCC-Marble Ceramic Center, Inc. v. Ceramica Nuova D'Agostino, 144 F.3d 1384 (11th Cir. 1998), *cert. denied*, 526 U.S. 1087 (1999); H. Bernstein & J. Lookofsky, Understanding the CISG in Europe 29 (1997).

[256] For an excellent analysis of the issue, see Flechtner, *The U.N. Sales Convention (CISG) and MCC-Marble Ceramic Center, Inc. v. Ceramica Nuova D'Agostino, S.P.A.: The Eleventh Circuit Weighs in on Interpretation, Subjective Intent, Procedural Limits to the Convention's Scope, and the Parol Evidence Rule*, 18 J. L. & Com. 259 (1999).

[B] Usages and Practices

Article 9 of the CISG spells out the circumstances in which established practices and trade usages are applicable in the international context.[257] The drafting of the provision reflects a necessary compromise. Established trading nations have long recognized and utilized usages because they reflect the legitimate expectations of the parties. While not denying this benefit, the developing nations concluded that the inclusion of usages would place traders in their countries, often new to international trade, at a disadvantage in that they might be held to usages of which they were unaware.

The compromise was to recognize usages but to restrict their availability in ways that would address the concerns that had been raised. Article 9(1) provides that "[t]he parties are bound by any usage to which they have agreed." The parties thus can incorporate a usage into their agreement by express assent. A usage not expressly assented to through a contract term is applicable if a court determines that the parties intended for it to apply.

Parties can also become bound to usages to which they have not expressly assented, subject to three restrictions set out in Article 9(2). First, the usage must be one that both parties knew or ought to have known about. This requirement addresses the concern that a party might be held to a usage of which it is justifiably unaware. Second, the usage must be widely known internationally to parties to contracts of the type involved in the particular trade concerned. This requirement further increases the prospect that the parties will know or have reason to know of a usage and is a hedge against an incorrect determination under the first requirement. The group to which the requirement applies consists of members of the trade involved under the contract in question, and the contracts to which the usage applies must be of the type of contract in question. Finally, the usage must be one that is regularly observed by members of this same group. In other words the usage must be one which in international trade is both known to and regular observed by parties in comparable transactions.

Regarding contract practices, Article 9(1) provides that "[t]he parties are bound . . . by any practices which they have established between themselves." The parties' conduct under earlier, comparable contracts provides the basis for establishing a practice between them, an approach that should not be objectionable to traders in developing nations because the reasonable expectations involved are created through their own prior actions and statements.

---

[257] In addition, Article 8(3) specifies that subsequent conduct of the parties to a contract is to be considered in determining intent.

[C]   Default Terms

As indicated previously, freedom of contract plays a central role in the CISG.[258] When the parties to a contract expressly or implicitly agree to a term, the term displaces the effect of a contrary provision of the CISG. In the absence of an express or implied term, the CISG, like Articles 2 and 2A, includes several provisions that supply missing terms.

[1]   Open-Price Terms

The CISG includes what appears to be a default provision on open-price terms. Article 55 provides that "[w]here a contract has been validly concluded but does not expressly or implicitly fix or make provision for determining the price, the parties are considered in the absence of any indication to the contrary to have impliedly made reference to the price generally charged at the time of the conclusion of the contract for such goods sold under comparable circumstances in the trade concerned." The provision has been construed, however, in a manner that significantly limits its influence. The discussion in a prior chapter of this book covers the issue.[259]

[2]   Delivery Terms

The CISG states the obligations of a seller as follows: "The seller must deliver the goods, hand over any documents relating to them and transfer the property in the goods, as required by the contract and this Convention."[260] The primary source of the seller's obligations will be the contract language, as supplemented by established practices and usages. Delivery terms are especially important in nearly all international sales transactions. Transportation costs can be high given the distances involved, and international sales involve licences, authorizations, and formalities necessary to comply with export-import trade requirements. Because of these considerations, the parties are likely to use explicit delivery terms rather than to rely on the default provisions of the CISG.

[a]   Incoterms

Parties to international sales contracts frequently use standardized trade terms in their agreements. The most commonly used trade terms are called "Incoterms." Incoterms is an acronym for the "international trade terms" that are prepared by the International Chamber of Commerce. The first statement of these terms was adopted in 1936 and the latest version became effective on July 1, 1990.[261] The International Chamber of Commerce is not a government entity, and Incoterms are not an international treaty or any form of legislation.

---

[258] Article 6 provides that "[t]he parties may exclude the application of this Convention or, . . . , derogate from or vary the effect of any of its provisions."

[259] *See* § 2.09[B] *supra*.

[260] CISG Art. 30.

[261] International Chamber of Commerce, Incoterms 1990 (I.C.C. Pub. No. 460) (1990) (hereinafter 1990 Incoterms).

Incoterms nevertheless have received widespread international acceptance, and most commentators believe that the meanings behind the terms qualify as trade usages. Parties generally are well advised, however, to incorporate the meaning of the term they use through a precise statement in their contract. For example, a term might state "FOB San Diego (Incoterms 1990 Revision)."

The 1990 revision of Incoterms includes thirteen trade terms that are grouped into four categories. They start with the single Group E term under which a seller makes the goods available to the buyer at the seller's place of business. This is the only term in which the use of a carrier is not specifically required. Under the Group F terms, the seller must deliver the goods to a carrier that the buyer employs to transport the goods. The Group C terms obligate the seller to make the contract for carriage and pay for it, but not to assume the risk of loss or additional costs that are incurred after shipment. Finally, the Group D terms impose all of the costs and risks attendant on delivering the goods to the country of destination on the seller. The 1990 version of Incoterms provides the following chart concerning these terms:[262]

INCOTERMS 1990

Group E Departure	**EXW**	Ex Works
Group F Main carriage unpaid	**FCA** **FAS** **FOB**	Free Carrier Free Alongside Ship Free on Board
Group C Main carriage Paid	**CFR** **CIF** **CPT** **CIP**	Cost and Freight Cost, Insurance and Freight Carriage Paid to Carriage and Insurance Paid to
Group D Arrival	**DAF** **DES** **DEQ** **DDU** **DDP**	Delivered at Frontier Delivered ex Ship Delivered ex Quay Delivered Duty Unpaid Delivered Duty Paid

For each of the thirteen trade terms, the Incoterms publication sets out ten topics that it uses to explain the term's meaning, and the ten topics appear in the same order after each term. The topics cover what the seller must do to deliver and what the buyer must do to take delivery, the parties' respective obligations regarding contracts for carriage and insurance, their obligations regarding licences and customs formalities, the transfer of the risk of loss, notice to the other party, inspections, the division of costs between the parties, and the provision and acceptance of documents. For each topic, the publication spells out the obligation of the seller and the corresponding obligation of the buyer. The format provides a convenient basis for understanding and comparing the terms, and it helps the parties decide which term to use.

For an example of the use of the topics, consider the term "FOB," which is used with a named port of shipment. The buyer must make the arrangements

---

[262] 1990 Incoterms, at 7.

and incur the expense for the carriage of goods from the port of shipment. The seller does not have any responsibility for the contract of carriage or for insurance during the voyage. The seller fulfills its delivery obligation when the goods pass over the ship's rail at the named port and the risk of loss then passes to the buyer. The seller must notify the buyer that the goods are on board. The seller must arrange and pay for any formalities required for export of the goods, and the buyer has the same responsibility regarding import. Because it is tied to vessels, the FOB term is appropriate only for ocean and inland waterway transport. Comparable allocations between the seller and the buyer are available through the FCA term, which can be used for any mode of transportation, including multimodal transport.[263] Under the FCA term the seller meets its obligation by handing over goods cleared for export to the carrier and at the place named by the buyer.

Compare the CIF term, which is used with a named port of destination. The seller must arrange for transport of the goods by water to the named port and must pay the cost of transport. The seller must, in addition, procure and pay for marine insurance to cover the buyer's risk of loss during transport from the port of shipment to the port of destination. The seller fulfills its delivery obligation when the goods are delivered on board the ship at the port of shipment, and the risk of loss then passes to the buyer. The seller must notify the buyer that the goods have been delivered on board the vessel. The seller has full responsibility for export costs and formalities; the buyer is responsible for import costs and formalities. As with FOB, the CIF term can only be used only for ocean and inland waterway transport. The comparable term applicable to any mode of transport is CIP.[264]

[b] Open-Delivery Terms

The CISG includes provisions concerning the seller's obligation to deliver "[i]f the seller is not bound to deliver the goods at any other particular place."[265] The most relevant of these provisions applies to a contract that involves carriage of the goods. The CISG requires the seller in these transactions to "make such contracts as are necessary for carriage to the place fixed by means of transportation appropriate in the circumstances and according to the usual terms for such transportation."[266] The seller satisfies its delivery obligation when, after making the appropriate contracts, the seller "hand[s] the goods over to the first carrier for transmission to the buyer."[267] The risk of loss also passes to the buyer at this point.[268]

---

[263] The FCA term is recommended for use in cases of roll-on/roll-off or container shipping in which the ship's rail does not have a practical purpose. 1990 Incoterms, at 39.

[264] If the buyer wants the seller to assume full responsibility for the goods and the cost of transport until they arrive at a designated port, it should bargain for a term from Group D.

[265] CISG Art. 31.

[266] CISG Art. 32(2).

[267] CISG Art. 31(a).

[268] CISG Art. 67(1).

If the transaction does not involve the carriage of goods and the seller does not have an obligation to deliver at another particular place, the CISG has a delivery provision that applies if the parties at the time of contracting knew where the goods were located or where they were to be produced.[269] A seller in these circumstances delivers by placing the goods at the buyer's disposal at that place. For example, a buyer that plans to travel internationally might pick up a purchased car in another country at the manufacturing plant. The seller is obligated to have the car available and ready for delivery at that location.

A residual provision of the CISG applies if the contract terms and any relevant practices and usages do not provide for delivery at a particular place and the other CISG delivery provisions do not apply. In these cases the seller's obligation to deliver consists of "placing the goods at the buyer's disposal at the place where the seller had his place of business at the time of the conclusion of the contract."[270] Due to the significance of the issue and its effect on the obligation to pay for shipping, insurance, and other costs, the parties are likely to provide express delivery terms rather than rely upon any of the CISG default provisions, let alone this residual provision.

[3]　Open-Payment Terms

The buyer in a transaction governed by the CISG "must pay the price for the goods . . . as required by the contract and this Convention."[271] Another provision amplifies the nature of the payment obligation as follows: "The buyer's obligation to pay the price includes taking such steps and complying with such formalities as may be required under the contract or any laws and regulations to enable payment to be made."[272] For example, a buyer might be required to make the necessary arrangements for the issuance of a letter of credit or to secure the administrative authorization required in several countries for payment to be made abroad.

In the unusual event that an agreement does not specifically provide for the time and place of payment, the CISG requires payment at the seller's place of business.[273] The requirement is consistent with the expectations of most sellers and protects the seller by ensuring that it receives payment at a practical location. An exception applies if "payment is to be made against the handing over of the goods or of documents;" in that case, payment is to be made at the place where the handing over occurs.[274] Another default rule requires the buyer to pay the price when the goods or the documents covering disposition of the goods are placed into the buyer's control.[275] Furthermore, "[t]he buyer is not

---

[269] CISG Art. 31(b).

[270] CISG Art. 31(c).

[271] CISG Art. 53.

[272] CISG Art. 54.

[273] CISG Art. 57(1)(a).

[274] CISG Art. 57(1)(b).

[275] CISG Art. 58(1).

bound to pay the price until he has had an opportunity to examine the goods."[276] The scheme of the convention is that the buyer is not required to pay for the goods until it attains control over them but, conversely, the seller is not required to pass control until the buyer makes payment.

[D] General Principles

Article 7(2), which addresses the issue of incomplete statutory coverage, provides as follows: "Questions concerning matters governed by this Convention which are not expressly settled in it are to be settled in conformity with the general principles on which it is based or, in the absence of such principles, in conformity with the law applicable by virtue of the rules of private international law." With respect to the transactions to which it applies, the CISG displaces domestic law with a new legal order that is solely international in its orientation and application.[277] The Convention mandates an autonomous interpretation that is freed from domestic law and placed on an international plane. Most significantly, it requires that matters that "are not expressly settled in it are to be settled in conformity with the general principles on which it is based."[278] Thus, even if the provisions of the CISG do not cover an issue, the applicable legal standard still must be found within the CISG through an examination of its underlying general principles.

An initial approach to ascertaining the CISG's general principles is through the process of analogy. It involves identifying the values that underlie the resolution of a particular issue and applying them to an analogous issue. An even more sophisticated form of analysis also is required: The premises upon which the individual provisions of the CISG are based must be identified in order to reveal the principles not stated directly in its text. This involves a process of reasoning back from a final substantive provision to the values that shaped it. By drawing out the value judgments reflected in each provision, the common features that emerge provide the core principles that can be applied in filling gaps within the structure of the CISG. Uncertainties thus are resolved by extending to them the same underlying values that prompted the development of the convention's specific provisions. Article 7 mandates this process.[279]

Scholars and adjudicators have made significant contributions in identifying general principles in the CISG. They include protection of the reasonable reliance of the parties, preservation of the contract, communicating with the other party throughout the transaction, the prevention of surprise, the observance of good faith, recognition of the principle of freedom of contract,

---

[276] CISG Art. 58(3). An exception on the timing for inspection of the goods applies when "the procedures for delivery or payment agreed upon by the parties are inconsistent with [the buyer] having such an opportunity [before being obligated to pay]." *Id.*

[277] By contract, Article 1 of the UCC provides that the prior legal order (common law) supplements Article 2 unless displaced by particular provisions of the Code. *See* § 1.05 *supra.*

[278] CISG Art. 7(2).

[279] Professor Van Alstine argues that Article 7 delegates the authority to courts to develop substantive law that addresses the gaps that emerge in the Convention's express provisions. Van Alstine, *Dynamic Treaty Interpretation*, 146 U. Pa. L. Rev. 678, 753-58 (1998).

fixing obligations and the distribution of risk, mitigation of damages, the principle of estoppel, full compensation following breach, and acting reasonably. Continued efforts by scholars will facilitate understanding in this critical area.

A real danger is that adjudicators will make a feeble effort with respect to general principles and revert back to national law.[280] The CISG allows resort to the rules of private international law, which constitute choice-of-law rules that result in the application of the law of a particular country, only "in the absence of such principles." Conclusory statements to the effect that relevant principles do not exist, however, should be viewed with skepticism. The principles are the values reflected in the CISG provisions, both individually and collectively, and sufficient values generally will be available to address most of the issues that arise. Recourse to private international law is available only after exhausting the prescribed methods of resolving the issue through the terms of the CISG *and* its underlying general principles.

---

[280] For a description of this "homeward trend" in the process of construing the language of the CISG, see § 1.07[D] *supra*.

Chapter 5

WARRANTY

§ 5.01 WARRANTIES IN GENERAL

Article 2 covers several types of warranties: express warranties, implied warranties of merchantability, implied warranties of fitness for a particular purpose, and implied warranties of title and against infringement.[1] The first three categories establish the seller's responsibility with respect to quality of the goods whereas the warranties of title and against infringement cover the extent of the property interest that the seller passes to the buyer. Warranties may arise

---

[1] Article 2A is comparable but, because title does not pass in a lease transaction, it replaces the warranty of title with a warranty of quiet possession.

through a seller's representations (express warranties) or by operation of law (implied warranties). They may also arise from a course of dealing or usage of trade.

Warranty liability is a type of strict liability. If the goods fail to live up to the seller's representations, are not of merchantable quality, or are not fit for the buyer's particular purpose, the reason for the failure is irrelevant. The buyer need only prove that the goods did not conform to the contract's quality standard.[2] Of course, the buyer must also prove that any damages it sustained were proximately caused by the breach and, even if the goods were defective, the seller may raise a number of affirmative defenses — that the warranty was disclaimed, that the buyer failed to give proper notice, that the statute of limitations had expired, that the parties were not in privity of contract, or that the buyer assumed the risk of harm. The material below covers each type of warranty and each of the affirmative defenses.

§ 5.02 TYPES OF WARRANTIES

[A]   Express Warranties [§ 2-313; § 2A-210]

The UCC recognizes three ways in which a seller or lessor can create an express warranty:

(1)   an affirmation of fact or promise relating to the goods that the seller or lessor makes to the buyer or lessee may create an express warranty that the goods will conform to the affirmation or promise;[3]

(2)   a description of the goods may create an express warranty that the goods will conform to the description;[4] and

(3)   a sample or model may create an express warranty that the whole of the goods will conform to the sample or model.[5]

Before any of these three methods creates an express warranty, an additional requirement must be met: The seller's representation (*i.e.*, affirmation, promise, description, sample, or model) must become "part of the basis of the bargain."

---

[2] *Vlases v. Montgomery Ward & Co., Inc.*, 377 F.2d 846, 4 UCC Rep. Serv. 164 (3d Cir. 1967), contains an excellent statement of the Code's strict liability approach. In that case, a buyer of diseased chickens sought to recover for breach of an implied warranty of merchantability and, in response to the seller's argument that it was blameless, the court stated as follows:

> The entire purpose behind the implied warranty sections of the Code is to hold the seller responsible when inferior goods are passed along to the unsuspecting buyer. What the Code requires is not evidence that the defects could or should have been uncovered by the seller but only that the goods upon delivery were not of merchantable quality. . . . The gravamen here is not so much with what precautions were taken by the seller but rather with the quality of the goods contracted for by the buyer.

377 F.2d at 849–50, 4 UCC Rep. Serv. at 168–69.

[3] UCC §§ 2-313(1)(a); 2A-210(1)(a).

[4] UCC §§ 2-313(1)(b); 2A-210(1)(b).

[5] UCC §§ 2-313(1)(c); 2A-210(1)(c).

The discussion below addresses this requirement after first covering each of the three methods of warranty creation.

Initially, consider the following background. Under the formerly applicable doctrine of *caveat emptor*, a seller's statement regarding the nature of the goods was generally taken as a statement of opinion and not as a warranty. For example, in the 1804 case of *Seixas v. Woods*,[6] a dealer described the wood it sold as "braziletto," valuable in a manufacturing process, when in fact it was worthless "peachum." The court held that the seller had not intended to make a warranty and that the description was merely a statement of opinion on a matter of which the seller and buyer were equally ignorant.[7] Under *caveat emptor*, a buyer that wanted a warranty had to bargain for it, and such a bargain was generally reflected in the use of formal words such as "warrant" or "guarantee." Unless formal words of warranty were used, the buyer took the risk that the goods were not as described. New York rejected this approach in 1872,[8] and Article 2, like the Uniform Sales Act that preceded it, also rejects it. Section 2-313(2) provides that "[i]t is not necessary to the creation of an express warranty that the seller use formal words such as 'warrant' or 'guarantee' or that he have a specific intention to make a warranty. . . ."[9] The essence of an express warranty is that the goods sold will conform to the seller's objective representations, not its subjective intent. To be actionable, the representations must be the kind that would be relied upon by a reasonable person in the circumstances of the buyer.

[1]   Affirmation of Fact, Promise, or Description

A seller can create an express warranty by making an affirmation of fact or a promise about the physical characteristics, quality, or performance capabilities of the goods. Article 2 does not distinguish in effect between an affirmation of fact and a promise, although "affirmation of fact" would seem to refer to the current characteristics of the goods and "promise" would seem to refer to their future characteristics. The drafters did not use both terms in order to make this distinction, however, but rather to repudiate a line of older cases that limited express warranties to situations in which the seller used words of promise.

To be actionable, an affirmation of fact or promise must become part of the basis of the bargain, a requirement that is discussed below.[10] It seems inevitable that an affirmation of fact or a promise included in a final writing would be part of the basis of the bargain. This suggests that the drafters primarily had in mind representations temporally removed from the time of formation. The Comments

---

[6] 2 Caines 48 (1804).

[7] If the seller had known that its description was inaccurate, the buyer could have sought a remedy based on the tort of deceit. Today, deceit (or fraud) is part of the broader doctrine of misrepresentation.

[8] Hawkins v. Pemberton, 51 N.Y. 198 (1872).

[9] Article 2A is comparable. UCC § 2A-210(2).

[10] *See* § 5.02[A][3] *infra*. This section also discusses the often fine line between an affirmation of fact or promise on the one hand and sales talk, or "puffing," on the other hand.

support this view[11] and the cases bear it out, finding express warranties formed by pre-sale advertising, brochures, catalogs, pre-contract proposals, letters and emails, statements of sellers or their agents and employees, and the like. The Comments even suggest that a court may find an express warranty based on a post-contract representation by a seller.[12]

In many cases, the issue is less the existence of a warranty than it is a dispute over the warranty's scope. For example, in *Rite Aid Corp. v. Levy-Gray*[13] a statement on an insert provided by a pharmacy with a prescription drug instructed the patient to take the drug with food or milk if an upset stomach occurred. This was held sufficient for the jury to conclude that the pharmacy had represented that the drug was compatible with food and milk. Similarly, in *Gooch v. E.I. Du Pont de Nemours & Co.*[14] the seller's statement that a herbicide would control the weeds listed on its label was held also to mean that it would do so without harming the crop to which it was applied. In *Knapp Shoes, Inc. v. Sylvania Shoe Manufacturing Corp.*,[15] a manufacturer's statement that it would fully warrant its shoes was held not to mean that every shoe would be defect free, but rather that its shoes would conform to industry standards establishing a permissible percentage of defective shoes.

If a description of the goods becomes part of the basis of the bargain, it creates an express warranty that the goods will conform to the description. In *Best Buick, Inc. v. Welcome*,[16] for example, a consumer who traded in a Mercedes on a new car told the dealer that it was a 1970 model when in fact it was a 1968 model. When the dealer sought damages for the discrepancy, the court held that the consumer had made an express warranty by description. Similarly, the court in *Hill Aircraft & Leasing Corp. v. Simon*[17] found that the description "Aero Commander, N-2677B, Number 135, FAA, Flyable" created a warranty that the aircraft could be fully certified under FAA regulations.

Although express warranties created by affirmation of fact or promise and express warranties created by description typically overlap,[18] a significant factor distinguishes the two categories. Under Section 2-313(1)(a), an affirmation or promise must be made *by the seller to the buyer* whereas this limitation does not appear in subsection (1)(b), meaning that a description may

---

[11] UCC § 2-313, Comment 7 states in part that "[t]he precise time when words of description or affirmation are made or samples are shown is not material."

[12] *Id.*

[13] 162 Md. App. 673, 876 A.2d 115, 57 UCC Rep. Serv.2d 951 (2005), *aff'd*, 391 Md. 608, 894 A.2d 563 (2006).

[14] 40 F. Supp. 2d 863, 38 UCC Rep. Serv. 2d 796 (W.D. Ky 1999).

[15] 72 F.3d 190, 28 UCC Rep. Serv. 2d 430 (1st Cir. 1995).

[16] 18 UCC Rep. Serv. 75 (Mass. App. Div. 1975); *see also* American Honda Motor Co., Inc. v. Boyd, 475 So. 2d 835, 41 UCC Rep. Serv. 410 (Ala. 1985) (seller liable for breach of express warranty where car described as new had been damaged in transit); Adam Metal Supply, Inc. v. Electrodex, Inc., 386 So. 2d 1316, 30 UCC Rep. Serv. 178 (Fla. Ct. App. 1980) (description of aluminum by brand name created an express warranty).

[17] 122 Ga. App. 524, 177 S.E.2d 803, 8 UCC Rep. Serv. 474 (1970).

[18] UCC § 9-313, Comment 3 states that "[i]n actual practice, affirmations of fact made by the seller during a bargain are regarded as part of the description of those goods. . . ."

come from a source other than the seller.[19] Buyers commonly describe the goods they wish to buy when they place an order and a seller that responds by delivering the goods extends a warranty that they conform to the buyer's description.[20] The Comments make the obvious point that a description may be by "[t]echnical specifications, blueprints and the like."[21]

The scope of an express warranty can be particularly difficult to assess when a description is extremely broad, such as "an automobile." The Comments indicate that "the whole purpose of the law of warranty is to determine what it is that the seller has in essence agreed to sell"[22] and in the context of broad descriptions this principle can face a major challenge. Given the array of components that make up an automobile, which ones must function and for how long? The Comments provide some guidance by noting that "in determining what they have agreed upon good faith is a factor and consideration should be given to the fact that the probability is small that a real price is intended to be exchanged for a pseudo-obligation."[23] Thus, the price required by the seller is a significant factor in determining the scope of the seller's obligations.[24]

The Comments also state that descriptions "must be read against the applicable trade usages with the general rules as to merchantability resolving all doubts."[25] This suggests that a broad description ordinarily carries with it an inference that the described goods will have some reasonable level of functionality. The issue arose in *Tacoma Boatbuilding Co., Inc. v. Delta Fishing Co., Inc.*,[26] in which the buyer purchased a used "marine engine" that wound up needing significant repairs in order to function. The buyer argued that the description created an express warranty that the engine would work to propel a boat across the water but the court, noting that the implied warranty of merchantability had been disclaimed, held for the seller. In doing so, the court noted that the buyer would have had a cause of action if the engine had in fact been a "wooden box." It is not clear how the court would have reacted if the seller had delivered a marine-engine shell containin g a mechanism beyond repair, but the cited Comment suggests that this too would have been a breach of an express warranty.

---

[19] Autzen v. John C. Taylor Lumber Sales, Inc., 280 Or. 783, 572 P.2d 1322, 23 UCC Rep. Serv. 304 (1977) (inadequate defense for seller to assert that survey of boat hull was conducted by a third party and thus statements were made by someone other than seller); Miles v. Kavanaugh, 350 So. 2d 1090, 22 UCC Rep. Serv. 911 (Fla. Dist. Ct. App. 1977) (description by appraiser became an express warranty when used in negotiations).

[20] Klein v. Sears Roebuck & Co., 733 F.2d 1421, 41 UCC Rep. Serv. 1233 (4th Cir. 1985) (buyer specified need for mower that would be safe on his rolling lawn).

[21] UCC § 2-313, cmt. 5.

[22] UCC § 2-313, cmt. 4.

[23] *Id.*

[24] Alan Wood Steel Co. v. Capital Equip. Enterprises, Inc., 39 Ill. App. 3d 48, 349 N.E.2d 627, 19 UCC Rep. Serv. 1310 (1976) (extremely low purchase price paid for used crane rebutted argument that description "75 ton Brownhoist" indicated that the crane would lift 75 tons).

[25] UCC § 2-313, cmt. 5.

[26] 28 UCC Rep. Serv. 26 (W.D. Wash. 1980).

Under Section 2-313(1)(a), an affirmation of fact or promise must relate to the goods in order to be actionable. The requirement is obvious at a theoretical level — if a representation does not relate to the goods it cannot be the basis of an obligation that the goods conform to it — but is not always so obvious in practice. The decision in *Royal Business Machines, Inc. v. Lorraine Corp.*[27] distinguished between representations that relate to the goods and those that do not. The buyer in that case purchased 128 photocopiers and later sued for breach of express warranties that it claimed arose from a number of representations. The court found that statements relating to the cost of supplies, the availability of replacement parts, the readiness of the copiers for marketing, and their capacity to earn substantial profits did not sufficiently relate to the goods to be the basis of an express warranty.

[2]   Sample or Model

Express warranties by sample or model arise when the seller provides the buyer with a tangible example of the goods. The Comments indicate that a sample must be drawn from the actual goods to be sold while a model is not drawn from those goods.[28] By providing the buyer with a sample or model, the seller warrants that the characteristics of the goods sold will be consistent with those of the sample or model.[29]

Like other express warranties, an express warranty that arises by sample or model may raise questions of scope. The Comments indicate the nature of the issue as follows:

> [T]here is no escape from the question of fact. . . . [I]n mercantile experience the mere exhibition of a "sample" does not of itself show whether it is merely intended to "suggest" or to "be" the character of the subject-matter of the contract. The question is whether the seller has so acted with reference to the sample as to make him responsible that the whole shall have at least the values shown by it. The circumstances aid in answering this question.[30]

This distinction could lead parties to dispute whether an express warranty was created by sample or model or, conceding the creation of the warranty, which attributes are included within its scope. A sample or model will not provide an express warranty if a reasonable buyer in the circumstances would believe that the seller was simply using it to suggest the characteristics of the goods rather adopting it as a description of the goods.[31]

---

[27] 633 F.2d 34, 30 UCC Rep. Serv. 462 (7th Cir. 1980).

[28] UCC § 2-313, cmt. 6.

[29] *Id.*

[30] UCC § 2-313, cmt. 6; *see also* Kopper Glo Fuel, Inc., v. Island Lake Coal Co., 436 F. Supp. 91, 22 UCC Rep. Serv. 1117 (E.D. Tenn. 1977) (sample shown only as representative of goods did not create express warranty).

[31] See Flynn v. Biomet, Inc., 21 UCC Rep. Serv. 2d 580 (E.D. Va. 1993) (doctor did not warrant strength of experimental hip prosthesis by slamming it against examining room table).

A sample that is above average in quality may bind the seller to a standard that is higher than that provided by the implied warranty of merchantability or fitness.[32] For example, Section 2-314(2)(b) requires that fungible goods be of "fair average quality," but a buyer directed to a sample might receive an express warranty that the goods exceed average quality. As the comparison can be a two-edged sword, however, an express warranty will provide less protection than the implied warranties if the sample on which it is based demonstrates that the goods will not be fit for their ordinary purposes or for the buyer's particular purpose. For example, in *Trans-Aire International, Inc. v. Northern Adhesive Co., Inc.*,[33] the seller sent the buyer samples of its adhesive, which the buyer intended to use to install fabric in recreational vehicles. The buyer then purchased a quantity of the adhesive, but it failed to perform the intended task. Because the final product was consistent with the sample, the seller did not breach the express warranty.

The Comments suggest that sellers should be given more leeway when using a model than when using a sample:

> If the sample has been drawn from an existing bulk, it must be regarded as describing values of the goods contracted for unless it is accompanied by an unmistakable denial of such responsibility. If, on the other hand, a model of merchandise not on hand is offered, the mercantile presumption that it has become a literal description of the subject matter is not so strong, and particularly so if modification on the buyer's initiative impairs any feature of the model.[34]

Because a sample must be drawn from the goods that are actually available for sale, it normally will be perceived as more inclusive than a model regarding the attributes of the goods to be delivered. Of course, the extent of detail and functionality of a model is an important factor in determining the extent to which it is truly representative of the goods.

[3] Basis of the Bargain

An express warranty cannot be created unless the representation (affirmation of fact, promise, description, sample, or model) becomes "part of the basis of the bargain." This requirement stands in contrast to the corresponding provision in Article 2's predecessor, the Uniform Sales Act, which stated that an affirmation of fact or promise could only constitute a warranty "if the natural tendency of such affirmation or promise is to induce the buyer to purchase the goods, and if the buyer purchases the goods relying thereon."[35] The Code's drafters consciously deleted the references to reliance and to the buyer's inducement and substituted the basis-of-the-bargain requirement, which they

---

[32] The same observation applies to descriptions and seller promises with respect to the goods that set a standard above average.

[33] 882 F.2d 1254, 9 UCC Rep. Serv. 2d 878 (7th Cir. 1989).

[34] UCC § 2-313, cmt. 6; *see* Blockhead, Inc. v. Plastic Forming Co., Inc., 402 F. Supp. 1017, 18 UCC Rep. Serv. 636 (D. Conn. 1975) (presumption that model is a literal description of goods is not strong).

[35] Uniform Sales Act § 12.

did not define. The Comments provide some insights to their thinking. For example, consider the following excerpt:

> The present section deals with affirmations of fact by the seller, descriptions of the goods or exhibitions of samples, exactly as any other part of a negotiation which ends in a contract is dealt with. No specific intention to make a warranty is necessary if any of these factors is made part of the basis of the bargain. In actual practice affirmations of fact made by the seller about the goods during a bargain are regarded as part of the description of those goods; hence no particular reliance on such statements need be shown in order to weave them into the fabric of the agreement. Rather, any fact which is to take such affirmations, once made, out of the agreement requires clear affirmative proof.[36]

The Comment suggests that a seller's representation may create an express warranty even though the buyer may not be able to show any particular level of reliance on it. The buyer does not have to prove that, but for the representation it would not have bought the goods; nor does it have to show that the representation was a material part of its decision. Section 2-313(1) requires only that the representation become *part* of the basis of the bargain. Consistent with the Comment, many courts have concluded that the requirement is a burden-shifting device pursuant to which a seller's representation is presumed to be part of the mix of reasons inducing its buyer to make a purchase, and only clear and affirmative proof of complete nonreliance can remove it from their agreement. Several other approaches have been developed by the courts, however, leading one court to agree with a scholar's statement that basis of the bargain is probably an indefinable concept.[37]

The burden-shifting approach was used in *Yates v. Pitman Manufacturing, Inc.,*[38] in which a seller certified that a crane met a specified ANSI (American National Standards Institute) standard and the buyer presented evidence at trial that it did not satisfy that standard. On appeal, the seller argued that the lower court had properly stricken the buyer's express-warranty claim because the buyer had not presented any evidence supporting its contention that the standard was part of the basis of the bargain. The appellate court reversed, pointing to the failure of the seller to present evidence that it had been excluded. Absent such evidence, the standard was presumed to be part of the basis of the bargain.

By contrast, the seller in *Hayes v. Bering Sea Reindeer Products*[39] successfully made the required showing. The buyer of a used aircraft asserted in that case that the seller had made express warranties by delivering an airworthiness certificate and by faxing a description of the aircraft. The trial court held for the seller and the Alaska Supreme Court affirmed. The Court conceded that the certificate and description ordinarily would have created express warranties but

---

[36] UCC § 2-313, cmt. 3.

[37] Torres v. Northwest, 949 P.2d 1004, 36 UCC Rep. Serv. 2d 378 (Haw. Ct. App. 1997) (citing 3 M. Foran, Williston on Sales § 17-7, at 12 (5th ed. 1994).

[38] 257 Va. 601, 514 S.E.2d 605, 38 UCC Rep. Serv. 2d 386 (1999).

[39] 983 P.2d 1280, 39 UCC Rep. Serv. 2d 372 (Alaska 1999).

held that under the circumstances of the case they did not. Prior to entering into the contract, the buyer's expert had spent two days thoroughly inspecting the aircraft and his report rendered an opinion on its airworthiness and noted numerous discrepancies between its actual condition and the description. Armed with this information, the buyer had negotiated a lower price and the seller had insisted that the written agreement refer to the extensive inspection and acknowledge that the purchase was being made without any warranties. The court concluded that the buyer did not rely on either the certificate or the description and therefore they did not become part of the basis of the bargain.[40]

Suppose that a buyer is unaware of its seller's representations until after the sale is consummated. Under the burden-shifting approach, proof of the lack of awareness would prevent the representations from becoming part of the basis of the bargain, and most courts have so held.[41] A few courts, however, have sided with buyers on the theory that the Code eliminates the reliance requirement altogether. Support for this position can be found in the following Comment:

> In view of the principle that the whole purpose of the law of warranty is to determine what it is that the seller has in essence agreed to sell, the policy is adopted of those cases which refuse except in unusual circumstances to recognize a material deletion of the seller's obligation.[42]

For example, in *Winston Industries, Inc. v. Stuyvesant Insurance Co., Inc.*,[43] a consumer buyer purchased a mobile home that proved to be defective. The buyer admitted that he had been unaware of the manufacturer's express warranty until after the breach, but the court upheld his claim nonetheless. The court was more concerned with what the seller thought was being sold than with what the buyer thought he was purchasing. The rationale for this approach is that two buyers, each of which pays the same price for the same product, should receive the same warranty protection from a merchant seller and the seller's responsibilities should not turn on what one of the buyers may have heard, seen, or read.

Other buyer-oriented courts have taken different approaches. For example, in *Massey-Ferguson, Inc. v. Laird*,[44] the seller's express warranty was not delivered to the buyer until after the sale. The buyer prevailed because he had been aware before the sale that the manufacturer gave express warranties, and

---

[40] *See also* Sylvia Coal Co. v. Mercury Coal & Coke Co., 156 S.E.2d 1, 4 UCC Rep. Serv. 650 (W. Va. 1967) (statements by seller stressing that the coal to be delivered would be inferior to sample provided to buyer prevented sample from becoming part of the basis of the bargain).

[41] *See, e.g.*, Ciba-Geigy Corp. v. Alter, 309 Ark. 426, 834 S.W.2d 136, 20 UCC Rep. Serv. 2d 448 (1992) (seller's advertising could not create an express warranty when buyer was unaware of it); Terry v. Moore, 448 P.2d 601 (Wyo. 1968) (post-sale statement by seller of well-drilling equipment regarding production capacity unenforceable); Schmaltz v. Nissen, 431 N.W.2d 657, 7 UCC Rep. Serv. 2d 1061 (S.D. 1988) (merchant seller of seeds not liable when buyer admitted he had not read the language on seed bags before consummating sale).

[42] UCC § 2-313, cmt. 4.

[43] 317 So. 2d 493, 17 UCC Rep. Serv. 924 (Ala. Ct. App. 1975); *see also* Villalon v. Vollmering, 676 S.W.2d 220, 39 UCC Rep. Serv. 80 (Tex. Ct. App. 1984); Jensen v. Seigel Mobile Homes Group, 105 Idaho 189, 668 P.2d 65, 35 UCC Rep. Serv. 804 (1983).

[44] 432 So. 2d 1259, 36 UCC Rep. Serv. 437 (Ala. 1983).

the court held that the fact that he was unaware of the precise scope of the warranty was not fatal to his claim. Suppose, however, that the buyer had been totally unaware of the warranty's existence until after the sale. A few courts would still have found in the buyer's favor, either on the no-reliance theory advanced in *Winston Industries* or on the theory that the contract had been modified. The modification rationale finds support in the following statement from the Comments:

> The precise time when words of description or affirmations are made or samples are shown is not material. The sole question is whether the language or samples or models are fairly to be regarded as part of the contract. If language is used after the closing of the deal (as when the buyer when taking delivery asks and receives an additional assurance), the warranty becomes a modification, and need not be supported by consideration if it is otherwise reasonable and in order (section 2-209).[45]

The modification approach is problematic. Section 2-209 applies to "[a]n agreement modifying a contract," and, even though modifications generally do not require consideration to be binding,[46] it is difficult to conceptualize a unilateral post-sale comment as an "agreement" absent consideration or reliance.[47] A slightly different approach would be to adopt an expansive reading of the word "bargain." In contrast to a "contract," which is usually formed at a particular time, the term "bargain" might be sufficiently elastic to encompass an ongoing consensual relationship such that representations made by the seller during the course of the relationship could qualify as part of the basis of the expanded bargain.[48]

Either of these approaches or the no-reliance approach could explain the result in *Rite Aid Corp. v. Levy-Gray*,[49] in which the court held a pharmacy liable for an affirmation of fact on an insert included with a prescription drug even though the buyer was unaware of the insert until after the sale. The affirmation was that the drug could safely be taken with food or milk, and the buyer relied on it to her detriment. This reliance might have sufficed to prove the existence of a modification, but the court instead stressed the fact that requiring actual knowledge at or before the time of sale would negate virtually all consumer warranties. Because the insert had been provided at the time the drugs were sold, the court held, using the language of the Comments, that the insert was fairly to be regarded as part of the contract even though the buyer did not become aware of it until later.

---

[45] UCC § 2-313, cmt. 7.

[46] UCC § 2-209(1).

[47] *See, e.g.*, Hrosik v. J. Keim Builders, 37 Ill. App. 3d 352, 345 N.E.2d 514, 19 UCC Rep. Serv. 472 (1976) (post-sale affirmations require new consideration to be binding).

[48] *See, e.g.*, Autzen v. John C. Taylor Lumber Sales, Inc., 280 Ore. 783, 572 P.2d 1322, 23 UCC Rep. Serv. 304 (1977) (seller's post-sale statement that a boat's hull was "very sound" was part of the parties' ongoing relationship as seller and buyer). *See generally* Murray, *Basis of the Bargain: Transcending Classical Concepts*, 66 Minn. L. Rev. 283 (1982).

[49] 894 A.2d 563, 59 UCC Rep. Serv. 2d 807 (Md. 2006). See also the discussion of this case in the text accompanying note 13 *supra*.

Another post-sale case is *Autzen v. John C. Taylor Lumber Sales, Inc.*,[50] in which the parties contracted for the sale of a 50-foot wooden boat. The seller had a survey conducted to determine the boat's soundness and the results, passed on to the buyer after the sale had been consummated, indicated that it was "very sound" and "should be well suited for its intended purpose." When the buyer discovered extensive dry rot and an insect infestation, he brought suit based on the survey and obtained a favorable verdict from the trial court. On appeal, the seller argued that the survey could not have been part of the basis of the bargain because it was not provided until after the contract had been formed. The appellate court affirmed, indicating that the seller had improperly confused the concepts of bargain and contract and explaining how the survey could have become part of the basis of the bargain:

> At the time Buyer was first informed of the Huhta survey results, he had not yet taken possession of the boat. While this description did not induce the actual formation of the contract, the jury might have found that it did induce and was intended by the Seller to induce Buyer's satisfaction with the agreement just made, as well as to lessen Buyer's degree of vigilance in inspecting the boat prior to acceptance.[51]

The argument in favor of post-sale liability is diminished if an affirmation is made long after the deal has been consummated, and in such cases the buyer with the best chance of prevailing is one that can prove reliance on the seller's representation. For example, the buyer in *Downie v. Abex Corp.*[52] testified that he refrained from making safety modifications to the goods because of the seller's post-sale representations and the court held in his favor on the ground that the contract had been modified.[53]

At least one court, applying Section 2-313 by analogy, has held that in some circumstances the basis-of-the-bargain requirement may be met even if the buyer is aware that its seller's representations are probably false. In *CBS, Inc. v. Ziff-Davis Publishing Co.*,[54] a case involving the purchase by CBS of a consumer magazine publishing business, CBS received financial information from the seller that assured the profitability of certain magazines, but then performed its own investigation and, by the time the deal was consummated, had substantial doubts as to the information's truthfulness. The court held that the critical question was not whether CBS relied on the truthfulness of the seller's representations but whether it relied on them being part of the contract. In

---

[50] 280 Or. 783, 572 P.2d 1322, 23 UCC Rep. Serv. 304 (1977).

[51] 572 P.2d at 1325–26.

[52] 741 F.2d 1235, 39 UCC Rep. Serv. 427 (10th Cir. 1984); *see also* Bigelow v. Agway, Inc., 506 F.2d 551, 15 UCC Rep. Serv. 769 (2d Cir. 1974) (farmer prevailed after relying on seller's statement that hay could be baled safely after being sprayed with seller's product).

[53] In some cases, an alternative approach may be available. Under Section 2-314(2)(f), goods are not of merchantable quality if they fail to "conform to the promises or affirmations of fact made on the container or label if any." The implied warranty of merchantability is discussed in § 5.02[B] *infra*. Unless this implied warranty is effectively disclaimed, a disappointed buyer can enforce affirmations made on the container or label without having to prove that they became part of the basis of the bargain. *See, e.g.,* Farmers Union Coop. Gin v. Smith, 9 UCC Rep. Serv. 823 (Okla. Ct. App. 1971).

[54] 75 N.Y.2d 496, 554 N.Y.S.2d 449, 553 N.E.2d 997 (N.Y. 1990).

effect, CBS bought a right of indemnification and was entitled to enforce it.

[4] The Affirmation/Opinion ("Puffing") Dichotomy

Section 2-313(2) insulates a seller whose expression constitutes puffing, meaning that the expression either is a statement of opinion or a commendation of the goods. Differentiating between affirmations of fact and promises on the one hand and puffing on the other hand is often difficult. The original Comments provided some help, and the Comments to amended Article 2 expanded on the issue in a helpful way. The Comments state as follows:

> Concerning affirmations of value or a seller's opinion or commendation under subsection (2), the basic question remains the same: What statements of the seller have in the circumstances and in objective judgment become part of the basis of the bargain? As indicated above, all of the statements of the seller do so unless good reason is shown to the contrary. The provisions of subsection (2) are included, however, since common experience discloses that some statements or predictions cannot fairly be viewed as entering into the bargain. Even as to false statements of value, however, the possibility is left open that a remedy may be provided by the law relating to fraud or misrepresentation.[55]

The Comments from amended Section 2-313 helpfully add the following:

> There are a number of factors relevant to determine whether an expression creates a warranty under this section or is merely puffing. For example, the relevant factors may include whether the seller's representations taken in context, (1) were general rather than specific, (2) related to the consequences of buying rather than the goods themselves, (3) were "hedged" in some way, (4) were related to experimental rather than standard goods, (5) were concerned with some aspects of the goods but not a hidden or unexpected nonconformity, (6) were informal statements made in a formal contracting process, (7) were phrased in terms of opinion rather than fact, or (8) were not capable of objective measurement.[56]

Note that Section 2-313(2) excludes only "an affirmation *merely* of the value of the goods or a statement purporting to be *merely* the seller's opinion or commendation of the goods."[57] At some point, a seller's expression transitions from mere puffing and becomes an express warranty.[58] The following Comment indicates that the transition occurs when the expression becomes part of the basis of the bargain, meaning that there is a linkage between that requirement and the puffing defense:

---

[55] UCC § 2-313, cmt. 8. The quoted language is reproduced as the first paragraph of amended UCC § 2-313, cmt. 10.

[56] Amended UCC § 2-313, cmt. 10.

[57] UCC § 2-313(2) (emphasis supplied).

[58] *See, e.g.*, Young & Cooper, Inc. v. Vestring, 214 Kan. 311, 521 P.2d 281, 14 UCC Rep. Serv. 916 (1974).

Concerning affirmations of value or a seller's opinion or commendation under subsection (2), the basic question remains the same: What statements of the seller have in the circumstances and in objective judgment become part of the basis of the bargain?[59]

Not surprisingly, disputes in this area are fact intensive and must be resolved on a case-by-case basis. In the leading case of *Interco, Inc. v. Randustrial Corp.*,[60] the buyer resurfaced its warehouse floor with Sylox, a floor covering manufactured by the seller. The product proved to be an impediment to warehouse traffic rather than an expedient because the floor shifted more than the covering could tolerate. The buyer argued that the following language from the seller's sales catalog created an express warranty: "Sylox is a hard yet malleable material which bonds firm to wood floors for smooth and easy hand-trucking. *Sylox will absorb considerable flex without cracking* and is not softened by spillage of oil, grease or solvents."[61] The seller, of course, characterized the language as a mere statement of opinion and the jury returned a verdict in its favor.

The appellate court concluded that the seller's statement was an attempt to affirm a particular fact — that Sylox would absorb a considerable amount of flex — rather than a statement of opinion. Noting that the buyer had no particular expertise in the field of floor coverings, the court stated, "[a]n important factor is whether the seller assumes to assert a fact of which the buyer is ignorant or whether the seller merely expresses an opinion on which the buyer may be expected to have an opinion and be able to express his own judgment."[62] The court nevertheless affirmed the jury's verdict because the seller's statement was too imprecise to set a quality standard. The jury had to determine whether the purchased Sylox conformed to the statement and, from the evidence presented, it could have concluded that the flex in the warehouse floor was more than "considerable" and thus more than what the seller indicated the product could handle. Many other courts have stressed that a representation, to be actionable, must be objective in nature, meaning that it must be verifiable or capable of being proven true or false.[63] If a representation is not verifiable or capable of being proven false, a reasonable person could not rely on it.

The relative sophistication of the buyer as a factor is illustrated by *Sessa v. Riegle*,[64] in which the court held that a seller's statement that a racehorse was "sound" merely stated an opinion. The court was influenced by the fact that the

---

[59]   UCC § 2-313, cmt. 8.

[60]   533 S.W.2d 257, 19 UCC Rep. Serv. 464 (Mo. Ct. App. 1976). The case demonstrates that express warranties can arise from pre-bargaining advertising. *See also* Crest Container Corp. v. R. H. Bishop Co., 111 Ill. App. 3d 1068, 67 Ill. Dec. 727, 445 N.E.2d 19, 35 UCC Rep. Serv. 1498 (1982) (catalog); Keith v. Buchanan, 173 Cal. App. 3d 13, 220 Cal. Rptr. 392, 42 UCC Rep. Serv. 386 (1985) (advertising).

[61]   533 S.W.2d at 260 (emphasis supplied).

[62]   *Id.* at 263.

[63]   *See, e.g.*, Boud v. SDNCO, Inc., 54 P.3d 1131, 48 UCC Rep. Serv. 2d 532 (Utah 2002) (picture in catalog showing yacht moving through water coupled with statements that it offered the "best performance" and "superb handling" could not be objectively verified).

[64]   427 F. Supp. 760, 21 UCC Rep. Serv. 745 (E.D. Pa. 1977).

buyer was a sophisticated horseman who had the horse inspected before sale by another, even more sophisticated, expert. Further, the seller's statement was made in the context of other statements that were obviously opinion, such as "the horse is a good one" and "you will like him." The statement regarding soundness fell within the penumbra of the seller's other statements and took on their coloring. In other cases, similar statements made to less sophisticated buyers have given rise to warranty liability.[65]

Balog v. Center Art Gallery-Hawaii, Inc.[66] also illustrates the degree to which the relative sophistication of the parties bears on the outcome. The seller, an art dealer, represented that a painting was an original work by Salvador Dali. The court noted that a sophisticated buyer would have understood this statement to be an opinion but concluded that, given the actual buyer's lack of expertise, it constituted an express warranty.[67]

Section 2-313(2) gives explicit protection to sellers that make statements regarding the value of their goods.[68] For example, in *Daughtrey v. Ashe*[69] the court held that a seller's appraisal of a diamond ring for insurance purposes was merely an opinion. However, the seller's statement in the same appraisal that the diamond was of "v.v.s." quality, one of the highest ratings used by gemologists, was held to be an actionable affirmation of fact. The Comments point out that even a statement of value might in some circumstances constitute fraud or misrepresentation.[70]

[B]   The Implied Warranty of Merchantability [§ 2-314; § 2A-212]

If a seller is a merchant with respect to goods of the kind being sold, Section 2-314(1) provides a gap-filler with regard to their quality. The quality standard is "merchantability," and subsection (2) spells out what it means. Section 2-314

---

[65] *See, e.g.,* Slyman v. Pickwick Farms, 15 Ohio App. 3d 25, 472 N.E.2d 380, 39 UCC Rep. Serv. 1630 (1984) (veterinarian's statement to the crowd at an auction that a racehorse was "sound" was an affirmation of fact); Yuzwak v. Dygert, 144 A.D.2d 938, 534 N.Y.S.2d 35, 7 UCC Rep. Serv. 2d 731 (1988) (court denied seller's motion for summary judgment on a seller's statement that a horse was a good one for children); Valley Datsun v. Martinez, 578 S.W.2d 485 (Tex. Ct. Civ. App. 1979) (seller's statement that six-year old Volkswagen camper was "in excellent condition" created express warranty; camper sustained burned out clutch and thrown rod two days and 120 miles after purchase).

[66] 745 F. Supp. 1556, 12 UCC Rep. Serv. 2d 962 (D. Haw. 1990).

[67] Although UCC § 2-313(2) provides that formal words of warranty are not necessary to the creation of an express warranty, a buyer that wants to be certain that a seller's statement of authenticity will be treated as a warranty should insist that formal words be used.

[68] UCC §§ 2-313(2), 2A-210(2).

[69] 243 Va. 73, 413 S.E.2d 336, 16 UCC Rep. Serv. 2d 294 (1992); *see also* Hall v. T. L. Kemp Jewelry, Inc., 71 N.C. App. 101, 322 S.E.2d 7, 39 UCC Rep. Serv. 1648 (1984). *But see* Goldman v. Barnett, 793 F. Supp. 28, 18 UCC Rep. Serv. 2d 55 (D. Mass. 1992) (whether dealer's appraisal of paintings constituted an express warranty was an issue of fact).

[70] UCC § 2-313, cmt. 8.

states in full:[71]

(1) Unless excluded or modified (Section 2-316), a warranty that the goods shall be merchantable is implied in a contract for their sale if the seller is a merchant with respect to goods of that kind. Under this section the serving for value of food or drink to be consumed either on the premises or elsewhere is a sale.

(2) Goods to be merchantable must be at least such as

   (a) pass without objection in the trade under the contract description; and

   (b) in the case of fungible goods, are of fair average quality within the description; and

   (c) are fit for the ordinary purposes for which such goods are used; and

   (d) run, within the variations permitted by the agreement, of even kind, quality and quantity within each unit and among all units involved; and

   (e) are adequately contained, packaged, and labeled as the agreement may require; and

   (f) conform to the promises or affirmations of fact made on the container or label, if any.

(3) Unless excluded or modified (Section 2-316) other implied warranties may arise from course of dealing or usage of trade.

[1] "Merchant with Respect to Goods of That Kind"

The implied warranty of merchantability does not apply to all sales: It arises only if the seller is a merchant with respect to goods of the kind being sold. The warranty is thus based on a principle of enterprise liability and applies if the seller has a professional status with respect to the goods.[72] Because such merchants are assumed to have specialized knowledge or skill with regard to the goods they sell,[73] they should be able to foresee the ordinary uses to which the goods are put and to provide compensation as part of the cost of doing business for the harm caused by the failure of the goods to be fit for those purposes.

Article 2 defines "merchant" as follows:

---

[71] Article 2A includes a comparable provision. UCC § 2A-212. The warranty is not made by a finance lessor.

[72] As a gap-filler, the warranty may be displaced by agreement of the parties. UCC § 2-316 places restrictions on the manner in which a modification or exclusion (disclaimer) of the implied warranty of merchantability or fitness may effectively be made. Implied-warranty disclaimers are discussed in § 5.03[B] *infra*.

[73] *See* UCC § 2-104, cmt. 2 ("Obviously this qualification restricts the implied warranty to a much smaller group than everyone who is engaged in business and requires a professional status as to particular kinds of goods.").

"Merchant" means a person who deals in goods of the kind or otherwise by his occupation holds himself out as having knowledge or skill peculiar to the practices or goods involved in the transaction or to whom such knowledge or skill may be attributed by his employment of an agent or broker or other intermediary who by his occupation holds himself out as having such knowledge or skill.

Under this definition, there are three types of merchants: (1) those that deal in goods of the kind sold, (2) those that hold themselves out as having knowledge or skill peculiar to the *goods* involved in the transaction, and (3) those that hold themselves out as having knowledge or skill peculiar to the *practices* involved in the transaction. Section 2-314(1)'s reference to merchants "with respect to goods of that kind" excludes only the third type of merchant. Most sellers found liable for breach of the implied warranty of merchantability have been dealers, but neither the definition nor the cases applying it are so limited.

A manufacturer is obviously a merchant,[74] as are dealers that sell the goods out of their inventory. What about other sellers? The Comments suggest that whether a particular person is a merchant turns on the quantity of goods sold by the person.[75] Sellers that make only isolated sales are not merchants for purposes of Section 2-314 even though they likely qualify as merchants under other Code provisions dealing with normal contract practices, such as Sections 2-201 (statute of frauds), 2-205 (firm offers), 2-207 (battle of the forms), and 2-209 (modification and rescission).[76] Applying this analysis, the court in *Cohen v. Hathaway*[77] held that commercial fishermen who sold their fishing vessel were not merchants with respect such vessels and therefore did not make an implied warranty of merchantability. The same reasoning protected a hardware dealer that sold a truck used in its business.[78]

As the *Cohen* case illustrates, sellers have a better chance of avoiding liability when the goods are not inventory,[79] but sellers other than manufacturers and dealers have occasionally been held to be merchants. For example, in *Ferragamo v. Massachusetts Bay Transportation Authority*,[80] the seller of used trolley equipment was found to be a merchant because it made such sales on a regular basis. By contrast, the seller in *Czarnecki v. Roller*[81] was not a merchant even though he sold five yachts over a period of several years. The court undoubtedly

---

[74] *See, e.g.*, Valley Iron & Steel Co. v. Thorin, 278 Or. 103, 562 P.2d 1212, 21 UCC Rep. Serv. 760 (1977) (foundry operator was merchant even though it was manufacturing a special tool for the first time).

[75] UCC § 2-314, cmt. 3.

[76] See UCC § 2-104, cmt. 2.

[77] 95 F. Supp. 575, 39 UCC Rep. Serv. 857 (D. Mass. 1984).

[78] Colton v. Decker, 540 N.W.2d 172, 30 UCC Rep. Serv. 2d 206 (S.D. 1995).

[79] *See, e.g.*, Siemen v. Alden, 34 Ill. App. 3d 961, 341 N.E.2d 713, 18 UCC Rep. Serv. 884 (1975) (sawmill that sold saw was not a merchant); Allen v. Nicole, Inc., 172 N.J. Super. 442, 412 A.2d 824, 28 UCC Rep. Serv. 982 (1980) (carnival operator who sold defective ride not a merchant).

[80] 395 Mass. 581, 481 N.E.2d 477, 41 UCC Rep. Serv. 304 (1985).

[81] 726 F. Supp. 832, 11 UCC Rep. Serv. 2d 829 (S.D. Fla. 1989).

was influenced by the fact that the seller was an individual selling yachts that he had used for consumer purposes.

Courts experience considerable trouble with cases involving farmers and ranchers. Most of the decisions have held such sellers to be merchants,[82] although a few cases have been decided to the contrary[83] and several states have enacted nonuniform amendments to the Code that insulate farmers and ranchers from merchant status.[84]

By its terms, Section 2-314 applies only to contracts for sale, meaning either a present sale of goods or a contract to sell goods in the future.[85] Subsection (1) resolves the pre-Code uncertainty on whether a restaurant that serves a meal engages in a sales transaction or a service transaction by stipulating that for purposes of the implied warranty of merchantability "the serving for value of food or drink to be consumed either on the premises or elsewhere is a sale." By contrast, in the case of blood transfusions, several states have precluded applicability of the warranty through case law or statutes that treat the transfusions as service transactions.[86]

The importance of the sale requirement is illustrated by *Evans v. Chrysler Corp.*,[87] in which the plaintiff paid a fee to enter a vehicle auction lot, started a car on the lot, and was injured when it surged forward and hit a truck. The court held that he could not recover for breach of an implied warranty of merchantability because he had neither bought nor entered into a contract to buy the car. By contrast, the court in *Blue v. Harris Teeter, Inc.*[88] held in favor of a customer who removed a bag of ice from a bin inside a self-service retail store. The bag broke, spilling ice and water onto the floor, and the customer slipped and injured his ankle. The decision is a stretch because the customer was in no way obligated to buy the ice when the injury occurred, but the court's inclination to provide relief to an injured person is understandable and the customer had initiated what might well have resulted in a sales transaction. A Comment to Section 2-313 provides support for the decision by suggesting that a court might appropriately expand the application of a particular warranty beyond the strict boundaries permitted by the Code's language.[89]

---

[82] *See, e.g.*, Fear Ranches, Inc. v. Berry, 470 F.2d 905, 12 UCC Rep. Serv. 27 (10th Cir. 1972).

[83] *See, e.g.*, Sparks v. Stich, 135 A.D.2d 989, 522 N.Y.S.2d 707, 5 UCC Rep. Serv. 2d 922 (1987) (farmers were not merchants in transaction involving sale of their house and 17 cows even though they regularly raised and sold such animals).

[84] *See, e.g.*, Kan. Stat. Ann. § 82-2-316 (1983), *overturning the result in* Musil v. Hendrich, 6 Kan. App. 2d 196, 627 P.2d 367, 31 UCC Rep. Serv. 432 (1981).

[85] UCC § 2-106(1).

[86] *See, e.g.*, Gibson v. Methodist Hospital, 822 S.W.2d 95, 17 UCC Rep. Serv. 2d 81 (Tex. Ct. App. 1991).

[87] 44 UCC Rep. Serv. 2d 1003 (Mass. Super. Ct. 2001).

[88] 130 N.C. App. 484, 506 S.E.2d 298, 36 UCC Rep. Serv. 2d 367 (1998) (unpublished).

[89] UCC § 2-313, Comment 2 provides as follows:

Although this section is limited in its scope and direct purpose to warranties made by the seller to the buyer as part of a contract for sale, the warranty sections of this Article are not designed in any way to disturb those lines of case law growth which have recognized that warranties need not be confined either to sales contracts or to the direct parties to

[2]   The Standard of Merchantability

Section 2-314 does not define merchantability but it does establish minimal standards for the concept by providing in subsection (2) that "[g]oods to be merchantable must be at least such as" pass six articulated criteria. The list is not exhaustive and additional criteria may apply through trade usage or case-law development.[90]

The most important standard — the one that establishes the essence of the implied warranty — is that goods must be "fit for the ordinary purposes for which such goods are used."[91] The seller need not tender the best possible goods, but they must be able to perform the ordinary tasks for which it they are used.[92] This standard may not satisfy all the expectations a particular buyer may have had when making a purchase. A seller can breach an express warranty relating to goods that are entirely adequate for their ordinary uses by overpromising, but it will not breach the implied warranty of merchantability unless the goods are defective. Consistent with the kinds of defects that may give rise to strict liability in tort,[93] breach of the implied warranty of merchantability may be predicated on design defects, defects in the manufacturing process, or defects in the instructions given to the buyer. The buyer must establish that the defect in the goods existed at the time they left the seller's possession or control.[94]

The most common defect is a flaw in the manufacturing process. In *Fredrick v. Dryer*,[95] for example, the buyer recovered for breach of an implied warranty of merchantability when the mobile home that he purchased proved to be a "lemon." The roof leaked, the doors would not latch, the electrical wiring was installed incorrectly, and the plumbing did not work. The merchantability standard is also breached, however, if the defect stems from a design error. For

---

such a contract. They may arise in other appropriate circumstances such as in the case of bailments for hire, whether such bailment is itself the main contract or is merely a supplying of containers under a contract for the sale of their contents.

The reference in the Comment to "this Article" indicates that it was intended to apply to more than just express warranties.

[90] UCC § 2-314(3) & cmt. 6.

[91] UCC § 2-314(2)(c). "Such goods" is a reference back to language modifying goods in paragraphs (a) and (b) and means goods within the contract description.

[92] The buyer bears the burden of proving that the use to which it put the goods was an ordinary purpose. *See, e.g.*, Derienzo v. Trek Bicycle Corp., 376 F. Supp. 2d 537, 57 UCC Rep. Serv. 2d 863 (S.D.N.Y. 2005) (although buyer's evidence supported a finding that jumping was an ordinary use of mountain bike, the more specific question of whether the type of jump performed by buyer was an ordinary purpose could not be answered on a motion for summary judgment); Bethlehem Steel Corp. v. Chicago Eastern Corp., 863 F.2d 508, 7 UCC Rep. Serv. 2d 399 (7th Cir. 1988) (buyer's claim of breach with regard to steel that was not suitable for use as side wall of grain bin failed because buyer did not present any evidence that this use was an ordinary purpose for the steel).

[93] Restatement (Third) of Torts § 402A.

[94] Olshansky v. Rehrig Internat'l, 872 A.2d 282, 57 UCC Rep. Serv. 2d 474 (R.I. 2005) (no recovery because plaintiffs did not satisfy their burden of establishing the condition of the allegedly defective shopping cart at the time it left the manufacturer's possession).

[95] 257 N.W.2d 835, 23 UCC Rep. Serv. 55 (S.D. 1977).

example, in *Valley Iron & Steel Co. v. Thorin*[96] the buyer was a retail dealer in forestry equipment and wanted to carry a line of hoedads, which are tools used to plant seedlings. The manufacturer, a foundry that had never produced a hoedad before, recommended that the tool be made of iron. The hoedads broke easily, producing a large volume of complaints, but hoedads subsequently manufactured from steel by a different foundry proved satisfactory. The court held that the manufacturer's design flaw constituted a breach of the implied warranty of merchantability.

Even if goods are properly designed and manufactured, they are not of merchantable quality if the seller's failure to give adequate instructions regarding their use results in harm to a buyer. For example, the buyer in *Hayes v. Ariens Co.*[97] recovered for his personal injuries because the manufacturer failed to warn of the danger of removing clogged snow from a snowblower without turning the motor off. Similarly, the court in *Stephens v. G. D. Searle & Co.*[98] held a prescription-drug manufacturer liable for failing to warn of the side effects of its products.

Goods are not defective merely because they will not perform the task for which they were purchased. For example, in *Computerized Radiological Services v. Syntex Corp.*[99] radiologists who had purchased an X-ray scanner complained that it was unfit to perform body scans. The machine, which was not defective, had been designed to perform head scans only. The court held that the machine was of merchantable quality but found for the radiologists under the implied warranty of fitness for particular purpose. Similarly, in *Whitson v. Safeskin Corp, Inc.*[100] a nurse suffered an allergic reaction from using a latex examination glove but could not recover under the standard of merchantability because the ordinary purpose of the glove was to protect the wearer from transmitting or being exposed to blood-borne pathogens. This ground is a bit narrow in that one would normally expect the glove to perform its ordinary task without causing harm to the wearer, and in this regard the court noted that the nurse had failed to provide any evidence to show that a normal user would be similarly affected.[101]

The fact that goods cause harm, even harm in the nature of personal injury, does not mean that they are unmerchantable. For example, in *Webster v. Blue Ship Tea Room*[102] the plaintiff was injured by a fish bone in her fish chowder. The court, siding with the seller, adopted a "foreign/natural" test and concluded

---

[96] 278 Or. 103, 562 P.2d 1212, 21 UCC Rep. Serv. 760 (1977).

[97] 391 Mass. 407, 462 N.E.2d 273, 38 UCC Rep. Serv. 48 (1984).

[98] 602 F. Supp. 379, 40 UCC Rep. Serv. 441 (E.D. Mich. 1985).

[99] 595 F. Supp. 1495, 40 UCC Rep. Serv. 49 (E.D.N.Y. 1984).

[100] 313 F. Supp. 2d 473, 53 UCC Rep. Serv. 2d 216 (M.D. Pa. 2004).

[101] *See also* Fiddler's Inn, Inc. v. Andrews Dist. Co., Inc., 612 S.W.2d 166, 31 UCC Rep. Serv. 1277 (Tenn. Ct. App. 1980) (implied warranty of merchantability not breached when buyer ordered heating units that were too small to keep buyer's rooms warm but there was nothing inherently wrong with the heaters). The implied warranty of fitness, discussed in § 5.02[C] *infra*, can be breached even though the goods are merchantable.

[102] 347 Mass. 421, 198 N.E.2d 309, 2 UCC Rep. Serv. 161 (1964).

that a buyer who is injured by a substance that is natural to the food cannot recover for breach of the implied warranty of merchantability. The buyer would have prevailed if she had been injured by a stone that had fallen into the chowder. A number of courts have abandoned the foreign/natural test in favor of a standard based on reasonable consumer expectations.[103] For example, in *Johnson v. CFM, Inc.*[104] a consumer became ill after drinking a cup of coffee that contained excessive grounds and recovered even though grounds are a natural product of coffee because the concentration level exceeded the expectations of a reasonable consumer. The buyer did not fare as well in *Morrison's Cafeteria of Montgomery, Inc. v. Haddox*,[105] in which the court held as a matter of law that a one-centimeter fish bone in a fish fillet was not inconsistent with reasonable consumer expectations.

The reasonable-consumer-expectations test is not limited to food and drink products. For example, a court applied it in favor of the buyer of a small utility vehicle, a Ford Bronco II, in *Denny v. Ford Motor Co.*[106] The buyer in that case suffered serious personal injuries when she slammed on the brakes to avoid hitting a deer and the vehicle rolled over, and she brought claims against Ford based on strict liability in tort and breach of an implied warranty of merchantability. Both theories were predicated on an allegation that the vehicle's short wheel base, high center of gravity, and narrow track width constituted a design defect that caused it to be unstable. With regard to the tort claim, the trial court had instructed the jury to apply a risk/utility test and the jury had found for Ford. On the warranty claim, the trial court had instructed the jury to apply a reasonable-consumer-expectations test and the jury had found for the buyer. In affirming the verdict, the New York Court of Appeals held that the application of different tests for defectiveness in tort and in contract was appropriate and that a reasonable consumer's expectations regarding the safety of a vehicle was an appropriate test for the contract claim.

The Comments indicate that the implied warranty of merchantability applies to used goods,[107] and most courts have agreed.[108] Of course, the goods must be judged under standards appropriate for used goods, and less is expected of used goods than is expected of new goods. Thus, a seller may be able to avoid liability

---

[103] The *Webster* court discussed this test in addition to the foreign/natural test, noting that fish bones were "to be anticipated" in fresh New England fish chowder.

[104] 726 F. Supp. 1228, 10 UCC Rep. Serv. 2d 1195 (D. Kan. 1990).

[105] 431 So. 2d 975, 35 UCC Rep. Serv. 1074 (Ala. 1983); *cf.* Goodman v. Wenco Management, 100 N.C. App. 108, 394 S.E.2d 832, 13 UCC Rep. Serv.2d 106 (1990) (consumer who chipped tooth on bone in hamburger recovered because size of bone exceeded consumer expectations).

[106] 87 N.Y.2d 248, 639 N.Y.S.2d 250, 662 N.E.2d 730, 28 UCC Rep. Serv. 2d 15 (Ct. App. 1995).

[107] UCC § 2-314, cmt. 3. See also § 2-314, Comment 7, which states, "In cases of doubt as to what quality is intended, the price at which a merchant closes a contract is an excellent index of the nature and scope of his obligation under the present section." This suggests that a buyer that pay s a rock-bottom price should have low expectations regarding quality.

[108] Only in Texas and Alabama have the courts held that section 2-314 is inapplicable to a merchant's sale of used goods. *See, e.g.,* Valley Datsun v. Martinez, 587 S.W.2d 485, 26 UCC Rep. Serv. 331 (Tex. Ct. Civ. App. 1979); Osborn v. Custom Truck Sales and Serv., 562 So. 2d 243, 12 UCC Rep. Serv. 2d 664 (Ala. 1990).

by showing that the product failed due to normal wear and tear.[109] On the other hand, buyers have recovered by tracing the failure of used goods to a design or manufacturing defect,[110] or by demonstrating that the goods were exposed to excessive wear and tear for their age.[111]

Although most of the reported cases have been decided under the "ordinary purposes" standard of Section 2-314(2)(c), the other standards set forth in Section 2-314(2) may also come into play. Under paragraph (a), for example, the goods must pass without objection in the trade under the contract description. This standard is illustrated by *Delano Growers' Cooperative Winery v. Supreme Wine Co., Inc.*,[112] in which a seller of California sweet wine incurred liability for selling wine that failed to meet industry standards due to the presence of too much purple nectar. Under paragraph (b), fungible goods must be of fair average quality, and in *T. J. Stevenson & Co., Inc. v. 81,193 Bags of Flour*[113] the buyer recovered when flour was found to contain an excessive level of beetle infestation.

Paragraph (e) requires that the goods be "adequately contained, packaged, and labeled as the agreement may require." The wording of the standard is problematic because a gap-filler would not be needed if the parties had reached agreement on the manner in which the goods were to be contained, packaged, or labeled. One possible interpretation is to limit the agreement language to labeling the goods and not apply it to containing or packaging them. However, the Comments indicate that the drafters intended something else: A situation "where the nature of the goods and of the transaction require a certain type of container, package or label."[114] Under paragraph (e), buyers have recovered when bottles have exploded,[115] when goods have broken during shipment,[116] when misleading labeling has made resale difficult,[117] and when inadequate labeling of cartons has caused confusion over the brand of appliances contained

---

[109] *See, e.g.*, Carey v. Woburn Motors, Inc., 29 UCC Rep. Serv. 1228 (Mass. Ct. App. 1980) (seller not responsible when used car broke down 29 days after purchase since failure was consistent with normal wear and tear).

[110] *See, e.g.*, Whittle v. Timesavers, Inc., 614 F. Supp. 115, 42 UCC Rep. Serv. 126 (W.D. Va. 1985).

[111] *See, e.g.*, Testo v. Dunmire Oldsmobile, Inc., 16 Wash. App. 39, 554 P.2d 349, 20 UCC Rep. Serv. 54 (1976) (used car failed within 200 miles of purchase and evidence showed that it had been raced by previous owner).

[112] 393 Mass. 666, 473 N.E.2d 1066, 40 UCC Rep. Serv. 93 (1985); *see also* Krack v. Action Motors Corp., 87 Conn. App. 687, 867 A.2d 86, 56 UCC Rep. Serv. 2d 368 (2005) (salvaged vehicle would not pass without objection in a sales contract in which it was described as used).

[113] 629 F.2d 338, 30 UCC Rep. Serv. 865 (5th Cir. 1980). The court actually relied on UCC § 2-314(2)(a), but § 2-314(2)(b) would have provided a more appropriate basis for the holding since it explicitly applies to fungible goods.

[114] UCC § 2-314, cmt. 10.

[115] *See, e.g.*, Seigel v. Giant Food, Inc., 20 Md. App. 611, 318 A.2d 874, 14 UCC Rep. Serv. 892 (1974).

[116] *See, e.g.*, Standard Brands Chemical Indus., Inc. v. Pilot Freight Carriers, Inc., 65 Misc. 2d 1029, 319 N.Y.S.2d 457, 9 UCC Rep. Serv. 422 (Sup. Ct. 1972).

[117] *See, e.g.*, Agricultural Services Ass'n v. Ferry-Morse Seed Co., 551 F.2d 1057, 21 UCC Rep. Serv. 443 (6th Cir. 1977).

within.[118] In *Gunning v. Small Feast Caterers, Inc.*,[119] a customer asserted a claim against a restaurant when a glass containing water exploded in his hand. The court held that the implied warranty of merchantability had been breached because the water had not been adequately contained and packaged.

Paragraph (f) operates in a manner that is fundamentally different from any of the other paragraphs. Paragraphs (a), (b), (d) and (e) are all subsets of the broader principle of paragraph (c) — that goods must be fit for their ordinary purposes. Paragraph (f) requires that goods "conform to the promises or affirmations of fact made on the container or label if any." For an example of the paragraph's operation, suppose a manufacturer makes representations (promises or affirmations of fact) on a label and then sells the goods to a retailer, which resells them to the public. By selling the goods, the retailer adopts the representations on the label as its own and, if they become part of the basis of the bargain, they constitute express warranties running from the retailer to its buyer. Even if they do not constitute express warranties, perhaps because the buyer did not read the container or label and a court holds that the representations did not become part of the basis of the bargain,[120] the buyer will have a cause of action for breach of the implied warranty of merchantability. If the buyer's express-warranty claim against the retailer is valid, the retailer will want to throw the loss back on the manufacturer. Whether the representations constitute express warranties running from the manufacturer to the retailer must be determined under Section 2-313. However, even if they do not, paragraph (f) will provide the retailer with a cause of action against the manufacturer for breach of the implied warranty of merchantability.[121]

[3] A Brief Comparison of the Implied Warranty of Merchantability and Strict Liability in Tort

A buyer that suffers harm because of a product defect may wish to pursue both a tort action and an action for breach of warranty. This section provides a brief comparison of the most commonly asserted tort and contract theories: strict products liability and the implied warranty of merchantability.

Under the Restatement (Third) of Torts, a person "engaged in the business of selling or otherwise distributing products who sells or distributes a defective product is subject to liability for harm to persons or property caused by the defect."[122] Liability attaches even though the seller has not been negligent in designing, manufacturing, or selling the goods, and in this respect the theory is similar to the theory that underlies the implied warranty of merchantability. As with that warranty, the types of product defects that may give rise to liability

---

[118] *See, e.g.*, Carnes Constr. Co. v. Richards & Conover Steel & Supply Co., 10 UCC Rep. Serv. 797 (Okla. Ct. App. 1972).

[119] 4 Misc. 3d 209, 777 N.Y.S.2d 268, 53 UCC Rep. Serv. 2d 502 (Sup. Ct. 2004).

[120] The basis-of-the-bargain requirement is discussed in § 5.02[A][3] *supra*.

[121] UCC § 2-314, Comment 10 states that paragraph (f) "follows from the general obligation of good faith which requires that a buyer should not be placed in the position of reselling or using goods delivered under false representations appearing on the package or container."

[122] Restatement (Third) of Torts: Products Liability § 1.

are design defects, defects in the manufacturing process, and defects in the instructions provided with the goods.[123]

Because strict products liability deals only with personal injury and property damage, it is generally unavailable when the loss is purely economic. The economic-loss doctrine, which precludes buyers from using tort theories to recover damages that are economic in nature, is discussed elsewhere in this chapter and the reader is referred to that material for a discussion of the types of cases to which the doctrine applies.[124] The current discussion assumes that the harm caused by the goods meets the threshold requirements for a tort action.

A number of differences distinguish an action based on strict products liability and an action based on breach of the implied warranty of merchantability. Because contract law allows parties to allocate risks while tort law performs a risk-sharing function, several contract defenses may not be available in tort. For example, parties may disclaim implied warranty liability[125] or limit the remedies available for breach.[126] Disclaimers and limitations of remedies are ordinarily ineffective to constrain strict products liability.[127]

Lack of contractual privity sometimes constitutes a valid defense to an action based on an implied warranty of merchantability,[128] but lack of privity is irrelevant to a claim based on strict products liability. The Restatement (Third) of Torts imposes liability on anyone who in a commercial context "transfers ownership [of a product] either for use or consumption or for resale leading to ultimate use or consumption. Commercial product sellers include but are not limited to, manufacturers, wholesalers, and retailers."[129]

Strict tort also precludes the contract defense that bars a buyer from any remedy if the buyer does not give notice of breach within a reasonable time after it discovers or should have discovered a defect.[130] The applicable statute of limitations also differs. The limitation period for breach of the implied warranty of merchantability is four years from tender of delivery of the goods,[131] and this period runs without regard to discovery of the defect that eventually causes the harm. Although the limitation period for strict products liability varies from state to state, the cause of action generally accrues at the time the defect is or should have been discovered.

---

[123] *See* § 5.02[B][2] *supra*; Restatement (Third) of Torts: Products Liability § 2.

[124] *See* § 5.08 *infra*; Restatement (Third) of Torts: Products Liability § 21.

[125] See UCC § 2-316, discussed in § 5.03[B] *infra*.

[126] See UCC § 2-719, discussed in § 5.04 *infra*.

[127] Restatement (Third) of Torts: Products Liability § 18. Comment d to that section states that the rule does not address whether a person "with full information and sufficient bargaining power, may contract with product sellers to accept curtailment of liability in exchange for concomitant benefits" or agree to an alternative dispute-resolution process.

[128] *See* § 5.06 *infra*.

[129] Restatement (Third) of Torts: Products Liability § 20.

[130] See UCC § 2-607(3)(a), discussed in § 7.03[B][3] *infra*.

[131] See UCC § 2-725(2), discussed in § 5.07 *infra*. The limitation period may be reduced by agreement to not less than one year but may not be extended by agreement. UCC § 2-725(1).

A jurisdiction's test for determining whether goods are merchantable may differ from the test for determining whether they are defective for purposes of strict products liability. The various tests for merchantability are discussed above.[132] Among the tests devised for tort defects are a consumer-expectations test and a risk/utility test. In *Denny v. Ford Motor Co.*[133] the court applied a consumer-expectations test to the plaintiff's warranty claim and a risk/utility test to her tort claim. The jury found that Ford had not committed a tort but was liable for breach of warranty. The drafters of amended Article 2 concluded that the application of inconsistent tests is inappropriate and stated in a Comment that "[w]hen recovery is sought for injury to person or property, whether goods are merchantable is to be determined by applicable state products liability law."[134]

[C] The Implied Warranty of Fitness for a Particular Purpose [§ 2-315; § 2A-213]

Although the implied warranty of fitness for a particular purpose can be made by any seller, not just a seller that is a merchant with respect to the goods,[135] it is much narrower in its application than the implied warranty of merchantability. It requires that the seller, at the time of contracting, have reason to know (1) of the particular purpose for which the buyer will be using the goods, and (2) that the buyer is relying on the seller's skill or judgment to select or furnish the goods.[136] These requirements are discussed below.

[1] Reason to Know Buyer's Particular Purpose

For the implied warranty of fitness to arise, the seller must have reason to know of the buyer's intended use of the goods. Article 2 does not define "reason to know" directly but its meaning can be gleaned from Section 1-202(a) dealing with notice. Under that provision, a person has " 'notice' of a fact if the person: 1) has actual knowledge of it; 2) has received a notice or notification of it; or 3) from all the facts and circumstances known to the person at the time in question, has reason to know that it exists." Based on paragraph (3), one can infer that a person has reason to know of a fact if, based on the universe of facts actually known[137] by the person, a reasonable person in the circumstances would have inferred the fact's existence. The Comments to Section 2-315 explain the reason-to-know requirement as follows:

---

[132] *See* § 5.02[B][2] *supra*.

[133] 87 N.Y.2d 248, 639 N.Y.S.2d 250, 662 N.E.2d 730, 28 UCC Rep. Serv. 2d 15 (Ct. App. 1995). The case is discussed in § 5.02[B][2] *supra*.

[134] UCC Amended § 2-314, cmt. 7.

[135] Because of the requirement that the buyer rely on the seller's skill or expertise in selecting or furnishing the goods, cases in which the seller is not a merchant with respect to the goods are relatively rare.

[136] UCC §§ 2-315, 2A-213.

[137] UCC § 1-202(b) provides that " '[k]nowledge' means actual knowledge. 'Knows' has a corresponding meaning." The Code's notice standard is not based on the concept of inquiry notice. That is, whether a seller has reason to know the ultimate fact is based on an inference from the facts known to the seller, not from the facts it might have known if it had inquired further.

Whether or not this warranty arises in any individual case is basically a
question of fact to be determined by the circumstances of the contracting. Under this section the buyer need not bring home to the seller
actual knowledge of the particular purpose for which the goods are
intended or of his reliance on the seller's skill and judgment, if the
circumstances are such that the seller has reason to realize the purpose
intended or that the reliance exists.[138]

In most cases, the buyer simply tells the seller why the goods are being
bought. For example, in *Computerized Radiological Services v. Syntex Corp.*,[139]
a group of radiologists told the seller they needed a machine for body scans. The
seller breached the implied warranty of fitness when it supplied a machine that
performed only head scans. In other cases, a seller lacking actual knowledge may
nevertheless incur liability. For example, in *Agricultural Services Association v.
Ferry-Morse Seed Co.*[140] a buyer purchased a quantity of seed that was obviously
too large for its personal use and the seller was found to have reason to know that
at least some of the seed would be resold. The implied warranty of fitness does
not arise if the buyer fails to communicate the purpose for which the goods are
being bought and the seller is unable to infer that purpose from the facts known
to it.[141]

[2] Particular Purpose vs. Ordinary Purpose

The implied warranty of fitness applies if the goods are used for a "particular
purpose." It appears that the drafters intended that the warranty not apply if
the buyer bought the goods for any of their ordinary purposes, although the
courts have not uniformly applied this distinction. The following statement from
the Comments makes the distinction clear:

A "particular purpose" differs from the ordinary purpose for which the
goods are used in that it envisages a specific use by the buyer which is
peculiar to the nature of his business whereas the ordinary purposes for
which goods are used are those envisaged in the concept of merchantability and go to uses which are customarily made of the goods in
question. For example, shoes are generally used for the purpose of
walking upon ordinary ground, but a seller may know that a particular
pair was selected to be used for climbing mountains.[142]

---

[138] UCC § 2-315, cmt. 1.

[139] 595 F. Supp. 1495, 40 UCC Rep. Serv. 49 (E.D.N.Y. 1984); *see also* Neilson Business
Equipment Center, Inc. v. Italo Monteleone, M.D., P.A., 524 A.2d 1172, 3 UCC Rep. Serv. 2d 1721
(Del. 1987) (seller that agreed to customize computer equipment to meet buyer's processing needs
gave warranty of fitness).

[140] 551 F.2d 1057, 21 UCC Rep. Serv. 443 (6th Cir. 1977).

[141] *See, e.g.*, Berryman Products, Inc. v. Additives, Inc., 2005 U.S. Dist. LEXIS 14472 (N.D. Tex.,
July 18, 2005) (third-party supplier did not have knowledge or reason to know that buyer planned to
use chemicals in aerosol cans); Hickham v. Chronister, 792 S.W.2d 631, 13 UCC Rep. Serv. 2d 132
(Mo. Ct. App. 1990) (seller of orthodontic molds not liable because orthodontist supplied the plans and
specifications).

[142] UCC § 2-315, cmt. 2.

Lewis v. Mobil Oil Corp.[143] is one of the leading cases on the "particular purpose" requirement. The seller recommended that the buyer, a sawmill operator, use a non-additive mineral oil in the sawmill's hydraulic system. Even though the oil was fit for its ordinary purposes, the buyer recovered because the oil failed to remedy the specific problem for which it had been selected. *Fiddler's Inn, Inc. v. Andrews Distributing Co., Inc.*[144] provides another example of a particular purpose. The buyer purchased heating units that failed to keep the rooms in its inn warm. The heaters were of merchantable quality but were too small for the buyer's rooms. Although use of the heaters in the large rooms qualified as a particular purpose, the seller avoided liability because the buyer had selected the heaters.

Most courts have understood that the implied warranty of fitness should not be invoked when goods are being used for an ordinary purpose. For example, in *Crysco Oilfield Services, Inc. v. Hutchison-Hayes International, Inc.*,[145] the court held that an implied warranty of fitness did not arise when shale shakers were used in oil fields for precisely the tasks for which they were manufactured. Similarly, in *Howard Construction Co. v. Bentley Trucking, Inc.*,[146] a buyer purchased sand to use in making cement and the court, finding that this use was an ordinary purpose, dismissed the buyer's claim for breach of the implied warranty of fitness.

A number of courts, undoubtedly influenced by the buyer's reliance on the seller's expertise, have essentially merged the implied warranty of merchantability and the implied warranty of fitness. These courts hold that a particular purpose is *any* purpose for which the buyer purchases the goods, including one of the ordinary purposes for which the goods are used. For example, *Renze Hybrids, Inc. v. Shell Oil Co.*[147] involved an insecticide that had been designed for use against a variety of insects. The buyer purchased the goods for use against one of these insects and the court held that this constituted a particular purpose. Similarly, the court in *Great Dane Trailer Sales, Inc. v. Malvern Pulpwood, Inc.*[148] held that when the buyer's particular purpose in purchasing the goods happens to be one of the ordinary purposes for which the goods were manufactured, the two warranties merge and the buyer can enforce either (assuming, of course, that for purposes of Section 2-314 the seller is a merchant with respect to the goods). The merger approach will be attractive to a buyer

---

[143] 438 F.2d 500, 8 UCC Rep. Serv. 625 (8th Cir. 1971).

[144] 612 S.W.2d 166, 31 UCC Rep. Serv. 1277 (Tenn. Ct. App. 1980).

[145] 913 F.2d 850, 12 UCC Rep. Serv. 2d 1019 (10th Cir. 1990); *see also* Fernandes v. Union Bookbinding Co., Inc., 400 Mass. 27, 507 N.E.2d 728, 5 UCC Rep. Serv. 2d 959 (1987) (warranty of fitness not breached when spacer-ply cutting press being used for its ordinary purpose caused personal injury); Solarz v. DaimlerChrysler Corp., 47 UCC Rep. Serv. 2d 969 (Pa. Ct. Com. Pl. 2002) (providing safe and reliable transportation is not the particular purpose of a minivan but rather its ordinary use).

[146] 186 S.W.3d 837 (Mo. Ct. App. 2006).

[147] 418 N.W.2d 634, 5 UCC Rep. Serv. 2d 1331 (Iowa 1988).

[148] 301 Ark. 436, 785 S.W.2d 13, 11 UCC Rep. Serv. 2d 875 (1990); *see also* Filler v. Rayex Corp., 435 F.2d 336, 8 UCC Rep. Serv. 323 (7th Cir. 1970) (young baseball player injured when flip-up baseball sunglasses shattered on being struck by a baseball).

whose seller is not a merchant with respect to the goods or whose seller has disclaimed the implied warranty of merchantability but not the implied warranty of fitness. It will also be attractive to a buyer that has not proved whether its purpose in buying the goods was ordinary or particular but that has otherwise proved the elements of Section 2-315.

In many cases the distinction between the implied warranties will be irrelevant. If the buyer has relied on the seller to select the goods, the seller likely will have stated expressly that they will do the job, giving rise to an express warranty. However, since the parol evidence rule[149] might preclude the buyer from introducing testimony of the express warranty, having an alternative theory based on an implied warranty might prove to be of critical importance.

[3]   Reason to Know of Buyer's Reliance

In addition to having reason to know of the buyer's particular purpose, the buyer must be relying on the seller's skill or judgment in selecting or furnishing the goods and the seller must have reason to know that fact.[150] For example, in *Light v. Weldarc Co., Inc.*[151] the buyer was blinded in one eye when his safety glasses slipped and he was struck by a flying object. The buyer admitted that he had been aware when he made the purchase that safety glasses are prone to slip and had accepted the pair in question even though they did not have a head strap. Under the circumstances the buyer's reliance was insufficient to invoke the implied warranty of fitness.[152]

Other buyers have lost because their own expertise undermined their claim of reliance. For example, in *O'Keefe Elevator Co., Inc. v. Second Avenue Properties, Ltd.*[153] the buyer of a wheelchair lift was found to have relied on its own knowledge rather than that of the seller. Another example is *Sylvia Coal Co. v. Mercury Coal & Coke Co.*,[154] in which a buyer claimed that the coal it purchased was unfit for making coke. The seller prevailed because it proved that it had no knowledge of the process for making coke and that the buyer was experienced in that regard.

[D]   The Warranties of Title and Against Infringement
[§ 2-312; § 2A-211]

The seller in a contract for the sale of goods impliedly warrants to the buyer that the seller has good title. Section 2-312(1) provides that:

(a)   the title conveyed shall be good, and its transfer rightful; and

(b)   the goods shall be delivered free from any security interest or other

---

[149] See UCC § 2-316(1) (express warranties subject to parol evidence rule), discussed in § 5.03[A] *infra*. For a general discussion of the parol evidence rule, see § 4.02 *supra*.

[150] The meaning of "reason to know" is discussed in § 5.02[C][1] *supra*.

[151] 569 So. 2d 1302, 14 UCC Rep. Serv. 2d 431 (Fla. Ct. App. 1992).

[152] The court did not address whether the buyer's use constituted a particular purpose.

[153] 216 Neb. 170, 343 N.W.2d 54, 37 UCC Rep. Serv. 1100 (1984).

[154] 151 W. Va. 818, 156 S.E.2d 1, 4 UCC Rep. Serv. 650 (1967).

lien or encumbrance of which the buyer at the time of contracting has no knowledge.

The seller need not be a merchant to breach the implied warranty of title. If the buyer loses its rights in the goods because of an adverse claim of ownership (as when the goods previously had been stolen, rendering the buyer's title void) or because of an enforceable security interest in the goods entitling the secured party to priority over the buyer, the warranty has been breached.

An exception to the warranty governs sales made in circumstances "which give the buyer reason to know that the person selling does not claim title in himself or that he is purporting to sell only such right or title as he or a third person may have."[155] Thus, the warranty of title does not arise for goods that are purchased at a sheriff's execution sale.[156] Prior to the adoption of revised Article 9, the exception also applied to goods purchased at a secured party's foreclosure sale. However, revised Section 9-610(d) reverses this result, and unless disclaimed[157] a secured party disposing of collateral at foreclosure makes "the warranties relating to title, possession, quiet enjoyment, and the like which by operation of law accompany a voluntary disposition of property of the kind subject to the contract."

Has the implied warranty of title been breached if a third party asserts a colorable claim to the goods that the buyer ultimately defeats? The Comments indicate that Article 2 has abolished any implied warranty of quiet possession,[158] suggesting that the seller is not liable for the costs that the buyer incurs in successfully defending against the claim. The Comments also state, however, that "[d]isturbance of quiet possession, although not mentioned specifically, is one way, among many, in which the breach of the warranty of title may be established" and that one of the purposes of the implied warranty of title is to ensure that the buyer "not be exposed to a lawsuit in order to protect [title]."[159] These statements suggest that the implied warranty of quiet possession still exists and has been merged into the implied warranty of title. The cases generally hold that the assertion by a third party of a claim that casts a substantial cloud on the buyer's title gives rise to a cause of action but that assertion of a frivolous claim does not.[160]

---

[155] UCC § 2-312(2).

[156] UCC § 2-312, cmt. 5.

[157] The warranty may be disclaimed as provided in UCC § 2-312 or under rules provided by UCC § 9-610(e) and (f).

[158] UCC § 2-312, cmt. 1.

[159] *Id.*

[160] *See, e.g.*, American Container Corp. v. Hanley Trucking Corp., 111 N.J. Super. 322, 268 A.2d 313, 7 UCC Rep. Serv. 1301 (1970) (casting of substantial shadow over buyer's title, regardless of the ultimate outcome, violates warranty of good title); C.F. Sales, Inc. v. Amfert, 344 N.W.2d 543, 38 UCC Rep. Serv. 844 (Iowa 1983) (to breach warranty of title, claim must be reasonable and colorable); Maroone Chevrolet, Inc. v. Nordstrom, 587 So. 2d 514, 15 UCC Rep. Serv. 2d 759 (Fla. Ct. App. 1991) (whether claim is substantial is an objective test, not predicated on the baseless anxiety of a hypersensitive buyer).

Article 2A does not include an implied warranty of title because the lessor does not deliver title to the goods to the lessee. Article 2A does, however, expressly recognize the implied warranty of quiet possession.[161] The Comments explain the warranty as follows:

> Inherent in the nature of the limited interest transferred by the lease-the right to possession and use of the goods-is the need of the lessee for protection greater than that afforded to the buyer. Since the scope of the protection is limited to claims or interests that arose from acts or omissions of the lessor, the lessor will be in position to evaluate the potential cost, certainly a far better position than that enjoyed by the lessee.[162]

Articles 2 and 2A protect the buyer and lessee from claims based on infringement of intellectual property rights if the seller or lessor is a merchant that regularly deals in goods of the kind.[163] In Article 2A, the warranty against infringement is not made by a finance lessor. Because the finance lessor does not participate in selection of the goods, it does not have any way to ensure that the goods in the lease do not infringe on patents of third parties. Liability, of course, does not extend to cases in which the buyer or lessee furnishes the specifications for the goods.[164]

§ 5.03 WARRANTY DISCLAIMERS [§ 2-316, § 2-312; § 2A-214]

Although Articles 2 and 2A provide buyers and lessees with a powerful array of express and implied warranty rights, they also include provisions that can be used to undercut significantly both the availability and the extent of warranty protection. Appropriate language in a sales or lease agreement can eliminate implied warranties, and a merger clause invoking the parol evidence rule can create a barrier to the enforcement of express warranties. Sections 2-316 and 2A-214 authorize "disclaimers"[165] of implied warranties, and, if a warranty is provided, Sections 2-719 and 2A-503 permit the parties by agreement to limit the available remedies. The discussion in this section addresses warranty disclaimers, while the next section covers modification of remedies.

---

[161] UCC § 2A-211(1).

[162] UCC § 2A-211, cmt.

[163] UCC §§ 2-312(3), 2A-211(2). "Merchant" is used more narrowly in these sections than in the sections dealing with the implied warranty of merchantability, which applies not only to merchants that are dealers but also to merchants that hold themselves out as having knowledge or skill with respect to the goods. See the discussion of merchants in § 5.02[B][1] *supra*.

[164] UCC §§ 2-312(3), 2A-211(3).

[165] Although the term "disclaimer" is commonly used, the Code actually speaks in terms of exclusion and modification of warranties. UCC §§ 2-316, 2A-214. These provisions, along with UCC § 2-312 dealing with warranties of title and against infringement, not only authorize disclaimers but also regulate the manner in which they may be made.

[A]   Express Warranty Disclaimers Not Effective

There is something inherently suspicious when a seller that has made an express warranty attempts to disclaim responsibility. Section 2-316(1) provides that if language or conduct tending to negate or limit the warranty is inconsistent with language or conduct relevant to its creation, the attempted negation or limitation is inoperative.[166] The Comments indicate that this rule protects buyers "from unexpected or unbargained language of disclaimer by denying effect to such language when inconsistent."[167]

Before finding an inconsistency, a court should attempt to find a practical construction that will harmonize and give effect to all the language and conduct.[168] On occasion, a seller has convinced a court to do so in a way that affords protection from the buyer's claim. In *Alan Wood Steel Co. v. Capital Equipment Enterprises, Inc.*,[169] the seller described the product as a "75 ton, 40 foot boom Brownhoist Steam Locomotive Crane" but also stated that all descriptions were approximations. The court held that the seller had not expressly warranted that the crane would lift 75 tons. In other cases, language that appears to limit or negate an express warranty sometimes has been construed so that it merely affects the extent of the warranty.[170]

As noted above, the statute provides that an attempted negation is inoperative if the language and conduct cannot be harmonized, and it is almost impossible to harmonize a representation that would constitute an express warranty with a broad statement purporting to disclaim all express warranties. For example, a pre-contract written statement that an irrigation system was trouble-free led the court to negate a blanket disclaimer of express warranties in *Whitaker v. Farmhand, Inc.*[171] Similarly, in *Fundin v. Chicago Pneumatic Tool Co.*[172] a blanket disclaimer did not protect a seller that had expressly warranted that a drilling rig could drill to a specified depth. In numerous other cases, courts have found blanket disclaimers or phrases like "as is" insufficient to negate express warranty claims.[173]

Section 2-316(1) includes a reminder that its provisions are subject to another potential limitation: The rule rendering disclaimers inoperative is subject to the

---

[166] UCC § 2A-214(1) is the same.

[167] UCC § 2-316, cmt. 1.

[168] UCC § 2-316(1) provides in part that "[w]ords or conduct relevant to the creation of an express warranty and words or conduct tending to negate or limit warranty shall be construed wherever reasonable as consistent with each other. . . ." Section 2A-214(1) includes nearly identical language.

[169] 39 Ill. App. 3d 48, 349 N.E.2d 627, 19 UCC Rep. Serv. 1310 (1976).

[170] In *Consolidated Papers, Inc. v. Dorr-Oliver, Inc.*, 153 Wis. 2d 589, 451 N.W.2d 456, 11 UCC Rep. Serv. 2d 492 (Ct. App. 1989), the seller warranted that a wood-processing machine was free from defects but also stated that decomposition by chemical action and wear did not qualify as a defect. Reading the language together, the court held that the seller had not warranted that the machine would not fail due to corrosion.

[171] 173 Mont. 345, 567 P.2d 916, 22 UCC Rep. Serv. 375 (1977).

[172] 152 Cal. App. 3d 951, 199 Cal. Rptr. 789, 38 UCC Rep. Serv. 55 (1984).

[173] *See, e.g.*, Perfection Cut, Inc. v. Olsen, 470 N.E.2d 94, 39 UCC Rep. Serv. 1237 (Ind. Ct. App. 1984).

parol evidence rule.[174] Consequently, a buyer may be precluded from introducing evidence of language or conduct that supports the existence of an express warranty, making a disclaimer unnecessary. For example, in *Investors Premium Corp. v. Burroughs Corp.*[175] the buyer alleged that the seller had made express warranties prior to the consummation of the sale. The court found that the parties had reduced their agreement to a final and complete writing that did not include the alleged warranty and granted summary judgment for the seller.[176] The application of the parol evidence rule to express warranties does not differ from its general application. The rule is discussed at length elsewhere in this book.[177]

[B]   Disclaiming the Implied Warranties of Merchantability and Fitness

The Code provides a number of mechanisms for disclaiming the implied warranties of merchantability and fitness. These warranties can be disclaimed by the use of certain "magic" words, by other language that is appropriate in the circumstances, by a buyer's conduct in examining the goods, or by a course of dealing, course of performance, or usage of trade. The ensuing subsections discuss these mechanisms.

[1]   Disclaimers Using "Safe-Harbor" Language

Sections 2-316(2) and 2A-214(2) provide that, to be effective, an exclusion or modification of the implied warranty of merchantability must use the word "merchantability."[178] To exclude or modify the implied warranty of fitness in a sale, the following language is suggested but not mandated: "There are no warranties which extend beyond the description on the face hereof."[179] In a lease, the suggested language is the following: "There is no warranty that the goods will be fit for a particular purpose." These provisions have generally been understood to create "safe harbors" for sellers and lessors.

---

[174] Section 2A-214(1) is similar.

[175] 389 F. Supp. 39, 17 UCC Rep. Serv. 115 (D.S.C. 1974).

[176] *See also* Valley Paving, Inc. v. Dexter & Chaney, Inc., 2000 Minn. App. LEXIS 897, 42 UCC Rep. Serv. 2d 433 (Aug. 22, 2000) (unpublished) (the court excluded evidence concerning an alleged oral warranty because the written agreement between the parties included a merger clause); Klickitat County Public Utility Dist. No. 1 v. Stewart & Stevenson Services, Inc., 59 UCC Rep. Serv. 2d 408 (E.D. Wash. 2006) (parol evidence rule precluded introduction of evidence relevant to existence of express warranty because parties adopted writing that was final and complete).

[177] *See* § 4.02 *supra*.

[178] Courts routinely permit sellers also to use the root word "merchantable," as in the phrase "there is no warranty that the goods will be merchantable."

[179] UCC § 2-316(2). Since the quoted language is just an example, phrases like "there is no warranty of fitness" or "there is no warranty that the goods will be fit for the particular purpose for which they were purchased" should also be effective. More general language may suffice as well, but its use is risky. *See, e.g.*, UCC § 2-316, cmt. 4; Thorman v. Polytemp, Inc., 2 UCC Rep. Serv. 772 (N.Y. Cty. Ct. 1965) (statement that express warranties were given "in lieu of all statutory or implied warranties" sufficient).

For sales transactions, the implied warranty of merchantability can be disclaimed orally, although only a foolish seller would attempt to do so. If the disclaimer is in a writing, it must be conspicuous. Any disclaimer of the implied warranty of fitness must be in a conspicuous writing. Article 2A does not make such a fine distinction, and disclaimers of both implied warranties must be in a conspicuous writing.[180]

Most of the litigation has centered on the conspicuousness requirement. The Code defines "conspicuous" as follows:

> 'Conspicuous', with reference to a term, means so written, displayed, or presented that a reasonable person against which it is to operate ought to have noticed it. Whether a term is 'conspicuous' or not is a decision for the court. Conspicuous terms include the following:
>
> (A) a heading in capitals equal to or greater in size than the surrounding text, or in contrasting type, font, or color to the surrounding text of the same or lesser size; and
>
> (B) language in the body of a record or display in larger type than the surrounding text, or in contrasting type, font, or color to the surrounding text of the same size, or set off from surrounding text of the same size by symbols or other marks that call attention to the language.[181]

The Comments offer the following additional guidance: "Although [paragraphs A and B] indicate some of the methods for making a term attention-calling, the test is whether attention can reasonably be expected to be called to it. The statutory language should not be construed to permit a result that is inconsistent with that test."[182] Put another way, the paragraphs do not create safe-harbors, and a disclaimer in microscopic font will not be made effective merely because the surrounding text is even smaller.

The definition creates an objective test, and the court must take into consideration the relative sophistication of the target group of buyers or lessees as opposed to the relative sophistication of the actual buyer or lessee. The words "reasonable person against which it is to operate" dictates this approach. More should be required to set off a disclaimer from the rest of a writing when the buyer is a consumer than when the buyer is a merchant.[183] Indeed, a court should find that each term of a writing is conspicuous if the contract was negotiated in detail by the attorneys for two sophisticated commercial entities.[184]

---

[180] UCC § 2A-214(2).

[181] UCC § 1-201(a)(10). The definition in the original version of Article 1 is less detailed.

[182] UCC § 1-201, cmt. 10.

[183] *See, e.g.,* Ellmer v. Delaware Mini-Computer Systems, Inc., 665 S.W.2d 158, 38 UCC Rep. Serv. 751 (Tex. Civ. App. 1983) (citing buyer sophistication as a factor in deciding whether a term is conspicuous).

[184] *See, e.g.,* American Elec. Power Co. v. Westinghouse Elec. Corp., 418 F. Supp. 435, 19 UCC Rep. Serv. 1009 (S.D.N.Y. 1976).

Courts frequently find disclaimers to be inconspicuous. In some cases sellers simply do not come close to compliance, as with a warranty disclaimer in the same type size, style, and color as the other language on a page of the seller's catalog.[185] Sometimes the headings used by the seller do not qualify. Examples include a case in which the court ruled that "Important Notice to Purchaser" was not conspicuous[186] and another in which the court held that "Factory Warranty" did not draw attention to the disclaimer set forth in the subsequent language because the heading suggested the creation of a warranty rather than its negation.[187] By contrast, a disclaimer was enforced because of a conspicuous paragraph heading that stated "Warranty, Disclaimers, and Limitation of Liabilities."[188]

A number of decisions deal with a disclaimer located on the reverse side of a standardized form. For example, in *Hunt v. Perkins Machinery Co., Inc.*[189] the front of the form made no reference to a disclaimer that was written in capital letters on the reverse side. Moreover, the form was attached to a pad and the buyer had no opportunity to examine the reverse side until after the contract was signed. The court had no difficulty invalidating the disclaimer. Sellers that use a reverse-side disclaimer should include a clear and conspicuous reference to the reverse side on the front of the form.[190] Of course, the disclaimer itself must also be conspicuous, and a conspicuous reference on the front of the form will not salvage an inconspicuous disclaimer on the back.[191]

In some instances, a court has upheld an inconspicuous disclaimer because the buyer was aware of it at the time of contracting. For example, in *Cates v. Dover Corp.*[192] the court denied summary judgment to the buyer of automotive lifts even though the disclaimer was inconspicuous because of a genuine issue regarding the buyer's knowledge of the disclaimer. This approach is troubling when the buyer is a consumer or a merchant that is unsophisticated relative to the seller. Making a disclaimer conspicuous is not difficult, and applying a

---

[185] Paper Mfgrs. Co. v. Rescuers, Inc., 60 F. Supp. 2d 869, 40 UCC Rep. Serv. 2d 146 (N.D. Ind. 1999).

[186] U.S. Steel v. Fiberex, Inc., 751 S.W.2d 638, 6 UCC Rep. Serv. 2d 1438 (Tex. Ct. App. 1988), *aff'd in part/rev'd in part*, 772 S.W.2d 442, 8 UCC Rep. Serv. 2d 991 (Tex. 1989).

[187] Blankenship v. Northtown Ford, Inc., 95 Ill. App. 3d 303, 420 N.E.2d 167, 31 UCC Rep. Serv. 480 (1981).

[188] Tulger Contracting Corp. v. Star Bldg. Sys., Inc., 52 UCC Rep. Serv. 2d 917 (S.D.N.Y. 2002).

[189] 352 Mass. 535, 226 N.E.2d 228, 4 UCC Rep. Serv. 281 (1967).

[190] *See, e.g.*, Moorer v. Hartz Seed Co., 120 F. Supp. 2d 1283, 43 UCC Rep. Serv. 2d 295 (M.D. Ala. 2000) (heading on invoices stated "ADDITIONAL TERMS, CONDITIONS, AND LIMITED WARRANTY ON BACK" just above the customer signature line plus a bold heading on the back stating "Limited Warranty" held conspicuous); Hamilton v. O'Connor Chevrolet, Inc., 399 F. Supp. 2d 860 (N.D. Ill. 2005) (conspicuous front-side references effective to call attention to terms on reverse-side); Massey-Ferguson v. Utley, 439 S.W.2d 57, 6 UCC Rep. Serv. 51 (Ky. Ct. App. 1969) (reference to reverse side in same color and type as other provisions on front of form held ineffective).

[191] *See, e.g.*, Norm Gershman's Things to Wear, Inc. v. Mercedes Benz of North America, Inc., 558 A.2d 1066, 9 UCC Rep. Serv. 2d 541 (Del. 1989).

[192] 790 S.W.2d 559, 12 UCC Rep. Serv. 2d 47 (Tex. Ct. Civ. App. 1990); *see also* Office Supply Co., Inc. v. Basic/Four Corp., 538 F. Supp. 776, 34 UCC Rep. Serv. 857 (E.D. Wis. 1982) (inconspicuous disclaimer effective because buyer's president was aware of it).

rigorous enforcement standard provides a strong incentive for compliance. Unless the buyer is a relatively sophisticated commercial entity, the court should invalidate an inconspicuous disclaimer.

[2]   Disclaimers Using Other Language

The safe-harbor rule of Section 2-316(2) is expressly made subject to Section 2-316(3), which reinforces the point by beginning with the words "Notwithstanding subsection (2)." The effect is clear — a disclaimer that is effective under subsection (3) need not comply with the formalities required for safe-harbor protection under subsection (2).

Subsection 3 contains three alternative methods for disclaiming implied warranties. Paragraph (a) states that, unless the circumstances indicate otherwise, a seller can disclaim all implied warranties by using expressions like " 'as is,' 'with all faults' or other language that in common understanding calls the buyer's attention to the exclusion of warranties and makes plain that there is no implied warranty."[193] The Comments state that "[s]uch terms in ordinary commercial usage are understood to mean that the buyer takes the entire risk as to the quality of the goods involved."[194] While the "magic words" of subsection (2) are effective in all circumstances, the alternative language of subsection (3)(a) is not a safe harbor and will not be effective if, in the circumstances, a buyer could not be expected to understand that it was intended to operate as a disclaimer. Because the statute refers to the "common understanding" of the language, what is important is not a particular buyer's understanding but the general understanding of the target group of buyers.

"As is" is included commonly in the sale of used goods, particularly automobiles,[195] but not in the sale of new goods. Thus, the court in *Gindy Manufacturing Corp. v. Cardinale Trucking Corp.*[196] held that the phrase did not disclaim the implied warranty of merchantability in a sale of new trucks. Even with used goods, a seller cannot be certain that an "as is" clause will be effective. For example, in *Knipp v. Weinbaum*[197] the court reversed summary judgment for a seller that used such a clause in connection with the sale of a used motorcycle. The fact that the buyer was an ordinary consumer might have convinced a jury that, under the circumstances, such a consumer would not have understood the meaning of the phrase.

Article 2 does not explicitly require clauses containing alternative language to be in a writing. It also does not require them to be conspicuous, and some courts

---

[193] UCC § 2A-214(3)(a) is the same. *See* Morningstar v. Hallett, 85 A.2d 125, 54 UCC Rep. Serv. 2d 716 (Pa. Super. Ct. 2004) ("as is" clause in contract disclaimed implied warranties but not express warranty that the horse being sold was eleven years old).

[194] UCC § 3-316, cmt. 7. The Comment suggests that "as they stand" is the equivalent of "as is" and "with all faults."

[195] The Federal Trade Commission Used Car Rule requires the use of "as is" to disclaim implied warranties. 16 CFR § 455.2(b).

[196] 111 N.J. Super. 383, 268 A.2d 345, 7 UCC Rep. Serv. 1257 (1970).

[197] 351 So. 2d 1081, 22 UCC Rep. Serv. 1141 (Fla. Ct. App. 1977).

have held inconspicuous language to be effective.[198] This approach is consistent with the Comments and with a literal reading of the provision, especially as compared with the immediately preceding subsection where the word "conspicuous" is used, but it may not be consistent with the underlying purpose of protecting the buyer from "unexpected and unbargained language"[199] and many courts have imposed a conspicuousness requirement.[200] Article 2A explicitly requires a conspicuous writing.[201]

[3] Examination of the Goods

If a buyer or lessee, before entering into a contract, has examined the goods or has refused a request that they be examined, "there is no implied warranty with regard to defects that an examination ought in the circumstances to have revealed."[202] The Code does not explicitly provide for the same result in the case of express warranties, but an examination in some contexts will preclude a valid claim based on an express warranty. Assume that a seller makes an affirmation of fact that the buyer completely disregards based on an examination of the goods. The seller can argue that under these circumstances the affirmation did not become part of the basis of the bargain and thus did not create an express warranty.

For the seller to avoid liability, the buyer must have actually examined the goods as fully as desired or must have refused to examine them. Refusal requires that the seller demand an examination, not merely give the buyer an opportunity for one.[203] Moreover, the examination or refusal must occur prior to contracting. Section 2-316(3)(b) refers to an "examination" rather than an "inspection." A buyer that receives goods generally has a right to inspect them before payment or acceptance,[204] but this has nothing to do disclaimers of warranties. If a post-contract inspection reveals a defect, it will justify rejection of the goods but will not operate to exclude warranty liability.[205]

The seller cannot prevail on the theory of warranty disclaimer through examination of the goods unless the defect is one that a reasonable examination would have revealed. Two factors bear on this issue: "[t]he particular buyer's

[198] *See, e.g.*, Joseph Charles Parrish, Inc. v. Hill, 173 Ga. App. 97, 325 S.E.2d 595, 40 UCC Rep. Serv. 1673 (1984) (inconspicuous phrase "I accept the above described car in its present condition" effective to disclaim all implied warranties); Harper v. Calvert, 687 S.W.2d 227, 39 UCC Rep. Serv. 1655 (Mo. App. 1984) (inconspicuous "as is" clause effective).

[199] UCC § 2-316, cmt. 1.

[200] *See, e.g.*, Fernandez v. Western R.R. Builders, Inc., 112 Idaho 907, 736 P.2d 1361, 5 UCC Rep. Serv. 2d 347 (1987); Board of Directors of Harriman v. Southwest Petroleum Corp., 757 S.W.2d 669, 7 UCC Rep. Serv. 2d 386 (Tenn. Ct. App. 1988); Lumber Mut. Ins. Co. v. Clarklift of Detroit, Inc., 224 Mich. App. 737, 569 N.W.2d 681, 33 UCC Rep. Serv. 2d 1105 (1997).

[201] UCC § 2A-214(3)(a).

[202] UCC §§ 2-316(3)(b), 2A-214(3)(b).

[203] *See, e.g.*, Calloway v. Manion, 572 F.2d 1033 (5th Cir. 1978); Agricultural Services Ass'n v. Ferry-Morse Seed Co., 551 F.2d 1057 (6th Cir. 1977); UCC § 2-316, cmt. 8.

[204] UCC § 9-513(1).

[205] *See, e.g.*, Murray v. Kleen Leen, Inc., 41 Ill. App. 3d 436, 354 N.E.2d 415, 20 UCC Rep. Serv. 298 (1976) (examination of pigs on delivery).

skill and the normal method of examining goods in the circumstances."[206]
Accordingly, professionals are held to a higher standard than buyers that have
no expertise with regard to the goods.[207]

[4] Post-Contracting Disclaimers

Sellers sometimes attempt to disclaim a warranty after the contract for sale
has been consummated. The disclaimer may be located on an invoice, or it might
be printed in a warranty booklet that is not turned over to the buyer until the
goods are delivered.[208] At an earlier time, courts routinely invalidated such
disclaimers on the ground that they represented unilateral attempts to modify
existing contracts.[209] This is less true today because in some contexts courts
today will enforce terms first disclosed after a buyer has made payment and
received the goods. The impact of these cases on post-contract disclaimers is
discussed elsewhere.[210]

Sellers frequently ask buyers to return postcards after the sale to register
the product for express-warranty purposes, and in doing so the seller may
attempt to use the postcard to show the buyer's assent to a contract
modification. This argument did not succeed in *Van der Broeke v. Bellanca
Aircraft Corp.*[211] The buyer, a commercial crop duster, ordered an airplane
manufactured by the defendant and several months later received a warranty
booklet containing a disclaimer. The buyer subsequently returned the warranty-
registration postcard to the manufacturer. The postcard did not make any
reference to the disclaimer and had not been signed by the buyer. The court
found the evidence to support a modification to be insufficient because the
postcard did not indicate the buyer's assent to the disclaimer. Even if there had
been a modification, the lack of a signature would probably have rendered it

---

[206] UCC § 2-316, Comment 8 refers to "[t]he particular buyer's skill and the normal method of
examining goods in the circumstances."

[207] *See, e.g.*, Hall Truck Sales, Inc. v. Wilder Mobile Homes, Inc., 402 So. 2d 1299, 32 UCC Rep.
Serv. 440 (Fla. Dist. Ct. App. 1981) (buyer of earth-moving machine should have discovered machine's
inability to grade soil); Twin Lakes Mfg. Co., Inc. v. Coffey, 222 Va. 467, 281 S.E.2d 864, 32 UCC Rep.
Serv. 770 (1981) (consumer buyer could not be expected to discover defect in mobile home's frame).

[208] Occasionally, a disclaimer is located in a security agreement that is executed after the contract
for sale has been consummated. Section 9-206(2) of original Article 9 made it clear that Article 2
governs the sales aspects of the transaction, and Comment 3 to that section stated that it "prevents
a buyer from inadvertently abandoning his warranties by a 'no warranties' term in the security
agreement when warranties have already been created under the sales arrangement." The scope of
Section 9-206 was extended beyond buyers and lessees of goods in revised Article 9 [§ 9-403(b)] and
thus the revision contains no counterpart to original Section 9-206(2). Nevertheless, the principle
remains unchanged.

[209] Kalmes Farms, Inc. v. J-Star Indus., Inc., 52 UCC Rep. Serv. 2d 845 (D. Minn. 2004)
(disclaimer in owner's manual provided to the buyer two months after installation of the silo
unloader); Nebraska Plastics, Inc. v. Holland Colors Am., Inc., 51 UCC Rep. Serv. 2d 1100 (D. Neb.
2003) (disclaimer included in material safety data sheet delivered to buyer after bargain had been
negotiated); Sithon Maritime Co. v. Holiday Mansion, 983 F. Supp. 977, 35 UCC Rep. Serv. 2d 108
(D. Kan. 1997) (disclaimer in maintenance manual for boat engines that was not received by buyer
until after entering into contract).

[210] *See* § 2.05 *supra*.

[211] 576 F.2d 582, 24 UCC Rep. Serv. 594 (5th Cir. 1978).

unenforceable under the statute of frauds.[212]

The court in *Tolmie Farms, Inc. v. Stauffer Chemical Co.*[213] upheld a post-contract disclaimer contained in an invoice. The court noted that such clauses generally are ineffective, but the parties had engaged in similar transactions over a long period of time and on each occasion the buyer had received an invoice containing the disclaimer. According to the court, the buyer had acquiesced to the seller's terms, giving rise to a course of dealing. The court's analysis is troubling. The evidence did not show that the buyer had been aware of the earlier disclaimers and, since material terms in confirmations generally are ineffective,[214] the buyer was justified on each occasion in not reading the invoice. It is difficult to see how a term that was ineffective in each instance could become effective through cumulative use unless the buyer had at some point become aware of it. The Code does provide for disclaimers through course of dealing, course of performance, or usage of trade,[215] but a prerequisite for a course of dealing is a common basis of understanding.[216] Since the buyer was unaware of the earlier disclaimers, the common basis was missing in *Tolmie Farms*.

[C]   Disclaiming the Warranties of Title, Quiet Possession, and Against Infringement [§ 2-312; § 2A-214]

Section 2-312(2) provides that the warranty of title may be excluded or modified by "specific language" but provides no further guidance. It includes no magic words or suggested language and makes no reference to conspicuousness. The text does not refer to the warranty as an "implied" warranty and thus Section 2-316(3)(a), which provides that language like "as is" may be effective to disclaim all implied warranties, does not apply.[217] Consistent with the language of Section 2-312(2), the courts generally have required a fairly high level of specificity. Thus, the court in *Rockdale Cable T.V. Co. v. Spadora*[218] held that a statement that the seller purported to transfer only such right title and interest as he might possess was insufficient. Section 2-312(3), which deals with disclaimers of the warranty against infringement, appears to require less by way of specificity, stating only that the warranty exists "[u]nless otherwise agreed." Nevertheless, a seller seeking to disclaim this warranty would be well

---

[212] UCC § 2-209(3). The statute-of-frauds provision governing modifications is discussed in § 3.06 *supra.*

[213] 124 Idaho 607, 862 P.2d 299, 23 UCC Rep. Serv. 2d 65 (1993).

[214] See the discussion of UCC § 2-207(2) in § 2.04[C] *supra.*

[215] UCC §§ 2-316(3)(c); 2A-214(3)(c). These concepts are discussed generally in § 4.03 *supra.*

[216] UCC § 2-205(1).

[217] UCC § 2-312, cmt. 6. Section 2-316(3)(a) is discussed in § 5.03[B][2] *supra.* Article 2A's warranty of quiet possession and the warranty against infringement found in both articles are likewise not "implied" warranties.

[218] 97 Ill. App. 3d 754, 423 N.E.2d 555, 33 UCC Rep. Serv. 176 (1981). The seller ultimately prevailed because the court found that in the circumstances it should have realized that the seller was not warranting title. *See also* Jones v. Linebaugh, 34 Mich. App. 305, 191 N.W.2d 142, 9 UCC Rep. Serv. 1187 (1971) (language common to quitclaim deed insufficient).

advised to use specific language. Section 2A-214(4) requires that to be effective language disclaiming both the warranty of quiet possession and the warranty against infringement must be specific.

Notwithstanding the lack of a statutory requirement, sellers should make their disclaimers conspicuous out of concern that courts, consistent with the rationale used by some courts to require conspicuousness with regard to "as is" disclaimers,[219] will impute such a requirement into the statute. With regard to lessees, Section 2A-214(4) explicitly requires that disclaimers of the warranty of quiet possession and the warranty against infringement "be by a writing, and be conspicuous."

Section 2-312(2) also provides that the warranty of title may be excluded or modified by circumstances "which give the buyer reason to know that the person selling does not claim title in himself or that he is purporting to sell only such right or title as he or a third person may have."[220] For example, the warranty does not arise for goods purchased at a sheriff's execution sale.[221] Prior to the adoption of revised Article 9, the same principle applied to goods purchased at a secured party's foreclosure sale. However, revised Section 9-610(d) reverses this result, and unless disclaimed[222] a secured party disposing of collateral at foreclosure makes "the warranties relating to title, possession, quiet enjoyment, and the like which by operation of law accompany a voluntary disposition of property of the kind subject to the contract."

Although not explicitly stated, surely the circumstances from which a disclaimer of the warranty of title may be inferred include a course of performance, course of dealing, or usage of trade. Again, Article 2A is explicit on the point, with Section 2A-214(4) permitting both the warranty of quiet possession and the warranty against infringement to be disclaimed by "circumstances, including course of performance, course of dealing, or usage of trade, [that] give the lessee reason to know that the goods are being leased subject to a claim or interest of any person." The same result clearly applies with regard to the Article 2 warranty against infringement because it is disclaimed if the parties otherwise agree and inferences from the three implied-in-fact sources would be part of the agreement.

[D]   Disclaimers and Unconscionability

Can a disclaimer that meets the requirements of Section 2-316(2) nevertheless fail under the unconscionability doctrine?[223] Several of the illustrations in the Comments to Section 2-302, the general unconscionability

---

[219] *See* § 5.03[B][2] *supra.*

[220] UCC § 2-312(2).

[221] UCC § 2-312, cmt. 5; *see also*, Spoon v. Herndon, 167 Ga. App. 794, 307 S.E.2d 693, 37 UCC Rep. Serv. 928 (1983) (fact that buyer received from seller certificate of title to car indicating another person as seller could have led a jury to conclude that buyer should have realized that seller was not warranting title).

[222] The warranty may be disclaimed as provided in UCC § 2-312 or under rules provided by UCC § 9-610(e) and (f).

[223] Unconscionability is discussed generally in § 4.05[A] *supra.*

section, involve warranty disclaimers.[224] Their inclusion suggests that the drafters thought that mere mechanical compliance with the Code's language and conspicuousness requirements would not be enough to insulate disclaimers from attack. On the other hand, Section 2-316 does not expressly mention unconscionability, as does its counterpart — Section 2-719 — dealing with limited-remedy clauses. Furthermore, the requirements of section 2-316(2) are precise and relatively easy to police, suggesting the absence of any need for the more general policing doctrine of unconscionability. Arguably procedural unconscionability should be difficult or impossible to show if the requirements of the section are met.[225]

A majority of courts have concluded that disclaimers are subject to the unconscionability doctrine,[226] although a number of decisions provide to the contrary.[227] Numerous states have resolved the issue by enacting nonuniform legislation forbidding disclaimers of implied warranties in consumer transactions.[228] In addition, the Magnuson-Moss Warranty Federal Trade Commission Improvement Act,[229] discussed elsewhere in this chapter,[230] precludes disclaimers in certain contexts.

§ 5.04 MODIFICATION OR IMPAIRMENT OF RIGHTS AND REMEDIES [§ 2-719; § 2A-503]

[A] Exclusive-Remedy Clauses

A seller that does not disclaim warranties may nonetheless seek to limit its exposure for their breach. The Code facilitates this approach by permitting the agreement to provide for remedies that are in addition to or in substitution for those that would otherwise be available, and to limit or alter the ordinary measure of damages.[231] Although either party may take advantage of Section 2-719, in practice it is sellers that typically make use of it and they almost invariably prefer to limit available remedies rather than provide additional

---

[224] UCC § 2-302, cmt. 1.

[225] The policy arguments are articulated in Leff, *Unconscionability and the Code — The Emperor's New Clause*, 115 U. Pa. L. Rev. (1967) (arguing that UCC § 2-316 preempts application of the unconscionability doctrine), and Phillips, *Unconscionability and Article 2 Implied Warranty Disclaimers*, 62 Chi.-Kent L. Rev. 199 (1985) (arguing that unconscionability should be used aggressively to invalidate disclaimers).

[226] *See, e.g.*, Rottinghaus v. Howell, 35 Wash. App. 99, 666 P.2d 899, 37 UCC Rep. Serv. 42 (1983); FMC Fin. Corp. v. Murphree, 632 F.2d 413, 30 UCC Rep. Serv. 496 (5th Cir. 1980).

[227] *See, e.g.*, Ohio Savings Bank v. H. L. Vokes Co., 54 Ohio App. 3d 68, 560 N.E.2d 1328, 13 UCC Rep. Serv. 2d 92 (1989) (UCC § 2-302 inapplicable to warranty disclaimers in a commercial setting); Ford Motor Co. v. Moulton, 511 S.W.2d 690, 14 UCC Rep. Serv. 312 (Tenn.), *cert. denied*, 419 U.S. 870 (1974).

[228] *See, e.g.*, Md. Com. Law Ann. § 2-316 (1982); Mass. Ann. Laws ch. 106, § 2-316A (1984); Kan. Stat. Ann. § 50-636(a) (1983).

[229] 15 U.S.C. § 2301 *et seq.*

[230] *See* § 5.09[B] *infra.*

[231] UCC § 2-719(1). Article 2A is comparable. UCC § 2A-503(1).

remedies. Without an exclusive-remedy clause, the buyer might have a right to reject nonconforming goods, revoke acceptance of them,[232] or keep them and recover direct, incidental, and consequential damages.[233]

A common technique used by sellers is to expressly warrant that the goods will be free from defects in material and workmanship for a stated period of time and then specify that the exclusive remedy for breach of this warranty is repair or replacement of the defective part or the defective product.[234] The seller also commonly provides that, at its option, it may refund the purchase price. The typical writing also disclaims all other express[235] and all implied warranties and provides that the writing is the complete and exclusive agreement of the parties, thereby invoking the parol evidence rule to preclude the buyer from testifying that the seller made other express warranties. A seller's success with this strategy requires careful drafting, and even then circumstances may cause the strategy to fail. To be effective, an exclusive-remedy clause must be agreed to by the parties[236] and must expressly state that the remedy or remedies are intended to be exclusive.[237] Even if carefully drafted, post-contracting events may cause the clause to fail its essential purpose,[238] in which case the buyer will have access to all of the ordinary Code remedies in addition to the contractual remedy. Finally, a limitation or exclusion of consequential damages may be held unconscionable.[239]

Although they both operate to limit a seller's exposure to liability and may even operate in tandem, warranty disclaimers and exclusive-remedy clauses address distinct legal issues. An effective disclaimer eliminates the affected warranty from the transaction, thereby precluding a cause of action that could otherwise have been brought based on breach of the warranty. The seller obviously does not need to limit the remedies available for breach of an effectively disclaimed warranty. By contrast, an exclusive-remedy clause is based on the assumption that the seller is in breach of warranty or another contractual obligation and limits the nature of the buyer's remedies or the amount of damages that the buyer can recover.[240] Based on this fundamental

---

[232] Rejection and revocation of acceptance are discussed in §§ 7.04, 7.05 *infra.*

[233] Monetary damages for breach of warranty are discussed in § 8.02[D] *infra.*

[234] Many sellers do not warrant the quality of the goods but rather promise it will repair or replace any part proven to be defective within a certain period of time after purchase. The distinction between an express warranty with a limited remedy clause and a repair-or-replace promise is discussed in § 5.07 *infra* on the statute of limitations.

[235] See § 5.03[A] *supra,* which discusses the general ineffectiveness of express-warranty disclaimers.

[236] UCC §§ 2-709(1)(a), 2A-503(1).

[237] UCC §§ 2-709(1)(b), 2A-503(2).

[238] UCC §§ 2-709(2), 2A-503(2); *see* discussion § 5.04[A][2] *infra.*

[239] UCC §§ 2-709(3), 2A-503(3); *see* discussion § 5.04[B] *infra.*

[240] *See, e.g.,* Iron Dynamics v. Alstom Power, Inc., 64 UCC Rep. Serv. 2d 201 (N.D. Ind. 2007). The text of Article 2 highlights the distinction between warranty disclaimers and exclusive-remedy clauses. UCC § 2-316, which deals generally with disclaimers, provides as follows in subsection (4): "Remedies for breach of warranty can be limited in accordance with the provisions of this Article on liquidation or limitation of damages and on contractual modification of remedy (Sections 2-718 and

distinction, the topic of exclusive-remedy clauses does not entirely fit within this chapter on warranties. We nevertheless discuss the topic at this point both to highlight the distinction between exclusive-remedy clauses and warranty disclaimers and to emphasize the combined role that the two types of provisions play in limiting a seller's exposure.

Unlike implied-warranty disclaimers under Section 2-316(2), the statute does not require that either an exclusive-remedy clause or a clause limiting or excluding consequential damages be conspicuous. This disparity has led most courts to refuse to impose such a requirement,[241] although some decisions are to the contrary.[242]

[1]   "Expressly Agreed to Be Exclusive"

Section 2-719(2)(b) provides that "resort to a remedy as provided is optional unless the remedy is expressly agreed to be exclusive, in which case it is the sole remedy." The provision creates a presumption that a contractually described remedy is cumulative with the other remedies available under Article 2.[243] For the stated remedy to operate as the exclusive remedy, the parties must express such an intent.

The courts have not required that the writing use the word "exclusive," only that the language make it clear that the stated remedy is the sole remedy and is not optional.[244] For example, in *Fredonia Broadcasting Corp. v. RCA Corp.*[245] a TV station was not permitted to recover monetary damages against a seller that sold it defective equipment. The contract stated that correction of defects by repair and replacement "shall constitute the fulfillment of all RCA's obligations in respect of the equipment furnished." On occasion, courts have been willing to

---

2-719)." The point is obvious, and Article 2A does not include a comparable provision.

[241] *See, e.g.*, McCrimmon v. Tandy Corp., 202 Ga. App. 233, 414 S.E.2d 15, 17 UCC Rep. Serv. 2d 1134 (1992) (limitation on consequential damages); Island Creek Coal Co. v. Lake Shore, Inc., 832 F.2d 274, 4 UCC Rep. Serv. 2d 1067 (4th Cir. 1987) (limitation on consequential damages); Lara v. Hyundai Motor America, 331 Ill. App. 3d 53, 264 Ill. Dec. 416, 770 N.E.2d 721, 47 UCC Rep. Serv. 2d 1379 (2002), *appeal denied*, 201 Ill. 2d 571, 271 Ill. Dec. 927, 786 N.E.2d 185 (2002) (limitation on consequential damages). Some courts, while not holding that there is a conspicuousness requirement, have nevertheless noted the fact that a limitation or exclusion of consequential damages is conspicuous in determining that it is enforceable. *See, e.g.*, Morgan Bldgs. and Spas, Inc. v. Humane Soc. of Southeast Texas, 65 UCC Rep. Serv. 2d 308 (Tex. Ct. App. 2008).

[242] *See, e.g.*, Moscatiello v. Pittsburgh Contractors Equip. Co., 407 Pa. Super. 363, 595 A.2d 1190, 16 UCC Rep. Serv. 2d 71 (1991) (exclusive-remedy clause); Stauffer Chem. Co. v. Curry, 778 P.2d 1083, 10 UCC Rep. Serv. 2d 342 (Wyo. 1989) (exclusive-remedy clause). A limitation on consequential damages must be conspicuous to be effective under the Magnuson-Moss Warranty-Federal Trade Commission Improvement Act, discussed in § 5.09[B] *infra*.

[243] UCC § 2-719, Comment 2 states that "[s]ubsection (1)(b) creates a presumption that clauses prescribing remedies are cumulative rather than exclusive. If the parties intend the term to describe the sole remedy under the contract, this must be clearly expressed."

[244] Ralston Purina Co. v. Hartford Accident & Indem. Co., 540 F.2d 915 (8th Cir. 1976) (contract term that provided that the buyer "may" make one of two elections held not to be mandatory in nature); Cannon v. Neal Walker Leasing, Inc., 1995 Ohio App. LEXIS 2839, 39 UCC Rep. Serv. 2d 1139 (June 28, 1995) (unpublished) (because the agreement did not indicate that the remedy was exclusive, it was in addition to other available remedies, including revocation of acceptance).

[245] 481 F.2d 781 (5th Cir. 1973).

construe ambiguous language in the seller's favor, particularly in commercial transactions. For example, in *Evans Manufacturing Corp. v. Wolosin*,[246] the court held that a statement that repair or replacement was provided in lieu of all other *warranties* was found to be exclusive. Other courts have required more clarity, and in *Ford Motor Co. v. Reid*[247] the court held that language almost identical to that in *Evans Manufacturing* did not create an exclusive remedy because the reference to other warranties did not make it clear that the *remedy* was to be exclusive.

[2] Failure of Essential Purpose

If an exclusive remedy fails its essential purpose, the buyer's right to pursue other remedies is restored. Most of the cases involve sellers that either fail to honor the exclusive remedy or try but cannot effectuate the remedy in a timely fashion. In *Select Pork, Inc. v. Babcock Swine, Inc.*,[248] the exclusive remedy specified return of the purchase price in the event of nonconformity. When the seller delivered the wrong kind of pigs and then refused to give a refund, the buyer's ordinary remedies were restored. In *Great Dane Trailer Sales, Inc. v. Malvern Pulpwood, Inc.*,[249] the court held that an exclusive repair-or-replace remedy failed its essential purpose when the seller's shoddy repair work left the buyer's trailer in an unsafe condition. The court in *Erection Specialists, Inc. v. Edwards Duetz Diesel, Inc.*[250] held that an unreasonable delay in providing parts for a repair made the manufacturer liable for damages proximately caused by the delay.[251] By contrast, the court in *Potomac Constructors, LLC v. EFCO Corp.*,[252] upheld an exclusive repair-or-replace clause in a contract to supply steel formwork for a bridge's support structure despite the significant delay in making needed repairs. The court stressed that the contract was between sophisticated commercial entities, the goods were of complex design, there was no allegation of bad faith, and the goods were actually repaired.

Numerous cases have dealt with "lemons." A lemon is goods that the seller cannot repair despite repeated attempts. In some cases, the same problem repeats itself; in others, the goods manifest a series of unrelated defects. In the typical case, the buyer eventually becomes frustrated and attempts either to

---

[246] 1 UCC Rep. Serv. 193 (Pa. Ct. C.P. 1957).

[247] 250 Ark. 176, 465 S.W.2d 80, 8 UCC Rep. Serv. 985 (1971).

[248] 640 F.2d 147, 30 UCC Rep. Serv. 839 (8th Cir. 1981). The contract also contained a clause excluding consequential damages, which the court found unconscionable under UCC § 2-719(3).

[249] 301 Ark. 436, 785 S.W.2d 13, 11 UCC Rep. Serv. 2d 875 (1990); *see also* Lara v. Hyundai Motor Am., 331 Ill. App. 3d 53, 47 UCC Rep. Serv. 2d 1379 (Ill. Ct. App. 2002) (trial court erred in granting summary judgment for a seller who allegedly failed after fourteen attempts over a two-year period to repair various parts of the buyer's vehicle).

[250] 2005 U.S. Dist. LEXIS 33047 (E.D. Tenn., June 28, 2005).

[251] *See also* Stone Transport, Inc. v. Volvo Trucks N. Am. Inc., 57 UCC Rep. Serv. 2d 77 (6th Cir. 2005) (repair-or-replace remedy failed of its essential purpose when purchasers of trucks were not able to have warranty work performed on the trucks away from the home dealership because other dealers of the trucks did not have adequate parts and because of recurrent problems due to the inability to repair certain defects).

[252] 530 F. Supp. 2d 731, 65 UCC Rep. Serv. 2d 731 (D. Md. 2008).

revoke acceptance or to recover damages. The seller, of course, insists on additional repair opportunities. The decisions in this area exhibit a disturbing lack of uniformity.[253] Clearly, the exclusive remedy will fail its essential purpose at some point, but the buyer must guess as to when that will occur.[254] Generally, consumer buyers are afforded more protection than commercial buyers, and sellers will be given more repair opportunities when the goods are complex than when they are simple.[255]

In a few cases, the exclusive remedy has failed its essential purpose even though the seller was willing to abide by it in a timely fashion. For example, in *Rudd Construction Equipment Co. v. Clark Equipment Co.*[256] a parts manufacturer's exclusive repair-or-replace remedy failed its essential purpose when a part caused the machine in which it was installed to catch fire. The court held that merely replacing the part would not provide the buyer with a "fair quantum" of a remedy. This approach finds support in the Comments, which state:

> [I]t is of the very essence of a sales contract that at least minimum adequate remedies be available. If the parties intend to conclude a contract for sale within this Article they must accept the legal consequences that there be at least a fair quantum of remedy for breach of the obligations or duties outlined in the contract.[257]

A few courts have invoked the essential-purpose test to invalidate clauses that give the buyer an unreasonably short period of time to assert a claim for breach of warranty. For example, in *Wilson Trading Corp v. David Ferguson, Ltd.*[258] a contract for the sale of yarn provided that no claims could be asserted more than ten days after receipt of the yarn. The problem was that the buyer could not discover the yarn's tendency to fade unevenly until after the yarn had been knitted into sweaters and washed, and because enforcement of the ten-day provision would have left the buyer without a remedy, the court held that the provision failed its essential purpose. The analysis is somewhat unsatisfying because it was not an exclusive remedy that failed but rather a problem caused by an unreasonable time limitation that had the effect of precluding all remedies,

---

[253] *Compare* Liberty Truck Sales, Inc. v. Kimbrel, 548 So. 2d 1379, 9 UCC Rep. Serv. 2d 908 (Ala. 1989) (repair remedy failed its essential purpose when new trucks needed four repairs), *with* Belcher v. Versatile Farm Equip. Co., 443 So. 2d 912, 37 UCC Rep. Serv. 706 (Ala. 1983) (repair remedy did not fail its essential purpose despite four attempts to repair).

[254] Most states address this problem for consumers buying new motor vehicles. Lemon laws are discussed in § 5.09[C] *infra*.

[255] *See, e.g.* Delmarva Power & Light Co. v. ABB Power T & D Co., Inc., 47 UCC Rep. Serv. 2d 1033 (Del. Super. Ct. 2002) (repair remedy did not fail of its essential purpose, despite the fact that repairs required two months, because the seller acted promptly and diligently in effecting the repair and the product sold was a sophisticated and complex piece of machinery that operated in conjunction with the generator of the utility).

[256] 735 F.2d 974, 38 UCC Rep. Serv. 873 (6th Cir. 1984); *see also,* Andover Air Ltd. Partnership v. Piper Aircraft Corp., 7 UCC Rep. Serv. 2d 1494 (D. Mass. 1989) (remedy worth $10 failed its essential purpose when buyer's losses exceeded $100,000).

[257] UCC § 2-719, cmt. 1.

[258] 23 N.Y.2d 398, 297 N.Y.S.2d 108, 244 N.E.2d 685, 5 UCC Rep. Serv. 1213 (1968).

thereby acting as an indirect disclaimer. Although not directly on point, the court appropriately referenced Article 1, which provides that "[w]henever [the Uniform Commercial Code] requires any action to be taken within a reasonable time, a time that is not manifestly unreasonable may be fixed by agreement."[259] Given the nature of the goods and the defect, the ten-day limitation in *Wilson Trading* was manifestly unreasonable.

[B]   Remedy Limitations and Unconscionability

The Comments to Section 2-719 provide the following reminder that the general unconscionability doctrine of Section 2-302 applies to exclusive-remedy clauses by stating that "any clause purporting to modify or limit the remedial provisions of this Article in an unconscionable manner is subject to deletion and in that event the remedies made available by this Article are applicable as if the stricken clause had never existed."[260]

Sellers often seek to limit their exposure to liability through clauses that limit or exclude consequential damages. Section 2-719(3) expressly sanctions such clauses, but here the drafters were not content to rely on the Comments and provided explicitly that such clauses are subject to an unconscionability test.[261] If the consequential damages consist of personal injuries caused by consumer goods,[262] a clause precluding the consumer from recovering for the injuries is prima facie unconscionable, a presumption that is virtually impossible to overcome.[263] When the product causes personal injury to someone other than a consumer, the presumption of unconscionability does not apply. Thus, the court in *Schlenz v. John Deere Co.*[264] correctly placed the burden of establishing unconscionability on the buyer, a farmer who was injured while using farm machinery. There is less here than meets the eye since a person whose personal injuries are caused by defective goods will typically have a cause of action in tort based on strict products liability.

Even without the presumption, a consumer buyer may be able to convince a court that a clause limiting or excluding consequential damages is unconscionable. For example, in *Fischer v. General Electric Hotpoint*,[265] a case in which a consumer sought to recover for food that spoiled when the purchased refrigerator failed, the court found that a clause excluding consequential damages was unconscionable. By contrast, an exclusionary clause was upheld in

---

[259] Unrevised UCC § 1-204(1) [revised § 1-302(1)].

[260] UCC § 2-719, cmt. 1. Unconscionability is discussed in § 4.05[A] *supra*.

[261] Section 2A-503(3) is the same.

[262] Although Article 2 does not expressly import the Article 9 definition of consumer goods, it no doubt is applicable. Under that definition, consumer goods are "goods that are used or bought for use primarily for personal, family, or household purposes." UCC § 9-102(a)(23).

[263] Martin v. American Med. Sys., Inc., 116 F.3d 102, 32 UCC Rep. Serv. 2d 1101 (4th Cir. 1997) (clause excluding damages unconscionable as applied to consumer injured by penile implant); Tuttle v. Kelly-Springfield Tire Co., 585 P.2d 1116, 24 UCC Rep. Serv. 1070 (Okla. 1978) (clause excluding damages unconscionable as applied to consumer injured after tire blowout).

[264] 511 F. Supp. 224, 31 UCC Rep. Serv. 1020 (D. Mont. 1981).

[265] 108 Misc. 2d 683, 438 N.Y.S.2d 690, 31 UCC Rep. Serv. 849 (Sup. Ct. 1981).

NEC Techs., Inc. v. Nelson,[266] a case involving a consumer's claim for loss suffered in a burglary when the seller's burglar alarm failed. The court emphasized the fact that the buyer understood the nature of the risk and chose not to insure against the risk of burglary.

When the buyer is a commercial entity, most courts have routinely upheld clauses limiting or excluding consequential damages,[267] although a few decisions favor the buyer. For example, in *Oldham's Farm Sausage Co. v. Salco, Inc.*[268] the buyer suffered over $200,000 in consequential losses when sausage-processing equipment failed to operate properly. The court held that the clause, which was buried in fine print, was unconscionable.

[C] Exclusive-Remedy Clauses and Clauses Limiting or Excluding Consequential Damages in Combination

Sellers frequently use both exclusive-remedy clauses and clauses limiting or excluding consequential damages. This approach provides them with two lines of defense: If effective, the exclusive-remedy clause will preclude the recovery of consequential damages, but if that clause fails its essential purpose the limit on consequential damages will still reduce the seller's overall exposure. Some courts have confounded a seller's expectations by holding that the failure of an exclusive-remedy clause also rendered the clause limiting consequential damages unenforceable.[269]

A majority of the decisions have analyzed the two clauses independently. For example, the leading case of *American Electric Power Co. v. Westinghouse Electric Corp.*[270] involved the sale of a $12 million generator to a public utility. The court analyzed the clauses independently because they were stated in separate sections of the contract, the transaction was between two large

---

[266] 267 Ga. 390, 478 S.E.2d 769, 31 UCC Rep. Serv. 2d 992 (1987).

[267] *See, e.g.*, Canal Elec. Co. v. Westinghouse Elec. Corp., 973 F.2d 988, 18 UCC Rep. Serv. 2d 391 (1st Cir. 1992) (limitation conscionable in contract for sale of power generators entered into by two large electric companies); Blevins v. New Holland North America, Inc., 97 F. Supp. 2d 747, 42 UCC Rep. Serv. 2d 97 (W.D. Va. 2000) (clause excluding consequential damages conscionable even though contained in terms delivered after sale and employee of buyer suffered personal injury); Monarch Nutritional Labs., Inc. v. Maximum Human Performance, Inc., 2005 U.S. Dist. LEXIS 36000 (D. Utah, July 18, 2005) (clause excluding consequential damages was effective automatically under UCC § 2-207(2) because it did not materially alter contract and was not unconscionable); Starr v. Dow Agrosciences LLC, 339 F. Supp. 2d 1097, 54 UCC Rep. Serv. 2d 563 (D. Or. 2005) (clause excluding consequential damages effective to preclude farmer from recovering lost profits caused by defective herbicide).

[268] 633 S.W.2d 177 (Mo. Ct. App. 1982); *see also*, A&M Produce Co. v. FMC Corp., 185 Cal. App. 3d, 186, Cal. Rptr. 114, 34 UCC Rep. Serv. 1129 (1982) (clause excluding consequential damages unconscionable in contract for sale of equipment to farmer).

[269] *See, e.g.*, Arabian Ag. Serv. Co. v. Chief Indus., Inc., 309 F.3d 479, 48 UCC Rep. Serv. 2d 1394 (8th Cir. 2002); Matco Mach. & Tool Co. v. Cincinnati Milacron Co., 727 F.2d 777, 37 UCC Rep. Serv. 1577 (8th Cir. 1984).

[270] 418 F. Supp. 435, 19 UCC Rep. Serv. 1009 (S.D.N.Y. 1978); *see also*, Blevins v. New Holland North America, Inc., 97 F. Supp. 2d 747, 42 UCC Rep. Serv. 2d 97 (W.D. Va. 2000); Sheehan v. Monaco Coach Co., 2006 U.S. Dist. LEXIS 5557 (W.D. Wis., Jan. 25, 2006).

commercial entities, the machinery was complex and somewhat experimental, and after the exclusive-remedy clause was struck the buyer still had a minimum adequate remedy — recovery of the purchase price.

Section 2-719(2), read in isolation, supports the interconnectedness of the clauses by stating that upon failure of an exclusive-remedy clause an aggrieved party is entitled to the remedies provided by Article 2, and these would include consequential damages in appropriate cases.[271] Nevertheless, the *American Electric* decision is correct. Section 2-719(2) applies the essential-purpose test only to exclusive-remedy clauses,[272] and deciding whether such a clause has failed is a fact determination that is based on the seller's post-contract behavior. The unconscionability test for determining the effectiveness of a clause limiting or excluding consequential damages is found in Section 2-719(3).[273] This issue is for the court and is based on circumstances existing at the time the contract is formed.[274]

This analysis does not deny a correlation between the failure of an exclusive-remedy clause and the unconscionability of a clause limiting or excluding consequential damages. The current trend is to approach the issue on a case-by-case basis, examining factors such as whether the clauses as drafted appear to be dependent upon each other, whether enforcing the clause limiting or excluding consequential damages would leave the buyer without a minimum adequate remedy, and whether the seller's willful or dilatory conduct in failing to effectuate the exclusive remedy proximately caused the consequential damages.[275] If upon examination the court determines that the consequential damages did not flow from the failure of the exclusive-remedy clause and that the contract adequately represents the parties' real understandings regarding the allocation of risks, the clause limiting or excluding consequential damages is enforced.[276] This approach applies even if the buyer is a small business or consumer rather than a sophisticated commercial entity.[277]

---

[271] UCC § 2-719, Comment 1 is to the same effect.

[272] UCC §§ 2-719(2), 2A-503(2).

[273] UCC § 2A-503(3) is the consistent.

[274] UCC § 2-302 provides in relevant part as follows: "If the court as a matter of law finds the contract or any clause of it to have been unconscionable *at the time it was made.* . . ." (emphasis supplied).

[275] *See, e.g.*, Employers Ins. Co. of Wausau v. Suwannee River Spa Lines, Inc., 866 F.2d 752, 8 UCC Rep. Serv. 2d 659 (5th Cir. 1989).

[276] *See, e.g.*, Piper Jaffray & Co. v. SunGard Sys. Internat'l, Inc., 57 UCC Rep. Serv. 2d 479 (D. Minn. 2005).

[277] *See, e.g.*, Sheehan v. Monaco Coach Corp., 2006 U.S. Dist. LEXIS 5557 (W.D. Wis., Jan. 25, 2006) (court relies in part on language in consumer contract providing that exclusive-remedy and exclusion-of-consequential damages clauses were to be construed independently).

§ 5.05   DEFENSES BASED ON THE CLAIMANT'S CONDUCT

In order to prevail on a breach-of-warranty claim, a buyer must establish more than the existence of the warranty and its breach by the seller. It must also show that it suffered a loss proximately caused by the breach.[278] In this regard the buyer must be able to withstand claims that its own misconduct caused the loss.

The text of the Code refers to proximate cause only in Section 2-715(2)(b), which provides that a buyer may recover consequential damages based on personal injury or property loss "proximately resulting from any breach." However, the fact that the words are not used elsewhere does not negate their applicability to damages generally. Section 2-715(2)(b) uses them to make warranty law congruent with tort law when the damages are cognizable in tort, but the concept applies equally to other types of consequential damages[279] and to direct damages as well. The following except from the Comments reveals the drafters' intention that proximate cause to be broadly applicable.

> In an action based on breach of warranty, it is of course necessary to show not only the existence of the warranty but the fact that the warranty was broken and that the breach of the warranty was the proximate cause of the loss sustained.[280]

Given the fundamental role of proximate cause in tort law, courts inevitably have drawn from tort concepts in assessing the effect of a buyer's misconduct on its claim for breach of warranty. Many courts, following the Comments, have addressed the issue using the language of causation.[281] Other courts have used terms like product misuse, contributory negligence, comparative negligence, and assumption of the risk. Much of the confusion in this area is the result of semantics since the core issue, however described, can be boiled down to causation.

Like tort claims based on strict products liability,[282] warranty claims do not depend on a seller's negligence and many courts have followed the approach of the Restatement (Second) of Torts, which categorically rejects contributory negligence as a defense.[283] By contrast and again consistent with the Second

---

[278] *See, e.g.*, Broucher v. Northeastern Log Homes, Inc., 57 UCC Rep. Serv. 2d 105 (D. Me. 2005), *recommendation adopted*, 365 F. Supp. 2d 1 (D. Me. 2005) (insufficient for buyer to show that goods were used and injury followed; buyer must also show that seller's breach of warranty caused the injury).

[279] Consequential damages are discussed generally in § 8.02[E] *infra*.

[280] UCC § 2-314, cmt. 13.

[281] *See, e.g.*, Johnson v. Monsanto Co., 48 UCC Rep. Serv. 2d 586 (Ohio Ct. App. 2002) (unpublished) (grant of summary judgment improper because genuine issue of material fact existed as to whether chemicals buyer mixed with the seller's herbicide before application constituted misuse and, in turn, whether seller's breach proximately caused buyer's loss).

[282] See § 5.02[B][3] *supra*, which contains a brief comparison between strict products liability and the implied warranty of merchantability.

[283] Regarding contributory negligence, Restatement (Second) of Torts § 402A, Comment n, provides that "[c]ontributory negligence of the plaintiff is not a defense when such negligence

Restatement, the courts have been receptive to the defense of assumption of the risk. The Second Restatement describes assumption of the risk as follows:

> [In contrast with contributory negligence generally], the form of contributory negligence which consists in voluntarily proceeding to encounter a known danger, and commonly passes under the name of assumption of risk, is a defense under this Section as in other cases of strict liability. If the user or consumer discovers the defect and is aware of the danger, and nevertheless proceeds unreasonably to make use of the product and is injured by it, he is barred from recovery.[284]

Although the distinction between conduct that constitutes mere negligence and conduct that constitutes assumption of the risk can be paper thin, if the approach described above is followed it makes all the difference in the world. Contributory negligence is not a defense at all; assumption of the risk is a complete defense.[285]

The Code does not refer to contributory negligence or assumption of the risk, but the drafters clearly understood that a buyer's conduct would have a bearing on the issue of causation. The Comments to Sections 2-314 and 2-715 address the proposition as follows:

> In such [a breach-of-warranty] action an affirmative showing by the seller that the loss resulted from some action or event following his own delivery of the goods can operate as a defense. . . . Action by the buyer following an examination of the goods which ought to have indicated the defect complained of can be shown as matter bearing on whether the breach itself was the cause of the injury.[286]

> Where the injury involved follows the use of goods without discovery of the defect causing the damage, the question of "proximate" cause turns on whether it was reasonable for the buyer to use the goods without such inspection as would have revealed the defects. If it was not reasonable for him to do so, or if he did in fact discover the defect prior to his use, the injury would not proximately result from the breach of warranty.[287]

These Comments suggest that a failure to inspect or a less-than-competent inspection goes to the issue of proximate cause and may even constitute a complete defense. A failure to inspect or a careless inspection would constitute contributory negligence rather than assumption of the risk under tort law; however, as noted above, most decisions have been consistent with the approach adopted by the Restatement (Second) of Torts. For example, the court in *Upjohn Co. v. Rachelle Lab., Inc.*[288] concluded that the buyer's loss was proximately

---

consists merely in a failure to discover the defect in the product or to guard against the possibility of its existence."

[284] *Id.*

[285] *See, e.g.,* Duff v. Bonner Bldg. Supply, Inc., 105 Ida. 123, 666 P.2d 650 (1983) (no defense on mere contributory negligence while conduct that constitutes misuse or assumption of the risk constitutes complete defense).

[286] UCC § 2-314, cmt. 13.

[287] UCC § 2-715, cmt. 6.

[288] 661 F.2d 1105, 32 UCC Rep. Serv. 747 (6th Cir. 1981); *see also,* Wallace v. Owens-Illinois, Inc.,

caused by a breach of warranty even though an inspection by the buyer would have revealed the defect. Although using the language of causation, the court rejected entirely the defense of contributory negligence.

Not every court has rejected contributory negligence as a defense. For example, the court in *Malul v. Capital Cabinets, Inc.*[289] held that the negligence of a buyer of kitchen cabinets who installed them too close to his stove could be considered in determining the proximate cause of the deformation of the cabinet doors but that it would not constitute a defense unless it was determined to be the sole cause. An occasional court has gone further and held that contributory negligence constitutes a complete defense.[290]

Again consistent with the Restatement (Second) of Torts, negligence that rises to the level of assumption of the risk has generally been accepted as a complete defense to a warranty action. For example, in *Krajewski v. Enderes Tool Co., Inc.*[291] a farmer who suffered eye injuries when a pry bar splintered brought an action against the manufacturer of the bar alleging breach of an implied warranty of merchantability and strict products liability. The evidence showed that the farmer had removed his safety goggles while using the bar even though he knew there might have been flying debris even if it had not splintered. Because he understood the danger and voluntarily exposed himself to it, he assumed the risk and was entirely precluded from recovering under either cause of action.

Concluding that the radically different results produced when assumption of the risk constitutes a complete defense and contributory negligence does not constitute a defense at all cannot be justified under tort law, a majority of states have adopted comparative fault for strict products liability actions. Recognizing this trend, the Restatement (Third) of Torts no longer distinguishes between contributory negligence and assumption of the risk; rather, it adopts the general principle of comparative fault and leaves it to the states to determine the mechanics of apportionment.[292] The shift is explained as follows:

> Section 402A of the Restatement, Second, of Torts, recognizing strict liability for harm caused by defective products, was adopted in 1964 when the overwhelming majority rule treated contributory negligence as a total bar to recovery. Understandably the [American Law] Institute was reluctant to bar a plaintiff's products liability claim in tort based on

---

300 S.C. 518, 389 S.E.2d 155, 11 UCC Rep. Serv. 2d 835 (Ct. App. 1989); Fernandes v. Union Bookbinding Co., 400 Mass. 27, 507 N.E.2d 728, 5 UCC Rep. Serv. 2d 959 (1987); Coulter v. American Bakeries Co., 530 So. 2d 1009, 7 UCC Rep. Serv. 2d 49 (Fla. Dist. Ct. App. 1988).

[289] 191 Misc. 2d 399, 740 N.Y.S.2d 828, 47 UCC Rep. Serv. 2d 502 (City Civ. Ct. 2002); *see also,* Ford Motor Co. v. Lee, 137 Ga. App. 486, 224 S.E.2d 168, 18 UCC Rep. Serv. 1184 (1976), *aff'd in part, rev'd in part,* 237 Ga. 554, 229 S.E.2d 379 (1976) (contributory negligence not a defense per se but jury permitted to consider buyer's negligence in determining causation).

[290] *See, e.g.,* Dewitt v. Eveready Battery Co., 144 N.C. App. 143, 550 S.E.2d 511 (2001) (buyer of batteries injured by battery acid).

[291] 396 F. Supp. 2d 1045, 59 UCC Rep. Serv. 2d 1 (D. Neb. 2005); *see also* Monsanto Co. v. Logisticon, Inc., 763 S.W.2d 371, 9 UCC Rep. Serv. 2d 934 (Mo. Ct. App. 1989) (assumption of risk complete defense to action based on breach of implied warranty of merchantability).

[292] Restatement (Third) of Torts: Products Liability § 17.

conduct that was not egregious. . . . Since then, comparative fault has swept the country. Only a tiny minority of states retain contributory negligence as a total bar.[293]

Courts have occasionally used a comparative fault analysis even in the absence of a statute. For example, in *Signal Oil & Gas Co. v. Universal Oil Products*[294] a refinery discovered that a piece of equipment had been assembled improperly two months before it caused a fire. The court held that the jury should have been instructed to allocate the loss between the parties based on a comparison of their fault.

A majority of states have adopted comparative fault by statute for at least some causes of action and the courts have had to determine the extent to which the statutes apply to warranty actions. For example, the court in *Correia v. Firestone Tire & Rubber Co.*[295] declined to apply a comparative-fault statute that by its terms was applicable to actions based on negligence to warranty actions and also declined to adopt the doctrine as a matter of common law. By contrast, the comparative-fault statute at issue in *Fiske v. MacGregor, Division of Brunswick*[296] referred to actions based on personal injury and the court held that it applied to a warranty claim. Citing a similar statute that applied comparative fault to personal injury actions, the court in *Little Rock Elec. Contractors, Inc. v. Okonite Co.*[297] declined to extend comparative fault to a case involving purely economic loss.

§ 5.06 PRIVITY

Lack of privity of contract created an impenetrable barrier for a party with a breach of warranty claim at common law.[298] This barrier meant that only a buyer could bring a warranty action, not a person other than a buyer that might be harmed by the goods, and the buyer's action could be brought only against its immediate seller. Courts generally interpreted the Uniform Sales Act, the Code's predecessor, as being in accord with this common-law tradition.

---

[293] *Id.*, cmt. a.

[294] 572 S.W.2d 320, 24 UCC Rep. Serv. 555 (Tex. 1978); *see also* Frazer v. A. F. Munsterman, Inc., 123 Ill. 2d 245, 527 N.E.2d 1248, 7 UCC Rep. Serv. 2d 121 (1988) (relying on UCC § 2-715, Comment 5, as basis for using comparative fault).

[295] 388 Mass. 342, 446 N.E.2d 1033 (1983).

[296] 464 A.2d 719, 36 UCC Rep. Serv. 1128 (R.I. 1983).

[297] 294 Ark. 399, 744 S.W.2d 381, 5 UCC Rep. Serv. 2d 978 (1988); *see also* Broce-O'Dell Concrete Products, Inc. v. Mel Jarvis Construction Co., Inc., 634 P.2d 1142, 32 UCC Rep. Serv. 762 (Kan. Ct. App. 1981) (statute required allocation of fault for personal-injury actions and court, reasoning by analogy to economic-loss doctrine, declined to apply principle to case in which breach of an express warranty led to purely economic loss); *Cf.* Dakota Grain Co., v. Ehrmantrout, 502 N.W.2d 234, 23 UCC Rep. Serv. 2d 402 (N.D. 1993) (allocation of fault appropriate in calculating purely economic damages because comparative fault statute referred to warranty actions).

[298] *See generally* Prosser, *The Fall of the Citadel (Strict Liability to the Consumer)*, 50 Minn. L. Rev. 791 (1966).

[A]   Horizontal and Vertical Privity Generally [§ 2-318; § 2A-216]

Privity problems comprise two different types of cases that may be classified as horizontal and vertical. The issue in a vertical privity case is which remote sellers in the chain of distribution qualify as proper defendants. The issue in a horizontal privity case is which persons other than a seller's immediate buyer qualify as proper plaintiffs. The following chart may help in understanding the terminology:

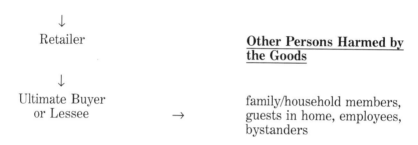

Chain of Distribution

Manufacturer

↓

Retailer   **Other Persons Harmed by the Goods**

↓

Ultimate Buyer
or Lessee   →   family/household members,
                                    guests in home, employees,
                                    bystanders

If the ultimate buyer brings an action against the manufacturer, the issue will be one of vertical privity. If the ultimate buyer's spouse brings an action against the retailer, the issue will be one of horizontal privity. An action by the spouse against the manufacturer raises issues of both horizontal (whether the spouse is a proper plaintiff) and vertical (whether the manufacturer is a proper defendant) privity.

The extent to which lack of privity should be eroded as a defense proved contentious when Article 2 began to be widely adopted in the states. Originally the drafters provided a uniform answer with regard to horizontal privity but were silent with regard to vertical privity. However, many state legislatures determined that the uniform provision was too restrictive and enacted nonuniform provisions, sometimes badly drafted. The nonuniform provisions sometimes were limited to horizontal privity and sometimes addressed vertical privity as well. Eventually, the Code was amended to provide three well-drafted alternatives. The original provision became Alternative A, with Alternatives B and C being progressively more expansive in describing the protected class for horizontal privity purposes. Alternatives B and C also eliminated the vertical-privity requirement for the protected class. Alternative A has been adopted by a majority of states, although many of them have made nonuniform changes to the language. Some states adopting Alternatives B and C have also made nonuniform changes. The three official alternatives state as follows:

Alternative A. A seller's warranty whether express or implied extends to any natural person who is in the family or household of his buyer or who is a guest in his home if it is reasonable to expect that such person may use, consume or be affected by the goods and who is injured in person by breach of the warranty. A seller may not exclude or limit the operation of this section.

Alternative B. A seller's warranty whether express or implied extends to any natural person who may reasonably be expected to use, consume or be affected by the goods and who is injured in person by breach of the warranty. A seller may not exclude or limit the operation of this section.

Alternative C. A seller's warranty whether express or implied extends to any person who may reasonably be expected to use, consume or be affected by the goods and who is injured by breach of the warranty. A seller may not exclude or limit the operation of this section with respect to injury to the person of an individual to whom the warranty extends.[299]

Each alternative treats members of the protected class as third-party beneficiaries. In the case of Alternative A, the class members are third-party beneficiaries only as to warranties made by the last seller in the distributive chain. Under Alternatives B and C, the class members are third-party beneficiaries of the warranties made by any seller in the chain.

Under Alternative A, the absence of privity still provides a defense if the plaintiff does not incur personal injuries,[300] is not in the buyer's family or household or a guest in the buyer's home, or could not reasonably be expected to use, consume, or be affected by the goods. Notably, the described class does not include bystanders, employees, and guests of the buyer outside the home (*e.g.,* passengers in the buyer's car). An important issue is whether the defined class should be treated as a floor or as a ceiling. In other words, are the courts free to extend protection to persons outside the class? Since the states adopting Alternative A, even when it was the only alternative available, were free to expand the class, the Code's Permanent Editorial Board concluded that the alternative creates a ceiling.[301] As might be expected, however, a few courts have determined otherwise.[302] Whether a claimant is a member of the protected class or not is less important than it may at first appear since a person who has suffered personal injuries usually will be able to recover on the tort theory of strict products liability, which has dispensed with all privity barriers.[303]

The last sentence of Alternative A precludes a seller from excluding or limiting the operation of Section 2-318. This does not mean that a seller may not

---

[299] UCC § 2-318. UCC § 2A-216 is comparable.

[300] Because the Alternative requires personal injury, a protected person must be a "natural person," meaning an individual rather than an entity. Alternative B is the same in this regard.

[301] Permanent Editorial Board for the Uniform Commercial Code, Rpt. No. 3, at 13 (1967).

[302] *Compare* Curlee v. Mock Enterprises, Inc., 41 UCC Rep. Serv. 63 (Ga. Ct. App. 1985) (guest on houseboat lacked standing), *and* Thompson v. Rockford Mach. Tool Co., 744 P.2d 357, 4 UCC Rep. Serv. 2d 1418 (Wash. Ct. App. 1987) (employee lacked standing), *with* Whitaker v. Lian Feng Mach. Co., 156 Ill. App. 3d 316, 509 N.E.2d 591, 4 UCC Rep. Serv. 2d 444 (1987) (employee had standing), *and* Reed v. City of Chicago, 263 F. Supp. 2d 1123, 50 UCC Rep. Serv. 2d 146 (N.D. Ill. 2003) (statutory class extended to cover prisoner who hanged himself using a paper gown that was designed to tear away).

[303] See § 5.02[B][3] *infra* for a comparison of strict products liability and liability based on an implied warranty of merchantability.

disclaim warranties or limit remedies for their breach. As noted above, a protected claimant is a third-party beneficiary and may assert only the rights of the person that received the warranty. What the last sentence means is that a seller that makes a warranty may not by contract prevent it from running to the members of the protected class.

As noted above, Alternatives B and C erode the privity barrier further than does Alternative A.[304] Alternative B still encompasses only personal injuries, but it expands the class of potential plaintiffs to include any natural person. Alternative C eliminates the limitation that restricts recovery to personal injury and expands the defined class to encompass any person, whether an individual or an entity. Like Alternative A, Alternatives B and C preclude a seller from excluding or limiting the operation of Section 2-318. However, Alternative C permits a seller to limit the operation of the section to persons who suffer personal injury, which would effectively make the class of protected persons the same as the class protected by Alternative B.

As noted above, Section 2-318 initially addressed only the issue of horizontal privity. This conclusion is clear from the language of Alternative A, the only choice originally provided to the states, permitting enforcement of a seller's warranty by a person "who is in the family or household of *his buyer* or who is a guest in *his* home."[305] Regarding vertical privity, the Comments state that:

> The first alternative expressly includes as beneficiaries within its provisions the family, household and guests of the purchaser. Beyond this, the section in this form is neutral and is not intended to enlarge or restrict the developing case law on whether the seller's warranties, given to his buyer who resells, extend to other persons in the distributive chain.[306]

Alternatives B and C do not have language similar to the "his buyer" and "his home" language of Alternative A and thus address vertical as well as horizontal privity issues. Also unlike Alternative A, they may be used by a buyer in the chain of distribution if the buyer falls within the described class.

Although the last seller in the chain of distribution is often the most convenient defendant, that seller may have gone out of business, may lack adequate resources to compensate the claimant, or may have effectively disclaimed its warranty liability, leaving an injured buyer or third party to pursue sellers higher up the chain. As noted above, Alternative A does not address this vertical-privity issue, but Alternatives B and C do. For example, in *Cruickshank v. Clean Seas Co.*[307] a commercial retailer bought marine paint from a distribu-

---

[304] Although all three of the alternatives define the class of potential plaintiffs differently, they all require that the members of the defined class must reasonably be expected to "use, consume or be affected by the goods."

[305] UCC § 2-318, alt. A (emphasis supplied).

[306] UCC § 2-318, cmt. 3.

[307] 346 B.R. 571, 60 UCC Rep. Serv. 2d 460 (D. Mass. 2006); *see also* Coverstar, Inc. v. Cooley, Inc., 60 UCC Rep. Serv. 2d 170 (D. Utah 2006) (Alternative C controlled breach-of-warranty claim brought by distributor against remote manufacturer of component part); Rampey v. Novartis Consumer Health, Inc., 867 So. 2d 1079, 51 UCC Rep. Serv. 2d 117 (Ala. 2003) (in denying recovery

tor, which in turn had bought the paint from the manufacturer. The retailer incurred liability to its customers when the paint proved to be defective, and it brought an action against the manufacturer seeking to enforce express and implied warranties made by the manufacturer to the distributor. The court held that Massachusetts's version of Section 2-318, which was nonuniform but similar to Alternative C, was the controlling law. The manufacturer prevailed because the court held that it could not have reasonably expected the retailer to use, consume, or be affected by the goods.

Because of the ready availability of the tort theory of strict products liability, vertical privity, like horizontal privity, is rarely needed when personal injury is involved. Indeed, in *Kramer v. Piper Aircraft Corp.*[308] the Florida Supreme Court held that injured airplane passengers could not assert a warranty claim against a remote manufacturer because of the availability of strict products liability. If relief in tort is not available, as when a state has not adopted the theory of strict products liability or the statute of limitations has run in tort but not in contract, most courts have dropped the vertical privity requirement.[309] For similar reasons most jurisdictions do not adhere to a privity requirement for claims involving the type of property damage cognizable in tort.[310]

The decisions vary more when the plaintiff's claim is for economic loss, meaning direct damages (*i.e.*, loss of value of the goods themselves) or consequential damages other than the types of property damage cognizable in tort (*e.g.*, lost profits). In the leading case of *Morrow v. New Moon Homes, Inc.*,[311] the buyers of a mobile home sued the remote manufacturer when the home proved to be seriously defective. The court permitted the action, observing that:

> A number of courts recently confronting this issue have declined to overturn the privity requirement in warranty actions for economic loss. One principal factor seems to be that these courts simply do not find the social and economic reasons which justify extending enterprise liability to the victims of personal injury or property damage equally compelling in the case of a disappointed buyer suffering "only" economic loss. There is an apparent fear that economic losses may be of a far greater magnitude in value than personal injuries, and being somehow less foreseeable these losses would be less insurable, undermining the risk spreading theory of enterprise liability.

---

to nonprivity buyer claiming economic damages, court noted that Alabama's version of UCC § 2-318, which is essentially the same as Alternative B, would have eliminated the privity barrier if the claim had been for personal injury).

[308] 520 So. 2d 37, 5 UCC Rep. Serv. 2d 301 (Fla. 1988); *see also*, Davis v. Ford Motor Co., 63 UCC Rep. Serv. 2d 445 (S.D. Fla. 2007) (vertical privity required to recover for personal injuries because of availability of strict products liability).

[309] *See, e.g.*, Roberts v. General Dynamics, Convair Corp., 452 F. Supp. 688, 21 UCC Rep. Serv. 565 (S.D. Tex. 1977); Williams v. West Penn Power Co., 467 A.2d 811, 36 UCC Rep. Serv. 107 (Pa. Super. 1983).

[310] The types of property damage for which recovery may be had in tort are discussed in § 5.08 *infra* on the economic-loss rule.

[311] 548 P.2d 279, 19 UCC Rep. Serv. 1 (Alaska 1976).

Several of the courts which have recently considered this aspect of the privity issue have found those arguments unpersuasive. We are in agreement and hold that there is no satisfactory justification for a remedial scheme which extends the warranty action to a consumer suffering personal injury or property damage but denies similar relief to the consumer "fortunate" enough to suffer only direct economic loss.[312]

Quite a few courts have followed *Morrow* in dropping the vertical privity barrier when the claim is for direct damages,[313] especially when the claimant is a consumer. There are, however, many decisions to the contrary.[314] Many of the courts that allow recovery for direct damages retain the privity barrier when the claim is for consequential damages.[315] The issue is not an easy one, but in the final analysis most courts have concluded that they should refrain from exposing sellers to losses for which they are unable to plan and against which they may be unable to insure.

An effective disclaimer of implied warranties by the last seller in the chain of distribution clearly precludes recovery on such warranties by parties that are statutory third-party beneficiaries. Does a disclaimer by a seller further up the chain that is effective against its immediate buyer also preclude recovery for breach of implied warranties by remote buyers and third parties? If the theory supporting recovery is that the claimant is a third-party beneficiary, the answer should be yes.[316] A third-party beneficiary steps into the shoes of the party in privity and is bound by the contract provisions that are effective against that party. However, some courts have held that a disclaimer between parties in privity is ineffective against remote parties, giving rise to what might be referred to as a common-law implied warranty that runs with the goods. For example, in *Patty Precision Products Co. v. Browne & Sharpe Manufacturing Co.*[317] the United States awarded a contract to the buyer for the manufacture of bomb

---

[312] 548 P.2d at 290–91, 19 UCC Rep. Serv. at 17–18.

[313] *See, e.g.*, Consumers Power Co. v. Mississippi Valley Structural Steel Co., 636 F. Supp. 1100, 1 UCC Rep. Serv. 2d 402 (E.D. Mich. 1986); Hyundai Motor America, Inc. v. Goodin, 822 N.E.2d 947, 56 UCC Rep. Serv. 2d 339 (Ind. 2005).

[314] *See, e.g.*, Tex Enterprises v. Brockway Std., Inc., 149 Wash. 2d 204, 66 P.3d 625, 50 UCC Rep. Serv. 2d 317 (2003) (remote buyer not permitted to recover because it could not prove it was an intended third-party beneficiary); Rampey v. Novartis Consumer Health, Inc., 867 So. 2d 1079, 51 UCC Rep. Serv. 2d 117 (Ala. 2003) (lack of privity barred consumer's economic-damage claim against drug manufacturer); Sylvan R. Shemitz Designs, Inc. v. Newark Corp., 60 UCC Rep. Serv. 2d 117 (Conn. Super. Ct. 2006) (lack of privity barred manufacturer of light fixtures from recovering from remote manufacturer of capacitor boots).

[315] *See, e.g.*, Mt. Holly Ski Area v. U.S. Electrical Motors, 666 F. Supp. 115, 4 UCC Rep. Serv. 2d 715 (1987); Blanco v. Baxter Healthcare Corp., 158 Cal. App. 4th 139, 70 Cal. Rptr. 3d 556, 64 UCC Rep. Serv. 2d 790 (2008) (lack of privity barred decedent's family from recovering from manufacturer of bileaflet mitral heart valve). For cases that have permitted recovery, see Crest Container Corp. v. R. H. Bishop Co., 111 Ill. App. 3d 1068, 445 N.E.2d 19, 35 UCC Rep. Serv. 1498 (1982); Spagnol Enterprises, Inc. v. Digital Equip. Corp., 390 Pa. Super. 372, 568 A.2d 948, 11 UCC Rep. Serv. 2d 49 (1990).

[316] Accordingly, an effective disclaimer by a remote seller against its immediate buyer should be effective against a person whose claim is based on UCC § 2-318. The drafters of Article 2A recognized this relationship and provided for that result in UCC § 2A-216.

[317] 846 F.2d 1247, 6 UCC Rep. Serv. 2d 692 (10th Cir. 1988).

racks. The seller purchased controls for the product from General Electric, which disclaimed the implied warranty of merchantability. When the bomb racks did not perform as expected, the buyer brought suit against the seller and General Electric. The appellate court reversed the trial judge's ruling that the disclaimers were relevant, holding that a disclaimer not revealed to a remote buyer cannot be effective against that buyer.[318] Other courts have held to the contrary.[319]

[B]   Special Considerations with Express Warranties

Although a person may be a statutory third-party beneficiary of an express warranty under Section 2-318,[320] most of the reported privity cases on express warranties have involved buyers asserting claims based on affirmations of fact or promises made directly to the buyer by the remote seller, in advertising or otherwise. Allowing a seller to use direct communications to induce buyers to purchase its goods and then to assert lack of privity when one of them brings a product dissatisfaction claim would be incongruous. The Comments provide support for applying the Code's warranty provisions by analogy in this context.[321]

The leading case on this issue, *Randy Knitwear, Inc. v. American Cyanamid Co.*,[322] held a seller of chemical resins used to treat fabric to be liable to a remote clothing manufacturer for breach of an express warranty when clothing made from the fabric shrank too much. The seller had placed advertisements in trade journals for clothing manufacturers, had sent direct mailers to the plaintiff, and had even furnished its immediate buyers with garment tags for delivery to clothing manufacturers stating that the treated fabric would not shrink. The plaintiff had sewed the tags into the clothing that it manufactured. The court noted that allowing a manufacturer to avoid liability after engaging in a heavy advertising campaign would be unrealistic and it overruled prior decisions requiring privity.

---

[318] Oklahoma, whose law applied in the decision, subsequently amended its version of UCC § 2-318 in an apparent attempt to reverse the result in *Patty Precision*. However, because Oklahoma had adopted Alternative A, which does not address issues of vertical privity, it is not clear that the amendment achieved its intended purpose.

[319] *See, e.g.*, Spagnol Enterprises v. Digital Eqpt. Corp., 390 Pa. Super. 372, 568 A.2d 948, 11 UCC Rep. Serv. 2d 49 (1989).

[320] *See* § 5.06[A] *supra*.

[321] *See* UCC § 2-313, cmt. 2.

[322] 11 N.Y.2d 5, 226 N.Y.S.2d 363, 181 N.E.2d 399 (1962); *see also* U.S. Tire-Tech, Inc. v. Boeran, 110 S.W.3d 194, 50 UCC Rep. Serv. 2d 780 (Tex. Ct. App. 2003) (privity not required for express warranty claim brought under Texas Deceptive Trade-Practices Consumer Protection Act); Nomo Agroindustrial Sa De CV v. Enza Zaden North America, Inc., 492 F. Supp. 2d 1175, 64 UCC Rep. Serv. 2d 165 (D. Ariz. 2007) (remote seed manufacturer liable for breach of express warranty because of written advertising materials provided to buyer); *cf.* Canadian Pacific Ry. Co. v. Williams-Hayward Protective Coatings, Inc., 57 UCC Rep. Serv. 2d 136 (N.D. Ill. 2005) (summary judgment for seller appropriate because there was no evidence that remote buyer received any brochures or catalogs from seller, nor had seller engaged in advertising aimed at remote buyer). *But see* Stewart v. Gainesville Glass Co., 233 Ga. 578, 212 S.E.2d 377 (1975) (manufacturer of special glass windows not liable to homeowner since its express warranties did not run to a clearly identified person).

As with implied warranty claims against remote sellers, the courts have been reluctant to permit buyers asserting express-warranty claims to recover consequential economic damages from remote sellers. For example, in *Beyond the Garden Gate, Inc. v. Northstar Freeze-Dry Manufacturing, Inc.*,[323] a manufacturer of a machine that freeze dried flowers made affirmations of fact about the quality of the machine to a person that contacted the manufacturer while considering whether to buy a used machine from a third party. When the machine failed to live up to the affirmations, the buyer sought direct and consequential economic damages. The jury awarded no direct damages but granted the buyer an award of $40,000 to compensate for its lost profits. The Iowa Supreme Court reversed, holding that nonprivity buyers asserting express warranty claims are limited to direct damages.

A buyer that is a statutory or intended third-party beneficiary of an express warranty may enforce the warranty even though unaware of its existence. For example, in *Harris Moran Seed Co., Inc. v. Phillips*[324] commercial tomato farmers bought "mountain fresh" tomato plants from a dealer. The plants had been grown from seeds sold by the defendant, which had warranted that plants grown from the seeds would be "true to type." Even though the farmers were unaware of the warranty when they bought the plants, the court affirmed a jury verdict in their favor on the ground that they were intended beneficiaries of the warranty because (1) the harm to them was foreseeable, (2) the contract between the defendant and the dealer referred in several places to end users, and (3) the language of the warranty conformed to language used in the Federal Seed Act,[325] which protects both buyers and end users. Nothing prevents a claimant from also being an intended third-party beneficiary of an implied warranty.

[C]   Finance Lessee as Beneficiary of Supply Contract [§ 2A-209]

In a statutory finance lease, the finance lessor acquires the goods from the supplier, by either sale or lease, and then leases them to the finance lessee.[326] The finance lessor does not make the implied warranties of merchantability or fitness and only rarely makes an express warranty. Accordingly, the finance lessee must look to the supplier for warranty protection. By operation of law, Article 2A makes the finance lessee the beneficiary of all warranties, express or implied, that the supplier has made to the finance lessor.[327]

The extension of warranty protection to the finance lessee does not modify the rights and obligations of the finance lessor and the supplier under the supply contract, nor does it create an inference that the finance lessee has assumed any

---

[323] 526 N.W.2d 305, 26 UCC Rep. Serv. 2d 140 (Iowa 1995).

[324] 949 So. 2d 916 (Ala. Ct. Civ. App. 2006).

[325] 7 U.S.C. § 1551 *et seq.*

[326] Finance leases are discussed generally in § 1.04[B] *supra*.

[327] UCC § 2A-209(1).

of the finance lessor's obligations.[328] Once the supplier receives notice that the goods are subject to a finance lease, the supply contract cannot be modified or rescinded. If the supplier and the finance lessor modify or rescind the supply contract before the supplier receives notice, the modification or rescission is effective against the finance lessee. In such a case the finance lessor is deemed to have assumed liability for any warranties that would have run to the finance lessee had the modification or rescission not occurred.[329]

The finance lessee's remedies are limited by the nature of the leasehold interest.[330] For example, if the goods are defective, the finance lessee can reject them and recover damages from the supplier, but the right to recover any money already paid accrues to the finance lessor. Nothing in Article 2A prevents the supplier from disclaiming warranties or limiting the available remedies.

§ 5.07 THE STATUTE OF LIMITATIONS [§ 2-725; § 2A-506]

The statute of limitations for both sales and leases expires four years after the cause of action accrues, although the parties may by the original sale or lease agreement reduce the period to as little as one year.[331] The limitations period begins upon accrual of the cause of action, and in sales transactions accrual occurs at the time of the breach without regard to the aggrieved party's knowledge of the breach.[332] Thus, a buyer has four years to sue a seller for such breaches as a defect in the manner of tender or a failure to install the goods and a seller has four years to sue a buyer for failing to make a payment when due.

Ordinarily, the breach of a warranty occurs when the seller tenders delivery,[333] thus making it possible for the limitations period to run before the buyer becomes aware of the defect. For example, in *Beckmire v. Ristokrat Clay Products Co.*[334] bricks that the buyer had purchased for the exterior of his home began to deteriorate after only six years. The buyer argued that the nature of bricks was such that the implied warranty of merchantability should run beyond six years. While not disagreeing, the court held that the statute of limitations had run even though the implied warranty might have been breached.

Certain events extend the statutory period. For example, while repairs alone will not toll the running of the statute,[335] the court in *Coakley & Williams, Inc. v. Shatterproof Glass Corp.*[336] held that the limitations period begins anew if the seller tenders replacement goods. If the seller installs the goods, several courts

---

[328] UCC § 2A-209(2).

[329] UCC § 2A-209(3).

[330] UCC § 2A-209(1).

[331] UCC §§ 2-725(1), 2A-506(1). The parties may not extend the limitations period by agreement.

[332] UCC § 2-725(2).

[333] *Id.*

[334] 36 Ill. App. 3d 411, 343 N.E.2d 530, 18 UCC Rep. Serv. 1218 (1976).

[335] *See, e.g.,* Poppenheimer v. Bluff City Motor Homes, 658 S.W.2d 106, 38 UCC Rep. Serv. 167 (Tenn. Ct. App. 1983).

[336] 706 F.2d 456, 36 UCC Rep. Serv. 87 (4th Cir. 1983).

have held that a cause of action for breach of warranty does not accrue until the installation is complete.[337]

The Code does not alter the common-law rules governing tolling of the statute.[338] For example, in *Balog v. Center Art Gallery-Hawaii, Inc.*[339] the seller's constant reiteration to the buyer that a painting was genuine prevented the buyer from discovering that it was a forgery, giving rise to an estoppel that tolled the running of the statute. Of course, fraud or concealment of a defect by the seller will also toll the statute.[340]

If a warranty explicitly extends to the future performance of the goods and the defect cannot be discovered until the time for performance arrives, accrual does not occur until the defect is or should be discovered.[341] For example, in *Perry v. Augustine*[342] the seller expressly warranted that the buyer's new furnace would heat his home to 75 degrees when the outside temperature fell to 20 degrees below zero. The court held that the warranty explicitly extended to future performance and thus the limitations period did not begin to run until conditions arose that allowed the promise to be tested. Because the reference to future performance must be explicit, none of the implied warranties can fall within the future-performance exception.[343]

Sellers frequently warrant that their products will be free from defects for a stated period of time, and such promises clearly extend to the future performance of the goods.[344] However, suppose a seller says nothing about the quality of the goods but instead promises that it will repair or replace any parts that prove to be defective during a stated period. The courts in these cases have split three ways. Some courts have held that the repair-or-replace promise is not an express warranty at all.[345] These courts rely on the language in Section 2-313(1)(a) providing that a qualifying affirmation of fact or promise "creates an express warranty that the goods shall conform to the affirmation or promise." The seller must carry out the repair-or-replace promise but the goods cannot conform to it. Since the promise is not a warranty, a cause of action does not accrue until the promise is breached. Other courts have held that the repair-or-replace promise constitutes an express warranty but that it extends to the future

---

[337] *See, e.g.*, Westinghouse Elec. Corp. v. Carolina Power & Light Co., 12 UCC Rep. Serv. 2d 127 (W.D. Pa. 1990).

[338] UCC §§ 2-725(4), 2A-506(4).

[339] 745 F. Supp. 1556, 12 UCC Rep. Serv. 2d 962 (D. Haw. 1990).

[340] Freiberg v. Atlas-Turner, Inc., 37 UCC Rep. Serv. 1592 (D. Minn. 1984).

[341] UCC § 2-725(2).

[342] 37 Pa. D.&C.2d 416, 3 UCC Rep. Serv. 735 (Pa. Ct. Com. Pl. 1965); *see also* Hillcrest Country Club v. N.D. Judds Co., 236 Neb. 233, 461 N.W.2d 55, 12 UCC Rep. Serv. 2d 990 (1990) (express warranty that acrylic finish on roofing material would last for 20 years extended to future performance).

[343] *See, e.g.*, Murphy v. Spelts-Schultz Lumber Co. of Grand Island, 240 Neb. 275, 481 N.W.2d 422, 17 UCC Rep. Serv. 2d 467 (1992).

[344] *See, e.g.*, Black Leaf Prods. Co. v. Chemisco, Inc., 678 S.W.2d 827, 39 UCC Rep. Serv. 508 (Mo. Ct. App. 1984).

[345] *See, e.g.*, Mydlach v. DaimlerChrylser Corp., 226 Ill. 2d 307, 314 Ill. Dec. 760, 875 N.E.2d 1047, 64 UCC Rep. Serv. 2d 44 (2007).

performance of the goods, thereby invoking the rule that a cause of action accrues when the defect is or should be discovered.[346] Although different in analysis, the first two approaches reach functionally the same result. The third approach is to hold that the promise is an express warranty but that it extends to the future performance of the seller and not to the future performance of the goods.[347] Thus, the cause of action accrues upon tender of delivery even though the repairs that become the subject of litigation may not occur until sometime in the future. The third approach is troubling in the context of long-term warranties because the seller's failure to perform may occur only a short time before the limitations period ends. It could even occur after the limitations period ends, but even a court that follows the third approach could not hold that a five-year repair-or-replace promise becomes unenforceable after four years.

Courts have split on whether to apply Article 2's statute of limitations to claims for indemnification. The typical case involves a manufacturer that sells goods to a retailer, which in turn resells them to an ultimate buyer. If the ultimate buyer sues the retailer for breach of warranty, the retailer will try to throw the loss back onto the manufacturer. Although the retailer's suit can be seen as a warranty action in its own right, it might also be properly viewed as an indemnification action. A right to indemnification arises when one party discharges a debt that should have been paid by another. Should Article 2's four-year provision apply to such actions or should the limitations period applicable to indemnification actions, which is typically longer, control?[348]

A number of courts, promoting a policy of repose, have applied the four-year provision.[349] Others, however, concerned about the fact that the retailer's suit could be precluded before the ultimate buyer's suit even commenced, have applied the general statute of limitations.[350] Perhaps the best approach is a compromise position articulated in *Sheehan v. Morris Irrigation, Inc.*[351] The court in *Sheehan* concluded that Article 2 applied because the indemnitee had sufficient time to bring its action before the four-year period expired. The court clarified, however, that it would have opted for the general statute of limitations had that not been the case.

Suppose the goods remain on the retailer's shelf for more than four years and the ultimate buyer later brings a suit for breach of warranty against the remote manufacturer. The few courts that have ruled on this issue have reached

---

[346] *See, e.g.*, Oulette Mach. Sys., Inc. v. Clinton Lindberg Cadillac Co., 60 S.W.3d 618, 45 UCC Rep. Serv. 2d 163 (Mo. Ct. App. 2001).

[347] *See, e.g.*, Flagg Energy Dev. Corp. v. General Motors Corp., 244 Conn. 126, 709 A.2d 1075, 35 UCC Rep. Serv. 2d 138 (1998).

[348] The drafters of Article 2A resolved this issue by providing that "[a] cause of action for indemnity accrues when the act or omission on which the claim for indemnity is based is or should have been discovered by the indemnified party, whichever is later." UCC § 2A-506(2).

[349] *See, e.g.*, Farmers Nat'l Bank v. Wickham Pipeline, 114 Idaho 565, 759 P.2d 71 (1990).

[350] *See, e.g.*, City of Wood River v. Geer-Melkus Constr. Co., 233 Neb. 179, 444 N.W.2d 305, 9 UCC Rep. Serv. 2d 957 (1989).

[351] 460 N.W.2d 413, 13 UCC Rep. Serv. 2d 145 (S.D. 1990).

different conclusions. In *Patterson v. Her Majesty Industries, Inc.*,[352] the court sided with the ultimate buyer, a consumer, and held that the cause of action accrued when the goods were purchased from the retailer. This approach, which is consistent with the drafters' intention that there be minimally adequate remedies available for breaches of warranty, makes sense. The need to protect the consumer is particularly acute when the retailer has disclaimed its own warranties at the time of sale and the consumer has relied on the apparent existence of the manufacturer's warranty. Some decisions, however, have rejected the *Patterson* approach.[353]

Because of the differing nature of lease transactions, Article 2A deviates from its statutory analogue with respect to the statute of limitations. Many lease transactions have a duration in excess of four years, and it is not uncommon for the lessor in a long-term lease to be responsible for maintenance and repairs. Accordingly, Article 2A provides that a cause of action accrues when the lessee should have discovered the breach, even in breach of warranty cases.[354]

§ 5.08 THE ECONOMIC-LOSS DOCTRINE

A variety of circumstances may motivate buyers and lessees of defective goods to prefer an action based on tort principles over a claim for breach of warranty. The primary objective is often to circumvent defenses that might otherwise be available to the defendant. The plaintiff might not have bargained for express-warranty protection or the duration of an otherwise applicable express warranty might have expired; implied warranties might have been disclaimed; the remedies available for breach of an express or implied warranty might have been limited; the statute of limitations might have expired; notice of breach might not have been given; or lack of contractual privity might preclude recovery. If any of these defenses jeopardize a warranty claim or threaten to severely reduce the available recovery, the plaintiff understandably will prefer a claim that is not burdened by them. Potential tort claims, depending on the facts, include strict products liability, negligence, and misrepresentation (including fraud).

Over the years, courts responding to these tort claims have developed what is called the "economic-loss doctrine" pursuant to which buyers are precluded from using tort theories to recover damages that are economic in nature. The courts generally restrict tort recovery to damages that result from injury to a person or to property other than the goods themselves. If a buyer or lessee suffers harm because the goods do not comply with their contract-based expectations, warranty law applies to the exclusion of tort remedies. The restriction applies to both direct economic loss (*i.e.*, loss of value of the goods themselves) and consequential economic loss (*e.g.*, lost profits).

---

[352] 450 F. Supp. 425, 23 UCC Rep. Serv. 1198 (E.D. Pa. 1978).

[353] *See, e.g.*, Thomas v. King Ridge, Inc., 771 F. Supp. 478, 16 UCC Rep. Serv. 2d 127 (D.N.H. 1991); Heller v. United States Suzuki Motor Co., 64 N.Y.2d 407, 488 N.Y.S.2d 132, 477 N.E.2d 434, 37 UCC Rep. Serv. 156 (1985).

[354] UCC § 2A-506(2).

A United States Supreme Court admiralty opinion, *East River S.S. Corp. v. Transamerica Delaval, Inc.*,[355] was highly influential in the development of the economic-loss doctrine, which the Court applied to foreclose tort claims against a manufacturer of a ship engine that required repairs when it did not function properly. Embracing the analysis of Justice Traynor in *Seely v. White Motor Co.*,[356] the Court concluded that the loss-spreading function of tort law should be confined to recovery for personal injury or property damage resulting from the introduction of defective products into the stream of commerce. It explained that economic loss can be addressed better through contract law because the parties can structure their expectations and respective liabilities through the bargaining process. By contrast, tort liability is best directed toward injuries associated with dangerous products. The Court was concerned that if tort liability were not so constrained, "contract law would drown in a sea of tort."[357]

Courts following *East River* see the UCC provisions as a legislative framework within which the parties may allocate the risk of economic losses resulting from sales transactions, and they view tort claims based on strict liability and negligence as disruptive of this carefully balanced system. Although some courts have been reluctant to apply the economic-loss doctrine when the affected buyer is a consumer, most courts have recognized that the reasoning that supports the doctrine in commercial transactions applies as well when the buyer is a consumer.

Limited exceptions to the economic-loss doctrine have been recognized in a minority of jurisdictions. One of these exceptions is to allow economic loss recovery in tort when a defect renders goods unreasonably dangerous even if personal injury or property damage has not occurred.[358] The rationale for this approach is that it will provide further incentive for manufacturers to exercise care in designing and producing their products. The exception has been rejected by most courts on the ground that strict tort liability already creates the necessary incentive because sellers cannot anticipate that injuries resulting from a dangerous defect will be limited to economic loss.

Another exception allows recovery in tort even if the damage is limited to the goods themselves if the damage is the result of a sudden, calamitous event caused by a defect in the goods.[359] A rationale advanced for this approach is that the value of the product is further reduced by the sudden event causing the harm, as distinct from a loss associated with a more gradual deterioration. Most courts have found this reasoning unpersuasive and apply the economic-loss doctrine to cases in which a defect causes harm to the goods themselves, whether gradually or calamitously, equating these cases with those in which the goods

---

[355] 476 U.S. 858 (1986).

[356] 63 Cal. 2d 9, 45 Cal. Rptr. 17, 403 P.2d 145, 2 UCC Rep. Serv. 915 (1965).

[357] 476 U.S. at 866.

[358] *See, e.g.,* Salt River Project Agr. Imp. & Power Dist. v. Westinghouse Elec. Corp., 143 Ariz. 368, 694 P.2d 198, 40 UCC Rep. Serv. 2d 418 (1984) (rotating blades in a gas turbine unit were destroyed by explosion and fire).

[359] *See, e.g.,* Capitol Fuels, Inc. v. Clark Equip. Co., 181 W. Va. 258, 382 S.E.2d 311, 9 UCC Rep. Serv. 2d 1229 (1989) (fire caused from leaks in the hydraulic fuel lines destroyed a vehicle).

simply fail to function as warranted or otherwise fail meet the buyer's expectations. Consider, for example, a defective truck that has to be repaired after it rolls over in an accident that did not cause personal injury or damage to any other real or personal property.[360] Most courts would apply the economic-loss doctrine to such a situation.

Plaintiffs sometimes seek to avoid the doctrine by arguing that the goods that failed were a component of a larger product and that the injury to the product constituted injury to "other property." In *Midwest Helicopters Airways, Inc. v. Sikorsky Aircraft*,[361] for example, the tail-rotor drive on a helicopter allegedly was defective and caused the helicopter to crash. The buyer argued that the resulting damage to the helicopter constituted damage to other property that was actionable under tort law but the court held otherwise, limiting the buyer to its contract remedies. In cases like this, most courts find that the buyer purchased an entire product, not simply a collection of component parts, and injury to the product caused by a defective component constitutes economic loss rather than property damage.

Some courts have applied the economic-loss doctrine even when there is injury to property other than the goods if the harm was within the contemplation of the parties at the time of contract formation. For example, in *Detroit Edison Co. v. NABCO, Inc.*[362] an electric utility brought an action against suppliers of power-plant pipe after a section of pipe exploded, destroying walls and damaging equipment, hydraulic lines, wires, and insulation throughout the plant. The appellate court affirmed the lower-court holding that under Michigan law the losses constituted economic loss that the parties could have allocated in the bargaining process and were therefore not recoverable in negligence or strict tort liability. Similarly, the court in *Dakota Gasification Co. v. Pascoe Building Systems*[363] barred tort recovery against suppliers of steel structural components used in a building for damage to the contents of the building caused by the collapse of its roof.

Rather than drawing the distinction between injury to the product itself and injury to other property, this line of cases focuses on the foreseeability of the property damage. If the resulting damages were foreseeable, they were within the contemplation of the parties when they entered the contract and the buyer could have used the bargaining process to insist upon greater protection through additional warranties. The court in *Dakota Gasification* explained that a different holding would be contrary to the underlying principles of the economic-loss doctrine because "[a]llowing tort remedies in a case such as this would perversely encourage contractors to 'bargain' for no warranty or insurance

---

[360] These facts led Justice Traynor to deny tort recovery in the landmark decision of *Seely v. White Motor Co.*, 63 Cal. 2d 9 45 Cal. Rptr. 17, 403 P.2d 145, 2 UCC Rep. Serv. 915 (1965).

[361] 849 F. Supp. 666 (E.D. Wis. 1994), *aff'd*, 42 F.3d 1391 (7th Cir. 1994).

[362] 35 F.3d 236, 24 UCC Rep. Serv. 2d 850 (6th Cir. 1994).

[363] 91 F.3d 1094, 30 UCC Rep. Serv. 2d 411 (8th Cir. 1996); *cf. Corsica Coop. Ass'n v. Behlen Mfg. Co., Inc.*, 967 F. Supp. 382, 35 UCC Rep. Serv. 2d 1116 (D. S.D. 1997) (although the court denied tort recovery for a corn-storage building that collapsed or for its contents, it allowed the tort claim for two vehicles parked outside that were damaged).

protection in exchange for a reduced purchase price, because they could rely on tort remedies as their 'warranty.' "[364]

Other courts, concluding that an approach based on the foreseeability of the property damage is too broad, have articulated a test based on the purchaser's expectations. The focus under this test is whether, given the anticipated function of the goods, a purchaser in the position of the plaintiff should have foreseen the risk that the goods would cause the harm sustained by the plaintiff. The Restatement (Third) of Torts rejects both foreseeability tests as too expansive, leaving the question of whether contracting parties may by express agreement disclaim or limit remedies for property damage to developing case law. It requires any exclusions or limitations to be discussed in the purchase contract.

The economic-loss doctrine thus is imposed to preserve the distinctive goals of recovery under tort and contract theories, with tort protection limited to cases in which there are safety concerns. Tort law does not require that goods satisfy the expectations of their buyers. Responsibility for the quality of the goods is the province of warranty law, which allows the parties to allocate the risk by contract. A disappointed buyer cannot escape the consequences of an unfavorable bargain by ignoring it and invoking tort law.

Buyers in sales transactions often have asserted claims based on misrepresentation, including fraud. Because these claims lie in tort, the defendants have responded that they are barred under the economic-loss doctrine. Because the supreme courts in many states have not decided the extent to which the doctrine should extend to these types of torts, the federal courts have been required in several cases to predict the likely position of the state courts on the issue. Competing arguments have been advanced but a consensus on some of the questions has not yet emerged.

The easiest cases appear to be the ones in which the seller allegedly makes a negligent misrepresentation which becomes part of the basis of the bargain, making it an express warranty. A buyer that is influenced by such a representation can make sure that the representation is reflected in any final writing, thereby preventing application of the parol evidence rule. Ignoring the requirements for a contract claim (*e.g.*, the basis-of-the-bargain requirement) simply by framing the claim in terms of negligent misrepresentation circumvents the policies underlying contract law in the same way that tort claims based on negligence or strict liability do. It is not surprising that the courts have generally applied the economic-loss doctrine to claims of negligent misrepresentation.

Courts differ on the extent to which the doctrine precludes claims for intentional misrepresentation, or fraud. One approach, represented by *Huron Tool and Engineering Co. v. Precision Consulting Services, Inc.*,[365] provides that all frauds claims cannot be banned categorically under the economic-loss doctrine. The doctrine bars claims that are intertwined with warranty and breach-of-contract claims, but certain claims based on fraud in the inducement are not barred. Thus, the court in *Huron Tool* restricted the plaintiff to its

---

[364] 91 F.3d at 1100.

[365] 209 Mich. App. 365, 532 N.W.2d 541, 26 UCC Rep. Serv. 2d 703 (1995).

contractual remedies because the fraudulent misrepresentation alleged by the plaintiff concerned the quality and character of the goods sold. In contrast, the buyer succeeded on its tort claim in *Kaloti Enterprises, Inc. v. Kellogg Sales Co.*[366] After the buyer in that case placed an order for food products that it intended to resell to large-market stores, the seller changed its practices by making direct sales to these same stores, thus shutting the buyer out of the very resale market that it had used in the past and expected to use again. The court adopted the exception articulated in *Huron Tool*, stating that the economic-loss doctrine does not apply if "the fraud concerns matters whose risk and responsibility did not relate to the quality or the characteristics of the goods for which the parties contracted or otherwise involved performance of the contract."[367]

Budgetel Inns, Inc. v. Micro Systems, Inc.[368] exemplifies the other approach to claims based on fraud. This approach precludes application of the economic-loss doctrine to fraud claims generally and is explained by the *Budgetel* court's statement that "[t]he tort, after all, is inducing someone to enter into a contract, so to say that it does not apply where the tort involves the contract or its subject matter analytically makes no sense."[369] Even if fraud is interwoven with a contract, it remains distinct in that it stems from a common-law duty and not from the contract itself. In the view of the *Budgetel* court, "[a]n outright lie to induce a party to enter a contract differs substantially from a broken contractual promise."[370] As further support for its position, the court noted that rather than enhancing freedom of contract, the effect of the economic-loss doctrine in this context hinders that freedom because parties cannot knowingly allocate risk if they cannot rely on the other party to speak truthfully during negotiations.

§ 5.09 OTHER LAWS

[A] Federal Preemption

Considerable litigation in recent years has addressed the extent to which provisions in certain federal statutes preempt state product-liability claims. The Federal Insecticide, Fungicide, and Rodenticide Act (FIFRA),[371] which regulates the packaging and labeling of these substances, contains an express provision under which state-law "requirements" that are additional to or different from those established by FIFRA are preempted.[372] In *Bates v. Dow*

---

[366] 2005 WI 110, 283 Wis. 2d 555, 699 N.W.2d 205 (2004).

[367] 699 N.W.2d at 219.

[368] 8 F. Supp. 2d 1137, 35 UCC Rep. Serv. 2d 1073 (E.D. Wis. 1998).

[369] 8 F. Supp. 2d at 1147.

[370] *Id.*

[371] 7 U.S.C.A. §§ 136–136y.

[372] Express preemption occurs when Congress, as in FIFRA, addresses preemption in the legislation. Implied preemption can arise when Congress creates a regulatory scheme that is sufficiently pervasive to bring it into conflict with state legislative or judicial doctrines. Courts must also determine whether Congress intended to preempt an entire field (field preemption) or intended merely to preempt conflicting provisions of state law (conflict preemption).

Agrosciences LLC,[373] the plaintiff sued for crop damage allegedly caused by the defendant's pesticide, asserting *inter alia* claims based on defective design, defective manufacture, negligent testing, and breach of an express warranty set forth on a label. The Supreme Court rejected the argument that the claims were preempted, holding that "requirements" as used in FIFRA means rules of law, including common-law rules, that must be obeyed, such as disclosures on a label mandated by government regulations, not events that might motivate an optional decision, such as the decision to place an express warranty on a label. The Court noted that the only provisions of FIFRA relevant to product-liability claims relate to labeling and packaging, and even in that area the only state-law requirements that are preempted are those that are in addition to or different from those mandated by the federal law. The Court stated the bottom line as follows: "Rules that require manufacturers to design reasonably safe products, to use due care in conducting appropriate testing of their products, to market products free of manufacturing defects, and to honor their express warranties or other contractual commitments plainly do not qualify as requirements for 'labeling or packaging'."[374] Even though the manufacturer's warranty appeared on the label and FIFRA deals with labeling, the plaintiff's claim for breach of the warranty was no more preempted than were his claims for defective design, defective manufacture, and negligent testing.

The plaintiff in *Bates* also brought claims for fraud and negligent failure to warn, and the Court indicated that these claims might be preempted because they alleged that the product's label contained false statements and inadequate warnings and were premised on common-law rules that constituted requirements. However, the Court could not determine whether the state-law requirements were additional to or different from those of FIFRA on the one hand, or parallel to them on the other hand. As long as its requirements are parallel to those of FIFRA, a state can provide remedies not available under FIFRA.[375] The Court remanded the case to the Court of Appeals for a determination of this issue.

The Court in *Bates* provided a succinct summary of the narrow range of the FIFRA preemptions provision, as follows:

> In the main, it pre-empts competing state labeling standards — imagine 50 different labeling regimes prescribing the color, font size, and wording of warnings — that would create significant inefficiencies for manufacturers. The provision also pre-empts any statutory or common-law rule that would impose a labeling requirement that diverges from

---

[373] 544 U.S. 431 (2005) (Justice Breyer concurs; Justices Thomas and Scalia concur in part and dissent in part).

[374] 544 U.S. at 444.

[375] The court noted support for this "parallel requirements" approach in its plurality ruling in *Medtronic, Inc. v. Lohr*, 518 U.S. 470 (1996), which involved a comparably-worded preemption provision in the Medical Device Amendments Act of 1976, 90 Stat. 1049, amending the Food, Drug and Cosmetics Act of 1938, 52 Stat. 1049, 21 U.S.C. §§ 360–360rr. 21 U.S.C. § 360k(a) (preemption provision).

those set out in FIFRA and its implementing regulations. It does not, however, pre-empt any state rules that are fully consistent with federal requirements.[376]

In other cases the Supreme Court has found federal preemption. In *Cipollone v Liggett Group, Inc.*[377] it held that any state-law requirements that established claims for failure to warn or that in any way undercut federally mandated warnings were preempted to the extent that they were based on anything included or omitted in advertising or promotions by a manufacturer.[378] In *Riegel v. Medtronic, Inc.*[379] it addressed the FDA regulations governing the pre-market approval of a medical device, which cover the design, manufacture, labeling, and any other attribute affecting safety or effectiveness. A majority held that common-law claims that concern safety or effectiveness were pre-empted to the extent that such state requirements are different from or add to the federal requirements. In 2009, the Court affirmed the ruling of the Vermont Supreme Court in *Levine v. Wyeth*[380] holding that the prescription-drug labeling regulations imposed by the Federal Food and Drug Administration on manu-facturers did not preempt state-law product liability claims when those claims alleged that different labeling was required to make the drugs reasonably safe for use.[381] The manufacturer had ample authority to include a stronger warning unilaterally concerning a dangerous method of administering its drug.

[B]   The Magnuson-Moss Act

Congress enacted the Magnuson-Moss Warranty Federal Trade Commission Improvement Act[382] (the "Act") in 1975, primarily addressing the treatment of a "written warranty" provided in connection with a "consumer product." Largely a disclosure statute, the Act requires a party that extends a written warranty to provide consumers with certain information.[383] The stated purpose of the Act is "to improve the adequacy of information available to consumers, prevent deception, and improve competition in the marketing of consumer products. . . ."[384]

Although most of the Act deals with the treatment of written warranties, it also creates a federal cause of action for breach of implied warranties on consumer products that arise under the Code even if the seller does not give a written warranty.[385] It has no application to a UCC express warranty that does

---

[376] 544 U.S. at 452.

[377] 505 U.S. 504 (1992).

[378] The case applied the Public health Cigarette Smoking Act of 1969, 15 U.S.C. § 1334(b).

[379] 128 S. Ct. 999, 169 L. Ed. 892 (2008).

[380] 183 Vt. 76, 944 A.2d 179 (2006), *cert. granted*, 128 S. Ct. 1118, 169 L. Ed. 2d 845 (2008), *aff'd*, 2009 U.S. LEXIS 1774 (Mar. 4, 2009).

[381] The case applies the Federal Food Drug, and Cosmetic Act, 21 U.S.C. § 301 *et seq.*

[382] 15 U.S.C. §§ 2301–12.

[383] 15 U.S.C. § 2302(a).

[384] 15 U.S.C. § 2302(a).

[385] 15 U.S.C. § 2310(d)(1).

not constitute a written warranty as that term is defined in the Act. Because "written warranty" is central to the Act, its definition is provided in full. The term means:

(A) any written affirmation of fact or written promise made in connection with the sale of a consumer product by a supplier to a buyer which relates to the nature of the material or workmanship and affirms or promises that such material or workmanship is defect free or will meet a specified level of performance over a specified period of time, or

(B) any undertaking in writing in connection with the sale by a supplier of a consumer product to refund, repair, replace, or take other remedial action with respect to such product in the event that such product fails to meet the specifications set forth in the undertaking,

which written affirmation, promise, or undertaking becomes part of the basis of the bargain between a supplier and a buyer for purposes other than resale of such product.[386]

Although the definition obviously borrows heavily from UCC Section 2-313, it is narrower and broader than that provision. It is narrower in that express warranties under the Code need not be written to be actionable. Also, although Article 2 recognizes express warranties that constitute mere descriptions of the goods, they will not qualify as written warranties under the Act. Even written express warranties that relate to the nature of the material or workmanship will not be written warranties under the Act if they do not constitute a commitment for a specified period of time that the goods will be defect free or will meet a specified level of performance.[387]

Rather than making a commitment regarding the quality of the goods, many sellers make commitments regarding the remedial actions they will take if the goods fail to meet certain specifications. Despite some decisions to the contrary, the best way to understand such promises is not as express warranties but as enforceable commitments that do not constitute warranties.[388] Here the category of written warranty under the Act is broader than express warranty under the Code because it includes a written promise by a seller to repair or replace any parts that do not meet stipulated specifications or to refund the purchase price in the event the goods fail to meet the specifications.[389]

---

[386] 15 U.S.C. § 2301(6). Because of the reference in the definition to the sale of a consumer product, application of the Act to lease transactions has proven to be highly controversial, with cases decided both ways. For a review of the cases, see W. Lawrence & J. Minan, The Law of Personal Property Leasing § 14:39 (2004 & Supp.).

[387] Lytle v. Roto Lincoln Mercury & Subaru, Inc., 167 Ill. App. 3d 508, 521 N.E.2d 201, 7 UCC Rep. Serv. 2d 1091 (Ill. Ct. App. 1988) (seller's form merely indicated that automobile had been prepared for delivery); Skelton v. General Motors Corp., 660 F.2d 311 (7th Cir. 1981) (written statement that transmission would meet a specified level of performance did not include a specified period of time).

[388] The issue is discussed in the context of the statute of limitations. See § 5.07 supra.

[389] Milicevic v. Fletcher Jones Imports, Ltd., 402 F.3d 912 (9th Cir. 2005) (failure of seller and manufacturer to remedy defective brakes and rear window seal constituted breach of written warranty to make any repairs or replacements necessary to correct defects in the automobile).

Application of the Act requires that the goods qualify as a "consumer product," defined in relevant part as "tangible personal property which is distributed in commerce and which is normally used for personal, family or household purposes."[390] Unlike UCC Article 9, under which the definition of consumer goods turns on the actual or intended use of the goods,[391] the buyer's actual use is irrelevant under the Act. It instead uses an objective standard of normal use. Sellers need to know whether the Act applies to their products, and focusing on the normal use of the goods promotes greater certainty. As a result, the occasional use by a consumer of goods normally used for a business purpose will not invoke application of the Act,[392] whereas sales of goods normally used for both consumer and commercial purposes are covered even though the particular buyer uses them in its business.[393]

Some additional terminology is necessary to understand fully the impact of the Act. As noted above, the Act creates a federal cause of action for breach of implied warranties. It does not create implied warranties but rather uses the term to mean any implied warranty arising under state law.[394] The Code's implied warranties of merchantability and fitness qualify. If a particular state provides that lack of privity is a defense to an implied-warranty action, there will be no implied-warranty claim for purposes of the Act.[395] Enforcement rights under written and implied warranties on consumer products run in favor of consumers, an expansive term that means a buyer of a consumer product for a purpose other than resale (including a person buying a consumer product for a business purpose, a person to whom the product is transferred during the duration of a written or implied warranty, and any other person entitled to enforce the warranty under state law). The last part of the definition is a reference to the statutory third-party beneficiaries along the horizontal privity line protected by the relevant state's version of UCC Section 2-318 and those remote buyers to whom express warranties run on a basis other than Section 2-318.[396]

Finally with regard to terminology, the Act uses the terms "supplier" and "warrantor" in a manner that is confusing at first glance. A supplier is "any person engaged in the business of making a consumer product directly or indirectly available to consumers"[397] and a warrantor is "any supplier or other person who gives or offers to give a written warranty or who is or may be obligated under an implied warranty."[398] To illustrate, suppose a manufacturer

---

[390] 15 U.S.C. § 2301(1).

[391] UCC § 9-102(a)(23).

[392] CAT Aircraft Leasing, Inc. v. Cessna Aircraft Co., 1990 U.S. Dist. LEXIS 14720 (D. Kan., Oct. 3, 1990) (12-passenger, twin-engine turbojet aircraft).

[393] Business Modeling Techniques, Inc. v. General Motors Corp., 474 N.Y.S.2d 258 (Sup. Ct. 1984) (Act applied to cars owned by corporation and used predominately for business purposes).

[394] 15 U.S.C. § 2301(7).

[395] Privity is discussed in § 5.06 *supra*.

[396] *See* § 5.06[A] (horizontal privity), [B] (additional rules for express warranties) *supra*.

[397] 15 U.S.C. § 2301(4).

[398] 15 U.S.C. § 2301(5).

sells a consumer product to a retailer, who resells it to a consumer. The manufacturer provides the consumer with a written warranty while the retailer provides only an express warranty of description[399] and effectively disclaims all implied warranties. Both the manufacturer and the retailer are suppliers, but only the manufacturer is a warrantor. If the retailer had not disclaimed the implied warranties, it too would be a warrantor. Application of the Act can be particularly significant because, as the discussion below explains, it permits a consumer to recover costs and expenses, including attorney fees.

Warrantors often provide express warranties that are restrictive in their scope, disclaim all implied warranties, and limit an aggrieved buyer's remedies to the seller's repair or replacement of goods that do not conform to the express warranties. Unsophisticated consumers tend to believe that they have received substantial warranty protection, when in reality their protection is less than the standard protection of an implied warranty and the general Article 2 remedies. Congress enacted the Magnuson-Moss Act to improve both warranty products made available to consumers and consumer understanding of warranties through the goals that Congress identified.

As noted above, the Act is primarily a disclosure statute, and it advances Congress' purpose of improving the availability of warranty information by empowering the Federal Trade Commission (FTC) to establish requirements that warrantors must meet in disclosing fully and conspicuously, in simple and readily understandable language, the terms and conditions of their written warranties.[400] Regulations issued by the FTC[401] require, in part, that any written warranty contain the following information: the parties to whom the warranty extends; the parts or products covered; what the warrantor will do in the event of a claim; step-by-step explanations for obtaining warranty service; information on any informal dispute-settlement procedures; and the commencement and duration of the warranty.[402] The FTC also has complied with the statutory mandate that it prescribe rules requiring that the terms of a written warranty be made available prior to the purchase of the goods.

The disclosure requirements kick in if the goods cost more than five dollars.[403] For goods costing more than ten dollars,[404] the Act also requires that a written warranty be designated either as a "full (statement of duration) warranty" or as a "limited warranty."[405] A warrantor that provides a full warranty undertakes to meet federal minimum standards set forth in the Act.[406] First, the standards require the warrantor to remedy any defect, malfunction, or failure of the product to conform within a reasonable period of time. Second, the warrantor

---

[399] Nothing in the Act requires that a supplier of a consumer product provide consumers with a written warranty. 15 U.S.C. § 2302(b)(2).

[400] 15 U.S.C. § 2306 contains disclosure requirements for service contracts.

[401] See 16 C.F.R. Parts 700–703.

[402] 16 C.F.R. § 701.3.

[403] 15 U.S.C. § 2302(e).

[404] 15 U.S.C. § 2303(d).

[405] 15 U.S.C. § 2303(a).

[406] 15 U.S.C. § 2304(a).

may not disclaim or limit the duration of any implied warranty even though the written warranty has a limited duration.[407] Third, the warranty may limit or exclude consequential damages for breach of a written warranty or an implied warranty but only by conspicuous language on the face of the warranty.[408] The Act conditions such limitations and exclusions on compliance with state law and, because some states prohibit the practice, an FTC regulation requires all written warranties containing a limitation or inclusion to include the following statement: "Some states do not allow the exclusion or limitation of incidental or consequential damages, so the above limitation or exclusion may not apply to you."[409] Fourth, a warrantor extending a full warranty that cannot remedy defects or malfunctions after a reasonable number of attempts must allow the consumer to elect a refund or a replacement product. If a written warranty is labeled "full," it is deemed to incorporate the federal minimum standards and any provision inconsistent with those standards, such as a requirement that a consumer pay the first $50 of any covered repair, is unenforceable.[410]

Congress hoped that the labeling requirement would advance the Act's objective of improving competition in the marketing of consumer products. Warrantors may choose to extend written warranties that do not meet all of the federal minimum standards but must designate them as limited warranties. Congress expected the term "limited warranty" to have a negative psychological effect on consumers, lessening their inclination to purchase products with the inferior designation. The goal has not been achieved. Because few suppliers use the full-warranty designation, limited warranties have become the norm and are not questioned by most consumers.

The Magnuson-Moss Act advances the Congressional objective to help prevent deception by excluding a right to disclaim any implied warranty when a supplier makes a full or limited written warranty to a consumer or enters into a service contract[411] with a consumer at the time of sale or within 90 days thereafter.[412] Even though UCC Section 2-316 provides mechanisms by which sellers may disclaim Article 2 implied warranties, doing so in violation of the Act is ineffective for all purposes, including state law.[413]

Although a supplier giving a limited written warranty or entering into a service contract at the time of sale or within 90 days thereafter may not disclaim

---

[407] The prohibition on limiting the duration of an implied warranty is in 15 U.S.C. § 2308(b).

[408] The Code does not require that a clause limiting or excluding consequential damages be conspicuous. *See* UCC § 2-719, discussed § 5.04 *supra*.

[409] 16 C.F.R. § 701.3(a)(8).

[410] 15 U.S.C. § 2304(e).

[411] A service contract differs from a seller's written warranty promising repair, replacement, or refund. The term refers to a separate written contract to maintain or repair a consumer product for a specified period of time. 15 U.S.C. § 2301(8). A service contract may be sold to a consumer by a person in the normal chain of distribution for the goods or by a person outside the chain.

[412] 15 U.S.C. § 2308(a).

[413] 15 U.S.C. § 2308(c); Ismael v. Goodman Toyota, 106 N.C. App. 421, 417 S.E.2d 290, 18 UCC Rep. Serv. 2d 101 (1992) (because dealer that sold used car violated Magnuson-Moss by disclaiming all implied warranties while at the same time entering into a service contract, the disclaimer was invalid).

implied warranties created by other law, it may limit their duration.[414] A regulation of the FTC, however, requires a provision that limits the duration of these warranties to be accompanied by the following statement: "Some states do not allow limitations on how long an implied warranty lasts, so the above limitation may not apply to you."[415] The limiting provision itself must comply with the requirements of the Act, meaning that the duration cannot be less than the duration of the written warranty which, in turn, must extend for a reasonable time. The limitation on duration must be displayed prominently on the face of the written warranty, set forth in clear and unmistakable language, and it must be conscionable.[416]

It is not entirely clear what limiting the duration of an implied warranty means. For an implied-warranty action to succeed, the claimant must prove that the defect existed when the goods left the seller's control.[417] This is not like the operation of a written warranty under the Act, where a seller promises either that no part will malfunction during a stated period of time without regard to whether the part was defective when it left the seller's control or that it will repair or replace any part that fails during the period. Presumably what is meant by a limitation on the duration of an implied warranty is that notice of a claim must be made before the stated period expires.

The Act provides for a variety of remedies and methods of enforcement. The Attorney General or the FTC can enforce its provisions. The Act also creates a private right of action for a consumer who is damaged by the failure of a supplier, warrantor, or service contractor to comply with its obligations under the Act or its obligations under a written warranty, implied warranty, or service contract.[418] Application of the remedial provisions of the Act to implied warranties even when no written warranty has been given provides a powerful incentive for warrantors of consumer products to live up to their obligations. A consumer who prevails in litigation is entitled to its costs and expenses, including attorney's fees based on actual time expended rather than a percentage of the value of the claim, unless the court in its discretion determines that costs and expenses should not be awarded.[419] Before suing, the consumer must go through an informal dispute-resolution procedure if the warrantor has established such a procedure

---

[414] 15 U.S.C. § 2308(b). A supplier giving a full written warranty may not even limit the duration of implied warranties created by other law. 15 U.S.C. § 2308(a).

[415] 16 C.F.R. § 701.3(a)(7).

[416] 15 U.S.C. § 2308(b).

[417] *See* § 5.02[B][2] *supra.*

[418] 15 U.S.C. § 2310(d). Even though the Act creates a federal cause of action, most litigation must occur in state court. The Act allows suit to be brought in any court of competent jurisdiction [15 U.S.C. § 2310(d)(1)(A)] but restricts access to the federal courts. Generally, for an action to be brought in federal district court the amount in controversy must be at least $50,000 and, in the case of a class action, there must be at least 100 named plaintiffs and the amount of each individual claim must be at least $25. 15 U.S.C. § 2310(d)(1)(B), (d)(3). A few courts have held that the class action limitations can be circumvented by asserting a claim under the Act using the procedures provided by the federal Class Action Fairness Act of 2005 (CAFA). *See, e.g.*, Chavis v. Fidelity Warranty Services, 415 F. Supp. 2d 620 (D.S.C. 2006).

[419] 15 U.S.C. § 2310(d)(2).

and stated in the written warranty that it must be used.[420] The consumer must also give the warrantor a right to cure the defect before bringing suit.[421]

[C]   State Consumer Protection Laws

Many states have implemented legislation to strengthen warranty protections given to consumers. Several of them have adopted non-uniform amendments to the Code that restrict the right to disclaim implied warranties and the right to modify the right to recover damages for their breach in consumer sales. For example, Massachusetts has amended Section 2-316 so that it does not apply to consumer sales.[422] Other states have adopted less pervasive changes. For example, a seller in Alabama may not use a disclaimer to avoid liability for personal injuries incurred in connection with a sale of consumer goods.[423] Disclaimers in a consumer sale in New Hampshire are ineffective unless the buyer signs a separate writing, provided before the sale, that contains statutorily mandated clauses.[424] Some states have adopted separate legislation that characterizes warranty violations as deceptive or unfair trade practices, thereby providing an additional potential source of protection for unsatisfied buyers.[425]

Several states have adopted detailed statutory schemes that address consumer warranty issues. For example, California's Song-Beverly Consumer Remedy Act[426] creates warranties of merchantability and fitness that have a maximum duration of one year. These warranties can be disclaimed only by a conspicuous writing, available prior to the sale, stating that the goods are being sold "as is" or "with all faults," that the entire risk as to their quality and performance is on the buyer, and that the buyer will be responsible for all repairs. In an approach that resembles the federal Magnuson-Moss Act, the Song-Beverly Act provides that the implied warranties created by it may not be disclaimed if express warranties of quality or performance are given. The Song-Beverly Act regulates express warranties by requiring that the warrantor be identified clearly and that the scope of the warranty be stated in readily understandable language. In addition to actual damages, breach of the Song-Beverly Act subjects a warrantor to costs and attorney fees, and to treble damages if the breach is willful.

The Kansas Consumer Protection Act[427] goes farther in protecting consumers. It prohibits attempts to exclude or otherwise limit the implied

---

[420]   15 U.S.C. § 2310(a)(3).

[421]   15 U.S.C. § 2310(e).

[422]   Mass. Gen. Law Ann. ch. 106, § 2-316A. Other states have adopted a similar approach. *See, e.g.,* Conn. Gen. Stat. Ann. § 42a-2-316(5); Me. Rev. Stat. Ann. tit. 11, § 2-316(5); Md. Code Com. Law § 2-316.1; D.C. Code § 28:2-316.01.

[423]   Ala. Code 1975 § 7-2-316(5).

[424]   N.H. Rev. Stats. Ann. § 382A:2-316(4).

[425]   *See, e.g.,* Ohio Rev. Code Ann. § 4165.01; Tex. Bus. & Com. Code Ann. § 17.41.

[426]   Cal. Civ. Code § 1790 *et seq.; see also* Minn. Stat. Ann. §§ 325.951–325.954; W. Va. Code §§ 46A-1-107, 46A-8-102; R.I. Gen. Laws § 6A-2-329.

[427]   Kan. Stat. Ann. § 50-623 *et seq.* West Virginia has a similar statute. W. Va. Code § 46A-6-107.

warranties of merchantability and fitness or to limit any remedy that would otherwise be available for a breach of either warranty. In addition to actual damages, it provides for the recovery of attorney fees and a civil penalty of up to $2,000 against any supplier in a consumer transaction that violates the statute by attempting to disclaim an implied warranty or limit a remedy. It also abolishes any remnants of the privity doctrine that might otherwise prevent an injured party from successfully pursuing a warranty claim.

To the extent permitted by law, probably every automobile manufacturer seeks to disclaim implied warranties and to limit an aggrieved buyer to a repair-or-replacement remedy for a fixed period of time if the vehicle breaks down. This approach places a disappointed consumer at the distinct disadvantage of having to prove, after a succession of unsuccessful repair attempts, that the exclusive remedy has failed its essential purpose.[428] Even if the remedy has failed its essential purpose, the consumer may face the additional dilemma that continued use of the vehicle after an attempted revocation of acceptance could undermine the availability of that remedy.[429]

Many states have addressed the problems in this area by enacting what are known as "lemon laws." Although the details vary from state to state, for the most part the statutes follow a basic pattern. A typical lemon law provides a remedy if the manufacturer does not satisfactorily repair defects that substantially impair the value, use, or safety of the vehicle within the stated warranty period or the first year following delivery, whichever is earlier. If a satisfactory repair is not accomplished within a specified number of attempts, typically four, or if the vehicle is out of service for thirty or more days during the applicable time period, the buyer may elect to receive either a new vehicle or a refund of the purchase price. Absence of privity between the consumer and the manufacturer is not a defense. Because most consumers cannot purchase another vehicle to use during the time it may take to resolve a claim, continued use of the vehicle does not bar a lemon-law remedy or constitute a waiver of the right to revoke acceptance.

§ 5.10   AMENDED ARTICLE 2

[A]   Remedial Promises

The amendments introduce the term "remedial promise" and use it to resolve a statute-of-limitations problem. The term means "a promise by the seller to repair or replace the goods or to refund all or part of the price of goods upon the happening of a specified event."[430] The Comments make it clear that repair, replacement, and refund are the only promises that qualify and that the seller has complete power to specify precisely the event that must occur for the promise to be triggered.[431] The remedial-promise concept was adopted to

---

[428] *See* § 5.04[a][2] *supra*.

[429] *See* Chapter 7 *infra*.

[430] UCC Amended § 2-103(1)(n).

[431] UCC Amended § 2-103, cmt. 9.

resolve a statute-of-limitations issue.[432] Under the amendments, a remedial promise is not an express warranty or warranty-like obligation and a cause of action for its breach does not accrue until the seller fails to perform the promise at the time performance is due.[433]

Section 2-313 as amended deals separately with express warranties and remedial promises, with the latter not subject to the basis-of-the-bargain test.[434] Similarly, Sections 2-313A and 2-313B apply to statutory obligations in the nature of express warranties and to remedial promises, and subsection (3) of each section contains tests that are analogous to the basis-of-the-bargain test for express warranties. These tests are not applicable to remedial promises.

As the Comments make clear, whether a remedial promise is an exclusive remedy is determined entirely by Section 2-719.[435] If it is expressly agreed to be exclusive and does not fail the essential-purpose test, it is the buyer's exclusive remedy; if it is not expressly agreed to be exclusive, or if it fails its essential purpose, the buyer may resort to any appropriate Code remedy. The official comment also provides that a post-sale promise made "to correct a problem with the goods that the seller is not obligated to correct that is made to placate a dissatisfied customer is not within the definition of remedial promise." Whether such a promise is enforceable at all turns on whether the requirements for modification have been met.

Bear in mind that a warranty and a remedial promise are distinct obligations, each with a separate limitations period. If a seller states that it will repair or replace any part that fails within a prescribed period of time, it is making a remedial promise but not an express warranty. If the seller states that no part will fail for a prescribed period, it is making an express warranty but not a remedial promise. If it states that no part will fail but if one does it will be repaired or replaced, it is making both an express warranty and a remedial promise. The express warranty will be governed by one limitations provision and the remedial promise by another. If the limitations period for the express warranty has expired, a subsequent breach of the remedial promise will not revive it, and vice-versa. Because the measure of damages may differ depending on the nature of the breach, the distinction can be of real significance.

[B]   Express Warranties and Similar Obligations

[1]   Express Warranties to Immediate Buyer

The rules regarding express warranties are essentially unchanged. Amended Section 2-313 contains a new subsection (1) that defines the term "immediate buyer" as "a buyer that enters into a contract with the seller," and express warranties are limited to obligations that meet the tests of subsection (2) and run from a seller to an immediate buyer. Other than the use of "immediate

---

[432] The problem is discussed in § 5.07 *supra*.

[433] UCC Amended § 2-725(2)(c).

[434] UCC Amended § 2-313(4).

[435] UCC Amended § 2-103, cmt. 9.

buyer," subsection (2) is unchanged from original subsection (1). The limitation of express warranties to parties in privity is not new, but the amendments highlight it in order to create a contrast with Sections 2-313A and 2-313B, which create new statutory obligations in the nature of express warranties that run directly from a seller to a remote purchaser rather than to the seller's immediate buyer.

[2]   Obligations to Remote Purchaser — Record Packaged with or Accompanying Goods

Amended Article 2 contains a new Section 2-313A that imposes an obligation in the nature of an express warranty that runs directly from a seller to a remote purchaser. It is designed to deal with what are sometimes called "pass-through" warranties — warranties that arise when a remote seller makes, in a record packaged with or accompanying new goods intended in the normal chain of distribution for a remote purchaser, an affirmation of fact, promise, description, or remedial promise that would be enforceable under Section 2-313 as an express warranty or remedial promise if made to an immediate buyer. Most pass-through warranties take the form of a card inside the packaging that contains the goods, but the section is not so limited. The information may be printed on the outside of the box, on a card inside the box, or in a booklet that is inside the box or that is turned over to the remote purchaser at or before the purchase (*e.g.*, an owner's manual turned over to the remote purchaser by a car dealer).

In the prototypical transaction, Manufacturer (M) sells the goods to which the record relates to Retailer (R), who resells or leases them to Remote Purchaser (RP). M is the seller, R is the immediate buyer, and RP is the remote purchaser. There must be a sale for the section to be triggered, a requirement that is satisfied by the transaction between M and R. "Purchaser" is used more narrowly here than in Article 1, where the term refers to a person that acquires a property interest pursuant to any type of voluntary transaction, including by gift or secured transaction.[436] For Section 2-313A to apply, the remote purchaser must acquire the goods in a transaction of sale or lease. If M "reasonably expects the record to be, and the record is, furnished to" RP, RP obtains the benefit of the section whether it acquires the goods by sale or lease.

"Normal chain of distribution" is not defined. The intent, as expressed in the Comments,[437] is to exclude goods such as "gray" goods, salvaged goods, and used goods sold as seconds. Another limitation is that the section only applies to transactions in goods that are new or are sold or leased as new.

The section uses the term "obligation" rather than "warranty," leaving warranty to describe relations between parties in privity. Nevertheless, the liability contemplated, other than liability arising from a remedial promise, is essentially the same as express warranty liability for affirmations of fact, promises, or descriptions under amended Section 2-313(2)(a) and (b). Similarly,

---

[436] UCC § 1-201(30), (29).

[437] UCC Amended § 2-313A, cmt. 1.

a remedial promise to a remote purchaser is identical in effect to a remedial promise to an immediate buyer under amended Section 2-313(4) — it creates an obligation that the promise will be performed upon the happening of the specified event. Section 2-313A does not contain a provision analogous to amended Section 2-313(1)(c), but the Comments indicate that it is not intended to overrule a decision imposing liability on a remote seller that distributes a sample or model.[438] The comment also notes that neither Section 2-313A nor 2-313B is "intended to overrule cases that impose liability on facts outside [their] direct scope."

Because there is no contract, and hence no "bargain," between the seller and the remote purchaser, the drafters decided not to use the term "basis of the bargain." Instead, they created a substitute test in subsection (3)(a) for affirmations of fact, promises, and descriptions: There is no liability if a reasonable person in the position of the remote purchaser would not believe that the particular representation created an obligation. The relationship between the reasonable-person test and the basis-of-the-bargain test is explained as follows in the Comments:

> Obligations other than remedial promises created under this section are analogous to express warranties and are subject to a test that is akin to the basis of the bargain test of Section 2-313(2). The seller is entitled to shape the scope of the obligation, and the seller's language tending to create an obligation must be considered in context. If a reasonable person in the position of the remote purchaser, reading the seller's language in its entirety, would not believe that an affirmation of fact, promise or description created an obligation, there is no liability under this section.[439]

While this test is clearly akin to the basis-of-the-bargain standard, it also appears to differ in a significant respect. An immediate buyer that is unaware of its seller's representation would generally be unable to establish that the representation became part of the basis of the bargain. A remote purchaser, on the other hand, would not need to have read the relevant language in the record, despite having it available because it had been furnished and the buyer reasonably expected to be furnished, because the test is based on what a reasonable person in the buyer's comparable situation would have believed. The substitute test in section 2-313A does not apply to remedial promises that the seller includes in the record because these promises are not subject to a basis-of-the-bargain test even when the seller has privity with the buyer.[440]

Subsection (4) contains a "puffing" test that is identical to the one set forth in amended Section 2-313(3),[441] and that, in turn, is identical to the test in original Section 2-313(2). Subsection (5)(a) permits the seller to use Section 2-719 to modify or limit the remedies available to the remote purchaser if the modification

---

[438] UCC Amended § 2-313A, cmt. 4.

[439] UCC Amended § 2-313A, cmt. 5.

[440] UCC Amended § 2-313A(3)(b); cf. UCC Amended § 2-313(4).

[441] See UCC Amended § 2-313, cmt. 10.

or limitation is furnished to the remote purchaser no later than the time of purchase or is set forth in the record that contains the actionable representation. Subsection (5)(b) further limits seller responsibility by providing that the remote purchaser may not recover consequential damages in the form of lost profits. In most cases these damages would not be available anyway under the foreseeability test of Section 2-715(2)(a), and at any rate the seller is likely to invoke its opportunity under Section 2-719(3) to exclude recovery of consequential damages by agreement. Thus, the statutory prohibition reflects reality. Beyond lost profits, incidental and consequential damages are available subject to the usual tests, and, under subsection (5)(c), direct damages may be calculated in any reasonable manner.

Subsection (6) provides that, for an obligation other than a remedial promise,[442] breach occurs if the goods fail to conform to the affirmation of fact, promise, or description at the time they leave the seller's control. This provision largely parallels the approach most courts have taken for warranty liability between parties in privity. The approach correlates with shifting of the risk of loss, which typically occurs when the goods are delivered to the immediate buyer.[443] Although breach occurs if the goods do not conform when they leave the seller's control, accrual of the remote purchaser's cause of action does not occur under amended Section 2-725(3)(b) until the remote purchaser receives them. This parallels the accrual rule — time of tender and completion of any agreed installation or assembly — for warranties between parties in privity. In another parallel, the cause of action does not accrue under amended Section 2-725(3)(c) until the remote purchaser discovers (or should have discovered) the breach if the obligation explicitly extends to the future performance of the goods and discovery must await the time for performance.

[3]   Obligations to Remote Purchaser — Advertising and Similar Communications to the Public

Like new Section 2-313A, new Section 2-313B imposes a direct obligation running from a seller to a remote purchaser, this time based on advertising or a similar communication to the public.[444] In most respects the section is identical to Section 2-313A, and the discussion in the preceding section of this book should be consulted with respect to such issues as terminology (immediate buyer, remote purchaser, new goods and goods sold as new, normal chain of distribution); remedial promise; the substitute for the basis-of-the-bargain test (a reasonable person in the position of the remote purchaser); and preclusion of recovery of lost profits. The major distinction is that Section 2-313B is predicated on advertising or a similar communication to the public by the

---

[442] The limitation period for breach of a remedial promise is the same without regard to whether the seller's obligation arises under UCC Amended §§ 2-313, 2-313A, or 2-313B. The limitations period for remedial promises is discussed in § 5.07 *supra*.

[443] UCC Amended § 2-509(3) no longer distinguishes between merchant and nonmerchant sellers.

[444] The phrase "similar communication to the public" is intended to mean a communication in the nature of advertising, such as a press release. UCC Amended § 2-313B, cmt. 5. It is not intended to apply to all information made public by a remote seller, and courts should interpret it to mean "advertising or the equivalent."

remote seller rather than on a record that accompanies the goods and is furnished to the remote purchaser.

The section adds an additional test for enforceability that is not found in Section 2-313A. That section does not require that the remote purchaser be aware of or have any expectations with regard to the record upon which liability is predicated; it merely requires that the record be furnished to a remote purchaser. Under Section 2-313B(3)(a), however, the remote purchaser must enter into the sale or lease with knowledge of the communication and with an expectation that the goods will conform to an affirmation of fact, promise, or description, or that the seller will perform a remedial promise. Noting a temporal aspect to advertising, Comment 4 recognizes that it would be highly unusual to be able to satisfy the required levels of expectation and belief based on an out-of-date communication. Comment 5 makes the obvious point that the communication at issue must be considered in light of all information known by the remote purchaser at the time of contracting:

> For example, a news release by a manufacturer limiting the statements made in its advertising and which are known by the remote purchaser, or a communication to the remote purchaser by the immediate seller limiting the statements made in the manufacturer's advertising must be considered to determine whether the expectation requirement applicable to the remote purchaser and the belief requirement applicable to the reasonable person in the position of the remote purchaser are satisfied.

[C]   Relationship Between Non-Merchantability and Defectiveness In Tort

Although the amendments do not make textual changes of consequence in Section 2-314, they include an important addition to the official comments. Because of the close parallel between strict products liability in tort and the implied warranty of merchantability, and because plaintiffs typically plead both theories in actions alleging personal injury or property damage, the drafters concluded that a court should not apply different standards to determine whether a product is non-merchantable under Article 2 and whether it is defective and unreasonably dangerous for tort purposes.[445] Accordingly, they drafted the following new Comment:

> Suppose that an unmerchantable lawn mower causes personal injury to the buyer, who is operating the mower. Without more, the buyer can sue the seller for breach of the implied warranty of merchantability and recover for injury to person "proximately resulting" from the breach. Section 2-715(2)(b).

> This opportunity does not resolve the tension between warranty law and tort law where goods cause personal injury or property damage. The primary source of that tension arises from disagreement over whether

---

[445] Section 5.02[B][3] *supra* contains a brief comparison between the implied warranty of merchantability and strict products liability.

the concept of defect in tort and the concept of merchantability in Article 2 are coextensive where personal injuries are involved, *i.e.*, if goods are merchantable under warranty law can they still be defective under tort law, and if goods are not defective under tort law can they be unmerchantable under warranty law? The answer to both questions should be no, and the tension between merchantability in warranty and defect in tort where personal injury or property damage is involved should be resolved as follows:

When recovery is sought for injury to person or property, whether goods are merchantable is to be determined by applicable state products liability law. When, however, a claim for injury to person or property is based on an implied warranty of fitness under Section 2-315 or an express warranty under Section 2-313 or an obligation arising under Section 2-313A or 2-313B, this Article determines whether an implied warranty of fitness or an express warranty was made and breached, as well as what damages are recoverable under Section 2-715.

To illustrate, suppose that the seller makes a representation about the safety of a lawn mower that becomes part of the basis of the buyer's bargain. The buyer is injured when the gas tank cracks and a fire breaks out. If the lawnmower without the representation is not defective under applicable tort law, it is not unmerchantable under this section. On the other hand, if the lawnmower did not conform to the representation about safety, the seller made and breached an express warranty and the buyer may sue under Article 2.[446]

Application of the principle enunciated in this comment would preclude the result in *Denny v. Ford Motor Company*,[447] in which the jury found that an off-road vehicle's utility outweighed the risk of roll-over in applying the state's risk/utility tort test but that it nevertheless was not fit for its ordinary purposes under Section 2-314. Under the Comment's rationale, the risk/utility test would have been applied to both the tort claim and the warranty claim. Whether that approach would have resulted in a different outcome in the actual case is speculative because the jury, given only that test, might have reached a different conclusion on the relative utility of the vehicle.

[D] Warranty of Title

The Comments to original Section 2-312 indicate that part of the concept of rightful transfer is that a buyer not be exposed to a lawsuit in order to protect its interest in the goods,[448] and the courts have generally recognized the validity of this principle. The amended section elevates the principle to the text by providing that a transfer must not only be rightful but also must not "unreasonably expose the buyer to litigation because of any colorable claim to or interest in the goods." Put another way, a buyer is entitled to marketable title.

---

[446] UCC Amended § 2-314, cmt. 7.

[447] 639 N.Y.S.2d 250 (1995). The case is discussed in § 5.02[B][3] *supra*.

[448] UCC § 2-312, cmt. 1.

For the warranty to be breached, the claim at issue must be reasonable and colorable, and until such a claim is resolved the market for the goods is impaired.

Section 2-312 has also been reorganized for clarity. The warranty against infringement has been moved from subsection (3) to subsection (2), and amended subsection (3) deals with disclaimers of both the warranty of title and the warranty against infringement. Thus, the rules for the creation of warranties appear first, followed by the rules for their disclaimer.

[E]   Disclaimers

The amendments to Section 2-316(2) on the disclaimer of implied warranties establish different standards based on whether the contract is a consumer contract. The term "consumer contract" itself is new to the amendments and is defined as a contract between a merchant seller and a consumer,[449] with the term "consumer" defined as "an individual who buys or contracts to buy goods that, at the time of contracting, are intended by the individual to be used primarily for personal, family, or household purposes."[450] A consumer-to-consumer contract is not a "consumer contract," but that exclusion is irrelevant for current purposes as the seller in such a contract would not make an implied warranty of merchantability.

Amended Section 2-316(2) requires different language than its predecessor for a disclaimer of the implied warranty of merchantability in a consumer contract. The new language is as follows: "The seller undertakes no responsibility for the quality of the goods except as otherwise provided in this contract." The word merchantability is not used, but the sentence conveys considerably more information to the average consumer than was previously conveyed by the word merchantable. A disclaimer using the consumer language is effective also in a nonconsumer contract. Otherwise, as under the original section, the language in a nonconsumer contract must mention merchantability. In addition, the amended subsection substitutes "record" for "writing" and, in the case of a consumer contract, eliminates oral disclaimers by requiring that the disclaimer be in a record.

With respect to disclaimers of the implied warranty of fitness for nonconsumer contracts, amended Section 2-316(2) provides the same language that is suggested rather than mandated in the original subsection. For consumer contracts, however, the following language is mandated: "The seller assumes no responsibility that the goods will be fit for any particular purpose for which you may be buying these goods, except as otherwise provided in the contract." As with a disclaimer of the implied warranty of merchantability, a disclaimer using the more expansive consumer language is also effective in a nonconsumer contract.

Amended Article 2 makes some clarifications to Section 2-316(3). In the case of a consumer contract evidenced by a record, the amended subsection requires

---

[449] UCC Amended § 2-103(1)(d).

[450] UCC Amended § 2-103(1)(c).

that a disclaimer through expressions like "as is" or "with all faults" be set forth conspicuously in the record.[451] Although there is no rule for other transactions, including oral consumer transactions, the inference is clear — there is neither a record nor a conspicuousness requirement. With respect to a disclaimer based on a buyer's examination of the goods, the amendments move the requirement that a seller make a demand before there can be a refusal to inspect by a buyer from the Comments to the text.[452]

[F]   Statutory Third-Party Beneficiaries

The amendments retain the three alternatives to original Section 2-318, with the only change being that each alternative now encompasses, in addition to express warranties under Section 2-313 and implied warranties under Sections 2-314 and 2-315, statutory obligations in the nature of warranties (Sections 2-313A and 2-313B) and remedial promises. Thus, under Alternative A, warranties, statutory obligations, and remedial promises extend to the same class of persons to whom warranties extended under prior law, and the same is true of Alternatives B and C.

[G]   Statute of Limitations

Amended Article 2 makes several relevant changes in the basic statute-of-limitations scheme. The general limitations period under amended Section 2-725(1) is four years after the cause of action accrues or one year after the breach is or should have been discovered, but in no event is it longer than five years after accrual. The period may be reduced to not less than one year in nonconsumer contracts but may not be reduced in consumer contracts. With regard to express (and implied) warranties, breach is now deemed to occur when the seller tenders delivery and completes any agreed upon installation or assembly.[453] A cause of action for breach of a remedial promise accrues when the promise is not performed at the time performance is due."[454]

§ 5.11   CISG

The CISG does not use the term "warranty" because it is generally not used in other countries. Nevertheless, the chapter of the CISG on obligations of the seller requires that the goods conform to the contract's requirements. Article 35(1) states as follows: "The seller must deliver goods which are of the quantity, quality and description required by the contract and which are contained or packaged in the manner required by the contract." In other words, the CISG imposes a basic obligation on the seller to deliver goods that meet the quality requirements of the contract.

---

[451] UCC Amended § 2-316(3)(a).

[452] UCC Amended § 2-316(3)(b).

[453] UCC Amended § 2-725(3)(a).

[454] UCC Amended § 2-725(2)(c).

Because the CISG does not use the term "warranty," obviously it does not differentiate between express and implied warranties. Article 35(1) clearly encompasses express terms related to the quantity, quality, and description of the goods, but that it is not limited to express terms is apparent from Article 35(2), which provides that "the goods do not conform with the contract unless" they meet four designated standards. The standards correlate with the implied warranties of merchantability and fitness and with the express warranty created by a sample or model.

One of the standards requires that the goods be "fit for the purposes for which goods of the same description would ordinarily be used."[455] Although the standard does not use the word "merchantable," it is clearly comparable to the Code's core requirement for merchantability.[456] Another standard, also similar to one of the Code's requirements for merchantability, is that the goods must be "contained or packaged in the manner usual for such goods or, where there is no such manner, in a manner adequate to preserve and protect the goods."[457]

Different domestic standards in the countries of the buyer and the seller pose issues concerning the benchmark for ordinary use. In one case, for example, mussels purchased by a German buyer from a New Zealand seller contained levels of cadmium that exceeded the levels recommended by the German Federal Health Department. The German Supreme Court sensibly held that a seller should not be held to the standards imposed by public law requirements in the buyer's country unless those requirements conform to the standards of the seller's country or the seller has been adequately informed of the buyer's unique domestic requirements.[458] In another case, the court relied upon a previous relationship between the parties in determining that German law applied to paprika with dangerous levels of toxins.[459]

Yet another CISG standard corresponds to the UCC's implied warranty of fitness for a particular purpose. The seller must deliver goods that "[a]re fit for any particular purpose expressly or impliedly made known to the seller at the time of the conclusion of the contract."[460] The seller can eliminate the obligation by showing that the buyer did not rely on the seller's skill and judgment to provide an appropriate product or that the buyer was not reasonable in its reliance on the seller. Under the final standard, the goods must "[p]ossess the qualities of goods which the seller has held out to the buyer as a sample or model."[461] This standard corresponds to the requirements of Section 2-313(1)(c) of the Code, which differs from other express warranties in that it rests on inferences rather than expressions.

---

[455] CISG Art. 35(2)(a).

[456] UCC § 2-314(2)(c).

[457] CISG Art. 35(2)(d); cf. UCC § 2-314(2)(e).

[458] [Germany] (08-03-1995) No. VIII ZR 159/94, Bundesgerichtof; full text available on Unilex, section D.1995.9.

[459] [Germany] (21-08-1995) 1 KfH O 32/95, Landgerich Ellwangen; full text available on Unilex, Daction D.1995.20.

[460] CISG Art. 35(2)(b).

[461] CISG Art. 35(2)(c).

The CISG also includes provisions that correspond with the UCC's warranties of title and against infringement. Article 41 states that "[t]he seller must deliver goods which are free from any right or claim of a third party, unless the buyer agreed to take the goods subject to that right or claim." Under this provision, the goods must be free from security interests and other forms of liens as well as from third-party claims of ownership. Article 42 deals with rights or claims of third parties based on industrial or other intellectual property. The article limits a seller's liability to rights or claims of which the seller, at the time of the conclusion of the contract, knew or could not have been unaware.

While the CISG does not address warranty disclaimers explicitly, it introduces Article 35(2)'s standards with the caveat "[e]xcept where the parties have agreed otherwise." Moreover, Article 6 is drafted broadly to permit the parties to derogate from or vary the effect of the convention's provisions. Thus, the CISG clearly permits disclaimers, but it does not include any requirements governing their form or language. Some commentators argue that Section 2-316 of the UCC should apply to transactions governed by the CISG because of the mandatory nature of the section and the public policy that supports its requirements. They bolster their argument by pointing to Article 4, which provides that the CISG is not concerned with the validity of the contract or any of its provisions or of any usage. In other words, freedom of contract permits the parties to disclaim the standards established by Section 35(2), but whether a particular disclaimer is valid must be determined by domestic law.

Other commentators argue that the language of Article 35(2) explicitly authorizing the parties to deviate from the standards on the conformity of the goods should be sufficient to trigger the Article 4 exception which permits the exclusion of validity "except as otherwise provided in this Convention." The proponents of this approach also believe that subjecting the validity of disclaimers to U.S. law would be an unsound public policy for international sales transactions. Language patterned after UCC Section 2-316(2) would be meaningless to many international traders because, like the CISG, many domestic legal systems do not utilize the terms "warranty," "disclaimer," or "merchantability," nor do they draw distinctions between express and implied warranties. If disclaimers are an issue of validity requiring the application of U.S. law, sellers will have to draft their disclaimers to satisfy both the CISG, U.S. law, and any relevant domestic law of the non-U.S. contracting party.

Chapter 6

RISK OF LOSS

§ 6.01   INTRODUCTION

The goods in a contract for sale or lease are susceptible to a variety of calamities. They may be lost, stolen, damaged, or completely destroyed. Goods are vulnerable during their manufacture, storage, and transit, and even after they have been received by a buyer or lessee. The transit stage is often the period of greatest exposure to loss because the goods are being moved from one location to another and third parties, such as carriers, often are involved. An issue of loss allocation arises when a loss occurs without the fault of either party to the sale or lease.

The Uniform Sales Act tied most of the rights and duties of the parties to a contract for sale, including loss-allocation principles, to the location of title.[1] This approach proved to be unsatisfactory in part because the location of title depended on the intent of the parties, which often was unclear. The Code greatly reduces the significance of title[2] and abandons it altogether as a basis for resolving many issues,[3] including loss allocation.

Articles 2 and 2A allocate losses only as between the parties to a sales or lease contract. Ultimate liability often lies with a third party, such as a bailee that incurs liability for breach of its duty of care with respect to goods in its possession, a third party that incurs liability for negligence that caused the loss, or an insurer that incurs liability under a policy of insurance. Other law determines the extent of third-party liability.

Allocation of the risk of loss affects the duties of the parties. If a loss occurs after the risk has passed to the buyer, the buyer must nevertheless pay for the goods.[4] By contrast, if the loss occurs before the risk passes to the buyer, the seller must make a substitute, conforming tender in order to avoid liability for nondelivery.[5] The loss-allocation principles effectively determine which party must proceed against any available third party with greater liability for the loss.[6]

---

[1] Uniform Sales Act § 22.

[2] Of course, the passage of title remains the signature feature of a sale. "A 'sale' consists in the passing of title from the seller to the buyer for a price." UCC § 2-106(1).

[3] "Each provision of this Article with regard to the rights, obligations and remedies of the seller, the buyer, purchasers or other third parties applies irrespective of title to the goods except where the provision refers to such title." UCC § 2-401; see, e.g., Martin v. Mellands, 27 UCC Rep. Serv. 94 (N.D. 1979) (trial court's use of title as relevant indicium for risk of loss was erroneous). Article 2A includes a comparable provision, adding that the provisions of the article apply without respect to who has possession of the goods. UCC § 2A-302.

[4] The buyer's obligation is to pay for the goods. UCC § 2-301; UCC § 2-709(1)(a) (seller's cause of action for price in risk-of-loss context); see § 9.04[A][2] infra; see also Rheinberg Kellerei GmbH v. Brookfield Nat'l Bank of Commerce, 901 F.2d 481, 11 UCC Rep. Serv. 2d 1214 (5th Cir. 1990) (seller entitled to recover from buyer for wine that deteriorated after remaining exposed at harbor).

[5] The seller's obligation is to transfer and deliver the goods. UCC § 2-301. On measures of damages for nondelivery, see §§ 8.02[B], [C], 8.04 infra. A seller sometimes will be excused from further performance, but excuse provides only a defense and the seller cannot affirmatively recover from the buyer. Excuse generally relates to the doctrines of impossibility and commercial impracticability. See § 7.08 infra.

[6] Windows, Inc. v. Jordan Panel Sys. Corp., 177 F.3d 114, 38 UCC Rep. Serv. 2d 267 (2d Cir. 1999) (buyer could sue carrier for damage to shipment caused by carrier's negligence but could not proceed against seller because the risk of loss had shifted to buyer).

§ 6.02   SALES

[A]   In the Absence of Breach [§ 2-509]

Section 2-509 allocates the risk of loss when neither party is in breach of the sales contract. Section 2-510 determines the effect, if any, that a breach by either party has upon that allocation.[7]

[1]   Agreement

Section 2-509(4) recognizes that the parties to a sales contract can agree between themselves on when the risk of loss passes to the buyer.[8] The agreement can be found in the express terms of the contract or by implication from an applicable trade usage, course of dealing, or course of performance.[9]

Parties that employ express terms should be careful to articulate their intentions clearly, as courts sometimes have held that the language used was not effective to pass the risk of loss. For example, the contract in *Caudle v. Sherrard Motor Co.*[10] contained a clause stating that neither loss nor destruction of a house trailer would release the buyer from its payment obligation. Thieves stole the trailer from the dealer's lot before the buyer took possession and the court interpreted the clause as fixing responsibility on the buyer only after he took possession. Placing the risk of loss on a buyer before delivery was so uncommon, in the view of the court, that the seller should have articulated such an intention more clearly.[11]

When goods are to be shipped by carrier, the parties often include express terms, consisting of abbreviations, that comprise a form of business shorthand designed to specify various requirements.[12] The use of these terms has consequences for risk-of-loss allocation. For example, in a shipment contract[13] between a San Francisco seller and a New York buyer that is created by a term stating "F.O.B. San Francisco $15,000," tender occurs in San Francisco and the seller incurs both the cost and the risk of putting the goods into possession of a

---

[7] *See* § 6.02[B] *infra.*

[8] Forest Nursery Co., Inc. v. I.W.S., Inc., 141 Misc. 2d 661, 534 N.Y.S.2d 86, 8 UCC Rep. Serv. 2d 923 (Dist. Ct. 1988) (risk of loss passed to buyer through terms stating "No Risk to Supplier" and "NOTICE: ALL SHIPMENTS TRAVEL AT RISK AND COST OF PURCHASER").

[9] UCC § 2-509, cmt. 5; Mercanti v. Persson, 160 Conn. 468, 280 A.2d 137, 8 UCC Rep. Serv. 969 (1971) (risk of loss of a mast being built for a boat owner could have passed to the owner if trade usage in the boat-building trade placed the risk of fire loss on the owner during work in progress, but the issue of trade usage had not been preserved for the record).

[10] 525 S.W.2d 238, 17 UCC Rep. Serv. 754 (Tex. Ct. App. 1975).

[11] *See also* Hayward v. Postma, 31 Mich. App. 720, 188 N.W.2d 31, 9 UCC Rep. Serv. 379 (1971) (clause requiring buyer to carry insurance on goods at all times insufficient to pass risk of loss on uninsured boat destroyed by fire on seller's premises).

[12] *See* UCC §§ 2-319 (F.O.B. and F.A.S terms), 2-320 (C.I.F. and C. & F. terms). See § 4.04[C][1] *supra* for a discussion of these terms.

[13] The distinction between shipment and destination contracts in the context of risk of loss is discussed further in § 6.02[A][2] *infra* and is discussed generally in § 4.04[C][1] *supra.*

carrier in that city.[14] If a collision destroys the goods while the seller is moving them across San Francisco to the rail terminal, the loss remains on the seller. If the loss results from a rail mishap during cross-country transit, the risk is on the buyer.[15] If the F.O.B. term creates a destination contract, as in "F.O.B. New York $15,000," the buyer attains more for the stated price.[16] The seller incurs the risk and expense of transporting the goods across the country to New York and thus bears the risk of the rail mishap.

F.O.B. terms can be much more specific than simply designating the relevant city for purposes of tender and passage of the risk of loss. For example, the term might designate a specific vehicle or vessel, in which case "the seller must in addition [to other responsibilities] at his own expense and risk load the goods on board."[17] Thus, in a shipment contract the risk remains on the seller if the goods are damaged when a crate breaks open during the loading process.

If the agreement of the parties does not allocate risk, one of the first three subsections of Section 2-509 governs the issue. These gap-filling provisions are discussed in the ensuing material.

[2] Shipment by Carrier

Section 2-509(1) allocates the risk of loss when the contract "requires or authorizes the seller to ship the goods by carrier"[18] and its rules correlate with the rules discussed above for F.O.B. contracts.[19] This ensures a consistent approach irrespective of whether the parties create a shipment or a destination contract through the use of an F.O.B. term, through another express term, or through an implied-in-fact term. If transportation by carrier is required, or if it is authorized and the seller chooses that option, and the parties have not agreed on a term creating a destination contract, Article 2 presumes a shipment contract.[20] The Comments explain that "[t]he seller is not obligated to deliver at a named destination and bear the concurrent risk of loss until arrival, unless he has specifically agreed so to deliver or the commercial understanding of the terms used by the parties contemplates such delivery."[21]

Section 2-509(1) provides as follows:

---

[14] UCC § 2-319(1)(a).

[15] See, e.g., Black Prince Distillery, Inc. v. Home Liquors, 148 N.J. Super. 286, 372 A.2d 638, 21 UCC Rep. Serv. 1037 (1977) (buyer liable for purchase price of liquor hijacked from carrier's truck).

[16] UCC § 2-319(1)(b).

[17] UCC § 2-319(1)(c). Consolidated Bottling Co. v. Jaco Equip. Corp., 442 F.2d 660, 8 UCC Rep. Serv. 966 (2d Cir. 1971) (the term "f.o.b. purchaser's truck" left the risk of loss on the seller until the truck was loaded).

[18] UCC § 2-509(1).

[19] See § 6.02[A][1] supra.

[20] Eberhard Mfg. Co. v. Brown, 61 Mich. App. 268, 232 N.W.2d 378, 17 UCC Rep. Serv. 978 (1975) (in the absence of an express or implied-in-fact term on delivery or risk of loss, a shipment contract was created); see also Pestana v. Karinol Corp., 367 So. 2d 1096, 25 UCC Rep. Serv. 1306 (Fla. Ct. App. 1979) (shipment contract created in the absence of delivery term).

[21] UCC § 2-503, cmt. 5.

Where the contract requires or authorizes the seller to ship the goods by carrier

> (a) if it does not require him to deliver them at a particular destination, the risk of loss passes to the buyer when the goods are duly delivered to the carrier even though the shipment is under reservation (Section 2-505); but

> (b) if it does require him to deliver them at a particular destination and the goods are there duly tendered while in the possession of the carrier, the risk of loss passes to the buyer when the goods are there duly so tendered as to enable the buyer to take delivery.

The first provision deals with shipment contracts. Risk of loss passes to the buyer when the seller duly delivers the goods to the carrier, and to determine when such a delivery occurs the provisions governing a seller's tender of delivery in such contracts must be consulted. The basic rules on tender are in Section 2-503, but in the case of a shipment contract Section 2-503(2) requires the seller to comply with Section 2-504.[22] Tender occurs under that section, and thus the risk of loss passes, when the seller places the goods in the possession of an appropriate carrier and makes a contract for their transportation that is reasonable under the circumstances, delivers or tenders to the buyer any documents necessary for the buyer to obtain possession of the goods from the carrier, and notifies the buyer of the shipment.[23]

In a destination contract the risk of loss passes upon the seller's tender of delivery, which occurs when the carrier tenders the goods to the buyer at the designated destination.[24] Under Section 2-503, which governs the manner of tender, the carrier, acting as the seller's agent, must put and hold conforming goods at the buyer's disposition, provide any necessary notification to the buyer, and tender any necessary documents.[25]

[3] Goods Held by a Bailee

Section 2-509(2) provides as follows:

> Where the goods are held by a bailee to be delivered without being moved, the risk of loss passes to the buyer

---

[22] Montana Seeds, Inc. v. Holliday, 178 Mont. 119, 582 P.2d 1223, 24 UCC Rep. Serv. 884 (1978) (because risk of loss passed to buyer on delivery of goods to carrier, the buyer had to pursue the carrier on its liability for delivering part of shipment to wrong address).

[23] Rheinberg-Kellerei GmbH v. Vineyard Wine Co., Inc., 53 N.C. App. 560, 281 S.E.2d 425, 32 UCC Rep. Serv. 96 (1981) (seller's failure to notify buyer directly or by forwarding shipping documents until after loss of shipment at sea did not facilitate buyer protecting its interest by insurance and left risk of loss on seller).

[24] UCC § 2-509(1)(b).

[25] UCC § 2-503(1), (3), (5); Baumgold Bros., Inc. v. Allan M. Fox Co., East, 375 F. Supp. 807, 14 UCC Rep. Serv. 580 (N.D. Ohio 1973) (tender did not occur when seller sent package containing diamonds by registered mail and it disappeared after postal worker left it on the counter of buyer's unattended store).

(a)   on his receipt of a negotiable document of title covering the goods; or

(b)   on acknowledgment by the bailee of the buyer's right to possession of the goods; or

(c)   after his receipt of a non-negotiable document of title or other written direction to deliver, as provided in subsection (4)(b) of Section 2-503.

The subsection covers the three possible scenarios with respect to goods that the seller has entrusted to a bailee. Paragraph (a) applies if the bailee issues a negotiable document for the goods. Because title to the goods is merged into such a document, the risk of loss passes when the buyer receives the document and thereby becomes the owner of the goods.[26]

Rather than issuing a negotiable document, a bailee might give the seller a nonnegotiable document, the scenario contemplated in paragraph (c). A nonnegotiable document does not represent title to the goods but rather functions as a mechanism for determining who has the right to take delivery from the bailee. Delivery of the document to the buyer does not establish the buyer's right to delivery unless it is named in the document as a person entitled to receive delivery. If the document instead names the seller, the seller can facilitate the buyer's right to possession by giving the buyer a written delivery order. This order, which itself constitutes a nonnegotiable document,[27] establishes the buyer's right to take possession of the goods.[28] Risk of loss does not pass to the buyer until it receives a writing establishing its right to possession and the buyer has a reasonable opportunity to present the writing to the bailee.[29] If the bailee refuses to honor the writing, the seller's tender is defeated and it retains the risk of loss.[30]

In the final scenario, the bailee does not give any type of document to the seller. Paragraph (b) provides the functional equivalent of paragraph (c) by indicating that risk of loss passes from the seller to the buyer when the bailee acknowledges the buyer's right to possession of the goods. For example, in *Whately v. Tetrault*,[31] the seller of a motorboat and trailer accompanied the buyer to a storage location and informed the bailee that the goods had been sold and would be picked up the following day by the buyer's agent. The court held that the agent's arrangement with the bailee to pick up the goods constituted the bailee's acknowledgment of the buyer's right to the goods and passed the risk of

---

[26] Henry Heide, Inc. v. Atlantic Mut. Ins. Co., 80 Misc. 2d 485, 363 N.Y.S.2d 515, 16 UCC Rep. Serv. 701 (Sup. Ct. 1975) (risk of loss for 200,000 pounds of sugar that disappeared from a warehouse had passed from the seller to the buyer with tender of the negotiable warehouse receipt).

[27] UCC § 1-201(16).

[28] UCC § 7-403(1),(4).

[29] UCC §§ 2-509(2)(c), 2-503(4)(b); Commonwealth Propane Co. v. Petrosol Int'l, Inc., 818 F.2d 522, 3 UCC Rep. Serv. 2d 1778 (6th Cir. 1987) (written delivery direction for stored propane).

[30] UCC § 2-503(4)(b).

[31] 29 Mass. App. Dec. 112, 5 UCC Rep. Serv. 838 (1964).

loss.[32]

Occasionally a seller tries to apply the literal language of subsection (b) to a case that does not involve a true bailment. For example, in *Caudle v. Sherrard Motor Co.*[33] the buyer left on business before he could take delivery of a house trailer that he had just purchased. The seller indicated that the buyer could return at his convenience for the trailer, but in the interim it was stolen from the seller's premises. The seller contended that the risk of loss passed to the buyer under Section 2-509(2)(b) because prior to the theft the seller had acknowledged the buyer's right to possession. In other words, the seller argued that it acted as a bailee in holding the goods for the buyer.

The court properly rejected the seller's position.[34] The seller had simply agreed to postpone the time when the buyer would take delivery of the goods and, even if title had passed, the characterization of the seller as a bailee would have been technically correct but not dispositive. Allowing a seller to pass the risk of loss to a buyer simply by acknowledging the buyer's right to take possession of the goods would defeat the underlying rationale of the Code's loss-allocation scheme. A seller that remains in possession of the goods continues to exert control over them and should be expected to maintain insurance on them.[35]

[4] All Other Cases

If none of the other rules of Section 2-509 apply, subsection (3) governs loss allocation in the absence of breach.[36] The subsection creates different rules depending on whether the seller is a merchant or a nonmerchant. If the seller is a merchant, risk of loss does not pass until the buyer receives the goods,[37] and receipt means taking physical possession of the goods.[38] By defining receipt in this manner, the drafters deprived the seller of arguments based on the buyer's

---

[32] *Cf.* O.C.T. Equip., Inc. v. Shepherd Mach. Co., 95 P.3d 197, 54 UCC Rep. Serv. 2d 327 (Okla. Ct. App. 2004) (risk of loss had not passed to the buyer because the bailee in possession of the tractor had not acknowledged to the buyer, prior to the time that the engine was destroyed, that the buyer had a right to possession).

[33] 525 S.W.2d 238, 17 UCC Rep. Serv. 754 (Tex. Ct. App. 1975).

[34] For similar holdings, see Conway v. Larsen Jewelers, Inc., 104 Misc. 2d 872, 429 N.Y.S.2d 378, 29 UCC Rep. Serv. 842 (Civ. Ct. 1980) (no bailment created with respect to piece of jewelry purchased on a lay-away plan); Courtin v. Sharp, 280 F.2d 345 (5th Cir. 1960), *cert. denied*, 365 U.S. 814 (1961) (seller of colt did not qualify as bailee for purposes of § 2-509(2)(b) by agreeing to board colt for the buyer).

[35] UCC § 2-509, cmt. 3.

[36] UCC § 2-509(3).

[37] National Plumbing Supply Co. v. Castellano, 118 Misc. 2d 150, 460 N.Y.S.2d 248, 36 UCC Rep. Serv. 814 (Just. Ct. 1983) (delivery of goods to unnamed individuals on a job site not under the control of the buyer did not pass the risk of loss).

[38] UCC § 2-103(1)(c). Ron Mead T.V. & Appliance v. Legendary Homes, Inc., 746 P.2d 1163, 6 UCC Rep. Serv. 2d 117 (Okla. Ct. App. 1987) (leaving appliances in unlocked garage from which they were stolen did not constitute buyer's physical possession necessary for "receipt"); *cf.* Hughes v. Al Green, Inc., 65 Ohio St. 2d 110, 418 N.E.2d 1355, 31 UCC Rep. Serv. 890 (1981) (risk for the damage resulting from a collision of a purchased automobile was on the buyer that had taken immediate possession).

constructive or symbolic possession. A merchant continues to exert control over the goods and prudently should continue to keep them insured.[39] Until the buyer takes physical possession of the purchased goods, therefore, the risk of loss remains on the merchant seller, and this result applies whether delivery occurs at its place of business[40] or pursuant to a destination contract in which the seller makes delivery using its own vehicle. In the latter case the rule of Section 2-509(1)(b) discussed above does not apply because it is limited to destination contracts involving the use of a carrier.

If the seller is not a merchant, risk of loss passes to the buyer on tender of delivery, which occurs when the seller puts and holds conforming goods at the buyer's disposition.[41] For example, suppose an individual agrees to buy several pieces of furniture from a neighbor who does not qualify as a merchant. If the neighbor agrees to hold the goods for the buyer while the buyer arranges to rent a trailer to move them, the risk of loss passes to the buyer even though it has not yet taken possession.[42] The seller may not have insurance covering the goods, and the buyer obtains an insurable interest upon identification of the goods to the contract[43] and thus has the ability to purchase insurance.

[B]   In the Event of Breach [§ 2-510]

A breach by either party to a sales contract might influence the risk-of-loss allocation. Section 2-510 includes three rules that govern the effect of a breach on risk of loss. Two of these rules concern breach by the seller; the last covers breach by the buyer.

[1]   Buyer's Right to Reject

If a seller's tender gives the buyer a right of rejection, the risk of loss "remains on the seller until cure or acceptance."[44] Since the provision requires only that the buyer have a right to reject, not that it make an effective rejection, its effect is to leave the risk on the seller even if the risk otherwise would have passed to the buyer.[45] For example, consider a shipment contract that requires the seller to ship goods by rail from Los Angeles to St. Louis but does not contain an F.O.B. term. If the seller ships conforming goods the risk of loss

---

[39] UCC § 2-509, cmt. 3. "The buyer, on the other hand, has no control of the goods and it is extremely unlikely that he will carry insurance on goods not yet in his possession." *Id.*

[40] UCC § 2-509, cmt. 3. Hayward v. Postma, 31 Mich. App. 720, 188 N.W.2d 31, 9 UCC Rep. Serv. 379 (1971).

[41] UCC § 2-503(1).

[42] *Cf.* Martin v. Melland's Inc., 283 N.W.2d 76, 27 UCC Rep. Serv. 94 (N.D. 1979) (seller who retained possession and use of his used truck and haystack mover under a contract agreement that allowed this arrangement until new equipment was available to him had not tendered delivery and thus bore the risk of loss when a fire destroyed the equipment).

[43] UCC § 2-501(1).

[44] UCC § 2-510(1). The various circumstances in which a buyer has a right of rejection are discussed in § 7.04 *infra.*

[45] *See, e.g.,* T. J. Stevenson & Co., Inc. v. 81,193 Bags of Flour, 629 F.2d 338, 30 UCC Rep. Serv. 865 (5th Cir. 1980) (delivery of unmerchantable flour gave buyer the right to reject and thus left the risk of loss on seller).

passes to the buyer under Section 2-509(1)(a) when the seller duly delivers the goods to the carrier.[46] If the seller ships defective goods, however, it retains the risk of loss because the buyer has a right to reject under the perfect tender rule of Section 2-601.[47] The same result follows if the goods are conforming but the seller materially breaches its obligation to make a reasonable contract for their transportation. The buyer then would have a right to reject under Section 2-504.

Section 2-510(1) ceases to apply if the goods are cured or the buyer accepts. Once either event occurs, loss allocation once more will be controlled by the agreement of the parties or by the default rules of Section 2-509. For example, suppose a merchant seller takes back nonconforming goods and effectuates a cure by repairing them. The buyer no longer has a right of rejection and thus Section 2-510(1) is no longer applicable. If the seller, rather than promptly taking back the goods, cures by delivering conforming replacement goods, the risk of loss with respect to the replacement goods passes to the buyer under the normal rules, but the loss with respect to the nonconforming goods remains on the seller.[48]

As with cure, acceptance by the buyer reinstates the normal risk-allocation rules.[49] Acceptance terminates a buyer's right to reject,[50] thus ending the applicability of Section 2-510(1). For example, suppose that a seller delivers nonconforming goods to a buyer, thus leaving the risk of loss on the seller. If the buyer waits too long to reject it will be deemed to have accepted.[51] If loss occurs thereafter Section 2-510(1) will no longer apply and, since the risk has already passed to the buyer under Section 2-509(3), the buyer bears the loss.[52]

[2]   Buyer's Revocation of Acceptance

Although a justifiable revocation of acceptance[53] by a buyer does not cause the risk of loss to shift back to the seller, it does determine the rights of the parties in the event that a loss occurs. Section 2-510(2) provides that "[w]here the buyer rightfully revokes acceptance he may to the extent of any deficiency in his effective insurance coverage treat the risk of loss as having rested on the seller from the beginning."

---

[46] UCC § 2-509(1)(a).

[47] *See, e.g.,* Larsen v. A.C. Carpenter, Inc., 620 F. Supp. 1084, 2 UCC Rep. Serv. 2d 433 (E.D. N.Y. 1985), *aff'd,* 800 F.2d 1128 (2d Cir. 1986) (risk of loss never passed to the buyer because seller put nonconforming seed potatoes into possession of carrier).

[48] "The 'cure' of defective tenders contemplated by subsection (1) applies only to those situations in which the seller makes changes in goods already tendered, such as repair, partial substitution, sorting out from an improper mixture and the like since 'cure' by repossession and new tender has no effect on the risk of loss of the goods originally tendered." UCC § 2-510, cmt. 2.

[49] The various circumstances in which acceptance occurs are discussed in § 7.03[A] *infra.*

[50] UCC § 2-607(2).

[51] UCC § 2-606(1)(b).

[52] The result would have been otherwise if the goods had been stolen or destroyed before the buyer's right of rejection had expired.

[53] Revocation of acceptance is discussed generally in § 7.05 *infra.*

Unlike the rule of Section 2-510(1), which is based on the *right* to reject, the aggrieved buyer must actually revoke in order to invoke this rule.[54] The distinction can be particularly significant in light of the requirement that a revocation must be made "before any substantial change in condition of the goods which is not caused by their own defects."[55] Thus if the goods are destroyed in a fire caused by their own defective wiring, the buyer may still be entitled to revoke acceptance and pursue other appropriate damages. By contrast, if a buyer with a right to revoke has not yet done so when a fire caused by something other than their own defect destroys the goods, the buyer bears the full risk of the loss even if it is uninsured.

For a case to be within Section 2-510(2), it will have passed previously through the circumstances described in Section 2-510(1). In other words, a defect that gives the buyer a right to revoke acceptance will have given it a right to reject, but the acceptance will have rendered Section 2-510(1) inapplicable and will have reinstated the normal risk-allocation rules. The risk under those rules almost certainly will be on the buyer by the time it revokes its acceptance. The revocation under Section 2-510(2) does not literally cause the risk to revert back to the seller, but rather allows the buyer to treat it as having been on the seller from the beginning to the extent the buyer lacks effective insurance coverage.[56] If the buyer's insurance fully covers the loss, it bears the entire risk. If the buyer has no insurance, it technically bears the risk but can place the entire loss on the seller.[57] If the buyer's insurance only partially covers the loss, it retains the risk but can place the uninsured portion of the loss on the seller.

Section 2-510(2) operates as an antisubrogation provision.[58] Upon paying the buyer for loss or damage to the goods, an insurer might wish to recoup the payment by subrogating itself to the buyer's claim against the seller for breach of contract. Indeed, the insurance contract might include a provision that entitles the insurer to subrogation. Section 2-510(2), however, defeats any opportunity for the insurer to assert a successful claim against the seller by leaving on the buyer the risk of any loss for which the buyer has effective insurance coverage. Because the buyer does not have a claim against the seller, and the seller lacks any basis for subrogation.

[3] Breach by the Buyer

Section 2-510(3), which deals with the effect of a buyer's breach on the allocation of loss, provides that "[w]here the buyer as to conforming goods already identified to the contract for sale repudiates or is otherwise in breach

---

[54] *See, e.g.*, Meat Requirements Coordination, Inc. v. GGO, Inc., 673 F.2d 229, 33 UCC Rep. Serv. 917 (8th Cir. 1982) (seller not liable for loss from meat spoilage when buyer did not revoke its acceptance within a reasonable time).

[55] UCC § 2-608(2).

[56] "The word 'effective' as applied to insurance coverage in those subsections is used to meet the case of supervening insolvency of the insurer. The 'deficiency' referred to in the text means such deficiency in the insurance coverage as exists without subrogation." UCC § 2-510, cmt. 3.

[57] Beal v. Griffin, 123 Ida. 445, 849 P.2d 118, 21 UCC Rep. Serv. 2d 244 (Ida. Ct. App. 1993).

[58] "This section merely distributes the risk of loss as stated and is not intended to be disturbed by any subrogation of an insurer." UCC § 2-510, cmt. 3.

before risk of their loss has passed to him, the seller may to the extent of any deficiency in his effective insurance coverage treat the risk of loss as resting on the buyer for a commercially reasonable time."[59] This rule may be useful to an underinsured seller if the buyer breaches the contract and a loss subsequently occurs before the risk of loss would otherwise have passed to the buyer under the normal risk-allocation rules.

Section 2-510(3) applies only if the buyer breaches the contract before the risk of loss passes under the normal rules and three additional conditions are satisfied: (1) the goods conform to the contract, (2) they were identified to the contract before the buyer's breach, and (3) the seller has a deficiency in its effective insurance coverage. As to the first condition, if the goods had been nonconforming the seller would have breached by tendering them, thereby giving the buyer a right to reject and leaving the risk of loss on the seller under Section 2-510(1). As to the second condition, until the goods are identified to the contract the buyer does not have an insurable interest in them and it would be unfair to allocate an uninsurable loss to the buyer.[60] The third condition operates as an antisubrogation provision in a manner comparable to Section 2-510(2), which applies when a loss occurs after a buyer justifiably revokes its acceptance.[61]

If the three conditions are met the aggrieved seller can treat the risk of loss as resting on the buyer, but only for a commercially reasonable time. The rationale for the limitation is that a breach by the buyer before the risk of loss passes will almost certainly take the form of a repudiation, a failure to take delivery, or a wrongful rejection, and in each instance the seller ultimately will be the owner of the goods and should, at some point, be fully responsible for what happens to them. Limiting the protection of Section 2-510(3) to a commercially reasonable time gives the seller an opportunity to purchase adequate insurance. The court in *Multiplastics, Inc. v. Arch Industries, Inc.*[62] held in favor of an aggrieved seller even though the loss occurred slightly more than a month after the buyer's breach and the seller had not yet purchased insurance. The court based its decision on principles of estoppel, stressing the fact that the buyer had repeatedly indicated that it would transmit delivery instructions to the seller and accept deliveries of the goods.[63]

---

[59] UCC § 2-510(3).

[60] UCC § 2-501(1). For a discussion of identification, see § 1.03[B] *supra.*

[61] *See* § 6.02[B][2] *supra.*

[62] 348 A.2d 618, 14 UCC Rep. Serv. 573 (Conn. 1974).

[63] *See also* Portal Gallaries, Inc. v. Tomar Products, Inc., 60 Misc. 2d 523, 302 N.Y.S.2d 871, 6 UCC Rep. Serv. 1047 (N.Y. Sup. Ct. 1969) (because more than a reasonable period of time passed for the seller to procure additional insurance to cover the entire loss, the breaching buyer of paintings was not liable for the deficiency in insurance coverage).

§ 6.03   LEASES

[A]   General Rule [§ 2A-219(1)]

Determining the risk of loss is easy under the general rule of Article 2A, which provides that "risk of loss is retained by the lessor and does not pass to the lessee."[64] The rule reflects the general practice in personal property leasing[65] and is based on an assessment of which party is more likely to insure the goods against loss. The most sensible approach generally is for the lessor to insure the goods and pass through the applicable portion of the cost to the lessee in the form of higher rent, particularly if the rental term is relatively short. Otherwise the lessor might have to insure the goods, drop the insurance on leasing them, and then reinsure when the lease ends.

[B]   Exceptions

[1]   Applicability

Article 2A recognizes two exceptions to the general rule allocating the risk of loss to the lessor. The parties can expressly agree to a different risk-allocation scheme, and the general rule does not apply to finance leases.

[a]   Express Agreement

The parties are free to determine risk-of-loss allocation pursuant to the principle of freedom of contract. Article 2 includes a specific provision that recognizes this right in the risk-of-loss context.[66] The drafters of Article 2A felt that an explicit provision was unnecessary because Article 2A is founded on freedom of contract.[67] The parties to a lease thus can decide for themselves which party will bear the risk of loss and when, if at all, it will pass to the lessee.[68] Passing the loss to the lessee might be sensible in a longer-term lease in which the lessee assumes the responsibility for care and maintenance of the goods.

Article 2A includes a unique provision on agreements concerning insurance: "The parties by agreement may determine that one or more parties have an obligation to obtain and pay for insurance covering the goods and by agreement may determine the beneficiary of the proceeds of the insurance."[69] This provision recognizes that an agreement to require the lessee to obtain insurance

---

[64] UCC § 2A-219(1).

[65] UCC § 2A-219, cmt.

[66] UCC § 2-509(4); *see* § 6.02[A][1] *supra.*

[67] UCC § 2A-219, cmt.

[68] Sunbelt Cranes Const. & Hauling, Inc. v. Gulf Coast Erectors, Inc., 189 F. Supp. 2d 1341 (M.D. Fla. 2002) (lessee expressly agreed to bear risk of loss of a leased crane under any circumstances, including acts of negligence of its own or others and acts of God).

[69] UCC § 2A-218(5).

will not necessarily be construed to allocate the risk of loss to the lessee.[70] In either event the lessee's failure to insure the goods would be a default that would entitle the lessor to damages for the resulting loss.[71]

[b] Finance Leases [§ 2A-219(1)]

Article 2A allocates the risk of loss differently in a finance lease.[72] It provides that "[i]n the case of a finance lease, risk of loss passes to the lessee."[73] The allocation of loss to the finance lessee is based on the role of the finance lessor. In a finance lease, the finance lessor is not involved in manufacturing, selecting, or supplying the goods; rather, it acts as a financing conduit enabling the finance lessee to acquire possession and use of the goods.[74] Although a finance lessor can take possession of the goods,[75] generally the manufacturer or supplier delivers them directly to the finance lessee. Finance leases also tend to be of relatively long duration, a circumstance that sometimes causes the parties to an ordinary lease to allocate the risk of loss to the lessee. Accordingly, in the absence of a contrary agreement, the risk of loss in a finance lease passes to the finance lessee.

[2] When Risk Passes

If the risk of loss is to pass to the lessee in a particular lease transaction, the time at which it passes must be ascertained. The issue is not relevant in most bipartite lease transactions because the risk of loss remains on the lessor. If the parties expressly agree that the risk will be borne by the lessee but do not agree on the time when the risk passes, the time of passage may have to be determined. Similarly, timing issues can arise when Article 2A shifts the risk of loss to the finance lessee under a finance lease.

Article 2A therefore provides rules that apply if "risk of loss is to pass to the lessee and the time of passage is not stated."[76] These rules follow the pattern of the Article 2 statutory analogue.[77] Thus, they draw a distinction between cases based on whether either party defaults. Not surprisingly, the Article 2A provisions apply only to ordinary lease transactions in which the parties have

---

[70] The issue has been litigated in the Article 2 context. Hayward v. Postma, 31 Mich. App. 720, 188 N.W.2d 31, 9 UCC Rep. Serv. 379 (1971) (language in secured sales agreement that buyer must "at all times keep the goods fully insured" held insufficient to apprise buyer that risk of loss had passed on goods buyer had not yet received).

[71] O/E Sys., Inc. v. Inacom Corp., 179 F. Supp. 2d 363 (D. Del. 2002) (when lessor proceeded directly against insurer, on policy on which lessee wrongfully failed to name lessor as loss payee, the court dismissed the claim because lessor was not a named insured or an intended third-party beneficiary or assignee the policy, nor was it yet a judgment creditor against the lessee).

[72] Finance leases are discussed generally in § 1.04[B] *supra.*

[73] UCC § 2A-219(1). Liberty Capital Resources, Inc. v. Garcia, 57 UCC Rep. Serv. 2d 1 (Cal. Ct. App. 2005) (risk of loss on the finance lessee for a leased tow truck that was destroyed in a head-on collision).

[74] *See* § 1.04[B] *supra.*

[75] UCC § 2A-103, cmt. g.

[76] UCC § 2A-219(2).

[77] *See* UCC §§ 2-509, 2-510.

agreed to transfer the risk of loss to the lessee and to finance leases, and then only if the parties' agreement does not set the time at which the risk of loss passes.

[a]   In the Absence of Default [§ 2A-219(2)]

The first rules that determine when risk of loss passes in the absence of breach apply to cases in which the lessor is required or authorized to ship the goods by carrier[78] and they duplicate precisely the comparable Article 2 rules.[79] Thus, in a shipment contract the risk of loss passes to the lessee when the goods are duly delivered to the carrier, whereas in a destination contract the risk of loss does not pass until the goods are duly tendered to enable the lessee to take delivery from the carrier.[80]

Article 2A does not incorporate several of the Article 2 provisions that are needed to amplify these delivery concepts in order for the risk-of-loss provisions to work. It does not include the sections on F.O.B. provisions,[81] manner of tender of delivery,[82] or shipment by a carrier.[83] These provisions simply do not play a sufficient role in the leasing context to justify their inclusion, even in the context of risk allocation. Lease agreements commonly include express terms that determine the risk of loss, which narrows considerably the role of the Code's rules on shipment and destination contracts. The typical practice in finance leases in which the goods will be shipped directly by the supplier to the finance lessee is particularly relevant. The finance lease agreement generally requires the finance lessee to certify in writing that the goods have been received in good condition.

The second rule on when risk of loss passes to the lessee in the absence of a default applies when the goods are held by a bailee and are to be delivered without being moved. It provides that "the risk of loss passes to the lessee on acknowledgment by the bailee of the lessee's right to possession of the goods."[84] This rule also mirrors a provision of Article 2.[85] The other two options in this context that are included in Article 2 — dealing with the issuance of negotiable and nonnegotiable documents by the bailee — were omitted from Article 2A as they are not relevant to lease transactions.[86]

The final rule is the residual provision, and it is likewise comparable to Article 2.[87] Thus, if the lessor is a merchant the risk of loss passes to the lessee upon

---

[78] UCC § 2A-219(2)(a).

[79] UCC § 2-509(1)(a); *see* § 6.02[A][2] *supra.*

[80] For an explanation of shipment and destination contracts, see § 6.02[A][1], [2] *supra.*

[81] UCC § 2-319.

[82] UCC § 2-503.

[83] UCC § 2-504.

[84] UCC § 2A-219(2)(b).

[85] UCC § 2-509(2)(b); *see* § 6.02[A][3] *supra.*

[86] UCC § 2A-219, cmt.

[87] UCC § 2A-219(2)(c); *see* UCC § 2-509(3); § 6.02[A][4] *supra.*

receipt of the goods.[88] In the case of a finance lease, the same rule applies if the supplier is a merchant. Receipt of goods means "taking physical possession of them."[89] If the lessor is not a merchant, risk of loss passes to the lessee on tender of delivery.

[b]   In the Event of Default [§ 2A-220]

Article 2A follows the Article 2 format of stating additional rules on risk-of-loss allocation that apply when one of the parties is in default.[90] It incorporates precisely the same rules as Article 2 and thus are based on breach by the lessor as evidenced by the lessee having a right to reject or justifiably revoking acceptance, and on breach by the lessee.[91] Again, the rules apply only if the risk of loss passes to the lessee and the parties have not fixed the time for its passage.

The rules require some care in their application to finance leases. The Comments caution that the reallocation rule based on revocation does not "allow the lessee under a finance lease to treat the risk of loss as having remained with the supplier from the beginning."[92] A lessee can use the revocation provision only upon making an effective revocation of acceptance, and Article 2A strictly limits that right with respect to a finance lessee. For the most part, the obligations undertaken by a finance lessee become independent and irrevocable upon acceptance of the goods.[93] Any attempt to revoke in this context would not be rightful and thus would not invoke a risk reallocation.

§ 6.04   AMENDED ARTICLE 2

The major change in this area is the elimination of the residual rule on allocation of risk in cases in which the seller is not a merchant. Under original Section 2-509(3), risk of loss passes to a buyer on receipt of the goods if the seller is a merchant and on tender of delivery if the seller is a nonmerchant. Under the amended provision, the risk shifts when the buyer receives the goods without regard to the seller's status. The drafters concluded that the same rationale that underlies the merchant rule — that a seller in possession of goods is likely to be insured and a buyer that has not received possession is unlikely to be insured — applies equally to sales by nonmerchants.[94]

The rationale can be demonstrated through a simple illustration. Assume that a buyer enters into a contract to buy a seller's car and the parties agree that the buyer will pick the car up at noon on Wednesday. If the seller makes a

---

[88]   UCC § 2A-219(2)(c).

[89]   UCC § 2-103(1)(c). This section is cross-referenced by UCC § 2A-103(3).

[90]   UCC § 2A-220; *see* UCC § 2-510.

[91]   *See* § 6.02[B] *supra*; Fluid Concepts, Inc v. DA Apartments Ltd. Partnership, 159 S.W.3d 226, 56 UCC Rep. Serv. 2d 570 (Tex. Ct. App. 2005) (lessor could not utilize section 2A-220 because there was not any evidence of a deficiency in the lessor's insurance coverage).

[92]   UCC § 2A-220, cmt.

[93]   UCC § 2A-407(1); *see* § 7.05[F] *infra*.

[94]   UCC Rev. § 2-509, cmt. 1.

conforming tender at the agreed time but the buyer fails to show up and that night the car is stolen, original Section 2-509(3) places the risk of loss on the buyer even though the seller is likely to still be insured and the buyer is likely to be uninsured. The amended provision is more in line with reality. It leaves the risk on the seller pending receipt by the buyer and, because the buyer is in breach, under Section 2-510(3) the seller may for a commercially reasonable time treat the risk as resting with the buyer to the extent of a deficiency in the seller's effective insurance coverage.

§ 6.05   CISG

[A]   Contracts Involving Transit of the Goods

[1]   INCOTERMS

The risk-of-loss provisions of the CISG play a relatively limited role. Sales of goods in the international arena most commonly involve the use of carriers to transport the goods to the location desired by the buyer. INCOTERMS, the international commercial terms established by the International Chamber of Commerce, includes twelve terms applicable to sales involving the use of carriers. Many parties choose to use these terms because the terms enable them to determine many aspects of their reciprocal obligations, including the allocation of the risk of loss. Given the widespread acceptance of INCOTERMS, most parties in international sales avail themselves of the opportunity afforded by Article 6 to opt out of the CISG default provisions on risk of loss by including a specific term selected from INCOTERMS.

For each of the trade terms enumerated in INCOTERMS, ten topics are addressed and the fifth topic always deals with passage of the risk of loss to the buyer.[95] With the trade terms included in Group F,[96] the risk of loss passes when the seller makes an appropriate delivery of the goods to the carrier designated by the buyer.[97] The terms in Group C require the seller to make and pay for the contract for carriage, but the seller does not incur any further risk of loss after it makes an appropriate delivery of the goods to the carrier.[98]

---

[95] For an explanation of the organization of the topics in INCOTERMS, see § 4.07[C][2][a] *supra*.

[96] *Id.* (detailed discussion of the significance of trade terms and their groupings).

[97] The terms FAS and FOB can be used only for sea transport or inland waterway transport. Under FAS, the risk of loss passes on the seller's delivery of the goods to the side of the designated vessel at the loading place in the port of shipment, whereas under FOB the risk does not pass until the goods pass over the ship's rail during loading. The term FCA can be used with any mode of transportation, and risk of loss passes when the seller meets its obligation to deliver the goods by placing them into the custody of the carrier. The third of the ten topics addressed in INCOTERMS covers the acquisition and payment for insurance. None of the terms in Group F impose any responsibility for insurance on the seller.

[98] The terms CFR and CIF can be used only for sea or waterway transport. Risk of loss passes under both terms when the goods pass the ship's rail at the port of shipment. Whereas the seller does not incur any responsibility for insurance under CFR, CIF requires the seller to procure and pay for insurance for the benefit of the buyer. The terms CPT and CIP are comparable terms for any mode of transportation. Risk passes when the seller places the goods into the custody of the carrier. The

Under the terms in Group D, the seller incurs the costs and the risks of delivering the goods to the country of destination.[99]

[2] Default Terms

Article 67 of the CISG covers contracts in which the seller is to obligated to place the goods into the custody of a carrier. If that obligation requires the seller "to hand the goods over to a carrier at a particular place, the risk does not pass to the buyer until the goods are handed over to the carrier at that place."[100] Assume that a contract requires a seller located in San Diego to ship the goods on a designated ship from the port in Long Beach. If a collision on the freeway destroys the goods during their transport by truck from the seller's place of business to Long Beach, the risk of their loss remains on the seller without regard to whether the seller used its own truck or hired an independent trucking company. The seller's obligation was to hand the goods over to the carrier in Long Beach and the accident occurred before the seller complied.

If the seller in a contract involving carriage of the goods "is not bound to hand them over at a particular place, the risk passes to the buyer when the goods are handed over to the first carrier for transmission to the buyer."[101] The basis for the rule is recognition that international sales transactions often involve multi-modal transport. The use of several different forms of transportation, such as rail, ship, and truck, has proliferated with the increased use of containerized shipping. A contract might not specify a specific means of transport, or it might require the seller to ship the goods by sea without stating a particular ship's location. If the accident in the preceding illustration occurred under such a contract in a truck owned by an independent trucking company, risk would have passed to the buyer because the seller had turned the goods over to the first of the multi-modal transportation carriers. Risk would not have passed if the seller had used its own truck because it would not yet have turned the goods over to the first multi-modal carrier.

---

seller must procure and pay for insurance for the benefit of the buyer under CIP, but not under CPT.

[99] The terms DES and DEQ can be used only for sea and waterway transport. The risk of loss passes under DES when the goods are placed at the disposal of the buyer on board the vessel at the unloading point in the port of destination. The term DEQ delays risk passage until the goods are placed at the disposal of the buyer on the quay or wharf of the port of destination. Three of the terms in Group D can be used with any mode of transport. Risk passes under DAF when the goods at placed at the disposal of the buyer at the named place of delivery at the frontier. DDU establishes the place for availability at the named place in the country of importation, and DDP recognizes a comparable location but only after the goods have been cleared for importation. None of the terms in Group D impose any responsibility for insurance on the seller. On the other hand, because the seller bears the risk of loss for a substantial, if not all, of the transit by carrier, sellers generally choose to insure the goods for their own benefit.

[100] CISG Art. 67(1).

[101] CISG Art. 67(1).

[B]   Contracts Not Involving Transit of the Goods

If the contract does not require the seller to turn the goods over to a carrier, Article 69 governs allocation of the risk of loss.[102] If the buyer is bound to take over the goods at a location other than the seller's place of business, the risk passes when the buyer is aware that the goods have been placed at its disposal at the designated location.[103] This default rule covers a sale of goods held at a warehouse if the buyer must take delivery of the goods at the warehouse. In addition, the provision covers a delivery in the seller's own vehicle if the transit of the goods does not involve a common carrier. If the buyer is bound to take over the goods at the seller's place of business, the risk passes when the buyer complies by taking over the goods.[104] If the buyer breaches by failing to take over the goods in due time, the risk passes at the time the seller places the goods at the buyer's disposal and the buyer breaches.[105]

---

[102] The only INCOTERM that does not involve the transit of goods is Ex Works at the seller's premises. Risk of loss passes under this term when the seller places the goods at the disposal of the buyer at the named place and time, or if no place or time is stated, at the place and time that is usual for the delivery of such goods.

[103] CISG Art. 69(2).

[104] CISG Art. 69(1).

[105] A breach by the seller does not affect the risk-of-loss allocation unless the breach is fundamental. CISG Art. 70. With a fundamental breach the buyer retains the right to avoid the contract. For discussion of the concepts of fundamental breach and avoidance (comparable to rejection) in the CISG, see § 7.10[A][1][a] *infra*.

Chapter 7

PERFORMANCE AND BREACH

§ 7.01 OBLIGATIONS OF THE PARTIES GENERALLY [§ 2-301]

Article 2 states the general obligations of a seller and a buyer as follows: "The obligation of the seller is to transfer and deliver and that of the buyer is to accept and pay in accordance with the contract."[1] Although the structure of the sentence is awkward, the phrase "in accordance with the contract" should be read to modify the obligations of both seller and buyer. Stated more expansively, the seller's obligation is to transfer title[2] and deliver the goods in accordance with the contract, and the buyer's obligation is to accept the goods and pay for them in accordance with the contract. The reference to the contract incorporates the obligations created by the terms of the agreement and any obligations imposed by the gap-filling provisions of Article 2.[3]

Although Section 2-301 by its terms does not condition the seller's duty to deliver or the buyer's duty to pay, the section must be read in the context of other provisions that make it clear, absent agreement to the contrary, that the duties function as constructive concurrent conditions.[4] Thus, tender of delivery by the seller is a condition precedent to the buyer's duty to accept the goods[5] and tender of payment by the buyer is a condition precedent to the seller's duty to deliver.[6] Neither party can establish breach by the other without at least tendering its own performance.

---

[1] UCC § 2-301.

[2] A sale "consists in the passing of title from the seller to the buyer for a price." UCC § 2-106(1).

[3] See the discussion of "contract" and "agreement" in § 2.01 *supra*.

[4] This relationship is stated in other sections. UCC §§ 2-507(1) (delivery is a condition to the duty to pay); 2-511(1) (tender of payment is a condition to the duty to deliver). The parties can agree otherwise.

[5] UCC § 2-601. The mechanics of tender are discussed in § 4.04[C] *supra*.

[6] UCC § 2-511(1). The mechanics of payment are discussed in § 4.04[D] *supra*.

The foregoing statement of the duties of the parties is broad and general. An in-depth understanding of their duties requires an analysis of a number of interrelated provisions. The ensuing parts of this chapter provide that analysis.

§ 7.02 OVERVIEW OF ACCEPTANCE, REJECTION, AND REVOCATION OF ACCEPTANCE

When a seller tenders delivery of goods, a buyer has a choice.[7] If the goods or the manner in which they are tendered fail in any respect to conform to the contract, the buyer has a right to reject the goods, accept them, or accept some commercial units[8] and reject others.[9] If title has passed to the buyer,[10] rejection revests it in the seller,[11] and as a consequence a rejecting buyer in possession of the goods is a bailee rather than an owner. The buyer's duties as bailee are discussed below.[12]

If the goods and the manner of tender fully conform to the contract, the buyer is obligated to accept the goods and to pay for them according to the terms of the contract. The buyer nevertheless has the power (but not the right) to reject the goods and thereby revest title in the seller,[13] although in this instance the buyer's action will constitute a breach. Whether rightful or wrongful, rejection generally precludes acceptance, although a seller can treat its buyer as having accepted the goods if after rejection the buyer wrongfully does an act inconsistent with the seller's ownership.[14]

A buyer with a right to reject goods might nevertheless accept them, either with or without awareness of a nonconformity. In either event, acceptance precludes rejection but does not of itself impair any other remedy provided by Article 2,[15] such as a claim for breach of contract if the tender of delivery was nonconforming or a claim for breach of warranty if the goods are nonconforming. In limited circumstances, acceptance can be revoked.[16] Like rejection, a justified revocation revests title in the seller,[17] thereby placing the buyer back in the

---

[7] The same choice and concepts apply to a lessee upon tender by the lessor.

[8] " 'Commercial unit' means such a unit of goods as by commercial usage is a single whole for purposes of sale and division of which materially impairs its character or value on the market or in use." UCC § 2-105(6). The definition provides examples, including a suite of furniture and an assortment of sizes.

[9] UCC § 2-601. The section's "perfect tender" rule is discussed in depth in § 7.04[A] *infra*.

[10] "Unless explicitly agreed otherwise, title passes to the buyer at the time and place at which the seller completes its performance with reference to the delivery of the goods. . . ." UCC § 2-401(2).

[11] UCC § 2-401(4).

[12] *See* § 7.04[b][3] *infra*.

[13] UCC § 2-401(4) (rejection "whether or not justified" revests title in seller).

[14] UCC §§ 2-602(2)(a), 2-606(1)(c); *see* discussion § 7.03[A][3] *infra*.

[15] UCC § 2-607(2).

[16] *See* § 7.05[A] *infra*.

[17] An unjustified revocation does not revest title in the seller. UCC § 2-401(4). For some reason, Article 2 generally uses "rightful" when referring to rejections and "justifiable" when referring to revocations of acceptance. The adjectives have the same meaning: Whether rightful or justified, the

position it would have occupied if it had initially rejected the goods.[18]

Acceptance, rejection, and revocation of acceptance are thus three inconsistent buyer responses to a seller's tender.[19] Acceptance is the pivotal concept. It constitutes a basic contract obligation of the buyer if the goods and the tender conform to the contract. It is also relevant in determining whether the buyer has a right to reject or to revoke its acceptance. Rejection is a pre-acceptance concept, and once acceptance occurs rejection is no longer possible. Revocation of acceptance is a post-acceptance concept that, if justified, undoes the acceptance. Because of its pivotal role, acceptance is discussed first.

§ 7.03   ACCEPTANCE

[A]   Methods of Acceptance [§ 2-606; § 2A-515]

A buyer accepts tendered goods whenever any of the events listed in Section 2-606 occur. The section provides:

Acceptance of goods occurs when the buyer

(a)   after a reasonable opportunity to inspect the goods signifies to the seller that the goods are conforming or that he will take or retain them in spite of their non-conformity; or

(b)   fails to make an effective rejection (subsection (1) of Section 2-602), but such acceptance does not occur until the buyer has had a reasonable opportunity to inspect them; or

(c)   does any act inconsistent with the seller's ownership; but if such act is wrongful as against the seller it is an acceptance only if ratified by him.[20]

---

buyer's action is authorized by Article 2 and does not constitute a breach.

[18] UCC § 2-608(3) (revoking buyer has same rights and duties with regard to the goods as if it had rejected them).

[19] One commentator has dubbed these concepts the UCC's TARR Baby. *See* Whaley, *Tender, Acceptance, Rejection and Revocation — The UCC's TARR Baby*, 24 Drake L. Rev. 52 (1974).

[20] UCC § 2-606(1).

[1]   Buyer's Signification

Acceptance under Section 2-606(1)(a) requires a buyer to signify[21] to its seller that the goods conform to the contract[22] or that the buyer will take or retain them despite a known nonconformity.[23] However, acceptance does not occur under the provision unless the buyer has had a reasonable opportunity to inspect the goods. If it has had such an opportunity, its statement that the goods are conforming constitutes an acceptance even if it has not bothered to inspect them.[24]

The right to inspect is critical because it gives the buyer an opportunity to determine whether the goods conform to the contract before deciding whether to accept them. The parties can agree on the manner in which the buyer may exercise its inspection rights,[25] and if there is no agreement the general rule is that "the buyer has a right before payment or acceptance to inspect [the goods] at any reasonable place and time and in any reasonable manner."[26] The parties can agree that payment is to be made before inspection,[27] in which case the payment does not constitute an acceptance.[28] If the buyer later rightfully rejects the goods, its remedies will include a right to recover the payment.[29]

---

[21] Parties generally signify something through a statement, but nothing in the statute prevents them from doing it by conduct, such as paying for the goods after having an opportunity to inspect them. In this regard, UCC § 2-606, Comment 3 states that "[u]nder paragraph (a), payment made after tender is always one circumstance tending to signify acceptance but in itself it can never be more than one circumstance and is not conclusive." *See, e.g.,* Novacore Technologies, Inc. v. GST Communications Corp., 20 F. Supp. 2d 169, 37 UCC Rep. Serv. 2d 638 (D. Mass. 1998) (payment of most of purchase price most important factor in determining that buyer had accepted computer system).

[22] In re L&M Fabricators, 114 B.R. 100 (W.D. Pa. 1990) (message to seller noting that 2,214 delivered steel U-bolts were ready for heat treating).

[23] International Commodities Export Corp. v. North Pacific Lumber Co., 764 F. Supp. 608, 15 UCC Rep. Serv. 2d 825 (D. Or. 1991) (buyer aware that beans would not meet import standards); Plateq Corp. v. Machlett Laboratories, 189 Conn. 433, 456 A.2d 786, 35 UCC Rep. Serv. 1162 (1983) (on being assured that some remaining minor deficiencies would be corrected, buyer indicated it would send its truck to pick up custom-made steel tanks).

[24] *See* G & H Land & Cattle Co. v. Heitzman & Nelson, Inc., 102 Idaho 204, 628 P.2d 1038, 31 UCC Rep. Serv. 541 (1981) (buyer waived inspection right by failing to exercise it).

[25] UCC § 2-513(1); *see* Bevel-Fold, Inc. v. Bose Corp., 9 Mass. App. 576, 402 N.E.2d 1104, 28 UCC Rep. Serv. 1333 (1980) (agreement of parties allowed buyer of stereo cabinets to make a final quality inspection during its production process).

[26] UCC § 2-513(1). The subsection also provides that "[w]hen the seller is required or authorized to send the goods to the buyer, the inspection may be after their arrival." *Id.* UCC § 2-513(2) provides that the "[e]xpenses of inspection must be borne by the buyer but may be recovered from the seller if the goods do not conform and are rejected."

[27] The situation commonly arises when a buyer orders goods through a toll-free telephone number or over the Internet and as a condition to shipment the seller requires that the price be charged to the buyer's credit card. Most instances of payment against documents of title require payment before inspection. UCC § 2-513(3)(b). The once popular C.O.D. shipment, which means cash on delivery, also requires payment before inspection. UCC § 2-513(3)(a).

[28] UCC § 2-512(2); *see, e.g.,* Gragg Farms & Nursery v. Kelly Green Landscaping, 81 Ohio Misc. 2d 34, 674 N.E.2d 785, 32 UCC Rep. Serv. 2d 1119 (1996) (payment did not constitute acceptance because contract required payment before inspection).

[29] UCC § 2-711(1).

Before allowing a buyer to take possession of the goods, a seller may require the buyer to sign a form indicating that the buyer has inspected them and found them to be conforming. The effectiveness of the purported acceptance depends on the nature of the goods and the inspection opportunity actually afforded the buyer. The proverbial inspection by kicking the tires of a new car and taking it for a spin around the block is unlikely to convince most courts that the buyer had a reasonable opportunity to inspect with respect to mechanical difficulties that were not readily apparent and that manifested themselves shortly after delivery.[30]

[2]   Failure to Reject

Many acceptances by buyers result from their inaction and silence. Under Section 2-606(1)(b) a buyer that fails to effectively reject goods is deemed to have accepted them, again subject to a reasonable opportunity to inspect.[31] Under Section 2-602(1) rejection must be within a reasonable time, no doubt tied to the time for inspection, after delivery or tender of the goods, and it is ineffective if the buyer does not seasonably notify the seller. Failure to give the required notice results in automatic acceptance.[32] The mechanics of rejection are discussed in detail below.[33]

[3]   Conduct Inconsistent with Seller's Ownership

Under Section 2-606(1)(c) acceptance occurs when a buyer does an act inconsistent with the seller's ownership of the goods. The buyer's conduct might be rightful or wrongful. For an example of rightful conduct, suppose a buyer receives goods and without inspection makes fundamental changes to their nature, such as cutting delivered rolls of carpeting into smaller dimensions required for performance under an installation contract with a third party. Title to the goods typically vests in the buyer upon delivery and, as owner, the buyer has every right to work with them. By contrast, suppose a buyer effectively rejects delivered goods, whether rightfully or wrongfully, or justifiably revokes its acceptance of them, but afterward it uses the goods. The rejection or revocation revests title in the seller, converting the buyer into a bailee. Reflecting the buyer's status as bailee, Section 2-602(2)(a) provides that any

---

[30] *But see* Rozmus v. Thompson's Lincoln-Mercury Co., 209 Pa. Super. 120, 224 A.2d 782, 3 UCC Rep. Serv. 1025 (1966) (buyer's signed acceptance of new car upheld even though defects manifested themselves as he drove home from the dealership).

[31] DiDomenico Packaging Corp. v. Nails Again, Inc., 139 Misc. 2d 525, 527 N.Y.S.2d 676, 6 UCC Rep. Serv. 2d 119 (Civ. Ct. 1988) (acceptance resulted when buyer held shipment of paper cartons for several months without making a simple inspection that would have shown they were nonconforming because they did not include a printed customer guarantee).

[32] EPN-Delaval, S.A. v. Inter-Equip, Inc., 542 F. Supp. 238, 34 UCC Rep. Serv. 130 (S.D. Tex. 1982) (failure for 65 days to inspect and reject goods with defects that would be obvious to the buyer's quality control staff resulted in acceptance); Fablok Mills, Inc. v. Cocker Machine & Foundry Co., 125 N.J. Super. 251, 310 A.2d 491, 13 UCC Rep. Serv. 449 (1973) (purchaser notified seller of problems with knitting machines but having not rejected was held to an acceptance); Hudspeth Motors, Inc. v. Wilkinson, 238 Ark. 410, 382 S.W.2d 191, 2 UCC Rep. Serv. 273 (1964) (buyer held truck with defects for five months without any attempt to reject).

[33] *See* § 7.04 *infra*.

post-rejection exercise of ownership is wrongful as against the seller,[34] and under Section 2-606(1)(c) the seller may by ratification treat the buyer's conduct as an acceptance.[35]

Not every use of delivered goods is inconsistent with the seller's ownership. Some pre-rejection use may be necessary, either as part of or pending a timely inspection. Even in the post-rejection/revocation context, not every use of the goods will be inconsistent with the seller's ownership. Some use of the goods may be necessary to carry out the buyer's responsibility as bailee to take reasonable care of them. In addition, a rightfully rejecting or justifiably revoking buyer has a security interest in goods in its possession or control for any payments made on the price and for certain expenses,[36] and Article 9, which might be applied by analogy, explicitly permits a secured party to use or operate collateral for the purpose of preserving it or its value.[37] The court in *Jorgenson v. Pressnall*[38] found that buyers who continued to live in a mobile home after properly revoking their acceptance did so in order to preserve its value and therefore did not lose the benefit of their revocation.[39] As the discussion below demonstrates, other courts have gone beyond the rationale of *Jorgenson*, concluding that reasonable post-rejection/revocation use of goods, although inconsistent with the seller's ownership, does not undo the rejection or revocation.

[a]   Pre-Rejection Conduct

Regarding the level of pre-rejection conduct that will constitute an acceptance, the variety of fact patterns makes generalizations difficult. Consider actions by the buyer that irreversibly change the nature or condition of the goods. In *La Villa Fair v. Lewis Carpet Mills, Inc.*,[40] the court recognized that to determine whether delivered carpet was defective the buyer had no choice but to cut into some of the rolls. Accordingly, it held that rejection was appropriate because the cutting was a necessary part of the buyer's inspection.

---

[34] Although set forth in the section on rejection, UCC § 2-602(2)(a) applies also to revocations of acceptance by virtue of UCC § 2-608(3), which imposes on a revoking buyer the same duties as if the goods were being rejected.

[35] UCC § 2-606(1)(c). The seller's other options are to replevy the goods, which will be preferable to a monetary claim if the buyer is insolvent, or to treat the buyer's conduct as a conversion and recover their fair market value rather than the contract price. Replevin and conversion are discussed in § 10.01[A], n.12.

[36] UCC § 2-711(3). Covered expenses are those reasonably incurred in inspection, receipt, transportation, care, and custody of the goods.

[37] UCC § 9-207(b)(4)(A).

[38] 274 Or. 285, 545 P.2d 1382, 18 UCC Rep. Serv 1206 (1976). Compare *Bowen v. Young*, 507 S.W.2d 600, 14 UCC Rep. Serv. 403 (Tex. Ct. App. 1974), in which the buyer rejected a mobile home and, when the seller failed to refund his deposit, paid to have the heating system changed from electric to gas to conform to the contract and lived in it for a year. The court held that the buyer's conduct amounted to an acceptance and that instead of living in the home he should have recovered his money by foreclosing on his security interest.

[39] UCC § 2-608(3) provides that a revoking buyer has the same rights and duties as if it had rejected the goods.

[40] 219 Kan. 395, 548 P.2d 825, 19 UCC Rep. Serv. 120 (1976).

In *Intervale Steel Corp. v. Borg & Beck Division of Borg-Warner Corp.*[41] the buyer, after checking delivered steel for dimensional accuracy and chemical content, cut it into pieces that it intended to use later when filling orders for finished products. A few weeks later it continued the manufacturing process and discovered that the steel was too brittle for ordinary use; further examination revealed that the defect occurred because the steel was annealed only once, not twice as specified in the contract. The court held that the buyer had accepted the goods under Section 2-606(1)(b) by failing to make an effective rejection, concluding that a reasonable time for inspection had expired by the time the buyer discovered the defect. It rejected the argument that acceptance occurred when the buyer cut the steel into pieces because it concluded that Section 2-606(1)(c) only applies if the buyer uses the goods after learning that they are defective. The court's rationale makes sense in some contexts. For example, a commercial buyer that takes delivery of a truck and immediately begins making deliveries with it should not be deemed on the basis of that conduct alone, without knowledge of the defect, to have accepted it. The buyer should still have a reasonable time for inspection and if the truck breaks down shortly after delivery the option of rejecting it should be available.[42] On the other hand, the buyer in *Intervale Steel* fundamentally changed the nature of the steel and therefore should have been held to have accepted it even though it was unaware of the defect. The reason for the distinction is that rejection should revest in the seller title to goods in the same basic condition as when they were delivered, giving the seller the option of fixing the nonconformity and selling them or selling them in their defective condition and obtaining whatever it can for them.

The following is a sampling of cases in which courts have determined that a buyer has accepted by acting inconsistently with the seller's ownership rights: Commingling ten loads of grain with other grain,[43] destroying defective grass-catcher bags;[44] authorizing repairs to a boat;[45] adding shoes to inventory and selling nearly half of them;[46] making payment with knowledge of nonconformity;[47] installing kitchen units with readily apparent defects;[48] installing a hoist and dump bed on a truck;[49] processing potatoes into flakes and

---

[41] 578 F. Supp. 1081, 38 UCC Rep. Serv. 805 (E.D. Mich. 1984).

[42] *See, e.g.*, Zabriskie Chevrolet, Inc. v. Smith, 99 N.J. Super. 441, 240 A.2d 195, 5 UCC Rep. Serv. 30 (1968) (buyer held not to have completed inspection of a new car when a latent defect in the transmission made the car inoperable a short distance from the dealer's place of business).

[43] Veath v. Specialty Grains, Inc., 190 Ill. App. 3d 787, 546 N.E.2d 1005, 10 UCC Rep. Serv. 2d 771 (1989).

[44] C. R. Daniels, Inc. v. Yazoo Mfg. Co., Inc., 641 F. Supp. 205, 2 UCC Rep. Serv. 2d 481 (S.D. Miss. 1986).

[45] Tonka Tours, Inc. v. Chadima, 354 N.W.2d 519, 39 UCC Rep. Serv. 122 (Minn. Ct. App. 1984).

[46] Lorenzo Banfi di Banfi Renzo & Co. v. Davis Congress Shops, Inc., 568 F. Supp. 432, 36 UCC Rep. Serv. 1183 (N.D. Ill. 1983).

[47] Atlantic Aluminum & Metal Distributors v. Adams, 123 Ga. App. 387, 181 S.E.2d 101, 9 UCC Rep. Serv. 63 (1971).

[48] Cervitor Kitchens, Inc. v. Chapman, 82 Wash. 2d 694, 513 P.2d 25, 13 UCC Rep. Serv. 458 (1973).

[49] Park Co. Implement Co. v. Craig, 397 P.2d 800, 2 UCC Rep. Serv. 379 (Wyo. 1964).

selling them;[50] removing plants from their containers and planting them pursuant to a landscaping contract;[51] and driving, repairing, painting, and attempting to sell an automobile.[52] Circumstances that have been held insufficient to constitute an acceptance include using a machine with the objective of making it work rather than using it in production;[53] blanching peanuts in a process that did not substantially change them;[54] transshipping uninspected goods in their original, unopened packaging to another location;[55] and continuing to use carpet that had been affixed to the floor.[56]

[b]   Post-Rejection Conduct

As noted above, some courts have held that a buyer's reasonable post-rejection/revocation use of goods for a purpose other than satisfying a bailee's or secured party's duty does not undo its rejection or revocation of acceptance notwithstanding the clear language of Section 2-602(2)(a), which states that "any" such exercise of ownership is wrongful as against the seller, and Section 2-606(1)(c), which states that the seller may by ratification treat the buyer's wrongful conduct as an acceptance.[57] The Comments to amended Article 2 succinctly explain the rationale for the holdings:

> In general, a buyer that either rejects or revokes acceptance of the goods should not subsequently use the goods in a manner that is inconsistent with the seller's ownership. In some instances, however, the use may be reasonable. For example, a consumer buyer may have incurred an unavoidable obligation to a third-party financier and, if the seller fails to refund the price as required by this Article, the buyer may have no reasonable alternative but to use the goods (*e.g.*, a rejected mobile home that provides needed shelter). Another example might involve a commercial buyer that is unable immediately to obtain cover and must use the goods to fulfill its obligations to third parties.[58]

---

[50] Borges v. Magic Valley Foods, Inc., 102 Idaho 204, 616 P.2d 273, 29 UCC Rep. Serv. 1282 (1980).

[51] Oda Nursery, Inc. v. Garcia Tree & Lawn, Inc., 708 P.2d 1039, 42 UCC Rep. Serv. 164 (N.M. 1985).

[52] Fiat Auto U.S.A., Inc. v. Hollums, 185 Ga. App. 113, 363 S.E.2d 312, 5 UCC Rep. Serv. 2d 969 (1987).

[53] Distco Laminating, Inc. v. Union Tool Corp., 81 Mich. App. 612, 265 N.W.2d 768, 24 UCC Rep. Serv. 129 (1978).

[54] Stratton Industries, Inc. v. Northwest Georgia Bank, 191 Ga. 683, 382 S.E.2d 721, 10 UCC Rep. Serv. 2d 387 (1989).

[55] Columbia Can Co. of J.J., Inc. v. Africa-Middle East Marketing, Inc., 188 N.J. Super. 45, 455 A.2d 1143, 36 UCC Rep. Serv. 137 (1983).

[56] Garfinkel v. Lehman Floor Covering Co., 60 Misc. 2d 72, 302 N.Y.S.2d 167, 6 UCC Rep. Serv. 915 (D. Ct. 1969).

[57] *See generally* R. J. Robertson, Jr., *Rights and Obligations of Buyers with Respect to Goods in Their Possession After Rightful Rejection or Justifiable Revocation of Acceptance*, 60 Ind. L.J. 663 (1985).

[58] UCC Amended § 2-608, cmt. 8.

The cases generally reflect the approach suggested by the Comment; that is, the effectiveness of a rejection or revocation of acceptance is preserved if the subsequent use of the goods occurs because the seller's failure to refund the price leaves the buyer without an economically viable alternative[59] or because the buyer cannot promptly cover in the marketplace and must use the goods to mitigate its damages.[60] An example of a case in which both factors were present is *Deere & Co. v. Johnson*,[61] in which the court held that a farmer's continued use of a combine did not undo his revocation of acceptance because the combine was essential to his work, his financial commitment on the combine made purchasing a replacement difficult, and his conduct had the effect of mitigating his damages. The cases make clear that the buyer's continued use is limited to the duration of its exigent circumstances, and a number of buyers have lost because their use was found to be excessive.[62]

A seller is obligated to refund the full contract price after a rightful rejection or justifiable revocation of acceptance[63] even though the buyer's continued use benefits the buyer and may cause the goods to depreciate in value.[64] Some courts, applying principles of restitution, have awarded sellers a setoff for the value of the benefit to the buyer, typically measured in terms of the fair rental value of the goods in their defective condition.[65] This approach makes sense in that otherwise the buyer will have use of the goods for free, but in some instances

---

[59] *See, e.g.*, Liarikos v. Mello, 418 Mass. 669, 639 N.E.2d 716, 27 UCC Rep. Serv. 2d 136 (1994) (buyer with limited finances did not undo revocation by continuing to use car that was essential to running her business); McCullough v. Bill Swad Chrysler-Plymouth, Inc., 449 N.E.2d 1289, 36 UCC Rep. Serv. 513 (Ohio 1983) (revoking car buyer's financial position limited); *cf.* Mitchell v. Backus Cadillac-Pontiac, Inc., 274 Ga. App. 330, 618 S.E.2d 87, 58 UCC Rep. Serv. 2d 178 (2005) (buyer accepted car where he continued to use it and had a sunroof installed after revocation of acceptance).

[60] *See, e.g.*, Toshiba Machine Co. v. SPM Flow Control, Inc., 180 S.W.3d 761 (Tex. Ct. App. 2005), *review granted and remanded* 2006 Tex. LEXIS 251 (Mar. 31 2006); Minsel v. El Rancho Mobile Home Ctr., Inc., 188 N.W.2d 9, 9 UCC Rep. Serv. 448 (Mich. Ct. App. 1971) (buyers continued to occupy mobile home for six weeks following revocation because of their inability to find alternative housing).

[61] 271 F.3d 613, 46 UCC Rep. Serv. 2d 433 (5th Cir. 2001).

[62] *See, e.g.*, Computerized Radiological Services v. Syntex Corp., 786 F.2d 72, 42 UCC Rep. Serv. 1656 (2d Cir. 1986) (use of CAT scanner for 22 months following revocation constituted reacceptance because use continued longer than reasonably necessary to acquire another scanner); Barrett v. Brian Bemis Auto World, 408 F. Supp. 2d 539 (N.D. Ill. 2005) (buyer's use of car for over 37,000 miles after revoking acceptance unreasonable).

[63] UCC § 2-711(3).

[64] A similar situation may occur prior to revocation of acceptance. One commentator has argued that the Code's failure to provide sellers with a setoff in such circumstances is an obvious oversight. *See* Priest, *Breach and Remedy for the Tender of Nonconforming Goods Under the Uniform Commercial Code: An Economic Approach*, 91 Harv. L. Rev. 960, 979 (1978); *see also* Pavesi v. Ford Motor Co., 382 A.2d 954, 23 UCC Rep. Serv. 929 (N.J. Sup. Ct. 1978) (seller entitled to offset for benefit buyer received in driving car two years before revoking acceptance); North American Lighting, Inc. v. Hopkins Manufacturing Corp., 37 F.3d 1253, 24 UCC Rep. Serv. 2d 1061 (7th Cir. 1994) (seller of defective automobile headlight aiming system whose buyer used it for two years before revoking acceptance entitled to setoff measured by quantum meruit).

[65] *See, e.g.*, Johnson v. General Motors Corp., 668 P.2d 139, 36 UCC Rep. Serv. 1089 (Kan. 1983) (seller entitled to setoff for reasonable value of post-revocation use of truck); Lawrence v. Modern Mobile Homes, Inc., 526 S.W.2d 729, 24 UCC Rep. Serv. 874 (Mo. Ct. App. 1978) (seller entitled to introduce evidence of reasonable value of buyer's post-revocation use of mobile home).

a buyer may have suffered so much inconvenience that cannot be measured in monetary terms that a court would be justified in refusing to permit a setoff.

Article 2A does not include a direct counterpart to Section 2-606(1)(c), and the Comments indicate that the provision was omitted "as irrelevant given the lessee's possession and use of the leased goods."[66] This rationale makes no sense in the context of post-rejection/revocation use of the goods by a lessee, but Section 2A-515(1)(a), which states that acceptance occurs if a lessee "acts with respect to the goods in a manner that signifies to the lessor that the goods are conforming or that the lessee will take or retain them in spite of their nonconformity," provides a basis for reaching an appropriate result.

[B] Consequences of Acceptance [§ 2-607; § 2A-516]

Several consequences are tied to acceptance. A buyer that accepts goods will still have a monetary remedy for a nonconformity in the goods or the tender of delivery, but the buyer's ability to avoid paying the contract price by revesting title in the seller will be limited to situations in which revocation of acceptance is appropriate. With an exception for finance leases,[67] the same consequences apply to acceptance in both sale and lease contexts.

[1] Rejection and Revocation of Acceptance

Acceptance of the goods precludes rejection.[68] Even if rejection would have been rightful because of a nonconformity in the goods or the tender of delivery, the buyer's acceptance forecloses that remedy. As a consequence, the buyer winds up with title to the goods and its only opportunity to revest title in the seller is through revocation of acceptance. The right to revoke acceptance is significantly more restricted than the right to reject.[69] As the discussion on revocation of acceptance will demonstrate, a nonconformity that initially gave rise to a right to reject quite often will not justify a revocation.

[2] Obligation to Pay

A buyer that accepts goods must pay for them at the contract rate.[70] This requirement, operating together with the provisions that preclude rejection and limit revocation of acceptance, effectively binds the buyer to complete its contract obligations following an acceptance. The buyer may have a claim for monetary damages, but it typically will have lost the right to cancel the contract.[71]

---

[66] UCC § 2A-515, cmt.

[67] UCC § 2A-516(2); *see* § 7.05[F] *infra.*

[68] UCC § 2-607(2).

[69] *See* § 7.05[A] *infra.*

[70] UCC § 2-607(1). Articles 2 and 2A differ with regard to the extent to which a seller and a lessor can enforce this obligation. *See* § 9.04[A][1], [B] *infra.*

[71] "'Cancellation' occurs when either party puts an end to the contract for breach by the other. . . ." Its effect is to discharge the cancelling party from all executory obligations while preserving its remedies for breach of the whole contract or an unperformed balance. UCC § 2-106(4).

A buyer is particularly well-advised to reject nonconforming goods in a falling market. Acceptance obligates the buyer to pay the full contract price, and its monetary damages will be measured only by the difference in the value of the goods as warranted and their value as delivered.[72] This measure might be as little as the cost of replacing a defective component part.[73] By rejecting, the buyer is excused from paying the purchase price and can recover any part of the price already paid,[74] after which it can purchase comparable goods on the open market at the lower market price. Certain limits temper the buyer's ability to use the rejection remedy in this fashion; the seller might have a right to cure the defect and retender the goods,[75] or a court might find that the buyer rejected in bad faith by using the nonconformity as a mere pretext to avoid what had turned into a bad deal.[76]

[3] Notification

The requirement that an aggrieved buyer notify its seller of breach pervades Article 2. A rejection must be effectuated by notification,[77] and in certain contexts a failure to state in the notification a particular defect ascertainable by reasonable inspection will preclude the buyer from using the defect to justify the rejection or to establish breach for the purpose of recovering monetary damages.[78] After acceptance, a buyer seeking a remedy must notify its seller within a reasonable time after it discovers or should have discovered any breach, and here again the consequence of noncompliance is severe — the buyer is barred from any remedy.[79]

According to the following Comment, the contents of a post-acceptance notification need not state the nonconformity with the particularity of a notification effectuating a rejection:

The content of the notification need merely be sufficient to let the seller know that the transaction is still troublesome and must be

---

[72] UCC § 2-714(2). Upon notifying the seller, the buyer can set off damages resulting from the seller's breach of contract. UCC § 2-717. Adam Metal Supply Inc. v. Electrodex, Inc., 386 So. 2d 1316, 30 UCC Rep. Serv. 178 (Fla. Ct. App. 1980).

[73] See § 8.02[D][2][a] infra.

[74] UCC § 2-711(1).

[75] See § 7.04[C][1] infra.

[76] See § 7.04[C][2] infra.

[77] UCC § 2-602(1) (rejection ineffective unless buyer seasonably notifies seller).

[78] UCC § 2-605(1). The procedural aspects of rejection, including notification, are discussed in § 7.04[B] infra.

[79] UCC 2-607(3)(a); see, e.g., Hitachi Electronic Devices (USA), Inc. v. Platinum Technologies, Inc., 366 S.C. 163, 621 S.E.2d 38, 57 UCC Rep. Serv. 2d 883 (2005) (buyer's failure to provide timely notification of breach barred it from enforcing seller's promise to repair or replace defective goods); Adams v. Wacaster Oil Co., Inc., 81 Ark. App. 150, 98 S.W.3d 832, 50 UCC Rep. Serv. 2d 774 (2003) (buyer's failure to notify seller of breach justified summary judgment for seller that allegedly provided improper fuel for crop duster and caused it to crash); Fleet Maintenance, Inc. v. Burke Energy Midwest Corp., 11 Kan. App. 2d 523, 728 P.2d 408, 2 UCC Rep. Serv. 2d 904 (1986) (failure to notify seller of defective condition of engine barred buyer from any remedy, including revocation of acceptance and action for damages for breach of an implied warranty).

watched. There is no reason to require that the notification which saves the buyer's rights under this section must include a clear statement of all the objections that will be relied on by the buyer, as under the section covering statements of defects upon rejection (Section 2-605). Nor is there reason for requiring the notification to be a claim for damages or of any threatened litigation or other resort to a remedy. The notification which saves the buyer's rights under this Article need only be such as informs the seller that the transaction is claimed to involve a breach, and thus opens the way for normal settlement through negotiation.[80]

In addition to opening the way for settlement, courts and commentators have suggested the following rationales for providing notification: It gives the seller an opportunity to investigate and thereby determine the nature of the problem and its potential liability; it enables the seller to cure the problem with the buyer's consent or to make suggestions to the buyer regarding an appropriate cure, thereby mitigating the harm; it enables the seller to negotiate a settlement with the buyer or, if settlement efforts are unsuccessful, to prepare for litigation; and it protects the seller against stale claims that it can no longer investigate.[81]

If the post-acceptance remedy being sought is revocation of acceptance rather than monetary damages, "[m]ore will generally be necessary than the mere notification of breach required under [Section 2-607(3)]. On the other hand the requirements of [Section 2-605] on waiver of buyer's objections do not apply here."[82] The additional information required of a notification that the buyer is revoking acceptance is that the goods again belong to the seller.[83] Without this information, the seller will not know that it is expected to take back the goods and refund the contract price.[84]

Although the courts generally follow the Comments and do not require particularization of the defect that forms the basis of the buyer's claim, there is some variance regarding phrasing. For example, compare the holdings in *Zeigler v. Sony Corp. of America*[85] and *Marvin Lumber and Cedar Co. v. PPG*

[80] UCC 2-607, cmt. 4.

[81] *See* W. Lawrence & W. Henning, *A Unified Rationale for Section 2-607(3) Notification*, ____ S.D. L. Rev. ____ (forthcoming 2009) (arguing that some of the rationales are unconvincing and a buyer should not be deprived of remedies unless a delay in notification results in prejudice to the seller).

[82] UCC § 2-608, cmt. 5. The notification requirement for revocation of acceptance is discussed generally in § 7.05[B] *infra.*

[83] Notwithstanding the fact that UCC § 2-605, which requires particularization in certain contexts, is limited to rejection, some courts have required a revoking buyer to particularize any defects that substantially impair the value of the goods to it. *See, e.g.*, Solar Kinetics Corp. v. Joseph T. Ryerson & Son, Inc., 488 F. Supp. 1237, 29 UCC Rep. Serv. 85 (D. Conn. 1980); *see also* Phoenix Color Corp. v. Krause America, Inc., 46 UCC Rep. Serv. 2d 442 (4th Cir. 2001) (unpublished) (particularization not required because buyer's complaints prior to notification made clear to seller the nature of the defect).

[84] *See, e.g.*, Sipe v. Fleetwood Motor Homes of Pennsylvania, Inc., 66 UCC Rep. Serv. 2d 655 (D. Minn. 2008) (buyer's statement that seller could take motor home and "shove it up his ass" insufficient to advise seller that it again owned the motor home).

[85] 48 Conn. Supp. 397, 36 Conn. L. Rptr. 531, 849 A.2d 19 (Super. Ct. 2004).

Industries, Inc.[86] In the former case, the court held that a notification must at least state that a warranty has been breached; in the latter, the court held that there is no need to state explicitly that the problem constitutes a breach of warranty. Cases following the *Zeigler* approach typically involve merchant buyers[87] and base their holding on the language from the quoted Comment to the effect that a proper notification must be such as "informs the seller that the transaction is claimed to involve a breach."

Is notification required if the seller is already aware of the breach? For example, if a seller makes a late delivery, a fact of which it is aware, should the buyer's right to damages be conditioned on giving timely notification? The court in *Jay V. Zimmerman Co. v. General Mills, Inc.*[88] answered the question in the negative, noting that the purpose of notification is to bring the fact of breach to the seller's attention, which is unnecessary when the seller already knows of its breach.[89] By contrast, the court in *Eastern Air Lines, Inc. v. McDonnell Douglas Corp.*,[90] focusing on the importance of notification in enabling a seller to attempt to negotiate a settlement and prepare for litigation, held that notification is required even if the seller knows it breached the contract.

Under the Code, whether an action is taken within a reasonable time "depends on the nature, purpose, and circumstances of the action."[91] Given the fact-intensive nature of the test, the cases not surprisingly reflect a wide disparity in the acceptable time for giving a notification. Many courts have indicated a more lenient attitude if the seller is not prejudiced by the delay. For example, the court in *Hays v. General Electric Co.*[92] held that a delay by a commercial buyer of over

---

[86] 401 F.3d 901, 57 UCC Rep. Serv. 2d 18 (8th Cir. 2005).

[87] *See, e.g.*, Eastern Air Lines, Inc. v. McDonnell Douglas Corp., 532 F.2d 957, 19 UCC Rep. Serv. 353 (5th Cir. 1976) (merchant buyer must notify seller that its claim states a breach, citing UCC § 2-104(1)(b)'s requirement that merchants, to be in good faith, must observe reasonable commercial standards of fair dealing).

[88] 327 F. Supp. 1198, 9 UCC Rep. Serv. 680 (E.D. Mo. 1971); *see also* Arcor, Inc. v. Textron, Inc., 960 F.2d 710, 32 UCC Rep. Serv. 2d 475 (7th Cir. 1992).

[89] Section 1-202(d) provides support for this argument, stating that a person notifies another "by taking such steps as may reasonably be required to inform the other person in ordinary course. . . ." If the seller already knows the fact at issue, no steps would be required to so inform it.

[90] 532 F.2d 957, 19 UCC Rep. Serv. 353 (5th Cir. 1976); *see also* Brookings Municipal Utilities, Inc. v. Amoco Chemical Co., 103 F. Supp. 2d 86, 34 UCC Rep. Serv. 2d 1024 (N.D.N.Y. 2000).

[91] UCC § 1-205(a). "Whenever [the Uniform Commercial Code] requires an action to be taken within a reasonable time, a time that is not manifestly unreasonable may be fixed by agreement." UCC § 1-302(b). *See, e.g.*, Bailey v. Monaco Coach Corp., 350 F. Supp. 2d 1036, 55 UCC Rep. Serv. 2d 539 (N.D. Ga. 2004) (seller not liable for breach of repair-or-replace remedy because buyer failed to give notification within five days after discovering breach as required by contract). A contractual requirement that imposes on the buyer a time limit for notification that expires before a defect manifests itself may be found to be manifestly unreasonable. *See, e.g.*, Q. Vandenberg and Sons, N.V. v. Siter, 204 Pa. Super. 392, 204 A.2d 494, 2 UCC Rep. Serv. 383 (1964) (jury question whether term requiring notification within eight days after delivery of tulip bulbs was manifestly unreasonable as applied to warranty that bulbs would bloom after planting).

[92] 151 F. Supp. 2d 1001, 45 UCC Rep. Serv. 2d 449 (N.D. Ill. 2001). An unexplained delay in giving notification is likely to prove fatal to the buyer's claims if the goods are destroyed during the delay, thereby precluding the seller from performing tests that might have pinpointed the cause of the problem. *See, e.g.*, Cole v. Keller Industries, Inc., 872 F. Supp. 1470, 25 UCC Rep. Serv. 2d 709 (E.D.

eight months in notifying the seller that the motors in its exercise treadmills were overheating and burning out did not preclude the buyer from pursuing a remedy because the seller was not prejudiced by the delay; that is, the delay did not undermine any of the policies underlying the notification requirement. The Comments indicate that a more liberal standard is appropriate for consumer buyers: "'A reasonable time' for notification from a retail consumer is to be judged by different standards so that in his case it will be extended, for the rule of requiring notification is designed to defeat commercial bad faith, not to deprive a good-faith consumer of his remedy."[93]

The Comments suggest that a statutory third-party beneficiary of a warranty under Section 2-318 should be relieved of any obligation to discover defects, but they go on to state that "the reason of this section does extend to requiring the beneficiary to notify the seller that an injury has occurred."[94] The courts have generally agreed,[95] although several courts, noting that Section 2-607(3)(a) imposes the notification requirement on the "buyer," have ignored the Comment and excused third-party beneficiaries from the requirement, especially where personal injuries are involved.[96]

[4] Burden of Establishing Breach

Since tender of conforming goods is a condition precedent to a buyer's duty to accept,[97] a seller has the burden of establishing that a buyer's rejection was wrongful.[98] By contrast, a buyer that has accepted goods and seeks a remedy has the burden of establishing that the seller is in breach.[99] The significance of the distinction between rejection and acceptance can be overstated: If a rejecting buyer wishes not only to cancel the contract but also to recover monetary damages, it will bear the burden of establishing the seller's breach.

Va. 1994) (delay of four months unreasonable when during interim ladder was partially destroyed by buyer's testing and rivets relevant to determining whether it was defective were lost).

[93] UCC § 2-607, cmt. 4; *see, e.g.*, Riley v. Ken Wilson Ford, Inc., 109 N.C. App. 163, 426 S.E.2d 717, 20 UCC Rep. Serv. 2d 74 (1993) (delay of over two years by consumer buyer of car not unreasonable). A few courts have even held that the filing of a complaint by a consumer constitutes reasonable notification. *See, e.g.*, In re Bridgestone/Firestone, Inc. Products Liability Litigation, 155 F. Supp. 2d 1069, 45 UCC Rep. Serv. 2d 516 (S.D. Ind. 2001).

[94] UCC § 2-607, cmt. 5. The Comment also states that the extended time for notification to be afforded consumer buyers should also be afforded third-party beneficiaries who are consumers. For discussion of statutory third-party beneficiaries of a warranty, see § 5.06[A] *supra*.

[95] *See, e.g.*, Maldonado v. Creative Woodworking Concepts, Inc., 296 Ill. App. 3d 935, 694 N.E.2d 1021, 35 UCC Rep. Serv. 2d 501 (1998) (injured employee of purchaser required to give notification).

[96] *See, e.g.*, Yates v. Pitman Mfg. Co., 257 Va. 601, 514 S.E.2d 605, 38 UCC Rep. Serv. 2d 386 (1999) (injured employee of purchaser not required to give notification to manufacturer because UCC § 2-607(3)(a) imposes the requirement on "buyers").

[97] UCC § 2-601.

[98] "'Burden of establishing' a fact means the burden of persuading the trier of fact that the existence of the fact is more probable than its nonexistence." UCC § 1-201(b)(8).

[99] UCC 2-607(4).

Allocation of the burden of proof was outcome determinative in *Miron v. Yonkers Raceway, Inc.*,[100] a case in which the buyer of a thoroughbred racehorse warranted to be sound discovered after the horse was delivered to him and he had it transported to his barn that one of its leg bones had a hairline fracture. The court held that because a reasonable time to inspect had expired before the horse was transported, the buyer's attempted post-delivery rejection was ineffective and he was deemed to have accepted the horse. The parties presented evidence that tended to show both that the fracture occurred prior to the sale and that it occurred during or after transport. The buyer failed on its claim for breach of warranty because it could not meet its burden of establishing that the injury occurred before the horse left the seller's control.

§ 7.04   REJECTION

[A]   Perfect Tender Rule [§ 2-601; § 2A-509(1)]

A buyer is entitled to exercise the remedy of rejection "if the goods or the tender of delivery fail *in any respect* to conform to the contract."[101] Goods and any part of a performance conform to the contract "when they are in accordance with the obligations under the contract."[102] With a rightful rejection the buyer may cancel the contract, thereby excusing it from further performance, recover any part of the purchase price that has been paid, and recover damages for total breach measured either by the difference between the contract price and the price of a substitute transaction or the difference between the contract price and the market price of the goods.[103] The standard for rejection differs significantly from the general contract-law requirement, which is that there must be a material breach before the aggrieved party is entitled to cancellation and damages for total breach.[104] Under the literal wording of Section 2-601, a buyer may reject if the manner in which tender of delivery is made or the quality of the goods constitutes anything less than exact compliance with the seller's contractual obligations.[105] The standard of exact compliance is commonly referred to as the "perfect tender rule."[106] Instead of rejecting, a buyer faced

---

[100] 400 F.2d 112, 5 UCC Rep. Serv. 673 (2d Cir. 1968); *see also* Alliance Wall Corp. v. Ampat Midwest Corp., 17 Ohio App. 3d 59, 477 N.E.2d 1206, 41 UCC Rep. Serv. 377 (1984) (buyer unable to establish whether damage to aluminum panels occurred in manufacturing process or in transit).

[101] UCC § 2-601 (emphasis supplied). A lessee's right to reject is patterned precisely on this provision. UCC § 2A-509(1).

[102] UCC § 2-106(2).

[103] UCC § 2-711(1).

[104] E. A. Farnsworth, Contracts § 8.15 (2d ed. 1990). Printing Center of Texas, Inc. v. Supermind Pub. Co., Inc., 669 S.W.2d 779, 39 UCC Rep. Serv. 127 (Tex. Ct. App. 1984) (complete performance rather than substantial performance required).

[105] *See, e.g.*, Ramirez v. Autosport, 88 N.J. 277, 440 A.2d 1345, 33 UCC Rep. Serv. 134 (1982); Moulton Cavity & Mold, Inc. v. Lyn-Flex Indus., Inc., 396 A.2d 1024, 25 UCC Rep. Serv. 1026 (Me. 1979).

[106] Courts in some instances have declined to adhere to the rule. *See, e.g.*, D. P. Technology Corp. v. Sherwood Tool, Inc., 751 F. Supp. 1038, 13 UCC Rep. Serv. 2d 686 (D. Conn. 1990) (holding that the Connecticut Supreme Court would require that a delay in delivery of specially manufactured

with a nonconforming tender may accept the goods notwithstanding the nonconformity, or it may reject some commercial units and accept the rest.[107]

The drafters of Article 2 concluded that the reasoning that led common-law courts to limit the right to cancel to cases of material breach did not justify a similar limitation on the right to reject a nonconforming tender.[108] The common-law developed the concept of constructive conditions to determine the order in which the promises of the parties had to be performed if they did not establish their own schedule,[109] but applied literally the concept would have been unduly harsh. The result of a failure of condition generally is forfeiture — the person in whose favor the condition operates is excused from performance — and the common-law rule is that a true condition fails if it is not fully satisfied. If the same requirement were applied to constructive conditions, the party required to perform first would forfeit all rights under the contract if it tendered anything less than full performance. The forfeiture risk is particularly poignant in situations, like construction contracts, in which labor and materials expended in an attempt to perform that falls short of full performance cannot be returned to the contractor.

Common-law courts mitigated the potential for harshness by developing the substantial performance standard for satisfying constructive conditions.[110] A less-than-perfect but nevertheless substantial performance results in a nonmaterial breach,[111] but the constructive condition is satisfied, preventing

---

goods must be substantial in order for the buyer to reject and remanding for determination of whether 16-day delay was substantial); Clark v. Zaid, Inc., 282 A.2d 483, 9 UCC Rep. Serv. 1014 (Md. 1971) (in determining the right of a buyer to reject furniture, the court must consider factors such as the nature and extent of damage and whether the furniture could be repaired); National Fleet Supply, Inc. v. Fairchild, 450 N.E.2d 1015, 36 UCC Rep. Serv. 480 (Ind. Ct. App. 1983) (court states in *dictum* that it is generally understood that rejection is not available when tender is deficient in some small respect).

[107] A commercial unit is "such a unit of goods as by commercial usage is a single whole for purposes of sale and division of which materially impairs its character or value on the market or in use." UCC § 2-105(6); *see, e.g.*, Salinas Lettuce Farmers Coop. v. Larry Ober Co., Inc., 28 UCC Rep. Serv. 684 (U.S. Dept. Agric. 1980) (commercial unit consisted of entire truckload of vegetables and attempt to reject cartons of decaying vegetables while accepting undamaged cartons constituted acceptance of the entire unit).

[108] For more detailed elaboration on the rationales underlying the perfect tender rule, see Lawrence, *Appropriate Standards for a Buyer's Refusal to Keep Goods Tendered by a Seller*, 35 William & Mary L. Rev. 1635 (1994); Lawrence, *The Prematurely Reported Demise of the Perfect Tender Rule*, 35 U. Kan. L. Rev. 557 (1987). For a different perspective, see Sebert, *Rejection, Revocation, and Cure Under Article 2 of the Uniform Commercial Code: Some Modest Proposals*, 84 Nw. U. L. Rev. 375 (1990).

[109] *See* Jones v. Barkley, 99 Eng. Rep. 434, 437-38 (K.B. 1781) (paraphrasing Lord Mansfield's opinion in *Kingston v. Preston*, 2 Doug. 689, 99 Eng. Rep. 437 (K.B. 1773)). *See generally* Patterson, *Constructive Conditions in Contracts*, 42 Colum. L. Rev. 903 (1942).

[110] Boone v. Eyre, 126 Eng. Rep. 160(a) (K.B. 1777).

[111] Substantial performance and material breach are essentially two sides of the same coin. If performance is substantial but not complete, the unperformed duties constitute a nonmaterial breach. If performance is insubstantial, the unperformed duties constitute a material breach. Damages apply for either a material or nonmaterial breach but cancellation is reserved for material breach.

cancellation by the aggrieved party.[112] The reason the drafters did not extend the substantial performance rule to cases of rejection was because the ability of the buyer to return the rejected goods to the breaching seller for the most part avoids forfeiture. The drafters thought that the rights of an aggrieved buyer would be better protected under the perfect tender rule because the standard provides more certainty in its application than is possible under the substantial performance rule.[113] If the parties do not wish to be bound by the rule, they can establish their own performance standards.

[B]   Procedural Aspects [§ 2-602; § 2A-509(2)]

Rejection never occurs automatically. The automatic consequence is quite the opposite — the buyer is held to an acceptance if it does not reject the goods after having a reasonable opportunity to inspect them,[114] with the attendant consequence of terminating the right of rejection.[115] Thus, the right of rejection is waived if it is not exercised.[116]

The basic procedural requirements for rejection include two elements: "Rejection of goods must be within a reasonable time after their delivery or tender" and it "is ineffective unless the buyer seasonably notifies the seller."[117] The Code thus distinguishes between the right to reject and the effectiveness of an attempted rejection. The right to reject is waived if it is not effectively exercised by meeting the procedural requirements. Alternatively, exercising the procedures creates a rejection that is effective even in the absence of a right to do so. Such action by the buyer results in breach, but it nevertheless revests title to the goods in the seller[118] and precludes acceptance as a matter of right.[119]

[1]   Timeliness

An effective rejection must occur within a reasonable time after delivery of the goods or their tender, and "[w]hether time for taking an action required by [the Uniform Commercial Code is reasonable depends on the nature, purpose,

---

[112] Jacob & Youngs, Inc. v. Kent, 129 N.E. 889 (N.Y. 1921).

[113] The decision of whether a breach is material requires consideration of multiple criteria. Restatement (Second) of Contracts § 241. An aggrieved party that errs in balancing these criteria and proceeds to cancel the contract for an immaterial breach commits a material breach. Walker & Co. v. Harrison, 81 N.W.2d 352 (Mich. 1957).

[114] UCC § 2-606(1)(b); see § 7.03[A][2] supra.

[115] UCC § 2-607(2); see § 7.03[B][1] supra.

[116] See, e.g., Robinson v. Jonathan Logan Fin., 277 A.2d 115, 9 UCC Rep. Serv. 57 (D.C. Ct. App. 1971) (right to reject and intention to do so are irrelevant if buyer fails to comply with procedural requirements for rejection).

[117] UCC § 2-602(1). The Article 2A provision on leases is comparable. UCC § 2A-509(2).

[118] UCC § 2-401(4). In some instances, as when delivery is to occur at the seller's place of business and the buyer rejects before taking physical possession of the goods, title may not have passed at the time of rejection. In such a case the provision on revesting of title is superfluous.

[119] See, e.g., Integrated Circuits Unlimited v. E. F. Johnson Co., 875 F.2d 1040, 8 UCC Rep. Serv. 2d 695 (2d Cir. 1989).

and circumstances of such action."[120] The surrounding circumstances vary greatly from case to case,[121] but as a rule prompt detection of a deficient tender is desirable because the nature and extent of the problem can be investigated sooner, responsibility for the deficiency can be ascertained more readily, a cure by the seller can be effectuated more quickly, and the goods can be returned to the seller more quickly if the deficiency is not going to be cured. These benefits have the effect of mitigating the adverse consequences of the breach for both the buyer and the seller.

The time for rejection must be considered in light of the buyer's right to inspect because a failure to make an effective rejection after having had a reasonable opportunity to inspect constitutes an automatic acceptance.[122] This does not mean that a reasonable time for rejection and a reasonable opportunity to inspect are co-extensive; after all, if an inspection reveals a problem the buyer should have an opportunity to decide what action to take and, if it decides to reject, to prepare and send a notification to that effect. Nevertheless, a buyer that engages in significant delay after having a reasonable opportunity to inspect runs a significant risk that it will be deemed to have accepted.

The time for rejection was exceptionally short in *Miron v. Yonkers Raceway, Inc.*,[123] a case in which the buyer sought to reject a racehorse after discovering a fracture in one of its legs less than twenty-four hours after taking delivery. The court noted that the injury could have been ascertained in an inspection by a veterinarian and that such an inspection is customarily made prior to taking delivery of a racehorse. After taking delivery the buyer had the horse transported to his barn, and such a fragile and spirited animal might well have injured itself during transport. On the basis of these factors the court held that the buyer had accepted the horse by not giving notification of rejection before the horse was transported.

Comparing cases provides a sense of the factors that courts consider in resolving the timeliness issue. In *Hartz Seed Co. v. Colman*[124] the court held that rejection of soybeans after one month was timely because testing was required to discover the defect and the time taken for testing was reasonable. On the other hand, seven weeks to reject undersized steel was held to be unreasonable in *Michael M. Berlin & Co. v. T. Whiting Mfg., Inc.*[125] because of the ease with which the steel could have been measured. Rejection a month and a half after delivery was timely in *Badger Produce Co., Inc. v. Prelude Foods International, Inc.*[126] because the rejected frozen crabmeat was kept in cold storage and was only semiperishable, whereas rejection of pork roasts for excessive fat only three hours after inspection was untimely in *Max Bauer Meat*

---

[120] UCC 1-205(1).

[121] The other two factors — nature and purpose of the action — are inherent in the policies that underlie the right of rejection generally.

[122] UCC § 2-606(1)(b).

[123] 400 F.2d 112, 5 UCC Rep. Serv. 112 (2d Cir. 1968).

[124] 271 Ark. 756, 612 S.W.2d 91, 30 UCC Rep. Serv. 944 (1981).

[125] 5 UCC Rep. Serv. 357 (N.Y. Sup. Ct. 1968).

[126] 130 Wis. 2d 230, 387 N.W.2d 98, 1 UCC Rep. Serv. 2d 422 (Ct. App. 1986).

Packer, Inc. v. United States[127] because placing the meat in a deep freeze during the delay froze it too much to permit reworking or reinspection. Rejection of carpeting nine months after delivery was held to be reasonable in *La Villa Fair v. Lewis Carpet Mills, Inc.*[128] because the seller knew the carpeting would be stored until needed for installation in an apartment-construction project delayed by strike. As these cases demonstrate, the courts place a great deal of emphasis on the difficulty of discovering the defect, the perishability of the goods, and the extent to which the delay prejudices the economic interests of the seller.

[2] Contents of Notification

Rejection is effectuated by notification, and the notification must be sufficiently specific to indicate that the buyer is rejecting the goods. Several courts have invalidated a purported rejection because the notification merely advised the seller of a problem.[129] While such a notice might be sufficient to preserve the buyer's breach of warranty claim,[130] it is not enough to support a rejection. The seller needs to know that the buyer is not just dissatisfied with the transaction but is actually rejecting the goods. Upon receipt of this information, the seller can determine an appropriate response.

In many but not all circumstances, the notification of rejection must particularize the reason for the rejection. Section 2-605(1) provides as follows:

> The buyer's failure to state in connection with rejection a particular defect which is ascertainable by reasonable inspection precludes him from relying on the unstated defect to justify rejection or to establish breach
>
> (a)   where the seller could have cured it if stated seasonably; or
>
> (b)   between merchants when the seller has after rejection made a request in writing for a full and final written statement of all defects on which the buyer proposes to rely.[131]

The rationale for particularization where the defect can be cured is obvious. The seller must decide whether to propose a cure, and it cannot make this determination without knowing the nature of the problem. Curable[132] defects must always be particularized; other defects need not be particularized unless both parties are merchants and the seller makes a written request for a full and

---

[127]   458 F.2d 88, 10 UCC Rep. Serv. 1056 (Ct. Cl. 1972).

[128]   219 Kan. 395, 548 P.2d 825, 19 UCC Rep. Serv. 120 (1976).

[129]   *See, e.g.*, Integrated Circuits Unlimited, Inc. v. E. F. Johnson Co., 875 F.2d 1040, 8 UCC Rep. Serv. 2d 695 (2d Cir. 1989); CMI Corp. v. Leemar Steel Co., 733 F.2d 1410, 38 UCC Rep. Serv. 798 (10th Cir. 1984).

[130]   Post-rejection notification is discussed in § 7.03[B][3] *supra*.

[131]   The comparable provision for lease transactions is UCC § 2A-514(1).

[132]   Read literally, UCC § 2-605(1)(a) applies if the defect is curable without regard to whether the seller has a right to cure under § 2-508. The drafters of the amendments revised the language to make it clear that the provision is not triggered unless the seller has both the right and the capacity to cure.

final written statement listing all defects on which the buyer intends to rely. In cases where the defect cannot be cured and the seller does not request a full and final statement, the drafters chose a policy of "permitting the buyer to give a quick and informal notice of defects in a tender without penalizing him for omissions in his statement."[133]

The consequences of a failure to particularize when required are dramatic: The buyer cannot rely on the unstated defect to justify its rejection, and it also cannot rely on it as a basis for a post-acceptance remedy such as monetary damages or revocation of acceptance. The preclusion rule applies to all defects that could have been ascertained by reasonable inspection. The rationale for this rule is that the seller should be advised of all curable defects in the first instance and should not run the risk of curing a stated defect only to have the goods rejected after retender because of another defect that the buyer could have discovered previously. Thus, a buyer that intends to reject is well advised to complete its inspection and complain of every defect that it reasonable can identify at the time it sends its notification.

[3] Rights and Duties of Buyer

Section 2-711(3) provides that a buyer has a security interest in rightfully rejected goods in its possession or control for any payments made on their price and for certain expenses, and a buyer may foreclose its security interest by selling the goods under the resale procedures established for aggrieved sellers under Section 2-706.[134] If the buyer does not have a security interest, it has the duties of a bailee, meaning that it must "hold [the goods] with reasonable care at the seller's disposition for a time sufficient to permit the seller to remove them."[135]

The buyer generally has no further duties if it rejected the goods rightfully.[136] However, Section 2-603 adds further obligations in some circumstances. If the buyer is a merchant and the seller has neither an agent nor a place of business in the market where the rejection occurs, the buyer must follow any reasonable instructions from the seller regarding the goods. Instructions are deemed unreasonable as a matter of law if the seller does not provide indemnity for expenses after the buyer demands it. If, under the circumstances described above, the seller does not provide instructions and the goods are perishable or threaten to decline in value speedily, the buyer must proceed unilaterally "to make reasonable efforts to sell them for the seller's account."[137] A buyer that sells the goods under this provision is entitled to reimbursement from the seller or out of the proceeds of sale for reasonable expenses incurred in caring for the goods or in selling them, including a

---

[133] UCC § 2-605, cmt. 1.

[134] The procedures are discussed in § 9.01[A] *infra*.

[135] UCC § 2-602(2)(b). Section 2A-512(1)(a) is comparable.

[136] UCC § 2-603(2)(c). Section 2A-512(1)(c) is comparable.

[137] UCC § 2-603(1); Traynor v. Walters, 342 F. Supp. 455, 10 UCC Rep. Serv. 965 (M.D. Pa. 1972) (Christmas trees).

reasonable sales commission.[138] A buyer that executes these obligations in good faith is protected from liability based on acceptance or conversion.[139]

Section 2-604 applies to all buyers. Subject to the duties of a merchant buyer under Section 2-603, the buyer "may store the rejected goods for the seller's account or reship them to him or resell them for the seller's account."[140] If the buyer chooses to resell the goods for the seller's account, it is entitled to reimbursement in the same manner as a merchant buyer selling perishables under Section 2-603.[141]

Article 2A adds a provision that does not appear in Article 2.[142] It protects the interest of a person that purchases goods in good faith from a lessee that is disposing of the goods following a rightful rejection. The purchaser "takes the goods free of any rights of the lessor and [in a finance lease] the supplier even though the lessee fails to comply" with some of the procedural requirements of Article 2A.

[C]   Limitations on and Exceptions to the Perfect Tender Rule

[1]   The Cure Limitation [§ 2-508; § 2A-513]

The most significant factor ameliorating the effect of the perfect tender rule is the seller's right to cure.[143] Cure following rejection is not an absolute right,[144] but when properly invoked it gives the seller a second opportunity to tender the goods and thereby impose on the buyer an obligation to accept and pay for them. Section 2-508 provides in its entirety as follows:

---

[138] UCC §§ 2-603(2). The buyer may recover as a commission either an amount that is usual in the trade or, if none, to a reasonable amount not in excess of 10%. *Id.*

[139] UCC §§ 2-603(3). Without this provision, a seller might argue that the buyer's conduct amounts to a wrongful exercise of ownership under UCC § 2-602(2)(a) and constitutes a conversion or, if ratified by the seller, an acceptance under UCC § 2-606(1)(c).

[140] UCC § 2-604. Section 2A-512(1)(b) is comparable. *See, e.g.,* Broglie v. Mackay-Smith, 26 UCC Rep. Serv. 87 (4th Cir. 1979) (buyer's sale of horse); Pacific Marine Schwabacher, Inc. v. Hydroswift Corp., 525 P.2d 615, 15 UCC Rep. Serv. 354 (Utah 1974).

[141] UCC § 2-603(1). Section 1-107 makes section captions part of the Code, and the captions to Sections 2-603 and 2-604 indicate that they are limited to rightfully rejected goods even though the language of the sections does not contain such a limitation. Some provisions should be so limited (*e.g.,* a buyer's right under Section 2-603(1) to demand indemnity for expenses or under Sections 2-603(2) and 2-604 to be reimbursed for expenses of sale and to receive a commission). However, the duties under Section 2-603 to follow instructions and to sell perishables and the buyer's options under Section 2-604 should apply whether the rejection is rightful or wrongful. Amended Article 2 clarifies the sections in this regard.

[142] UCC § 2A-511(4).

[143] UCC § 2-508. Cure rights for a lessor are comparable. UCC § 2A-513.

[144] Notwithstanding the language of Section 2-508, which refers to rejection but not to revocation of acceptance, some courts have found a right to cure following revocation. *See* § 7.05[C] *infra.* In addition, at least one court has found a statutory right to cure even though the buyer neither rejected the goods nor revoked its acceptance. Inter-Americas Ins. Corp., Inc. v. Imaging Solutions Co., 185 P.3d 963, 66 UCC Rep. Serv. 2d 234 (Kan. Ct. App. 2008).

(1) Where any tender or delivery by the seller is rejected because non-conforming and the time for performance has not yet expired, the seller may seasonally notify the buyer of his intention to cure and may then within the contract time make a conforming delivery.

(2) Where the buyer rejects a non-conforming tender which the seller had reasonable grounds to believe would be acceptable with or without money allowance the seller may if he seasonally notifies the buyer have a further reasonable time to substitute a conforming tender.

The elements of cure are explained below.[145] The right to cure in the context of an installment contract is discussed below, in the material dealing with installment contracts generally.[146]

[a]   Time During Which to Cure

The time of the seller's post-cure retender determines the applicability of Section 2-508's two subsections. The first subsection applies only if retender occurs within the time for performance established by the contract.[147] For example, a seller might deliver a refrigerator on Wednesday under a contract that requires delivery no later than Friday. If the buyer rejects the refrigerator because it is the wrong color, the seller has a right to cure by making a conforming tender no later than Friday. The theory of the subsection is that a conforming retender within the contractual time for performance gives the buyer everything in its bargain.[148] Notification by the seller of its intent to cure with time remaining for performance precludes the buyer from treating the early defective tender as an anticipatory repudiation.[149]

If the parties do not specify a time for the seller's performance, Section 2-309(1) provides that delivery must occur within a reasonable time. The Comments to that section state that the obligation of good faith requires reasonable notification before the buyer can treat the contract as breached because of the expiration of a reasonable time and that when both parties permit an originally reasonable time to expire in silence their course of conduct may have the effect of extending the time.[150] Arguably, if the seller actually makes a tender of delivery, the delivery itself fixes the time for delivery, meaning that

---

[145] More extensive analysis of cure under Section 2-508 is provided in Lawrence, *Cure Under Article 2 of the Uniform Commercial Code: Practices and Prescriptions*, 21 UCC L.J. 138 (1988). Analysis of cure in additional contexts is provided in Lawrence, *Cure in Contracts for the Sale of Goods: Looking Beyond Section 2-508*, 21 UCC L.J. 333 (1989).

[146] *See* § 7.04[C][3] *infra.*

[147] *See, e.g.*, Marlowe v. Argentine Naval Comm'n, 808 F.2d 120, 2 UCC Rep. Serv. 2d 1226 (D.C. Cir. 1986) (failure to cure within the remaining time for contract performance).

[148] *See, e.g.*, Meads v. Davis, 22 N.C. App. 479, 206 S.E.2d 868, 15 UCC Rep. Serv. 40 (1974) (problem discovered during installation of carpet, but contract included installation).

[149] If a seller actually repudiates, Section 2-508(1) does not provide a right to cure. *See* Neptune Research & Dev., Inc. v. Teknics Indus. Sys., Inc., 235 N.J. Super. 522, 563 A.2d 465, 10 UCC Rep. Serv. 2d 107 (1989) (cure provisions do not govern seller's right to retract an anticipatory repudiation).

[150] UCC § 2-309, cmt. 5.

the seller in an indefinite-time contract cannot qualify for cure under Section 2-508(1). The seller could qualify by giving a prior reasonable notification that fixes a future date for performance.

Section 2-508(2), which applies if retender occurs after the contractual time for performance has expired, is of greater importance to most sellers. It effectively modifies the contract by extending the seller's tender obligation for a further reasonable time. The rationale for allowing additional time is based on a balancing of the interests of the parties. The extension of time protects the seller from the forfeiture of its contract rights that otherwise would occur under the high standard imposed by the perfect tender rule. The buyer's right to a perfect tender suffers only marginal interference because the tender following cure must conform to the contract in all respects except for the time at which it occurs.[151]

Based on the need to achieve this balance, a breaching seller that is granted a further reasonable time to substitute a conforming tender must act expeditiously. A seller should not be allowed to lock a disappointed buyer into an extended waiting period but rather should correct the nonconformity promptly. Unreasonable delay in investigating and correcting the problem should cause the cure effort to fail.[152] Further, the right to cure should be contingent on the seller's ability to accomplish it, meaning the right does not exist if a prompt cure is impossible[153] and the right should be terminated by repeated, unsuccessful cure efforts.[154] The seller's right to cure must be contingent on the buyer's needs, and thus the further reasonable time will be vanishingly short if the buyer's need for the goods is so immediate that it must either have them at once or enter into a cover transaction with another seller.

A few courts have inappropriately tied the additional time for cure under Section 2-508(2) to a determination of whether the buyer materially changed its position following notification of the seller's intent to cure.[155] The seller's notification should preclude the buyer from engaging in such strategic conduct, and after receiving a notification the buyer must allow the seller a further reasonable time, however long that may be. Use of a changed-position criterion to reduce a seller's post-notification time for cure might have the undesirable effects of prompting the buyer to act precipitously to limit the seller's cure

---

[151] See § 7.04[C][1][d] *infra* on the requirements for an effective tender following cure.

[152] *See, e.g.*, Mobile Housing, Inc. v. Stone, 490 S.W.2d 611, 12 UCC Rep. Serv. 235 (Tex. Ct. App. 1973) (no repair work commenced on mobile home until nearly two months after rejection).

[153] *See, e.g.*, Johannsen v. Minnesota Valley Ford Tractor Co., 304 N.W.2d 654, 31 UCC Rep. Serv. 558 (Minn. 1981) (dealer indicated to buyer on August 3 that he could not fix hydraulic leak problem on new tractor until replacement parts became available the following April).

[154] *See, e.g.*, General Motors Acceptance Corp. v. Grady, 27 Ohio App. 3d 321, 501 N.E.2d 68, 2 UCC Rep. Serv. 2d 887 (1985) (reasonable time to cure passed when seller's response to numerous attempts by buyer to have new car repaired indicated unwillingness or inability to cure promptly); Steele v. Pacesetter Motor Cars, Inc., 267 Wis. 2d 873, 672 N.W.2d 141, 2003 WI App. 242, 52 UCC Rep. Serv. 2d 405 (2003) (trial court erred in ruling that after repeated unsuccessful attempts at cure buyer had to give seller one last chance).

[155] *See, e.g.*, Ramirez v. Autosport, 88 N.J. 277, 440 A.2d 1345, 33 UCC Rep. Serv. 134 (1982); Bartus v. Riccardi, 55 Misc. 2d 3, 284 N.Y.S.2d 222, 4 UCC Rep. Serv. 845 (Sup. Ct. 1967).

opportunity and of allowing the seller to retain its right to cure until the buyer takes an affirmative step to cut it off.

[b]   Seasonable Notification

The right to cure is implemented by a seasonable notification to the buyer of the seller's intent to cure. To be effective the notification must clearly state the seller's intent to cure.[156] To be seasonable the notification must be given within an agreed time or, absent agreement, within a reasonable time.[157] The determination of a reasonable time, of course, depends on the nature, purpose, and circumstances of the action.[158] The nature of the right to cure and the purpose for which it was created suggest that the time for notification should be relatively short. Although the seller should have enough time to investigate the circumstances to determine whether the tender was in fact nonconforming and to decide whether to attempt a cure, the aggrieved buyer should not be required to speculate long concerning the seller's intent. The extent to which the buyer has reasonably changed its position before receiving the seller's notification,[159] as by entering into a cover transaction, is of particular importance in this context. The obligation of good faith is relevant here, and it should, for example, preclude a buyer in a declining market from attempting to cut off the seller's right to cure by precipitously entering into a cover transaction at the prevailing market price.

The requirement of a seasonable notification of an intent to cure necessarily implies that the buyer must, absent exigent circumstances that force it to act quickly, give the seller a reasonable opportunity to ascertain the existence and extent of the alleged nonconformity. For example, in *Wilson v. Scampoli*[160] a color television delivered by the seller had a reddish tinge that the service representative could not adequately diagnose while examining the set in the buyer's home. Rather than allowing the chassis to be taken to the seller's facility for examination, the buyer's daughter insisted on receiving a different set. The appellate court reversed a trial court verdict for the buyer and awarded the seller the purchase price because the daughter's response inappropriately interfered with the seller's decision-making process regarding whether and how to implement its right to cure.[161]

---

[156] *See, e.g.*, National Fleet Supply, Inc. v. Fairchild, 450 N.E.2d 1015, 36 UCC Rep. Serv. 480 (Ind. Ct. App. 1983) (seller did not properly notify buyer that it intended to cure when its president, upon being notified that buyer was rejecting defective engine, told buyer to return engine for a refund and did not unambiguously indicate an intent to cure until two months later).

[157] UCC § 1-205(2).

[158] UCC § 1-205(1).

[159] *See, e.g.*, National Fleet Supply, Inc. v. Fairchild, 450 N.E.2d 1015, 36 UCC Rep. Serv. 480 (Ind. Ct. App. 1983) (buyer paid to have old engine repaired and installed in truck before receiving seller's notification).

[160] 228 A.2d 848, 4 UCC Rep. Serv. 178 (D.C. Ct. App. 1967).

[161] *See also* Olson v. Ford Motor Co., 258 Ga. App. 848, 575 S.E.2d 743, 50 UCC Rep. Serv. 2d 166 (2002) (buyer's insistence that another dealership perform warranty work and his refusal to let dealer fix problem improperly interfered with seller's right to cure); Terrell v. R & A Mfg. Partners, Ltd., 835 So. 2d 216, 50 UCC Rep. Serv. 2d 151 (Ala. Ct. Civ. App. 2002) (buyer that rejected trailer

[c] Reasonable Grounds to Believe Tender Acceptable

A seller does not have an automatic right to cure when its time for performance has passed; rather, the seller must have had reasonable grounds to believe that the tender would be acceptable to the buyer. The Comments indicate that the drafters included the requirement to balance the interests of the seller and the buyer:

> Subsection (2) seeks to avoid injustice to the seller by reason of a surprise rejection by the buyer. However, the seller is not protected unless he has "reasonable grounds to believe" that the tender would be acceptable.[162]

The right to cure in these cases protects the seller from surprise rejections, and the reasonable-grounds requirement protects the buyer from improper allegations of surprise. The requirement must be viewed in light of the drafters' goal of limiting the risk of forfeiture inherent in the perfect tender rule. Cure forces a modification of the contract to give the seller a second opportunity to perform by granting additional time to make a perfect retender, but its availability is conditioned on the seller's bona fide initial effort to comply. A seller may not obtain an automatic extension of time by forcing a rejection through a deliberately nonconforming tender or by performing initially in any other manner that it cannot reasonably believe will be acceptable to the buyer.

In practice a seller is not entitled to cure unless it reasonably believes that its tender fully conforms to the contract or, knowing its tender is nonconforming, reasonably believes that the buyer will accept anyway, perhaps with a reduction in price to reflect the reduced value resulting from the nonconformity.[163] In either situation the buyer's rejection will come as a surprise. If a seller has reason to know that rejection is likely, it cannot claim to have been surprised and therefore does not have a right to cure.

A seller always has adequate grounds to believe its tender will be acceptable if it has no reason to know of a nonconformity, a point that is illustrated by *Wilson v. Scampoli*,[164] one of the landmark opinions in this area. The buyer in that case rejected a color television set that the seller delivered in a factory-sealed carton because the color did not look right, and the court specifically found that the seller had "reasonable grounds to believe that merchandise like color television sets, new and delivered as crated at the factory, would be acceptable as delivered. . . ."[165] While generally true, the statement is overbroad. The

---

because it did not have dual controls as required by contract refused to give the manufacturer an opportunity to remedy the defect).

[162] UCC § 2-508, cmt. 2.

[163] Unfortunately, too many courts applying § 2-508(2) have simply ignored the "reasonable grounds to believe" requirement. *See* Schmitt & Frisch, *The Perfect Tender Rule-An "Acceptable" Interpretation*, 13 U. Tol. L. Rev. 1375, 1380 (1980) (suggesting that more cases have ignored this element than have addressed it).

[164] 228 A.2d 848, 4 UCC Rep. Serv. 178 (D.C. Ct. App. 1967).

[165] 228 A.2d at 849.

result might have been different if the seller had received a recall order on the television from the manufacturer or if similar televisions delivered to other buyers had resulted in a significant number of complaints. The seller's expert witness in *Wilson* testified that removal of a television chassis was frequently necessary with new sets to determine the cause of a color malfunction and the extent of adjustment or correction needed to achieve full operational efficiency. Depending on the degree of frequency involved, the seller reasonably might have been expected to check the color quality prior to delivery.

The proposition that a seller with knowledge that its tender does not conform to the contract has a right to cure if it has a commercially reasonable basis for assuming the tender will be acceptable can be illustrated by language in the trial court opinion in *Joc Oil USA, Inc. v. Consolidated Edison of New York, Inc.*[166] The contract in that case required the seller to deliver a shipment of oil with a maximum sulfur content of 0.5%, and it tendered oil certified by a refinery to have a sulfur content of 0.52%. Con Ed rejected when a post-delivery test showed that the sulfur content was really 0.92%. Not coincidentally, the price of oil had dropped by about 25% between the time the parties entered into the contract and the time the seller delivered the oil. The seller knew that Con Ed was authorized to use oil with up to a 1% sulfur content and that it mixed shipments, some in excess of 1%, in order to stay within its guidelines. Noting that the price of oil had fallen significantly between the time of contract formation and the time of delivery, the court stated that "although it had no predelivery knowledge of the.92% sulfur content . . . [the seller] would still have believed that such a shipment would have been acceptable to Con Ed based upon its prior knowledge of Con Ed purchase and use practices during this period of oil scarcity and volatile pricing."[167] In other words, even if the seller had known of the high sulfur content, it would have had reasonable grounds to believe that its tender would be acceptable, at least with a money allowance to reflect the lower market price of the inferior oil.[168] The court found that Con Ed was in breach for rejecting the seller's offer to cure by delivering a shipment conforming to the original contract.

In another well-known case, *Zabriskie Chevrolet, Inc. v. Smith*,[169] the transmission on the buyer's new car failed after his wife drove it off the dealer's

---

[166] 434 N.Y.S.2d 623, 30 UCC Rep. Serv. 426 (Sup. Ct. 1980), *aff'd sub nom*, T.W. Oil, Inc. v. Consolidated Edison of New York, Inc., 84 A.D.2d 970, 447 N.Y.S.2d 572 (App. Div. 1981), *aff'd*, 57 N.Y.2d 574, 457 N.Y.S.2d 458, 443 N.E.2d 932, 35 UCC Rep. Serv. 12 (1982).

[167] *Id.*, 434 N.Y.S.2d at 630. The court applied comparable reasoning to reach a different result in *McKenzie v. Alla-Ohio Coals, Inc.*, 29 UCC Rep. Serv. 852 (D.C.D.C. 1979), a case in which the seller delivered coal with an ash content ranging between 13.5% and 16% under a purchase order specifying that the ash content was not to exceed 7.5%. Addressing the reasonableness of the seller's belief, the court noted that "it is unlikely that a reasonable seller in plaintiff's position would be ignorant of such drastic variances in the quality of the coal . . . [and] similarly, no evidence of trade custom in the record indicate[d] that coal with such high ash content would be suitable for use as metallurgical coal, the purpose for which it was purchased." *Id.* at 857.

[168] The court rejected Con Ed's argument that the "with or without money allowance" language in the statute indicates that the seller must have in mind the possibility of a money allowance in order to have a right to cure and therefore cannot qualify for the right unless it knows of the nonconformity at the time of tender. If this argument had prevailed, the seller would have lost on the actual facts of the case.

[169] 99 N.J. Super. 441, 240 A.2d 195, 5 UCC Rep. Serv. 30 (1968).

lot and went 0.7 miles. After the buyer rejected the car, the dealer repaired it by replacing the transmission with one taken off another new car in its inventory. The buyer rejected the repaired car. The court never held directly that the seller did not have a right to cure, only that its proffered cure was ineffective, but in *dictum* it noted that the dealer did not have reasonable grounds to believe that a new car with a defective transmission would be acceptable. The point is obvious but irrelevant: Testimony indicated that before tender the dealer had put the car through a 70-point check that included the transmission and also included a road test, so it had every reason to believe that the actual car tendered to the buyer would be acceptable.

Some courts have improperly applied a magnitude-of-the-defect test in assessing the reasonableness of the seller's belief that the goods will be acceptable to the buyer.[170] This test precludes cure if the nonconforming tender involves a major defect. Use of the test constitutes an unwarranted rewriting of the statutory standard, substituting the nature of the breach for the requirement that the seller believe that its tender will be acceptable. A seller's right to cure is not eliminated just because the defect in the tender is material; nor is a seller automatically entitled to cure just because the defect is immaterial.

[e]   Conforming Retender

The fact that a seller invokes its right to cure does not alter its contractual obligations except to the extent Section 2-508(2) provides it with additional time in which to perform. Thus, a seller's tender after cure remains subject to the perfect tender rule.

Following notification of an intent to cure, one of three things will happen: The seller will at some point abandon its attempt to cure and will not retender the goods; the seller will cure and make a conforming retender; or the seller's attempted cure will be unsuccessful and it will make a nonconforming retender. In the first situation, the buyer's original rejection remains effective and no further action on its part is necessary. In the second situation, the conforming retender reimposes on the buyer an obligation to accept and pay for the goods. In the third situation, the buyer's initial rejection covered only the first tender and it must again reject the goods within a reasonable time or be deemed to have accepted them.

The issue of a cure's adequacy often arises when a seller attempts to repair nonconforming goods rather than replace them. Repair should be allowed, provided that it results in goods that conform fully to the contract. As the court in *Wilson v. Scampoli*[171] noted, the buyer should not be required "to accept patchwork goods or substantially repaired articles in lieu of flawless merchandise." The seller did not meet the standard in *Worldwide RV Sales &*

---

[170] *See, e.g.*, Johannsen v. Minnesota Valley Ford Tractor Co., 304 N.W.2d 654, 31 UCC Rep. Serv. 558 (Minn. 1981); Jones v. Abriani, 169 Ind. App. 556, 350 N.E.2d 635, 19 UCC Rep. Serv. 1102 (1967).

[171] 228 A.2d 848, 850, 4 UCC Rep. Serv. 178 (D.C. Ct. App. 1967). The case is discussed in § 7.04[C][1][c] *supra*.

Service v. Brooks,[172] a case in which the contract for a motor home required "dual roof air conditioning" but the vehicle that was tendered and rejected had only one roof air conditioner, located in the center. The seller offered to cure by placing air conditioning units in the roof at the front and back of the vehicle, but removing the central unit would have left a hole in the roof. The court easily concluded that the proposed cure was inadequate.

The case that is probably cited most often for adequacy of repair is *Zabriskie Chevrolet, Inc. v. Smith*,[173] a case in which the seller of a new car attempted to cure a defective transmission by installing the transmission from another new car on its lot. In holding that the attempted cure was inadequate, the court noted that cure "does not, in the court's opinion, contemplate the tender of a new vehicle with a substituted transmission, not from the factory and of unknown lineage from another vehicle in plaintiff's possession."[174] The decision is debatable. On the one hand, the substitute transmission was from a new car, but on the other hand it was not necessarily from the same model as that purchased by the buyer. As the quoted language suggests, the decision might have been different if the defective transmission had been replaced with a new one from the factory. Perhaps the most that can be said is that the seller failed to convince the court that its attempted cure provided the buyer with the equivalent of a new car in terms of durability and value.[175]

The *Zabriskie* court reinforced its reasoning with what has become known as the "shaken-faith" doctrine, which considers the effect that knowledge of the original defect and repair has on the disappointed buyer. The court stated:

> For a majority of people the purchase of a new car is a major investment, rationalized by the peace of mind that flows from its dependability and safety. Once their faith is shaken, the vehicle loses not only its real value in their eyes, but becomes an instrument whose integrity is substantially impaired and whose operation is fraught with apprehension.[176]

The shaken-faith doctrine is an appropriate consideration, provided it is not applied on the basis of the specific buyer's subjective concerns. Whether goods conform to the contract is determined objectively, and thus the acceptability of a repair as a method of cure should be determined from the perspective of a reasonable buyer. If knowledge of the circumstances of a repair would leave a reasonable buyer with safety concerns, the buyer is not being tendered what was bargained for and the repair is not an adequate cure.[177] The *Zabriskie* court may

---

[172] 534 N.E.2d 1132, 8 UCC Rep. Serv. 2d 386 (Ind. Ct. App. 1989).

[173] 99 N.J. Super. 441, 240 A.2d 195, 5 UCC Rep. Serv. 30 (1968). The case is discussed in § 7.04[C][1][c] *supra*.

[174] 99 N.J. Super. 441, 458, 240 A.2d 195, 205 (1968).

[175] Sinco, Inc. V. Metro-North Commuter R. Co., 133 F. Supp. 2d 308, 44 UCC Rep. Serv. 2d 137 (S.D.N.Y. 2001) (as with original tender, seller has burden of establishing that goods conform to the contract on retender following cure).

[176] *Id.*

[177] Hemmert Agric. Aviation, Inc. v. Mid-Continent Aircraft Corp., 663 F. Supp. 1546, 4 UCC Rep. Serv. 2d 726 (D. Kan. 1987) (discomfort and fear from the handling of a crop-dusting aircraft and repeated efforts to correct the problem).

have yielded excessively to the buyer's subjective complaints in that shaken faith seems to have been assumed and its reasonableness unexplored. To the extent that the doctrine is applied uncritically, it may be used improperly as leverage to extract the form of cure that the buyer prefers, which is typically replacement.[178]

Better reasoning under the shaken-faith doctrine is provided in *Bayne v. Nall Motors, Inc.*,[179] a case in which the differential on a new car locked up four days after delivery. The seller attempted to cure by replacing the differential but the evidence showed that it had not checked to see whether damage had been done to other parts of the car, such as the drive train, and this prevented it from meeting its burden of proof. The court noted as follows:

> The fact that the dealer and manufacturer and their employees strongly believe in the quality of the repaired auto does not make this vehicle as acceptable as a similar automobile that has not experienced the same tremendous internal impact and a reasonable buyer could not be expected to be satisfied under the facts herein.[180]

In another helpful case, *Sinco, Inc. v. Metro-North Commuter R. Co.*,[181] the seller agreed to provide a fall-protection system to be used by employees doing renovation work on Grand Central Station. After the system was installed, the seller conducted a training session during which critical components failed. The buyer rejected the system and also rejected the seller's offer to cure the defect with replacement parts, indicating that its employees had such a lack of confidence in the system that they would not use it. The court held for the buyer, noting that an effective cure would require the seller to provide the buyer and its employees with convincing evidence that the system was now safe.

[f]   Consensual Cure

Even if Article 2 does not provide a breaching seller with a statutory right to cure unless the buyer rejects the goods, the right can be obtained consensually. The seller might offer to correct a nonconformity, or the buyer might request or even demand a cure. Neither party can force the other to acquiesce, but mutual assent modifies the original contract and creates cure rights that otherwise would not have applied.[182] The parties can specify the nature of the seller's

---

[178] *See* Asciolla v. Manter Oldsmobile-Pontiac, Inc., 117 N.H. 85, 370 A.2d 270, 21 UCC Rep. Serv. 112 (1977) (court upheld buyer insistence on replacement of automobile rather than just the transmission).

[179] 12 UCC Rep. Serv. 1137 (Iowa Dist. Ct. 1973).

[180] *Id.* at 1141. Two additional well-reasoned cases on this point are *Champion Ford Sales, Inc. v. Levine*, 49 Md. App. 547, 433 A.2d 1218, 32 UCC Rep. Serv. 108 (Ct. Spec. App. 1981) (difference between a car with a new factory-built and installed engine and a repaired car with a shop-rebuilt engine), and *Ford Motor Co. v. Mayes*, 575 S.W.2d 480, 24 UCC Rep. Serv. 1057 (Ky. Ct. App. 1978) (pickup truck frame was twisted and "diamonded," which would cause unusual stress and wear to various moving parts of the truck).

[181] 133 F. Supp. 2d 308, 44 UCC Rep. Serv. 2d 137 (S.D.N.Y. 2001).

[182] *See, e.g.*, Ranta Construction, Inc. v. Anderson, 66 UCC Rep. Serv. 2d 200 (Col. Ct. App. 2008) (owners who revoked acceptance and then agreed that seller could cure defect obligated to give seller an opportunity to do so before bringing action for breach of warranty); Cardwell v. International Housing, 282 Pa. Super. 498, 423 A.2d 355, 31 UCC Rep. Serv. 512 (1980) (buyer who agreed to

corrective action and the length of time that will be given to effectuate the cure.

Consensual cure can arise any time after tender, even before rejection has occurred. For example, in *Havas v. Love*[183] the buyer of a motor bus observed smoke coming from the air-conditioning unit and allowed the seller an opportunity to fix the unit, but when he then noticed smoke and fumes coming from the motor, he rejected. The court did not address the basis for the cure opportunity relating to the air conditioning unit, but clearly it was consensual in nature.

A buyer considering consensual cure should require prompt agreement with the seller; otherwise, it runs the risk of failing to reject within a reasonable time and thereby being deemed to have accepted. This delay would not prevent consensual cure, but it would preclude rejection. If the parties agree, the buyer can make its acceptance expressly conditional upon a defined cure.[184] If the condition fails, the acceptance is ineffectual and the buyer is entitled to reject.[185]

[2]   The Good-Faith Limitation [§ 1-203]

Rejection is not a self-executing right; rather, the buyer must take action in order to effectuate a rejection and thereby enforce its contract rights.[186] Consequently, the right to reject is limited by the buyer's duty to act in good faith.[187]

The good-faith limitation is an important mechanism for helping the courts fairly apply the perfect tender rule. The primary complaint about the rule is that it affords an opportunity for a buyer that has become dissatisfied with its bargain to nitpick the seller's tender in order to find an inconsequential defect that can be used as an excuse to reject the goods and cancel the contract. Both the right to cure and the duty of good faith have the effect of constraining such opportunistic behavior.

Contract performance should fulfill the legitimate expectations of the parties.[188] Notwithstanding the literal language of Section 2-601, a buyer that receives the full measure of what was bargained for, in the sense of fulfilling these expectations, has no right to use some insignificant deviation from the precise contract specifications as a pretext for cancelling a contract that it no

---

delivery of mobile home model different from the one specified in the written contract abandoned right to reject goods as nonconforming to original contract).

[183] 89 Nev. 458, 514 P.2d 1187, 13 UCC Rep. Serv. 466 (1973).

[184] North Am. Steel Corp. v. Siderius, 75 Mich. App. 391, 254 N.W.2d 899, 22 UCC Rep. Serv. 62 (1977) (subject to price adjustment).

[185] Christopher v. Larson Ford Sales, Inc., 557 P.2d 1009, 20 UCC Rep. Serv. 873 (Utah 1976) (seller's promise that buyers could return motor home if problems persisted entitled buyers to reject when the condition to their acceptance failed).

[186] UCC § 2-602(1); *see* § 7.04[B] *supra*.

[187] Section 1-304 provides that "[e]very contract or duty within the [Uniform Commercial Code] imposes an obligation of good faith in its performance and enforcement." The duty of good faith is discussed generally in § 4.05[B] *supra*.

[188] E. A. Farnsworth, Contracts 562 (2d ed. 1990).

longer finds advantageous.[189] It is dishonest, or at least inconsistent with reasonable commercial standards of fair dealing,[190] to feign dissatisfaction with the seller's performance when the true motive for rejecting the goods is based on another factor, such as a desire in a falling market to acquire the goods elsewhere at a lower price.[191] If the buyer is using an insignificant defect as a pretext for its rejection, the rejection is wrongful and the seller should not be required to cure the defect in order to retain the benefit of its bargain.

[3]   The Installment Contract Exception [§ 2-612; § 2A-510]

Section 2-612 governs a buyer's right under an installment contract to reject a nonconforming tender of an installment and the right of either party to cancel the contract.[192] The section does not incorporate the perfect tender rule except with regard to documents that must be tendered in order for a buyer to take delivery from a bailee. With regard to individual installments, Section 2-612(2) provides as follows:

> The buyer may reject any installment which is non-conforming if the non-conformity substantially impairs the value of that installment and cannot be cured or if the non-conformity is a defect in the required documents; but if the non-conformity does not fall within subsection (3) and the seller gives adequate assurance of its cure the buyer must accept that installment.

Substantial impairment is the same as material breach at common law, a point made clear by the Comments to another section that uses the same concept.[193] The installment contract creates a continuing relationship between the buyer and the seller that extends beyond the single nonconforming delivery, and the buyer is not entitled to cancel that relationship easily. What is substantial for

---

[189] *See, e.g.*, Printing Center of Texas, Inc. v. Supermind Pub. Co., Inc., 669 S.W.2d 779, 39 UCC Rep. Serv. 127 (Tex. Ct. App. 1984) (evidence of circumstances indicating that buyer's motivation in rejecting goods was to escape bargain would support finding of bad-faith rejection).

[190] Prior to the 2001 revision of Article 1, the standard of good faith was bifurcated. Original Section 1-201(19) defined the term as "honesty in fact in the conduct or transaction concerned." Section 2-103(1)(b) overrode this definition for merchants by requiring both "honesty in fact and the observance of reasonable commercial standards of fair dealing in the trade." Revised Section 1-201(b)(20) requires both elements, but several states have amended their versions of the revised article to leave the original definition in place, thus perpetuating the bifurcation between merchants and non-merchants.

[191] *See, e.g.*, Neumiller Farms, Inc. v. Cornett, 368 So. 2d 272, 26 UCC Rep. Serv. 61 (Ala. 1979) (claim of dissatisfaction with subsequent deliveries of chipping potatoes after market price declined substantially held to be made in bad faith, making the rejection a breach). For a study on buyer attempts to reject during a falling market, see generally Eno, *Price Movement and Unstated Objections to the Defective Performance of Sales Contracts*, 44 Yale L.J. 782 (1935).

[192] "An 'installment contract' is one which requires or authorizes the delivery of goods in separate lots to be separately accepted, even though the contract contains a clause 'each delivery is a separate contract' or its equivalent." UCC § 2-612(1).

[193] "The most useful test of substantial value is to determine whether material inconvenience or injustice will result if the aggrieved party is forced to wait and receive an ultimate tender minus the part or aspect repudiated." UCC § 2-610, cmt. 3 (addressing anticipatory repudiation).

purposes of rejecting an installment "can turn not only on the quality of the goods but also on such factors as time, quantity, assortment, and the like. It must be judged in terms of the normal or specifically known purposes of the contract."[194]

Unlike single-delivery cases, a buyer's rightful rejection of an installment does not of itself give the buyer a right to cancel the contract. Under Section 2-612(3), cancellation is justified only if "non-conformity or default with respect to one or more installments substantially impairs the value of the whole contract. . . ." In other words, rejection of an installment requires a material breach as to that installment; cancellation requires a material breach of the contract taken as a whole.[195]

A seller in an installment contract has a more generous right to cure than a seller in a single-delivery contract. Unlike Section 2-508, Section 2-612(2) does not create different standards for cure depending on whether the contract time for performance has expired. Section 2-508 applies only after rejection, whereas Section 2-612(2) precludes the buyer from rejecting if the seller gives adequate assurances of cure. Section 2-612(2) does not contemplate a retender which would give the buyer an opportunity to discover whether the seller has effectively cured the nonconformity; instead, the buyer must accept the original tender solely on the strength of the seller's assurances, a rule that is particularly appropriate given the continuing nature of the parties' relationship. Section 2-612(2) omits all reference to the requirement of Section 2-508(2) that the seller have reasonable grounds to believe that its tender will be acceptable, and the Comments suggest that the omission is no mistake by stating that a buyer must accept an installment delivery if the nonconformity is curable and the seller gives adequate assurances that cure will be forthcoming.[196] The Comments also indicate that a seller in an installment contract may cure by giving the buyer a price break, something that would be outside the scope of Section 2-508, which requires that the seller make a conforming retender.[197] The extent of the inconsistencies shows that the two sections do not interact.[198]

[4]　　The Shipment Contract Exception [§ 2-504]

Section 2-504 establishes the proper manner for a seller's tender of delivery in a shipment contract.[199] The section imposes obligations on the seller in three respects: placing conforming goods in the possession of such a carrier and

---

[194] UCC § 2-612, cmt. 4; *see also* Restatement (Second) of Contracts § 241.

[195] The right to cancel an installment contract is discussed in more detail in § 7.07[A][4] *infra*.

[196] UCC § 2-612, cmt. 5.

[197] *Id.*

[198] Some courts addressing cure rights with respect to installment contracts have failed to perceive these distinctions. *See, e.g.*, Bodine Sewer, Inc. v. Eastern Ill. Precast, Inc., 143 Ill. App. 3d 920, 493 N.E.2d 705, 1 UCC Rep. Serv. 2d 1480 (1986); Arkla Energy Resources v. Roye Realty & Development, Inc., 9 F.3d 855, 22 UCC Rep. Serv. 2d 155 (10th Cir. 1993) (seller's right to cure in installment contract subject also to § 2-508).

[199] A shipment contract is one in which "the seller is required or authorized to send the goods to the buyer and the contract does not require him to deliver them at a particular destination." UCC § 2-504; *see* § 4.04[C][1] *supra*. Article 2A does not have a comparable provision.

making such a contract for their transport as is reasonable in the circumstances; obtaining and tendering such documents as may be necessary to enable the buyer to obtain possession of the goods from the carrier; and notifying the buyer of the shipment. The final sentence of the section eliminates the perfect tender rule for two of these obligations, providing that, "[f]ailure to notify the buyer [as required] or to make a proper contract [as required] is a ground for rejection only if material delay or loss ensues."

The drafters probably adopted this exception to the perfect tender rule as a reaction to earlier case law in which buyers rejected goods because of some technical noncompliance with shipping arrangements even though they did not suffer any perceivable injury. For example, in *Filley v. Pope*[200] the seller shipped pig iron to New Orleans from Leith, Scotland under a contract calling for shipment from Glasgow. The seller shipped from Leith because the only ship available was discharging its cargo there and a vessel would not be available from Glasgow for several weeks. The Supreme Court upheld the buyer's refusal to accept the tendered iron, considering itself "bound to give effect to the terms which the parties have chosen for themselves" and to have "neither the means, nor the right, to determine why the parties in their contract specified 'shipment from Glasgow.' "[201]

The material breach standard of Section 2-504 precludes decisions like *Filley*. Regarding the requirement that the contract for transport be reasonable, the Comments are instructive:

> Whether or not the shipment is at the buyer's expense the seller must see to any arrangements, reasonable in the circumstances, such as refrigeration, watering of live stock, protection against cold, the sending along of any necessary help, selection of specialized cars and the like for paragraph (a) is intended to cover all necessary arrangements whether made by contract with the carrier or otherwise. There is, however, a proper relaxation of such requirements if the buyer is himself in a position to make the appropriate arrangements and the seller gives him reasonable notice of the need to do so. It is an improper contract under paragraph (a) for the seller to agree with the carrier to a limited valuation below the true value and thus cut off the buyer's opportunity to recover from the carrier in the event of loss, when the risk of shipment is placed on the buyer by his contract with the seller.[202]

Section 2-504 preserves the perfect tender rule for the seller's obligation to obtain and promptly tender any necessary documents. This approach is consistent with Section 2-612(2), which generally limits the right to reject an installment to a nonconformity that "substantially impairs the value of that installment" but applies the perfect tender rule "if the non-conformity is a defect in the required documents." These provisions reflect the mercantile custom

---

[200] 115 U.S. 213 (1885).

[201] *Id.* at 220.

[202] UCC § 2-504, cmt. 3.

requiring strict compliance in documentary transactions.[203] Scholars have long recognized the justifications for preserving the free marketability of documents and protecting buyers in cash sales from the risks associated with securing a refund from the seller.[204]

§ 7.05 REVOCATION OF ACCEPTANCE [§ 2-608; § 2A-517]

The effect of a justifiable revocation of acceptance[205] is the same as the effect of a rightful rejection: Title to the goods is revested in the seller;[206] the buyer becomes a bailee and has the same rights and duties regarding the goods as if it had rejected;[207] and the buyer is entitled to cancel[208] the contract, recover so much of the price as has been paid,[209] and recover monetary damages for breach.[210] The procedural aspects of a revocation are comparable to rejection in that it is effectuated by notification, but unlike rejection the buyer has the burden of establishing that the grounds for revocation are present and that the goods are sufficiently defective to justify the remedy.[211] Notwithstanding the similarities, the right to revoke is much more constrained than the right to reject, as the following discussion will demonstrate.

[A] The Right

[1] Limited Circumstances

A buyer has a right to revoke only in limited circumstances that relate to whether the buyer knew the goods were nonconforming at the time of acceptance. A buyer that knows of a defect prior to acceptance can only revoke if it accepts on the reasonable assumption that the nonconformity will be cured and it is not seasonably cured.[212] For example, in *North American Lighting, Inc. v. Hopkins Manufacturing Corp.*[213] a buyer of an automobile headlight

---

[203] *See* Honnold, *Buyer's Right of Rejection*, 97 U. Pa. L. Rev. 457, 467 (1949).

[204] *Id.* at 478–79; Llewellyn, *On Warranty of Quality and Society: I*, 36 Colum. L. Rev. 699, 730–31 (1936).

[205] UCC § 2-608. With the exception of some specialized provisions dealing with finance leases, which are covered separately in this text, the provisions for leases are comparable. UCC § 2A-517.

[206] UCC § 2-401(4).

[207] UCC § 2-608(4).

[208] UCC § 2-711(1).

[209] UCC § 2-711(3). The seller may be entitled to a setoff based on restitutionary principles for the buyer's benefit in using the goods. *See* § 7.03[A][3][b] *supra.*

[210] UCC § 2-711(1).

[211] UCC § 2-607(4); *see* discussion § 7.03[B][4] *supra.*

[212] UCC § 2-608(1)(a). A common situation in which sellers have been found to have given assurances is when they provide the buyer with a repair-or-replace remedy. If the seller is unable to repair and refuses to replace, the buyer may revoke its acceptance if all other requirements (*e.g.*, the requirement that the defect substantially impair the value of the goods to the buyer) are met. *See, e.g.*, Beal v. Griffin, 123 Idaho 445, 849 P.2d 118, 21 UCC Rep. Serv. 2d 244 (1993) (seller's failure to provide promised remedy justified revocation).

[213] 37 F.3d 1253, 24 UCC Rep. Serv. 2d 1061 (7th Cir. 1994).

aiming system was allowed to revoke two years after accepting. Even though the buyer knew at the time of acceptance that the system did not meet federal standards as required by the contract, it accepted on the basis of the seller's assurances that the system could be modified to meet the standards and it worked with the seller's experts until it became obvious that they could not succeed. By contrast, a buyer that knows of a nonconformity but accepts without a reasonable expectation of cure is entitled to monetary damages but lacks an equitable basis to insist on revocation.

Even if a buyer accepts without knowledge of a nonconformity, revocation is available only if acceptance was reasonably induced either by the difficulty of discovering the nonconformity or by the seller's assurances. The limitations create an incentive for buyers to be vigilant. Buyers are not deemed to have accepted until they have been afforded a reasonable opportunity to inspect the goods,[214] and a buyer that fails to inspect, or inspects but fails to discover a nonconformity that would have been revealed by a reasonable inspection, does not have a right to revoke its acceptance.[215] The right to reject that is lost because of a failure to conduct a reasonable inspection cannot be regained through revocation of acceptance.

Revocation of acceptance is permitted if an unknown nonconformity was too latent to be detected by a reasonable pre-acceptance inspection.[216] It is also permitted if the seller gives assurances of the goods' quality, thereby causing the buyer to relax its vigilance and fail to discover a nonconformity.[217]

[2]   Subjective Standard of Substantial Impairment

Even if a buyer can establish one of the limited circumstances justifying revocation, it still must establish that the nonconformity of a lot or commercial unit "substantially impairs its value to him."[218] The perfect tender rule does not

---

[214] UCC § 2-606(1)(a),(b); *see* 7.03[A] *supra*.

[215] *See, e.g.,* Campbell v. AG Finder Iowa, Nebraska, 683 N.W.2d 126, 53 UCC Rep. Serv. 2d 235 (Iowa Ct. App. 2004) (buyer could not revoke acceptance when reasonable pre-acceptance testing would have shown that soybeans were genetically modified); In re Barney Schogel, Inc., 12 B.R. 697, 34 UCC Rep. Serv. 29 (Bankr. S.D.N.Y. 1981) (buyer who did not discover defect in specially manufactured windows until after installation because of failure to inspect upon delivery precluded from revoking acceptance).

[216] *See, e.g.,* Atlantic Industries, Inc. v. O.E.M., Inc., 555 F. Supp. 184, 35 UCC Rep. Serv. 795 (W.D. Okla. 1983) (buyer required to undertake only inspection tests common in the industry); Kesner v. Lancaster, 378 S.E.2d 649, 9 UCC Rep. Serv. 2d 122 (W. Va. 1989) (test for revocation satisfied when buyer makes reasonable inspection and defect is not reasonably apparent or buyer does not have some special expertise).

[217] *See, e.g.,* Trinity Products, Inc. v. Burgess Steel, L.L.C., 486 F.3d 325, 62 UCC Rep. Serv. 2d 904 (8th Cir. 2007) (contract provision stating that buyer "unequivocally accepted" by failing to give notification of rejection within five days after delivery did not preclude buyer from revoking acceptance based on seller's assurances); GNP Commodities, Inc. v. Walsh Heffernan Co., 95 Ill. App. 2d 966, 420 N.E.2d 659, 31 UCC Rep. Serv. 1342 (1981) (buyer of pork bellies accepted in reliance on seller's assurances that their "freeze date" was appropriate for delivery against future short sales).

[218] UCC § 2-608(1). The limitation of revocation of acceptance to a defective lot or commercial unit differs from rejection, where a nonconformity in any of the tendered goods permits a buyer to reject all them. UCC § 2-601.

apply but, as explained below, the standard is not quite the same as material breach at common law.

Two noted commentators have identified several reasons why a buyer is required to meet the higher standard before being allowed to revoke its acceptance.[219] Goods are typically in the buyer's possession longer than in rejection cases, and the obligation to refund the purchase price becomes increasingly burdensome as they depreciate in value. Moreover, the buyer often benefits from its use of the goods, making the obligation to refund the full price inequitable absent a compelling rationale.[220] Finally, the chances increase that the defect will have been caused or exacerbated by the buyer but that the buyer will be able to convince the court that it is the seller's responsibility. These arguments, coupled with the fact that an aggrieved buyer that cannot revoke still has a remedy for monetary damages, justify the deviation from the perfect tender rule.

Although a defect that justifies revocation must substantially impair the value of the goods,[221] the level of impairment is judged on the basis of its impact on the actual buyer.[222] In other words, whether impairment is substantial depends solely on the personal circumstances of the buyer, not those of a hypothetical reasonable buyer.[223] The subjective nature of the standard is emphasized in the Comments: "The test is not what the seller had reason to know at the time of contracting; the question is whether the non-conformity is such as will in fact cause a substantial impairment of value to the buyer though the seller had no advance knowledge as to the buyer's particular circumstances."[224]

The use of a subjective standard is consistent with the drafters' desire to make it easier for an aggrieved buyer to determine the appropriate legal response. The buyer must assume the higher burden of showing substantial impairment to justify revocation, but the showing need be made only in the context of the buyer's own circumstances. Undoubtedly, cases in which goods substantially conform to a contract on an objective basis but are substantially defective as applied to a particular buyer are unusual, and courts must be able to distinguish between buyers that have valid reasons for considering a defect to be substantial and those that make a mountain out of a molehill. Nevertheless, the standard permits buyers to rely more confidently upon their own circumstances when determining whether to revoke and, in the event of litigation, they can focus the court's attention on how the breach impacted them.

---

[219] J. White & R. Summers, Uniform Commercial Code § 8-4 (5th student ed. 2000).

[220] Some courts have used restitutionary principles to provide the seller with a setoff for the value of the benefit the buyer received by using the goods. See § 7.03[A][3][b] supra.

[221] See, e.g., First Nat. Bank of Litchfield v. Miller, 56 UCC Rep. Serv. 2d 640 (Conn. Super. Ct. 2005) (blocked fuel line on new boat did not constitute substantial impairment).

[222] "The buyer may revoke his acceptance of a lot or commercial unit whose non-conformity substantially impairs its value to him." UCC § 2-608(1) (emphasis supplied).

[223] Waddell v. L.V.R.V. Inc., 125 P.3d 1160, 58 UCC Rep. Serv. 2d 654 (Nev. 2006) (substantial impairment turns on particular buyer's needs and circumstances and how the alleged defect impacts on its use of the goods in light of those needs and circumstances).

[224] UCC § 2-608, cmt. 2.

Whether goods are defective is determined objectively, on the basis of Article 2's warranty provisions, and a buyer must demonstrate that the goods are objectively defective before arguing about the impact of the defect on it.[225] The distinction is illustrated by *Fullerton Aircraft Sales & Rentals, Inc. v. Page Avjet Corp*,[226] a case in which the buyer complained of vibrations in a purchased aircraft. The court noted that other pilots did not notice excessive vibration and held that the buyer could not revoke its acceptance because it could not establish that its pilot was particularly sensitive to ordinary levels of vibration. The analysis is incorrect. The tendered aircraft complied with all express warranties and with the implied warranty of merchantability, and an implied warranty of fitness for the buyer's particular purpose had not been created. The goods thus conformed to the contract, and the buyer had neither a claim for breach of warranty nor a basis for revoking acceptance. Had a warranty related to the level of vibration been breached, the determination of whether it substantially impaired the value of the aircraft to the buyer would have been determined in light of its alleged idiosyncratic sensitivity.

The court properly applied the standard in *Colonial Dodge, Inc. v. Miller*,[227] a case involving a station wagon that required extra-wide tires because it came with a heavy-duty trailer package. The buyer noticed after acceptance that the spare tire required by the contract had not been included. When he asked the dealer for one, he was told that the spare had not been included because of a nationwide strike in the tire industry and that one would not be available for several months. He then revoked his acceptance. He established at trial that the defect was substantial to him because his job required him to drive as many as 150 miles a day on the Detroit freeways, often in the early morning hours, and he feared being stranded in a dangerous area. Even though the nonconformity might well have been trivial to an average buyer, the court properly upheld the buyer's revocation.

[B]   Procedural Aspects

Revocation, like rejection, is never self-executing; rather, the buyer must notify the seller for it to be effective.[228] The required contents, and the relationship of a notification required to effectuate a revocation and those required to effectuate a rejection or to preserve a right to monetary damages, are discussed elsewhere in this chapter.[229]

A revocation "must occur within a reasonable time after the buyer discovers or should have discovered the ground for it."[230] The reasons for requiring

---

[225] *See, e.g.*, Kelmar v. Mid-Michigan Freightliner, Inc., 52 UCC Rep. Serv. 2d 411 (Mich. Ct. App. 2003) (buyer may not justifiably revoke acceptance without nonconformity).

[226] 3 UCC Rep. Serv. 2d 1393 (4th Cir. 1987) (unpublished).

[227] 420 Mich. 452, 362 N.W.2d 704, 40 UCC Rep. Serv. 1 (1984).

[228] UCC § 2-608(2); *accord* UCC § 2A-517(4).

[229] *See* §§ 7.03[B][3] (post-acceptance notification generally), 7.04[B][2] (notification of rejection) *supra*.

[230] UCC § 2-608(2). Article 2A is comparable on the requirements of timeliness of revocation. UCC § 2A-517(4).

timeliness are comparable to the policies that underlie timely notice of rejection.[231] A "reasonable time" in the revocation context, however, often extends beyond the comparable standard of timeliness required in other contexts. The Comments explain as follows:

> "Since this remedy will be generally resorted to only after attempts at adjustment have failed, the reasonable time period should extend in most cases beyond the time in which notification of breach must be given, beyond the time for discovery of non-conformity after acceptance, and beyond the time for rejection after tender."[232]

If a buyer accepts goods on the reasonable assumption that a known nonconformity will be cured, it must of course give the seller a reasonable opportunity to effectuate the cure before revoking its acceptance. Even if the buyer accepted the goods with a latent defect, upon discovery of the defect it is likely to give the seller an opportunity to fix the problem before deciding to revoke, and courts should encourage this behavior by being tolerant of buyers that are working in good faith with their sellers.[233]

Revocation must occur "before any substantial change in the condition of the goods which is not caused by their own defects."[234] The seller is entitled to have the goods returned without substantial change or excessive deterioration while in the hands of the buyer, excluding normal wear and tear.[235] If the change or deterioration results from a defect in the goods, such as spoilage that spreads to additional fruit included as part of a lot, the substantial-change limitation does not apply.

A buyer that revokes acceptance has the same rights and duties with respect to the goods as one that rejects them.[236] These rights and duties have been discussed elsewhere in this chapter.[237]

[C]   Post-Revocation Cure

By its terms, Section 2-508 grants a right to cure only in cases of rejection. Nevertheless, some courts have found a right to cure following a revocation of acceptance, usually citing as authority Section 2-608(3), which provides that

---

[231]   *See* § 7.04[B][1] *supra.*

[232]   UCC § 2-608, cmt. 4.

[233]   *See, e.g.*, Waddell v. L.V.R.V. Inc., 125 P.3d 1160, 58 UCC Rep. Serv. 2d 654 (Nev. 2006) (notification of revocation 18 months after acceptance timely because buyer worked continuously with seller on attempts to repair defects).

[234]   UCC § 2-608(2); *see, e.g.*, Intervale Steel Corp. v. Borg & Beck Div., Borg-Warner Corp., 578 F. Supp. 1081, 38 UCC Rep. Serv. 805 (E.D. Mich. 1984) (cutting rolls of steel into parts); Western Paper Co. v. Bilby, 783 P.2d 980, 11 UCC Rep. Serv. 2d 503 (alteration of paper in custom printing process).

[235]   *See, e.g.*, Deere & Co. v. Johnson, 271 F.3d 613, 46 UCC Rep. Serv. 2d 433 (5th Cir. 2001) (normal wear and tear from use of combine did not constitute substantial change in its condition).

[236]   UCC § 2-608(3). Section 2A-517(5) is comparable.

[237]   *See* § 7.04[B][3] *supra.*

after revocation a buyer has the same rights and duties as if it had rejected.[238] The rationale is a stretch at best. The reference to a buyer's post-rejection rights and duties was almost certainly intended to mean those created or imposed by Section 2-602(2)(b) (buyer's duty to hold rejected goods with reasonable care), Section 2-603 (merchant buyer's rights and duties), and Section 2-604 (buyer's options as to salvage). None of these provisions remotely implicate a duty to allow the seller to cure. Moreover, Section 2-605 requires that a rejecting buyer's notification particularize the defect upon which the buyer is relying if the goods can be cured so that the seller will know what it must do before retendering the goods. If the drafters had intended a right to cure after revocation, surely Section 2-605 would have been expanded to cover that circumstance. Consistent with this analysis, most courts have concluded that the drafters' limitation of Section 2-508 to cases of rejection was intentional and have denied a post-revocation right to cure.[239]

One can debate whether granting sellers a post-revocation right to cure represents sound policy. The consequences of revocation are more adverse to a seller than the consequences of rejection because the goods are likely to have deteriorated or depreciated through use, yet the seller must refund the full purchase price.[240] If permitting cure would relieve the seller of this burden without unduly disadvantaging the buyer, perhaps it should be given that right. However, the buyer might be disadvantaged because of potential difficulties in applying the right. For example, what would the standard for retender be? The post-rejection standard — the perfect tender rule — is clear and the buyer is minimally disadvantaged by having to reaccept, but determining the appropriate standard after a seller repairs and retenders used goods would not be easy. Under no circumstances should the seller be permitted to effectuate a partial repair that renders a defect insubstantial but does not fully fix it and then demand that, because the standard for revocation can no longer be met, the buyer reaccept the goods. Such an approach would leave the buyer with nonconforming goods and only a right to money damages.

Another argument against providing a post-revocation cure right is that cure was created as a limitation on the perfect tender rule and to an extent reflects a concern that buyers will engage in opportunistic behavior to avoid contracts that they no longer find to be advantageous. A buyer's acceptance, coupled with the higher standard of impairment required for revocation, makes such opportunistic behavior much less likely. The parties can always agree that the seller can cure a defect and in so doing they can set the standard for repair.[241]

---

[238] *See, e.g.*, David Tunick, Inc. v. Kornfeld, 838 F. Supp. 848 (S.D.N.Y. 1993) (finding a right to cure after revocation of acceptance but holding that cure rights generally do not extend to a seller of an artist's prints).

[239] *See, e.g.*, Head v. Phillips Camper Sales & Rental, Inc., 234 Mich. App. 94, 593 N.W.2d 595, 37 UCC Rep. Serv. 2d 1033 (1999); U.S. Roofing, Inc. v. Credit Alliance Corp., 228 Cal. App. 3d 1431, 279 Cal. Rptr. 533, 14 UCC Rep. Serv. 2d 746 (1991); Grappelburg v. Landrum, 666 S.W.2d 88 (Tex. 1984); *see also* J. Sebert, *Rejection, Revocation, and Cure Under Article 2 of the Uniform Commercial Code: Some Modest Proposals*, 84 Nw. U.L. Rev. 375, 392-93 (1990).

[240] Some courts have used restitutionary principles to provide the seller with a setoff for the value of the benefit the buyer received by using the goods. *See* § 7.03[A][3][b] *supra*.

[241] *See* § 7.04[C][1][e] *supra*.

Leaving the matter to the agreement of the parties enhances an aggrieved buyer's leverage in dealing with a recalcitrant seller.

Extending the cure right in one class of revocation cases clearly would be unjustified. A buyer that accepts goods while aware of a nonconformity is entitled to revoke only if the buyer accepted "on the reasonable assumption that its non-conformity would be cured and it has not been seasonably cured."[242] This provision implicitly gives the seller a right to cure before revocation of acceptance,[243] and giving a seller that has tried but failed a second bite at the apple would be unjustifiably burdensome to the buyer.

[D]   Wrongful Revocation

A buyer that is not entitled to reject may nevertheless do so by notifying the seller of its rejection within a reasonable time after delivery or tender. The rejection is wrongful and the seller is entitled to cancel the contract and recover damages,[244] but it is effective to preclude acceptance[245] and to revest title to the goods in the seller. The latter point is clear from Section 2-401(4), which states in relevant part as follows:

> A rejection or other refusal by the buyer to receive or retain the goods, whether or not justified, or a justified revocation of acceptance revests title to the goods in the seller.

Note that in the case of a revocation of acceptance, title does not revest in the seller unless the revocation is justified. The statutory provision establishes a significant difference in the treatment of wrongful rejections and wrongful revocations of acceptance.

Economic efficiency provides the rationale that underlies recognition of a wrongful but effective rejection. The seller is generally in a better position than the buyer to dispose of the rejected goods and to minimize damages. Even if the rejection is wrongful, the burden is on the seller to utilize its superior resale position and to satisfy itself with damages against the breaching buyer.

The same rationale has some merit in the revocation context but is outweighed by other considerations. The goods are more likely to have deteriorated or depreciated after they were tendered and the seller's superior ability to dispose of them might diminish as their quality changes. Furthermore, the policy reasons that support making revocation of acceptance less readily available than rejection[246] also justify a refusal to recognize the effectiveness of a wrongful revocation. Section 2-703 states that the seller may cancel the contract in the event of a wrongful revocation, but the seller would also be justified in ignoring

---

[242]   UCC § 2-608(1)(a).

[243]   Champion Ford Sales, Inc. v. Levine, 433 A.2d 1218, 1222, 32 UCC Rep. Serv. 108 (Md. Ct. Spec. App. 1981) (seller has right to cure when "buyer accepts nonconforming goods with the expectation that the nonconformity will be remedied").

[244]   UCC § 2-703.

[245]   Integrated Circuits Unlimited v. E. F. Johnson Co., 875 F.2d 1040, 8 UCC Rep. Serv. 2d 695 (2d Cir. 1989).

[246]   See § 7.05[A] *supra*.

the attempted revocation and allowing the acceptance to stand. Because Article 2 does not fully articulate the consequences of a wrongful revocation, the issue is in considerable doubt.

[E]   Revocation and Privity

Whether a buyer that has incurred a direct economic loss can assert a monetary claim for breach of warranty against a remote manufacturer is a complex question that is discussed in detail elsewhere in this book.[247] If the buyer can do so, the question arises whether it can also revoke its acceptance against the manufacturer.

The overwhelming majority of courts have held against such a right.[248] The rationale is partly technical: The buyer accepted the immediate seller's tender and revocation of that acceptance necessarily implies an action against the same seller. The rationale also is based on the policy determination that requiring a remote manufacturer that probably sold the goods at wholesale to refund the retail price paid by the ultimate buyer would be unfair.

A few courts have shown a willingness to extend the traditional bounds by allowing revocation against a remote manufacturer. Most of the cases involve the breach of an express warranty extended by the manufacturer,[249] and another factor that has influenced some courts has been the insolvency of the immediate seller. *Durfee v. Rod Baxter Imports, Inc.*[250] involved both factors — a repair-or-replace promise from the manufacturer that failed its essential purpose and the insolvency of the dealer — and the Minnesota Supreme Court permitted the buyer to revoke his acceptance against the manufacturer.[251]

[F]   Irrevocable Promises in Finance Leases [§ 2A-407]

The right to revoke an acceptance is severely constrained in the finance-lease context. The finance lessor acts merely as a financing conduit to facilitate the lessee's acquisition of the goods from the supplier. The warranties of the manufacturer or supplier extend to the finance lessee, so in the event of a problem with the goods, the finance lessee's remedy is to pursue the manufacturer or the supplier. The finance lessee generally does not have an option to revoke acceptance or even to set off its damages against rental payments due under the lease. Section 2A-407(1) provides that in a finance lease that is not also a consumer lease "the lessee's promises under the lease contract

---

[247] *See* § 5.06 *supra.*

[248] *See, e.g.,* Mydlach v. DaimlerChrysler Corp., 226 Ill. 2d 307, 314 Ill. Dec. 760, 875 N.E.2d 1047, 64 UCC Rep. Serv. 2d 44 (2007); Zanger v. Gulf Stream Coach, Inc., 60 UCC Rep. Serv. 2d 490 (E.D. Mich. 2005).

[249] *See, e.g.,* Gochey v. Bombardier, Inc., 153 Vt. 607, 572 A.2d 921, 11 UCC Rep. Serv. 870 (1990).

[250] 262 N.W.2d 349, 22 UCC Rep. Serv. 945 (Minn. 1977).

[251] A later decision by the Minnesota Court of Appeals indicated that *Durfee* should be limited to its facts and denied a right to revoke acceptance against a remote manufacturer because the dealer was not insolvent. Smith v. The Mobility Group, Inc., 66 UCC Rep. Serv. 2d 6 (Minn. Ct. App. 2008).

become irrevocable and independent upon the lessee's acceptance of the goods."[252]

Section 2A-407(1) must be read *in pari materia* with Section 2A-517(1)(b), which grants a right of revocation in a finance lease if acceptance was induced by assurances of the finance lessor.[253] The finance lessee's reliance on assurances from the finance lessor can reduce the lessee's vigilance in inspecting the goods and is thus the basis for granting the finance lessee the right to revoke. Revocation is precluded for finance lessees in the two other circumstances in which revocation would be available to a buyer or ordinary lessee:[254] The finance lessee cannot look to the finance lessor for cure, so it cannot revoke an acceptance that was induced on the assumption that a nonconformity would be cured; and since a finance lessor does not participate in selecting the goods, a finance lessee may not revoke due to an unknown nonconformity that could not have been discovered by a reasonable pre-acceptance inspection.

§ 7.06 WHAT CONSTITUTES BREACH

[A] Article 2 [§ 2-711, § 2-703]

Article 2 does not purport to provide a comprehensive list of the events that might constitute a breach by either a seller or a buyer. Section 2-711 is an "index" provision that contains a partial list of an aggrieved buyer's remedies, and in accomplishing this task it states four circumstances in which a seller's breach will justify cancellation and provide the buyer with access to the cover and market remedies of Sections 2-712 and 2-713. The four articulated breaches are a seller's failure to make delivery, a seller's repudiation, a buyer's rightful rejection, and a buyer's justifiable revocation of acceptance.[255]

Not only does Section 2-711 not list all of the circumstances that might constitute a breach that entitles the buyer to monetary damages, it does not even list all the circumstances that might justify cancellation. A seller might breach by failing to install the goods as promised, by failing to provide technical support as promised, by failing to fulfill its obligations under a limited remedy clause, or by failing to perform any other contractual obligation. While

---

[252] The provision is a statutory enactment having the effect of a "hell or high water" clause common in finance leases. *See, e.g.,* Stewart v. United States Leasing Corp., 702 S.W.2d 288 (Tex. Ct. App. 1985) (lessee that signed acceptance certificate liable to lessor despite nondelivery of equipment from supplier). The colorful name of the clause indicates the lessee's responsibility to continue making rental payments after acceptance no matter what happens.

[253] UCC § 2A-517(1)(b).

[254] *See* § 7.05[A][1] *supra.*

[255] Section 2-711(2) provides in addition that two of the articulated events — failure to deliver and repudiation — provide a basis for recovering the goods from the seller under Section 2-502 (seller's insolvency) or for obtaining a decree of specific performance or replevying the goods under Section 2-716.

monetary damages are available for any of these breaches, presumably cancellation requires, as at common law, that the breach be material.[256]

Section 2-703 is an index provision that contains a partial list of an aggrieved seller's remedies, and it parallels Section 2-711 in articulating four circumstances in which a buyer's breach will justify cancellation and provide the seller with access to the cover, market, and lost-profit remedies of Sections 2-706 and 2-708, as well as certain other statutory remedies. The four articulated breaches are a buyer's wrongful rejection, a buyer's wrongful revocation of acceptance, a buyer's failure to make a payment due on or before delivery, and a buyer's repudiation. As with the buyer's index provision, the section does not attempt to list all the circumstances that might constitute breach by the buyer.

[B]   Article 2A [§ 2A-501, § 2A-508, § 2A-523]

Part 5 of Article 2A, which deals with default generally, is divided into three subparts. Subpart A, which states fundamental principles applicable to both lessors and lessees, is patterned to an extent on the approach adopted by Article 9, which deals with default in the context of secured transactions.[257] Following a default by the lessor or the lessee, the aggrieved party has the rights and remedies provided in Article 2A and in the lease agreement.[258] Whereas Article 9's rights and remedies predominantly favor secured parties whose debtors are in default, Article 2A is more evenhanded and provides an extensive array of remedies for both lessors and lessees. The difference in approach is justified by the fact that the obligations under a lease agreement tend to be more bilateral in nature than the obligations under a security agreement.[259]

Also consistent with the approach of Article 9, Section 2A-501(3) establishes that on default by the lessor or the lessee "the party seeking enforcement may reduce the party's claim to judgment, or otherwise enforce the lease contract by self-help or any available judicial procedure or nonjudicial procedure, including administrative proceeding, arbitration, or the like." This provision is an expanded version of Section 9-601(a), which reflects the procedures available to a foreclosing secured party. Consequently, some of the options, particularly self-help, have the greatest relevance when the lessee is in default.

In determining what constitutes default, Article 2A resembles Article 9 in some respects but differs substantially in others. Neither article specifically defines default. Article 9 does not address the matter at all, leaving it to the parties to determine in their security agreement what events will constitute default.[260] Article 2A goes further, providing in section 2A-501 that "[w]hether

---

[256] The right to reject for "any" nonconformity and the right to revoke acceptance if a nonconformity substantially impairs the value of the goods to the buyer, as opposed to substantial impairment measured objectively, are exceptions to the general requirement of contract law that cancellation be predicated on a material breach.

[257] See UCC § 9-601(a) (after default secured party has rights and remedies provided by Article 9 and by agreement of the parties).

[258] UCC § 2A-501(2).

[259] UCC § 2A-101, cmt.

[260] See W. Lawrence, W. Henning, & R. Freyermuth, Understanding Secured Transactions Ch.

the lessor or the lessee is in default under a lease contract is determined by the lease agreement and this Article."[261] Certain events of default are established by index provisions similar to those in Article 2. Like Sections 2-711 and 2-703, Sections 2A-508 and 2A-523 are index provisions that identify statutory remedies available to aggrieved lessees and lessors and identify the types of breaches that will justify application of the listed remedies.[262]

§ 7.07 PROSPECTIVE IMPAIRMENT OF EXPECTATIONS

In addition to the basic obligations imposed on buyers and sellers to perform their respective duties when they become due, Article 2 aligns with the common law in recognizing an obligation that arises immediately upon contract formation: "A contract for sale imposes an obligation on each party that the other's expectation of receiving due performance will not be impaired."[263] The provision requires that neither party prospectively impair the reasonable expectations of the other party. Articles 2 and 2A each include provisions on anticipatory repudiation and the right to demand adequate assurances of performance to deal with problems associated with prospective impairment. Another relevant provision determines when an aggrieved party may cancel the executory portion of an installment contract.

[A] Anticipatory Repudiation [§ 2-610; § 2A-402]

The Code provisions on anticipatory repudiation closely parallel common law doctrine, which can be traced back to the famous case of *Hochster v. De La Tour*.[264] The court in that case permitted an employee to sue his employer for breach of contract even though the time for the employee to start work had not yet arrived. The doctrine of anticipatory repudiation thus provides an aggrieved party with immediate remedies even though the other party's performance obligation is not yet due.

---

17 (4th ed. 2007). The courts have generally held that, in the absence of a clause in the security agreement defining events of default, only nonpayment by the debtor will constitute a default; *see, e.g.*, Cofield v. Randolph Cty. Comm'n, 90 F.3d 468, 30 UCC Rep. Serv. 2d 374 (11th Cir. 1996).

[261] UCC § 2A-501(1). Common contractual events of default by a lessee include failure to fulfill a requirement to insure the goods or to provide regular maintenance service. Common contractual events of default by a lessor include failure to maintain or repair the goods.

[262] Section 2A-508(a) on the lessee's remedies refers to a lessor's failure to deliver the goods in conformity with the lease contract, repudiation by the lessor, and rightful rejection or justifiable revocation of acceptance by the lessee. Section 2A-523(a) on the lessor's remedies refers to wrongful rejection or revocation of acceptance by the lessee, failure by the lessee to make a payment when due, and repudiation by the lessee.

[263] UCC § 2-609(1). Section 2A-401(1) is comparable.

[264] 2 El. & B. 678, 118 Eng. Rep. 922 (Q.B. 1853).

[1]   What Constitutes a Repudiation

The Code does not define what constitutes a repudiation but follows an approach consistent with the common law. The Comments state that "anticipatory repudiation centers upon an overt communication or an action which renders performance impossible or demonstrates a clear determination not to continue with performance."[265] A statement by a party that it cannot or will not perform clearly qualifies[266], as does an action that precludes its ability to perform, such as selling to a third party goods that are the subject matter of a contract.[267] With respect to such actions, the Comments advise that "[i]t is not necessary for repudiation that performance be made literally and utterly impossible;"[268] rather "repudiation can result from action which reasonably indicates a rejection of the continuing obligation."[269] Thus, the fact that the seller in the prior example could theoretically repurchase the goods from the third party and perform its contractual obligations will not prevent its conduct from constituting a repudiation. All that is required is that the statement or action clearly and definitely indicate that the person providing it does not intend to perform.[270]

In order to invoke the doctrine of anticipatory repudiation, a repudiation must "substantially impair the value of the contract to the other."[271] Consistent with its usage in Section 2-612 on installment contracts,[272] the concept of substantial impairment correlates with the material breach standard of the common law.[273] The Comments specify that the "most useful test of substantial value is to determine whether material inconvenience or injustice will result if the aggrieved party is forced to wait and receive an ultimate tender minus the part or aspect repudiated."[274]

---

[265] UCC § 2-610, cmt. 1.

[266] Barclays Am. Business Credit Inc., v. E & E Enters., Inc., 697 S.W.2d 694, 42 UCC Rep. Serv. 706 (Tex. Ct. App. 1985) (statement by seller/assignor to buyer/account debtor that the plant was closing and would not deliver orders constituted a repudiation).

[267] *See* Red River Commodities, Inc. v. Eidsness, 459 N.W.2d 811, 13 UCC Rep. Serv. 2d 1084 (N.D. 1990) (sale of harvested sunflowers to a third party was repudiation).

[268] UCC § 2-610, cmt. 2.

[269] *Id.*

[270] *See, e.g.*, Lantec, Inc. v. Novell, Inc., 306 F.3d 1003, 49 UCC Rep. Serv. 2d 147 (10th Cir. 2002) (voice-mail message that two executives of the manufacturer wanted to terminate the contractual relationship with the plaintiffs not definite enough to constitute a repudiation); Gatoil (USA), Inc. v. Washington Metro. Area Transit Auth., 801 F.2d 451, 2 UCC Rep. Serv. 2d 151 (D.C. Cir. 1986) (communications to buyer about difficulties obtaining a supplier did not constitute repudiation by seller).

[271] UCC § 2-610.

[272] *See* § 7.07[A][4] *infra.*

[273] UCC § 2-10, cmt. 3. *See, e.g.*, Neptune Research & Dev., Inc. v. Teknics Indus. Sys., Inc., 235 N.J. Sup. 522, 563 A.2d 465, 10 UCC Rep. Serv. 2d 107 (1989) (the court applied the criteria of Section 214 of the Restatement (Second) of Contracts to determine if the breach was material).

[274] UCC § 2-610, cmt. 3.

[2]   Options of the Aggrieved Party

The aggrieved party has several options following an anticipatory repudiation. One option is simply to await performance by the other party.[275] It can wait silently, or it can urge that the repudiation be retracted. It can wait as long as it wishes — an aggrieved party is not required to resort to a remedy — but if it waits more than a commercially reasonable time the mitigation-of-damages principle may limit its recovery. For example, in *Oloffson v. Coomer*[276] a farmer agreed to grow 40,000 bushels of corn and deliver it to a grain merchant in two equal installments in October and November. The spring was too wet for planting and the farmer repudiated the contract in early June. Instead of entering into a cover transaction right away,[277] the merchant kept insisting that the farmer deliver. The court determined that since the farmer's statement was unequivocal and since there was a readily accessible market for corn, a commercially reasonable time to await a retraction expired on the same day as the repudiation. The merchant's failure to cover on that day constituted a failure to mitigate and limited its damages to the difference between the market price on that day and the contract price, or about 3 cents a bushel.[278]

Instead of waiting for performance, an aggrieved party may resort to any remedy for breach, as provided in Section 2-711 (aggrieved buyer) and Section 2-703 (aggrieved seller).[279] Both sections recognize repudiation as a breach that justifies cancellation of the contract and the recovery of damages or, in an appropriate case in which the aggrieved party is a buyer, specific performance. The aggrieved party can resort to a remedy at any time, even if it has notified the repudiating party that it would await performance and has urged a retraction of the repudiation. The only limitation on the right to resort to a remedy is the duty of good faith, which the Comments explain in this context as follows: "[T]he aggrieved party is left free to proceed at any time . . . unless he has taken some positive action which in good faith requires notification to the other party before the remedy is pursued."[280]

An aggrieved party that chooses not to cancel the contract may suspend its own performance while it awaits performance or retraction by the repudiating party.[281] Thus, in *Unique Systems, Inc. v. Zotos International, Inc.*,[282] after the

---

[275] UCC § 2-610(a).

[276] 11 Ill. App. 3d 918, 296 N.E.2d 871, 12 UCC Rep. Serv. 1082 (1973).

[277] "Cover" is a transaction in which an aggrieved buyer purchases substitute goods. Under UCC § 2-712(2), a covering buyer's direct damages are the difference between the cost of cover and the contract price. The cover remedy is discussed in § 8.02[B] *infra*.

[278] Section 2-713 determines an aggrieved buyer's market-based damages. *See* § 8.02[C] *infra*. The merchant in *Olaffson* eventually covered at an average price of roughly 30 cents per bushel over the contract price.

[279] UCC § 2-610(b).

[280] UCC § 2-610, cmt. 4.

[281] UCC § 2-610(c). *See, e.g.*, Created Gemstones, Inc. v. Union Carbide Corp., 417 N.Y.S.2d 905, 391 N.E.2d 987, 26 UCC Rep. Serv. 712 (1979) (repudiation by seller entitled buyer to suspend payments on gems previously delivered).

[282] 622 F.2d 373, 28 UCC Rep. Serv. 1340 (8th Cir. 1980).

buyer repudiated by refusing to proceed until market tests not required in the contract were conducted and produced satisfactory results, the seller was entitled to suspend its efforts to develop and manufacture hair-spray systems for the buyer.

A person that has reasonable grounds for insecurity may demand adequate assurances of performance under Section 2-609. This device is not really needed after an actual repudiation, but is sometimes used in this context, especially if the aggrieved party is not entirely certain that a court will conclude that the other party's language or conduct meets the stringent standards for a repudiation. The section is described in detail below.[283]

[3]   Retraction [§ 2-611; § 2A-403]

A repudiating party sometimes can retract the repudiation and thereby reinstate the contract. The retraction must occur before the next performance is due and before the aggrieved party has "canceled or materially changed his position or otherwise indicated that he considers the repudiation final."[284] The occurrence of any of these events prior to retraction terminates the right to retract.[285] Courts have found that aggrieved parties have materially changed their position by *inter alia* purchasing the goods from another source[286] or by ceasing to advertise the seller's products.[287] Absent cancellation or material change of position, it makes sense to allow a retraction since the interests of the aggrieved party will not have been prejudiced; in fact, the aggrieved party may have been waiting to see whether a retraction would be forthcoming. The Code protects the aggrieved party's interests by reinstating the contract "with due excuse and allowance to the aggrieved party for any delay occasioned by the repudiation."[288]

A repudiating party can retract "by any method which clearly indicates to the aggrieved party that the repudiating party intends to perform."[289] It can manifest this intention through words or conduct.[290] A retraction, however, cannot include conditions to which the repudiating party is not entitled.[291] Upon retraction, the aggrieved party may make justifiable demands for adequate

---

[283]   *See* § 7.07[B] *infra*.

[284]   UCC § 2-611(1). Section 2A-403 is comparable.

[285]   Neptune Research & Dev., Inc. v. Tecknics Indus. Sys., Inc., 235 N.J. Super. 522, 563 A.2d 465, 10 UCC Rep. Serv. 2d 107 (1989) (attempted retraction later the same day as repudiation was too late because buyer canceled the contract in the interim).

[286]   Bonebrake v. Cox, 499 F.2d 951, 14 UCC Rep. Serv. 1318 (8th Cir. 1974) (bowling alley equipment).

[287]   Record Club of Am., Inc. v. United Artists Records, Inc., 643 F. Supp. 925, 2 UCC Rep. Serv. 2d 1310 (S.D. N.Y. 1986).

[288]   UCC § 2-611(3).

[289]   UCC § 2-611(2).

[290]   Gibbs, Nathaniel (Can.) Ltd. v. International Multifoods Corp., 804 F.2d 450, 2 UCC Rep. Serv. 2d 1312 (8th Cir. 1986) (agreement by buyer to accept subsequent delivery); Fast v. Southern Offshore Yachts, 587 F. Supp. 1354, 38 UCC Rep. Serv. 1569 (D. Conn. 1984) (buyer's execution of proposed escrow agreement for balance due on sale served as retraction).

[291]   Pittsburgh-Des Moines Steel Co. v. Brookhaven Manor Water Co., 532 F.2d 572, 18 UCC Rep.

assurances of performance under Section 2-609.

[4]   Installment Contracts [§ 2-612(3); § 2A-510(2)]

The Code uses the substantial-impairment test to determine whether an aggrieved party in an installment contract can treat a nonconformity or default in delivery of one or more individual installments as a default with respect to the entire contract. Section 2-612(3) provides that "[w]henever non-conformity or default with respect to one or more installments substantially impairs the value of the whole contract there is a breach of the whole." With substantial impairment of the value of the whole contract, the aggrieved party can treat the defaults with respect to the individual installments as if it were an anticipatory repudiation of the whole contract.[292]

The Comments indicate that the issue is the actual effect of the defaults, not the extent to which they are a reliable predictor of future problems. The Comments make the point as follows:

> Whether the non-conformity in any given installment justifies cancellation as to the future depends, not on whether such non-conformity indicates an intent or likelihood that the future deliveries will also be defective, but whether the non-conformity substantially impairs the value of the whole contract.[293]

Application of the substantial-impairment standard is illustrated by *Holiday Manufacturing Corp. v. BASF Systems, Inc.*,[294] a case involving a contract for the manufacture of six million cassettes to be delivered at the rate of 500,000 per month. The initial deliveries contained substantial defects but the court found that the defects did not substantially impair the value of the whole contract. It based its conclusion on the buyer's ability to cure the defects and its lack of protest about the delays required in order to effectuate the cures. By contrast, the court in *SJ Groves & Sons Co. v. Warner Co.*[295] found that substantial impairment resulted from the seller's failure to deliver adequate supplies of concrete at the scheduled times because the failures caused delays in construction and heavy overtime expenses.[296]

Serv. 931 (7th Cir. 1976) (seller indicated it would begin construction of a large water tank on receipt of personal guarantee of payment by buyer's president).

[292] A similar rule applies to installment lease contracts. UCC § 2A-510(2).

[293] UCC § 2-610. cmt. 6. *Compare* KCA Electronics, Inc. v. Legacy Electronics, Inc., 2007 Cal. App. Unpub. LEXIS 6107 (July 26, 2007) (a 6% failure rate on a computer component substantially impaired the value of the whole contract because the incorporation of that many defective components would tarnish the reputation of the buyer's new product and because the inspection process to detect the defective components was costly and tied up the production line), *with* Precision Master, Inc. v. Mold Masters Co., 63 UCC Rep. Serv. 2d 400 (Mich. Ct. App. 2007) (because the amount of the unpaid invoice was such a small portion of the total value of the contract, it provided an insufficient basis to cancel the contract with respect to the specific purchase order, let alone the entire contract).

[294] 380 F. Supp. 1096, 15 UCC Rep. Serv. 820 (D.C. Neb. 1974).

[295] 576 F.2d 524, 24 UCC Rep. Serv. 1 (3d Cir. 1978).

[296] *See also* Graulich Caterer Inc. v. Hans Holterbosch, Inc., 101 N.J. Super. 61, 243 A.2d 253, 5 UCC Rep. Serv. 440 (1968) (substantial impairment when seller could not deliver quality food

Several cases have involved a seller's refusal to deliver further installments because of the buyer's failure to make timely payment for earlier installments. The Comments provide the following insight: "If only the seller's security in regard to future installments is impaired, he has the right to demand adequate assurances of proper performance but has not an immediate right to cancel the entire contract."[297] As with cases of seller breach, the standard for cancellation is whether there has been substantial impairment of the value of the whole contract, and the Comments indicate that the standard cannot be met unless the aggrieved seller demands adequate assurances of performance.[298] If such assurances are not forthcoming within a commercially reasonable time, the buyer's failure to pay ripens into an anticipatory repudiation.[299] Under this approach, withholding further shipments without first demanding assurances constitutes a breach by the seller.[300]

Notwithstanding the Comments, a seller sometimes may cancel the whole contract without first demanding assurances. In *Cherwell-Ralli, Inc. v. Rytman Grain Co.*,[301] the buyer, substantially behind on its payments and becoming concerned about the effect this would have on future deliveries, sought assurances from the seller. The seller indicated that it would continue making delivery if the buyer substantially reduced the amount of the delinquency. The buyer sent a check but then changed its mind and stopped payment when it became concerned that the amount of the check would not suffice. The seller then cancelled and the court upheld its action. As the Comments note, breaches as to installments have a cumulative effect,[302] and at some point the threshold of substantial impairment is reached.

[B]   Demand For Assurances of Performance [§ 2-609; § 2A-401]

[1]   The Right

If a party to a sales contract becomes concerned that the other party will not perform even though there has not been a repudiation, the concerned party may demand assurances of performance,[303] in which case the failure of the other party to provide an adequate response causes the concern to ripen into a

---

comparable to samples used to form the contract and buyer needed the food daily for its World's Fair pavilion).

[297] UCC § 2-610, cmt. 6.

[298] *See, e.g.,* Cassidy Podel Lynch, Inc. v. Snyder General Corp., 944 F.2d 1131, 15 UCC Rep. Serv. 2d 1225 (3d Cir. 1991) (seller not entitled to cancel because it did not demand adequate assurances of performance).

[299] *See* § 7.07[C] *infra.*

[300] *See, e.g.,* Gulf Chem. & Metallurgical Corp. v. Sylvan Chem. Corp., 122 N.J. Super. 499, 300 A.2d 878, 12 UCC Rep. Serv. 117 (1973).

[301] 433 A.2d 984, 29 UCC Rep. Serv. 513 (Conn. 1980).

[302] UCC § 2-612, cmt. 6.

[303] UCC § 2-609. Section 2A-401 is comparable.

repudiation.[304] Under the common law, the concerned party would be in a dilemma because it could not justifiably cancel the contract.[305] Section 2-609 helps alleviate the dilemma.

Section 2-609(1) provides for the demand as follows:

> When reasonable grounds for insecurity arise with respect to the performance of either party the other may in writing demand adequate assurance of due performance and until he receives such assurance may if commercially reasonable suspend any performance for which he has not already received the agreed return.

Because of the significant consequences of failing to respond to a demand and because of the signaling role that formalities can play, the demand must be in writing.[306] The Comments also indicate that a demand is not proper without a significant degree of impairment: "If either the willingness or the ability of a party to perform declines materially between the time of contracting and the time for performance, the other party is threatened with the loss of a substantial part of what he has bargained for."[307] A person that suspends its own performance after sending a demand not justified by the circumstances runs the risk that its conduct will constitute a repudiation or at least give the other party reasonable grounds for insecurity.

Decided cases provide a contextual basis for understanding the types of concerns that will justify a demand. Courts found that reasonable grounds for insecurity existed in the following instances: A seller's failure to provide roof trusses on a regular basis as required on a construction project,[308] the delivery of a high percentage of defective goods in a prior installment,[309] a seller's indication of its intention to alter the terms of the contract unilaterally,[310] a buyer known to be in financial difficulties,[311] and a buyer's breach on another

---

[304] *See* UCC § 2-609(4).

[305] *See* J. Calamari & J. Perillo, The Law of Contracts 12-2 (3d ed. 1987); Robertson, *The Right to Demand Adequate Assurance of Due Performance under UCC Section 2-609 and Restatement (Second) of Contracts Section 251*, 38 Drake L. Rev. 305 (1989).

[306] *See, e.g.*, Continental Grain Co. v. McFarland, 628 F.2d 1348, 29 UCC Rep. Serv. 512 (4th Cir. 1980). *But see* AMF, Inc. v. McDonald's Corp., 536 F.2d 1167, 19 UCC Rep. Serv. 801 (7th Cir. 1976) (UCC § 2-609 triggered even though there was not a written demand, and apparently not even an oral demand).

[307] UCC § 2-609, cmt. 1. Section 2-609(2) provides that if both parties are merchants the reasonableness of the grounds for insecurity are to be determined according to commercial standards.

[308] Universal Builders Corp. v. United Methodist Convalescent Homes of Conn., 7 Conn. App. 318, 508 A.2d 819, 1 UCC Rep. Serv. 2d 763 (1986).

[309] T&S Brass & Bronze Works, Inc. v. Pic-Air, Inc., 790 F.2d 1098, 1 UCC Rep. Serv. 2d 433 (4th Cir. 1986).

[310] Copylease Corp. of Am. v. Memorex Corp., 403 F. Supp. 625, 18 UCC Rep. Serv. 317 (S.D.N.Y. 1975).

[311] Lubrication & Maintenance, Inc. v. Union Resources Co., 522 F. Supp. 1078, 32 UCC Rep. Serv. 1117 (S.D.N.Y. 1981).

grain contract with the seller.[312] By contrast, reasonable grounds for insecurity were not present in the following instances: A merchant's delay in forwarding papers in a sale of heifers,[313] a buyer's uncertainty about performance by its principal supplier when there were several other suppliers that could deliver,[314] and a low balance in the bank account of a buyer with substantial assets.[315]

The Code does not provide guidance on the specific wording of a demand, but the cases generally require that it be specific enough to communicate to the other party that its failure to provide adequate assurances will be treated as a repudiation.[316] Inadequate demands have included a request for information,[317] an indication that a buyer wished to meet with the seller,[318] and a request for acceleration of payment for the first shipment of goods.[319]

Some courts have restricted the scope of a proper demand unduly by not permitting a concerned party to insist on more than the party is entitled to under the terms of the contract.[320] Because the concerned party necessarily learns of the grounds for insecurity after the contract has been formed, the concerns were not within its contemplation at the time of formation. Sometimes the only viable means of removing the insecurity is through measures that exceed the contract's requirements. For example, the court in *Brisbin v. Superior Valve Company*[321] rejected the buyer's argument that the magistrate judge erred in finding that the seller's demand for an immediate partial payment was reasonable, arguing that under the terms of the contract the seller was not yet entitled to the payment. Dilatory behavior and changing positions on product testing by the buyer had caused the seller to worry that the buyer would not give all the necessary approvals, which would leave the seller unable to recoup its startup costs.

---

[312] National Farmers Org. v. Bartlett & Co., 560 F.2d 1350, 22 UCC Rep. Serv. 658 (8th Cir. 1977).

[313] Cole v. Melvin, 441 F. Supp. 193, 22 UCC Rep. Serv. 1154 (D.S.D. 1977).

[314] In re Coast Trading Co., Inc, 26 B.R. 737, 35 UCC Rep. Serv. 1180 (D. Or. 1982).

[315] Pittsburgh-Des Moines Steel Co. v. Brookhaven Manor Water Co., 532 F.2d 572, 18 UCC Rep. Serv. 931 (7th Cir. 1976).

[316] *But see* AMF, Inc. v. McDonald's Corp., 536 F.2d 1167, 19 UCC Rep. Serv. 801 (7th Cir. 1976) (Section 2-609 triggered even though nothing in the communications of the parties indicated that the insecure party was about to take action that could lead to cancellation).

[317] SPS Indus., Inc. v. Atlantic Steel Co., 186 Ga. App. 94, 366 S.E.2d 410, 6 UCC Rep. Serv. 2d 122 (1988) (letter requesting information as to why shipment was late).

[318] Penberthy Electromelt Int'l, Inc. v. U.S. Gypsum Co., 38 Wash. App. 514, 686 P.2d 1138, 39 UCC Rep. Serv. 891 (1984).

[319] National Ropes, Inc., v. National Diving Serv., Inc., 513 F.2d 53, 16 UCC Rep. Serv. 1376 (5th Cir. 1975).

[320] Scott v. Crown, 765 P.2d 1043, 7 UCC Rep. Serv. 2d 464 (Colo. Ct. App. 1988).

[321] 398 F.3d 279, 56 UCC Rep. Serv. 2d 152 (3d Cir. 2005).

[2] Effect of the Demand

After receiving a justified demand, a party has a reasonable time not exceeding thirty days in which to provide adequate assurances of due performance.[322] If provided, the assurances eliminate the insecurity and the concerned party must continue with its performance.[323] Failure to provide adequate assurances escalates a concern that initially created only reasonable grounds for insecurity into a full-fledged repudiation.[324]

Sometimes a party demanding assurances insists that they take a particular form; however, all the statute requires is that the assurances be "adequate in the circumstances of the particular case."[325] In other words, they must be sufficient to alleviate the insecurity of a reasonable person in the position of the person making the demand.[326] The Comments indicate that sometimes nothing more is necessary than a verbal commitment by a reputable person indicating that the matter is receiving appropriate attention.[327] Often, however, verbal assurances will not suffice. Even absent a statutory right to insist that assurances take a particular form, courts have sustained demands for an escrow deposit,[328] correction of quantity and quality control problems,[329] confirmation of intent to receive shipments,[330] and a contractual guarantee coupled with a letter of credit.[331]

---

[322] UCC § 2-609(4).

[323] American Bronze Corp v. Streamway Prods., 8 Ohio App. 3d 223, 456 N.E.2d 1295, 37 UCC Rep. Serv. 687 (1982) (buyer responded to demand concerning payment by tendering a check for all outstanding accounts and agreeing to the demand to make prompt payment of new accounts); Precision Master, Inc. v. Mold Masters Co., 63 UCC Rep. Serv. 2d 400 (Mich. Ct. App. 2007) (even though seller demanded payments C.O.D. rather than on credit, the court determined that the buyer's offer to secure a letter of credit with a bank to assure payments within the original terms of the contract provided an adequate assurance).

[324] UCC § 2-609(4); Rad Concepts, Inc. v. Wilks Precision Instr. Co., Inc., 167 Md. App. 132, 891 A.2d 1148 (2006) (failure to provide reasonable assurances led to repudiation).

[325] UCC § 2-609(4); see, e.g., U.S. v. Great Plains Gasification Assocs., 819 F.2d 831, 4 UCC Rep. Serv. 2d 1442 (8th Cir. 1987) (purchaser of natural gas not justified in seeking assurances of long-term sales under contract that allowed seller to terminate in good faith); GJP Enterprises, Inc. v. Performance Contracting, Inc., 2006 U.S. Dist. LEXIS 57351 (N.D. Ohio, Aug. 16, 2006) (seller's demand excessive because, rather than a demand for assurances that it would be paid, it demanded full payment in advance).

[326] UCC § 2-609(2) provides that if both parties are merchants the adequacy of the assurances is to be determined according to commercial standards.

[327] UCC § 2-609, Comment 4 provides that "where the buyer can make use of a defective delivery, a mere promise by a seller of good repute that he is giving the matter his attention and that the defect will not be repeated, is normally sufficient."

[328] Kunian v. Development Corp. of Am., 165 Conn. 300, 334 A.2d 427, 12 UCC Rep. Serv. 1125 (1973) (insecurity based on failure to make payments or abide by subsequent promises to pay).

[329] LNS Inv. Co., Inc. v. Phillips, 66 Co., 731 F. Supp. 1484, 12 UCC Rep. Serv. 2d 113 (D. Kan. 1990) (insecurity based on unacceptable quantity and quality of goods ordered).

[330] USX Corp. v. Union Pac. Resources Co., 753 S.W.2d 845, 7 UCC Rep. Serv. 2d 100 (Tex. Ct. App. 1988).

[331] Creusot-Lorie Int'l, Inc. v. Coppus Eng'g Corp., 585 F. Supp. 45, 39 UCC Rep. Serv. 186 (S.D.N.Y. 1983) (insecurity based on similar goods failing when provided to other buyers).

§ 7.08 EXCUSE

[A] Fundamental Versus Incidental

Even though a sales or lease contract imposes fixed obligations on the parties, the Code recognizes defenses based on unanticipated contingencies; that is, post-contracting events that make a required performance considerably more difficult or even impossible.[332] The defenses reflect the common-law defense of excuse based on impossibility of performance[333] and extend beyond the doctrine by embracing excuse based on commercial impracticability.[334]

The sales provisions on excuse cover casualty to identified goods, substituted performance, and failure of presupposed conditions. Section 2-613 provides for excuse if identified goods suffer casualty. Section 2-614 permits substituted performance if the agreed method of delivery becomes impracticable or the agreed method of payment fails because of governmental regulation. Section 2-615 excuses a seller's performance that becomes impracticable because of the occurrence of a contingency the nonoccurrence of which was a basic assumption on which the contract was made or because of good-faith compliance with a governmental regulation. Comparable provisions cover lease transactions.[335]

The following Comment suggests that Section 2-614 was placed between Sections 2-613 and 2-615 for a specific reason:

> This section appears between Section 2–613 on casualty to identified goods and the next section on excuse by failure of presupposed conditions, both of which deal with excuse and complete avoidance of the contract where the occurrence or non-occurrence of a contingency which was a basic assumption of the contract makes the expected performance impossible. The distinction between the present section and those sections lies in whether the failure or impossibility of performance arises in connection with an incidental matter or goes to the very heart of the agreement.[336]

Generally, the essential aspects of a sales agreement — in the language of the Comment, failures that go to the "very heart" of the agreement — are the seller's delivery of the goods and the buyer's payment. Incidental aspects deal with the methods by which the essential aspects are achieved. An event that makes performance of an essential duty impossible or commercially impracticable may result in a complete excuse of performance, whereas an event that impedes a party's ability to perform an incidental duty has a more limited effect: It excuses the party from using the required method but imposes on it an obligation to use a commercially reasonable substitute method.

---

[332] *See generally* Wladis, *Impracticability as Risk Allocation: The Effect of Changed Circumstances Upon Contract Obligations for the Sale of Goods*, 22 Ga. L. Rev. 503 (1988).

[333] *See* Taylor v. Caldwell, 122 Eng. Rep. 309 (K.B. 1863).

[334] The leading pre-Code case on commercial impracticability is *Mineral Park Land Co. v. Howard*, 172 Cal. 289, 156 P. 458 (1916). The doctrine has never gained much favor at common law.

[335] UCC §§ 2A-221, 2A-404, 2A-405.

[336] UCC § 2-614, cmt. 1.

[B]   Casualty to Identified Goods [§ 2-613; § 2A-221]

The common law excuses performance if the subject matter of the contract is destroyed without the fault of either party, and Section 2-613 reflects that approach.[337] Several requirements must be satisfied for the excuse defense to apply. First, the parties must have presupposed the continued existence of the goods,[338] and for that reason the goods must have been identified to the contract at the time it was formed. Thus, destruction of a soybean crop by weather did not excuse the farmer/seller in *Bunge Corp. v. Recker*[339] because the contract merely described the type and quantity of soybeans to be delivered without identifying the specific goods. Identification occurs with crops upon planting if they are to be harvested within the next twelve months or the next growing season, whichever is longer, and since the farmer had planted his crops when he entered into the contract, he would have been excused if the contract had required delivery of soybeans being grown by him. The fact that Section 2-613 is inapplicable does not mean that a person may not be excused, but the analysis shifts to the commercial-impracticability provision, Section 2-615.[340] Although the court in the *Bunge* case did not discuss the application of that section, the fact that the farmer could readily obtain soybeans elsewhere would have made a successful defense unlikely.

The second requirement for excuse under Section 2-613 is that the loss must occur without the fault of either party. Fault is a "wrongful act, omission or breach;"[341] it includes negligence as well as intentional conduct.[342] The third requirement is that the loss must occur before the risk of loss passes to the buyer.[343] Upon passage of the risk of loss, the buyer assumes the consequences of an event that destroys the goods.[344]

If all three requirements are met, the contract is avoided if the loss is total and the seller's only remaining obligation is to return any payments that have been made.[345] If the loss is partial, the buyer may inspect the goods and either

---

[337] UCC § 2-613. Section 2A-221 is comparable.

[338] UCC 2-613, cmt. 1; Emery v. Weed, 494 A.2d 438, 41 UCC Rep. Serv. 115 (Pa. Super. 1985) (existence of Corvettes similar to the one stolen was irrelevant since the one stolen had been identified in the contract).

[339] 519 F.2d 449, 17 UCC Rep. Serv. 400 (8th Cir. 1975); *see also* Valley Forge Flag Co., Inc. v. New York Dowel & Moulding Import Co., Inc., 395 N.Y.S.2d 138, 21 UCC Rep. Serv. 1320 (Civ. Ct. 1977) (Section 2-613 not applicable to shipboard loss of dowels during a heavy storm while in transit from Malaysia because the goods were not identified at time of contracting).

[340] Commercial impracticability is discussed in § 7.08[D] *infra*.

[341] UCC § 1-201(b)(17).

[342] UCC § 2-613, cmt. 1.

[343] Salines v. Flores, 26 UCC Rep. Serv. 1159 (Tex. Civ. App. 1979) (in sale of watermelons "by the patch" risk of loss passed to the buyer at time of contracting, so contract was not avoided by destruction of the watermelons in hailstorm). For the applicable provisions on risk of loss, see UCC §§ 2-509 and 2-510 and the discussion in § 6.02 *supra*.

[344] The buyer is liable for the purchase price even if the goods are destroyed. UCC § 2-709(1)(a).

[345] Conway v. Larsen Jewelers, Inc., 429 N.Y.S.2d 378, 29 UCC Rep. Serv. 842 (Civ. Ct. N.Y.C. 1980) (claimant not entitled to increased market value of necklace purchased on lay-away plan that was subsequently stolen from seller's store).

accept them or elect to treat the contract as avoided. If it accepts the goods, its only right against the seller is a reduction in the contract price to reflect the lessened quantity or quality of the goods.

[C]   Substituted Performance [§ 2-614; § 2A-404]

Only partial excuse is available under Section 2-614, which deals with substituted performance. The section excuses exact compliance with incidental aspects of the contract that have failed or become commercially impracticable.[346] The rationale behind the section is that delivery and payment normally can be performed in an alternate manner without seriously jeopardizing the reasonable expectations of either party.

With respect to delivery, the substituted-performance rule applies when "without fault of either party the agreed berthing, loading, or unloading facilities fail or an agreed type of carrier becomes unavailable or the agreed manner of delivery otherwise become commercially impracticable."[347] Under these circumstances, if a commercially reasonable substitute is available, it must be tendered and accepted. If a commercially reasonable substitute is not available, the seller may be excused under Section 2-615.[348]

The Code does not allocate the increased costs that may be associated with a substituted method of delivery. A court addressed this issue in *Jon-T Farms, Inc. v. Goodpasture, Inc.*,[349] and imposed the costs on the seller. When it became clear that shipment by rail would be delayed because of a rail-car shortage, the parties agreed that the seller would ship some of the purchased grain in trucks. The court based its decision on the fact that the contract placed some transportation costs on the seller — the cost of transporting the grain to the railhead for loading — and none on the buyer.

Section 2-614 also applies if a governmental regulation precludes use of an agreed method of payment. If the contract is still fully executory, the seller may withdraw if the buyer cannot provide a substantially equivalent method of payment. If the buyer has already taken delivery, it may pay in accordance with the terms of the regulation unless it is discriminatory, oppressive, or predatory.

[D]   Commercial Impracticability [§ 2-615; § 2A-405]

[1]   General

Section 2-615 provides, in part, as follows:

Delay in delivery or non-delivery in whole or in part by a seller who complies with paragraphs (b) and (c) is not a breach of his duty under a contract for sale if performance as agreed has been made impracticable by the occurrence of a contingency the non-occurrence of which was a

---

[346] UCC §§ 2-614, 2A-404.

[347] UCC § 2-614(1).

[348] UCC § 2-615; *see* § 7.08[D] *infra.*

[349] 554 S.W.2d 743, 21 UCC Rep. Serv. 1309 (Tex. Ct. App. 1977).

basic assumption on which the contract was made or by compliance in good faith with any applicable foreign or domestic governmental regulation or order whether or not it later proves to be invalid.[350]

Two elements must be established to invoke the defense: (1) a supervening event that affects an essential aspect of a contract (*i.e.*, the occurrence of a contingency the nonoccurrence of which was a basic assumption of the contracting parties) or a supervening governmental regulation, and (2) resulting commercial impracticability.

The defense under Section 2-615 is usually referred to as "commercial impracticability," although the Code text does not use the term. The caption of the section is "Excuse by Failure of Presupposed Conditions" and the text refers only to contingencies that make performance impracticable, not commercially impracticable. The Comments use the term, stating that "[t]his section excuses a seller from timely delivery of goods contracted for, where his performance has become *commercially impracticable* because of unforeseen supervening circumstances not within the contemplation of the parties at the time of contracting."[351] The Comments further indicate that commercial impracticability, rather than impossibility or frustration of purpose, is used "in order to call attention to the commercial character of the criterion chosen by this Article."[352]

Section 2-615 by its terms applies only to sellers and the Code text does not articulate the related doctrine of frustration of purpose, which would be raised by buyers. Nevertheless, the Comments indicate that the rationale of the section is equally applicable to buyers[353] and some courts have followed the Comments' invitation.[354]

[a]   Supervening Event

An important element in determining whether a supervening event[355] is a sufficient basis for excuse is the extent to which the event is foreseeable.[356] The more foreseeable the event, the less likely it is to be an appropriate basis for

---

[350] UCC § 2-615(a). Section 2A-405 is comparable.

[351] UCC § 2-615, cmt. 1 (emphasis supplied).

[352] UCC § 2-615, cmt. 3.

[353] UCC § 2-615, cmt. 9.

[354] *See, e.g.*, International Minerals & Chemical Corp. v. Llano, Inc., 770 F.2d 879, 41 UCC Rep. Serv. 347 (10th Cir. 1985) (buyer excused from long-term requirements contract for natural gas); Northern Indiana Public Service Co. v. Carbon County Coal Co., 799 F.2d 265, 1 UCC Rep. Serv. 2d 1505 (7th Cir. 1986) (recognizing the defense of frustration of purpose but declining to excuse the buyer).

[355] The term "supervening event" is used for the sake of simplicity. UCC § 2-615 (a) technically requires "the occurrence of a contingency the nonoccurrence of which was a basic assumption on which the contract was made." The event may constitute the manifestation of a condition that existed prior to the time of contract formation but of which the parties were unaware, a situation sometimes referred to as "existing impracticability." The event may also be the nonoccurrence of something that the parties expected to occur.

[356] *See* Farnsworth, *Disputes over Omissions in Contracts*, 68 Colum. L. Rev. 860 (1968); *see also* Mextel, Inc. v. Air-Shields, Inc., 56 UCC Rep. Serv. 2d 6 (E.D. Pa. 2005) (the inclusion of a termination provision dealing with eventuality of a failure to meet design specification clearly

excuse.[357] The Comments specifically state that excuse of a seller results "where his performance has become commercially impracticable because of unforeseen supervening circumstances not within the contemplation of the parties at the time of contracting."[358]

Courts consistently deny requests for excuse based on an event that was reasonably foreseeable when the parties entered the contract. For example, the contract in *Eastern Air Lines, Inc. v. Gulf Oil Corp.*[359] required Gulf to meet Eastern's needs for jet fuel in certain cities for a five-year period and included a price-escalation clause intended to make increases in Eastern's price per gallon directly proportional to increases in Gulf's costs per barrel of crude oil. The clause used the price of West Texas Sour oil as an indicator. OPEC imposed an embargo on oil produced by its member nations, leading to an energy crisis in the United States. Gulf claimed excuse when the price of the oil it used to make jet fuel soared in relation to the price of West Texas Sour, making the contract highly unprofitable. The court denied the defense because the events leading up to the embargo were reasonably foreseeable at the time of contract formation. The court pointed to prior use of oil as a political weapon by oil-producing nations, repeated interruptions in the crude oil trade, and volatility in the foreign oil market.[360]

Similarly, a milk supplier in *Maple Farms, Inc. v. City of Elmira*[361] sought to be excused from a milk supply contract with a school district. The supplier attributed the 23% increase in market price over the contract price for the milk to unexpected crop failures and the sale of grain to Russia. The court determined, however, that the price increases were foreseeable. The court noted the general inflation prevalent at the time and the fact that milk prices had risen significantly prior to the time of contract formation.

The impracticability defense succeeded in *Florida Power & Light v. Westinghouse Electric Corp.*[362] Westinghouse agreed to provide Florida Power

---

demonstrated foreseeability); Leanin' Tree, Inc. v. Thiele Tech., Inc., 48 UCC Rep. Serv. 2d 991 (10th Cir. 2002) (unpublished) (manufacturer of carton-packing machine not excused when contract did not reflect any basic assumptions concerning the design of the cartons that the machine would pack and in any event seller should have foreseen that machine would be incompatible with the cartons actually used by the buyer).

[357] At some level all events are foreseeable, so a standard based on foreseeability is inherently difficult to apply. One suggestion for an alternate approach is that the losses imposed by a supervening event should be borne by the party that can in the circumstances most efficiently bear the risk. R. Posner & A. Rosenfeld, *Impossibility and Related Doctrines in Contract Law: An Economic Analysis*, 6 J. Leg. Stud. 83 (1977). Another suggestion is that excuse should be granted if the event was so remote that the parties did not provide for it in their agreement and either could not or did not insure against it. S. Walt, *Expectations, Loss Distribution, and Commercial Impracticability*, 24 Ind. L.J. 65 (1990).

[358] UCC § 2-615, cmt. 1. Comment 4 also refers to unforeseen contingencies.

[359] 415 F. Supp. 429, 19 UCC Rep. Serv. 721 (S.D. Fla. 1975).

[360] For another decision holding that the consequences of the oil situation in the Middle East were foreseeable, see Publicker Indus. v. Union Carbide Corp., 17 UCC Rep. Serv. 989 (E.D. Pa. 1975).

[361] 76 Misc. 2d 1080, 352 N.Y.S.2d 784, 14 UCC Rep. Serv. 722 (Sup. Ct. 1974).

[362] 826 F.2d 239 (4th Cir. 1987); *see generally* Joskow, *Commercial Impossibility, the Uranium Market and the* Westinghouse *Case*, 6 J. Legal Stud. 119 (1977).

with uranium for its nuclear power plants for ten years at a fixed price and, under an option selected by Florida Power, it agreed to dispose of the spent fuel. The parties anticipated that the spent fuel would be sent to a reprocessing plant but government policy changed and the anticipated reprocessing plants were not built. The court relieved Westinghouse of its obligation to take the spent fuel, which effectively passed the cost of storage to Florida Power.

The courts have decided a number of cases involving crop failure.[363] The Comments suggest the following guidelines:

> The case of a farmer who has contracted to sell crops to be grown on designated land may be regarded as falling either within the section on casualty to identified goods or this section, and he may be excused, when there is a failure of the specific crop, either on the basis of the destruction of identified goods or because of the failure of a basic assumption of the contract.[364]

Following this approach, the court in *Dunavant Enterprises, Inc. v. Ford*[365] excused a cotton farmer because of flooding on the land specified by the contract as the source of the cotton to be delivered. If a contract does not specify the land on which the crop will be produced, as in *Wickliffe Farms, Inc. v. Owensboro Grain Co.*,[366] the courts generally have refused to allow relief. The underlying assumption is that the parties did not contract for a specific source of crops, so the seller's obligation must be met by acquiring the required quantity from another source at the market price, which may be much higher.[367] The same reasoning generally applies to suppliers that are not farmers.[368]

To serve as a basis for excuse, the supervening event must be beyond the seller's control. As applied to contracts requiring the seller to obtain the goods from a particular source, the Comments describe the requirement as follows: "There is no excuse under this section, however, unless the seller has employed all due measures to assure himself that his source will not fail."[369] Thus, in *Nissho-Iwai Co. v. Occidental Crude Sales, Inc.*[370] the seller was not excused when its failure to pay taxes and other fees to the government of Libya resulted in an embargo that left it unable to deliver oil. Similarly, the court in *Roth Steel*

---

[363] *See generally* Bugg, *Crop Destruction and Forward Grain Contracts: Why Don't Sections 2-613 and 2-615 of the UCC Provide More Relief?*, 12 Hamline L. Rev. 669 (1989).

[364] UCC § 2-615, cmt. 9.

[365] 294 So. 2d 788, 20 UCC Rep. Serv. 667 (Miss. 1974).

[366] 684 S.W.2d 17, 39 UCC Rep. Serv. 195 (Ky. Ct. App. 1984) (drought adversely affected corn crop).

[367] The courts have generally not excused performance merely because of an increase in cost. *See* § 7.08[D][1][c] *infra*.

[368] Bliss Produce Co. v. AE Albert & Sons, Inc., 35 Agri. Dec. 742, 20 UCC Rep. Serv. 917 (1976).

[369] UCC § 2-615, cmt. 5. The requirement is consistent with the influential opinion of Justice Cardozo in *Canadian Industrial Alcohol Co. v. Dunbar Molasses Co.*, 258 N.Y. 194, 179 N.E. 383 (Ct. App. 1932) (supplier of molasses to be obtained from specific refinery not excused because it failed to take steps to assure its source of supply).

[370] 729 F.2d 1530, 38 UCC Rep. Serv. 1237 (5th Cir. 1984).

Products v. Sharon Steel Corp.[371] did not excuse a seller that caused its own problems by accepting too many purchase orders for raw materials that it knew were in short supply.

[b]   Governmental Regulation

A supervening governmental regulation that precludes performance may provide a basis for excuse. For example, newly promulgated environmental regulations have had the effect of excusing performance by a party required to comply with them.[372] Enactment of the Federal Water Pollution Control Act Amendments of 1972 excused a contract obligation in *Kansas City, Missouri v. Kansas City, Kansas*[373] to accept a city's sewage because compliance with the new treatment requirements of the federal law would have imposed a substantial, unreasonable burden on the defendant. Whether a governmental regulation is an appropriate basis for excuse is subject to the foreseeability test applied to supervening events generally. For example, the court in *Sabine Corp. v. ONG Western, Inc.*[374] denied a buyer's request for excuse based on a regulation that caused the price of natural gas to rise because the regulation was foreseeable to a person in the industry.

[c]   Resulting Commercial Impracticability

To be excused, a seller that can establish an unforeseeable supervening event or governmental regulation also must establish that the event or regulation caused commercial impracticability. This element generally translates into either impossibility or the increased financial hardship that continued performance will impose. With respect to increased costs, one court stated the issue as follows: "Whether 'grave injustice' would result from failure to excuse performance is merely an inquiry used to assess whether the cost to the contracting party of performing the contract is so excessive and unreasonable as to warrant the conclusion that performance has become impracticable."[375] The Comments address the impact of increased cost as a basis for the defense.

> Increased cost alone does not excuse performance unless the rise in cost is due to some unforeseen contingency which alters the essential nature of the performance. Neither is a rise or a collapse in the market in itself a justification, for that is exactly the type of business risk which business contracts made at fixed prices are intended to cover. But a severe shortage of raw materials or of supplies due to a contingency such as war, embargo, local crop failure, unforeseen shutdown of major sources

[371] 705 F.2d 134, 35 UCC Rep. Serv. 1435 (6th Cir. 1983).

[372] International Minerals & Chem. Corp. v. Llano, Inc., 770 F.2d 879, 41 UCC Rep. Serv. 347 (10th Cir. 1985), *cert. denied*, 475 U.S. 1015 (1986). Since it was the buyer that was excused, the case is outside the literal language of UCC § 2-615 and is an example of what the common law calls frustration of purpose. See text accompanying notes 353 and 354 *supra*.

[373] 393 F. Supp. 1 (W.D. Mo. 1975).

[374] 725 F. Supp. 1157, 11 UCC Rep. Serv. 2d 83 (W.D. Okla. 1989).

[375] Sabine Corp. v. ONG Western, Inc., 725 F. Supp. 1157, 1176, 11 UCC Rep. Serv. 2d 83 (W.D. Okla. 1989).

of supply or the like, which either causes a marked increase in cost or altogether prevents the seller from securing supplies necessary to his performance, is within the contemplation of this section.[376]

The courts have consistently taken a strict view for excuse claimed on the basis of increased costs.[377] Terminology such as severe, extreme, excessive, or unreasonable is common in the opinions, and few sellers have been successful.[378] For example, in *Louisiana Power & Light Co. v. Allegheny Ludlum Industries, Inc.*[379] the seller sought excuse from a contract to supply condenser tubing for construction of a nuclear plant because shortages of critical raw materials and increased labor costs increased the seller's costs of performance by about 38%. The unsympathetic court noted that both the overall corporate structure of Allegheny and the division intended to supply the tubing would make profits that year. The court also noted that while a loss resulting from contract performance is not pleasant, it is a fact of commercial life and not a sufficient basis for invoking the doctrine of commercial impracticability.[380]

In addition to finding that increases in the price of crude oil related to the Arab oil embargo were foreseeable, the court in *Eastern Air Lines, Inc. v. Gulf Oil Corp.*[381] found that Gulf did not establish that the increased cost of crude oil needed to produce the jet fuel required by the contract resulted in the requisite hardship. Gulf did not present evidence that showed its real costs; rather, it submitted costs that had been inflated by internal profits added at various stages of the importation and refining process. The year the energy crisis began in this country had been Gulf's most profitable year to date, and the following year was even more profitable.

The most dramatic application of commercial impracticability came in *Aluminum Co. of America v. Essex Group, Inc.*[382] The parties entered into a long-term contract under which Alcoa converted raw material supplied by Essex into molten aluminum and returned it to Essex.[383] The contract included carefully negotiated price-escalator provisions but they proved to be inadequate

[376] UCC § 2-615, cmt. 4.

[377] Although many commentators believe that the drafters devised Section 2-615 to improve the availability of the law on excuse, the courts have not pursued such a course. *See* Hurst, *Freedom of Contract in an Unstable Economy: Judicial Reallocation of Contractual Risks under UCC Section 2-615*, 54 N.C. L. Rev. 545, 555 (1976).

[378] D.S. Simmons, Inc. v. Steel Group, LLC, 65 UCC Rep. Serv. 2d 320 (E.D. N.C. 2008) (defendant's allegations that the increase in its cost of steel were unprecedented held insufficient to excuse its obligation to deliver structural steel).

[379] 517 F. Supp. 1319, 32 UCC Rep. Serv. 847 (E.D. La. 1981).

[380] *See also* Iowa Elec. Light & Power Co. v. Atlas Corp., 467 F. Supp. 129, 23 UCC Rep. Serv. 1171 (N.D. Iowa 1978) (rather than focusing on a nearly sevenfold increase in market price of uranium, the court addressed seller's costs of production and found that a 50-80 percent increase was not sufficient for excuse).

[381] 415 F. Supp. 429, 19 UCC Rep. Serv. 721 (S.D. Fla. 1975).

[382] 499 F. Supp. 53, 29 UCC Rep. Serv. 1 (W.D. Pa. 1980). The foreseeability aspect of the case is discussed in § 7.08[D][1][a] *supra*.

[383] The case is not within the scope of Article 2 because it was a contract for services; Alcoa was simply processing and returning goods that Essex already owned.

in the face of massive increases related to an energy crisis and pollution-control requirements. Alcoa contended that it would lose $75 million in performing the remainder of the contract and sought relief. The court found that the price increase constituted commercial impracticability but, instead of excusing Alcoa, it reformed the contract by establishing a new price for its services.[384]

[2] Duties of the Seller

A seller claiming excuse under Section 2-615 must comply with certain procedural requirements. It must give the buyer timely notification of a delay or of the fact that the goods will not be delivered.[385] If only a portion of the seller's capacity to perform is affected, it must allocate production and deliveries under a plan that is fair and reasonable[386] and notify the buyer of its estimated quota under the plan.[387] The plan can include regular customers not then under contract and may provide for the seller's own requirements.[388]

Section 2-616 provides that upon receiving notification of a material or indefinite delay or of an allocation plan, a buyer has a choice.[389] As to any affected delivery, it may by written notification terminate the contract and thereby be excused from its executory obligations[390] or, in the case of a proposed allocation plan, it may by written notification modify the contract by agreeing to take the proposed quota rather than the contractually required quantity.[391] If it fails to notify the seller of its intentions within a reasonable time not exceeding thirty days, the contract lapses with respect to the affected deliveries.[392] The provisions of Section 2-616 may not be modified unless the modification imposes greater obligations on the seller.[393]

---

[384] For differing perspectives on the *Alcoa* decision, see Dawson, *Judicial Revision of Frustrated Contracts: The United States*, 64 B.U. L. Rev. 1 (1984) (sharply critical); Speidel, *Court-Imposed Price Adjustments under Long-Term Supply Contracts*, 76 Nw. U. L. Rev. 369 (1981) (approves court adjustments).

[385] UCC § 2-615(c).

[386] UCC § 2-615(b). *See generally* White, *Allocation of Scarce Resources under Section 2-615 of the UCC: A Comparison of Some Rival Models*, 12 U. Mich. J. L. Ref. 503 (1979); *see also* Cosden Oil & Chem. Co. v. Karl O. Helm Aktiengesellschaft, 736 F.2d 1064, 38 UCC Rep. Serv. 1645 (5th Cir. 1984) (failure of seller of polystyrene to include buyer made allocation plan unfair); Terry v. Atlantic Richfield Co., 72 Cal. App. 3d 962, 140 Cal. Rptr. 510, 22 UCC Rep. Serv. 669 (1977) (allocation plan based on percentage of prior purchases upheld because it was fairly drawn with respect to customers as a whole).

[387] UCC § 2-615(c).

[388] Roth Steel Products v. Sharon Steel Corp., 705 F.2d 134, UCC Rep. Serv. 134 (6th Cir. 1983) (allocation plan that included subsidiary of seller that had not been a previous customer of seller was not fair and reasonable).

[389] UCC § 2-616. Section 2A-406 is comparable, except that the modification option is not available in a finance lease that is not also a consumer lease.

[390] UCC § 2-616(1)(a). If the prospective deficiency substantially impairs the value of the whole with respect to an installment contract, the buyer may terminate as to the whole.

[391] UCC § 2-616(1)(b).

[392] UCC § 2-616(2).

[393] UCC § 2-616(3).

§ 7.09 AMENDED ARTICLE 2

[A] Acceptance, Rejection, and Revocation of Acceptance

[1] Effective But Wrongful Rejection

A buyer clearly can make an effective but wrongful rejection under original Section 2-602, but the caption to the section refers to "rightful" rejections and thus is confusing. The word "rightful" in the captions to Sections 2-603 and 2-604 causes similar confusion. Unlike most legislation, the section captions are deemed to be part of the Uniform Commercial Code.[394] The amendments remove the word "rightful" from the captions and clarify in the text, particularly in Section 2-603, that a buyer can effectively reject goods even though the rejection is wrongful.

In the case of a merchant buyer, Section 2-603 states that, subject to any security interest, the buyer "is under a duty after rejection of goods in the buyer's possession or control to follow any reasonable instructions received from the seller with respect to the goods and in the absence of such instructions to make reasonable efforts to sell them for the seller's account if they are perishable or threaten to decline in value speedily." Because the caption to the section no longer contains the word "rightful," this duty clearly applies to an effective rejection without regard to whether it was rightful or wrongful. On the other hand, the familiar rule that instructions from the seller regarding disposition of the goods are not reasonable if, on demand by a merchant buyer, indemnity for expenses is not forthcoming, has been amended to apply only to cases of rightful rejection. Also, subsection (2), which permits the buyer to obtain reimbursement for reasonable expenses from the proceeds of sale and also deals with the buyer's commission, applies only if the rejection was rightful. Finally, and again consistent with the rest of the changes in this area, the removal of "rightful" from the caption to Section 2-604 indicates that any rejecting buyer, whether merchant or nonmerchant and without regard to the rightfulness of the rejection, has the right in appropriate circumstances to sell the goods for salvage.

[2] Notice of Breach

The drafting committee considered original Section 2-607(3)(a), which bars the buyer from any remedy if it fails to give timely notice, to be excessive. They amended the section to retain the requirement that the buyer give notice of breach to the seller within a reasonable time but also to provide that "failure to give timely notice bars the buyer from a remedy only to the extent that the seller is prejudiced by the failure." The change conforms Article 2 with the common law.[395]

---

[394] UCC § 1-107.

[395] *See* Restatement (Second) of Contracts § 229.

[3]   Continued Use of Goods After Rejection or Revocation of Acceptance

On occasion after a rightful rejection or justified revocation of acceptance, often when the seller is unwilling to live up to its responsibility to refund the price, a buyer will have no rational economic choice other than to continue to use the goods for a limited time. Under the literal language of the original article, any exercise of ownership by a buyer following rejection or revocation of acceptance is wrongful against the seller, and the seller can ratify the conduct as an acceptance.[396] Thoughtful courts have been able to find ways around the language in appropriate circumstances, and consistent with the better-reasoned cases, amended Sections 2-602, 2-606, and 2-608 now permit such use, but only to the extent that it is reasonable. If the use is reasonable, the buyer will, in most instances, be obligated to the seller for the reasonable value of its use of the defective goods.

[4]   The Standard for Rejection in an Installment Contract

An amendment to Section 2-612(2) makes the standard for rejection of a single installment consistent with the standard for revocation of acceptance under Section 2-608. In other words, a right to reject does not arise unless the nonconformity "substantially impairs the value of that installment to *the buyer.*"[397] The test accordingly is not what would be substantial to a reasonable buyer but what is substantial to the actual buyer given its specific circumstances.

[B]   Cure

[1]   Cure After Revocation of Acceptance

Original Section 2-508 does not, by its terms, provide a right to cure following a revocation of acceptance. Despite the limitation, a few courts have found that such a right exists.[398] Amended Article 2 follows the lead of these cases by granting sellers a right to cure following revocation of acceptance under Section 2-608(1)(b), but not under Section 2-608(1)(a). The latter provision applies only if the buyer accepted the goods on the reasonable assumption that they would be cured and they have not been cured. The seller has already had an opportunity to cure and failed, and thus does not deserve an additional opportunity. Section 2-608(1)(b), by contrast, applies if the buyer accepted the goods without discovering the nonconformity, either because of the difficulty of discovering it before acceptance or because of the seller's assurances regarding the quality of the goods.

---

[396] Original UCC §§ 2-602(2)(a), 2-608(3), and 2-606(1)(c).

[397] UCC Amended § 2-612(2) (emphasis supplied).

[398] *See* § 7.05[C] *supra.*

Amended Section 2-508 denies a right to cure following revocation of acceptance in a consumer contract. The drafting committee's reasoning was that parties can always agree to a consensual cure and that having an absolute right to revoke would enhance consumers' bargaining leverage.

The amended section clarifies the right to cure in installment contracts. Section 2-612(2) provides that a buyer must accept a nonconforming installment if the defect is curable and the seller gives reasonable assurances of cure. Amended Section 2-508 overcomes the remaining doubt of whether a seller has a statutory right to cure following rejection of an installment by explicitly stating that it has such a right.

[2] Early Tender

Amended Section 2-508(1) deals with a seller's right to cure if the buyer rejects or revokes acceptance and the agreed time for the seller to perform has not yet expired. The original provision predicates the right on seasonable notification to the buyer of the seller's intent to cure and the retender of conforming goods within the agreed time. The amended provision makes express two concepts that are implicit in the original provision: (1) The seller's right to cure is predicated on its good-faith performance in making the initial tender, and (2) the cure must be at the seller's expense. The amended provision also states that the buyer has a right to recover reasonable expenses caused by the seller's breach and subsequent cure.

[3] Additional Time for Performance

Original subsection (2) is designed to prevent surprise rejections, a concept implemented by the requirement that the seller have "reasonable grounds to believe [the goods or tender] would be acceptable with or without money allowance." This vague, subjective standard has led to a long line of confusing decisions, and the amended provision scraps it as unworkable. Instead, the standard for the seller is the familiar standard of good-faith performance in making the initial tender. In addition, the amended test focuses on the needs of the buyer by requiring that the second tender be "appropriate and timely in the circumstances." As with amended Section 2-508(1), the buyer is granted a right to recover reasonable expenses caused by the seller's breach and subsequent cure.

[4] Effect of Buyer's Failure to Particularize Defects

Amended Article 2 makes several changes to Section 2-605(1), which deals with the effect of a buyer's failure to notify the seller of defects with particularity. The buyer's notification is the event that triggers an effective rejection or revocation of acceptance and that alerts the seller to its need to initiate a cure.

Under the original rule, a buyer that fails to state in connection with rejection a defect ascertainable by reasonable inspection is precluded from relying on the unstated defect to justify rejection or to establish breach if the seller could have cured the defect. The provision does not explicitly require the seller to have a right to cure, only that it have the ability. As amended, a failure to state in connection with a rejection or a revocation of acceptance under Section 2-608(1)(b) a defect ascertainable by reasonable inspection precludes the buyer from relying on the unstated defect to justify rejection or revocation of acceptance only if the seller has both a right to cure the defect and the ability to do so.

A failure to particularize no longer precludes the buyer from relying on an unstated defect to establish breach under amended Section 2-605. The Official Comments make the point that the change does not eliminate the requirement that the buyer notify the seller of the breach to preserve the buyer's right to damages.

[C]   Repudiation

Questions of when a party can be considered to have repudiated a contract have long vexed and will continue to challenge courts. In an attempt to add some guidance, a new subsection has been added to Section 2-610:

> Repudiation includes language that a reasonable person would interpret to mean that the other party will not or cannot make a performance still due under the contract or voluntary, affirmative conduct that would appear to a reasonable person to make a future performance by the other party impossible.[399]

This new subsection does not purport to be an exclusive statement of when a repudiation has occurred and the change should not result in any difference of analysis by the courts, as its examples are consistent with general contract law.

§ 7.10   CISG

[A]   Avoidance of the Contract

The CISG refers to the right of an aggrieved party to put an end to a contract based on breach by the other party as "avoidance" rather than cancellation.[400] Avoidance allows the aggrieved party to end the contractual relationship and pursue a damages claim for the loss inflicted by the other party. In the absence of a right of avoidance, the aggrieved party must continue with the contract and rely on other remedies to protect its interests.

[1]   When Available

Article 49(1) states the circumstances under which a buyer may declare a contract avoided as follows:

> The buyer may declare the contract avoided:

---

[399] UCC Amended § 2-610(2).

[400] *See* CISG Arts. 49 (buyers), 64 (sellers). CISG Art. 72 also creates a right for an aggrieved party to avoid a contract in the context of an anticipatory repudiation. *See* § 7.10[B][1] *infra*.

(c)   If the failure by the seller to perform any of his obligations under the contract or this Convention amounts to a fundamental breach of contract; or

(d)   In case of non-delivery, if the seller does not deliver the goods within the additional period of time fixed by the buyer in accordance with paragraph (1) of article 47 or declares that he will not deliver within the period so fixed.[401]

The CISG does not recognize the Code's concepts of acceptance, rejection, and revocation of acceptance.

[a]   Fundamental Breach

Under Article 49(1)(a), a buyer may avoid a contract because of breach by the seller only if the breach is "fundamental." Article 25 defines fundamental breach as follows:

A breach of contract committed by one of the parties is fundamental if it results in such detriment to the other party as substantially to deprive him of what he is entitled to expect under the contract, unless the party in breach did not foresee and a reasonable person of the same kind in the same circumstances would not have foreseen such a result.

The definition focuses on the extent to which the affected party is deprived of its expectation under the contract, and to be fundamental the deprivation must be substantial.

Students of American contract law may be tempted to equate fundamental breach with the common-law requirement of material breach. Under the common-law, an aggrieved party may not cancel a contract unless the breach is material. The analogy, however, is imperfect. The delegates were concerned that imposing an excessively burdensome requirement would be inappropriate: Their objective was more to eliminate avoidance for lower-level types of breaches than to restrict it to the highest level of breach. They were concerned with the impact that avoidance can have in the international sphere, where transportation costs are often quite significant and arranging for an alternative disposition of goods when they have been shipped to a foreign country can be considerably more difficult and expensive than doing so in a domestic setting. Thus, to the extent that materiality is helpful in understanding fundamental breach, it must be considered through the lens of internationality and in furtherance of the delegates' goals.

Like Article 2, the CISG has two cure provisions: One for cases of early delivery, the other for cases in which an extension of the contract's performance date will be required.[402] Article 37 deals with cases of early delivery as follows:

If the seller has delivered goods before the date for delivery, he may, up to that date, deliver any missing part or make up any deficiency in the

---

[401] CISG Art. 64 establishes the right of a seller to avoid a contract under circumstances comparable to CISG Art. 49.

[402] *See* § 7.04[C][1][a] *supra.*

quantity of the goods delivered, or deliver goods in replacement of any non-conforming goods delivered or remedy any lack of conformity in the goods delivered, provided that the exercise of this right does not cause the buyer unreasonable inconvenience or unreasonable expense.[403]

The provision does not require a breaching seller that delivers early to notify the buyer of its intent to cure and thus, absent a clear indication that the seller will not cure, the buyer cannot safely declare the contract avoided because the seller might cure the breach even if it is fundamental. The only limitation on the seller's right to cure under Article 37 is that the cure cannot cause unreasonable expense or inconvenience to the buyer.[404]

Article 48(1) deals as follows with cases in which cure will require an extension of the seller's time for performance:

> Subject to article 49, the seller may, even after the date for delivery, remedy at his own expense any failure to perform his obligations, if he can do so without unreasonable delay and without causing the buyer unreasonable inconvenience or uncertainty of reimbursement by the seller of expenses advanced by the buyer.[405]

Even though cure in this context imposes some inconvenience on the buyer, it is permitted in order to lessen the impact of forfeiture and waste that otherwise might accompany a fundamental breach and subsequent avoidance by the buyer.

A literal reading of Articles 48 and 49 suggests that a buyer that acts promptly can preempt the seller's Article 48 cure rights. Article 48(1) expressly makes its provisions "[s]ubject to article 49." Article 49(1)(a) empowers a buyer to declare the contract avoided in the case of a fundamental breach by the seller. A cure effort by the seller thus would appear to be too late if the buyer, following an otherwise fundamental breach by the seller, declares the contract to be avoided before the seller cures.

An assessment of the underlying policy implications suggests a different approach. Consider the situation posed when a seller delivers a complex piece of machinery that does not work at all because of a defective computer chip for which the seller has an exclusive license. Obviously the inability of the machine to operate would pose such a detriment as substantially to deprive the buyer of what it was entitled to expect under the contract. With such a fundamental breach, the buyer would be entitled under Article 49(1)(a) to declare the contract avoided. The buyer in such a situation might be inclined to pursue this course for a variety of reasons, including a reassessment of its need for the machine, the impact of the purchase price on its changed economic conditions, the availability of comparable machines elsewhere at less cost, or an emotional response to the seller's breach. Although the defective computer chip has a major impact on the

---

[403] "[T]he buyer retains any right to claim damages as provided for in [the] Convention." CISG Art. 37. The CISG includes a comparable provision that allows a cure in the conformity of documents that are handed over before the time required in the contract. CISG Art. 34.

[404] For example, a delivered machine might have been installed in an assembly line and efforts to repair it might unreasonably interfere with the buyer's assembly operations.

[405] The buyer again retains a claim for any allowable damages. CISG Art. 48(1).

buyer, the seller should be able to remedy it easily and promptly. When considered from the seller's perspective, the seriousness of the breach is significantly lessened.

The drafting history of the CISG suggests that an offer to cure is relevant to the assessment of whether a breach is fundamental. Delegates to the Convention clearly expressed their concern that an aggrieved buyer not be able to cut off the seller's right to cure by making a precipitous declaration of avoidance. The language chosen to advance protection of the cure right, however, is very unfortunate. Article 49 does not impose a requirement on an aggrieved buyer to afford the seller an opportunity to cure before declaring avoidance. Reading such a requirement into Article 49 deprives the cross-reference in Article 48 of much of its meaning. Despite the cross-reference and the authority that it suggests for buyers to pursue avoidance without an opportunity to cure, buyers should be aware of the strong policy implications that might lead a court to consider an offer to cure in determining whether a seller's breach is fundamental.

[b]   Notice Under Article 47(1)

Article 47(1) provides that if a seller breaches in any manner "[t]he buyer may fix an additional period of time of reasonable length for performance by the seller of his obligations." A buyer that sends such a notice may not resort to any remedy for breach during the period fixed unless the seller sends a notice indicating that it will not perform during that period.[406] If the seller tenders performance during the period, the buyer must accept it but may recover damages caused by the delay.[407]

Notice under Article 47(1) resembles a device known under German law as a *"Nachfrist"* notice. German law allows an aggrieved party to establish a reasonable period of time for a breaching party to perform and to notify the breaching party that performance will not be acceptable after that period. The aggrieved party may terminate the contract if the breaching party fails to perform within the established time without regard to the nature of the breach.[408] Article 47(1) parallels the concept of *Nachfrist* notice in that it broadly permits a buyer to fix an additional time for performance following any breach by the seller.[409] Unlike German law, however, a buyer's right under the CISG to avoid a contract because of a seller's failure to perform during the period established by an Article 47(1) notice is limited to cases in which the seller initially failed to deliver the goods and does not deliver them during the notice period.[410]

---

[406] CISG Art. 49(2).

[407] *Id.*

[408] German (F.R.G.) Civil Code § 326.

[409] In order to avoid the contract, the notice under CISG Art. 47(1) must fix a period of time that is reasonable in length and must make clear to the seller that the fixed period operates as a final deadline for delivery.

[410] CISG Art. 49(1)(b). Article 64(1)(b) limits a seller's right to avoid a contract based on comparable notice to cases where, during the additional time fixed by the seller under Article 63, the buyer does not perform its "obligation to pay the price or take delivery of the goods." If the buyer

[2]   Notice of Avoidance

Article 26 provides that "[a] declaration of avoidance of the contract is effective only if made by notice to the other party."[411] Notification apprizes the other party of the aggrieved party's position and can help eliminate economic waste in some instances. For example, a seller should consider not shipping the goods if the buyer has already provided a declaration of avoidance. Communication of the buyer's position also may provide a catalyst for a negotiated settlement.

[B]   Prospective Impairment of Expectations

The CISG includes provisions that address the appropriate response when a party to a sales contract says or does something prior to the time for performance that creates uncertainty about whether that party will perform its obligations. Article 71 states when the aggrieved party can suspend its own performance and Article 72 states when it can avoid the contract. Article 73 deals with comparable issues under contracts that require delivery of the goods in installments. The relief available under these articles applies equally to buyers and sellers.

[1]   Avoidance of the Contract

As discussed above,[412] the general rule under the CISG is that a fundamental breach by a party entitles the other party to avoid the contract. Article 72 uses fundamental breach to determine whether a party can avoid the contract before the other party's performance is due. Article 72(1) provides as follows: "If prior to the date for performance of the contract it is clear that one of the parties will commit a fundamental breach of contract, the other party may declare the contract avoided."[413]

The clearest case of fundamental breach in this context is when a party states unequivocally that it cannot or will not perform its obligations. Even though the party making the statement might later change its mind, the statement satisfies the standard of Article 72. Most other situations pose a risk for the party seeking to avoid the contract as that party must prove that it was certain that the other party would have committed a fundamental breach. If the showing is inadequate, the declaration of avoidance can constitute an anticipatory breach entitling the other party to avoid the contract.

Although Article 72(2) was included to further constrain the avoidance power, it actually can alleviate some of the uncertainty for a party that believes it has grounds for avoidance. The provision states that "[i]f time allows, the party intending to declare the contract avoided must give reasonable notice to the

---

fails to comply with its other obligations, such as failing to get an import license or to arrange for shipping, the seller can avoid the contract only if the failure rises to the level of a fundamental breach.

[411] CISG Art. 26.

[412] *See* § 7.10[A][1][a] *supra*.

[413] The right to avoid a contract by using an Article 47(1) notice, *see* § 7.10[A][2] *supra*, is not available in this context.

other party in order to permit him to provide adequate assurance of his performance."[414] This provision permits a party to communicate an intention to avoid the contract before making an actual declaration of avoidance. Although a failure to respond in itself does not satisfy the standard of Article 72(1), a party that avoids the contract after giving the notice will likely be in a better position to establish that the other party would have committed a fundamental breach. If the party to which the notice is sent provides adequate assurances of performance, the assurances eliminate any basis to believe that a fundamental breach will occur, thereby precluding the need for avoidance prior to the date for performance.

[2]   Suspension of Performance

Article 71 provides an aggrieved party faced with a prospective impairment of expectations with a less drastic response than avoidance: The aggrieved party may simply withhold any further part of its own performance pending performance by the other party. Article 71(1) establishes the right to suspend performance as follows:

> A party may suspend the performance of his obligations if, after the conclusion of the contract, it becomes apparent that the other party will not perform a substantial part of his obligations as a result of:
>
> (a)   a serious deficiency in his ability to perform or in his creditworthiness; or
>
> (b)   his conduct in preparing to perform or in performing the contract.[415]

Like the right of avoidance under Article 72, the right to suspend performance focuses on what the other party will not do in the future. Whereas Article 72 is based on a determination that the other party "will commit a fundamental breach of contract," Article 71 is based on a determination that the other party "will not perform a substantial part of his obligations." While the two statements are similar, the Article 71 standard apparently requires something less than a showing of prospective fundamental breach. However, the difference between the standards is a question of degree and is difficult to isolate.

The element of certainty required under the two articles also appears to be closely comparable, even though stated differently. Article 72 requires that the prospective fundamental breach be "clear," whereas Article 71 requires that it "[become] apparent." The use of different language suggests that different standards apply, but they too are difficult to distinguish.

---

[414] CISG Art. 72(2). The notice is not required "if the other party has declared that he will not perform his obligations." CISG Art. 72(3).

[415] CISG Article 71(3) provides that "[a] party suspending performance, whether before or after dispatch of the goods, must immediately give notice of the suspension to the other party and must continue with performance if the other party provides adequate assurance of his performance."

[3]   Installment Contracts

Article 73 covers the right to avoid a contract that calls for delivery of the goods in installments. Article 73(1) entitles an aggrieved party to avoid the contract with respect to a particular installment if the other party's failure to perform constitutes a fundamental breach with respect to that installment.[416] The provision simply applies the basic rules of fundamental breach to an individual installment.[417] Avoidance rights with respect to future installments are covered in Article 73(2), which provides that an aggrieved party may declare the contract avoided if the failure of the other party with respect to any installment gives the aggrieved party "good grounds to conclude that a fundamental breach of contract will occur with respect to future instalments."

[C]   Exemption From Damages

The CISG refers to an excuse from performance based on intervening circumstances as an "exemption." Article 79(1) states the basic rule as follows:

> A party is not liable for a failure to perform any of his obligations if he proves that the failure was due to an impediment beyond his control and that he could not reasonably be expected to have taken the impediment into account at the time of the conclusion of the contract or to have avoided or overcome it or its consequences."

The provision, which is available to both buyers and sellers, requires the party claiming exemption to establish three elements: (1) the failure to perform was due to an impediment beyond the control of the claiming party; (2) the claiming party could not reasonably have been expected to have taken the impediment into account when the contract was formed; and (3) the claiming party could not have avoided or overcome either the impediment or its consequences.

The application of Article 79 is one of the most challenging aspects of the CISG. Probably every national sales law recognizes the principle of excuse based on intervening situations. Just as probable, each nation struggles in trying to apply the principle to the variety of circumstances in which relief is sought. The lack of certainty in the domestic arenas only exacerbates the difficulties in the international arena, and the parties are well advised to include in their agreement express terms addressing the consequences of unanticipated events.

An example based on one aspect of Article 79 illustrates the point. Although the article does not expressly state that an impediment justifying exemption must not have been foreseeable, its requirement that the claiming party establish that it could not reasonably have been expected to take account of the impediment comes close to incorporating a foreseeability standard. If the claiming party reasonably could have foreseen the impediment, it could have considered the risks associated with its occurrence and contracted accordingly.

---

[416] CISG Art. 73(1).

[417] *See* CISG Arts. 49 & 64; *see also* § 7.10[A][1][a] *supra*. Unlike Article 49, however, which recognizes buyer avoidance on grounds of fundamental breach or noncompliance with an Article 47(1) notice in cases of nondelivery, Article 73 recognizes only fundamental breach as grounds for avoidance in installment contracts.

Article 79(5) states that "[n]othing in this article prevents either party from exercising any right other than to claim damages under this Convention." In other words, the contract does not become a nullity; rather, the party that qualifies for the exemption is freed from liability for any damages caused by its nonperformance resulting from the impediment. The other party retains all of its other rights.

The fact that a party is exempted under Article 79 does not alter the fact that its failure to perform is a breach. Although the exempted party is not liable for damages, the aggrieved party may declare the contract avoided if it has grounds for avoidance.[418] For example, the initial impact of an impediment might cause a fundamental breach, or the delays occasioned by the impediment might ripen over time into a fundamental breach. A justified declaration of avoidance invokes certain rights under the CISG.[419] Most importantly, it allows each party to recover whatever it supplied or paid under the contract.[420] If the impediment prevents a seller from delivering the goods to the buyer, avoidance permits the buyer to recover any part of the purchase price already paid. Similarly, an avoiding seller can recover any goods that it delivered before an impediment prevented the buyer from paying for them.

Suppose that a seller claims an exemption on the grounds that its reputable supplier could not provide the goods in a timely manner. The seller may argue that, because of the supplier's reputation, it could not reasonably have been expected to take the impediment into account and that it was powerless to overcome the impediment or its consequences. Without more, the seller would be entitled to an exemption. Article 79, however, includes another provision that must be satisfied in this context: In addition to the ordinary elements, the seller must establish that the supplier would have been exempt if the same elements had applied to it.[421] If the supplier would have been exempt from a claim by the seller for damages, and if the seller qualifies for an exemption in its own right, the impediment is attributable to the supplier's failure to deliver the goods to the seller. On the other hand, if the seller could recover damages from the supplier it is liable to its own buyer for damages.

---

[418] *See* CISG Arts. 49, 64, 72 & 73; *see also* § 7.10[A] *supra.*

[419] *See* CISG Arts. 81-84.

[420] CISG Art. 81(2).

[421] CISG Art. 79(2).

Chapter 8

REMEDIES OF BUYERS AND LESSEES

§ 8.01 GENERAL

Articles 2 and 2A include indices of remedy provisions available to aggrieved parties in sale and lease transactions.[1] Article 2 generally uses the word "breach" for the event that triggers a remedy whereas Article 2A, reflecting the approach of Article 9, generally uses "default."[2] Each article provides for both monetary and nonmonetary remedies.

An aggrieved buyer's rights of rejection and revocation of acceptance are discussed in Chapter 7.[3] The primary focus of this chapter is on an aggrieved buyer's or lessee's monetary remedies, although nonmonetary remedies, notably specific performance, are covered as well. Two relevant concepts also are explained at the outset: The cumulative nature of the applicable remedies, and, with respect to Article 2A, the requirement that each method of measuring monetary damages requires an adjustment to account for the time value of money.

[A]　Cumulation of Remedies

The rights and remedies stated in Articles 2 and 2A are cumulative.[4] In other words, by electing a particular remedy an aggrieved party does not forfeit the right to pursue other appropriate remedies. The Comments to Article 2 state: "This Article rejects any doctrine of election of remedy as a fundamental policy and thus the remedies are essentially cumulative in nature and include all of the available remedies for breach."[5] The Comments to Article 2A also indicate a rejection of the election doctrine.[6]

The cumulative approach is consistent with the mandate that remedies be "liberally administered to the end that the aggrieved party may be put in as good a position as if the other party had fully performed."[7] The Comments elaborate as follows:

> Therefore, cumulation of, or selection among, remedies is available to the extent necessary to put the aggrieved party in as good a position as it would have been in had there been full performance. However,

---

[1]　UCC §§ 2-703, 2-711, 2A-508, 2A-523.

[2]　*See* § 7.06[A] (sales), [B] (leases) *supra.*

[3]　*See* §§ 7.04 (rejection), 7.05 (revocation of acceptance) *supra.*

[4]　UCC §§ 2-703, cmt. 1, 2A-501(4).

[5]　UCC § 2-703, cmt. 1.

[6]　UCC §§ 2A-508, cmt. 2, 2A-523, cmt. 1.

[7]　UCC § 1-106(1).

cumulation of, or selection among, remedies is not available to the extent that the cumulation or selection would put the aggrieved party in a better position than it would have been in had there been full performance by the other party.[8]

[B]　Time Value of Money

Monetary damages in lease cases must be reduced to present value. Even though in a lease transaction the performance of the parties will extend over a period of time, often measured in years, a judgment awarding damages must reflect a single amount and the time value of money must be reflected in that amount. Put another way, a successful claimant will receive a right to current payment, whereas if the lease had continued to the end each party would have performed its obligations (the lessee paying rent and the lessor permitting possession and use of the goods) with dollars and benefits of gradually decreasing value. Early payment in the form of damages enables a successful claimant to invest the money and earn a present rate of return.

In order to reflect the time value of money, the lease formulas reduce damages awards to present value. "Present value" means "the amount as of a date certain of one or more sums payable in the future, discounted to the date certain."[9] The damages formulas in Article 2A include the necessary dates for application of the discount. Reducing each element to present value determines the amount of money that would have to be invested now at the applicable rate of return to produce the indicated amount at the stated time in the future.

Calculating present value requires the use of a discount rate. The definition of present value includes the following provision concerning selection of a discount rate:

> The discount is determined by the interest rate specified by the parties if the rate was not manifestly unreasonable at the time the transaction was entered into; otherwise, the discount is determined by a commercially reasonable rate that takes into account the facts and circumstances of each case at the time the transaction was entered into.[10]

The party claiming damages benefits from a lower discount rate because this will increase the present recovery. A higher discount rate will lower the recovery.

---

[8]　UCC § 2A-501, cmt. 4.

[9]　UCC § 2A-103(1)(u).

[10]　*Id.*

§ 8.02 MONETARY REMEDIES

[A] Recovery of Payments Made [§ 2-711(1); § 2A-508(1)(b)]

If an aggrieved buyer does not receive the goods from the seller, or receives but does not retain them, the buyer is entitled to recover any part of the purchase price that has been paid.[11] Recovery of payments is thus appropriate if the seller fails to make delivery[12] or repudiates,[13] or if the buyer rightfully rejects tendered goods[14] or justifiably revokes its acceptance of them.[15] If a buyer accepts the goods and does not revoke its acceptance, it must pay the purchase price even if the goods are defective[16] and thus may not recovery any payments that have been made. The appropriate remedy in the case of accepted goods is monetary damages.[17]

The comparable remedy is not as absolute in the lease context. An aggrieved lessee that does not retain the goods for the full lease term may "recover so much of the rent and security as has been paid and is just under the circumstances."[18] The limitation on recovery imposed by the "justness" standard is in recognition of the fact that a lessee might appropriately cancel a lease contract after having used the goods for a considerable period of time and thus return of all rental payments might be unfair.[19] For example, a lessee entitled to revoke acceptance after having successfully used the goods for most of the lease term might not be entitled to much, if any, of the rent paid.[20] By contrast, a lessee generally should recover all prepaid rent if the goods are not delivered or are promptly rejected.

---

[11] UCC § 2-711(1).

[12] *See, e.g.*, June G. Ashton Interiors v. Stark Carpet Corp., 142 Ill. App. 3d 100, 491 N.E.2d 191, 2 UCC Rep. Serv. 2d 74 (1986).

[13] *See, e.g.*, Government of Republic of China v. Compass Communications Corp., 473 F. Supp. 1306, 28 UCC Rep. Serv. 393 (D.D.C. 1979).

[14] *See, e.g.*, Hollingsworth v. The Software House, Inc., 32 Ohio App. 3d 61, 513 N.E.2d 1372, 4 UCC Rep. Serv. 2d 1400 (1986).

[15] *See, e.g.*, S&R Metals, Inc. v. C. Itoh & Co. (America), Inc., 859 F.2d 814, 7 UCC Rep. Serv. 2d 61 (9th Cir. 1988).

[16] UCC § 2-607(1); *see* § 7.03[B][2] *supra*.

[17] *See* UCC § 2-714; § 8.02[D] *infra*. Damages are available only if the buyer gives the seller notification as required by UCC § 2-607(3)(a). *See* UCC § 2-714(1); § 7.03[B][3] *supra*.

[18] UCC § 2A-508(1)(b).

[19] UCC § 2A-508, cmt. 2.

[20] A comparable issue arises in the sales context when a buyer uses goods for a significant period of time before revoking acceptance. Article 2 does not provide for a seller to be compensated for the use but several courts have required payment based on principles of restitution. *See* § 7.03[A][3][b] *supra*.

[B] Cover [§ 2-712; § 2A-518]

The preferred monetary recovery for a buyer that does not receive goods from the seller, or that rightfully rejects or justifiably revokes acceptance of tendered goods, is based on a substitute "cover" transaction.[21] The buyer covers by purchasing comparable goods from another seller and, if the price of the substitute goods is higher, using the difference between that price and the original contract price as the measure of damages.[22] Cover is the preferred remedy because it comes the closest to meeting the Code's objective of placing an aggrieved party in the same economic position it would have occupied if the contract had been performed.[23] Cover facilitates this objective by basing damages on the actual cost of acquiring goods from a substitute source rather than on a hypothetical substitute acquisition based on market values.[24]

[1] Sales

Section 2-712(2) states the measure of cover damages as follows: "The buyer may recover from the seller as damages the difference between the cost of cover and the contract price,[25] together with any incidental or consequential damages as hereinafter defined (section 2-715), but less expenses saved in consequence of the seller's breach." The formula awards the buyer the difference between the actual price of the substitute goods and the original contract price along with any incidental and consequential damages.[26] An example of expenses saved as a result of the breach, which must be deducted, is the cheaper cost of transporting the substitute goods as compared with the cost of transporting the original goods.[27]

Not every substitute transaction will qualify for use in calculating damages. Section 2-712(1) provides as follows: "After a breach within the preceding section the buyer may 'cover' by making in good faith and without unreasonable delay any reasonable purchase of or contract to purchase goods in substitution

---

[21] Traditional common law did not recognize the cover measure of damages. Farnsworth, *Legal Remedies for Breach of Contract*, 70 Colum. L. Rev. 1145, 1191-92 (1970).

[22] Hessler v. Crystal Lake Crysler-Plymouth, Inc., 338 Ill. App. 3d 1010, 788 N.E.2d 405, 50 UCC Rep. Serv. 2d 330 (2003) (purchase of a limited production vehicle for about $30,000 over the contract price was an appropriate cover transaction because it represented the going market price for the vehicle).

[23] "The remedies provided by [the Uniform Commercial Code] must be liberally administered to the end that the aggrieved party may be put in as good a position as if the other party had fully performed." UCC § 1-305(a).

[24] Although the Code is silent on the point, a buyer that covers should not be allowed to use the market price/contract price measure of UCC § 2-713 to obtain higher damages as that tactic violates the objective of UCC § 1-305(a). *See, e.g.*, Neibert v. Schwenn Agri-Production Corp., 219 Ill. App. 3d 188, 579 N.E.2d 389, 16 UCC Rep. Serv. 2d 681 (1991).

[25] Allied Semi-Conductors Int'l, Ltd. v. Pulsar Components Int'l, Inc., 907 F. Supp. 618, 28 UCC Rep. Serv. 2d 543 (E.D. N.Y. 1995) (court rejected buyer's argument that it was entitled to cover damages after having covered at a price considerably lower than the original contract price).

[26] Incidental and consequential damages are discussed in § 8.02[E] *infra*.

[27] Melms v. Mitchell, 266 Or. 208, 512 P.2d 1336, 13 UCC Rep. Serv. 223 (1973) (expenses saved by buyers not having to cut the dry wood they purchased in cover had to be deducted).

for those due from the seller."[28] The aggrieved buyer thus must (1) cover in good faith, (2) do so in a timely manner, meaning without unreasonable delay, and (3) make substitute purchase that is reasonable.

The standards of good faith and timeliness ensure that an aggrieved buyer does not increase the seller's liability for damages unnecessarily. A buyer may not intentionally select the most expensive means of cover available, or cover in a manner that advances its own special interests.[29] Because inflationary pressure tends to cause prices to rise over time, a lengthy delay may increase the cost of cover. The two standards thus protect sellers from excessive recoveries.[30]

Two caveats must be considered in applying the standards. First, both standards are highly sensitive to surrounding circumstances. Appropriate action in one context may not be acceptable under different circumstances. For example, waiting thirty-eight days to cover in a rapidly rising market would ordinarily fail to satisfy the standards, but the court in *Dangerfield v. Markel*[31] approved such a delay because under the circumstances the buyer was unable to cover sooner.[32] The facts of each case must be analyzed carefully.

The other caveat is that the two standards are only general guidelines. The Comments make this point clear: "The test of proper cover is whether at the time and place the buyer acted in good faith and in a reasonable manner, and it is immaterial that hindsight may later prove that the method of cover was not the cheapest or most effective."[33] Consequently, the court held that the school district in *Huntington Beach Union High School Dist. v. Continental Information Systems Corp.*[34] had acted reasonably even though it allowed bids

---

[28] UCC § 2-712(1).

[29] In *Oloffson v. Coomer*, 11 Ill. App. 3d 918, 296 N.E.2d 871, 12 UCC Rep. Serv. 1082 (1973), the seller notified the buyer that he could not plant corn because the ground was too wet. Rather than covering quickly in the recognized market for corn, the buyer waited until the delivery date, which was several months later. The court justifiably did not allow the cover. Permitting such a delay would enable buyers to speculate, at the expense of their sellers, in hopes that the market price would drop below the contract price.

[30] This concern led the court in *American Carpet Mills v. Gunny Corp.*, 649 F.2d 1056, 31 UCC Rep. Serv. 964 (5th Cir. 1981), to uphold cover transactions made during a period extending from March to September. Because prices on the spot market for the goods declined steadily during this period, the delays accrued to the seller's benefit.

[31] 278 N.W.2d 364, 26 UCC Rep. Serv. 419 (N.D. 1979).

[32] *See also* Erie Casein Co., Inc. v. Anric Corp., 217 Ill. App. 3d 602, 577 N.E.2d 892, 15 UCC Rep. Serv. 2d 1240 (1991) (not covering until prices had risen significantly was justified because buyer encountered the same problems as seller in attempting to obtain the goods).

[33] UCC § 2-712, cmt. 2. The seller in *Rockland Indus., Inc. v. E+E (US) Inc.*, 991 F. Supp. 468 (D. Md. 1998), argued unsuccessfully that the buyer covered too soon given that prices had risen dramatically during a period of scarcity but there were indications at the time of the cover transaction that prices would decline in a few months, which in fact they did. The court stressed that the buyer had to make its determination at the time of the breach without the benefit of hindsight. The goods were critical to the buyer's business and the price volatility suggested that immediate cover was prudent.

[34] 621 F.2d 353, 29 UCC Rep. Serv. 112 (9th Cir. 1980).

from other sellers to expire and this ultimately led to a higher cost of cover.[35]

A few courts have addressed whether a buyer, rather than acquiring substitute goods from a third party, can cover by providing the goods itself. The seller in *Dura-Wood Treating Co. v. Century Forest Industries, Inc.*[36] argued unsuccessfully that the Code does not contemplate a buyer covering in this manner. The court upheld the cover because the buyer had taken price quotations and ultimately had determined that it could produce substitute goods at a price lower than it could acquire them from another supplier.[37] On the other hand, the court in *Kiser v. Lemco Industries, Inc.*[38] determined that a mere statement by the buyer that it had purchased a quantity of its own wheat at a stated price, without more, did not establish the requisite good faith.

For the cover remedy to apply, the buyer's purchase must constitute a reasonable substitute for the goods described in the contract. The requirement is met if the buyer purchases identical goods, but a buyer might be inclined, or even forced by circumstances, to purchase goods that differ from the described goods in some respect. The Comments clarify that what is envisioned is "goods not identical with those involved but commercially usable as reasonable substitutes under the circumstances of the particular case."[39] The closer the substitute goods are to the described goods, the more likely it is that the cover transaction will withstand scrutiny.[40] The question remains, however, as to the factors that courts should consider in determining how to accommodate cover goods that differ from the described goods.

Assuming good faith and timeliness, if a cover transaction is for goods that are inferior to the described goods, the court should ordinarily be willing to approve the transaction. Thus the purchase of a boat with smaller engines and ten percent fewer features for about $25,000 more than the original contract price qualified as a cover transaction in *Meshinsky v. Nichols Yacht Sales, Inc.*[41] because the buyer had not improved its economic position with the replacement.

---

[35] *See also* Farmer's Union Co-op Co. of Mead, Neb. v. Flamme Bros., 196 Neb. 699, 245 N.W.2d 464, 20 UCC Rep. Serv. 77 (1976) (co-op purchase of corn from its regular customers over two-week period at varying prices rather than immediate purchase of full amount on open market upheld as being in good faith and timely).

[36] 675 F.2d 745, 33 UCC Rep. Serv. 1201 (5th Cir. 1982).

[37] *See also* Cives Corp. v. Callier Steel Pipe & Tube, Inc., 482 A.2d 852, 39 UCC Rep. Serv. 1705 (Me. 1984) (it did not appear that buyer profited from in-house manufacture of substitute tubular steel).

[38] 536 S.W.2d 585, 19 UCC Rep. Serv. 1134 (Tex. Civ. App. 1976).

[39] UCC § 2-712, cmt. 1.

[40] *Compare* Goodell v. KT Enters., Ltd., 394 So. 2d 1087, 31 UCC Rep. Serv. 129 (Fla. Ct. App. 1981) (purchase of belt-conveyor system for use in pizza-freezing business constituted cover because it was of same general type as unit first ordered), *with* Valley Die Cast Corp. v. A. C. W., Inc., 25 Mich. App. 321, 181 N.W.2d 303, 8 UCC Rep. Serv. 488 (1970) (buyer did not cover by purchasing a more expensive car-wash system that operated on entirely different principle from pressure system purchased under original contract).

[41] 110 N.J. 464, 541 A.2d 1063, 6 UCC Rep. Serv. 2d 1144 (1988).

In some instances, a court should approve a cover transaction even though the substitute goods are superior to the described goods. For example, the buyer in *In re Lifeguard Industries, Inc.*[42] entered into a cover contract for aluminum siding with features that were superior to those of the described siding because it had a contract to install siding of a certain type and the cover seller was the only other manufacturer that produced that type of siding. If a qualifying cover transaction provides goods with higher quality and the value of the additional quality can be calculated with reasonable certainty, the court should deduct that value from the cost of cover unless the buyer will not benefit from the additional quality. Using the facts of *In re Lifeguard Industries* as a hypothetical, if the buyer could have charged its customer more for installing the substitute siding because of its superior features, the cover price should have been adjusted downward to reflect the benefit to the buyer. On the other hand, if the buyer was contractually required to install the siding at a fixed price, it would not benefit from the additional quality and an adjustment would be inappropriate.

[2]   Leases

The Article 2A provisions on cover are based on those of Article 2 but have been modified to reflect special considerations raised by substitute lease transactions. Article 2A authorizes an aggrieved lessee to cover by buying or leasing,[43] but only a substitute lease will qualify for the purpose of using the cover measure of damages.[44] The payment obligation incurred in buying substitute goods cannot be compared appropriately with the payment obligation in the original lease because of the inherently different nature of the transactions.

Even a substitute lease transaction may have significantly different terms — such as duration, insurance coverage, maintenance requirements — that can affect the lessee's payment obligation. Thus, in addition to the requirements that the lessee cover in good faith and in a commercially reasonable manner,[45] the substitute lease agreement must be "substantially similar to the original lease agreement."[46] A lessee that buys substitute goods or enters into a nonqualifying substitute lease has the same right to damages as a lessee that elects not to cover.[47] Although the Comments indicate that the "substantially similar" requirement is not a familiar one, it is comparable to the Article 2 mandate that a qualifying cover be a reasonable substitute purchase.[48] In both sales and lease transactions, the terms that affect cost and value under the

---

[42] 42 B.R. 734 (E.D. Ohio 1983).

[43] UCC § 2A-518(1).

[44] UCC § 2A-518(2).

[45] Whereas UCC § 2-712(1) requires that cover occur without unreasonable delay, UCC § 2A-518(1) reflects the approach of Article 9, which permits a secured party to dispose of collateral in any commercially reasonable manner. *See* § UCC 9-610(a), (b).

[46] UCC § 2A-518(2).

[47] See UCC § 2A-519(1), discussed in § 8.02[C] *infra.*

[48] UCC § 2-712(1), discussed in § 8.02[B][1] *supra.*

original contract and under the cover contract must be sufficiently comparable to legitimize using them as a basis for calculating damages.[49]

Because variations among leases are so likely,[50] the Comments to Article 2A articulate the need for courts to make necessary adjustments to the amounts that would otherwise be produced through the cover formula. They state that "[i]f the differences between the original lease and the new lease can be easily valued, it would be appropriate for a court to adjust the difference in rental to take account of the difference between the two leases, find that the new lease is substantially similar to the old lease, and award cover damages under this section."[51] The Comments go on to identify two tests that courts should apply in determining whether a substitute lease is substantially similar– the terms of the two contracts must be commercially comparable, and the court must be able to make fair apportionments.[52]

With regard to a difference in the duration of the original lease and the substitute lease, the cover formula works as follows: Rent under the original lease contract is deducted from rent under the new lease agreement, but only for the period of time that performance under the two lease terms coincide.[53] The Comments clarify that the lessee is entitled to consequential damages to compensate for the loss of use of the goods during the period between default on the original lease and commencement of the substitute lease.[54]

[C]   Market Price/Contract Price Differential [§ 2-713; § 2A-519(1), (2)]

Section 2-713 provides an alternative to cover as a method for measuring damages.[55] As with cover, it applies if a buyer either does not receive goods from the seller or if it rightfully rejects or justifiably revokes acceptance of tendered goods. The section awards an aggrieved buyer the difference between

---

[49] The Comments suggest this focus:

> [T]he various elements of the new lease agreement should also be examined. Those elements include the presence or absence of options to purchase or release; the lessor's representations, warranties and covenants to the lessee, as well as those to be provided by the lessee to the lessor; and the services, if any, to be provided by the lessor or by the lessee. All of these factors allocate cost and risk between the lessor and the lessee and thus affect the amount of rent to be paid.

UCC § 2A-518, cmt. 5.

[50] For example, unless the lessor repudiates a substitute lease cannot cover precisely the same period of time as the original lease.

[51] UCC § 2A-518, cmt. 5.

[52] UCC § 2A-518, cmt. 7.

[53] The Article 2A general measure for cover damages is "the present value, as of the date of the commencement of the term of the new lease agreement, of the rent under the new lease agreement applicable to that period of the new lease term which is comparable to the then remaining term of the original lease agreement minus the present value as of the same date of the total rent for the then remaining lease term of the original lease agreement." UCC § 2A-518(2).

[54] UCC § 2A-518, cmt. 2.

[55] Article 2A is comparable. UCC § 2A-519(1), (2).

the market price for the goods and the contract price.[56] Even though the section does not measure damages as accurately as does cover, its inclusion is necessary because the cover measure is unavailable if the buyer does not cover or if it attempts to do so but the substitute transaction does not qualify for use under Section 2-712.[57] In the absence of cover, the drafters had to rely on the marketplace to determine damages.[58]

[1] Election

May a buyer that covers elect to ignore Section 2-712 and have its damages calculated under Section 2-713? The Code gives mixed signals. On the one hand, Section 2-711(1) states that an aggrieved buyer may cover and calculate damages under Section 2-712 or recover damages under Section 2-713. At least one noted commentator has read this to support giving a covering buyer a choice of measures.[59] On the other hand, the Comments to Section 2-713 indicate that the section "provides a remedy which is completely alternative to cover under the preceding section and applies only when and to the extent that the buyer has not covered."[60]

Obviously a buyer will argue for election only if market-based damages exceed cover damages. There is a strong policy reason for limiting a covering buyer to the damages provided by Section 2-712. The goal of the Code's remedies is to place an aggrieved party in the same economic position it would have occupied if the other party had fully performed,[61] and the cover measure does this with precision. Permitting a covering buyer to opt for a greater recovery would lead to overcompensation. The few cases on point have generally not allowed an election,[62] and the drafters of Article 2A made the same choice: Section 2A-519(1) provides that market-based damages are available only if "a lessee elects not to cover or a lessee elects to cover and the cover is by a lease

---

[56] UCC § 2-713(1). *See, e.g.*, Gawlick v. American Builders Supply, Inc., 519 P.2d 313, 13 UCC Rep. Serv. 1031 (N.M. Ct. App. 1974) (buyer entitled not only to return of purchase price of vehicle with defective title but also to difference between purchase price and market value of vehicle with clear title). The Article 2A formula is stated in terms of the difference between the present value of market rent less the present value of the original rent. UCC § 2A-519(1). Under both formulas, incidental and consequential damages are added, and expenses saved as a consequence of the breach are deducted. *See, e.g.*, Ralston Purina Co. v. McFarland, 550 F.2d 967, 21 UCC Rep. Serv. 136 (4th Cir. 1977) (incorrectly holding that seller could not introduce evidence of buyer expenses saved because buyer did not introduce evidence of incidental or consequential damages).

[57] Interior Elevator Co. v. Limmeroth, 278 Or. 589, 565 P.2d 1074, 22 UCC Rep. Serv. 69 (1977) (market-based damages available to buyer that did not cover).

[58] *See generally* Childres, *Buyer's Remedies: The Danger of 2-713*, 72 Nw. U. L. Rev. 837 (1978).

[59] *See* Peters, *Remedies for Breach of Contract Relating to the Sale of Goods Under the Uniform Commercial Code: A Roadmap for Article Two*, 73 Yale L.J. 199, 260 (1963) (buyer should be able to choose between cover and market-based measures).

[60] UCC § 2-713, cmt. 5.

[61] UCC § 1-305(a).

[62] *See, e.g.*, Cosden Oil & Chem. Co. v. Karl O. Helm Aktiengesellschaft, 736 F.2d 1064, 38 UCC Rep. Serv. 1645 (5th Cir. 1984) (buyer would not have been allowed to seek higher market-based damages but jury found that it had in fact not covered); Flood v. MP Clark, Inc., 335 F. Supp. 970 (E.D. Pa. 1971) (market-based damages not available if buyer has covered).

agreement that for any reason does not qualify for treatment under [the cover provision], or is by purchase or otherwise."

Neither Article 2 nor Article 2A requires an aggrieved buyer or lessee to cover, and each article contains a provision that preserves the right to other remedies for a party that chooses not to cover or enters into a nonqualifying substitute transaction.[63] Thus whether to cover is a business judgment.[64] In deciding whether to cover, consideration should be given to the fact that covering might mitigate consequential damages and that a failure to do so might limit or eliminate the right to recover such damages.[65]

[2]   Selecting the Market

With market price an essential element in the damages formula, there must be a means to identify the applicable market. Market identity can become complex in sales and lease transactions because tender of the goods and their receipt can occur at different times and places. Consequently, the drafters had to provide a means of identifying the appropriate place and time at which to determine market price. If it is difficult to prove the market price at the designated time and place, a court may consider evidence of the price in a comparable market or at a reasonable time before or after the designated time.[66]

[a]   Place

Under both Articles 2 and 2A, "[m]arket price is to be determined as of the place for tender or, in cases of rejection after arrival or revocation of acceptance, as of the place of arrival."[67] The reasoning behind this choice is stated in the Comments: "The general baseline adopted in this section uses as a yardstick the market in which the buyer would have obtained cover had he sought that relief."[68] The drafters thus made assumptions about where a buyer would cover in a case in which the seller and buyer are located in different markets. If the goods arrive and are then rejected, if they arrive and are accepted but acceptance is subsequently revoked, or if a seller fails to ship goods under a destination contract or they are lost or destroyed in transit pursuant to such a contract,[69] the assumption is that the buyer would cover in its local

---

[63] UCC §§ 2-712(3), 2A-518(3). The Comments to these sections stress that cover is not mandatory. UCC §§ 2-712, cmt. 3, 2A-518, cmt. 1.

[64] "The decision to cover is a function of commercial judgment, not a statutory mandate replete with sanctions for failure to comply." UCC § 2A-518, cmt. 1.

[65] UCC § 2-715(2)(a), discussed § 8.02[E][2] *infra; see also* Neal-Cooper Grain Co. v. Texas Gulf Sulphur Co., 508 F.2d 283, 16 UCC Rep. Serv. 7 (7th Cir. 1974) (failure by buyer to cover does not bar any remedy except consequential damages that could have been prevented).

[66] UCC § 2-723(2).

[67] UCC §§ 2-713(2), 2A-519(2).

[68] UCC § 2-713, cmt. 1.

[69] In a destination contract, tender of the goods occurs after they reach their destination. By contrast, in a shipment contract tender occurs at the place from which the goods are shipped. Destination and shipment contracts are discussed in § 4.04[C] *supra.*

market because it would not have time to wait for a reshipment of goods from the seller's market. On the other hand, if a seller breaches by repudiation or by not properly tendering the goods to a carrier under a shipment contract, the assumption is that, with time for shipment still available, the buyer would most likely return to the seller's market for a cover transaction.

The validity of the drafters' assumptions is debatable. They are speculative in that they hypothesize a cover transaction that the aggrieved buyer or lessee did not pursue. On the other hand, the drafters felt the need to articulate principles to prevent aggrieved parties from simply "market shopping." Because cover is the preferred remedy, they sought to approximate, to the extent possible, the damages that would have resulted if a qualifying cover transaction had occurred.

The court in *Bliss Produce Co. v. A. E. Albert & Sons, Inc.*[70] ignored the clear language of the statute and instead followed the rationale articulated by the Comments. The contract required an Arizona seller to deliver goods to a North Carolina buyer under a shipment contract, meaning that tender was to occur in Arizona and, unless the goods reached North Carolina, that was the market for determining price. The seller failed to ship the potatoes. The court used the market value in North Carolina, reasoning that potatoes do not grow in Arizona and therefore the buyer most likely would have covered locally. The decision is interesting and might even have produced a more fair result; however, the statute is mandatory and the Comments merely provide its rationale, not a basis for deviating from it.

The drafters' assumptions can affect more than simply a determination of the market price for the goods: They can also affect a determination of transportation costs, perhaps requiring a downward adjustment to the damages because of expenses saved as a result of the breach. An aggrieved buyer that, after arrival, rejects or revokes acceptance of goods delivered under a shipment contract would presumably cover in the local market and thus should be deemed to have saved the expense of transporting the goods from the seller's market. If the goods had not been shipped, the buyer presumably would have covered in the seller's market and, as it would not have saved transportation expenses, no adjustment would be made.[71]

[b] Time

Section 2-713(1) provides that market price is to be determined "at the time when the buyer learned of the breach."[72] Just as the rules determining the relevant market are intended to approximate the market in which a hypothetical cover transaction would occur, the rule governing the relevant time is intended to approximate the time of such a cover transaction. A buyer cannot cover until it is aware of the breach and presumably will do so shortly thereafter.

---

[70] 35 Agric. Dec. 742, 20 UCC Rep. Serv. 917 (1976).

[71] The court in *Productora E Importadora De Papel, S.A. De C.V. v. Fleming*, 376 Mass. 826, 383 N.E.2d 1129, 25 UCC Rep. Serv. 729 (1979), misapplied the provision by deducting transportation costs even though the goods were never shipped under a shipment contract.

[72] UCC § 2-713(1).

The rule has led to considerable confusion in cases of anticipatory repudiation.[73] Does a buyer learn of the breach when it learns of the repudiation, or do "breach" and "repudiation" mean different things in this context such that a buyer cannot learn of the breach until the time for performance has arrived?

Section 2-723 suggests that, in cases of anticipatory repudiation, the drafters may have had different times in mind. The section provides:

> If an action based on anticipatory repudiation comes to trial before the time for performance with respect to some or all of the goods, any damages based on market price (Section 2-708 or Section 2-713) shall be determined according to the price of such goods prevailing at the time when the aggrieved party learned of the repudiation.[74]

The section is superfluous if "learned of the breach" in Section 2-713(1) means the same thing as "learned of the repudiation." Furthermore, to be consistent with the seller's analogous remedy, which is stated in Section 2-708, the language in Section 2-713 would have to mean the time for the seller's performance.[75] Despite the strong arguments in its favor, however, few courts have adopted this interpretation.[76]

A number of courts have held that "learned of the breach" means the same thing as "learned of the repudiation."[77] Although problematic in light of Section 2-723, the interpretation is conceptually sound. Section 2-609(1) provides that a contract for sale imposes an obligation not to impair the expectations of the other party and a repudiation constitutes a breach of this obligation. A buyer learns of this breach when it learns of the repudiation.

Yet a third approach has evolved in some courts: The market is measured a commercially reasonable time after the buyer learns of the repudiation.[78] The approach cannot be called an interpretation because the language of Section 2-713(1) cannot reasonably yield the desired result, but arguably it leads to fairer

---

[73] *See generally* Jackson, *Anticipatory Repudiation and the Temporal Element of Contract Law: An Economic Inquiry into Contract Damages in Cases of Prospective Nonperformance*, 31 Stan. L. Rev. 69, 104-06 (1978); Sebert, *Remedies Under Article Two of the Uniform Commercial Code: An Agenda for Review*, 130 U. Pa. L. Rev. 360, 372-73 (1981).

[74] UCC § 2-723(1).

[75] Section 2-708(1) measures the market price for the seller's damages at the time and place for tender. *See* § 9.02[B][1] *infra.*

[76] *See, e.g.,* Hess Energy, Inc. v. Lightning Oil Co. Ltd., 338 F.3d 357, 51 UCC Rep. Serv. 2d 1 (4th Cir. 2003) (holding that repudiation under the Code is distinct from breach and date for measuring market is date for performance); Cargill, Inc. v. Stafford, 533 F.2d 1222 (10th Cir. 1977) (in the absence of clearer statutory intent, using time of performance is appropriate because it corresponds to common-law approach); *see also* Roth Steel Prods. v. Sharon Steel Corp., 705 F.2d 134 (6th Cir. 1983).

[77] *See, e.g.,* Chronister Oil Co. v. UNOCAL Refining & Marketing, 34 F.3d 462, 24 UCC Rep. Serv. 2d 485 (7th Cir. 1994); Neal-Cooper Grain Co. v. Texas Gulf Sulphur Co., 508 F.2d 283, 16 UCC Rep. Serv. 7 (7th Cir. 1974); Fredonia Broadcasting Corp., Inc. v. RCA Corp., 481 F.2d 781, 12 UCC Rep. Serv. 1088 (5th Cir. 1973).

[78] *See, e.g.,* Cosden Oil & Chem. Co. v. Karl O. Helm Aktiengesellschaft, 736 F.2d 1064, 38 UCC Rep. Serv. 1645 (5th Cir. 1984).

outcomes. The justification for the approach is that it is consistent with and reinforces a right afforded a party responding to a repudiation. Section 2-610(a) provides that, for a commercially reasonable period of time, an aggrieved party may await performance by the repudiating party.[79] The aggrieved party may choose to wait in the hope that the repudiating party will change its mind and may even encourage it to do so, and during the delay the repudiating party may retract the repudiation and thereby reinstate the contract.[80] Fixing market damages before the end of a commercially reasonable time after the repudiation has the effect of undermining the incentive to pursue the option of waiting.

A commercially reasonable time might be quite short, measured perhaps in hours. For example, *Oloffson v. Coomer*[81] involved a forward contract in which a farmer agreed to sell the buyer a quantity of corn to be delivered after the harvest. The planting season was exceptionally wet and the farmer notified the buyer that he could not get his planting done and thus would not fulfill his contractual commitments. The contract did not require the corn to be grown by the farmer, and thus he was not excused from his delivery obligation.[82] Rather than covering quickly, the buyer waited to do so until the delivery date, which was several months later and at a time when the prices were higher. The court determined that the cover transaction did not occur within a reasonable time and limited the buyer to market-based damages. It held that under Section 2-713(1) the market is to be measured a commercially reasonable time after the buyer learns of the repudiation, but given the definiteness of the farmer's repudiation, which indicated that waiting would be futile, and the ready availability of corn in the commodities market, the commercially reasonable time was only a few hours. The measuring date used by the court was the date of the repudiation.

[3]   Relation to Code's General Remedial Policy

Occasionally the damages yielded by Section 2-713 will be disproportionately high in relation to the damages needed to satisfy the Code's general remedial policy, which is to place an aggrieved party in the same economic position it would have occupied if the contract had been performed.[83] When that occurs, the court must decide whether to award the buyer the full market-based measure of damages or to reduce them to an amount consistent with the policy. The argument for reducing the damages is obvious: It advances a fundamental Code policy. The argument for allowing the buyer the full market-based measure of damages is that Section 2-713 functions to provide statutory liquidated damages. Courts have split on the issue.

In *TexPar Energy, Inc. v. Murphy Oil USA, Inc.*,[84] the buyer contracted to purchase 15,000 tons of asphalt at $53 per ton, and on the same day it contracted

---

[79] UCC § 2-610(a).

[80] *See* § 7.07[B][2] *supra.*

[81] 11 Ill. App. 3d 918, 296 N.E.2d 871, 12 UCC Rep. Serv. 1082 (1973).

[82] *See* § 7.08[D][1][a] *supra.*

[83] UCC § 1-305(a).

[84] 45 F.3d 1111, 25 UCC Rep. Serv. 2d 759 (7th Cir. 1995); *see also* Tongish v. Thomas, 251 Kan. 728, 840 P.2d 471, 20 UCC Rep. Serv. 2d 936 (1992).

to sell the asphalt for $56 per ton. The buyer thus stood to gain $3 per ton. The price of asphalt rose to $80 per ton and the seller refused to make delivery. Eventually, the buyer arranged for the seller and the ultimate buyer to negotiate directly, and this resulted in the seller agreeing to sell the asphalt to the ultimate buyer for $68.50 per ton. The buyer agreed to reimburse the ultimate buyer for the additional $12.50 per ton that it had to pay, and thus the amount necessary to place the buyer in the same position it would have occupied if there had been no breach was $15.50 per ton ($12.50 for the cost of reimbursing the ultimate buyer plus $3 profit). The buyer sought instead the difference between the $80 market value and the contract price, or $27 per ton. The seller argued that giving the full market-based measure would constitute a windfall for the buyer, but the court was persuaded otherwise. It reasoned that awarding damages based on the market price would discourage sellers from repudiating their contracts in rising markets and would promote uniformity and predictability in commercial transactions. In effect, Section 2-713 operated as a statutory liquidated-damages provision.

The court in *Allied Canners & Packers, Inc. v. Victor Packing Co.*[85] reached the opposite conclusion. The seller was obligated to deliver a large quantity of raisins at 29.75 cents per pound minus a 4% discount, and the buyer contracted to resell the raisins at 29.75 cents per pound. Thus, the buyer stood to gain only the 4% discount, and its total anticipated profit was roughly $4,500. Due to heavy rains, the market price rose to 87 cents per pound and the seller breached. The buyer did not cover and this ordinarily would have exposed it to a damages claim from the ultimate buyer, but it was protected by a hold-harmless clause in the contract. The buyer sued for damages based on the difference between the market price of 87 cents per pound and the contract price of 29.75 cents per pound, or a total of roughly $150,000. The court concluded that Section 2-713 does not operate as a statutory liquidated-damages provision and limited the buyer's recovery to its lost profits.

[D]   Damages When Buyer Accepts the Goods [§ 2-714; § 2A-519(3), (4)]

Damages measured by the cover/contract or market/contract price differential are alternative methods of protecting a buyer's expectation interest in cases in which the buyer has not accepted the goods, or has accepted them and later justifiably revoked its acceptance. The remedy differs if a buyer accepts goods and does not revoke its acceptance.[86] A consequence of acceptance is that the buyer must pay at the contract rate, and this is true even if the tender was nonconforming and the buyer could have rejected the goods.[87] An aggrieved buyer that accepts and does not revoke acceptance cannot cancel

---

[85] 162 Cal. App. 3d 905, 209 Cal. Rptr. 60, 39 UCC Rep. Serv. 1567 (Cal. Ct. App. 1984).

[86] *Cf.* Kelly v. Olinger Travel Homes, Inc., 200 Or. App. 635, 117 P.3d 282, 59 UCC Rep. Serv. 2d 1173 (2005) (buyers who justifiably revoked acceptance of motor home did not have a cause of action under UCC § 2-714).

[87] UCC § 2-607(1); *see* § 7.03[B][2] *supra.*

the contract,[88] and since it has a duty to pay at the contract rate it cannot recover any part of the price that has been paid. The buyer's remedy is limited to a claim for monetary damages.

[1] Recovery of Ordinary Loss

Section 2-714(1), which provides a broad basis for recovering damages in the case of accepted goods, states as follows:

> Where the buyer has accepted goods and given notification (subsection (3) of Section 2-607) he may recover as damages for any non-conformity of tender the loss resulting in the ordinary course of events from the seller's breach as determined in any manner which is reasonable.[89]

In addition, incidental and consequential damages may be recovered.[90]

The measure covers any nonconformity related to tender.[91] For example, a seller's failure to make timely delivery constitutes a nonconformity of tender, as does a seller's failure to comply with shipping instructions.[92] It would appear that a tender of nonconforming goods also falls within the scope of the provision, but another provision — Section 2-714(2) — states the measure of recovery in such a case.[93]

[2] Breach of Warranty

[a] The Standard Formula

A buyer's recovery for a breach of warranty is calculated as follows:

> The measure of damages for breach of warranty is the difference at the time and place of acceptance between the value of the goods as accepted and the value they would have had if they had been as warranted, unless special circumstances show proximate damages of a different amount.[94]

---

[88] UCC § 2-711(1).

[89] UCC § 2-714(1). The Article 2A provision is comparable. UCC § 2A-519(3).

[90] UCC § 2-714(3).

[91] "The 'non-conformity' referred to in subsection (1) includes not only breaches of warranties but also any failure of the seller to perform according to his obligations under the contract." UCC § 2-714, cmt. 2.

[92] *See* Arcon Constr. Co. v. South Dakota Cement Plant, 349 N.W.2d 407 (S.D. 1984) (in action for failure to deliver concrete in timely manner brought by highway builder, court measured damages by rental value of equipment idled as a result of delay).

[93] *See* § 8.02[D][2] *infra*. An occasional court deciding a breach of warranty case with facts that do not fit within the standard formula of UCC § 2-714(2) has cited UCC § 2-714(1) as controlling. *See, e.g.*, Hill v. BASF Wyandotte, 280 S.C. 174, 311 S.E.2d 734, 38 UCC Rep. Serv. 1254 (S.C. 1984); Triple E, Inc. v. Hendrix & Dail, Inc., 344 S.C. 186, 543 S.E.2d 245, 43 UCC Rep. Serv. 2d 533 (S.C. Ct. App. 2001). It is not clear why the courts did not instead cite the "special circumstances" language at the end of UCC § 2-714(2) and discussed in § 8.02[D][2][c] *infra*.

[94] UCC § 2-714(2). Article 2A is comparable. UCC § 2A-519(4).

Stated another way, the standard formula is the difference in the value the goods should have had and the value they actually have.[95] An aggrieved buyer may also recover incidental and consequential damages.[96]

The contract price is strong evidence of the value the goods would have had if they had been as warranted.[97] Using the contract price recognizes the tendency of parties that bargain during the contract formation process to gravitate towards a price that reflects market values.[98] The contract price is not conclusive and,[99] for example, a buyer that can establish that the value of the goods would have exceeded the contract price if they had been as warranted is entitled to the benefit of its bargain. Thus, in *Chatlos Systems, Inc. v. National Cash Register Corp.*,[100] the court affirmed an award of damages that was more than four times the total contract price of roughly $46,000. The market value of a computer that would have performed as warranted was determined to be roughly $207,000, while the actual value of the defective computer was only $6,000. The buyer was entitled to roughly $201,000 in damages.

If at the time of tender the market value of conforming goods is less than the contract price, a buyer will usually be better off rejecting nonconforming goods.[101] Rejection enables the buyer to use the fortuity of the seller's breach to escape a bad bargain; with acceptance, damages will be based on the difference between the lower market value of conforming goods and the actual value of the accepted goods.

A common method used to establish the difference in value between the goods as warranted and as delivered is to prove the cost to repair the nonconformity.[102] Proof of the cost of repair shows the expenditure needed to give the buyer goods that conform to the contract.[103] Adjustments sometimes will be necessary in this

---

[95] JHC Ventures, L.P. v. Fast Trucking, Inc., 94 S.W.3d 762, 49 UCC Rep. Serv. 2d 167 (Tex. Ct. App. 2002) (because belly-dump door on dump trucks purchased with dual-dump feature did not operate but the back-dump feature did work, evidence showing the value of back-dump trucks was admissible to establish the value of the goods as delivered).

[96] UCC § 2-714(3).

[97] Arcor, Inc. v. Textron, Inc., 960 F.2d 710, 17 UCC Rep. Serv. 2d 475 (7th Cir. 1992) (contract price is evidence of fair market value of the goods if they had been as warranted).

[98] Heersema v. Dave Altman's R.V. Centers, Inc., 57 UCC Rep. Serv. 2d 728 (Cal. Ct. App. 2005) (unpublished) (although the buyer argued that market value should be manufacturer's suggested retail price rather than lesser amount actually paid by buyer, court ruled otherwise because seller's willingness to sell at actual price without any haggling suggested that true market value might have been even lower).

[99] Canterra Petroleum, Inc. v. Western Drilling & Mining Supply, 418 N.W.2d 267, 5 UCC Rep. Serv. 2d 1002 (N.D. 1987) (contract price may be strong but not conclusive evidence of value of goods).

[100] 670 F.2d 1304, 33 UCC Rep. Serv. 934 (3d Cir. 1982).

[101] Courts have held that a buyer that uses a minor nonconformity as a pretext for rejection when its real motivation is to avoid a bad bargain is in breach of the duty of good faith. *See* § 7.04[2] *supra*.

[102] Nelson v. Logan Motor Sales, Inc., 370 S.E.2d 734, 7 UCC Rep. Serv. 2d 116 (W. Va. 1988) (buyer's repair bills admissible); Jones v. Abriani, 169 Ind. App. 556, 350 N.E.2d 635, 19 UCC Rep. Serv. 1102 (1976) (estimated cost of repairs).

[103] Fassi v. Auto Wholesalers of Hookset, 145 N.H. 404, 762 A.2d 1034, 43 UCC Rep. Serv. 2d 291 (N.H. 2000) (seller contended that award of $2,000 for faulty transmission constituted windfall for

approach, however, to achieve the aim of placing the buyer in the same position it would have occupied if the seller had not breached. If repair will not make the goods the equivalent of conforming, unrepaired goods, damages measured solely by the cost of repair will undercompensate the buyer. The buyer should recover an additional amount that reflects the difference in value between conforming goods and the repaired goods.[104] A buyer alternatively might be overcompensated through repair, as when used goods are repaired with new parts and the useful life of the goods is extended. In such a case, the buyer's damages should be adjusted downward to adjust for the additional benefit.[105]

If the cost-to-repair method of valuation is not available because the goods cannot be repaired, an aggrieved buyer must take a different approach. With deficiencies so extensive that the goods essentially have no viable use, salvage value can be used to establish actual value.[106] If the nonconforming goods have more than salvage value, actual value might be established by resale.[107] In other cases, an aggrieved buyer will have to establish actual value through it own testimony or the testimony of an expert witness.[108] Although most courts recognize that the owner of personal property generally may testify as to its market value, most consumer buyers fail in the effort because they are unable to establish an adequate foundation of personal knowledge to support their lay assessment.[109]

---

buyers because they could still operate vehicle and court did not require them to use award to make repair; court properly ruled that the buyers were entitled to the benefit of their bargain, they presented valid evidence to show that cost of repair would be $2,000, and upon receiving award they would not be obligated to actually make repair); GFSI, Inc. v. J-Loong Trading, Ltd., 505 F. Supp. 2d 935 (D. Kan. 2007) (because defective polo shirts shrank by a full size, buyer's cost of repair was properly based on its expenditures for labels, having shirts re-labeled, color pressing, and freight).

[104] *See, e.g.,* Hartzell v. Justius Co., Inc., 693 F.2d 770, 34 UCC Rep. Serv. 1594 (8th Cir. 1982); Soo Line Ry. Co. v. Fruehauf Corp., 547 F.2d 1365, 20 UCC Rep. Serv. 1181 (8th Cir. 1977).

[105] *See, e.g.,* Tennessee Carolina Transp., Inc. v. Strick Corp., 283 N.C. 423, 196 S.E.2d 711, 12 UCC Rep. Serv. 1055 (1973) (court should instruct jury that damages under Section 2-714 should be reduced by the amount, if any, by which repairs enhanced value of goods).

[106] *See, e.g.,* Massey-Ferguson Credit Corp. v. Webber, 841 F.2d 1245, 6 UCC Rep. Serv. 2d 63 (4th Cir. 1988).

[107] *See, e.g.,* ITT-Industrial Credit Co. v. Mile Concrete Co., Inc., 31 N.C. App. 450, 229 S.E.2d 814, 20 UCC Rep. Serv. 1067 (1976) (resale price constituted some evidence of value of goods); HCI Chems. (USA), Inc. v. Henkel KGaA, 966 F.2d 1018, 18 UCC Rep. Serv. 2d 436 (5th Cir. 1992) (contract price was evidence of fair market value of goods if they had been as warranted and resale price was evidence of fair market value of goods as delivered).

[108] Sawyer v. Mercedes-Benz USA, LLC, 2007 Cal. App. Unpub. LEXIS 5885 (June 20, 2007) (buyer's expert witness based his opinion regarding diminished value of vehicle on his years of experience in automobile industry, the repair records, and Kelly Blue Book values).

[109] *See, e.g.,* Razor v. Hyundai Motor Am., 222 Ill. 2d 75, 854 N.E.2d 607, 58 UCC Rep. Serv. 2d 961 (2006) (overturning jury award on the grounds that it was conjecture and speculation given buyer's failure to establish a sufficient basis for award); Monroe v. Hyundai Motor Am., Inc., 270 Ga. App. 477, 606 S.E.2d 894 (2004) (because buyer's testimony did not indicate that his past vehicle purchases included vehicles with the same purported defects, his testimony was only his opinion on the value of the car to him and not on the impact of the defect on the fair market value of the vehicle). Buyer's attorney in *Deitrick v. National RV, Inc.*, 2007 Cal. App. Unpub. LEXIS 8708 (Oct. 29, 2007), asked buyer: "How have the water leaks in the motor home decreased the value of this motor home to you?" The relevant inquiry is the fair market value of the goods in their defective condition, not the subjective value of the goods to the buyer.

[b]   Time and Place for Valuation

The standard formula for measuring breach-of-warranty damages provides that the difference in values should be determined "at the time and place of acceptance."[110] This represents the time and place at which the buyer gains control and use of the goods. Considerable time may pass between the time a buyer enters into a contract and the time of acceptance and thus, as the court in *Chatlos Systems, Inc. v. National Cash Register Corp.*[111] pointed out, the difference in value between the goods as warranted and as accepted may increase between the time they are ordered and the time they are tendered. Of course, the converse is true as well.

[c]   Special Circumstances

The standard formula for breach-of-warranty damages applies "unless special circumstances show proximate damages of a different amount."[112] Courts have used the special-circumstances provision most frequently to deviate from the time of tender as the appropriate time for determining the applicable values. For example, if a buyer does not discover a defect until after acceptance, some courts have measured the value of the goods as accepted at the time the buyer discovered or should have discovered the breach rather than at the time of tender.[113] This approach generally increases the buyer's recovery because the goods usually depreciate in value. The Comments provide the following guidance: "If the non-conformity is such as would justify revocation of acceptance, the time and place of acceptance under this section is determined as of the buyer's decision not to revoke."[114]

Courts also have found special circumstances when there is a breach of the warranty of title. These cases generally measure the value of the goods if they had been as warranted as of the time the buyer has to give them up[115] because this approach most accurately reflects the buyer's actual loss. If the goods have depreciated in value after acceptance, the buyer has enjoyed their use until relinquishment and thus should be compensated only for the remaining lost value.[116] If the goods have appreciated in value, as often happens with art

---

[110] UCC § 2-714(2); *see, e.g.,* Maybery v. Volkswagen of Am., Inc., 271 Wis. 2d 258, 678 N.W.2d 357, 52 UCC Rep. Serv. 2d 912 (Ct. App. 2004), *aff'd* 278 Wis. 2d 38, 692 N.W.2d 226, 56 UCC Rep. Serv. 2d 214 (2005) (lower court committed error because valuations must be made at time and place of acceptance of defective vehicle, not at later time at which buyer traded in vehicle).

[111] 670 F.2d 1304, 33 UCC Rep. Serv. 934 (3d Cir. 1982).

[112] UCC § 2-714(2).

[113] *See, e.g.,* Harlan v. Smith, 507 So. 2d 943, 4 UCC Rep. Serv. 2d 1452 (Ala. Ct. App. 1986) (mobile home valued as of time buyer discovered defects).

[114] UCC § 2-714, cmt. 3; *see, e.g.,* Smith v. Penbridge Assoc., Inc., 440 Pa. Super. 410, 655 A.2d 1015, 26 UCC Rep. Serv. 2d 273 (1995) (court used increased value of a purported breeding pair of emus on date buyer first discovered that both emus were male).

[115] *See, e.g.,* Itoh v. Kimi Sales, 74 Misc. 2d 402, 345 N.Y.S.2d 416, 13 UCC Rep. Serv. 64 (Cir. Ct. 1973) (automobile valued as of time it was taken from buyers by police).

[116] *See, e.g.,* Metalcraft, Inc. v. Pratt, 65 Md. Ct. App. 281, 500 A.2d 329, 42 UCC Rep. Serv. 14 (1985) (value of goods on date of dispossession even though effects of depreciation made goods less valuable than when accepted).

objects, basing value on the time of relinquishment appropriately gives the buyer the benefit of the appreciation.[117]

[E] Incidental and Consequential Damages [§ 2-715; § 2A-520]

In addition to the ordinary damage measures of Sections 2-712 through 2-714, an aggrieved buyer may recover incidental and, in appropriate circumstances, consequential damages.[118] Even though the Code provides that an aggrieved buyer is entitled to both types of damages, distinguishing between them is sometimes important. One reason is that economic consequential damages are subject to a foreseeability test that limits their availability whereas incidental damages are not subject to the test. Also, sellers often exclude consequential damages but frequently fail to do the same for incidental damages.[119]

[1] Incidental Damages

Section 2-715(1) describes a buyer's incidental damages as follows:

> Incidental damages resulting from the seller's breach include expenses reasonably incurred in inspection, receipt, transportation and care and custody of goods rightfully rejected, any commercially reasonable charges, expenses or commissions in connection with effecting cover and any other reasonable expense incident to the delay or other breach.[120]

Although illustrative only,[121] the list is fairly comprehensive.

Incidental damages must result from a seller's breach, and this is another way of saying that they must be a consequence of the breach. Thus, they may be thought of as a subset of consequential damages. The Code creates a separate category for them because economic consequential damages are subject to a foreseeability test based on the famous English case of *Hadley v. Baxendale*[122] whereas incidental damages are not. As discussed below,[123] *Hadley* bifurcates damages into those that occur naturally and those that occur because of the buyer's circumstances. The foreseeability test applies only to the latter category

---

[117] *See, e.g.,* Jeanneret v. Vichey, 541 F. Supp. 80, 34 UCC Rep. Serv. 56 (S.D.N.Y. 1982) (proper to fix damages based on appreciated value of painting); Menzel v. List, 24 N.Y.2d 91, 298 N.Y.S.2d 979, 246 N.E.2d 742, 6 UCC Rep. Serv. 330 (1969) (buyer forced to give up painting entitled to use $22,500 as value of painting than $4,000 paid for it more than ten years earlier).

[118] UCC §§ 2-712(2) (cover), 2-713(1) (market price/contract price differential), 2-714(3) (accepted goods); *see also* Quality Business Forms of Minneapolis, Inc. v. Secured Choice, Inc., 51 UCC Rep. Serv. 2d 447 (Minn. Ct. App. 2003) (unpublished) (contrary to seller's position, UCC § 2-714(2) entitled buyer to consequential damages in the form of lost profits in addition to direct damages).

[119] For a discussion of the enforceability of a term excluding consequential damages, see § 5.04[B], [C] *supra.*

[120] Article 2A is comparable. UCC § 2A-520(1).

[121] UCC § 2-715, cmt. 1.

[122] 156 Eng. Rep. 145 (Ex. 1854).

[123] *See* § 8.02[E][2] *infra.*

whereas incidental damages are so common and predictable that they belong in the former category.

Incidental damages include only expenses, charges, and commissions, and a consequence of this limitation is that lost opportunities, such as lost profits, do not qualify and must be recovered, if at all, as consequential damages. Incidental damages include costs imposed on a buyer by a seller's breach, such as the mandatory duties with respect to tendered goods that a buyer must assume following a rightful rejection or justifiable revocation of acceptance.[124] Incidental damages also include costs that a buyer incurs in order to exercise its own rights, either under the contract itself or in pursuit of an appropriate remedy. Damages in the former category include the cost of inspecting goods that are rightfully rejected;[125] damages in the latter category include the cost of arranging for a cover transaction.[126]

[2]   Consequential Damages

Section 2-715(2) provides for consequential damages as follows:

> Consequential damages resulting from the seller's breach include
>
> (a)   any loss resulting from general or particular requirements and needs of which the seller at the time of contracting had reason to know and which could not reasonably be prevented by cover or otherwise; and
>
> (b)   injury to person or property proximately resulting from any breach of warranty.[127]

Consequential damages are losses resulting from a seller's breach that are neither within the definition of incidental damages nor within the ordinary damage measures of Sections 2-712 through 2-714. As noted above,[128] the court in *Hadley* distinguished between two types of damages: Those that occur

---

[124] *See* UCC §§ 2-602(2) (general duties upon rejection), 2-608(3) (upon revocation of acceptance, buyer has same general duties as if it had rejected), 2-603 (special duties of merchant buyer); §§ 7.04[B][3] (rejection), 7.04[B] (revocation of acceptance) *supra*; *see also* Lanners v. Whitney, 247 Or. 223, 429 P.2d 398, 4 UCC Rep. Serv. 369 (1967) (buyer who revoked acceptance of airplane entitled to recover money spent to preserve it); Indeck Energy Serv., Inc. v. NRG Energy, Inc., 54 UCC Rep. Serv. 2d 990 (N.D. Ill. 2004) (costs to re-ship goods, prepare them for storage, and store them).

[125] The inclusion of this expense is consistent with UCC § 2-513(2), which provides that "[e]xpenses of inspection must be borne by the buyer but may be recovered from the seller if the goods do not conform and are rejected."

[126] *See, e.g.*, Happy Dack Trading Co. Ltd. v. Agro-Indus., Inc., 602 F. Supp. 986, 41 UCC Rep. Serv. 1718 (S.D.N.Y. 1984) (inspection costs included buyer's travel and testing expenses); Consolidated Data Terminals v. Applied Digital Data Sys., Inc., 708 F.2d 385, 36 UCC Rep. Serv. 59 (9th Cir. 1983) (expenses incurred in inspecting, shipping, handling, and storing defective computer terminals). *But see* Fryatt v. Lantana One, Ltd., 866 So. 2d 158, 53 UCC Rep. Serv. 2d 543 (Fla. Dist. Ct. App. 2004) (buyer of computer system could not recover for value of services of employee who tried to get system to operate properly because buyer never showed how employee's productivity had been affected or whether buyer incurred a loss).

[127] Article 2A is comparable. UCC § 2A-520(2).

[128] *See* § 8.02[E][1] *supra*.

naturally and in the ordinary course from the breach such that they should be anticipated no matter the circumstances of the aggrieved party, and those that occur from the breach because of the aggrieved party's circumstances. The Code's ordinary damage measures implement, in a rough way, the "naturally occurring" side of *Hadley*. Evidence of this may be found in the statement in Section 2-714(1) that, in the case of accepted goods, damages for nonconformity of tender are "the loss *resulting in the ordinary course of events* from the seller's breach."[129] Recovery under an ordinary measure does not require a showing that the seller had any information about the buyer's circumstances.

For losses that fall outside the ordinary measures, Section 2-715(2)(a) limits liability by requiring that they result from general or particular requirements or needs of the buyer that the seller had reason to know of at the time of contracting.[130] The seller need not have knowledge of the buyer's circumstances, although that is typically the case.[131] Indeed, the Comments make clear that the potential for damages need not have been within the actual contemplation of the parties at all by stating that "[i]t is not necessary that there be a conscious acceptance of an insurer's liability on the seller's part, nor is his obligation for consequential damages limited to cases in which he fails to use due effort in good faith."[132] In practical effect, the reason-to-know test is a foreseeability requirement.[133]

Lost profits is the type of economic-loss claim most frequently litigated.[134] Courts also have allowed recovery for the cost of wasted labor in processing nonconforming goods,[135] restoration of a roof after removal of defective solar panels,[136] the cost of leasing software for use with a defective bookkeeping

---

[129] UCC § 2-714(1) (emphasis supplied).

[130] *Compare* Venture Indus. Corp. v. Himont U.S.A., Inc., 54 UCC Rep. Serv. 2d 161 (6th Cir. 2004) (buyer could not recover when it presented no evidence to show that seller had reason to know that buyer contemplated an extension of its contract with a third-party buyer), *with* Mississippi Chem. Corp. v. Dresser-Rand Co., 287 F.3d 359, 47 UCC Rep. Serv. 2d 244 (5th Cir. 2002) (seller had reason to know that malfunction in goods would cause ammonia plant to close and that ammonia was necessary for buyer's manufacturing process).

[131] *See, e.g.,* Sun Maid Raisin Growers v. Victor Packing Co., 146 Cal. App. 3d 787, 194 Cal. Rptr. 612, 37 UCC Rep. Serv. 148 (1983) (sellers knew that buyer was in business of reselling raisins and therefore was liable when its failure to provide raisins caused lost profits).

[132] UCC § 2-715, cmt. 3.

[133] *See, e.g.,* Precision Pine & Timber, Inc. v. U.S., 72 Fed. Cl. 460, 60 UCC Rep. Serv. 2d 1261 (2006) (it was foreseeable that stopping timber sale contracts with Forest Service would cause buyer to suffer lost profits).

[134] *See, e.g.,* Burrus v. Itek Corp., 46 Ill. App. 3d 350, 360 N.E.2d 1168, 21 UCC Rep. Serv. 1009 (1977) (lost profits established based on decrease in printing work following purchase of printing press); Franklin Grain & Supply Co v. Ingram, 44 Ill. App. 3d, 385 N.E.2d 922, 21 UCC Rep. Serv. 53 (1976) (loss of buyer's wheat crop due to late delivery of fertilizer).

[135] Atlantic Indus., Inc. v. O.E.M., Inc., 555 F. Supp. 184, 35 UCC Rep. Serv. 795 (W.D. Okla. 1983).

[136] Lanham v. Solar Am. of Cincinnati, Inc., 28 Ohio App. 3d 55, 501 N.E.2d 1245, 2 UCC. Rep. Serv. 2d 1545 (1986) (characterized by court as incidental damages).

machine,[137] loss of corollary sales,[138] and the cost of substitute accommodations during a delay in the delivery of a mobile home.[139] In the leading case of *Lewis v. Mobil Oil Corp.*,[140] the court held that the seller breached an implied warranty of fitness for a particular purpose by supplying an inappropriate oil for the buyer's hydraulic sawmill machinery. Problems persisted with the machinery over a long period of time until finally a more knowledgeable person in the seller's organization prescribed the correct oil. The court allowed the buyer to recover the profits it lost during the period when it used the inappropriate oil.

Consequential damages within the scope of Section 2-715(2)(a) are limited to those "which could not reasonably be prevented by cover or otherwise." This requirement reflects the basic mitigation principle under which damages are limited to those that the aggrieved party could not reasonably have avoided. The principle does not impose a duty on the buyer to mitigate, such as by entering a cover transaction; rather, it precludes the buyer from recovering for any part of the damages that could have been mitigated.[141] Mitigation most commonly occurs by cover, but the principle has been successfully invoked in other contexts.[142]

The foreseeability test does not apply if the loss takes the form of personal injury or property damage. Instead, the test for recovery is whether the harm was the proximate result of a breach of warranty.[143] The Comments explain as follows:

> Where the injury involved follows the use of goods without discovery of the defect causing the damage, the question of "proximate"cause turns on whether it was reasonable for the buyer to use the goods without such inspection as would have revealed the defects. If it was not reasonable for him to do so, or if he did in fact discover the defect prior to his use, the injury would not proximately result from the breach of warranty.[144]

---

[137] Acme Pump Co., Inc. v. National Cash Register Co., 32 Conn. Supp. 69, 337 A.2d 672, 16 UCC Rep. Serv. 1242 (1974).

[138] Migerobe, Inc. v. Certina USA, Inc., 924 F.2d 1330, 14 UCC Rep. Serv. 2d 59 (5th Cir. 1991).

[139] Long v. Quality Mobile Home Brokers, Inc., 248 S.E.2d 311, 25 UCC Rep. Serv. 470 (S.C. 1978).

[140] 438 F.2d 500, 8 UCC Rep. Serv. 625 (8th Cir. 1971).

[141] Hayes v. Hettinga, 228 N.W.2d 181, 16 UCC Rep. Serv. 983 (Iowa 1975) (buyer could not recover for lost profits because it failed to show the loss could not have been avoided by cover); Erection Specialists, Inc. v. Edward Deutz, Inc., 2005 U.S. Dist. LEXIS 33407 (E.D. Tenn., June 28, 2005) (buyer of crane failed to mitigate damages when it simply parked the crane, thereby allowing it to deteriorate because of neglect and non-use, whereas by expending $20,000 for a replacement engine, the buyer could have increased its annual revenue by $100,000 to $150,000).

[142] *See, e.g.*, V. Zappala & Co. v. Pyramid Co., 81 A.D.2d 983, 439 N.Y.S.2d 765 (1981) (buyer of discolored concrete blocks could not recover cost of coating blocks every five years after refusing seller's offer to replace defective blocks, as the refusal to accept replacements meant that the consequential damages were not proximately caused by the seller's breach); Chatlos Sys., Inc. v. National Cash Register Corp., 479 F. Supp. 738, 27 UCC Rep. Serv. 647 (D. N.J. 1979), *aff'd on other grounds*, 635 F.2d 1081 (3d Cir. 1980) (buyer refused to allow seller further access to computer to attempt to program it properly).

[143] UCC § 2-715(2)(b).

[144] UCC § 2-715, cmt. 5; Erdman v. Johnson Bros. Radio & TV Co., 260 Md. 190, 271 A.2d 744,

Personal injury and property damage are types of losses generally cognizable in tort, and limiting liability through a proximate-cause test is consistent with the strict-liability approach that underlies warranty liability.[145]

At common law, a buyer must prove consequential damages with a reasonable degree of certainty. Although the text of Section 2-715 does not include this requirement, it does not abrogate it and therefore the requirement supplements the certainty principle.[146] The Comments make clear that the certainty principle does not impose a technical standard of precise exactitude:

> The burden of proving the extent of loss incurred by way of consequential damage is on the buyer, but the section on liberal administration of remedies rejects any doctrine of certainty which requires almost mathematical precision in the proof of loss. Loss may be determined in any manner which is reasonable under the circumstances.[147]

The issue tends to have the most relevance in claims for lost profits[148] because the claims of buyers are sometimes sheer speculation.[149] Many courts apply the established-business rule, which limits recovery for lost profits to businesses with past experiences from which prospective profits can be extrapolated.[150] Today, most courts reject the idea that a lack of past experience is an absolute bar to recovering lost profits and instead follow an approach that assesses whether there is a rational basis for inferring an appropriate measure.[151] For

---

8 UCC Rep. Serv. 656 (1970) (buyer who had seen television set smoke and give off sparks but nevertheless left it plugged in could not hold seller liable for value of his house when set caught fire and burned the house).

[145] *See* discussion § 5.02[B][2] *supra*.

[146] UCC § 1-103.

[147] UCC § 2-715, cmt. 4.

[148] Courts also consider the issue in other contexts. *See, e.g.*, Hangzhou Silk Import & Export Corp. v. P.C.B. Internat'l Indus., Inc., 48 UCC Rep. Serv. 2d 1367 (S.D.N.Y. 2002) (consequential damages for loss of goodwill of buyer's retail customers allegedly caused by nonconforming garments delivered by defendant could not be recovered because buyer failed to show that termination of several of its retail accounts had anything to do with defendant's breach); H.A.S. of Fort Smith, LLC v. J.V. Mfg., Inc., 54 UCC Rep. Serv. 2d 1007 (Ark. Ct. App. 2004) (wages paid to employees who worked with seller in trying to correct defects in delivered equipment recoverable). Courts generally have denied recovery for factors like mental suffering. Carpel v. Saget Studios, Inc., 326 F. Supp. 1331, 9 UCC Rep. Serv. 82 (E.D. Pa. 1971) (no recovery for mental suffering for photographer's failure to deliver wedding pictures).

[149] General Supply & Equip. Co. v. Phillips, 490 S.W.2d 913, 12 UCC Rep. Serv. 35 (Tex. Ct. App. 1972) (florist speculated by estimating lost profits based on production and earnings per unit greater than he had ever realized).

[150] Gerwin v. Southeastern Cal. Ass'n of Seventh Day Adventists, 14 Cal. App. 3d 209, 92 Cal. Rptr. 111, 8 UCC Rep. Serv. 643 (1971) (lost profits could not be recovered for used bar equipment that buyer planned to use in a cocktail lounge because buyer did not have comparable business experience).

[151] Hardesty v. Andro Corp.–Webster Div., 555 P.2d 1030, 20 UCC Rep. Serv. 352 (Okla. 1976) (established profit experience of similar businesses); Corestar Internat'l Pte., Ltd v. LPB Communications, Inc, 2007 U.S. Dist. LEXIS 75324 (D.N.J., Oct. 10, 2007) (plaintiff's contracts for resale of goods that it agreed to purchase from supplier provided sufficient evidence to support its claim for lost profits).

example, in *Griffith v. Clear Lakes Trout Co., Inc.*,[152] the plaintiffs bought small trout from the defendant under a five-year contract that required them to raise the trout to market size and then sell them back to the defendant. Because of changes in the market for trout, the defendant insisted that they reach a larger size than required by the contract before it would accept them back. The delays required the plaintiffs to feed and care for the trout longer than anticipated and led to overcrowded conditions that stressed the trout, resulting in higher mortality rates than anticipated. The plaintiffs sued for lost profits for the fourth and fifth years of the contract and the appellate court affirmed the lower court's holding in their favor. The court accepted the comparative analysis that an accountant prepared using costs and mortality rates during the second and third years of the contract as sufficiently definite to support the plaintiffs' claim.

[F]   Breaching Buyer's Right to Restitution [§ 2-718(2)]

Section 2-718(2) deals with whether a buyer that makes a down payment[153] and then breaches in a manner that justifies the seller in withholding delivery may recover all or part of the down payment. In some instances, the seller will be entitled to all or part of the money because of an enforceable contract term liquidating damages.[154] Without such a term, two opposing principles are in play: Forfeitures are to be avoided, but a breaching party should be denied restitution. The Code strikes a compromise under which, subject to a seller's right to damages as liquidated or otherwise determined, the buyer may recover all but a statutorily defined portion of its down payment.

The statute allows the buyer to recover the amount by which its down payment exceeds either the amount established by an enforceable term liquidating damages[155] or the smaller of two sums: 1) $500, or 2) 20% of the value of the buyer's total performance under the contract.[156] In most instances, the value of the buyer's total performance will be the price of the goods in money, but sometimes a buyer will agree to pay with goods, other property, or services and the value of its performance will have to be determined.[157]

To illustrate the operation of Section 2-718(2), suppose that a buyer agrees to pay $5,000 for goods and gives the seller a $2,000 down payment. The buyer then repudiates and the seller, which has not yet delivered the goods, cancels the contract. If there is an enforceable term liquidating damages at $1,200, the

---

[152]   143 Ida. 733, 152 P.3d 604, 61 Serv. 2d 926 (2007).

[153]   The term used in the text is down payment, but the contract may instead used terms like prepayment or security deposit. If the down payment takes the form of goods that have been traded in and the seller resells them before it has notice of the buyer's breach, the amount received by the seller constitutes a down payment for purposes of UCC § 2-718(2). If the seller has notice of the buyer's breach while it still has the traded goods, it must resell them under the provisions of UCC § 2-706, which are discussed in § 9.01[A] *infra*.

[154]   Whether a term liquidating damages is enforceable or unenforceable as a penalty is discussed in § 9.07 *infra*.

[155]   UCC § 2-718(2)(a).

[156]   UCC § 2-718(2)(b).

[157]   "The price can be made payable in money or otherwise." UCC § 2-303(1).

buyer may recover $800 in restitution. If the term is unenforceable as a penalty or there is no such term, the buyer may recover in restitution the excess over the smaller of $500 or 20% of $5,000, which is $1,000. As $500 is smaller, the buyer may recover $1,500. It might simplify the formula to look at it this way: If the price of the goods is $2,500 or more, the seller may keep $500; if it is less than $2,500, the seller may keep 20% of the price.

A buyer's right to restitution is subject to offset to the extent the seller establishes a right to damages or establishes that it provided the buyer with a direct or indirect benefit under the contract. The right of offset may be illustrated by the facts of *Neri v. Retail Marine Corp.*,[158] where the buyer agreed to pay roughly $12,500 for a new boat and the repudiated after making a deposit of $4,250. The seller established that the breach caused a loss of roughly $3,250 and the court awarded the buyer roughly $1,000 — the amount of the deposit less the amount of the seller's damages. If the seller had not been able to establish damages, the buyer would have been entitled to restitution of roughly $3,750 — the amount of the deposit less $500.

§ 8.03   NONMONETARY REMEDIES

[A]   Cancellation [§ 2-711(1); § 2A-508(1)(a)]

Article 2 provides that " '[c]ancellation' occurs when either party puts an end to the contract for breach by the other."[159] Cancellation has the same effect as termination "except that the cancelling party also retains any remedy for breach of the whole contract or any unperformed balance."[160] An aggrieved buyer may both cancel the contract, thereby discharging its executory performance obligations, and recover money damages for the seller's breach.[161]

Cancellation is appropriate in any of the circumstances in which the seller's breach entitles the buyer to a refund of any part of the purchase price that has been paid.[162] The circumstances are those in which the buyer does not receive, or rightfully chooses not to retain, the goods; that is, cases in which the seller fails to deliver or repudiates, or the buyer rightfully rejects or justifiably revokes acceptance. A buyer may not cancel for nonconforming goods it has accepted and as to which it has not revoked acceptance, even if the nonconformity is substantial. In an installment contract, a seller's breach as to one or more installments does not justify cancellation as to subsequent installments unless the breach substantially impairs the value the whole contract.

---

[158] 30 N.Y.2d 393, 285 N.E.2d 311, 334 N.Y.S.2d 165 (1972).

[159] UCC § 2-106(4). Article 2A is comparable. UCC § 2A-103(1)(b).

[160] *Id.* " 'Termination' occurs when either party pursuant to a power created by agreement or law puts an end to the contract otherwise than for its breach." UCC § 2-106(3). Article 2A is comparable. UCC § 2A-103(1)(z); *see* Vending Credit Corp. v. Trudy Toys Co., 5 Conn. Cir. Ct. 629, 260 A.2d 135 (1969) (lessee required to exercise option to terminate lease agreement within time stipulated in lease agreement).

[161] Lanners v. Whitney, 247 Or. 223, 428 P.2d 398, 4 UCC Rep. Serv. 369 (1969).

[162] UCC §§ 2-711(1), 2A-508(1)(b); *see* § 8.02[A].

Although the Code is silent on the point, cancellation should also be available under common-law principles if the seller materially breaches the contract in a manner unrelated to the circumstances discussed above. Examples might include breaches related to installation or technical support obligations.

[B]   Specific Performance and Replevin [§ 2-716; § 2A-521]

Rather than monetary damages, buyers and lessees sometimes are entitled to delivery of the goods themselves through a decree of specific performance. Courts in their discretion may award specific performance under Articles 2 and 2A if "the goods are unique or in other proper circumstances."[163]

The requirement that the goods be unique perpetuates the traditional basis for granting a decree of specific performance. The remedy is equitable in nature and generally has not been granted when monetary damages can provide the aggrieved buyer with an adequate remedy at law, as is the case with ordinary goods. The Code expands on what is "unique," and the Comments explain the expansion as follows:

> In view of this Article's emphasis on the commercial feasibility of replacement, a new concept of what are "unique" goods is introduced under this section. Specific performance is no longer limited to goods which are already specific or ascertained at the time of contracting. The test of uniqueness under this section must be made in terms of the total situation which characterizes the contract.[164]

The drafters thus clearly rejected pre-Code cases in which the courts, perpetuating a meaning of unique that is consistent with one-of-a-kind heirlooms,[165] denied specific performance in cases of market shortages.[166] The intent is to make market realities a relevant consideration in requests for specific performance.[167] For example, when pollution control equipment failed to operate as warranted, the court in *Colorado-Ute Electrical Association v. Envirotech Corp.*[168] court rejected a monetary award based on the cost of a chemical additive that would bring performance up to state standards because of uncertainty about whether the state would continue to allow its use. The court instead awarded specific performance, finding that the equipment was unique and that the buyer

[163] UCC §§ 2-716(1), 2A-521(1).

[164] UCC § 2-716, cmt. 2.

[165] An Article 2 case consistent with this standard is *Gay v. Seafarer Fiberglass Yachts, Inc.*, 14 UCC Rep. Serv. 1335 (N.Y. Sup. Ct. 1974) (yacht with special hull design manufactured exclusively by defendant was unique).

[166] McAllister v. Patten, 214 Ark. 293, 215 S.W.2d 701 (1948) (dealer refusal to deliver promised new car during period of critical market shortages due to the war effort).

[167] S.W.B. New England, Inc., v. R.A.B. Food Group, LLC, 2008 U.S. Dist. LEXIS 14892 (S.D.N.Y., Feb. 27, 2008) (distributor established right to specific performance by showing that it tailored its business around supplier's dominant market brand and that other kosher-food brands were not adequate replacements in the relevant market).

[168] 524 F. Supp. 1152 (D. Colo. 1981).

would be harmed irreparably if it had to shut down because of a violation of clean-air standards.[169]

The Code further expands the circumstances in which specific performance is appropriate by authorizing the remedy in "other proper circumstances." The drafters did so with the explicit intent of liberalizing the availability of the remedy: "[W]ithout intending to impair in any way the exercise of the court's sound discretion in the matter, this Article seeks to further a more liberal attitude than some courts have shown in connection with the specific perfor-mance of contracts of sale."[170] Their only suggestion of what constitutes "other proper circumstances" is the cryptic indication that "inability to cover is strong evidence of 'other proper circumstances.' "[171]

Perhaps the most expansive application of the standard occurred in *Stephan's Machine & Tool, Inc. v. D & H Machinery Consultants, Inc.*[172] The seller breached a promise to deliver a replacement for defective machinery after the buyer made financial commitments for the purchase, and the buyer could not finance the purchase of a substitute. The court awarded specific performance because of the buyer's financial situation.

In *Laclede Gas Co. v. Amoco Oil Co.*,[173] the buyer successfully enjoined the seller from breaching a long-term supply contract for propane. Prices had risen dramatically as a result of an energy crisis and as a consequence the buyer could not find a seller that would enter into a substitute contract of comparable duration. The contract term, rather than the goods, was unique and the court considered this a proper circumstance in which to decree specific performance.

Although a decree of specific performance is within the discretion of the court, buyers may also be able to recover goods through an action in replevin. Section 2-716(3) provides that "[t]he buyer has a right to replevin for goods identified to the contract if after reasonable effort he is unable to effect cover for such goods or the circumstances reasonably indicate that such effort will be unavail-ing. . . ."[174] Unlike specific performance, replevin is a legal remedy and a buyer that cannot cover is entitled to it if the goods are identified.[175] An advantage of replevin is that it is a pre-judgment remedy that is simpler and less expensive to obtain than specific performance, and buyers generally prefer it. An advantage

---

[169] *See also* Copylease Corp. of Am. v. Memorex Corp., 408 F. Supp. 758 (S.D.N.Y. 1976) (product may be unique if other brands available are "distinctly inferior" in quality); *cf.* I.Lan Sys., Inc. v. Netscout Serv. Level Corp., 183 F. Supp. 2d 328, 46 UCC Rep. Serv. 2d 287 (D. Mass. 2002) (specific performance denied because mass-produced software that could perform same functions on ordinary computers was readily available).

[170] UCC § 2-716, cmt. 1.

[171] UCC § 2-716, cmt. 2. International Casings Group, Inc. v. Premium Standard Forms, Inc., 358 F. Supp. 2d 863, 56 UCC Rep. Serv. 2d 736 (W.D. Mo. 2005) (buyer's inability to find cover goods for supplier's hog casings led to an order for specific performance).

[172] 65 Ohio App. 2d 197, 417 N.E.2d 579 (1979).

[173] 522 F.2d 33, 17 UCC Rep. Serv. 447 (8th Cir. 1975).

[174] UCC § 2-716(3). Article 2A is comparable. UCC § 2A-521(3).

[175] Slidell, Inc. v. Millennium Inorganic Chem., Inc., 53 UCC Rep. Serv. 2d 829 (D. Minn. 2004) (replevin not available if buyer could cover and obtain substitute machines that would be adequate replacements).

of specific performance is that the court can fashion its decree in order to do justice and accomplish the goals of the contract. Thus, Section 2-716(2) provides that a decree of specific performance "may include such terms and conditions as to payment of the price, damages, or other relief as the court may deem just."

[C]   Buyer's Right to Goods on Seller's Insolvency [§ 2-502; § 2A-522]

In limited circumstances, a buyer that would ordinarily not be entitled to specific performance or replevin because it cannot meet the requirements of Section 2-716 may nevertheless have a right to recover the goods from the seller. The right is tightly circumscribed by Section 2-502(1), which provides that the buyer must have paid all or part of the price, must have a special property interest in the goods under Section 2-501(1),[176] and must make and keep good a tender of any unpaid part of the price. Even if the buyer meets these requirements, it may only recover the goods if: "(a) in the case of goods bought for personal, family, or household purposes, the seller repudiates or fails to deliver as required by the contract; or (b) in all cases, the seller becomes insolvent[177] within ten days after receipt of the first installment on their price."[178] The right of recovery will generally be exercised through a replevin action.[179]

The original provision, which dealt only with cases of insolvency, resolved for certain cases the question of whether a seller's insolvency constituted a basis for granting relief.[180] The drafters were aware that sellers in financial distress would sometimes "load up" by taking down payments from buyers to whom they never intended to deliver the goods. The requirement that the seller be insolvent at or within ten days after payment of the first installment is a rough and ready way of identifying the circumstances in which the seller is most likely to be engaged in this kind of fraudulent conduct.

As part of the Article 9 revision process, Section 2-502(1) was amended to extend beyond insolvency to situations in which a seller repudiates or fails to deliver consumer goods.[181] At the same time, a new subsection (2) was adopted providing that in these cases the recovery right vests when the buyer acquires a special property interest in the goods. The Comments explain that the effect of

---

[176] A buyer acquires a special property interest in goods, as well as an insurable interest, when the goods become identified to the contract for sale. UCC § 2-501(1). The time at which identification occurs is discussed in § 1.03[B] *supra*.

[177] Under the Code a person is insolvent if it has ceased paying debts not subject to a bona fide dispute in the ordinary course of its business, is unable to pay its debts as they come due, or is insolvent as the term is defined in bankruptcy law. UCC § 1-201(b)(23). Bankruptcy law limits insolvency to a balance-sheet test; whether at a fair valuation a person's debts exceed its assets. 11 U.S.C. § 101(32).

[178] UCC § 2-502(1). Section 2A-522 provides for qualifying lessees to recover identified goods if the lessor becomes insolvent within ten days after receipt of the first installment of rent and security.

[179] *See* § 10.01[A] n.12 *infra.*

[180] *See* A. Corbin, Contracts § 1156 (1964).

[181] Article 9 defines consumer goods as "goods that are used or bought for use primarily for personal, family, or household purposes." UCC § 9-102(a)(23).

the new provisions is to make the buyer's recovery right superior to the rights of a secured party that acquires a security interest in the goods through an agreement with the seller entered into after the recovery right vests.[182] For example, suppose a consumer gives a seller part of the price of a sofa that the seller agrees to hold on a layaway plan. The seller later grants a bank a security interest in all its inventory as collateral for a loan. If the seller defaults on the loan and the secured party repossesses all its inventory, the buyer may recover the sofa by tendering to the secured party the remaining part of the price.

§ 8.04 AMENDED ARTICLE 2

[A] Market Price/Contract Price Differential

Original Section 2-713(1) provides that the time for measuring market damages is "when the buyer learned of the breach." For cases of nondelivery, rightful rejection, or justifiable revocation of acceptance, the section was amended to provide that the market is to be measured "at the time for tender."[183] This brings the section into conformity with the rule that has always applied to aggrieved sellers.[184] In cases of repudiation, the measure is "the difference between the market price at the expiration of a commercially reasonable time after the buyer learned of the repudiation, but no later than [the time for tender]."[185]

The Comments to original Section 2-713 indicate that a covering buyer may not choose a market-based recovery because doing so would put the buyer in a better position than it would have occupied if the seller had fully performed and thus would constitute a windfall.[186] The principle is retained in the amendments and the rationale is explained more clearly in the Comments.[187]

[B] Specific Performance and Replevin

Reflecting modern commercial practice, amended Section 2-716(1) provides that, except in the case of a consumer contract, the parties may explicitly allocate the risk of specific performance in their agreement. The provision abrogates the historic rule that specific performance is unavailable if there is an adequate legal remedy.

---

[182] UCC § 2-501, cmt. 3.

[183] UCC Amended § 2-713(1)(a).

[184] UCC § 2-708(1).

[185] Amended UCC §§ 2-713(1)(b) and 2-708(1), discussed in § 9.09[A] *infra*, provide the same rule for aggrieved sellers in cases of buyer repudiation.

[186] UCC § 2-713, cmt. 5.

[187] Amended UCC § 2-713, Comment 7, explains that "[t]o award an additional amount because the buyer could show the market price was higher than the contract price would put the buyer in a better position than performance would have. Of course, the seller would bear the burden of proving that cover had the economic effect of limiting the buyer's actual loss to an amount less than the contract price-market price difference."

Because of the equitable origins of the remedy, the amended provision does not require a court to honor an agreement for the remedy of specific performance but rather invites it to do so. The Comments make the point as follows: "Nothing in this section constrains the court's exercise of its equitable discretion to decide whether to enter a decree for specific performance or to determine the conditions or terms of the decree."[188] The amendments further provide that specific performance may not be decreed if the breaching party's sole remaining obligation is the payment of money.

With regard to replevin and similar remedies provided for in original Section 2-716(3), the amendments add a new subsection (4) which provides that "[t]he buyer's right under subsection (3) vests upon acquisition of a special property, even if the seller had not then repudiated or failed to deliver." The Comments explain as follows:

> Subsection (4) provides that a buyer's right to replevin or a similar remedy vests upon the buyer's acquisition of a special property in the goods (Section 2-501) even if the seller has not at that time repudiated or failed to make a required delivery. This vesting rule assumes application of a "first in time" priority rule. In other words, if the buyer's rights vest under this rule before a creditor acquires an *in rem* right to the goods, including an Article 9 security interest and a lien created by levy, the buyer should prevail.[189]

§ 8.05   CISG

[A]   Measuring Damages

The CISG provisions on monetary damages apply equally to aggrieved buyers and sellers. Article 74 states the general rule, and Articles 75 and 76 provide alternatives for cases of contract avoidance.[190] Article 77 requires that damages be mitigated, and Article 78 allows for the recovery of interest.

The general rule of Article 74 is that "[d]amages for breach of contract consist of a sum equal to the loss, including loss of profit, suffered by the other party as a consequence of the breach." An aggrieved party thus may recover both direct and consequential damages if it can establish causation. The article addresses the concern that damages might be too remote by recognizing the principle of foreseeability: "Such damages may not exceed the loss which the party in breach foresaw or ought to have foreseen at the time of the conclusion of the contract, in the light of the facts and matters of which he then knew or ought to have known, as a possible consequence of the breach of contract."

---

[188] UCC Amended § 2-716, cmt. 3.

[189] UCC Amended § 2-716, cmt. 5. There is a similar new vesting rule in amended UCC § 2-502(2), which deals with the buyer's right to the goods in the event of the seller's insolvency, repudiation, or failure to deliver.

[190] Contract avoidance is addressed in Article 49 (avoidance by buyer), Article 64 (avoidance by seller), Article 72 (anticipatory breach), and Article 73 (installment contracts). The topics are discussed in § 7.10[A], [B] *supra*.

Articles 75 and 76 provide alternative measures in cases of avoidance that are more detailed than the general rule of Article 74. Article 75 provides as follows: "If the contract is avoided and if, in a reasonable manner and within a reasonable time after avoidance, the buyer has bought goods in replacement or the seller has resold the goods, the party claiming damages may recover the difference between the contract price and the price in the substitute transaction as well as any further damages recoverable under article 74." The provision enables an aggrieved buyer that enters into a cover transaction to measure its direct losses by the difference between the contract price and the price it actually paid to obtain the goods elsewhere. Similarly, an aggrieved seller may resell the goods elsewhere and recover the difference between the contract price and the resale price. The requirement that a substitute transaction occur within a reasonable time after avoidance and be made in a reasonable manner protects the breaching party from excessive damages. Article 75 permits an aggrieved party to recover consequential damages as provided in Article 74.

Article 76(1), which provides an alternative measure of direct damages based on the current market price, states in part as follows: "If the contract is avoided and there is a current price for the goods, the party claiming damages may, if he has not made a purchase or resale under article 75, recover the difference between the price fixed by the contract and the current price at the time of avoidance as well as any further damages recoverable under article 74." The measure is available if an aggrieved party elects not to enter into a substitute transaction or its substitute transaction does not qualify under Article 75. The time for determining the current price is "the time of avoidance" unless "the party claiming damages has avoided the contract after taking over the goods," in which case the current price is determined "at the time of such taking over."[191] In the latter case, the selection of the earlier date prevents a buyer that takes over the goods from delaying a declaration of avoidance in hopes of a favorable change in the market. The place for determining the current price is "the place where delivery of the goods should have been made or, if there is no current price at that place, the price at such other place as serves as a reasonable substitute, making due allowance for differences in the cost of transporting the goods."[192] As with Section 75, an aggrieved party may recover consequential damages as provided in Article 74.

Article 77, which recognizes the principle of mitigation, provides that "[a] party who relies on a breach of contract must take such measures as are reasonable in the circumstances to mitigate the loss, including loss of profit, resulting from the breach." If an aggrieved party fails to take reasonable steps which, if implemented, would lessen its loss, the breaching party "may claim a reduction in the damages in the amount by which the loss should have been mitigated."

The drafters of the CISG encountered major difficulties in addressing the concept of interest. A strong consensus supported the recovery of interest as necessary to fully compensate an aggrieved party for its loss but could not agree

---

[191] CISG Art. 76(1).

[192] CISG Art. 76(2).

on how to determine the appropriate rate because of widespread differences along political, economic, and religious lines. As a result the CISG includes a broad pronouncement that "[i]f a party fails to pay the price or any other sum that is in arrears, the other party is entitled to interest on it, without prejudice to any claim for damages recoverable under article 74" but neither provides a rate nor indicates how a tribunal should determine a rate. As a result, determining the appropriate rate has proven to be a highly controversial issue, with courts and commentators divided among multiple approaches.

[B]   Price Reduction

Article 50, which permits an aggrieved buyer that wishes to retain nonconforming goods to reduce the purchase price, provides that "[i]f the goods do not conform with the contract and whether or not the price has already been paid, the buyer may reduce the price in the same proportion as the value that the goods actually delivered had at the time of delivery bears to the value that conforming goods would have had at that time." The article precludes price reduction if the seller successfully exercises its right to cure the nonconformity or if the buyer refuses to accept an appropriate cure.[193]

Article 50 reflects a civil-law tradition under which "damages" generally are available only if a seller's conduct is negligent or fraudulent. Price reduction developed as a remedy based on the premise that even though a seller is not liable for damages, it should not be able to recover the full price for defective goods. Even though the CISG eliminates seller negligence as a necessary component of a buyer's claim for damages,[194] the drafters included the price-reduction remedy because of the insistence of civil-law nations and because it reduces the need to refer to other sources for principles of restitution.[195]

Although price reduction is in some respects comparable to the common-law right of setoff, its application may be quite different. In implementing the remedy "the buyer may reduce the price in the same proportion as the value that the goods actually delivered had at the time of the delivery bears to the value that conforming goods would have had at that time."[196] Thus, an aggrieved buyer must first establish a ratio based on the values, on the delivery date, of the goods actually delivered and of conforming goods, and it must then apply the ratio to the contract price. For example, in a stable market in which the value of conforming goods is the contract price, the delivery and acceptance of nonconforming goods worth 90% of the contract price would entitle the buyer to reduce the price by 10%. Suppose, however, that the contract price per unit is $50, the market price has dropped to $40 by the time of delivery, and the nonconforming goods have a market value of $30. Direct damages under Section 74 would be $10 per unit — the difference between the value of the actual goods

---

[193] For a discussion of a seller's right to cure, see CISG Arts. 37 & 48 and § 7.10[A][1][a] *supra*.

[194] *See* CISG § 45(1).

[195] Whereas civil-law systems require courts to determine the difference through the use of expert advise, Article 50 leaves the determination up to the buyer. A breaching seller should be able to challenge a buyer's erroneous calculation.

[196] CISG Art. 50.

delivered and the value they would have had if they had been conforming — and factoring in those damages would leave the buyer with an obligation to pay $40 (the contract price of $50 less damages of $10). In this situation, price reduction would be more advantageous for the buyer. The ratio would be the $30 value of the goods delivered divided by the $40 value of conforming goods on the delivery date, or 3/4. Applied to the contract price of $50, price reduction would yield a price per unit of $37.50.[197]

[C]   Specific Performance

Article 46(1) contains a broad general rule that, on its face, grants buyers a nearly unfettered right to demand full performance: "The buyer may require performance by the seller of his obligations unless the buyer has resorted to a remedy which is inconsistent with this requirement."[198] As a practical matter, buyers are unlikely to pursue specific performance very often. Sellers sometimes willingly correct deficiencies in order to maintain good business relations or to preclude avoidance of the contract. In addition, because litigation in pursuit of specific performance may be protracted, an aggrieved buyer may prefer to acquire needed goods elsewhere and to pursue a claim for damages if necessary. Beyond these practical considerations, the CISG contains several exceptions that limit a buyer's right to require performance.

The first exception is the proviso quoted above under which a buyer is not entitled to specific performance if it has resorted to an inconsistent remedy.[199] For example, a buyer may not declare a contract avoided and subsequently demand delivery of the goods. The seller likely would rely on the declaration of avoidance and should not be burdened by a later change in the buyer's position.

Another exception is found in Article 46(2), which provides that "[i]f the goods do not conform with the contract, the buyer may require delivery of substitute goods only if the lack of conformity constitutes a fundamental breach of contract and a request for substitute goods is made either in conjunction with notice given under article 39 or within a reasonable time thereafter."[200] Requiring sellers to replace goods with relatively minor defects would impose excessively costly obligations on sellers and thus promote economic waste. Even with a fundamental breach, a buyer's request for substitute goods must be given in conjunction with, or within a reasonable time after, it gives the seller notice specifying the nature of the lack of conformity under Article 39. The reasonable-

---

[197] "Put another way, expectation damages are designed to preserve for an aggrieved party the benefit of her bargain; reduction in price under Article 50 attempts to preserve the *proportion* of her bargain." Flechtner, *More U.S. Decisions on the U.N. Sales Convention: Scope, Parol Evidence, "Validity," and Reduction of Price Under Article 50*, 14 J. Law & Com. 153, 174 (1995) (emphasis supplied).

[198] Article 62, which gives an aggrieved seller a comparably broad right to require performance, provides that "[t]he seller may require the buyer to pay the price, take delivery or perform his other obligations, unless the seller has resorted to a remedy which is inconsistent with this requirement."

[199] CISG Art. 46(1).

[200] CISG Art. 46(2).

time limitation allows an aggrieved buyer some additional time after giving an Article 39 notice to decide whether to request substitute goods or pursue a different remedy.

Article 46(3), which contains yet another exception, provides in part that "[i]f the goods do not conform with the contract, the buyer may require the seller to remedy the lack of conformity by repair, unless this is unreasonable having regard to all the circumstances." As with a request for substitute goods, a request for repair must be given in conjunction with, or within a reasonable time after, the buyer gives the seller notice under Article 39. Because repair often will involve less expense than delivering substitute goods, a buyer may require repair even if the breach is not fundamental. The buyer, however, does not have completely unfettered rights with respect to this option because the demand must be reasonable in the circumstances. For example, if the buyer can make adequate repairs itself, or if they can be accomplished locally at less expense than requiring the seller's involvement, a demand for repair would be unreasonable.

The remedy of specific performance provoked considerable conflict in the efforts to develop an international law of sales. Legal systems following the common law generally start from a premise that remedies should be substitutional — that is, in the form of money damages — rather than specific. Consequently they tend to allow specific performance only in cases in which the monetary measure of damages would be inadequate to protect the aggrieved party's interests. In theory civil-law systems provide for more expansive rights to specific performance; however, there are significant variations even among civil-law jurisdictions, and in particular many of them do not permit coercive measures like imprisonment for contempt as readily as do some common-law systems. A few nations do not have any domestic-law mechanisms for enforcing an order of specific performance.

As a result of a perceived need for flexibility on this matter, Article 28 contains a provision that can on occasion preclude specific performance altogether: "If, in accordance with the provisions of this Convention, one party is entitled to require performance of any obligation by the other party, a court is not bound to enter a judgment for specific performance unless the court would do so under its own law in respect of similar contracts of sale not governed by this Convention." In other words, even though Article 46 gives a buyer the right to require performance, Article 28 allows a court to defer to its own domestic law in a case in which that law would not require specific performance.[201] If both Article 46 and the domestic law of the jurisdiction require specific performance, Article 28 has no effect and the CISG binds the court to award specific performance.[202]

---

[201] Courts in the United States thus are free to follow the provisions of UCC § 2-716 in determining whether to require the delivery of goods to a party to a sale governed by the CISG.

[202] The domestic rules would also be irrelevant when the right to specific performance is not available under the provisions of the CISG.

Chapter 9

REMEDIES OF SELLERS AND LESSORS

[C] Liquidated Damages

§ 9.10 CISG

[A] Unified Provisions on Damages

[B] Seller's Right to Specific Performance

§ 9.01 DAMAGES BASED ON SUBSTITUTE TRANSACTIONS

[A] Contract Price/Resale Price Differential [§ 2-706]

If a buyer breaches by repudiation, by failing to make a payment due on or before delivery, or by wrongful rejection or revocation of acceptance, under Section 2-706 the seller may resell the goods to another buyer and use the resale price as the basis for recovering monetary damages.[1] If the resale qualifies under criteria explained below, the starting point for calculating damages is "the difference between the resale price and the contract price."[2]

The contract/resale differential is the preferred remedy for an aggrieved seller because it best meets the objective of remedies under the Code generally — to place the nonbreaching party in the same economic position it would have occupied if the other party had fully performed.[3] By using the resale price, Section 2-706 measures an aggrieved seller's direct damages precisely.[4]

To qualify for use in calculating damages, a seller's resale must be made in good faith and in a commercially reasonable manner.[5] These criteria are consistent with mitigation principles and protect the buyer's interests: The seller cannot deliberately resell at a reduced price or thoughtlessly sell at any price offered and expect to be made whole under Section 2-706. It must pay enough attention to the resale to receive a fair price. Sellers that sell goods on their own behalf are motivated by their own economic self-interest to bargain for a fair purchase price and they must use the same level of effort when in effect selling goods on the buyer's behalf.

Section 2-706(2) grants sellers considerable leeway in determining the details of a resale, providing that it may be by public or private sale, may occur by way of one or more contracts, and may even be made by identifying the goods being resold to an existing contract. The goods may be sold as a unit or in parcels and the sale may occur at a time and, subject to a limitation for public sales discussed below, place of the seller's choosing. However, an overarching principle must be satisfied: "[Ev]ery aspect of the sale including the method,

---

[1] UCC § 2-703(d).

[2] UCC § 2-706(1).

[3] UCC § 1-305(a) (remedies provided by UCC "must be liberally administered to the end that the aggrieved party may be put in as good a position as if the other party had fully performed").

[4] Damages based on a seller's resale transaction are comparable to damages based on a buyer's cover transaction. *See* § 8.03 *supra*.

[5] UCC § 2-706(1).

manner, time, place and terms must be commercially reasonable."[6] The Comments articulate the intended interplay between seller discretion and the "commercially reasonable" requirement: "Subsection (2) frees the remedy of resale from legalistic restrictions and enables the seller to resell in accordance with reasonable commercial practices so as to realize as high a price as possible in the circumstances."[7] The Comments also state that the objective is "to enable the seller to dispose of the goods to the best advantage."[8]

A qualifying resale must reasonably be identified as referring to the contract that was breached by the buyer, but the goods do not have to be in existence.[9] For example, if a buyer repudiates before the seller completes manufacture, the seller can resell the goods and then complete them for the resale buyer.[10] Alternately, the seller may, if it exercises reasonable commercial judgment, complete the manufacture and then conduct its resale.[11] Similarly, existing goods need not have been identified to the contract with the breaching buyer to be the subject of a qualifying resale.[12]

Apex Oil Co. v. Belcher Co. of New York, Inc.[13] explores whether a seller that has identified goods to the contract with the breaching buyer can use a sale of comparable goods for purposes of calculating resale damages. The buyer in the case breached a contract for the sale of heating oil and the seller resold the oil that had been identified to the contract the next day. Six weeks later the seller sold the same amount of comparable oil to another buyer at a substantially lower price and sought to use that price in calculating its damages. It argued that its initial identification did not preclude it from using comparable goods for purposes of resale. The court agreed with the seller's basic proposition but held that the delay before the second resale was unreasonable given the volatility of the market. Therefore, the first resale fixed the price for purposes of Section 2-706.

Suppose in *Apex Oil* that, at the time of the breach, the seller had multiple contracts to sell heating oil. Could it have simply selected the contract at the

---

[6] UCC § 2-706(2); Coast Trading Co. v. Cudahy Co., 592 F.2d 1074, 25 UCC Rep. Serv. 1037 (9th Cir. 1978) (fictitious "wash" sale was designed to inflate damage claim); McMillan v. Meuser Material & Equip. Co., 60 Ark. 422, 541 S.W.2d 911, 20 UCC Rep. Serv. 110 (1976) (14-month delay in resale held unreasonable).

[7] UCC § 2-706, cmt. 4.

[8] UCC § 2-706, cmt. 6.

[9] UCC § 2-706(2).

[10] UCC § 2-704(1)(b) requires that the unfinished goods be demonstrably intended for the breaching buyer. UCC § 2-704(2) permits the seller, as long as it exercises reasonable commercial judgment, either to complete the manufacture and identify the goods to the contract or to cease manufacture and resell for scrap or salvage value.

[11] UCC § 2-704(2). The seller may also, again in the exercise of reasonable commercial judgment, cease manufacture and resell the goods for scrap or salvage value or proceed in any other reasonable manner. A seller that ceases manufacture will be entitled to damages based on its lost profits under UCC § 2-708(2).

[12] UCC § 2-706(2); *see also* UCC § 2-704(1)(a) (permitting seller to identify to the breached contract goods in its possession or control at the time it learned of the breach).

[13] 855 F.2d 997, 6 UCC Rep. Serv. 2d 1025 (2d Cir. 1988).

lowest price, identified it as referring to the broken contract, and used it as the basis for calculating damages? The Code gives no clear answer and the question for the court is whether the seller acted in good faith and in a commercially reasonable manner. The line between acting in good faith and manipulating the situation to unfairly inflate damages can be quite thin.

In order for a resale to qualify for use in the calculation of the seller's damages it must meet certain procedures that differ depending on whether the seller selects a public or private resale. A public sale is an auction and a private sale is any other sale.[14] The only requirement for a private sale is that the seller give the breaching buyer reasonable notification of its intent to resell.[15] More stringent procedures apply for a public sale. It must be conducted at a place or market that is usual for a public sale if one is reasonably available and, unless haste is required because the goods are perishable or threaten to decline speedily in value, the seller must give the breaching buyer reasonable notice of the time and place of the sale.[16] The statute assumes that the public will also be notified of the time and place — an auction could hardly be commercially reasonable otherwise — and if the goods will not be within the view of those attending the sale the notification must state where they are located and provide for reasonable inspection by prospective bidders.[17] Only identified goods may be sold at an auction unless they are sold in a recognized market for auctions of future goods of the kind.[18] The seller is free to participate in the bidding.[19] Failure to follow the proper procedures precludes a seller from using Section 2-706 in calculating its damages.[20]

[B]   Contract Price/Re-lease Price Differential [§ 2A-527]

Following a default by a lessee, a lessor may dispose of the goods in any manner it wishes — by lease, sale, or any other method.[21] It may dispose of goods that it has rightfully refused to deliver, goods that it repossesses from the lessee, and even goods that remain in the lessee's possession. As a practical matter, a lessor typically will want to reacquire possession from the lessee; otherwise, the purchaser might have to replevy the goods from an uncooperative lessee and this possibility undoubtedly will influence the price the purchaser is willing to pay.

If a lessor wants to use the proceeds of disposition as a basis for calculating damages, the disposition must meet certain criteria. Like a resale under Section 2-706, it must be made in good faith and in a commercially reasonable manner.

---

[14]   UCC § 2-607, cmt. 4.

[15]   UCC § 2-706(3); *See, e.g.*, Alco Standard Corp. v. F & B Mfg. Co., 51 Ill. 2d 186, 281 N.E.2d 652, 10 UCC Rep. Serv. 639 (1972) (notice need only indicate intention to resell).

[16]   UCC § 2-706(4)(b).

[17]   UCC § 2-706(4)(c).

[18]   UCC § 2-706(4)(a).

[19]   UCC § 2-706(4)(d).

[20]   *See, e.g.*, Cole v. Melvin, 441 F. Supp. 193, 22 UCC Rep. Serv. 1154 (D.S.D. 1977) (failure to notify buyer prior to public and private resales precluded use of resale prices to fix damages.)

[21]   UCC § 2A-527(1).

In addition, the disposition must be by lease and the substitute lease agreement must be substantially similar to the original lease agreement.[22] The original agreement and the substitute agreement must be sufficiently comparable to justify using the price differential as a basis for calculating damages.[23] However, precise correlation on all terms is unlikely in the lease context, and therefore the guiding premise is that the courts should adjust the damages formula to reflect the value of the differences and thus enable the substitute lease to qualify, provided that the differences can be valued with reasonable certainty.[24]

The damages formula has three elements.[25] First, the lessor is entitled to all accrued rent that is unpaid on the date the substitute lease commences. The lessor will need some time to negotiate the substitute lease and cutting off its rights under the first lease before the commencement date of the substitute lease would unfairly diminish its damages. The second element is the differential between the remaining rental under the original lease agreement and the rental for the comparable term under the new lease agreement. The future rents under both leases must be reduced to present value. The third element adds incidental damages and deducts expenses saved as a result of the breach.

[C]   Comparing Disposition Requirements for Sales, Leases, and Secured Transactions

Sellers, lessors, and secured parties all may need to dispose of assets when their contracting counterparts are in breach. In the case of a seller or lessor, the assets are the goods that are the subject matter of the sales or lease contract; in the case of a secured party, the assets are collateral for an obligation and may or may not be goods. Articles 2, 2A, and 9 give the disposing party broad discretion in selecting the method of disposal. If a seller or lessor wishes to use the disposition price in calculating its damages, it must proceed in a commercially reasonable manner; otherwise, it may dispose of the goods in any manner it wishes and recover damages based on a contract/market differential or, in an appropriate case, on lost profits. There is no requirement that a seller resell or that a lessor re-lease — if they wish, they can simply retain the goods for their own use. By contrast, a secured party must select a commercially reasonable method of disposition and each aspect of the disposition must be commercially

---

[22] These are the same requirements that Article 2A uses to determine the qualification of a substitute lease as a valid cover transaction for the purpose of determining the damages of an aggrieved lessee. *See* § 8.03[C] *supra.*

[23] In most lease cases decided before Article 2A, the courts required that the proceeds of a lessor's disposition be deducted from the amounts due under the lease. Fisher Trucking, Inc. v. Fleet Lease, Inc., 304 Ark. 451, 803 S.W.2d 888, 14 UCC Rep. Serv. 2d 887 (1991); Deutz-Allis Credit Corp. v. Jensen, 458 N.W.2d 163, 12 UCC Rep. Serv. 2d 512 (Minn. Ct. App. 1990). The dispositions in these cases, however, were by sale of the goods. A sale covers not only the value of the remaining lease term but the lessor's residual value in the goods as well. A sale is not sufficiently comparable to the original lease to provide a valid basis for comparison.

[24] UCC § 2A-527, cmt. 5.

[25] UCC § 2A-527(2).

reasonable.[26] In each of the situations in which a disposing party must proceed in a commercially reasonable manner, the Code sets out specific requirements that must be followed, and in each situation good-faith purchasers are encouraged to participate by a provision that shields them from claims asserted by the party in breach even if the disposing party fails to comply with the requirements.[27]

A secured party's interest in collateral is limited by the outstanding indebtedness and it must account to the debtor, or perhaps a junior lienor, for the amount by which the disposition proceeds exceed that indebtedness.[28] The surplus represents the debtor's equity and it, or a junior lienor, may redeem the collateral prior to disposition by paying the outstanding indebtedness.

A lessor holds the residual interest in the leased goods and consequently need not account to the lessee for any profit made on disposition.[29] Put another way, the lessee does not have any equity in the goods.[30] A disposition sale can never serve as a sufficiently comparable transaction for purposes of calculating the lessor's damages; only a substitute lease will suffice. The substitute lease must be entered into in good faith and conducted in a commercially reasonable manner, but the specific procedural rules governing resales under Section 2-706 were omitted from Section 2A-527. The reason is that the drafters, recognizing that lessors have multiple variables to negotiate and often face rapid changes in the market, determined not to draft with specificity.[31]

Like a lessor, a seller is not required to account to a breaching buyer for any profit realized upon resale of the goods.[32] Article 2 divorces issues related to resale from the location of title to the goods[33] and, in the unusual case in which title is technically located in the breaching buyer, the resale has the effect of transferring it to the resale buyer. Thus, the breaching buyer has no equity. The sole purpose of requiring the seller to act in good faith, in a commercially reasonable manner, and in accordance with the specific requirements for public and private sales is to mitigate the breaching buyer's damages by assuring that the resale price is reasonable.

If a buyer or lessee rightfully rejects or justifiably revokes acceptance, it has a security interest in goods in its possession or control as collateral for payments made and certain expenses.[34] A buyer may foreclose on its security interest by selling the goods according to the same procedures required of an

---

[26] UCC § 9-610(a). A secured party that fails to dispose of collateral in a commercially reasonable manner is liable for the loss caused by its failure. UCC § 9-625(b).

[27] UCC §§ 2-706(5), 2A-527(4), 9-617(b).

[28] UCC § 9-615(a), (d)(1). The outstanding indebtedness includes certain expenses related to the foreclosure process.

[29] UCC § 2A-527(5).

[30] UCC § 2A-527, cmt. 10.

[31] UCC § 2A-527, cmt. 4.

[32] UCC § 2-706(6); see, e.g., Mott Equity Elevator v. Svihovec, 236 N.W.2d 900, 18 UCC Rep. Serv. 388 (N.D. 1975).

[33] UCC §§ 2-401, 2-706, cmt. 11.

[34] UCC §§ 2-711(3), 2A-508(5).

aggrieved seller under Section 2-706;[35] a lessee may foreclose by disposing of the goods in any commercially reasonable, good-faith manner.[36] The interest of the buyer or lessee is limited to the secured obligation and thus it must account to the seller or lessor for any amount recovered in excess of that obligation.[37]

§ 9.02 CONTRACT PRICE/MARKET PRICE DIFFERENTIAL [§ 2-708(1); § 2A-528(1)]

[A]   The Measure

Article 2 retains the pre-Code method of calculating seller damages, which is the difference between the contract price and the market price.[38] As with the contract/resale measure, incidental damages are added and expenses saved in consequence of the buyer's breach are deducted. Although not as precise as the contract/resale measure, a method for calculating damages based on market value is necessary. Aggrieved sellers are not required to enter into a resale transaction, and only resales that satisfy the standard of commercial reasonableness qualify for use in calculating damages. The alternative measure is typically used when a reliable resale price is not available.

As with the contract/resale measure, market-based damages in the lease context consist of three elements.[39] The first element is the unpaid rent that has accrued under the lease, and the second element is the present value of the difference for the remainder of the lease term between the original rent and the market rent.[40] The final element adds incidental damages and deducts expenses saved as a result of the breach. The point of demarcation between the first two elements is the date of default if the lessee never took possession of the goods; otherwise it is the earlier of the date on which the lessor repossesses the goods or the date on which the lessee tenders them back.

A question not addressed by the Code is whether a seller that resells can ignore Section 2-706 and recover damages under Section 2-708(1). For example, in *Tesoro Petroleum Corp. v. Holborn Oil Co., Ltd.*,[41] after its buyer repudiated a contract to buy ten million gallons of gasoline at $1.30 per gallon the seller somehow managed to resell it for $1.10 per gallon even though the market price had plunged to $.80 per gallon. The seller claimed that it was entitled to the contract/market measure, or $5 million, because otherwise the buyer would be

---

[35] UCC § 2-711(3).

[36] UCC § 2A-508(5).

[37] UCC § 2-706(6); *see, e.g.*, Texpor Traders, Inc. v. Trust Co. Bank, 720 F. Supp. 1100, 10 UCC Rep. Serv. 2d 1227 (S.D.N.Y. 1989); UCC § 2A-527(5).

[38] UCC § 2-708(1).

[39] UCC § 2A-528(1).

[40] Info. Leasing Corp. v. Pall, Inc., 156 Ohio App.3d 378, 806 N.E.2d 178, 53 UCC Rep. Serv. 2d 260 (Ohio Ct. App. 2004) (lower court erred in not awarding lessor the present value of future rent minus the present value of the market rent for the remaining term of the lease).

[41] 145 Misc. 2d 715, 547 N.Y.S.2d 1012, 10 UCC Rep. Serv. 2d 814 (Sup. Ct. 1989).

the one to profit from its ability to arrange a favorable resale.[42] The buyer argued that the seller would recover a windfall if its damages were not limited to the contract/resale measure, or $2 million. After discussing the relevant authorities and finding no clear answer regarding the drafters' intent, the court concluded that awarding the larger market-based measure would violate the basic premise of placing the seller in the same economic position it would have occupied if the buyer had fully performed and limited recovery to the contract/resale measure.[43]

[B]   Determining the Market

[1]   Sales

Although a seller's contract/market remedy is comparable to a buyer's contract/market remedy,[44] the drafters were not consistent in establishing the methods for determining the applicable market price. The buyer's remedy ascertains market time based on when the buyer learned of the breach and establishes market place based on some poorly conceived rules that supposedly designate the place where the buyer most likely would have covered had that option been pursued.[45] The comparable seller's remedy is much simpler: Market price is determined "at the time and place for tender."[46] The drafters did not identify the criteria they used in selecting this approach.

[2]   Leases

The drafters of Article 2A took a more thoughtful approach. An aggrieved lessor can recover unpaid rent that accrues under the lease until the lessor could have entered into a substitute lease transaction, after which the differential between the original rent and the market rent, reduced to present value, applies to the remainder of the lease term. The opportunity to re-lease is thus the primary factor controlling the market date used in applying the remedy. Use of the differential reflects the principle of mitigation, giving the defaulting lessee the benefit of the market value that the lessor could have attained by entering into a substantially similar lease. The lessor's opportunity to enter into a substitute lease is tied to its possession of the goods, but it cannot extend its right to rent under the lease simply by delaying repossession. The lessee can fix the market date by retendering the goods to the lessor.

Article 2A establishes the market place as the place where the goods are located at the time the contract/market differential begins to apply. The premise

---

[42] The seller cited UCC Section 2-703 Comment 1, which states that seller's remedies are cumulative and that the doctrine of election of remedies does not apply. The Comment is not as clear cut as the seller suggested because it goes on to state that "[w]hether the pursuit of one remedy bars another depends entirely on the facts of the individual case."

[43] For a case permitting market-based recoveries larger than the resale-based measure, see *Wendling v. Puls*, 227 Kan. 780, 610 P.2d 580, 28 UCC Rep. Serv. 1362 (1980).

[44] *See* UCC § 2-713, § 8.04 *supra*.

[45] *See* § 8.04[B] *supra*.

[46] UCC § 2-708(1).

is that this location generally will be the most economically efficient place for the lessor to dispose of the goods.

§ 9.03   LOST PROFITS [§ 2-708(2); § 2A-528(2)]

Section 2-708(2) provides a different formula if the measure based on market price "is inadequate to put the seller in as good a position as performance would have done." Article 2A includes the same provision for lessors.[47] The Article 2 formula begins with "the profit (including reasonable overhead) which the seller would have made from full performance by the buyer." The formula allows for incidental damages and also provides for "due allowance for costs reasonably incurred and due credit for payments or proceeds of resale." The parenthetical reference to overhead means that the seller is entitled to be repaid for overhead costs directly allocable to the breached contract but not for indirect overhead costs that it would have paid without regard to the contract. In a typical case indirect overhead would include such things as rent and utilities. Compensation for out-of-pocket expenses that are not part of overhead is permitted by the phrase "due allowance for costs reasonably incurred."

Application of the provision has evolved into recognition of certain categories of sellers that may not be adequately protected by the other damages measures. The "lost-volume seller" is the most readily apparent category. The seller, which can be a manufacturer, retailer, or middleman, has a ready supply of goods available to meet the demand from buyers.[48] It will typically resell the goods intended for the breaching buyer to someone else following the breach, but if the goods are standard-priced, it will not recover any damages under the contract/ resale measure.[49] The seller's true interest in entering into a transaction is the profit associated with the transaction, and if it has excess capacity, meaning that it has or can obtain enough goods to supply all of its reasonably foreseeable buyers, it presumably would have made the second sale and earned the additional profit even if the buyer had not breached. The seller is entitled to the profit it would have made on the sale to the buyer.[50]

A case that has become influential in this area is *R. E. Davis Chemical Corp. v. Diasonics, Inc.*[51] After the buyer repudiated a contract for the purchase of an

---

[47] UCC § 2A-528(2).

[48] *See, e.g.*, Ragen Corp. v. Kearney & Trecker Corp., 912 F.2d 619 (3d Cir. 1990) (seller not entitled to lost-profit recovery because it could not have supplied goods for a second buyer).

[49] Even though Section 2-708(2) begins by stating the "[i]f the measure of damages provided in subsection (1) is inadequate. . . . ," the seller's resale measure in Section 2-706 is really the one that is inadequate to place the aggrieved seller in the same position as performance would have done. Most courts recognize this anomaly and apply Section 2-708(2) even though the lost-volume seller has resold the goods.

[50] *See, e.g.*, Islamic Republic of Iran v. Boeing Co., 771 F.2d 1279, 41 UCC Rep. Serv. 1178 (9th Cir. 1985); Snyder v. Herbert Greenbaum & Assocs., 38 Md. App. 144, 380 A.2d 618, 22 UCC Rep. Serv. 1104 (1977). For a case in the leasing context, see *Collins Entertainment Corp. v. Coats & Coats Rental Amusement*, 368 S.C. 410, 629 S.E.2d 635, 59 UCC Rep. Serv. 2d 402 (2006) (lessor qualified as lost-volume lessor because it established that it had more supply of video-poker machines than it had demand for them.)

[51] 826 F.2d 678 (7th Cir. 1991).

MRI machine, the seller resold it to a third party for the same price. The buyer sued to recover its down payment[52] and the seller counterclaimed for its lost profits. The Seventh Circuit established the following three-part test to determine whether a seller qualifies as a lost-volume seller: (1) the seller must possess the capacity to produce or acquire the additional goods for the second sale; (2) the second sale would have been profitable and therefore the seller would have produced or acquired the additional goods; and (3) the second buyer would have bought the additional goods if it had not been offered the goods intended for the breaching buyer. Since the seller in the case qualified under this test, it was entitled to its lost profits.

The statutory formula for measuring lost profits cannot be applied literally in the case of a lost-volume seller because the formula requires that the buyer be given a credit for proceeds of resale. Deduction of the proceeds of resale would simply wipe out any recovery. The deduction makes sense in the context of other types of buyers for which Section 2-708(2) was intended and courts, recognizing its inappropriateness, have not applied it to lost-volume sellers.[53]

Another class of persons for which the lost-profit measure is available is component-part manufacturers, meaning manufacturers that assemble goods for sale or lease. If a buyer or lessee repudiates before the manufacturing process is complete, the manufacturer must decide what to do.[54] If it justifiably decides not to complete the goods, its loss of the anticipated profit from the transaction cannot be recouped from a substitute transaction and thus it is entitled to recover under Section 2-708(2).[55] The entire damages formula operates properly in this context: Costs reasonably incurred in manufacturing and incidental damages are added to the basic lost-profit measure, which includes reasonable overhead, and payments or proceeds received from resale, which might be for salvage value, are deducted.[56]

An occasional case arises in which Section 2-708(1) overcompensates the seller. Can the buyer in such a case preclude application of Section 2-708(1) and thereby relegate the seller to damages for lost profits? In the first case to address the issue, *Nobs Chemical, U.S.A., Inc. v. Koppers Co., Inc.*,[57] the buyer

---

[52] A breaching buyer's right to recover a down payment is discussed in § 8.02[A] *supra*.

[53] New England Dairies, Inc. v. Dairy Mart Convenience Stores, Inc., 47 UCC Rep. Serv. 2d 480 (D. Conn. 2002); Teradyne, Inc. v. Teledyne Indus., Inc., 676 F.2d 865, 33 UCC Rep. Serv. 1669 (1st Cir. 1982).

[54] UCC §§ 2-704(2), 2A-524(2); *see* § 9.01[A] *supra*.

[55] Bead Chain Mfg. Co. v. Saxton Prods., Inc., 183 Conn. 266, 439 A.2d 314, 31 UCC Rep. Serv. 91 (1981) (manufacturer granted lost profits on incomplete electrical components for which no resale market existed); Timber Access Industries Co. v. U.S. Plywood-Champion Papers, Inc., 263 Or. 509, 503 P.2d 482, 11 UCC Rep. Serv. 994 (1972) (same for undelivered logs).

[56] More extensive analysis of the lost-profit measure and the controversies that have developed may be found in Goetz & Scott, *Measuring Seller's Damages: The Lost Profits Puzzle*, 31 Stan. L. Rev. 323 (1979); Harris, *A General Theory for Measuring Seller's Damages for Total Breach of Contract*, 60 Mich. L. Rev. 577 (1962); Speidel & Clay, *Seller's Recovery of Overhead Under UCC Section 2-708(2): Economic Cost Theory and Contract Remedial Policy*, 57 Cornell L. Rev. 681 (1972).

[57] 616 F.2d 212, 28 UCC Rep. Serv. 1039 (5th Cir. 1980).

entered into a contract to buy a fixed quantity of a motor-fuel additive for $540 per ton and breached when the market price fell to $220 per ton. The seller had arranged to acquire the additive from a foreign supplier for $445 per ton, but it was not contractually required to and did not make the purchase because of the buyer's breach. If the buyer had performed the seller would have made a profit of $95 per ton, whereas its market-based damages were $320 per ton. The Fifth Circuit limited the seller to its lost profits, reasoning that this fully protected the benefit of its bargain.[58] In *Trans World Metals, Inc. v. Southwire Co.*,[59] the Second Circuit distinguished *Nobs Chemical* on factual grounds and allowed recovery under 2-708(1). The seller agreed to supply aluminum at a fixed price and the buyer repudiated when the market for aluminum dropped dramatically. Unlike the seller in *Nobs Chemical*, the seller in *Trans World* did not have a fixed-price contract with a supplier. Because the seller had accepted the risk that the market price would rise, the court thought it would be inappropriate to limit its recovery to lost profits when the market moved in the other direction.

§ 9.04   ACTION FOR PRICE OR RENT [§ 2-709; § 2A-529]

In limited circumstances a seller can bring an action for any part of the price of goods that remains unpaid. The remedy is analogous to an aggrieved buyer's action for specific performance and, like specific performance, it has limited availability.[60] The reason for the limitations is that a seller in the business of selling goods of the type involved in the contract is typically better situated than the buyer to resell them. Thus, the ordinary recovery for an aggrieved seller is the contract/resale differential, or sometimes the contract/market differential or lost profits. Section 2-709(1) states the circumstances in which an action for the price is available.

A seller that recovers a judgment for the price must hold for the buyer any of the goods that have been identified to the contract and that are still within its control.[61] Payment of the judgment entitles the buyer to the goods.[62] If resale becomes possible before the judgment is collected, the seller can resell the goods and credit the proceeds to the buyer.[63]

---

[58] *See also*, Diversified Energy, Inc. v. Tennessee Valley Auth., 339 F.3d 437 (6th Cir. 2003).

[59] 769 F.2d 902, 41 UCC Rep. Serv. 453 (2d Cir. 1985).

[60] Although the seller's action for the price is comparable in several respects to a buyer's claim for specific performance, it also differs substantially. A seller's success results in a money judgment and, unlike the equitable decree used with specific performance, it is not a court order that is punishable by contempt if it goes unheeded.

[61] UCC § 2-709(2).

[62] *Id.*

[63] *Id.*

[A] Limited Applicability

[1] Accepted Goods

One of the consequences of a buyer's acceptance of tendered goods is that it must pay for them at the contract rate.[64] The requirement makes sense because the buyer's retention of the goods prevents the seller from reselling them to another buyer.[65] If the buyer does not fulfill its payment obligation for accepted goods, the seller can recover the price.[66] Conversely, if the buyer does not accept the goods, the seller usually does not have a right to the price.[67] Whether the buyer repudiates the contract or wrongfully refuses to take delivery or rejects the goods, the seller will retain possession or control of them and thus be in a superior position to mitigate its damages by disposing of them.

Cases often turn on whether acceptance occurred.[68] For example, in *Integrated Circuits Unlimited v. E.F. Johnson Co.*,[69] the buyer wrongfully rejected some of the lots of electronic parts shipped by the seller. Although wrongful, the rejection effectively revested title in the seller, precluded acceptance, and precluded recovery on the seller's action for the price.[70] The court in *McClure Oil Corp. v. Murray Equipment, Inc.*[71] held that the buyer's letter indicating that it was "having problems" with delivered pumps was not a rejection. Having accepted the goods, the buyer was liable for their price. In *Solar Kinetics Corp. v. Joseph T. Ryerson & Sons, Inc.*[72] the court held that the buyer's failure to comply with the procedural requirements for revoking acceptance left it still bound by its acceptance, entitling the seller to the unpaid balance of the price.[73]

---

[64] UCC § 2-607(1); *see* § 7.03[B][2] *supra*.

[65] The seller is entitled to the price even if the buyer asserts a claim for breach of warranty. The claims of the parties in such a case will be netted out in determining the final award of damages.

[66] UCC § 2-709(1)(a); *see, e.g.*, Indeck Energy Serv., Inc. v. NGR Energy, Inc., 54 UCC Rep. Serv. 2d 990 (N.D. Ill. 2004).

[67] *See, e.g.*, Wings Mfg. Corp. v. Lawson, 58 UCC Rep. Serv. 2d 836 (Tenn. Ct. App. 2005) (because buyer never accepted the goods, it was not required to pay for them and thus was entitled to recover the amount that seller wrongfully drew against its letter of credit).

[68] For explanations of acceptance, and the related concepts of rejection and revocation, see §§ 7.04, 7.05 *supra*.

[69] 875 F.2d 1040, 8 UCC Rep. Serv. 2d 695 (2d Cir. 1989).

[70] The procedural effects of a rejection are discussed in § 7.04[B] *supra*.

[71] 515 N.E.2d 546, 5 UCC Rep. Serv. 2d 1354 (Ind. Ct. App. 1987).

[72] 488 F. Supp. 1237, 29 UCC Rep. Serv. 85 (D. Conn. 1980).

[73] The court's suggestion that a buyer can make a wrongful but effective revocation of acceptance is subject to considerable doubt and is discussed in § 7.05[D] *supra*. Section 2-709(3) refers to a wrongful revocation, but the Comments indicate that an action for price for goods accepted includes "only goods as to which there has been no *justified* revocation of acceptance, for such a revocation means that there has been a default by the seller which bars his rights under this section." UCC § 2-709, cmt. 5 (emphasis added). Although the drafting is unclear, the preferable position is to deny the effectiveness of a wrongful revocation.

[2]   Goods Lost or Damaged

An exception to the general principle that limits a seller's right to the price to cases of acceptance applies when "conforming goods [are] lost or damaged within a commercially reasonable time after risk of their loss has passed to the buyer."[74] Loss or destruction of the goods after the risk of loss has passed means that the buyer must pay for them,[75] because the seller's opportunity to resell them will have become limited or nonexistent. The seller obviously cannot resell goods that have been lost or destroyed, and goods that have been damaged most likely will differ from the goods that the seller typically sells.

Application of the exception requires application of the Code provisions on allocating the risk of loss.[76] Most of the cases concerning risk of loss and actions for the price have involved goods shipped by common carrier. For example, the contract in *Ninth St. East, Ltd. v. Harrison*[77] provided for shipment F.O.B. the seller's location[78] and the goods suffered casualty while in transit to the buyer's location. The risk of loss passed to the buyer upon the seller's proper delivery of the goods to the carrier,[79] leaving the buyer liable for the price. Risk of loss passed to the buyer in *Rheinberg Kellerei GmbH v. Brooksfield Nat'l Bank of Commerce Bank*[80] after tendered wine arrived at the destination harbor and was made available for the buyer to take delivery.[81] The wine deteriorated substantially when it remained at the harbor too long because of the buyer's failure to pay the amount due upon presentment of a letter of collection, and the buyer was liable for the purchase price. In *Multiplastics, Inc. v. Arch Industries*[82] the buyer breached by failing to take delivery of the goods as required by the contract and they were destroyed by fire while still in the seller's possession. Although the risk of loss technically had not passed to the buyer, the seller was entitled to treat the loss as resting with the buyer to the extent of a deficiency in its insurance coverage.[83] Because the seller did not have any insurance, the buyer was liable for the full purchase price.

The seller is only entitled to the price of goods that have been lost or destroyed for a commercially reasonable time after the risk of loss passes to the buyer. For example, suppose a buyer wrongful rejects goods after they have been delivered and thus after the risk of loss passes. The rejection revests title in the seller and ordinarily it would arrange to regain possession of the goods

---

[74] UCC § 2-709(1)(a).

[75] For a discussion on allocation of the risk of loss under Articles 2 and 2A, and the legal consequences of the allocation, see Chapter 6.

[76] See UCC §§ 2-509, 2-510, discussed in Chapter 6 *supra*.

[77] 5 Conn. Cir. Ct. 597, 259 A.2d 772, 7 UCC Rep. Serv. 171 (1968).

[78] The risk of loss passed because the contract was a "shipment" contract, meaning that the seller was not required to deliver the goods to a particular destination. *See* discussion § 6.02[A][2] *supra*. Any claim on behalf of the buyer would be against the carrier or the buyer's insurance company.

[79] *See* UCC §§ 2-319(1)(a), 2-509(1)(a).

[80] 901 F.2d 481, 11 UCC Rep. Serv. 2d 1214 (5th Cir. 1990).

[81] *See* UCC § 2-509(1)(b).

[82] 166 Conn. 280, 348 A.2d 618 (1974).

[83] See UCC § 2-510(3), discussed in § 6.02[B][3] *supra*.

and then resell them. Limiting the seller's right to recover the price to a commercially reasonable time encourages it to take possession promptly, or at least to obtain casualty insurance. If it fails to do either, it loses the right to recover the price.[84]

[3] Goods Not Readily Resalable

The other exception to the general principle limiting sellers' right to the price to cases of acceptance applies to "goods identified to the contract if the seller is unable after reasonable effort to resell them at a reasonable price or the circumstances reasonably indicate that such effort will be unavailing."[85] The rationale for denying the seller the price simply does not apply in this context: A seller that cannot resell custom goods because there is no market is in no better position to dispose of them than the buyer. Furthermore, relegating the seller to damages based on market price would unfairly allocate to it the burden of establishing that price, which would be difficult or impossible given the nature of the goods.

Sellers of custom goods should make and document efforts to resell them. The seller in *Continental-Wirt Electronics Corp. v. Sprague Electric Co.*[86] successfully recovered the price after making several unsuccessful efforts to resell the goods. By contrast, the appellate court in *Multi-Line Manufacturing, Inc. v. Greenwood Mills, Inc.*[87] reversed a grant of summary judgment in favor of a fabric seller that provided only the opinion of its merchandise manager that it could not have resold the fabric for more than 50% of its value.[88]

[B] Recovery of Rent

The drafters of Article 2A originally followed the Article 2 approach precisely with regard to a lessor's right to recover the rent that the lessee promised to pay.[89] They ultimately adhered to the sales model with respect both to lost or damaged goods and to goods that the lessor cannot reasonably dispose of, but they made a significant change regarding accepted goods.[90]

Allowing a lessor to recover rent for any goods that have been accepted posed problems with respect to mitigation of damages because the lessor could repossess the goods and still recover the present value of future rent as long as

---

[84] The limitation to a commercially reasonable time reflects the same policy as the limitation to a commercially reasonable time in UCC § 2-510(3), discussed in § 6.02[B][3] *supra.*

[85] UCC § 2-709(1)(b).

[86] 329 F. Supp. 959, 9 UCC Rep. Serv. 1049 (E.D. Pa. 1971).

[87] 123 Ga. App. 372, 180 S.E.2d 917, 9 UCC Rep. Serv. 80 (1971).

[88] *Cf.* Precision Mirror & Glass v. Nelms, 8 Misc.3d 339, 797 N.Y.S.2d 720, 57 UCC Rep. Serv. 2d 258 (Civ. Ct. 2005) (seller entitled to price of custom-cut glass table top with unique shape and design because seller could not reasonably resell table top in ordinary course of its business).

[89] UCC § 2A-529(1) (1987).

[90] Article 2A also includes provisions comparable to Article 2 concerning the lessor's holding goods available to the lessee, the lessee's right to use of the goods for the remaining lease term on payment of the judgment, and the lessor's right to dispose of the goods prior to collection of the judgment. UCC § 2A-529(3),(4).

it held the goods for the lessee. The approach failed to recognize a fundamental distinction between sales and lease transactions: An unsecured seller cannot retake possession of goods that a buyer has accepted. If a sale is secured, the seller can repossess the goods, but it must dispose of them in a commercially reasonable manner and apply the proceeds to the outstanding indebtedness, remitting any surplus to the buyer.[91] In a lease, however, the lessor may repossess the goods following a default by the lessee[92] and, because it holds the residual interest, is not required to dispose of them.[93] Allowing a lessor to recover the rent after repossessing the goods eliminates any incentive it might have to enter into a substitute lease agreement and thereby mitigate its damages.[94]

Because of this concern, the drafters decided that "it is not economically sound to both allow recovery of the full rent and the goods to go unused,"[95] and they amended Section 2A-529(1)(a) so that future rent can be recovered for accepted goods only if the lessor has not repossessed them or the lessee has not tendered them back.[96] If a lessor leaves the lessee in possession of the goods following a default and the lessee chooses to retain them, the lessor is entitled to the rent because the lessee continues to enjoy the beneficial use of the goods. If either party chooses to terminate the lessee's possession, however, the lessor cannot recover future rent merely because the lessee initially accepted the goods. The lessee's damages will be mitigated to the extent of either the actual rent that the lessor attains through a qualifying substitute lease or of the market rent determined through the contract/market differential.[97] If the goods are custom goods for which there is no reasonable market, the lessor can still recover the price.

§_9.05   INCIDENTAL DAMAGES [§ 2-710; § 2A-530]

Each of the sellers' damages provisions provides that a seller may recover incidental damages, which are defined as follows:

> Incidental damages to an aggrieved seller include any commercially reasonable charges, expenses or commissions incurred in stopping delivery, in the transportation, care and custody of goods after the buyer's breach, in connection with return or resale of the goods or otherwise resulting from the breach.[98]

---

[91] *See* § 9.01[C] *supra.*

[92] UCC § 2A-525.

[93] UCC § 2A-527, cmt. 1.

[94] *See* Industrial Leasing Corp. v. Thomason, 96 Ida. 574, 532 P.2d 916 (1974) (pre-Article 2A case stating the nature of the problem).

[95] National Conference of Commissioners on Uniform State Law, Amendments to Uniform Commercial Code Article 2A, Leases § 2A-529, Drafting Note (July 13, 1990).

[96] UCC § 2A-529(1)(a). "The rule in Article 2 that the seller can recover the price of accepted goods is rejected" in Article 2A. UCC § 2A-529, cmt. 1.

[97] The alternative damage measures are discussed in § 9.02[B] *supra.*

[98] UCC § 2-710.

The description is a non-exclusive list of additional damages that commonly flow from a buyer's breach.[99] Article 2A includes a comparable provision for lessors.[100] As noted in the discussion of buyers' remedies,[101] incidental damages are a subset of consequential damages that are so common that they are not subjected to a foreseeability test. If damages are within the definition, the key issue is whether they are reasonable.[102]

The courts have readily recognized certain types of expenditures by a seller as incidental damages. The seller in *Afram Export Corp. v. Metallurgiki Halyps, S.A.*[103] recovered incidental damages for freight charges, inspection, and certification on resale of the goods. In *Lee Oldsmobile, Inc. v. Kaiden*[104] the seller recovered commissions on the resale of an automobile and transportation charges for delivering it to the place of resale. The court in *Servbest Foods, Inc. v. Emessee Industries, Inc.*[105] awarded incidental damages for the cold storage of meat.

Unlike the buyers' and lessees' remedy provisions, which explicitly refer to both incidental and consequential damages, the sellers' and lessors' remedy provisions omit any mention of consequentials. Admittedly, consequential damages are far more rare for sellers and lessors than they are for buyers and lessees, as the latter parties often incur lost profits or suffer harm resulting from defective goods.[106] The general measures of a seller's or lessor's direct damages take lost profits into account and usually provide adequate protection. These parties nevertheless may suffer consequential harm, and the question arises whether they can recover under supplementary principles imported from the common law under Section 1-103(b).[107] The courts have looked in this regard to Section 1-305(a), which provides that consequential damages may not be recovered "except as specifically provided in [the Uniform Commercial Code] or by other rule of law," and at the fact that consequential damages are explicitly provided for buyers but not for sellers, and have concluded that sellers are not entitled to such damages.[108] The result is not inevitable — the reference to other rules of law could provide a basis for a recovery and interests of fairness suggest

---

[99] UCC § 2-710, cmt.

[100] UCC § 2A-530.

[101] *See* § 8.02[E][1] *supra.*

[102] *See, e.g.*, Stamtec, Inc. v. Anson Stamping Co., 346 F.3d 651, 51 UCC Rep. Serv. 2d 1048 (6th Cir. 2003) (a claim of $800,000 to store two presses for slightly more than two years was not recoverable because seller did not prove reasonableness of amount).

[103] 772 F.2d 1358, 41 UCC Rep. Serv. 1709 (7th Cir. 1985).

[104] 56 Md. App. 556, 363 A.2d 270, 20 UCC Rep. Serv. 117 (1976).

[105] 82 Ill. App. 3d 662, 403 N.E.2d 1, 29 UCC Rep. Serv. 518 (1980).

[106] *See* § 8.06[B] *supra.*

[107] The common law generally permits recovery of consequential damages, subject to certain limitations. Restatement (Second) of Contracts § 351.

[108] *See, e.g.*, Nina Indus., Ltd. v. Target Corp., 56 UCC Rep. Serv. 2d 138 (S.D.N.Y. 2005); Sprague v. Sumitomo Forestry Co., Ltd., 144 Wash. 2d 751, 709 P.2d 1200, 42 UCC Rep. Serv. 202 (1985). *But see* Associated Metals & Minerals Corp. v. Sharon Steel Corp., 590 F. Supp. 18, 39 UCC Rep. Serv. 892 (S.D.N.Y. 1983), *aff'd*, 742 F.2d 1431 (2d Cir. 1983) (consequential damages may be recovered by applying supplementary principles derived from common law).

İMI

this approach — but sellers have met with a singular lack of success.

In the absence of a specific provision authorizing their recovery, sellers and lessors have had to be resourceful in trying to recover consequential damages. The most obvious approach is to argue that their damages are not consequential at all but rather are within the definition of incidental damages. In particular, they rely on the language at the end of the definition referring to "any commercially reasonable charges . . . otherwise resulting from the breach."[109] While open-ended, the language is somewhat limiting because of the reference to "charges." Thus, the court in *Nobs Chemical, USA, Inc. v. Koppers Co., Inc.*[110] properly held that the seller's loss of a volume discount with its supplier caused by the buyer's breach did not constitute incidental damages. Also, because incidental damages must be the result of a buyer's breach, a seller may not recover for pre-breach expenses.[111]

Courts have struggled to define the line between the categories. Some courts have suggested that losses involving dealings with third parties are generally consequential. For example, the court in *Petroleo Brasileiro, SA v. Ameropan Oil Corp.*[112] held that the seller was not entitled to recover penalty charges incurred because the buyer's breach caused it to default on a bank loan.[113] Other courts have indicated that incidental damages are generally unavoidable while consequential damages often may be avoided or mitigated, leaving them appropriate candidates for a foreseeability test. Judge Posner used this analysis in *Afram Export Corp. v. Metallurgiki Halyps, S.A.*,[114] a case in which the buyer of scrap metal refused to take delivery when the market price fell. The seller claimed as incidental damages $40,000 in interest that it incurred between the time of the breach and the time of resale on a $2.5 million loan, about $2 million of which was spent to acquire the metal. The court hypothesized a seller forced into bankruptcy as a result of a buyer's breach and indicated that the costs of the bankruptcy would be consequential damages. The seller should not have arranged its business in such a way that breach of a single contract would have such a catastrophic effect and, as consequential damages, the buyer would not be liable unless the bankruptcy was foreseeable to it. By contrast, it should be obvious to any buyer that a seller will incur interest charges like those claimed by the seller and thus the charges ordinarily would be recoverable, but in the actual case the seller lost because it failed to establish that it would have repaid all or any part of what was in effect a general business loan if the buyer had accepted and paid for the metal.[115] Thus, the seller was in effect complaining about its lost-opportunity cost, meaning the amount it would have earned on the

---

[109] UCC § 2-710; *see also* UCC § 2A-530.

[110] 616 F.2d 212, 28 UCC Rep. Serv. 1039 (5th Cir. 1980).

[111] *See, e.g.*, Serna, Inc. v. Harman, 742 F.2d 186, 39 UCC Rep. Serv. 481 (5th Cir. 1984) (seller not entitled to pre-breach cost of feeding and caring for cattle).

[112] 372 F. Supp. 503, 14 UCC Rep. Serv. 661 (E.D.N.Y. 1974).

[113] *See also* S.C. Gray, Inc. v. Ford Motor Co., 92 Mich. App. 789, 286 N.W.2d 34, 29 UCC Rep. Serv. 417 (1979) (seller not entitled to recover for high interest charges incurred when buyer's breach forced it to borrow money to carry on business).

[114] 772 F.2d 1358, 41 UCC Rep. Serv. 1709 (7th Cir. 1985).

[115] In this regard, see *New England Dairies, Inc. v. Dairy Mart Convenience Stores, Inc.*, 47

money if it had been paid. Lost-opportunity costs, as opposed to interest charges on a loan for the goods that are incurred pending resale and repayment of the loan, are consequential rather than incidental in nature.[116]

§ 9.06 INJURY TO LESSOR'S RESIDUAL INTEREST [§ 2A-532]

Article 2A adds a right of recovery to protect a lessor's residual interest. Section 2A-532 provides that "[i]n addition to any other recovery permitted by this Article or other law, the lessor may recover from the lessee an amount that will fully compensate the lessor for any loss of or damage to the lessor's residual interest in the goods caused by the default of the lessee." A lessee might fail to return the goods to the lessor at the end of the lease term, or the goods might be returned in a damaged condition beyond the normal wear and tear from the lessee's use that would be permitted.[117] The provision entitles the lessor to compensation for the impairment of its residual interest.

§ 9.07 LIQUIDATED DAMAGES

[A]   Sales [§ 2-718(1)]

Parties to a sales contract may choose to avoid the uncertainty of measuring damages in the event of a breach by agreeing to a liquidated-damages clause. An enforceable liquidated-damages clause determines the amount of damages, thereby removing their assessment from the purview of the court and the jury. Such a clause provides an efficient means to establish damages and serves to inform the parties about the extent of their liability in the event of breach.

Despite the inherent advantages of providing for liquidated damages, the courts historically have been concerned about their potential for abuse. Article 2 reflects this concern by authorizing agreement on a liquidated amount but subjecting the agreement to three limitations. Section 2-718(1) states:

> Damages for breach by either party may be liquidated in the agreement but only at an amount which is reasonable in the light of the anticipated or actual harm caused by the breach, the difficulties of proof of loss, and

---

UCC Rep. Serv. 2d 480 (D. Conn. 2002) (seller has burden of establishing that incidental damages were actually incurred).

[116] *See, e.g.*, Nina Indus., Ltd. v. Target Corp., 56 UCC Rep. Serv. 2d 138 (S.D.N.Y. 2005) (lost opportunity to use and invest cash flow that seller should have received not recoverable). With regard to interest charges on a loan for the goods pending resale, see, *e.g.*, *Masters Mach. Co., Inc. v. Brookfield Athletic Shoe Co., Inc.*, 4 UCC Rep. Serv. 2d 749 (1st Cir. 1986) (post-breach interest on loan in connection with contract that was actually paid by seller recoverable as incidental damages), and *Bulk Oil (USA), Inc. v. Sun Oil Trading Co.*, 697 F.2d 481, 35 UCC Rep. Serv. 23 (2d Cir. 1983) (post-breach interest payments on bank loan incurred by seller to finance acquisition of goods allowed as incidental damages).

[117] Puckett v. Kenesaw Leasing, Inc., 2006 U.S. Dist. LEXIS 54427 (E.D. Ark., Aug. 3, 2006) (although lessee assumed that lessor had picked up leased trailer following lessee's default, lessee incurred liability when trailer could not be located).

the inconvenience or nonfeasibility of otherwise obtaining an adequate remedy. A term fixing unreasonably large liquidated damages is void as a penalty.

The first limitation is actually more expansive than the approach generally followed at common law,[118] which scrutinizes the reasonableness of a liquidated amount only prospectively; that is, the damages must be reasonable in light of the harm that the parties, at the time of contracting, anticipated would flow from a breach. Article 2 allows reasonableness to be tested either by the anticipated harm or by the harm that actually results from a breach. In *California & Hawaiian Sugar Co. v. Sun Ship, Inc.*[119] the court upheld liquidated damages totaling $4.4 million dollars for an eight-month delay in building a barge because the damages were reasonable in light of the anticipated harm that could result from the loss of charter opportunities.[120] In *Lafayette Stabilizer Repair, Inc. v. Machinery Wholesalers Corp.*[121] the court focused on the harm that actually resulted from a breach in holding that a clause limiting damages to a $6,900 allowance for repairs was not reasonable when the goods proved to be unusable and beyond repair. Although explainable on other grounds,[122] the decision is facially troubling because it focuses entirely on the relationship between the liquidated amount and the actual damages without discussing whether the liquidated amount might have been a reasonable forecast of the harm. The most obvious use of the actual damages proviso is to validate clauses in light of the actual harm when it turns out that it was unreasonable as a forecast.

The alternative application of the tests was demonstrated in *Equitable Lumber Corp v. I.P.A. Land Development Corp.*[123] A contract provision required that, in the event of breach, the buyer would be required to pay reasonable attorneys' fees, which were defined as thirty percent of any amount collected. The court said that the reasonableness of the provision could be determined either (1) in light of the anticipated damages, which would require an assessment of its relationship to the fee that an attorney would normally charge for collection of the seller's claim, or (2) based on a comparison with the actual fee arrangement agreed upon by the seller and its attorney.

Although most clauses that are held unreasonable involve liquidated damages that are excessive, an occasional court, like the court in *Lafayette Stabilizer Repair*, has refused to uphold a clause because the liquidated damages are too

---

[118] *See generally* Comment, *Liquidated Damages: A Comparison of the Common Law and the Uniform Commercial Code*, 45 Fordham L. Rev. 1349 (1977).

[119] 794 F.2d 1433, 1 UCC Rep. Serv. 2d 1211 (9th Cir. 1986).

[120] The actual damages proved by the buyer at trial were only $368,000, the amount it spent for an alternative means of shipping its crop. The buyer also suggested that it had suffered harm of more than $3 million from lost charter opportunities but the evidence was not sufficient to support such a finding.

[121] 750 P.2d 1290, 40 UCC Rep. Serv. 122 (5th Cir. 1985).

[122] The court was reviewing an arbitral award and the arbitrator had determined that the loss was the fault of both parties.

[123] 38 N.Y.2d 516, 381 N.Y.S.2d 459, 344 N.E.2d 391, 8 UCC Rep. Serv. 273 (1976).

low. The case most often cited in this regard is *Varner v. BL Lanier Fruit Co.*,[124] in which a buyer of fruit breached after picking only some of the crop from the seller's trees and the seller was unable to sell the remainder of its fruit. The contract provided as liquidated damages that the seller would retain the advance payment that the buyer had made for some of the fruit. The court was concerned that the buyer would not have to pay damages for any of the unpicked fruit and thus found the clause unenforceable.

The second limitation on the validity of a liquidated-damages clause is that the amount stipulated must be reasonable in light of the difficulties involved in proving the loss.[125] This requirement appears to follow the common-law approach of determining difficulty of estimation as of the time of contract formation and tends to preclude liquidating damages when actual damages can be reasonably estimated at that time.[126] Application of the limitation can be illustrated by the facts of *Ray Catena Motor Car Corp. v. Curto*,[127] a case in which the buyer of a new car falsely certified that the used car he delivered to the dealer in trade had never been in a flood. After the trial court granted the dealer summary judgment on its breach-of-warranty claim,[128] the buyer placed lettering on the back window of his new car that stated, "I GOT ROYALLY SCREWED BY RAY CATENA" and parked it across from the dealer's lot. The parties negotiated a settlement of the warranty claim and also agreed that the buyer would pay the dealer an additional $150 per day if the lettering was not removed. When the buyer failed to remove the lettering for twenty-four days, the dealer sued to recover the liquidated amount. The appellate court reversed the lower court's refusal to enforce the agreement, finding that it was a valid liquidated-damages provision rather than a penalty. Actual damages would have been virtually impossible to establish and the agreement, which followed extensive negotiations, appeared to be a reasonable, good-faith effort to estimate the dealer's daily loss.

The third limitation is that liquidated damages are to be measured against the inconvenience or nonfeasibility of otherwise obtaining an adequate remedy. Apparently this requirement extends the focus beyond simply the difficulty of estimating money damages to a consideration of other available remedies as well. For example, the availability of specific performance in the event of a breach might be used to preclude enforcement of a liquidated-damages clause.

The second sentence of Section 2-718(2) states that unreasonably large liquidated damages are penalties and not enforceable. Several courts have

---

[124] 370 So. 2d 61, 26 UCC Rep. Serv. 716 (Fla. Dist. Ct. App. 1979).

[125] *See, e.g.*, Baker v. International Record Syndicate, Inc., 812 S.W.2d 53, 15 UCC Rep. Serv. 2d 875 (Tex. Ct. App. 1991) (liquidated damages of $1,500 per negative for photographer reasonable given the difficulty of determining value of work of art, potential for fame, and long-term earning power of photographs).

[126] *See, e.g.*, Lee Oldsmobile, Inc. v. Kaiden, 32 Md. App. 556, 363 A.2d 270, 20 UCC Rep. Serv. 117 (1976) (liquidated damages provision inapplicable because actual damages were capable of accurate estimation at time of contract formation).

[127] 2007 WL 3239015 (N.J. App. Div., Nov. 5, 2007) (unpublished).

[128] *See* UCC § 2-304(1) (if price "payable in whole or in part in goods each party is a seller of the goods which he is to transfer").

decided cases under this provision, often without indicating whether the characterization as a penalty is an independent test or the consequence of applying the other requirements.[129] It would seem that the requirements for an enforceable clause are established by the first sentence and that the second sentence is redundant. It is also misleading in that it refers to unreasonably large damages and omits any reference to damages that are unreasonably small.

A question that sometimes arises, most often in the oil and natural gas industries, is the effect of what are called "take-or-pay" clauses. Under such a clause the buyer must either take an agreed quantity at the contract price or pay for it anyway. Viewed as a liquidated-damages clause, a take-or-pay clause appears to be unreasonable; after all, a seller whose buyer repudiates or fails to take delivery of marketable goods is not entitled to the contract price[130] and the relevant methods of measuring its damages would typically produce a smaller amount than the price. Most courts, however, have understood that the clause is a risk-allocation device rather than a liquidated-damages clause.[131] The purpose of the clause is to apportion the risk of production and sale in volatile markets. The seller bears the risks associated with production and to compensate for these risks the buyer agrees either to take a minimum quantity or, if it fails to do so, to pay the price anyway. This arrangement assures a seller in a falling market of a steady source of revenue so that it can maintain its production capacity. Viewed from this perspective, taking and paying are simply alternative methods by which the buyer can perform its obligations under the contract.

[B]   Leases [§ 2A-504]

The Article 2A provision on liquidated damages is based on Article 2, but it deletes most of the requirements included in the sales provision. Section 2A-504(1) states:

> Damages payable by either party for default, or any other act or omission, including indemnity for loss or diminution of anticipated tax benefits or loss or damages to lessor's residual interest, may be liquidated in the lease agreement but only at an amount or by a formula that is reasonable in light of the then anticipated harm caused by the default or other act or omission.

---

[129] *See, e.g.*, Welch v. K-Beck Furniture Mart, Inc., 3 Ohio App. 3d 171, 444 N.E.2d 48, 35 UCC Rep. Serv. 474 (1981) (terms of furniture lay-away agreement, under which buyer who defaulted could forfeit over 40 percent of price, unenforceable as penalty); Hertz Commercial Leasing Corp. v. Dynatron, Inc., 37 Conn. Supp. 7, 427 A.2d 872, 30 UCC Rep. Serv. 770 (1980) (in lease case decided under Article 2, liquidated-damages provision was harsh and penal and subjected lessee to forfeiture). *But see* Coast Trading Co., Inc. v. Parmac, Inc., 21 Wash. App. 896, 587 P.2d 1071, 25 UCC Rep. Serv. 1047 (1978) (demonstration by seller that actual damages exceeded 15% of purchase price disposed of buyer's contention that 15% cancellation fee was a penalty).

[130] *See* § 9.04[A] *supra*.

[131] *See, e.g.*, Sabine Corp. v. ONG Western, Inc., 725 F. Supp. 1157, 11 UCC Rep. Serv. 2d 83 (W.D. Okla. 1989).

The sole standard is reasonableness of the damages, and it must be determined prospectively with respect to the anticipated harm.[132] Liquidated-damages provisions are common in lease agreements and focus primarily on default by the lessee. The drafters eliminated the other standards in order to facilitate this practice.[133]

Article 2A also eliminates the Article 2 provision that "[a] term fixing unreasonably large liquidated damages is void as a penalty."[134] The Comments explain the reason for the deletion:

> Further, . . . the expansion of subsection (1) to enable the parties to liquidate the amount payable with respect to an indemnity for loss or diminution of anticipated tax benefits resulted in another change: the last sentence of Section 2-718(1), providing that a term fixing unreasonably large liquidated damages is void as a penalty, was also not incorporated. The impact of local, state and federal tax laws on a leasing transaction can result in an amount payable with respect to the tax indemnity many times greater than the original purchase price of the goods. By deleting the reference to unreasonably large liquidated damages the parties are free to negotiate a formula, restrained by the rule of reasonableness in this section. These changes should invite the parties to liquidate damages.[135]

The Article 2A provision also reflects prior law in authorizing the use of a formula to establish liquidated damages. The Comments include several examples.[136] One formula, for example, adds overdue lease payments, accelerated future lease payments, and the estimated residual value, from which it deducts the net proceeds from the lessor's disposal of the goods by sale or re-lease. Tax indemnities, costs, interest, and attorneys' fees are also often added. Any formula that entitles the lessor to accelerated future lease payments should require mitigation by the lessor through sale or re-lease of the goods.[137] Future rents should also be reduced to present value.[138]

---

[132] Ames Linen Serv. v. Katz, 8 A.D.3d 945, 779 N.Y.S.2d 600 (App. Div. 2004) (liquidated-damages clause upheld against assertion that it was disproportionate to lessor's actual loss because lessor established that it had already replaced some of original inventory as it wore out during lease term prior to lessee's breach and that some inventory could not be re-leased to other customers).

[133] "Thus, consistent with the common law emphasis upon freedom to contract with respect to bailments for hire, this section has created a revised rule that allows greater flexibility with respect to leases of goods." UCC § 2A-504, cmt.

[134] UCC § 2-718(1); see § 9.07[A] supra.

[135] UCC § 2A-504, cmt. Some courts nevertheless continue to apply the penalty standard to liquidated-damages provisions in the lease context. See, e.g., TAL Fin. Corp. v. CSC Consulting, Inc., 446 Mass. 422, 844 N.E.2d 1085 (2006).

[136] UCC § 2A-504, cmt.

[137] Frank Nero Auto Lease v. Townsend, 64 Ohio App. 2d 65, 411 N.E.2d 507 (1979) (agreement allowing lessor to repossess vehicle and accelerate future rents but with no provision to mitigate damages allows double payment and is contrary to public policy).

[138] See, e.g., Goodin v. TBF Fin., LLC, 53 UCC Rep. Serv. 2d 265 (Ky. Ct. App. 2004) (stipulated damages that entitled lessor to entire amount of remaining balance under lease, without any adjustment to present value, and that gave lessor the additional right to return of leased equipment

§ 9.08   NON-MONETARY REMEDIES

[A]   Cancellation [§ 2-703(f); § 2A-523(1)(a)]

Cancellation occurs when a party justifiably ends a contract because of the other party's breach.[139] Executory obligations on both sides are discharged upon cancellation, but the nonbreaching party retains its right to pursue an appropriate remedy for breach of the whole contract or any unperformed balance.[140] The Code states specific circumstances in which cancellation is appropriate: Repudiation by the buyer, failure to make a payment due on or before delivery, and wrongful rejection or revocation of acceptance.[141] Presumably, a seller or lessor may also cancel a contract for other substantial breaches, as is the case at common law.

[B]   Withholding Delivery [§ 2-703(a); § 2A-523(1)(c)]

Although the contract obligations of a seller are to transfer and deliver conforming goods,[142] it nevertheless can withhold delivery in some circumstances. Lessors have comparable withholding rights. The right applies generally in the same circumstances in which cancellation is allowed; *i.e.*, when a buyer or lessee breaches or defaults by wrongfully rejecting or revoking, by failing to make a payment due on or before delivery, or by repudiating.[143] In addition, a seller may refuse to deliver except for cash upon discovering that the buyer is insolvent.[144] A lessor's rights are similar, except that a lessor does not have to deliver if an insolvent lessee pays cash.[145] Requiring the lessor to deliver goods to an insolvent lessee that could somehow scrape up the cash for the first payment due under the lease would leave the lessor in peril with respect to subsequent payments. An insolvent lessee would also lack the financial capability to satisfy such lease requirements as insuring the goods or providing repair and maintenance services.

---

without any requirement of mitigation not a reasonable estimation).

[139] UCC §§ 2-106(4), 2A-103(1)(b). Contrast termination, which occurs when a party ends a contract otherwise than for its breach (*i.e.*, because of a contractual power or rule of law). After termination, executory obligations are discharged and rights based on prior breach or performance survive. UCC §§ 2-106(3), 2A-103(1)(z).

[140] *Id.*

[141] UCC §§ 2-703(f), 2A-523(1)(a). In the case of an installment contract, cancellation requires that the breach go to the whole contract. *See* § 7.07[B][4] *supra.* Whether a revocation of acceptance can be effective even though wrongful is debatable. *See* § 7.05[D] *supra.*

[142] UCC § 2-301.

[143] UCC §§ 2-703(a), 2A-523(1)(c). As a practical matter a seller or lessor usually will have delivered prior to rejection.

[144] UCC § 2-702(1). A person is insolvent if it has ceased paying debts not subject to a bona fide dispute in the ordinary course of its business, is unable to pay its debts as they come due, or is insolvent as the term is defined in bankruptcy law. UCC § 1-201(b)(23). Bankruptcy law limits insolvency to a balance-sheet test; whether at a fair valuation a person's debts exceed its assets. 11 U.S.C. § 101(32).

[145] UCC § 2A-525(1).

If a buyer or lessee is insolvent, the seller or lessor also has a right to stop delivery of goods in the possession of a carrier or other bailee.[146] Even if the goods have been shipped when insolvency is discovered, there may still be time to change the carrier's delivery instructions. Timely instructions to a warehouse similarly can prevent the delivery of stored goods.

Even without insolvency, delivery by a bailee can be stopped if the buyer or lessee has repudiated or failed to make a payment due before delivery, or if the seller or lessor for any other reason has a right to withhold or reclaim the goods.[147] The right to stop delivery under these circumstances, however, is limited to shipments the size of a carload, truckload, planeload, or larger. The drafters decided that the imposition of stop-delivery orders for smaller shipments would impose an undue burden on carriers.[148] They did not consider the burden on the carrier with respect to large shipments to be sufficient to overcome the interests of the seller or lessor in withholding the goods from insolvent buyers or lessees.

Articles 2 and 2A specify time limitations on the effectiveness of a stop-delivery order: The seller or lessor must stop delivery before the buyer or lessee receives the goods and before negotiation to the buyer of any negotiable document covering the goods.[149] A stop-delivery order must also be made before a bailee other than a carrier acknowledges to the buyer or lessee that it holds the goods for it.[150] In the case of a carrier, the stoppage must occur before the carrier makes a comparable acknowledgment by reshipment or as a warehouse.[151]

The stop-delivery order must be sufficient to enable the bailee, through the exercise of reasonable diligence, to prevent delivery.[152] After implementing the order, the bailee must hold the goods and deliver them according to the directions of the seller or lessor. The seller or lessor, however, is liable to the bailee for any charges or damages that result.[153]

---

[146] UCC §§ 2-705(1), 2A-526(1).

[147] UCC §§ 2-705(1), 2A-526(1); *see, e.g.*, Amoco Pipeline Co. v. Admiral Crude Oil Corp., 490 F.2d 114, 13 UCC Rep. Serv. 1019 (10th Cir. 1974) (buyer's check for crude oil dishonored by drawee bank). A seller's or lessor's right to reclaim delivered goods is discussed in § 9.08[C][1] (seller) and [2] (lessee) *infra.*

[148] UCC § 2-705, cmt. 1.

[149] UCC §§ 2-705(2)(a),(d), 2A-526(2)(a) (a negotiable document of title would not be issued to a lessee); *see, e.g.*, Amoco Pipeline Co v. Admiral Crude Oil Corp., 490 F.2d 114, 13 UCC Rep. Serv. 1019 (10th Cir. 1974) (oil in possession of pipeline company had not been delivered to buyer).

[150] UCC §§ 2-705(2)(b), 2A-526(2)(b).

[151] UCC §§ 2-705(2)(c), 2A-526(2)(c).

[152] UCC §§ 2-705(3)(a), 2A-526(3)(a).

[153] UCC §§ 2-705(3)(b), 2A-526(3)(b).

[C]   Retaking Possession [§ 2-702(2), § 2-507(2), § 2-511(3); § 2A-525]

[1]   Seller

A credit seller generally does not have a right to repossess delivered goods if the buyer fails to pay for them. The seller transferred title in exchange for a promise and has no more rights in the goods than any other unsecured creditor of the buyer. Consequently, the seller must reduce its claim for nonpayment to a judgment and, if necessary, execute on the judgment. A seller that wants the right to repossess the goods must retain a security interest in them. Even then, the security interest is a limited property interest and repossession will not serve to convey title back to the seller. Rather, the seller must dispose of the goods in a commercially reasonable manner and must account to the buyer for any amount by which the proceeds of disposition exceed the sum of its expenses and the outstanding debt.[154]

A credit seller actually may reclaim the goods in one narrowly circumscribed situation. If the seller discovers that the buyer was insolvent when it received the goods, the seller may reclaim them if it demands return of the goods within ten days after the buyer receives them.[155] The rationale is that receiving goods on credit while insolvent is a tacit misrepresentation of solvency and constitutes a fraud against the seller.[156] The requirement that demand be made within ten days after receipt is inapplicable if the buyer gave the seller a written misrepresentation of solvency within three months before delivery.[157] The seller's right of reclamation is subject to the rights of a buyer in ordinary course of business or other good faith purchaser from the buyer.[158] Successful reclamation excludes all other remedies with respect to the goods.[159]

In the case of a cash sale,[160] Article 2 basically incorporates the common-law cash-sale doctrine.[161] Section 2-507(2) provides that "[w]here payment is due and demanded on the delivery to the buyer of goods or documents of title, his

---

[154] See the discussion of security interests in § 9.01[C] *supra.*

[155] UCC § 2-702(2); *see, e.g.*, Eastman Cutting Room Sales Corp. v. Ottenheimer & Co., Inc., 221 Ga. App. 659, 472 S.E.2d 494, 32 UCC Rep. Serv. 2d 465 (1996) (because Section 2-103(1)(c) defines "receipt" of goods as "taking physical possession of them," court rejected seller's argument that ten-day period did not commence until after installation of goods).

[156] UCC § 2-702, cmt. 2.

[157] Section 2-702(2) is the exclusive source for a seller's right of reclamation based on fraud or misrepresentation of solvency or intent to pay. "Except as provided in this subsection the seller may not base a right to reclaim goods on the buyer's fraudulent or innocent misrepresentation of solvency or of intent to pay." UCC § 2-702(2).

[158] UCC § 2-702(3). The rights of good faith purchasers and buyers in ordinary course of business generally are discussed in § 10.01[A] (purchasers) and [B] (buyers) *infra.*

[159] UCC § 2-702(3).

[160] A cash sale involves a contemporaneous exchange of goods for cash or a check. "[P]ayment by check is conditional and is defeated as between the parties by dishonor of the check on due presentment." UCC § 2-511(3); *see also* UCC § 3-310(b).

[161] UCC § 2-507, cmt. 3.

right as against the seller to retain or dispose of them is conditional upon his making the payment due." This provision must be read in context with Section 2-511(3), which provides that "payment by check is conditional and is defeated between the parties by dishonor of the check on due presentment." Thus, a seller may reclaim goods if the buyer's check bounces. Even though the text is silent on the point, the original Comments indicated that, as with credit sellers, a cash seller's right of reclamation was conditional on demand made within ten days after the buyer's receipt of the goods. Most courts followed the Comments in this regard.[162] After amendments in 1990 the Comments now state as follows:

> There is no specific time limit for a cash seller to exercise the right of reclamation. However, the right will be defeated by delay causing prejudice to the buyer, waiver, estoppel, or ratification of the buyer's right to retain possession. Common law rules and precedents governing such principles are applicable (Section 1-103).[163]

The amended Comments also indicate that, like a credit seller, a cash seller's right of reclamation is subject to the rights of good faith purchasers.[164]

[2] Lessor

A lessor's right to repossess the goods is patterned more on the rights of a secured party than on those of a seller; that is, default terminates a lessee's right to possession.[165] Unlike a seller, which parts with the entire interest in the goods, the lessor retains a residual interest and the right to repossess the goods protects that interest. The analogy to Article 9 is limited however: Whereas a secured party that repossesses goods does not own them and therefore must dispose of them and account to the debtor for any amount by which the proceeds of disposition exceed the sum of its expenses and the outstanding debt, the lessor owns the residual interest and is not required to dispose of the goods or to pay to the lessee any of the proceeds if it chooses to dispose of them.

A lessor has several options following default by the lessee:

> If the lessor or the lessee is in default under the lease contract, the party seeking enforcement may reduce the party's claim to judgment, or otherwise enforce the lease contract by self-help or any available judicial procedure or nonjudicial procedure, including administrative proceeding, arbitration, or the like, in accordance with this Article.[166]

Judicial action to enforce a lessor's right to take possession of the goods can lead to injunctive relief.[167] In most jurisdictions a lessor can proceed through a

---

[162] *See, e.g.,* Szabo v. Vinton Motors, 630 F.2d 1, 29 UCC Rep. Serv. 737 (1st Cir. 1980). *But see* Burk v. Emmick, 637 F.2d 1172, 29 UCC Rep. Serv. 1489 (8th Cir. 1980) (rejecting ten-day requirement and imposing instead a reasonableness requirement).

[163] UCC § 2-507, cmt. 3.

[164] *Id.*

[165] UCC § 2A-525.

[166] UCC § 2A-501(3) (based on UCC § 9-601(a)).

[167] UCC § 2A-525, cmt. 3, citing Clark Equip. Co. v. Armstrong Equip. Co., 431 F.2d 54 (5th Cir. 1970), *cert. denied,* 402 U.S. 909 (1971).

summary approach like a replevin action.[168]

A lessor need not go to court if repossession can be accomplished without a breach of the peace.[169] The lessor has the superior right to possession, but society has a paramount interest in avoiding confrontations that might escalate into violence.[170] If a breach of the peace is threatened, the lessor must proceed by judicial action. The lessor is also well advised to proceed by judicial action if its claim that the lessee is in default is subject to challenge. Taking possession in the absence of default leaves the lessor vulnerable to claims based on breach of contract and conversion, and the latter opens the prospect of a demand for punitive damages.[171]

§ 9.09 AMENDED ARTICLE 2

[A] Monetary Remedies

Amended Article 2 makes a number of changes to the provisions on sellers' damages. Most of the changes are not major in scope but rather tighten the looseness of some of the original drafting.

The amendments to Section 2-706 add a new subsection providing that "[f]ailure of a seller to resell under this section does not bar the seller from any other remedy."[172] This addition makes it clear that a seller is under no duty to attempt a resale in order to mitigate its damages. Curiously, original Section 2-712(3) dealing with buyers' cover includes a parallel provision and the omission of the provision in original Section 2-706 was no doubt an oversight.

The Comments to Section 2-706 have been revised significantly. One of the most helpful additions is the following excerpt that specifies when a seller is entitled to utilize the contract/resale measure of damages.

> The right of resale under this section arises when a seller reclaims goods under Section 2-507 or a buyer repudiates or makes a wrongful but effective rejection. In addition, there is a right of resale if the buyer unjustifiably attempts to revoke acceptance and the seller takes back the goods. However, the seller may choose to ignore the buyer's unjustifiable attempt to revoke acceptance, in which case the appropriate remedy is an action for the price under Section 2-709.[173]

Amended section 2-708(1) changes the measure of damages when a buyer makes an anticipatory repudiation. The measure of damages provided "is the

---

[168] Replevin is discussed in § 10.01[A] n.12 *infra*.

[169] UCC § 2A-525(3).

[170] The standard is the same as the standard for self-help repossession in Section 9-609(b)(2), and a wealth of Article 9 cases define what is meant by breach of the peace.

[171] *See* Mitchell v. Ford Motor Credit Co., 688 P.2d 42, 38 UCC Rep. Serv. 1812 (Okla. 1984) (award of only $1,000 actual damages but additional $60,000 punitive damages against Article 9 secured party that converted collateral).

[172] UCC Amended § 2-706(7).

[173] UCC Amended § 2-706, cmt. 2.

difference between the contract price and the market price at the place for tender at the expiration of a commercially reasonable time after the seller learned of the repudiation, but no later than the time [for tender under the contract]."[174] The drafters chose this time for determining market price because it is consistent with a seller's remedial rights following a repudiation under Section 2-610 and because it approximates the time at which a typical seller would resell the goods.[175]

The amendments also address the drafting problems in original Section 2-708(2). They expand the scope of the provision appropriately to encompass cases in which the measure of damages under Section 2-706 is inadequate, as well as similar cases under 2-708(1). They also delete the last clause of the original provision, thereby making it clear that the proceeds of resale do not have to be deducted from a lost-volume seller's damages.

Original Article 2 provides for buyers' consequential damages but makes no mention of consequential damages for sellers. Under amended Article 2 the various monetary-damage sections — amended Sections 2-706, 2-708, and 2-709 — permit the recovery of consequential damages as provided in amended Section 2-710, and that section in turn provides in subsection (2) that "[c]onsequential damages resulting from the buyer's breach include any loss resulting from general or particular requirements and needs of which the buyer at the time of contracting had reason to know and which could not reasonably be prevented by resale or otherwise."

Amended Section 2-710(3) states that consequential damages may not be recovered in consumer contracts. To emphasize that the subsection means what it says, the Official Comments indicate that this rule is nonwaivable.[176]

[B]   Nonmonetary Remedies

With regard to a seller's right of reclamation in a credit sale, original Section 2-702 requires that the seller make demand on the buyer within ten-days after the buyer's receipt of the goods (three months if the buyer had made a misrepresentation of solvency). Under the amended section the seller always has a reasonable time under the circumstances to make its demand, without regard to whether there has been a misrepresentation of solvency. The relaxation of the ten-day rule will have a limited impact because if the buyer has declared or been forced into bankruptcy, the seller will have to comply with Section 546(c) of the Bankruptcy Code, which includes a ten-day limitation. The drafters were aware that relaxation of the rule might be a trap for the unwary and placed a warning in the Comments.[177] A minor change to Section 2-702(3) makes it clear that only a bona fide purchaser *for value* cuts off a seller's right

---

[174] UCC Amended § 2-708(1)(b).

[175] UCC Amended § 2-708, cmt. 4. The provision correlates with a comparable remedy for buyers when the seller repudiates. *See* UCC Amended § 2-713(1)(b); § 8.04 *supra*.

[176] UCC Amended § 2-710, cmt. 3.

[177] UCC Amended § 2-702, cmt. 2.

of reclamation. The word "value" was omitted from the original section and is necessary because technically a donee is a purchaser[178] but should not cut off a right of reclamation.

If a sales transaction is intended to be for cash but the payment mechanism fails (*e.g.*, a check is dishonored), original Section 2-507 allows a seller to reclaim the goods, but the original drafting addresses the issue from the buyer's perspective by making its right to retain possession conditional upon payment. The amendments restate the proposition in terms of the seller's right of reclamation: "The seller may reclaim the goods delivered upon a demand made within a reasonable time after the seller discovers or should have discovered that payment was not made."[179] Section 2-507 was also amended to add a provision corresponding to Section 2-702(3) under which a seller's right of reclamation is cut off by a bona fide purchaser for value.[180]

Under original Section 2-705 a seller may stop delivery if a buyer repudiates the contract or fails to make a payment when due. The right is limited to bulk quantities of a "carload, truckload, planeload or large shipments of express or freight." The original drafters based the limitation on the assumption that it would be difficult to quickly isolate smaller quantities for purposes of requesting a stoppage from a carrier. Acknowledging that modern shipping practices with electronic tracking provide carriers with an efficient and effective way to track any size of shipment, the amendments remove the limiting language.

[C]   Liquidated Damages

Under original Section 2-718(1) a party seeking to enforce a liquidated-damages term must demonstrate the difficulty of proving the loss and the inconvenience or non-feasibility of obtaining an adequate remedy. The amendments eliminate these requirements for commercial contracts but retain them for consumer contracts. The amendments thus respect party autonomy while still requiring that the term be reasonable in light of the anticipated or actual harm.

Original Section 2-718(1) also states that an unreasonably large liquidated-damages term is void as a penalty. The amendments eliminate this language because it is unnecessary and misleading. If the liquidated damages are reasonable the term is enforceable for that reason, and thus the penalty language in the original provision is redundant. The original provision is misleading because of its emphasis on unreasonably large damages; a liquidated-damages term that provides for damages that are unreasonably small is likewise unenforceable.

---

[178] UCC § 1-201(b)(30) (defining "purchaser"), (29) (defining "purchase").

[179] UCC Amended § 2-507(2).

[180] UCC Amended § 2-507(3).

§ 9.10 CISG

[A] Unified Provisions on Damages

Unlike the UCC, which has separate damages provisions for buyers and sellers, the CISG has damages provisions that are common to both.[181] An explanation of these provisions is provided in Chapter 8[182] on buyers' damages and should be consulted also with respect to sellers' damages.

[B] Seller's Right to Specific Performance

The CISG gives a seller a broad right to require performance by a breaching buyer. Article 62 provides that "[t]he seller may require the buyer to pay the price, take delivery or perform his other obligations, unless the seller has resorted to a remedy which is inconsistent with this requirement." Article 62 eliminates the limitations that are included in Article 46 on the buyer's right to specific performance, as the concepts of substitute goods and repairs to goods are not relevant in the context of a buyer's breach.[183]

Article 28, however, potentially limits a seller's right to specific performance. That article permits a court that would not award specific performance in a domestic case to deny the remedy in any case in which "one party is entitled to require performance of any obligation by the other party."[184] Article 62 entitles the seller to require performance by the buyer. Thus, depending on the domestic law of the jurisdiction, the court may not be required to award specific performance to the seller.[185]

---

[181] CISG Arts. 74-77.

[182] *See* § 8.05[A] *supra.*

[183] *See* § 8.05[C] *supra.*

[184] An action for the price under UCC § 2-709 results in a money judgment rather than a decree in equity ordering payment that, if disobeyed, might result in contempt of court. Despite the difference in terminology, the Article 62 remedy should be subject to limitations on the remedy under the domestic law of the forum jurisdiction.

[185] Even courts in countries following the civil-law approach observe many limitations on the availability of this remedy.

Chapter 10

THIRD-PARTY INTERESTS

§ 10.01 RIGHTS OF THIRD PERSONS BASED ON PRIORITY RULES

[A]   Derivative Title; Apparent Authority; Voidable Title [§ 2-403(1); § 2A-304(1), § 2A-305(1)]

At common law, a person could not convey better title to goods than the person had, a concept captured by the Latin phrase *nemo dat quod non habet* (one cannot give what one does not have). This statement meant that a person to whom goods were transferred voluntarily acquired the property rights of the transferor and no more, a concept known as the doctrine of derivative title. The first sentence of Section 2-403(1) codifies the doctrine as follows: "A purchaser of goods acquires all title which his transferor had or had power to transfer except that a purchaser of a limited interest acquires rights only to the extent of the interest purchased."[1]

The reference to "power to transfer" incorporates agency principles, including the concept of apparent or ostensible authority.[2] The law initially took the position that ownership was sacrosanct, but this position began to erode

---

[1] "Purchaser" is broader than "buyer" and includes a person acquiring a property interest by means of any type of voluntary transaction, including by sale, lease, or security interest. UCC §§ 1-201(b)(30) (purchaser), 1-201(b)(29) (purchase). Even a donee qualifies as a purchaser.

[2] UCC § 2-403, Comment 1 states in part as follows: "[T]he policy of this Act expressly providing for the application of supplementary general principles of law to sales transactions wherever appropriate [UCC § 1-103(b)] joins with the present section to continue unimpaired all rights acquired under the law of agency or apparent agency or ownership or other estoppel, whether based on statutory provisions or on case law principles."

with the development of mercantile interests that inevitably accompanied the expansion of markets. Owners more and more entrusted their goods to commercial agents known as factors, and it was not uncommon for factors to sell entrusted goods for their own benefit. In the early part of the nineteenth century, states began to adopt "factors acts" under which a buyer relying on a factor's possession of goods and without notice of limitations on the factor's authority acquired good title.[3] Courts reached the same result under the doctrine of apparent authority: An owner, having clothed an agent with indicia of ownership, had so participated in misleading a bona fide purchaser into believing that the agent could rightfully transfer title that the purchaser acquired good title notwithstanding the agent's lack of actual authority.

The first sentence of Section 2-403(1) recognizes that a purchaser may seek to acquire only a limited interest in goods, in which case its rights will be limited to the interest purchased. An example of a limited interest is a leasehold interest of a lessee under Article 2A.[4] Title remains in the lessor[5] and the lessee acquires the right to possession and use of the goods.[6] Another example of a limited interest is a security interest[7] acquired by a secured party under Article 9.[8] As an illustration, suppose an owner of goods borrows money and by contract grants its lender a security interest in its goods. Title remains in the owner and the lender's interest in the goods is that they serve as collateral for the obligation. If the owner defaults, the lender may dispose of the goods through a process in which title is divested from the owner by operation of law and revested in a purchaser.[9]

The second sentence of Section 2-403(1) constitutes a partial codification[10] of the equitable doctrine of voidable title.[11] The concept initially arose in cases in which a buyer fraudulently acquired title and possession of goods from their owner and then conveyed them to a bona fide purchaser. As discussed above in the context of dishonest agents, the needs of the marketplace required subordination of the owner's interest, and voidable title became the vehicle for achieving this result. Courts applying the doctrine distinguished between cases

---

[3] UCC § 2-403, Comment 1 states that "[t]he section leaves unimpaired the powers given to selling factors under the earlier Factors Acts."

[4] UCC § 2A-103(1)(m) defines "leasehold interest" as "the interest of the lessor or the lessee under a lease contract."

[5] UCC § 2A-103(1)(q) (lessor's residual interest).

[6] UCC § 2A-103(1)(j) (definition of lease).

[7] The definition of security interest is complex but for current purposes it means "an interest in personal property or fixtures which secures payment or performance of an obligation." UCC § 1-201(b)(35).

[8] Article 9 governs, *inter alia*, security interests acquired by contract. UCC § 9-109(a)(1).

[9] UCC §§ 9-610 (secured party's right to dispose of collateral after default), 9-617(a)(1) (transferee at disposition acquires debtor's rights in collateral).

[10] It is a partial codification in that it provides a rule if a person has voidable title but does not articulate the circumstances giving rise to voidable title.

[11] The courts applied the doctrine of voidable title to dishonest buyers and the doctrine of apparent authority to dishonest agents, but the doctrines are based on the same principles. Voidable title is inapt as applied to agents because they do not acquire title.

in which a thief stole goods and those in which an owner clothed a fraudulent buyer with indicia of ownership. A thief did not acquire title and therefore could not convey good title irrespective of the innocence of the purchaser.[12] The thief's title was void, not voidable.

By contrast, a fraudulent buyer acquired voidable title, meaning that the owner could rescind the transaction and recover the goods from the buyer, but its rights in the goods would be cut off if they were resold to a bona fide purchaser.[13] To illustrate, suppose a buyer convinced an owner to sell goods on credit but never intended to pay. Title passed to the buyer, but if the owner discovered the fraud it could rescind the transaction and recover the goods.[14] However, if the goods were resold to a bona fide purchaser the owner's claim to the goods was cut off. The second sentence of Section 2-403(1) provides for this result as follows: "A person with voidable title has power to transfer a good title to a good faith purchaser for value."[15] Since a person with voidable title has the power to convey rights greater than its own, the voidable-title concept is an exception to the doctrine of derivative title.

As the common law developed, curious distinctions emerged. For example, if a fraudulent buyer paid with a check that was later dishonored, some courts considered the transaction the equivalent of a cash sale, meaning a sale in which the parties did not intend for title to pass until the cash was paid.[16] This meant

---

[12] This concept is still with us: If a thief steals goods and conveys them, the owner may recover the goods in a replevin action or their value in a conversion action. Even a good-faith purchaser for value cannot take good title through a thief.

Replevin, sometimes called "claim and delivery," is an action to recover possession of goods by a person claiming a greater right to possession. Conversion is a tort defined by Restatement (Second) of Torts § 222 as "an intentional exercise of dominion or control over a chattel which so interferes with the rights of another to control it that the actor may justly be required to pay the owner the full value of the chattel." A person acting in good faith can nevertheless incur conversion liability by intentionally exercising dominion or control over another's chattel.

[13] The seminal case is *Parker v. Parker*, 101 Eng. rep. 99 (K.B. 1793), and the first American case was *Mowrey v. Walsh*, 8 Cowen 238 (N.Y. Sup. Ct. 1828). As with the rights of bona fide purchasers, courts of equity created the owner's right of rescission. When the rights of the two parties were in conflict, the equities generally weighed more heavily in favor of the bona fide purchaser.

[14] In the example in the text, the right of rescission is predicated on fraud at the time of contract formation. If the buyer intended to pay at the time of formation but later defaulted, the seller would not have a right of rescission. The seller could protect itself against default by retaining an Article 9 security interest in the goods. In limited circumstances an unpaid credit seller will have a right to reclaim goods from a buyer but this right will be cut off by a good-faith purchaser for value. UCC § 2-702(2) (seller's right of reclamation), (3) (rights of good-faith purchaser). *See* discussion § 9.08[C][1] *supra*.

[15] Article 2A is in accord with Section 2-403(1). Section 2A-304(1) deals with a subsequent lease of goods by a lessor while an existing lease is still in effect and provides that the subsequent lessee obtains the leasehold interest that the lessor had or had power to transfer; however, a lessor with voidable title has power to transfer a good leasehold interest to a good faith subsequent lessee for value. Section 2A-305(1) deals with conveyances by a lessee and provides that a buyer or sublessee obtains the leasehold interest that the lessee had or had power to transfer; however, a lessee with a voidable leasehold interest has power to transfer a good leasehold interest to a good faith buyer or sublessee for value. Sections 2A-304(1) and 2A-305(1) are subject to Section 2A-303, which governs voluntary and involuntary transfers of rights and duties under a lease contract.

[16] *See, e.g.*, Ellis v. Nelson, 68 Nev. 410, 233 P.2d 1072 (1951). The Code provisions dealing with

that the buyer's title was void and it could not convey good title to a bona fide purchaser.[17] In another odd distinction, courts sometimes differentiated between impersonation in person and impersonation through a medium such as a telephone or the mail. If an impersonator acquired goods in a face-to-face transaction, the courts assumed that the owner's intent was to pass title to the impersonator, who was thereby vested with voidable title. On the other hand, if the impersonator acted through a medium it was assumed that the owner intended to transfer title only to the person being impersonated and not to the impersonator, who received void title.[18]

The third sentence of Section 2-403(1) expands the doctrine of voidable title by overruling some of the common-law distinctions. Thus, a person to whom goods have been delivered in a transaction of purchase has power to transfer good title to a good-faith purchaser for value even though "(a) the transferor was deceived as to the identity of the purchaser, or (b) the delivery was in exchange for a check which is later dishonored, or (c) it was agreed that the transaction was to be a 'cash sale', or (d) the delivery was procured through fraud punishable as larcenous under the criminal law."

[B]   Entrustment [§ 2-403(2); § 2A-304(2), § 2A-305(2)]

The concept of voidable title cannot be used when an owner delivers goods to a bailee because it is the very essence of a bailment transaction that the owner retains title to the goods.[19] The common-law protects a bailor's ownership by providing that goods in the hands of a bailee are not subject to the claims of the bailee's creditors and that the bailee lacks power to transfer good title even to a good-faith purchaser for value. However, as we saw with apparent authority and voidable title, the market's need to protect certain kinds of purchasers eventually trumped the law's interest in protecting ownership. The Code calls the vehicle by which the protection was provided the entrustment doctrine.[20]

"Entrusting" is defined in Section 2-403(3) to include "any delivery [of goods to a bailee] and any acquiescence in retention of possession [by the bailee]. . . ." "Delivery" is defined as the voluntary turnover of possession for certain types of assets dealt with under other articles of the Code but the definition does not apply to goods.[21] Despite the omission, delivery of goods undoubtedly means the same thing — the voluntary transfer of possession. An entrustment can also arise through acquiescence in a bailee's retention of possession. For example, in *Simon v. Moon*[22] a buyer bought a truck from a

---

the rights of a seller that receives a bad check are discussed in § 9.08[C][1] *supra.*

[17] *See, e.g.,* Handley Motor Co. v. Wood, 237 N.C. 318, 75 S.E.2d 312 (1953).

[18] *See, e.g.,* Newberry v. Norfolk & So. R.R., 135 N.C. 45, 45 S.E. 356 (1903).

[19] *See* R. Brown, The Law of Personal Property § 10.1 (W. Raushenbush 3d ed. 1975).

[20] For a discussion of the relationship of agency law principles to the entrustment concept, see Lawrence, *The "Created by His Seller" Limitation of Section 9-307(1): A Provision in Need of an Articulated Policy,* 60 Ind. L.J. 73 (1984).

[21] UCC § 1-201(b)(15).

[22] 137 Ga. App. 82, 222 S.E.2d 873, 18 UCC Rep. Serv. 1191 (1975), *case dismissed,* 236 Ga. 786, 225 S.E.2d 314 (1976).

dealer but left it with the dealer so that wrecker equipment could be installed. When the dealer sold it a second time, the court held that the first buyer's acquiescence in the dealer's retention of possession constituted an entrustment.

The definition of entrustment is broad enough to cover almost any type of bailment, but the substantive rule of Section 2-403(2) is limited to an "entrusting of possession to a merchant who deals in goods of that kind." Delivery of goods to, or acquiescence in the retention of possession by, a person in the business of, *inter alia*, repairing, storing, or transporting such goods constitutes an entrustment, but the entruster does not run the risk of being divested of its property rights. However, an entrustee that is a merchant that deals in goods of that kind has the power to transfer all of the entruster's rights to a buyer in ordinary course of business.[23] A buyer in ordinary course of business is a type of good-faith purchaser, the basic definition being "a person that buys goods in good faith, without knowledge that the sale violates the rights of another person in the goods, and in the ordinary course from a person, other than a pawnbroker, in the business of selling goods of that kind."[24] The typical buyer in ordinary course is an innocent buyer of a dealer's inventory. An example is the second buyer of the truck left with the dealer by the first buyer in *Simon v. Moon*, discussed above. The dealer's sale to the second buyer effectively cut off the rights of the first buyer.

The following example illustrates the application of Section 2-403(2) and differentiates it from the voidable-title rule of Section 2-403(1), which protects all good-faith purchasers for value. Assume an owner of two expensive watches takes them to a jeweler for repair. Whether fraudulently or by accident, the watches wind up in the jeweler's inventory. One of the watches is sold to a buyer in ordinary course of business.[25] The jeweler grants a bank a security interest in all its inventory as collateral for a loan and, when it defaults, the bank repossesses the other watch and sells it to a buyer at a foreclosure sale. The owner has no rights in the first watch because the jeweler had power to transfer the owner's rights in that watch to the buyer. The bank is a purchaser for value[26] and would take free of the owner's rights if Section 2-403(1) were applicable. However, the jeweler had neither voidable title nor apparent authority to grant the security interest.[27] Good-faith purchasers other than

---

[23] Article 2A is in accord. Under UCC § 2A-304(2), a subsequent lessee in ordinary course of business takes free of an initial lease contract if the initial lessee entrusts the goods to a lessor that is a merchant dealing in goods of that kind. Under UCC § 2A-305(2), a buyer or sublessee in ordinary course of business of goods entrusted by a lessor to a lessee that is a merchant dealing in goods of that kind takes free of the existing lease contract.

[24] UCC § 1-201(9). The definition contains other qualifications, including that the buyer must take possession of the goods or have a right to possession under Article 2 and must not acquire the goods in bulk or as security for or in satisfaction of a money debt. The definition of "lessee in ordinary course of business" is similar. UCC § 2A-103(1)(o).

[25] The facts as regards the buyer of the first watch are based loosely on the influential pre-Code case of *Zendman v. Harry Winston, Inc.*, 305 N.Y. 180, 111 N.E.2d 871 (1953).

[26] The bank would be a purchaser for value even if it acquired its interest in the jeweler's inventory before the jeweler acquired the watches. Value includes acquiring rights as security for a preexisting claim. UCC § 1-204(2).

[27] The theory underlying UCC § 2-403(2) is that an entruster clothes a merchant that deals in

buyers in ordinary course of business are not protected by Section 2-403(2) and thus the bank's interest was subordinate to that of the owner. What about the foreclosure-sale buyer? It will qualify as a buyer in ordinary course of business if the secured party sold the watch through a merchant that deals in watches, but even so the buyer will not be protected by Section 2-403(2) because the owner did not deliver the watch to, or acquiesce in retention of possession by, the merchant. The owner can replevy the watch from the buyer or recover its value in a conversion action.

Perhaps the most difficult problem in the entrustment area is the relationship between Section 2-403(2) and state certificate-of-title laws. Such laws often provide that a transfer of title to goods for which a state-issued certificate of title is required, such as automobiles, is not effective absent compliance with the procedures established by the law. The procedures vary from state to state but in general require that a buyer of used goods obtain the existing certificate of title[28] so that it can be surrendered to the state and a new certificate can be issued indicating the name of the new owner. An issue that has divided the courts is whether the failure of a buyer to comply with such procedures prevents the buyer from taking advantage of the entrustment doctrine.

Some courts have held that the more specific provisions of a certificate-of-title law prevail over the Code's more general provisions relating to title. For example, in *Kaminsky v. Karmin*[29] the defendant placed a used car with a dealer for sale on consignment but never gave the dealer the existing certificate of title. The dealer sold the car to the plaintiff for less than the authorized price and the defendant later claimed that the car still belonged to him. The plaintiff's request for a judgment declaring that the defendant's rights in the car had been transferred to him under Section 2-403(2) was denied. By not acquiring the certificate, the plaintiff had failed to comply with New York's certificate-of-title law and this precluded the plaintiff from taking advantage of the entrustment doctrine. Other courts, especially in cases where a consumer is the ultimate buyer, have held that Section 2-403(2) trumps a certificate-of-title law. For example, the court in *In re Cohen*[30] held that consumer car buyers who did not receive certificates of title from the dealer that sold to them nevertheless took free of the rights of the owners that entrusted the cars to the dealer.

---

goods of the kind with apparent authority to sell to a buyer in ordinary course of business. The provision leaves in place the common-law rule protecting a bailor from a bailee's creditors.

[28] The laws typically require that an assignment form pre-printed on the certificate be filled out showing the name of the new owner and that the assignment be signed by the existing owner as shown on the certificate. Most dealers don't have used cars titled in their names, and they typically require that a seller sign the assignment form on the certificate with the space for the new buyer's name left blank. The dealer fills in the blank space with the name of the person that buys from it and turns the certificate over to that person.

[29] 187 A.D.2d 488, 589 N.Y.S.2d 588, 19 UCC Rep. Serv. 2d 1073 (Sup. Ct. 1992).

[30] 199 B.R. 709 (9th Cir. App. Pan. 1996).

[C]   Estoppel

The doctrines of apparent authority, voidable title, and entrustment are based on estoppel principles, and those principles have occasionally been invoked to protect a buyer in a case not directly within the scope of Section 2-403. For example, in *Tumber v. Automation Design and Manufacturing Corp.*[31] a lessee sold leased equipment to the plaintiff and the lessor later claimed that the equipment still belonged to it. The lease transaction qualified as an entrustment but the plaintiff could not make use of Section 2-403(2) because the lessee was not a dealer in goods of the kind.[32] However, the lessor had acquiesced in the use of the equipment by two persons other than the lessee and had left the equipment with the lessee well beyond the end of the lease term. On those facts, the court held that the lessor had sufficiently clothed the lessee with indicia of ownership that it should be estopped from asserting its rights in the equipment.

§ 10.02   ASSIGNMENT AND DELEGATION

[A]   Sales [§ 2-210]

Under modern law most rights are assignable and most duties are delegable.[33] Article 2 confirms these principles by recognizing both assignment and delegation "as normal and permissible incidents of a contract for the sale of goods."[34]

While the general rule is that rights are freely assignable,[35] there is an exception for assignments that materially prejudice the rights of the other party to the sales contract. Section 2-210(2) provides that an assignment that "would materially change the duty of the other party, or increase materially the burden or risk imposed on him by his contract, or impair materially his chance of obtaining return performance" is ineffective. The situations in which these limitations will apply are relatively rare.[36] A seller's assignment of a right to payment that has been earned by performance should always be assignable, but an assignment of an unearned right to payment might decrease the seller's incentive to perform and thus increase the buyer's risk of nonperformance.[37]

---

[31] 130 N.J. Super. 5, 324 A.2d 602 (1974).

[32] The decision pre-dates Article 2A but the facts are also not within that article's relevant entrustment provision, Section 2A-305(2).

[33] Restatement (Second) of Contracts §§ 317(2), 318(1).

[34] UCC § 2-210, cmt. 1; *see, e.g.*, First Nat'l Bank of Milltown v. Schrader, 375 N.E.2d 1124, 24 UCC Rep. Serv. 219 (Ind. Ct. App. 1978) (error for trial court to dismiss assignee's action to recover balance of purchase price on grounds that assignor/seller was real party in interest because seller's contract rights were assignable).

[35] UCC § 2-210(2).

[36] For an example outside the sales sphere, a promise to care for a person for that person's life may not be assigned because doing so would materially change the promisor's duties. *See* Restatement (Second) of Contracts § 317, cmt. d, illus. 3.

[37] Most assignments of a seller's right to payment, whether earned or unearned, are governed by

Similarly, a buyer's assignment of a right to receive a fixed quantity of goods should be freely assignable, but an assignment of a buyer's rights under a requirements contract could materially increase the seller's risk. A few cases have discussed whether a buyer's assignment of warranty rights materially increases the seller's risks and burdens, with most of the decisions upholding the assignment.[38]

As with assignments of rights, the general rule is that duties are freely delegable.[39] However, the right to render performance through a delegate is precluded if the person to whom the duty is owed has a substantial interest in having the original promisor perform or control the acts required by the contract.[40] For a non-sales example, the duty to sing at a scheduled event is not delegable because of the personal nature of the performance.[41] By comparison, the court in *Buckeye Ag-Center, Inc. v. Babchuk*[42] held that a seller's duty to supply a specified quantity of corn was delegable. A delegation of performance may raise a concern in the mind of the person to whom performance is to be rendered, and that person may treat the delegation as creating reasonable grounds for insecurity and demand assurances of performance from the delegatee under the rules of Section 2-609.[43]

An effective delegation does not relieve the delegating party of its duty to perform or of liability for breach.[44] The delegation substitutes another party to perform the duty but the original party's obligation remains in effect until it is

---

UCC § 9-406, discussed this section, *infra*. Subsection (f) of that section overrides legal restrictions on assignment. Consistent with § 9-406, § 2-210(3) provides that the creation, attachment, perfection, or enforcement of a security interest in a seller's rights is not an assignment that materially prejudices the buyer unless, and then only to the extent that, enforcement by the secured party results in a delegation of the seller's duty to perform. Even then all aspects of the security interest remain effective, but the seller is liable to the buyer for damages that cannot be mitigated and the buyer may apply to the court for other relief, such as cancelling the contract or enjoining enforcement of the security interest.

[38] *See, e.g.*, Collins Co., Ltd. v. Carboline Co., 125 Ill. 2d 498, 127 Ill. Dec. 5, 532 N.E.2d 834, 7 UCC Rep. Serv. 2d 616 (1988); Sharrard, McGee & Co., P.A. v. Suz's Software, Inc., 100 N.C. App. 428, 396 S.E.2d 815, 12 UCC Rep. Serv. 2d 1006 (1990). The courts in Georgia have held that a buyer's assignment of a warranty materially increases the seller's obligations as a matter of law, Kaiser Aluminum & Chem. Corp. v. Ingersoll-Rand Co., 519 F. Supp. 60, 32 UCC Rep. Serv. 1369 (S.D. Ga. 1981), but even in that state an existing claim for damages for breach of warranty may be assigned. Irvin v. Lowe's of Gainesville, Inc., 165 Ga. App. 828, 302 S.E.2d 734, 36 UCC Rep. Serv. 450 (1983).

[39] UCC § 2-210(1). Section 2-210(4) contains a rule of construction that supports the principle that delegation is the norm. An assignment of "the contract" or "all my rights under the contract" or an assignment using comparably broad language constitutes an assignment of rights and, unless the language or circumstances indicate otherwise, a delegation of duties.

[40] UCC § 2-210(1); *accord* Restatement (Second) of Contracts § 318 (1979).

[41] Restatement (Second) of Contracts § 318, cmt. c, illus. 6; *see also* Restatement (Second) of Contracts § 318, cmt. c, illus. 7 ("A contracts with B that A will *personally* cut the grass on B's meadow. A cannot effectively delegate performance of the duty to C, however competent C may be" (emphasis supplied)).

[42] 533 N.E.2d 179, 9 UCC Rep. Serv. 2d 76 (Ind. Ct. App. 1989).

[43] UCC § 2-210(6). Making a demand for assurances does not prejudice the promisee's rights against the delegator. *Id.* UCC § 2-609 is discussed generally in § 7.07[B] *supra*.

[44] UCC § 2-210(1); *see also* Restatement (Second) of Contracts § 318(3); C.I.T. Corp. v. Jonnet, 3 UCC Rep. Serv. 321 (Pa. Ct. Com. Pl. 1965), *aff'd*, 419 Pa. 435, 214 A.2d 620, 3 UCC Rep. Serv. 968

discharged by performance or otherwise.[45] *Midwest Precision Services, Inc. v. PTM Industries Corp.*,[46] in which the seller of a machine sued the buyer for breach when the buyer's lessee wrongfully rejected the machine, illustrates this consequence. The buyer attempted to avoid liability by pointing to a provision in its contract with the seller that delegated to the lessee the buyer's duties with respect to acceptance and rejection, but the appellate court appropriately affirmed the trial court's determination that the provision did not insulate the buyer from liability if the lessee wrongfully rejected the machine. Similarly, in *Tarter v. MonArk Boat Co.*[47] the assignment by a seller of a contract to construct and sell a houseboat that included a delegation of the construction duty did not relieve the seller of liability for breach by the assignee.

An assignee's acceptance of a delegation of duties constitutes a promise by the assignee to perform the duties that is enforceable by both the assignor and the other party to the contract with the assignor.[48] For example, in *McKinnie v. Milford*[49] the court held that both the original seller of a horse and his buyer could enforce a duty assumed by a subsequent buyer. The original sales contract entitled the seller to use the horse for two breedings each year for as long as the horse lived, and the subsequent buyer purchased the horse with full awareness of these breeding rights.

Under Section 2-210 agreements prohibiting assignment and delegation are generally enforceable, but the right to prohibit a delegation by agreement is unfettered[50] while the right to prohibit an assignment is subject to an exception for rights to recover money for obligations that are no longer executory. Specifically, a right to damages for breach of a whole contract or a right to payment resulting from full performance may be assigned notwithstanding an agreement to the contrary.[51] Following a breach of the whole, an aggrieved party may cancel the contract, leaving the breaching party without an equitable basis to assert the validity of an anti-assignment provision. Similarly, if an assignor has fully performed, the other party will not have a convincing basis to object to a requirement that it tender performance to an assignee. Permitting assignment notwithstanding agreement to the contrary is justified in part because the absence of any executory obligations on the part of the assignor means that the assignment will not raise any questions regarding delegation.[52] A rule of construction that reflects the policy of leaving assignments less

(1965) (buyer's assignment of its rights to goods purchased under installment sales contract does not relieve buyer of its contract liability).

[45] Restatement (Second) of Contracts § 316, cmt. c.

[46] 887 F.2d 1128, 9 UCC Rep. Serv. 2d 1169 (1st Cir. 1989); *see also* Plastech Engineered Prods. v. Grand Haven Plastics, Inc., 56 UCC Rep. Serv. 2d 910 (Mich. Ct. App. 2005).

[47] 430 F. Supp. 1290, 22 UCC Rep. Serv. 33 (E.D. Mo. 1977).

[48] *Id.*; *see, e.g.*, De La Rosa v. Tropical Sandwiches, Inc., 298 So. 2d 471, 15 UCC Rep. Serv. 595 (Fla. Ct. App. 1974) (purchaser of restaurant's assets did not assume obligation of promissory note given in previous transaction and was therefore not liable for balance due on note).

[49] 597 S.W.2d 953, 29 UCC Rep. Serv. 430 (Tex. Ct. App. 1980).

[50] UCC § 2-210(1); *accord* Restatement (Second) of Contracts § 318(1).

[51] UCC § 2-210(2); *accord* Restatement (Second) of Contracts § 317(2)(c).

[52] UCC § 2-210, cmt. 3.

fettered than delegations provides that a prohibition on assignment of "the contract" precludes only a delegation of performance unless the circumstances indicate otherwise.[53]

Section 2-210(2), which as we have seen validates certain contractual limitations on assignment and creates certain legal limitations, is subject to Section 9-406, which invalidates the limitations if the right being assigned is a seller's right to future payment.[54] Section 2-210(2) thus only limits sellers in the small number of transactions that fall outside the scope of Article 9.[55] An agreement between a seller and a buyer is ineffective under Section 9-406(d) to the extent it "prohibits, restricts, or requires the consent of the [buyer]" to an assignment and also to the extent that it provides that an assignment constitutes a default by the seller or otherwise gives the buyer a basis for obtaining relief from the seller. For example, a buyer and seller might agree that the seller will not assign its right to be paid and that it will be liable to the buyer for liquidated damages if it breaches the agreement. Both the agreement not to assign and the agreement to pay liquidated damages are invalid. Similarly, legal rules that prohibit assignment or provide that an assignment provides the buyer with a basis for obtaining relief are invalid under Section 9-406(f).

[B] Leases [§ 2A-303]

As with Article 2, assignment and delegation are normal incidents of a lease contract under Article 2A. Section 2A-303(2) states the general rule that a transfer[56] is effective between the transferor and transferee notwithstanding a provision in a lease agreement that prohibits it.[57] If transfer is not prohibited but is instead made an event of default, the other party to the contract is entitled to all the statutory and contractual rights and remedies generally available to aggrieved parties under Section 2A-501(2).[58] Conversely, if transfer

---

[53] UCC § 2-210(3).

[54] Under Article 9 a right to payment for goods that have been sold on unsecured credit, whether or not the right has been earned by performance, is an account, and the right to payment for goods sold on secured credit is chattel paper. *See* UCC § 9-102(a)(2), (11). Article 9 generally applies whether the assignment provides the assignee with collateral for an obligation or constitutes a sale of the payment right. *See* UCC § 9-109(a)(1), (4).

[55] Article 9 does not apply to an assignment that occurs as part of a sale of the seller's business, § 9-109(d)(4), an assignment for the purpose of collection only, § 9-109(d)(5), an assignment to an assignee that is also obligated to perform under the contract, § 9-109(d)(6), or an assignment in full or partial satisfaction of a pre-existing debt if the assignment is of the right to payment under a single contract. UCC § 9-109(d)(7).

[56] Whereas Article 2 uses "assignment of rights" and "delegation of duties," Article 2A uses the term "transfer" throughout and differentiates between a transfer of rights and a transfer that is a delegation of duties.

[57] This is true whether the transfer is voluntary or occurs involuntarily, as by attachment, levy, or another judicial process, and it is true whether the transfer constitutes a sale, sublease, creation or enforcement of a security interest, or another type of disposition.

[58] UCC § 2A-303(4)(a). The general approach of making a transfer effective notwithstanding agreement to the contrary but enforcing a clause making the transfer an event of default is consistent with the general approach of Article 9. UCC § 9-401.

is prohibited but not made an event of default, the other party may recover damages caused by the transfer that cannot reasonably be mitigated and may apply to the court for other relief, such as cancellation of the lease contract or an injunction against the transfer.[59] The last rule applies even without an express prohibition if the transfer materially prejudices the other party, as by impairing its prospect of obtaining return performance, materially changing its duties, or materially increasing its burden or risk.[60]

The general rules set forth above are subject to limitations and exceptions. Under Section 2A-303(7), a term in a consumer lease prohibiting transfer or making it an event of default "must be specific, by a writing, and conspicuous." Under Section 2A-303(3), a provision in a lease contract that prohibits transfer of a right to damages for breach of the whole contract or of a right to payment resulting from full performance of the transferor's obligation, or a provision that makes such a transfer an event of default, is unenforceable.[61] Moreover, such a transfer does not materially prejudice the other party such that a remedy might be available even in the absence of a contractual provision.[62] Under this provision, a transfer by a lessor of its right to future rental payments is free from all contractual and legal restraints if the transferor has fully performed its duties under the lease contract, as will always be the case with finance lessors. Regarding other lessors, the Comments[63] distinguish between a potential duty, such as a promise to repair or replace in the event a warranty is breached, and an affirmative duty, such as a promise to maintain and service the goods or to provide upgrades. In the former case, a transfer of future payments may be made free of all contractual and legal restraints; in the latter case, Section 2A-303(2) applies and, although the transfer is effective, remedies are available to the other party to the lease contract.[64]

Like Article 2, Article 2A provides a rule of construction under which a transfer of "the lease" or "all my rights under the lease" constitutes a transfer of rights and, unless the language or circumstances indicate to the contrary, a

---

[59] UCC § 2A-303(4)(b).

[60] By contrast, under Article 2 such an assignment is ineffective between the assignor and the assignee. UCC § 2-210(2).

[61] UCC § 2A-303(3).

[62] Id.

[63] UCC § 2A-303, cmt. 3.

[64] UCC § 9-407 contains other exceptions to the general rules applicable to transactions within the scope of Article 9. Regarding a transfer of a lessor's interest under a lease contract or of its residual interest in the goods, UCC § 9-407(c) provides that the creation, attachment, perfection, or enforcement of a security interest is not a transfer that materially prejudices the lessee "unless, and then only to the extent that, enforcement actually results in a delegation of material performance of the lessor." Regarding a transfer of a lessee's interest under a lease contract, a term in the contract prohibiting the transfer is ineffective but a term making it an event of default is enforceable. The latter rule is subject to UCC § 2A-303(7), discussed in the text *supra*.

For purposes of Article 9, a lessor's right to future payment is called "chattel paper." UCC § 9-102(a)(11) (chattel paper defined). Transfers of chattel paper are within the scope of Article 9 whether the transfer is a sale or is to provide security for an obligation. UCC § 9-109(a)(1), (a)(3). Transfers of chattel paper are excluded from Article 9 in the same circumstances in which assignments of accounts (*i.e.*, a seller's right to future payment) are excluded. *See* n.55 *supra*.

delegation of duties.[65] Acceptance of the transfer constitutes a promise by the transferee to perform the duties that may be enforced by either the transferor or the other party to the lease contract,[66] and unless otherwise agreed by the lessor and lessee the transferor is not relieved of its performance obligations or of liability for their breach.

§ 10.03 AMENDED ARTICLE 2

The amendments to Section 2-210 do not change its basic policies; rather, they were designed to better integrate the section with revised Article 9. Subsection (1)(a) continues the familiar rule that all rights of a seller or buyer may be assigned unless the assignment would materially prejudice the other party, and it also continues the familiar rule that "[a] right to damages for breach of the whole contract or a right arising out of the assignor's due performance of its entire obligation may be assigned despite an agreement otherwise."

Subsection (a) is subject to Section 9-406,[67] which contains sweeping language invalidating contract terms and legal rules restricting assignment or making it an event of default, and to subsection (1)(b), which is the same as original Section 2-210(3).

Subsections (2), (3), and (4) do not differ substantively from the original section. The rules have been reorganized for clarity, with the substantive rules on delegation in subsection (2) and rules of construction regarding both assignment and delegation in subsections (3) and (4).

---

[65] UCC § 2A-303(5). The Article 2 counterpart is UCC § 2-210(5).

[66] *Id.*

[67] UCC § 9-406 is discussed in n.37 *supra.*

TABLE OF CASES

[References are to pages.]

[References are to pages.]

[References are to pages.]

[References are to pages.]

[References are to pages.]

[References are to pages.]

[References are to pages.]

[References are to pages.]

[References are to pages.]

[References are to pages.]

TABLE OF STATUTES

[References are to pages.]

[References are to pages.]

[References are to pages.]

Uniform Commercial Code (UCC) —Cont.

Uniform Commercial Code (UCC) —Cont.

[References are to pages.]

[References are to pages.]

[References are to pages.]

[References are to pages.]

[References are to pages.]

INDEX

[References are to pages.]

A

B

C

[References are to pages.]

[References are to pages.]

[References are to pages.]

[References are to pages.]

[References are to pages.]

[References are to pages.]